PENGUIN BOOKS

AESTHETICS,
METHOD, AND EPISTEMOLOGY

Michel Foucault was born in France in 1926. He served as director at the Institut Français in Hamburg and the Institut de Philosophie at the Faculté des Lettres in the University of Clermont-Ferrand. In 1970 he was appointed Professor of History of Systems of Thought at the Collège de France, where he taught for fourteen years. Himself a controversial intellectual presence, his lectures were often radically unconventional. His public life involved militant and courageous campaigning on behalf of prisoners, dissidents and homosexuals.

At the time of his death in 1984, Michel Foucault was without doubt France's most prominent thinker. His profoundly original studies of madness, crime, sexuality and methods of classification influenced disciplines as diverse as history, philosophy, sociology, medical history and literary criticism. He set new agendas for research in political theory, stimulated debates over gender identity, and raised questions about the meaning of truth and reason through the analysis of knowledge and power systems.

His many publications include *Madness and Civilisation* (1961); *The Order of Things* (1966); *The Archaeology of Knowledge* (1972); *The Birth of the Clinic* (1973); *Discipline and Punish* (1975) and three volumes of *The History of Sexuality* (1976, 1984, 1984). Many of his books are published by Penguin. *Ethics*, the first part of the three-volume *Essential Works* of Michel Foucault, is also published by Penguin. *Power*, part three, was recently published by Allen Lane.

James Faubion is a professor of anthropology at Rice University in Houston, Texas. He is the author of *Modern Greek Lessons: A Primer in Historical Constructivism*.

Series Editor Paul Rabinow is a professor of anthropology at the University of California at Berkeley. His previous books include *The Foucault Reader* and *Michel Foucault: Beyond Structuralism and Hermeneutics* (with Herbert L. Dreyfus).

MICHEL FOUCAULT

AESTHETICS,
METHOD, AND EPISTEMOLOGY

Edited by
JAMES FAUBION

Series Editor
PAUL RABINOW

Translated by
ROBERT HURLEY AND OTHERS

ESSENTIAL WORKS OF
FOUCAULT
1954–1984

VOLUME TWO

PENGUIN BOOKS

PENGUIN BOOKS

Published by the Penguin Group
Penguin Books Ltd, 80 Strand, London WC2R 0RL, England
Penguin Putnam Inc., 375 Hudson Street, New York, New York 10014, USA
Penguin Books Australia Ltd, 250 Camberwell Road, Camberwell, Victoria 3124, Australia
Penguin Books Canada Ltd, 10 Alcorn Avenue, Toronto, Ontario, Canada M4V 3B2
Penguin Books India (P) Ltd, 11 Community Centre, Panchsheel Park, New Delhi – 110 017, India
Penguin Books (NZ) Ltd, Cnr Rosedale and Airborne Roads, Albany, Auckland, New Zealand
Penguin Books (South Africa) (Pty) Ltd, 24 Sturdee Avenue, Rosebank 2196, South Africa

Penguin Books Ltd, Registered Offices: 80 Strand, London WC2R 0RL, England

www.penguin.com

Selections from *Dits et écrits, 1954–1984* edited by Daniel Defert and François Ewald,
with the assistance of Jaques Lagrange, first published by Editions Gallimard 1994
This selection first published with new translations in the USA by The New Press 1998
First published in Great Britain by Allen Lane The Penguin Press 1998
Published in Penguin Books 2000

021

Printed and bound in Great Britain by Clays Ltd, Elcograf S.p.A.

www.greenpenguin.co.uk

CONTENTS

ACKNOWLEDGMENTS

A special thanks to Robert Bledsoe, for help with Hölderlin; to Robert Hurley, from whom I have learned much; and to my perennial critics and collaborators, William R. Dull and Paul Rabinow.

Michel Foucault provides a splendid definition of work: "That which is susceptible of introducing a significant difference in the field of knowledge, at the cost of a certain difficulty for the author and the reader, with, however, the eventual recompense of a certain pleasure, that is to say of access to another figure of truth."[1] Diverse factors shape the emergence, articulation, and circulation of a work and its effects. Foucault gave us intellectual tools to understand these phenomena. In *Essential Works of Foucault 1954-1984* we use these very tools to understand his own work. Though he intended his books to be the core of his intellectual production, he is well known for having made strategic use of a number of genres—the book and the article to be sure, but also the lecture and the interview. Indeed, few modern thinkers have used such a wide array of forms in so skillful a fashion, making them an integral component in the development and presentation of their work. In this light, our aim in this series is to assemble a compelling and representative collection of Foucault's written and spoken words outside those included in his books.

Foucault died on June 25, 1984, at age fifty-seven, of AIDS, just days after receiving the first reviews of the second and third volumes of *The History of Sexuality* in the hospital. A year previous to his death, when he was showing no signs of illness, he had written a letter indicating that he wanted no posthumous publications; through the course of complex negotiations between those legally responsible to him, intellectually engaged with him, and emotionally close to him, it was decided that this letter constituted his will. He left behind, as far as we know, no cache of unpublished texts; we must conclude, then, that his papers were "in order." Ten years later, Editions Gallimard published *Dits et écrits*, well over three thousand pages of texts, organized chronologically. The editors, Daniel Defert and François Ewald, sought to collect all Foucault's published texts (his prefaces, introductions, presentations, interviews, articles, interventions, lectures, and so on) not included in his books. We have made a selection, eliminating overlapping or repetition of different versions of similar materials.

Likewise, a number of the lectures and courses will in time be published separately in English.

What we have included in these three volumes are the writings that seemed to us central to the evolution of Foucault's thought. We have organized them thematically. Selecting from this corpus was a formidable responsibility that proved to be a challenge and a pleasure. Many of these texts were previously unavailable in English. In broad lines, the organization of the series follows one proposed by Foucault himself when he wrote: "My objective has been to create a history of the different modes by which, in our culture, human beings are made subjects. My work has dealt with three modes of objectification which transform human beings into subjects."[2] In Volume One, following his course summaries from the Collège de France, which provide a powerful synoptic view of his many unfinished projects, the texts address "the way a human being turns him- or herself into a subject."[3] Volume Two is organized around Foucault's analysis of "the modes of inquiry which try to give themselves the status of the sciences."[4] Science, for Foucault, was a domain of practices constitutive of experience as well as of knowledge. Consequently, this volume treats the diverse modes of representations, of signs, and of discourse. Finally, Volume Three contains texts treating "the objectivizing of the subject in dividing practices,"[5] or, more generally, power relations.

Paul Rabinow

NOTES

1 Foucault, "Des Travaux," in *Dits et écrits* (Paris: Gallimard, 1994), vol. 4, p. 367.

2 Foucault, "The Subject and Power," in *Michel Foucault: Beyond Structuralism and Hermeneutics*, ed. Hubert Dreyfus and Paul Rabinow (2d ed., Chicago: University of Chicago Press, 1983), p. 208.

3 Ibid.

4 Ibid.

5 Ibid.

INTRODUCTION

Who, or what, is Michel Foucault? The possibilities already seem endless: structuralist, idealist, neoconservative, post-structuralist, antihumanist, irrationalist, radical relativist, theorist of power, missionary of transgression, aestheticist, dying man, saint, or, if nothing else, "postmodern." But, in fact, the most accurate label may simply be "Foucauldean." In accord with the precedent that Paul Rabinow set in his introduction to the first volume of this series, I will try to present the Foucauldean within those horizons immanent in Foucault's own writings: in his own puzzlings and assertions, his own speculations, his own references and allusions to other writers and other texts, to objects and events.

The papers and interviews included in this volume have been selected with this aim in mind. Spanning virtually all of Foucault's career, they reveal the remarkable scope of his philosophical attention, which ranges over painting and music, architecture and film, literature and historiography, mathematics and linguistics, the life sciences and the behavioral sciences; over ancient Greece, the European Renaissance, the Enlightenment (or "Classical age"), the Romantic period, the early (and the late) twentieth century. They reveal his most enduring philosophical "interlocutors," past and present: Plato and G. W. F. Hegel, whom he consistently opposed; Immanuel Kant, whom he both resisted and admired; Friedrich Nietzsche and Gilles Deleuze, neither of whom he could wholly embrace but both of whom provided him with critical and conceptual examples and important tools; and Georges Canguilhem, his mentor. The first volume of this series is devoted to Foucault's treatment of ethical action; the third will be devoted to his treatment of power relations and modes of domination. This, the second, volume brings together a more abstract collection of postulates and positions which informs Foucault's engagement and concern with ethics and power alike. Accordingly, some of the writings included here focus on madness and the shifting normative articulation of the boundary between reason and unreason, between valid and invalid experience, between normal and abnormal behavior. Others focus on the self, or "subject," and its shifting sociocultural constitution. Many more focus on knowledge and the shifting historical configuration of the practices of speculation and research thought, in the past or in the present, to produce truth.

Last but by no means least are a few of Foucault's retrospective reflections on his own work. The essay entitled "Foucault" (see pp. 459–63)[1] – extracted from an early version of what would become the preface to volume two of *The History of Sexuality*, submitted for publication in an edition in the French *Dictionary of Philosophers*, and signed pseudonymously "Maurice Florence" – is of special note for its clarity. It describes Foucault, its author, as belonging to the "critical tradition" of such philosophers as Immanuel Kant, and presents his project as a "critical history of thought." That project has two guiding questions. The first: At any historical moment, what kinds of conditions come into play in determining that a particular subject is the legitimate executor of a certain kind of knowledge? The second: At any historical moment, what conditions come into play in determining that a particular object is the appropriate object of a particular kind of knowledge? These are general questions, but Foucault declared that he was always interested only in specific sectors of the broader field of which they might be posed. His interest lies in those sectors where the subject, the bearer and executor, of a certain kind of knowledge is also posited as the object of that very same kind of knowledge. Hence his explorations of the "human sciences" and, later, his investigations of the history of ethics.

Foucault read himself quite accurately. Yet it is also worth noting that – in "Foucault," at least – he only alludes to the great number of twists and turns that even such a "restricted" project had taken, the conceptual revisions and methodological reworkings it underwent in its two decades. It might finally be noted that "Foucault" makes no mention whatever of its author's many investigations into avant-gardist art. Those investigations, to which I shall shortly turn, are intimately related to Foucault's project, but his omission of them is not a matter of simple oversight. Although they may not have been an integral part of what the project had become, they nevertheless were its "ontological preliminary." Or, more simply, they formed an inquiry into the very nature, the very being, of thought, but of thought before, or beyond – or, better, outside – "the subject."

AISTHĒSIS AND EXPRESSIBILITY

Chronologically preliminary as well: Foucault wrote his most sustained essays on literature and other "works of imagination" very early in his career, between 1962 and 1969. In 1966 he published *Les Mots et les choses*, which opens with a celebrated analysis of Velásquez's *Las Meninas*.[2] This book includes the earliest version of his well-known essay on René Magritte (see pp. 187-203), which appeared in 1968. Yet, for all the historical and generic range of the examples on which he draws, Foucault developed his early ontological resolutions most fully through his treatment of late nineteenth-century and early twentieth-century avant-gardist literature. In 1963 he published a monograph on the French experimental novelist Raymond Roussel.[3] For the first time in 1964 he participated in several literary colloquia, most of which included one or more of the leading members of the emerging elite associated with Philippe Sollers and the journal *Tel quel*.[4] He was not in search of beauty: he was not an aesthetician but a student of what the ancient Greeks called *aisthēsis*, "feeling," "experience," "felt experience." In the works of Roussel (see pp. 21-32), in the Surrealists (see pp. 123-35 and 171-74), in Georges Bataille (see pp. 69-87) and in Maurice Blanchot (see pp. 147-69) among others, he finds an obscure but articulate engagement with experiences that many modern philosophies of *aisthēsis* would prefer to ignore. It was, for him, the precedent and the inspiration for the first and one of the most urgent aims of his enterprise: a critique of the strictures, the exclusions, and the errors of what he often calls "humanism"—the doctrine that, behind history or beyond it, looms the singular nature or the singular essence of the human subject.[5]

It would be misleading to ascribe even to the early Foucault the intent to "transcend" either humanism or its ponderous subject. The avant-garde itself taught Foucault less about transcendence than about its limits. Among the most instructive of the literary characters he discerned, in one version or another, in the work of such writers as Roussel, Bataille, Gustave Flaubert,[6] Blanchot, Jorge-Luis Borges,[7] and Alain Robbe-Grillet,[8] is that of the latter-day Scheherazade. Like its predecessor, this character too is a spinner of tales: it tells tales in order to avoid confronting the intolerable, to defer the moment of its own destruction or death. It does not however, seek merely to add to what it has already composed. Its goal is less exhausting, if no less futile—to construct tales the last words of which are also the first, to tell stories that repeat and recount themselves over and over, ad infinitum (see pp. 91–92). This is one of the hallmarks of a literature that Foucault follows Marthe Robert in characterizing as "a certain relation to self, complex, multilateral, simultaneous, in which the fact of coming after (of being new) cannot at all be reduced to the linear law of succession."[9] It suggests, first, "an ontology of literature" for which Flaubert's infinite library is an apt metaphor (see pp. 103–122), and for which processes of doubling, or reiteration, and of recursion are very much of the literal essence (pp. 92–93).

Such an ontology must be antimimetic: it must run counter to every effort, from that found in Plato's *Republic* onward, to reduce the essence of literature to that of an "imitation of the real."[10] Notwithstanding the importance it seems to assign to the horror of death, it must also run counter to any attempt to locate the source of literature in the emotions. For the Rousseau of *La nouvelle Héloïse*, fiction has its cause in raw desire. It is the refined, the cultivated articulation of a primal cry of pain, of lust, of longing.[11] For Foucault, fiction has multiple and heterogeneous causes; it serves multiple and heterogeneous purposes. Among other things, it can be a means of intellectually and emotionally deferring the writer's encounter with his or her own finitude. Neither the causes nor the functions of fiction, though, reveal its being as clearly as the opposite, the fundamental *alter*, against which it stands. Questions of motive aside, the presence of fiction is the absence of death.[12] Its presence fills, or seeks to fill, a horrible expressive vacuum.

Fiction, a domain constituted against that vacuum, that "void,"[13] has usually counted among its "fundamental categories" that of the "speaking subject."[14] Beginning with the works of Sade, Foucault detected another category developing, which would need two centuries to mature. It denotes not an entity but a process, which Foucault initially names "thinking speech."[15] It informs an array of avant-gardist themes and expressive techniques. Death is its structural and logical *alter*, and it is a category of subjectivity and of experience; yet its difference lies in its lack of further strictures, especially those which might be imposed by any subject—any personage or personality—whether transcendental or historical. Unlike the Cartesian *cogito* ("I think"), thinking speech is manifest only as language: it owes its freedom to the structural permissiveness of language, but it has no existence outside of language itself. True, it appears in the guise of an "I" who speaks in and through the fiction of such writers as Blanchot (see pp. 147–48), but it is not an "author"–this presumptive character to whom interpreters appeal in arguing for the distinctive spirit or intention of a work.[16] It is not a self: Descartes's "I" is referential, but the "I" who speaks in and through Blanchot's fiction is only a placeholder. This "I" serves as an index for the expression and exploration of experiences that put our own ontological integrity–our "subjecthood"–into question or carry us beyond its limits. Only the "I speak" of fiction can serve as the index for thinking about our ontological "outside" (pp. 149–50).

Blanchot, for his part, is Foucault's definitive avant-gardist. More than a mere contributor or one among many "witnesses," Blanchot is "the real presence, absolutely distant, shimmering, invisible, the necessary destiny, the inevitable law, the calm, infinite, measured strength" of "thought of the outside," and so of fiction itself (p. 151). Foucault, crediting Blanchot with making discourse about fiction possible, describes him as "the last writer,"[17] a literary consummation and literary summum. Blanchot is a master at the construction of simulacra–the "copies without original" that Foucault sees as among the avant-garde's most subversive weapons[18]–and the definitive cartographer of fictional space. He systematically conflates genres and conflates "fiction" with philosophical "reflection." His novels are critical; his criticism narrative and novelistic (p. 154). He makes systematic–if never a dialectical–use of negation and contradiction (p. 152). His characters are often curiously absent, either soon to come or recently departed. They speak, but without stable voices or identities (pp. 165–67). The arena in which they act is the "equivocal hollow" of a dénouement always in the offing, of an origin forever lost (p. 154). The discursive space they inhabit has no end, no truth, no mask, no affirmation: it is "free of every center, unfettered to any native soil." It has no subjects: it is the ontological outside, and it permits movement in only a single direction, further out (p. 153).

Is this a space of transcendence? Far from it. It is the singular locus that allows the expression of all those experiences emanating from, or tending toward, self-dissolution. In Nietzsche, Foucault suggests, it is the space of "force" (p. 154). In Roussel, it is the space of the fantasy of self-annihilation and the erosive process of dying. In Bataille, it is the space of the transgression of the boundaries of the self in erotic transport. In Blanchot, it is the space of "attraction":

> It is necessary to be clear about what the word designates: "attraction," as Blanchot means it, does not depend upon any charm. Nor does it break one's solitude or found any positive communication. To be attracted is not to be beckoned by the allure of the exterior; it is rather to suffer [*éprouver*] – in emptiness and in destitution – the presence of the outside and . . . the fact that one is irremediably outside the outside. Far from calling on interiority to draw close to another, attraction makes it imperiously manifest that the outside is there, open, without depth, without protection or reserve . . . but that one cannot gain access to that opening. . . . (p. 154)

Thus, two ancient figures reemerge and become entrenched in Blanchot's oeuvre. The first is that of the Sirens, "the elusive and forbidden form of the alluring voice" (p. 160). The other is Eurydice, whose lover's hungry gaze would spell her eternal inaccessibility, her eternal condemnation to the underworld (pp. 161–62). They are all bitter reminders that transcendence must remain always out of reach.

This attraction is not tantamount to an enduring and unrequited longing. Instead, it is a single-minded condition, a state of fixation or obsession, the inextricable companion of "negligence." Attracted, the self cannot bother to maintain either appearances or its own boundaries. Attracted (and so, distracted) the self inevitably exceeds itself and the boundaries of the ordinary world – its meanings and laws and orders. Like Bataille's fictional space, Blanchot's is also a space of "transgression" (pp. 157–58). Within the two spaces, however, transgression is not at all the same. Bataille pushes Foucault toward paradox:

> [D]oes transgression not exhaust its nature when it violates the limit, being nothing beyond this point in time? And this point, this curious intersection of beings that do not exist outside it but totally exchange what they are within it – is it not also everything that overflows from it on all sides? It serves as a glorification of what it excludes: the limit opens violently onto the limitless, finds itself suddenly carried away by the content it had rejected, and fulfilled by this alien plenitude that invades it to the very core of its being. (p. 73)

With Blanchot, the paradox disappears. His dramatis personae may both obey and violate "public decrees," but they remain uniformly distant from "the law" (pp. 157–58). In Blanchot, law is not the "internal principle or prescription of conduct, but rather the outside that envelops it." It is always "invisible" (p. 158) and unattainable. Transgression has the same status – is indeed the structural and functional equivalent – of attraction itself. It is a disposition or a reaching-out that must remain unfulfilled.

In 1964 Foucault remarked on "the general form of transgression of which madness has for centuries been the visible face."[19] Yet he never mentions the relation between transgression and madness, or even madness at all, in his essay on Blanchot. This apparent omission, if surprising at first notice, already has its rationale in Foucault's doctoral dissertation – submitted in 1958, published in French in 1961, and published much abridged in English in 1965 as *Madness and Civilization*: "There is no madness except as the final instance of the work of art – the work endlessly drives madness to its limits; *where there is a work of art, there is no madness;* and yet madness is contemporary with the work of art, since it inaugurates its time of truth."[20] This phrasing is intentionally paradoxical, yet it has the status of an interpretive commandment. Where there is a work, there is no madness; where there is madness, there is no oeuvre: Foucault reiterates this at the conclusion of his introduction to an edition of Jean-Jacques Rousseau's *Dialogues*, published in 1962 (pp. 50–51). He reiterates it again in a favorable review of Jean Laplanche's *Hölderlin et la question du père* (see p. 18). With it, he summarizes his objectives to any interpretive approach that pretends to reveal or explicate the madness in or of any oeuvre, work of imagination, or work of thought. In 1964, offering a rare homage to Freud, Foucault offered this rationale:

> It will be necessary one day to pay this justice to Freud: he did not make a madness *speak* that had, for centuries, precisely been a language (excluded language, loquacious inanity, speech flowing indefinitely outside of the reflective silence of reason). On the contrary, he emptied out the unreasonable Logos. He dried it up. He made words go back to their source – to this blank [*blanche*] region of self-implication in which nothing is said.[21]

As every Scheherazade somehow knows, death is the experiential *alter* of thinking speech. "Madness" is Foucault's designation of the semiological and performative *alter* of thinking speech: madness says, it communicates nothing; it does nothing except "open an empty reserve [*réserve lacunaire*], which indicates the hollow in which language and speech implicate one another [and] are formed, the one out of the other. . . ."[22]

AISTHĒSIS AND ITS LIMITS

In several of the texts included in this volume Foucault notes that the literary quest for experiential and expressive frontiers—a mission of discovery that leads beyond referentiality, beyond imitation, beyond "reason," beyond the established generic bounds of disciplined invention, to the edges of coherence and interpretability just short of madness[23]—has come at a considerable cost: it has obliged literature to share some portion of the fate of madness itself. Even before the advent of industrial capitalism, madness held the status of "excluded speech."[24] By the nineteenth century, it took on an even more singular status as the purest negation of an ascendant practical logic of production and productivity.[25] It became a veritable sickness, a quintessentially disorderly incapacity that demanded new technologies of containment and a new legion of specialists dedicated to specifying its causes, symptomatologies, and cure.[26] Throughout this period, literature always had greater liberty and commanded greater epistemic respect. But with its avant-gardist pioneers, it gradually infiltrated epistemic regions that differed from those of madness only in degree, but not in kind; though not altogether "invalid," avant-gardist literature did come to attract an ever-greater number of its own psychoanalysts. It came to seem increasingly "symptomatic"; and, with madness, it increasingly was relegated to the "neutral space" (p. 149) of the most remote epistemic margins.

Foucault's study of those margins has the character of an epistemological rehabilitation; even more, though, it has the character of ontological reconnaissance. It explores those far reaches of expression which hold the greatest potential to illuminate the nature of thought, because they express nothing but thought. The study owes its very possibility to a particularly portentous event—the beginnings of the liberation of madness from its long-standing conflation with "mental illness," and the beginnings of the dissolution of the long-standing "anthropological unity" from which the bond between madness and mental illness had, for at least two centuries, derived much of its strength.[27] No longer definitively pathological, madness might at last be seen as purely psychical. Foucault, however, made few predictions as to what experiential or expressive epiphanies might lie ahead. The most pivotal conclusion he was willing to draw rests on the established example of both madness and the literary avant-garde. It is skeptical in tenor: finding no good reason to believe that the boundary between madness (as thoughtless speech or as the unspeakable) and thinking speech (or expressible experience) is anything but historically contingent and historically variable, he was dubious not only of Kant's analytic but of any similarly finitistic analytic that purports to resolve the "necessary conditions of any possible experience" without having every possible experience at its disposal. Hence his resistance to phenomenology from Edmund Husserl through Jean-Paul Sartre and Maurice Merleau-Ponty.[28] Even for the early Foucault, the necessary conditions of any possible experience already look far less stringent than what Kant and his successors presumed them to be; they look likely to be determinable only at infinity (and so, essentially indeterminable).

If the individual human consciousness, which is necessarily finite, is thus unlikely to provide a structurally adequate foundation for a philosophy of thought, it is even less likely to serve as an adequate repository of thought itself. Foucault extracts his alternative from Flaubert among many others: language, not consciousness, is at once the matrix of thought and its potentially infinite storehouse.[29] Yet what of thought as a process, as an event? In 1969 Foucault published *The Archaeology of Knowledge*, a long, somewhat troubled, but not altogether unsuccessful attempt to establish the co-determinacy of those "discursive events" he would call *énoncés*–"statements" or "pronouncements"–and the discursive formations that comprise them. In 1970 he appeared to strike an ontological alliance with the premier French philosopher of events–his friend and contemporary, Gilles Deleuze. Stress "appears": Foucault's brief review of two of Deleuze's treatises has become famous for its speculation that "perhaps one day, the century will be known as Deleuzian" (p. 343). Understood in this way, the speculation is as awkward in French as it is in English. It is, in fact, a *double entendre*, and it reads and translates more elegantly in its covert signification: "Some day, the in-crowd will be Deleuzian."[30] It is not a profession of full discipleship. However, the review provides an important bridge between Foucault's aesthetics and the ethics he later developed, by providing an important reminder of the conceptual and practical expanse separating them: though dense and difficult, it asserts clearly enough two principles that Deleuze and Foucault shared. The first establishes the general ontological priority of the event over the object; the second establishes the specific ontological priority of thought as an event over thought as *any* structure or system—notably over structures and systems of humanist design.

Foucault's Deleuze is a "reverse Platonist" (p. 344): he opens the door to all the alleged "imitations" and all the alleged "imitators" that Plato so distrusted. Plato urges the thinker to ascend from the world of transitory "appearance" to a sublime world of eternal and perfect Forms;[31] Deleuze urges the thinker to look down. He subverts Plato with his meticulous scrutiny of "a crop of hair or the dirt under its fingernails" (p. 346). He "perverts" Plato in inclining toward "the Sophists' spitefulness, the unmannerly gestures of the Cynics, the arguments of the Stoics, and the fluttering chimeras of Epicurus." He makes us want to read that most unmannerly of Cynics, Diogenes Laërtes. Deleuze is a philosopher of "all this swarming of the impalpable," a philosopher of emanations and phantasms that "topologize the materiality of the body." He escapes "the dilemmas of truth and falsehood and of being and nonbeing," and lets his phantasms "conduct their dance . . . act out their mime, as 'extrabeings'" (pp. 346–47). Deleuze teaches us how to think about the "pure event," and about the relation between the pure event and the phantasm. The former has no extension, either in space or in time; the latter is the event "in play," contracted or expanded to fit the scale, the pace, and the import of the story of which it is part.

Though Deleuze's inspirations include Spinoza, most analytical philosophers would probably see him as arguing less for Spinoza's "psychophysical parallelism" than for an ontology grounded exclusively in the incorporeal—and so they would label him a "mentalist."[32] Deleuze may or may not be a mentalist, but he certainly recognized in his own turn that Foucault, however preoccupied with the self-referential mechanisms of fiction or the self-constructive mechanisms of discourse, is neither a Kantian nor a mentalist. Deleuze's formidable *Foucault* has its faults,[33] but it does have the virtue of underscoring that Foucault always regards the psyche as being in, and of, a wider world. Nor is the Foucauldean psyche simply

passive: it is both the partial effect and the partial cause of its sur-
roundings. And it is both the partial effect and the partial cause of
certain aspects of itself.

However, Foucault finds in Deleuze terms immediately adequate to
define only the latter of the psyche's dynamics, its production and
reproduction of itself.[34] The pure event is "the thought," or "the object
of thought" [*le pensé*]; the phantasm is "thought" [*la pensée*]. In order
to grasp both their difference and their symbiosis, Foucault proposes
that

> we must conceptualize not the synthesizing and synthesized subject but
> rather a certain insurmountable fissure. Moreover, we must conceptu-
> alize a series, without any original anchor, of simulacra, idols, and
> phantasms which, in the temporal duality in which they are formed are
> always the two sides of the fissure from which they are made signs and
> are put in place as signs. The fissure of the I and series of signifying
> points do not form a unity that permits thought to be both subject and
> object, but they are themselves the event of thought [*la pensée*] and
> the incorporeality of what is thought [*le pensé*], the object of thought
> [*le pensé*] as a problem (a multiplicity of dispersed points) and thought
> [*la pensée*] as mime (repetition without a model). (pp. 353–54)

There is no unity of subject and object, nor possibility of that sort of
transcendence. What Deleuze instead allows Foucault to add to the
results of his aesthetic investigations is the specification of a psychic
"radical"—not yet another alter of thought, not its origin or first principle, but its productive and reproductive "moment." The ancient
Greeks knew that moment as an *aporia*–a "difficulty," or more literally, a thing that "stops us in our tracks." Foucault identifies it here as
the "object of thought," and that object as a *problem*.

Deleuze further allows Foucault to supplement, and to begin to
reorient, the conceptual apparatus out of which he had recently constructed his archaeology. Consider one of the most indispensable elements of that apparatus, the "archive":

> Instead of seeing, on the great mythical book of history, lines of words
> that translate in visible characters thoughts that were formed in some
> other time and place, we have, in the density of discursive practices,
> systems that establish statements as events (with their own conditions
> and domain of appearance) and things (with their own possibility and

XXII   *Introduction*

field of use) . . . all these systems of statements (whether of events or things) . . . [are] the archive.[35]

In *The Archaeology of Knowledge* Foucault objects that too many historians have privileged grand and conventional notions such as "evolution" or "development," "the spirit of an age" or the "mentality" of a civilizational "tradition." These privileges all too often signal an overemphasis on historical continuity at the expense of discontinuity and disruption, and methodological devaluation of the event itself.[36] However, the concept of the archive is open itself to very much the same objection: it, too, renders events subordinate to the "systems" of which they are a part. The concept of the object of thought as problem in fact holds the potential to effect an inversion of that subordination; but as a concept only of the dynamics of *aisthēsis*, and only of the seemingly vacant Deleuzean "point," it remains of quite limited analytical use. It demands both expansion and extension. Five years passed before, suitably altered, it began to reappear in Foucault's writings as "problematization."[37] Another five years passed before it became the conceptual centerpiece of his twin investigations of ethics and governmentality. In the interim, Foucault largely left behind his investigations of the thought of the outside in order to clarify, for his growing audience (and also for himself), those other dynamics of the psyche, within which limits can be quite palpable, and within which transgression is always also moral. Such were what he came to call the dynamics of "subjectivation," of thought very much in, and of, a wider world of regimes that would marshal it and of wills that would require of it not what it might inherently afford—the truth—but rather what it might be taxed to offer up, "knowledge."

METHOD AND MAN

For Foucault as for Ludwig Wittgenstein, language is never private, but its public "games" are irreducibly plural in form and function.[38] Between those discourses fashioned sheerly for the expression of experience and those fashioned for the production of knowledge, there is little common ground. The latter traffic in "facts." Between facts and knowledge, between knowledge and truth, Foucault clearly presumed a systematic relation. He did not, however, have a "theory" of knowledge; he never offered an account of the necessary and sufficient conditions for knowledge. As he said in a 1981 interview: "I'm not an analytical philosopher. Nobody's perfect."[59] If pressed, he might at least have agreed with those analytical philosophers who argue that knowledge is always defeasible, that claims to know perfectly justifiable in one context might turn out to be both unjustified and false in another. Any finitistic theory of knowledge would, for Foucault, in any case require a prioris. If valid at all, its validity could only be normative.

The starting point of Foucault's investigation of discursive and extradiscursive knowledge-producing practices is not normative; instead, it is descriptive and interpretive. Its potential domain comprises all those practices, past and present, which have been proposed or presumed to systematically generate the truth: put simply, it potentially includes all such "games of truth." Foucault is too often read as a relentless epistemological relativist, a disbeliever in the truth—which is odd, because he is entirely prepared to take a great many would-be purveyors of truth more or less at their word. In his 1968 "Response" to the Paris Epistemology Circle (see pp. 297–333), as in *The Archaeology of Knowledge*, he specifies four general criteria that mark the degree of systematicity and the objective epistemic authority of any game of truth. Between the "Response" and the *Archaeology*, his terms differ, but the criteria remain constant. Citing the latter text:

> The moment at which a discursive practice achieves individuality and autonomy, the moment therefore at which a single system for the formation of statements is put into operation, or the moment at which this system is transformed, might be called the *threshold of positivity*. When, in the operation of a discursive formation, a group of statements is articulated, claims to validate (even if unsuccessfully) norms of verification and coherence, and when it exercises a dominant function (as a model, a critique, or a verification) over knowledge, we will say that the discursive formation crosses a *threshold of epistemologization*. When the epistemological figure thus outlined obeys a number of formal criteria, when its statements comply not only with archaeological rules of formation, but also with certain laws for the construction of propositions . . . it has crossed a *threshold of scientificity*. And when this scientific discourse is able, in turn, to define the axioms necessary to it, the propositional structures that are legitimate to it, and the transformations that it accepts, when it is thus able, taking itself as a starting-point, to deploy the formal edifice that it constitutes . . . it has crossed the *threshold of formalization*.[40]

Foucault sees these criteria as indices of degrees of systematicity. His use of them highlights "levels, thresholds, and ruptures" between *and* within discursive practices—a much more complex and qualitatively ambiguous motility than Thomas Kuhn's distinction between "revolutionary" and "normal" science can capture.[41] Foucault's use of these criteria also highlights the temporal irregularity of the constitution of the scientific domain: in his judgment, only a single science—mathematics—has ever crossed all four thresholds simultaneously. The history of mathematics can thus be a history of an "ideality" which "has been questioned only to be repeated and purified."[42] The history of all other sciences, from physics to psychopathology, must at least as much be a history of "gropings and failures" as of resounding or stable success.[43]

Yet the historian should not treat mathematics as either a normative or a diagnostic model: "if one takes the establishment of mathematical discourse as a prototype for the birth and development of all the other sciences, one runs the risk of homogenizing all the unique forms of historicity, of reducing to the authority of a single rupture all the different thresholds that a discursive practice may cross, and reproducing endlessly, at every moment in time, the question of origin: the rights of historico-transcendental analysis would thus be reinstated."[44] The ontologist should also heed the warning: if relatively few discursive practices have crossed all four thresholds even at present, not all should ever be expected to cross any more than the first two or three. The "fault" of these inevitably less formal approaches might lie not only with their (relative lack of) internal resolution but also with the constitution of their objects. Numbers are one sort of thing; the psyche, and its history, are quite another. For Foucault, as for Wilhelm Dilthey and Hans-Georg Gadamer, knowledge is plural, at least in part because being is itself plural.[45]

In the "Response," Foucault announced his debt to an elder generation of historians of philosophy and of science who refused to privilege continuity over "rupture"—Gaston Bachelard, Martial Gueroult, and Georges Canguilhem (p. 299). Foucault's rejection of historical continualism may recall his own anti-Kantian aesthetics but his concern in the "Response" is not with the self-productive psyche alone: "The desire to make historical analysis the discourse of continuity, and make human consciousness the originating subject of all knowledge and all practice, are two faces of one and the same system of thought. Time is conceived in terms of totalization, and revolution never as anything but a coming to consciousness [*prise de conscience*]" (p. 301). Foucault called for the historiography of the psyche to disburden itself of its enchantment with the originary subject and all of its conventional proxies, from "tradition" and "mentality" to "evolution" and the "spirit of an age [*époque*]" (pp. 302-3). He also called for the renunciation of historicism, for which every beginning is merely apparent, and all manifest discourse secretly based upon an "already said" (p. 305). The psyche repeats itself only at infinity; so, too, its history. There can be no a priori delimitation of the possible variety of its multiple trains.[46]

On ontological grounds alone, then, one would have to conclude that the historiographer could never be confident of being able to specify every last axiom necessary to his or her practice, and historiography never confidently be able to cross Foucault's fourth threshold, the threshold of formalization. At best, it might aspire to cross the threshold of scientificity. But should it aspire to cross even that? The question certainly troubled Foucault throughout his career, not least because most of the inquiries that occupied him from about 1966 forward are themselves historiographic in character. No less troubling is the question of history's epistemological status, the epistemological authority it commands. He posed both questions to himself in dialogue with himself at the conclusion of *The Archaeology*. His answers are quite preliminary; they are also subtle. Their subtlety plays out in his usage not only of *histoire archéologique* and *épistème* but of two other terms—*connaissance* and *savoir*—whose ambiguities are easily lost under the single English rubric of "knowledge."

"What archaeology tries to describe," Foucault writes, "is not the specific structure of science, but the very different domain of *knowledge* [*savoir*]."[47] His *histoire archéologique*—"archaeological history"—has as its "point of attack the threshold of epistemologization—the point of cleavage between discursive formations defined by their positivity and epistemological figures that are not necessarily all sciences (and which may never, in fact, succeed in becoming sciences)." At this level," he adds, "scientificity does not serve as a norm . . . what one is trying to uncover are discursive practices insofar as they give rise to a corpus of knowledge [*savoir*], in so far as they assume the status and role of a science."[48] Such a corpus is made up—largely if not exclusively—of that typically scattered field of what Foucault calls a discourse.[49] Discourses are neither less nor more orderly than the conventional archaeological "site"; they may be rather "basic." They should not, however, be confused either with some "ordinary language" or with the ordinary language of everyday experience. They are, rather, that particular linguistic matrix which allows the archaeological historian to "reveal, between positivities, knowledge [*savoir*], epistemological figures, and sciences, a whole set of differences, relations, gaps, independences, autonomies, and the way in which they articulate their own historicities on one another."[50] Hence the possibility of the analysis of an *épistème*, an "episteme":

> the total set of relations that unite, at a given period, the discursive practices that give rise to epistemological figures, sciences, and possibly formalized systems. . . . The episteme is not a form of knowledge [*connaissance*] or type of rationality which, crossing the boundaries of the most varied sciences, manifests the sovereign unity of a subject, a spirit, or a period; it is the totality of relations that can be discovered, for a given period, between the sciences when one analyzes them at the level of discursive regularities.[51]

Although the episteme constrains discourse, it is always discursively open. It is not some "system of postulates that governs all the branches of knowledge [*connaissance*]."[52] It is, rather, "a constantly moving set of articulations, shifts, and coincidences that are established only to give rise to others."[53]

"Archaeological history" and the "episteme" belong to Foucault's technical vocabulary. *Savoir* and *connaissance* take on technical nuances of their own (though these nuances are never at great variance with ordinary French). *Savoir* is at once a verbal and a nominal form—"to know" as well as "knowledge." Its general sense is perhaps that of "awareness" or "cognizance" (compare the English "savvy"). One might, in this sense, know the Pythagorean theorem or the time of day, know that Beijing is in China or that the hydrogen atom has only a single electron, know of a continent called "Asia" or a diagram called the "periodic table," know of someone that she is kind or an heiress, know about a certain item of news, about a theory, about a rumor. *Savoir* can be quite abstract, or it can be quite concrete: one might know that a certain flower is fragrant from having smelled it. Such knowledge is not genuine if its object is nonexistent or false. It need not, however, be grounded in any principle. It need not be the product of a reliable method or a reliable pedagogy. It cannot be completely without justification, but its justification does not need to be precise or definitive. It can fall far short of proof. Hence, for Foucault, the general domain of *savoir*: a domain not of things known but of things to be known, one way or another, with less or with greater rigor from one instance to the next. Within such a general domain, there may be (and typically are) many subdivisions, many *savoirs*, each the constellation of a particular discursive practice, however scientific it may or may not be.

The verbal form of *connaissance* is *connaître*. Both are linked to the general concept that might best be rendered in English as "acquaintance." Thus one makes the acquaintance of (*fait la connaissance de*) or is acquainted with (*connaît*) another person. One is acquainted with, familiar with, a museum to which one has paid two or three visits. One is familiar with, perhaps even well versed in, Baroque painting (recall the "connoisseur") or economics or Boolean algebra. One has learned, and so knows, Mandarin or Sanskrit. One has learned, perhaps memorized, and so knows how to play Mozart's Sonata in C on the piano. *Connaissance* and *connaître* are ambiguous in French in very much the same way that "acquaintance" and "to be acquainted with" are ambiguous in English. They may signify a relatively superficial mode of knowledge, grounded in incomplete information or incomplete research, "knowledge" of minimal degree. But this knowledge might always be enriched; acquaintance might be cultivated and transformed into intimacy, into expertise. Hence the other significative side of both terms: *connaissance* can sometimes only be translated as "cognition," sometimes only as "learning," and its plural sometimes only as "a body of learning," indeed sometimes only as "expertise." *Connaître* sometimes demands translation as "to comprehend" or "to have mastered." Foucault's more technical usage of both of these terms always favors this latter side; it consistently evokes modes of knowledge tied to highly developed apparatuses of justification and modes of competence supported by well-crystallized apparatuses of "background training." In his more technical usage, *connaissance* always has its closest affinities with science. In his "Response," Foucault thus locates *savoir* "between" experience and science. "*Connaissance*," in contrast, "confers on experience the charge of giving an account of the effective existence of science. . . . The

thematic of understanding [*connaissance*] is tantamount to a denegation of knowledge [*savoir*]" (p. 332).

How close are *connaissance* and archaeological history? The imaginary interlocutor at the conclusion of *The Archaeology* remarks: "one
must at least deduce that your archaeology is not a science. . . . Yet
another of those discourses that would like to be taken as a discipline
still in its early stages, no doubt; which gives their authors the double
advantage of not having to establish their explicit, rigorous scientificity, and of opening up for it a future generality that frees it from the
hazards of its birth."[54] Foucault does not reject the accusation or pretend to be plying a "science." He does not expect archaeological history ever to attain scientificity.[55] What he claims for it, instead, is an
established domain of positivity: "it is related to the sciences that are
already constituted and establish their norms in the knowledge
[*savoir*] archaeologically described; for the archaeological enterprise,
these sciences are so many *science-objects*."[56] He suggests that it can
appeal to "generative grammar" for some at least of its analytical
standards.[57] He points to "social formations" as those "correlative
spaces" in which it might seek controls for, and the corroboration of,
at least some of its results. Finally, he proposes that it might some day
be able to call upon a "general theory of productions" as its own "enveloping theory."[58] Archaeology is neither a science nor a guarantor
of *connaissance*; it can only offer *savoir*; but it might some day be able
to cross the threshold of epistemologization, to call a regulative epistemological figure its own.

Could a general theory of productions, a general theory of how
historical (and psychic) differences are made, be the ultimate epistemological figure not just of archaeological history but also of historiography as a whole? Foucault does not say so; the tentative tone of his
conclusion to *The Archaeology* does not suggest that he encourages
any such inference. But he may be inclined toward the position all the
same. What form would a theory of productions take? Again, he does
not say, but surely it cannot be yet another transcendentalism, yet
another specification of the necessary and sufficient conditions either
of historical process or of historical events. He surely cannot expect it
even to take the form of a statistical or probabilistic modeling of such
conditions. Yet Foucault's venturing of the very idea of a general
theory of productions, which might at least postulate the necessary
(or, in their lieu, the sufficient) conditions of historical practice, or

postulate the general relation between discursive and extradiscursive practices, underscores his reluctance to adopt, even provisionally, any principle of the fundamental plurality or heterogeneity of historiographical diagnosis and historiographical method themselves. It underscores his central ambition, as historiographer and as methodologist, from *Madness and Civilization* through the first volume of *The History of Sexuality*: not merely to describe but to provide a corrective to the vast error that has its realization in the philosophy of the "constituting subject" (p. 437) and in "the human sciences," the sciences of "man."

ENVISIONING REVISION

In *Les Mots et les choses*, published in French in 1966 and translated into English four years later as *The Order of Things: An Archaeology of the Human Sciences*, Foucault argues that our "modern" conception of "man" is only some hundred and fifty years old. This new "man" is a being that makes the world, but it is also a creature, a being made from the world in which it lives. It is at once the subject of knowledge and the object within which the conditions of all possible knowledge lie.[59] It makes its philosophical appearance in the simultaneously transcendental and empirical analyses of Hegel's *Phenomenology of Spirit*.[60] It retains a central role in all those philosophical traditions to which Hegel is ancestral—in subsequent phenomenologies, but also in Marxism. It makes its scientific appearance when, in the early nineteenth century, "natural history becomes biology, when the analysis of wealth becomes economics, [and] when, above all, reflection upon language becomes philology."[61] In all these new sciences, "man" is an essentially finite being, an ephemeral expression of the laws of the various natural systems into which it is born and within which it is bound to die; but it is also a being who, for all its finitude, is somehow able to grasp its own nature, to comprehend all that it has ever been and all that it ever might be.[62]

"Man," in short, is a mystery. It is a being of paradoxes. It has, Foucault thinks, had its day. His conclusion to *The Order of Things* once again recalls what he has seen in Blanchot:

[T]he whole of the modern episteme . . . was bound up . . . with the shift of language towards objectivity, and with its reappearance in multiple form. If this same language is now emerging with greater and greater insistence in a unity that we ought to think but cannot as yet do so, is this not the sign that the whole of this configuration is now about to topple, and that man is in the process of perishing as the being of language continues to shine ever brighter upon our horizon?[63]

Foucault soon came to regret such grand and epochal pronouncements.[64] He never, however, abandoned his suspicion of either phenomenology or Marxism.[65] Though far from indicting all the discourses and practices that now constitute biology and economics and philology, he never abandoned his suspicion of any discourse or practice founded in a determinate axiomatics of "human nature." And he never abandoned the question that fiction might inspire but could never answer: "Does man really exist?"[66] Plainly, Foucault does not think so. But the question must then be: What has encouraged so many people to believe the contrary for so long?

That people should be in error is not itself odd. In a lengthy homage, Foucault credits Canguilhem with leading him to recognize, instead, that "life . . . is that which is capable of error" (p. 476). Error, in its turn, is generative of both "human thought and its history":

> The opposition of the true and the false, the values that are attributed to the one and the other, the power effects that different societies and different institutions link to that division – all this may be nothing but the most belated response to that possibility of error inherent in life. If the history of the sciences is discontinuous – that is, if it can be analyzed only as a series of "corrections," as a new distribution that never sets free, finally and forever, the terminal moment of truth – the reason, again, is that "error" constitutes not a neglect or a delay of the promised fulfillment but the dimension peculiar to the life of human beings and indispensable to the duration [*temps*] of the species. (p. 476)

Following Canguilhem, Foucault is not a pragmatist but a fallibilist, or better, a philosopher of fallibility.[67] The history of thought is a history of trials, an open-ended history of multiple visions and revisions, some more enduring than others.

A pragmatist might settle for an intellectualist analysis of how durable any particular vision or revision is, however much in error. Foucault is a much more complex "psychologist," and his treatment of the endurance of error is by no means limited to the pragmatist notation of the absence of any "stronger argument." In *The Archaeol-*

ogy, he already specified that dimension of his treatment which became central to his research through the seventies. He notes the "rarity" of statements, the considerable gap between the indefinite number of statements that might be generated within any discourse and the relatively few that actually end up constituting it. The gap evinces the "costliness" of such statements, the considerable capital that is required for their production and the price they accordingly bear. It evinces their "value," but a value that cannot be defined "by their truth." The value of statements resides, rather, in their presumptive truth, their presumptive authority, and so in their actual instrumental potential. In its rarity, the presumptively authoritative statement is "an asset—finite, limited, desirable, useful—that has its own rules of appearance, but also its own conditions of appropriation and operation; an asset that consequently, from the moment of its appearance (and not only in its 'practical applications'), poses the question of power; an asset that is, by nature, the object of a struggle, a political struggle."[68] Hence the rationale for a frankly functionalist investigation of the interaction of two separate forces: *pouvoir* and *savoir*, "power" and "knowledge."[69]

In a 1967 interview Foucault suggests that his archaeology "owes more to Nietzschean genealogy than to structuralism" (p. 294). Only in 1971, with "Nietzsche, Genealogy, History" (see pp. 369–91), did he further elaborate his debt, or perhaps *hint* would be more accurate. Here as elsewhere, it would be incautious to conflate his explication of another writer's position as in any sense a straightforward explication of his own. The essay on Nietzsche nevertheless marks another important turning of Foucauldean discourse—away from the archaeology of knowledge and toward a genealogy of "power–knowledge," as well as away from archaeological history and toward a history of the "dynastics of knowledge."[70] Genealogy remains a historiography of epistemic discontinuities, of epistemic ruptures; yet it introduces an additional dimension. It combines a diagnostics of the interior systematicity and structural productivity of discourses, of discursive formations, and of epistemes with a diagnostics of "descent": of "the accidents, the minute deviations—or conversely, the complete reversals—the errors, the false appraisals, and the faulty calculations that gave birth to those things which continue to exist and have value for us" (p. 374). It thus can reveal that "there is 'something altogether different' behind things, not a timeless and essential secret but the secret that they have no essence, or that their essence was fabricated in a piecemeal fashion from alien forms" (p. 371). It unmasks pretensions to "naturalness." It exposes the apparently simple as actually complex. It reveals that the things of history—historical things—are, at base, disparate (see p. 372). If archaeology attends to discursive practices, genealogy assumes a much broader vantage. It looks behind discursive practices to their extradiscursive setting, to the milieux from which they are excluded or in which their products are deployed. It looks not just for the descent of things but also for the emergence of the boundaries between them. What it confronts are "forces" and the "hazardous play of dominations" (p. 376). To aesthetic or archaeological analyses of the relations among forms, genealogy unites an analysis of those "relations of contrary forces" which constitute the actual stuff of history, actual events. What it finds are neither mechanisms nor final destinations. It instead finds chance, "the luck of the battle [*hasard de la lutte*]" (p. 381).

Foucault does not merely slip into prioritizing the system over the event in formulating his archaeology; he also imposes a severe phenomenological limit on it. Archaeology must always be a history of the past, because the archives available to us can only be past, can only be other than the one "within whose rules" we speak and which "gives to us what we can say."[71] At least by 1970, however, he began to recognize in his own past example an "ethnographic" strategy that might allow at least the outlines of the present to become clear. The historian may not be able to grasp the present in its totality. But a historian attentive to the shifting boundary dividing the normal from the abnormal, the historian of what the ethnographer would call the "deviant" and the "taboo," might be able even so to discern the general "modality" of the present to which he or she belongs (p. 335). Foucault reiterated the virtues of such a strategy—on which he never ceased to rely—much later in his career, even as he continued to advise "modesty" toward the present (p. 449). The strategy is nothing more than the synchronic phase of genealogy itself, its review of the state of subjects, of objects, and of the relations between them not through time but, instead, at any particular moment of time. From 1971 forward, Foucault favored genealogy not simply for its prioritization of events over systems but also for its programmatization of a history no longer constrained to be a history of the past but capable of being a "history of the present."[72]

Genealogy has yet another advantage over archaeology. It continues to treat archaeological phenomena – discourses and discursive formations; extradiscursive practices and organizations; the heterogeneous amalgams of discursive and extradiscursive practices and their technological accoutrements that Foucault occasionally refers to as "apparatuses" [*dispositifs*].[75] Like archaeology, it remains detached from those individual human intentions to which the classic historiographer or the phenomenologist might have appeal. Hence it neither lionizes nor blames. Unlike archaeology, though, it expands its focus beyond the internal generativity of discourses, to a much wider domain of interaction: between the proponents and the antagonists of any discourse or discursive formation; between discursive formations and their functional milieux. Archaeology – at least in its diagnostic "purity" – is a method suitable for rendering historical discontinuities and ruptures, but only at the expense of historical continuities and enduring historical conduits. Genealogy has its focal ground in the luck of battle, the unpredictable turns of victory and defeat. Like archaeology, it too is concerned with disruption. Precisely in its far more refined localism, though, it opens onto the regions above or beyond the fray, regions perhaps longer or more briefly at peace. It allows Foucault to characterize the historical process neither as discontinuous nor as continuous but, rather, as "a multiplicity of time spans that entangle and envelop one another" (p. 430). It allows him to conceive of history as a plurality of encounters and temporalities.

However, genealogy too has its shortcomings. It informs Foucault's approach to an extraordinarily diverse array of events and practices and institutions, from a peasant's confession of murder to the coalescence of "governmentality," but throughout, its methodological status is curiously indefinite.[74] It is of great service in illuminating the various historicities of the "sciences of man." But Foucault's remark in *Discipline and Punish* that certain sciences have managed to detach themselves from the conditions of their discursive emergence, to distance themselves from the play of power – knowledge, suggests that genealogy might prove of much less service to the historian of physics or mathematics.[75] What, moreover, of genealogy itself? Does it somehow preserve a privilege that other historical methodologies lack? Is it alone liberated from the scrutiny to which it subjects other informal knowledges? Foucault certainly never claimed that genealogy is itself beyond genealogical analysis, or that genealogy is beyond any involvement with power; if anything, he believed the contrary. Nor would a genealogy of genealogy inevitably undermine the virtues of the method or inevitably negate its results. Genealogical critique, whatever its object, is not the same as disproof. It is not a reductio ad absurdum. However, it does tend to leave its objects under a persistent aura of suspicion.

Might genealogy itself thus be suspect? Perhaps; but the answer would depend less on an inquiry into what it renders positive and what it excludes than on the quality of the forces that drive it. Foucault was convinced that the sciences of man emerge in error, in the mistaken postulate of a stable, definable, suprahistorical human essence, a fixed human nature. But, however grave, the error does not preclude discovery or the amassing of a great many particular truths about human beings. It persists in part because it has so many apparent corroborations. It persists in greater part, however, because of its virtually perfect accord with the norms of conceptual formation and the grand ambitions of a particular modality of reason, a particular rationalism, increasingly dominant in Europe and elsewhere from the early nineteenth century forward. Emphasizing its affinities with capitalist practices and the capitalist ethos, Max Weber would characterize such rationalism as "technical," as "calculative" and "instrumental."[76] Foucault, emphasizing its intellectual pragmatism, tends to write of it as the prevailing modern expression and prevailing modern instrument of *la volonté de savoir*, "the will to know."[77] Is genealogy an expression and an instrument of the same will?

If so, it would be a conceptually ill-formed, a very poor instrument. At least in its Foucauldean deployment, it would also seem consistently to lead to results quite contrary to those which would satisfy any managerial passion. It belongs apparently to another rationalism, another will. Yet genealogy leaves other rationalisms, other wills, largely obscure. Its constant point of departure and return is power–knowledge. Its critique has the will to know as its constant object. Its history is a history of strategies, of tactics, of battles. Were it a total, a universal method, it would surely be guilty of promulgating a reductive image of history and the psyche alike. Even restricted, it would seem to run the risk of picturing the sciences of man as nothing more than so many instrumentalist fantasies, nothing more than so many excrescences of the same acquisitive and inquisitional spirit. It would thus seem to run the risk of perpetuating the monotony of the very sort of "critique of ideology" to which Foucault is most opposed.

Not until the early eighties did Foucault settle on a more generous regard for both history and possible foci of genealogical research. In the interim, he developed a friendship with one of his former students, the classicist and philosopher Paul Veyne. At Berkeley and elsewhere, he also embarked upon an extensive philosophical exchange with Paul Rabinow and philosopher Hubert Dreyfus, and at last began to embrace the inevitable plurality, the inevitable heterogeneity, of historiographical diagnosis and historiographical method.[78] Adopting Veyne's term, Foucault spoke, first in 1979, of the necessity of historiographical "nominalism."[79] Veyne's nominalism, for its part, has much in common with Hayden White's "metahistory" and with many other recent narratologies:[80] it construes history as an ever-passing human spectacle, "not scientist but sublunary."[81] As spectacle, history lacks "elementary facts, because each fact has meaning only within its own plot and has reference to an indefinite number of plots."[82] No single plot can claim pride of place over any other; and no finite grouping of plots can claim to be exhaustive of any "event-worthy field."[83] It is somewhat unlikely that Foucault, who so pointedly objected to Jacques Derrida's excessive "textualization of discursive practices" (p. 416), could wholeheartedly embrace Veyne's own textualist rendering of the historical "fact." But he came at least to accept that what a nominalist would say of any particular technique of emplotment, any particular method, should be said of genealogy itself: it never tells the "whole story."

But of what might genealogy be able to tell at least part of the story? Especially in the aftermath of the publication of the first volume of *The History of Sexuality*, Foucault became increasingly interested in ethics and in that reflexive exercise of power through which human beings can, if always within limits, undertake to envision and to revise themselves. A history of such "practices of freedom" can be genealogical, but it is not, or not only, a history of battles. It is not, or not only, a history of the will to know. It evokes other relations, and other forces. One of these latter—though Foucault mentions it only rarely—is the *volonté de vérité*, the "will to truth," a will not strategic but curious. To another of them, Foucault never quite gave a name, but it might roughly be called the "will to become," a "poetic" will that exercises itself on the psyche, on the self, for the sake of self-realization.

With its application to ethics, genealogy itself becomes internally plural. In the early eighties, Foucault began to expand and to redefine its fulcrum. Deleuze returns, with the relevant changes being made. From a 1984 interview:

> For a long time, I have been trying to see if it would be possible to characterize the history of thought in distinguishing it from the history of ideas – that is, the analysis of systems of representations – and from the history of mentalities – that is, the analysis of attitudes and schemes of behavior. It seemed to me that there existed an element that was of a nature to characterize the history of thought: what one could call problems or, more exactly, problematizations. . . . Thought is not what dwells within an instance of behavior and gives it a meaning; it is rather what allows for a step back from that manner of doing or reacting, for putting it forward as a thought-object and interrogating it about its meaning, its conditions, and its ends. Thought is liberty in relation to what one does, the movement by which one detaches oneself from it, constitutes it as an object and reflects on it as a problem.[84]

In the same month, Foucault offered to another interviewer that "the notion that serves as a common form" to his studies, from *Madness and Civilization* forward, is precisely that of problematization, however long it might have taken him "to isolate it."[85]

What, then, provokes problematization? A historical hodgepodge, to consider only the evidence that Foucault himself has left to us. It includes the will to know, the will to truth, and the will to become. It includes the urge to administer both men and things. It includes the failure of the best-laid plans and the unexpected success of irresponsible frivolities. It includes the always-nagging inevitability of death, war, contagion. It includes demographic explosion and decline, rationalization, bureaucratization, industrialization, moral paradox, and experiential anomaly. It includes the eerie trenchancy of the mad and the inexplicable cry of a small child. It includes all that might ever trouble or startle us – not least, the occasional, unsummoned coalescence of our own idle musing.

What is the "form" of problematization? A certain distance, perhaps, between the psyche and its milieu, a distance that, in each case, has its own stimuli, its own consequences, and its own historicity. A hiatus in which the most unrestrained fantasy and the most rigorous reason might have equal exercise. A gap in which thought first of all mimics nothing but itself. A space of vision, and the constant test and trial of revisions, within which Foucault's philosophical and historical imagination, his personal *daimōn*, would always reside.

The *daimōn* lives. Had Foucault himself lived, his notion of problematization would undoubtedly have grown more rigorous, more refined. His genealogy of problematization would have grown even more copious and even more diverse. What remains is at once an incomplete and an imposing precedent. With it, there are many tasks, some of which to call, perhaps, our own.

> I would say that the work of the intellectual is in a sense to say what is, while making it appear able not to be, or not to be as it is. . . . What reason experiences [*éprouve*] as its necessity, or rather what the different forms of rationality put forward as their necessary being–one can perfectly well undertake a history of that and recover the network of contingencies from which it emerged. Which does not mean, however, that those forms of rationality were irrational: it means that they rest upon a base of human practice and human history; and since the latter were made, they can be unmade, provided one knows how they were made.[86]

JAMES D. FAUBION

NOTES

1 Here and throughout the introduction, internal citations refer to pages in this volume.

2 Foucault, *The Order of Things: An Archaeology of the Human Sciences*, trans. Alan Sheridan (New York: Random House, 1970), pp. 5–16.

3 See Foucault, *Raymond Roussel: Death and the Labyrinth*, trans. Charles Ruas (New York: Doubleday, 1984).

4 Founded in 1960 by the novelist and critic Philippe Sollers, *Tel quel* was devoted for more than two decades to the publication of avant-gardist literature and was especially important as a venue for "new novelists" such as Alain Robbe-Grillet.

5 See Foucault, "Entretien avec Madeleine Chapsal," in *Dits et écrits*, ed. Daniel Defert and François Ewald, with the assistance of Jacques Lagrange (Paris: Gallimard, 1994), vol. 1, pp. 516–17; "Qui-êtes-vous, professeur Foucault?," in *Dits et écrits*, vol. 1, pp. 615–19; and "Entretien sur la prison," in *Dits et écrits*, vol. 2, pp. 751–52.

6 Gustave Flaubert (1821–1880) is often regarded as among the first "modern" French writers. His best-known works are *Madame Bovary* (trans. Alan Russell [Baltimore: Penguin, 1950]) and

Sentimental Education (trans. Robert Baldick [Middlesex: Penguin, 1964]). See also pp. 103–122, below.

7 Jorge Luis Borges (1899–1986) was a celebrated Argentine writer and essayist. See, for example, *Labyrinths: Selected Stories and Other Writings*, trans. Donald A. Yates and James E. Irby (New York: New Directions, 1962).

8 Alain Robbe-Grillet (1922–) was the early leader of a generation of "new novelists" that included Nathalie Sarraute and Nobel laureate Claude Simon. His fictional works include *Jealousy* (trans. Richard Howard [London: J. Calder, 1959]), *The Erasers* (trans. Richard Howard [New York: Grove Press, 1964]), and the screenplay for Alain Resnais's *Last Year at Marienbad* (1962).

9 Marthe Robert, *L'Ancien et le nouveau* (Paris: Grasset, 1963). See Foucault, "Distance, aspecte, origine," in *Dits et écrits*, vol. 1, p. 278.

10 See Plato, *Republic*, trans. G. M. A. Grube (Indianapolis: Hackett, 1974), bks. 2–3, 377c–405c (pp. 47–73).

11 Jean-Jacques Rousseau, *Julie: ou, La nouvelle Héloïse* [1760], ed. René Pomeau (Paris: Garnier frères, 1960), introduction [Julie; or, The New Eloise, trans. Judith H. Howell (University Park, Pa.: University of Pennsylvania Press, 1968)].

12 See David Carroll, *Paraesthetics: Foucault/Lyotard/Derrida* (New York: Methuen, 1987).

13 See Foucault, "Distance, aspecte, origine," p. 285.

14 Foucault, "Le *Mallarmé* de J.-P. Richard," in *Dits et écrits*, vol. 1, pp. 423–33.

15 Foucault, "Débat sur le roman," in *Dits et écrits*, vol. 1, p. 340.

16 See pp. 214–15, below. Hence Foucault can argue consistently that avant-garde fiction reveals writing as the *alter* of the writer's death, and that it characteristically spells the death of the "author."

17 Foucault, "Folie, littérature, société," in *Dits et écrits*, vol. 2, p. 123.

18 On the simulacrum, see also Foucault's essay on the writer Pierre Klossowski, "The Prose of Actaeon," pp. 123–35, below; and see Jean Baudrillard, *For a Critique of the Political Economy of the Sign*, trans. Charles Levin (St. Louis: Telos, 1981), and *Simulations*, trans. Paul Foss, Paul Hutton, and Philip Beitchman (New York: Semiotext(e), 1983).

19 Foucault, "La Folie, l'absence d'oeuvre," in *Dits et écrits*, vol. 1, p. 415.

20 This quote comes from the closing pages of the text; emphasis is in the original. *Madness and Civilization*, trans. Richard Howard (New York: Random House, 1965), pp. 288–89.

21 Foucault, "La Folie, l'absence d'oeuvre," p. 418.

22 Ibid.

23 Ibid., p. 419; see also p. 275, below.

24 Ibid., p. 417.

25 Foucault, "La Folie et la société," in *Dits et écrits*, vol. 3, pp. 496–98.

26 Ibid., p. 498.

27 Foucault, "La Folie, l'absence d'oeuvre," p. 420.

28 Phenomenology, the philosophical study of the "structure" of experience, has two chief founders: G. W. F. Hegel (1770–1831) and Edmund Husserl (1859–1938). For Hegel, see especially *The Phenomenology of Spirit*, trans. A. V. Collins (Oxford, Eng.: Oxford University Press, 1977);

for Husserl, see *Ideas: General Introduction to Pure Phenomenology*, trans. W. R. Boyce Gibson (New York: Collier Books, 1962) and *Cartesian Meditations. An Introduction to Phenomenology*, trans. Dorion Cairns (The Hague: Nijhoff, 1977).

29 This sounds "structuralist." The Foucault who in a 1968 interview remarked that anthropologist Claude Lévi-Strauss, psychologist Jacques Lacan, political theorist Louis Althusser, literary critic Roland Barthes, and he, converge at least in "putting the importance of the human subject, human consciousness, human existence into question" might agree that it is indeed structuralist, as far as it goes. See "Interview avec Michel Foucault," in *Dits et écrits*, vol. 1, p. 655.

30 This alternate reading hangs on *siècle*—"century," but also, if more rarely, a circle of courtiers. My thanks to Paul Rabinow for pointing out the ambiguity to me.

31 See Plato, *Republic*, bks. 6–7.

32 A general discussion of mentalism—a vaguely defined doctrine ranging from the position that there are such things as mental things to the position that there are only such things as mental things—can be found in Daniel Dennett, *Brainstorms: Philosophical Essays on Mind and Psychology* (Cambridge, Mass.: MIT Press, 1981), pp. 54–61.

33 See Gilles Deleuze, *Foucault*, trans. Sean Hand (Minneapolis: University of Minnesota Press, 1988).

34 For the most wide-ranging and most rigorous discussion of Foucault's interpretive approach, see Hubert Dreyfus and Paul Rabinow, *Michel Foucault: Beyond Structuralism and Hermeneutics* (Chicago: University of Chicago Press, 1982).

35 Foucault, *The Archaeology of Knowledge, and the Discourse on Language*, trans. Alan Sheridan Smith (New York: Pantheon, 1982), p. 128.

36 Though Foucault is careful not to name names here, it is clear that he has many of the *Annaliste* historians in mind. For an excellent discussion of the School, and of some of the aspects of Foucault's complex relation to it, see Jacques Revel's introduction to *Histories: French Constructions of the Past*, vol. 1: *Postwar French Thought*, ed. Jacques Revel and Lynn Hunt (New York: New Press, 1995), pp. 1–63.

37 Foucault, "La Politique de la santé au XVIII⁰ siècle," in *Dits et écrits*, vol. 3, p. 14 ["The Politics of Health in the Eighteenth Century," in *Power/Knowledge: Selected Writings, 1972–1977*, ed. Colin Gordon, trans. Colin Gordon et al. (New York: Pantheon, 1980), p. 167].

38 Ludwig Wittgenstein, *Philosophical Investigations*, trans. G. E. M. Anscombe (3d ed.), (London: Basil Blackwell and Mott), pp. 2–35, 82–103.

39 Foucault, "Sexuality and Solitude," in *Essential Works of Foucault*, vol. 1: *Ethics: Subjectivity and Truth*, ed. Paul Rabinow (New York: New Press, 1997), p. 176.

40 Foucault, *Archaeology of Knowledge*, pp. 186–87.

41 See Thomas Kuhn, *The Structure of Scientific Revolutions* (2d ed., Chicago: University of Chicago Press, 1970), pp. 35–42; compare Foucault's comment on "normal science," p. 473 below.

42 Foucault, *Archaeology of Knowledge*, pp. 188–89.

43 Ibid.

44 Ibid.

45 This point is merely comparative. Though it is clear that Foucault knew at least some of Dilthey's work, it is much less clear whether or not he was familiar with Gadamer's.

46 Foucault sometimes speaks of "historical a prioris" (as at *The Archaeology of Knowledge*, p. 206), but these are of a different order. They refer to the "formative rules" that, at any given historical period, govern the production of one or another discourse or discursive formation. They are thus historical rather than transhistorical.

47 Foucault, *Archaeology of Knowledge*, p. 195 (emphasis in the original).

48 Ibid., p. 190.

49 Ibid., pp. 107–8.

50 Ibid., 191.

51 Ibid.

52 Ibid.

53 Ibid., p. 192.

54 Ibid., p. 206.

55 Ibid.

56 Ibid., p. 207.

57 This is a rather surprising remark from Foucault, who is usually opposed to the postulation of "deep structures" of any sort. Generative grammar, which postulates precisely such structures as the mental (or perhaps neurophysiological) ground of linguistic competence, was first formulated by Noam Chomsky (see his *Aspects of the Theory of Syntax* [Cambridge, Mass.: MIT Press, 1965]).

58 Foucault, *Archaeology of Knowledge*, p. 207.

59 Foucault, *Order of Things*, pp. 312–35.

60 Ibid., p. 331.

61 Ibid., p. 312.

62 Ibid., p. 320. For an especially vigorous rejection of the postulation of human essences, see also "Michel Foucault: Les Réponses du philosophe," in *Dits et écrits*, vol. 2, p. 817.

63 Foucault, *Order of Things*, pp. 385–86.

64 See *Archaeology of Knowledge*, p. 158.

65 Though Foucault never embraced phenomenology, he was something of a reformed Marxist: see Didier Eribon, *Michel Foucault*, trans. Betsy Wing (Cambridge, Mass.: Harvard University Press, 1991), pp. 50–58.

66 Foucault, *Order of Things*, p. 322.

67 The rather widespread impression that Foucault is a pragmatist stems largely from a remark to be found in a 1972 dialogue published under the title "Les Intellectuels et le pouvoir" (see *Dits et écrits*, vol. 2, pp. 306–15.). The remark runs as follows: "That's it: a theory is like a box of tools; nothing to do with the signifier." The words are not in fact Foucault's but those of his interlocutor, Gilles Deleuze. For all that, Foucault seems ready to offer his assent to them. What should not be overlooked, however, is the theme and the context of the dialogue. Neither has to do with theory in its relation to, say, physics (or even anthropology); both have to do with theory in its technical Marxist sense – as a set of universal guidelines for revolutionary praxis. In their discussion, neither Deleuze nor Foucault is espousing a position similar to that of James Dewey, William James, or any of their neopragmatist successors. Instead, each is rejecting the possibility of a single, a universally applicable, theory of revolutionary praxis.

68 Foucault, *Archaeology of Knowledge*, p. 120.

69 For Foucault these two forces are in no sense identical. Consider his comments during a 1983 interview: "when I read – and I know that it has been attributed to me – the thesis that 'Knowledge is power' or 'Power is knowledge,' I begin to laugh, since studying their *relation* is precisely my problem. If they were identical, I would not have to study them and I would be spared a lot of fatigue as a result. The very fact that I pose the question of their relation proves clearly that I do not identify them" ("Structuralism and Post-structuralism," p. 455 below).

70 Foucault, "De l'Archéologie à la dynastique," p. 406.

71 Foucault, *Archeology of Knowledge*, p. 130.

72 In "Structuralism and Post-structuralism, Foucault says, "I don't use the term 'archaeology' any longer" (p. 444). For what, to my knowledge, is Foucault's first published reference to the idea of a "history of the present," see *Discipline and Punish: The Birth of the Prison* [1975], trans. Alan Sheridan (New York: Vintage, 1979), p. 31.

73 See, for example, *Discipline and Punish*, p. 216, with reference to "the police."

74 See *I, Pierre Rivière, Having Slaughtered My Mother, My Sister, and My Brother: A Case of Parricide in the Nineteenth Century*, ed. Michel Foucault, trans. Frank Jellinek (Lincoln: University of Nebraska Press, 1982); and "On Governmentality," trans. Rossi Braidotti, *Ideology and Consciousness* 6 (Autumn 1979), pp. 5 – 21.

75 Foucault, *Discipline and Punish*, pp. 226 – 27.

76 See Max Weber, Author's Introduction [1915], in *The Protestant Ethic and the Spirit of Capitalism*, trans. Talcott Parsons (New York: Scribner's, 1958), pp. 13 – 31.

77 "The Will to Know" is also the subtitle of the first volume of *The History of Sexuality*. On that will, see pp. 387 – 88 in this volume. See also Foucault, "L'Occident et la vérité du sexe," in *Dits et écrits*, vol. 3, p. 105; and "Michel Foucault: la sécurité et l'état," in *Dits et écrits*, vol. 3, p. 385.

78 Veyne's book was published in French in 1971 and in English, as *Writing History: Essay on Epistemology*, trans. Mina Moore-Rinvolucri (Middletown, Conn.: Wesleyan University Press, 1984).

79 See Foucault, "The Birth of Biopolitics," in *Essential Works*, vol. 1, pp. 73 – 74; see also preface to *The History of Sexuality*, vol. 2, in *Essential Works*, vol. 1, p. 200.

80 See Hayden White, *Metahistory: The Historical Imagination in the Nineteenth Century* (Baltimore: Johns Hopkins University Press, 1973).

81 Veyne, *Writing History*, p. 42.

82 Ibid., pp. 42 – 43.

83 Ibid., p. 43.

84 "Polemics, Politics, and Problematizations: An Interview with Michel Foucault," in *Essential Works*, vol. 1, p. 117.

85 Foucault, "Le souci de la vérité," in *Dits et écrits*, vol. 4, p. 669.

86 Foucault, "Structuralism and Poststructuralism," p. 450 in this volume.

This volume comprises texts that span virtually the whole of Foucault's career. Like the first volume, this one includes several selections already available, if sometimes in truncated form, in English. Just short of half the selections appear here in English for the first time. All of the latter have been translated by Robert Hurley.

The editorial policy that governed the first volume remains in force. Here, too, as light as possible a hand has been exercised. The aim has been to render Foucault's vocabulary and expression with as much consistency as his own texts warrant, and the more literal translation has always been given preference over the less literal. The texts published in *Dits et écrits* have remained the standard against which all translations have been judged. Many of the translations already available in English have accordingly been subject only to minor mechanical and stylistic emendations. Several others, however, have been extensively modified, whether because of their inaccuracies or because they were either abridgments of, or included supplements to, their counterparts in *Dits et écrits*. Annotations indicate the extent of such modifications from one case to the next.

French terms used in a technical sense, and those terms which have proven particularly resistant to precise translation, are often placed in brackets after their English glosses. In this as in the first volume, *connaissance* (acquaintance, cognition, learning, expertise, knowledge), *savoir* (knowledge), and their cognates thus appear quite frequently. I have also included a general discussion of the usage of *connaissance* and *savoir* (in French, and in Foucault) in my Introduction. One further term merits special attention. Foucault's *énoncé* is consistently rendered here as "statement." It should not be confused with an utterance: the statement may be produced both in writing and orally; the utterance only in the latter mode. Nor should it be confused with a proposition: the statement is always a thing produced, always a historical event; the proposition is a purely formal entity, belonging to the sphere of logic. Foucault also sometimes uses the term *énonciation* in referring to a set, or a mode of the production, of *énoncés*. At the cost of losing the aural and visual link the French preserves, *énonciation* is regularly translated in this volume as "enunciation."

PART ONE

AESTHETICS

THE FATHER'S "NO"*a

T he *Hölderlin Jahrbuch* has been extremely important; since 1946, it has managed patiently to dislodge Hölderlin's texts from the accumulated weight of a half century of interpretations obviously inspired by the disciples of Stefan George. Friedrich Gundolf's analysis of *The Archipelago* stands as an excellent example of this latter approach,[1] given its emphasis on the sacred, circular presence of nature, the visible proximity of the gods who metamorphose into lovely bodies, their coming to light in the cycles of history, and their ultimate return heralded by the fleeting presence of the Child—the eternal and perishable guardian of fire. Caught up in the lyricism of a fulfilling time, all of these themes served to stifle what Friedrich Hölderlin had announced in the vitality of a rupture. Following the thematics of Stefan George, the young hero of "The Fettered River," torn from the stupefied bank in a theft that exposes him to the boundless violence of the gods, is transformed into a tender, soft, and promising child. The hymn commemorating cyclical process had silenced Hölderlin's words, the hard words that divide time. It was obviously necessary to recapture his language at its source.

A number of studies (some rather early and others more recent) have significantly altered the traditional reference points of the Hölderlin chronology. Heinrich Lange's simple scheme,[2] which placed all the "obscure" texts (like the *Grund zum Empedokles*) in a pathologi-

---

*This essay, a review of Jean Laplanche's *Hölderlin et la question du père* (Paris: Presses Universitaires de France, 1961), first appeared in *Critique* 178 (1962), pp. 195–209. This translation, by D. F. Bouchard and S. Simon, has been slightly amended.

cal calendar originating with the Bordeaux episode, was considerably modified some time ago; it was necessary to alter its dates so that the enigma of Hölderlin's madness could arise earlier than had been previously supposed (all the drafts of *Empedokles* were completed before Hölderlin left for France). But, in an inverse sense, the obstinate erosion of meaning proliferated; Friedrich Beissner tirelessly investigated the last hymns and the texts of madness; Leopold Liegler and Andreas Müller examined the successive configurations that developed from the same poetic core (*The Wanderer* and *Ganymede*).[5] The escarpment of mythic lyricism, the struggle at the limits of language from which it grows, its unique expression and perpetually open space, are no longer the last rays of light escaping from the growing darkness. They arise, on the level of meaning and of time, in that central and profoundly embedded point where poetry talks freely to itself in the words [*la parole*] that are proper to it.

Adolf Beck's clarifications with respect to the biography have also led to a whole series of reevaluations.[4] His studies bear in particular on two episodes: the return from Bordeaux (1802), and the eighteenmonth period of Hölderlin's tutorship at Waltershausen from the end of 1793 to the middle of 1795 and the departure from Jena. This period is especially important for the light it sheds on relationships that were previously neglected or misunderstood. This is the time in which Hölderlin met Charlotte von Kalb; the period of his relations, at once close and distant, with Friedrich Schiller; of Johann Fichte's influence; and of his abrupt return to his mother's house. But, most important, it is a time of strange anticipations, repetitions against the grain that present in up-beat what will, in the aftermath or in other forms, be restored as a down-beat. Charlotte von Kalb obviously prefigures Diotima and Susette Gontard; equally, Hölderlin's fervent attachment to Schiller, who, from afar, watches over, protects, and, from the heights of his reserve, pronounces the Law, delineates from the outside and within the order of events the terrible presence of the "unfaithful" gods from whom Oedipus (because he dared infringe on their territory) will turn away through the gesture in which he blinds himself: "a traitor in the realm of the sacred."[5] And the flight to Nürtingen, far from Schiller, from legislative Fichte, and from an already-deified Goethe mute before silent Hölderlin—is there not, in the dotted line of vicissitudes, the decipherable figure of this return home which will later be opposed, as balance, to the categorical turning-away of the gods? Yet other repetitions are introduced into the already-dense situation at Jena – invariably at Jena – but these according to the simultaneity produced by mirrors: on the level of Hölderlin's dependencies, his now established intimacy with Wilhelmine Marianne Kirms forms the double of the enchanted and inaccessible union in which, like gods, Schiller and Charlotte von Kalb are joined; the teaching position as a young tutor, which he accepts with enthusiasm and in which he showed himself rigorous and demanding to the point of cruelty, presents in relief the inverted image of the accessible and loving master he sought in Schiller but in whom he only found discreet concern, a constant, unbreachable distance, and deaf incomprehension.

We are indeed fortunate that the *Hölderlin Jahrbuch* has remained alien to the babbling of psychologists – doubly fortunate that they have not seen fit to investigate its findings. The gods were with us; they removed the temptation of submitting Hölderlin and his madness to a stricter form of that discourse which so many psychologists (Karl Jaspers first and foremost)[6] perpetually and pointlessly repeat: this approach, pursued to the very heart of madness, is based on the assumption that the meaning of a work, its themes and specific domain, can be traced to a series of events whose details are known to us. The question posed by this nonconceptual eclecticism, as it derives from "clinical" psychology, is whether a chain of significations can be formed to link, without discontinuity or rupture, an individual life to a life's work, events to words, and the mute forms of madness to the most essential aspects of a poem.

In fact, this possibility prescribes, to anyone who attends to it without being taken in by it, a different course. The old problem, concerned with the point at which a work ends and madness begins, is meaningless when posed in a context of uncertain dates and a maze of overlapping phenomena. Instead of assuming that a work collapses in the shadows of a pathological event once it achieves its secret truth, it is necessary to follow the movement in which a work gradually discloses the open and extended space of schizophrenic existence. At this extreme limit, we find a revelation that no language could have expressed outside of the abyss that engulfs it and that no fall could have demonstrated if it were not at the same time a conquest of the highest peaks.

This is the direction taken by Jean Laplanche in his book. He begins by adopting the discreet style of a "psychobiography." From this opening, he crosses his chosen field diagonally and discovers, approaching his conclusion, the nature of the problem which had informed his text from the start and from which it derived its prestige and mastery: how can language apply a *single and identical* discourse to poetry and madness? Which syntax functions *at the same time* on the level of declared meaning *and* on that of interpreted signification?

But, perhaps, in order to illuminate the particular powers of systematic inversion that animate Laplanche's text, we should at least pose—if not resolve—this question in its original form: what source gives rise to the possibility of this language and why, for the longest time, has it appeared so "natural" to us, that is, oblivious to its proper enigma?

As a Christianized Europe first began to name its artists, their lives were accorded the anonymous form of the hero, as if the name could only adopt the colorless role of chronological memory within the cycle of perfect recommencements. Vasari's *Vite* sets as its goal the evocation of an immemorial past, and its proceeds according to an ordained and ritual order. Genius makes itself known from infancy, not in the psychological form of precocity, but by virtue of its intrinsic right to exist in advance of time and to make its appearance only in its consummation. Genius is not born, but appears without intermediary or duration in the rift of history; similar to the hero, the artist sunders time so as to reestablish its continuity with his own hands. The manifestations of genius, however, are accompanied by a series of vicissitudes: one of the most frequent episodes concerns the passage from misrecognition to recognition. Giotto was a shepherd sketching sheep on a rock when Cimabue found him and paid homage to his hidden majesty (as the prince in medieval tales, living among peasants who adopted him, is suddenly recognized by a mysterious mark). An apprenticeship follows this experience, but it is more symbolic than real since it can invariably be reduced to the singular and unequal confrontation between the master and his disciple—the older man thought he was giving everything away to a youngster who already possessed all the older man's powers. The clash that ensues reverses their relationship: the child, set apart by a sign, transforms the master into a disciple, and the master, whose reign was merely a usurpation, suffers a symbolic death by virtue of the inviolable rights possessed by the anonymous shepherd. After Leonardo da Vinci painted the angel in the *Baptism of Christ,* Verrochio abandoned his career and, similarly, the aging Ghirlandaio withdrew in favor of Michelangelo. The artist has yet to attain his full sovereignty; another secret test awaits him, but this one is voluntary. Like the hero who fights in black armor, his visor covering his face, the artist hides his work and reveals it only upon completion. This was Michelangelo's procedure with the *David* as it was with Uccello's fresco above the gates of San Tommaso. Finally, the artist receives the keys to the kingdom, the keys of Demiurgy. He produces a world that is the double, the fraternal rival, of our own. In the instantaneous ambiguity of illusion, it takes its place and passes for it—the monsters painted by Leonardo on the roundel of Ser Piero are as horrifying as any found in nature. Through this return to nature, in the perfection of identity, a promise is fulfilled: man is freed, as the legend recounts that Filippo Lippi was actually liberated on the day he painted a supernatural resemblance of his master.

The Renaissance attitude towards the artist's individuality conflated an epic perception which derived from the already archaic form of the medieval hero with the Greek themes of the initiatory cycle, and at their boundary appeared the ambiguous and overdetermined structures of enigma and discovery, of the intoxicating force of illusion, of a return to nature that is basically *other,* and of an access to new lands revealed as *the same.* The artist was able to emerge from the age-old anonymity of epic singers only by usurping the power and meaning of the same epic values. The heroic dimension passed from the hero to the one whose task it had been to represent him at a time when Western culture itself became a world of representations. A work no longer achieved its sole meaning as a monument, a memory engraved in stone which was capable of surviving the ravages of time; it now belonged to the legend it had once commemorated; it became in itself an "exploit" because it conferred eternal truth upon men and upon their ephemeral actions and also because it referred to the marvellous realm of the artist's life as its "natural" birthplace. The painter was the first subjective inflection of the hero. His self-portrait was no longer merely a marginal sign of the artist's furtive participation in the scene being represented, as a figure hidden at the corner of the canvas; it became, at the very center of the work, the totality of the painting where the beginning joins the ending in the absolute heroic transformation of the creator of heroes.

In this fashion, for the artist, a relationship of the self to itself was tied up in the interior of the exploit that the hero could never experience. The heroic mode became the primary manifestation—at the boundary of the things that appear and their representations, for oneself and for others—of the singleness of approach to the truth of the work. This was nevertheless a unity both precarious and ineradicable, and one that disclosed, on the basis of its essential constitution, the possibility of a series of dissociations. Among the most characteristic were: the "distraught hero" whose life or passions were continually in conflict with his work (this is Filippo Lippi who suffered from the torments of the flesh and, unable to possess the lady whose portrait he was painting, was forced to "stifle his passion"); the "alienated hero," losing himself in his work and also losing sight of the work itself (plainly Uccello, who "could have been the most elegant and original painter since Giotto had he devoted to human and animal figures the time lost in his studies of perspective"); the "misunderstood hero," scorned by his peers (like Tintoretto who was driven away by Titian and spurned throughout his life by the Venetian painters). These avatars, which gradually traced the dividing line between the artist's deeds and the deeds of heroes, give rise to the possibility of an ambiguous stance (maintained through a composite vocabulary) which embraces *both* the work and what the work is not. The space cleared in the decline of heroism, a space whose nature was suspected by the sixteenth century, and one that our present culture cheerfully investigates in keeping with its basic forgetfulness, is ultimately occupied by the "madness" of the artist; it is a madness that identifies the artist with his work in rendering him alien to others—from all those who remain silent—and it also situates the artist outside his work when it blinds him to the things he sees and makes him deaf to even his own words. This state can no longer be understood as a Platonic ecstasy that protects him from illusion and exposes him to the radiant light of the gods, but as a subterranean relationship in which the work and what it is not construct their exteriority within the language of dark interiority. Given these conditions, it became possible to envisage the strange enterprise we call the "psychology of the artist," a procedure always haunted by madness even when the pathological dimension is absent. It is inscribed on the beautiful heroic unity that gave names to the first painters, but as an index of their separation, negation, and oblivion. The psychological dimension in our culture is the negation of epic perceptions. If we hope to understand the artists of the past, we can only do so by following this diagonal and illusive path on which the older, mute alliance between the work and the "other" of the work whose tales of heroic rituals and immutable cycles were commemorated by Vasari is at once caught sight of and lost.

In keeping with our discursive understanding, we have tried to construct the language of this unity. But is it lost to us? Or so fully incorporated in other discourses, in the monotony generated by discourses on "the relationship of art and madness," that is nearly impossible to unravel? This unity makes possible such discourses of reassessment (I think of Jean Vinchon) and misery (I think of Jean Fretet and many others).[7] At the same time, it is constantly occulted, deliberately neglected, and scattered through these repetitions. It lies dormant within discourse and forced by it into stubborn oblivion. This unity can be given new life only through a rigorous and uncompromising discourse such as that developed by Laplanche, perhaps the only scion to be saved from a most inglorious dynasty. Laplanche's remarkable readings multiply the problems that schizophrenia has, of late, insistently posed for psychoanalysis.

What is the precise point of saying that the place left empty by the Father is the *same* place that Schiller occupied in Hölderlin's imagination and subsequently abandoned, the *same* place made radiant by the unfaithful presence of the gods of the last texts prior to leaving the Hesperians under the royal law of institutions? More simply, what is this *same* figure outlined in the *Thalia-Fragment* before the actual meeting with Susette Gontard which is then faithfully reproduced in the definitive version of Diotima? What is this "sameness" to which analysis is so readily drawn? Why is this "identity" so insistently introduced in every analysis; why does it seem to guarantee the easy passage between the work and what it is not?

Of the numerous paths which lead to this "identity," Laplanche's analysis undoubtedly follows the most secure; he moves from one approach to another without ever losing his way, without wavering in his pursuit of this "sameness" which obsesses him with its inaccessible presence and its tangible absence. These paths form, as it were, three methodologically distinct but convergent approaches: the assimilation of themes in the imagination; an outline of the fundamental forms of experience; and finally, the dividing line along which Hölderlin's work and his life confront each other, where they are balanced, and where they become both possible and impossible in relation to each other.

1. The mythical forces, whose strange and penetrating vitality is experienced both inside and outside of Hölderlin's poetry, are those in which divine violence penetrates mortals to create a proximity in which they are illuminated and reduced to ashes; these are the forces of the Jungling, of a river at its source, contained and sealed by ice, water, and sleep, which shatters its bonds in a single movement in order to find its profound and inviting homeland at a distance from itself, outside itself. Are they not *also* Hölderlin's forces as a child, forces confiscated out of avarice and withheld by his mother, forces of which he requested the "full and unimpaired use" as a paternal inheritance he could dispose of as he liked? And are they not *also* the forces Hölderlin opposed to those of his student in a struggle exacerbated by the recognition that they were mirror images? Hölderlin's experience is totally informed by the enchanted threat of forces that arose from within himself and from others, that were at once distant and nearby, divine and subterranean, invincibly precarious; and it is in the imaginary distances between these forces that their mutual identity and the play of their reciprocal symbolization are constructed and contested. Is the oceanic relationship of the gods to the unleashing of their new vitality the symbolic and luminous form of Hölderlin's relationship to the image of the mother, or its profound and nocturnal basis? These relationships are constantly being transposed.

2. This play of forces, without beginning or ending, is deployed within its natural space, one organised by the categories of proximity and distance. These categories regulated the immediately contradictory oscillations of Hölderlin's relationship to Schiller. In Jena, Hölderlin was exalted by his "closeness to truly great minds," but, in this attractive profusion, he experiences profound misery—a desertlike emptiness that distances him from others and that creates an internal and unbreachable gap within himself. As a result of his own barrenness, he develops an abundant capacity to absorb the fertility of the

others, of this other who, in maintaining his reserve, refuses to give of himself and deliberately keeps his distance. The departure from Jena becomes comprehensible in this context: Hölderlin left Schiller's vicinity because in being close to him, he felt that he held no value for his hero, that he remained infinitely distant from him. In trying to gain Schiller's affection, he was trying "to come closer to the Good" – that which is by definition out of reach. He left Jena to realize more closely this "attachment," which was degraded each time he tried to establish a link and made more distant by his approach. It is likely that this experience was for Hölderlin connected to that of the fundamental space in which the gods appear only to turn away. This space, in terms of its basic configuration, is that of the great circle of nature, the "divine All-in-One," but this perfect circle without fault or mediation only emerges in the now extinguished light of Greece; the gods are *here* only by being *there*. The genius of Hellas, "the first-born of lofty nature," must be located in the great return commemorated in *Hyperion* in its evocation of endless circles.[8] But in the *Thalia-Fragment*, which forms the first draft of the novel, Greece is not the land of glorious presence. When Hyperion leaves Melitus (visited for only a short time) to undertake a pilgrimage to the dead heroes on the banks of the Scamander, it too disappears and he is condemned to return to a native land where the gods are present and absent, visible and hidden, in the manifest reserve of the "supreme secret which gives life or death." Greece is the shore where gods and men intermingle, the land of mutual presence and reciprocal absence. From this derives its prestige as the land of light; it defines a distant luminosity (exactly opposed to Novalis's nocturnal proximity) which is traversed, like the flight of an eagle or a lightning flash, by the violence of an abduction that is both murderous and loving. The light of Greece is an absolute distance which is destroyed and exalted by the imminent force of the assembled gods. Against the certain flight of all things near, against the threatening shaft of the distant, what remedies are possible? Who will protect us? "Is space always to be this absolute and radiant departure, this abject volte-face?"[9]

3. The definitive wording of *Hyperion* is already a search for a fixed point: it seeks to anchor itself in the improbable unity of two beings as closely aligned as a figure and its reflection in a mirror. In this context, the limit assumes the shape of a perfect circle which includes all things, a state as circular and pure as Hölderlin's friendship with Su-

sette Gontard. The flight of the Immortals is arrested in the light that reflects two similar faces; "the divine is trapped by a mirror and the dark threat of absence and emptiness is finally averted. Language now advances against this space whose opening summoned it and it attempts to obliterate this space by covering it with the lovely images of immediate presence. The work of art becomes a measure of what it is not in the double sense that it traverses the entire surface of this other world, and then limits it through its opposition. The work of art installs itself as joy of expression and averted madness. This is the period spent in Frankfurt as a tutor for the Gontard family, a time of shared tenderness and mutual understanding. But Diotima dies; Alabanda leaves in search of a lost homeland, Adamas in search of an impossible Arcadia. The dual relationship of the mirror has been shattered by a supreme and empty form, a form whose emptiness devours the fragile reflection, a form which is nothing in itself but which designates the *Limit* in all its aspects: the inevitability of death, the unwritten law of human brotherhood, the inaccessible existence of mortals who were touched by the divine. In the pleasure of an artistic work, at the border of its language, a limit emerges whose function is to silence its language and bring the work to completion, and this is the limit which formed the work against all that was not itself. The shape of this balance is that of a precipitous cliff where the work finds completion only through those elements it subtracts from itself. The work is ruined by that which initially constituted it. The limit that balanced the dual existence with Susette Gontard and the enchanted mirror of *Hyperion* emerges as a limit *in* life (Hölderlin's "unexplained" departure from Frankfurt) and as a limit *of* the work (Diotima's death and Hyperion's return to Germany "like homeless, blind Oedipus to the gates of Athens").

We can now see that this enigma of the *same*, in which the work merges with all that it is not, assumes an exactly reversed form from that proposed by Vasari. It becomes situated at the very center of the work, in those forces which necessitate its destruction from the start. A work and its *other* can speak in the *same* language of the *same* things only on the basis of the limit of the work. Any discourse that seeks to attain the fundamental dimensions of a work must, at least implicitly, examine its relationship to madness: not only because of the resemblance between the themes of lyricism and psychosis, or because the structures of experience are occasionally isomorphic, but more fundamentally, because the work poses and transgresses the limit which creates, threatens, and completes it.

The gravitational pull that the greatest platitudes seem to exert on the majority of psychologists has led them for several years to the study of "frustrations"; the involuntary fasting of rats serves as their infinitely fertile epistemological model. It is because of his double grounding in philosophy and psychoanalysis that Laplanche was able to direct his study of Hölderlin to a profound questioning of the negative, in which the Hegelian *repetition* of Jean Hippolyte and the Freudian *repetition* of Jacques Lacan find themselves *repeated*: repeated, that is, by the very necessity of their destined itinerary and its conclusion.

German prefixes and suffixes (*ab-*, *ent-*, *-los*, *un-*, *ver-*) are particularly well suited (far better than in French) for expressing the specific forms of absence, hiatus, and distancing which are indispensable for the psychotic construction of the father's image and the weapons of virility. It is not a question of seeing in the father's "no" either a real or a mythical orphanage; nor does it imply the eradication of the father's characteristic traits. Hölderlin's case is apparently straightforward, but it becomes extremely ambiguous if examined in depth. He lost his father at the age of two and his mother was remarried to Gock, the burghermaster, two years later. After five years, Gock died, leaving the child with delightful memories that were apparently unaffected even by the existence of a half-brother. On the level of Hölderlin's memories, the father's place was occupied by a distinct and positive figure, and only through death did it become partially disturbed. Undoubtedly, the idea of absence will be found not in this interplay of presences and disappearances but in a context where speech is linked to a particular speaker. Jacques Lacan, following Melanie Klein, has shown that the father, as the third party in the Oedipal situation, is not only the hated and feared rival but the agent whose presence limits the unlimited relationship between the mother and child, and whose first, anguished image emerges in the child's fantasy of being devoured. Consequently, the father separates; that is, he is the one who protects when, in his proclamation of the Law, he links space, rules, and language within a single and major experience. At a stroke, he creates the distance along which will develop the scansion of presences and absences, the speech whose initial form is based on constraints, and finally, the relationship of the signifier to the signified which not only gives rise to the structure of language but also to the exclusion and symbolic transformation of repressed material. Thus, it is not in alimentary or functional terms of deficiency that we understand the gap that now stands in the Father's place. To be able to say that he is missing, that he is hated, excluded, or introjected, that his image has undergone symbolic transmutations, presumes that he is not "foreclosed" (as Lacan would say) from the start and that his place is not marked by a gaping and absolute emptiness. The Father's absence, manifested in the headlong rush of psychosis, is not registered by perceptions or images, but relates to the order of the signifier. The "no" through which this gap is created does not imply the absence of a real individual who bears the father's name; rather, it implies that the father has never assumed the role of nomination and that the position of the signifier, through which the father names himself and, according to the Law, through which he is able to name, has remained vacant. It is toward this "no" that the unwavering line of psychosis is infallibly directed; as it is precipitated inside the abyss of its meaning, it evokes the devastating absence of the father through the forms of delirium and phantasms and through the catastrophe of the signifier.

Beginning with the period in Homburg, Hölderlin devoted himself to this absence, which is constantly elaborated in the successive drafts of *Empedokles*. At first, the tragic hymn sets out in search of the profound center of things, this central "Limitless" where all determinations dissipate. To disappear into the fire of the volcano is to rejoin, at the point of its inaccessible and open hearth, the All-in-One—simultaneously, the subterranean vitality of stones and the bright flame of truth. But as Hölderlin reworked this theme, he modified the basic spatial relationships: the burning proximity of the divine (high and profound forge of chaos where all that has ended can begin anew) is transformed into the distant radiance of the unfaithful gods; Empedocles destroyed the lovely alliance by assuming the status of a mediator with divine powers. Thinking he had realized the "Limitless," he had, in fact, merely succeeded in driving the Limits farther away in a flaw that stood for his entire existence and that was the product of his "handiwork." And in this definitive distancing of limits, the gods had already prepared their inevitable ruse; the blinding of Oedipus will not proceed with open eyes on this deserted shore where. Language and the Law, in fraternal confrontation, await the garrulous parricide. In a sense, language is the site of the flaw; Empedocles profanes the gods in proclaiming their existence and releases the arrow of absence to pierce the heart of things. Empedocles' language is opposed by the endurance of its fraternal enemy whose role is to create, in the interval of the limit, the pedestal of the Law which links understanding to necessity and determinations to their destiny. This positivity is not the result of an oversight; in the last draft, it reappears as an aspect of Manes' character in his absolute power of interrogation ("tell me who you are, tell me who I am")[10] and as the unshakable will to remain silent–he is a perpetual question who never answers. And yet, having arisen from the depths of time and space, he acts as an unwavering witness to Empedocles' nature as the Chosen One, the definitive absence, the one through whom "all things return again and future events have already achieved completion."[11]

Two extreme possibilities–the most allied and most opposed–are presented in this final and closely fought struggle. First, we are given the categorical withdrawal of the gods to their essential ether, the Hesperians in possession of the terrestrial world, the effacement of the figure of Empedocles as the last Greek, the arrival from the depths of the Orient of the couple Christ-Dionysus, come to witness the tempestuous exit of the dying gods. Simultaneously, a zone is created where language loses itself in its extreme limits, in a region where language is most unlike itself and where signs no longer communicate, that region of an endurance without anguish: *"Ein Zeichen sind wir, deutungslos"* ("A sign we are, meaningless"). The expansion of this final lyric expression is also the disclosure of madness. The trajectory that outlines the flight of the gods, and that traces, in reverse, the return of men to their native land, is indistinguishable from this cruel line that leads Hölderlin to the absence of the father, that directs his language to the fundamental gap in the signifier, that transforms his lyricism into delirium, his work into the absence of a work.

At the beginning of his book, Laplanche wonders if Blanchot, in his discussion of Hölderlin, had not rejected the possibility of extending the unity of meaning to the end of his analysis, if he had not prematurely appealed to the opaque event of madness or unquestionably invoked the mute nature of schizophrenia.[12] In the name of a "unitary" theory, he criticizes Blanchot for introducing a rupture, the absolute catastrophe of language, when it was possible to extend–

perhaps indefinitely – the communication between the meaning of schizophrenic speech and the nature of the illness. But Laplanche is able to maintain this continuity only by excluding from language the enigmatic identity which permits it to speak at the same time of madness *and* of an artistic work. Laplanche has remarkable analytic powers: his meticulous and rapid discourse competently covers the domain circumscribed by poetic forms and psychological structures; this is undoubtedly the result of extremely rapid oscillations which permit the imperceptible transfer of analogical figures in both directions. But a discourse (similar to Blanchot's) that places itself within the grammatical posture of the "and" that joins madness *and* an artistic work, a discourse that investigates this indivisible unity and concerns itself with the space created when these two are joined, is necessarily an interrogation of the Limit, understood as the line where madness becomes, in a precise sense, a perpetual rupture.

These two forms of discourse obviously manifest a profound incompatibility, even though an identical content is put to profitable use in either discourse; the simultaneous unraveling of poetic and psychological structures will never succeed in reducing the distance that separates them. Nevertheless, they are extremely close, perhaps as close as a possibility is to its realization. This is because the *continuity of meaning* between a work and madness can only be realized if it is based on the *enigma of similarity*, an enigma that gives rise to the *absolute nature of the rupture*. The dissolution of a work in madness, this void to which poetic speech is drawn as to its self-destruction, is what authorizes the text of a language common to both. These are not abstractions, but historical relationships that our culture must examine if it hopes to find itself.

"Depression at Jena" is the term that Laplanche applies to Hölderlin's first pathological episode. We could allow our imagination to play on this depressing event: in keeping with the post-Kantian crisis, the disputes of atheism, August Schlegel's and Novalis's speculations, the clamor of the Revolution which was understood as the promise of another world, Jena was certainly the arena where the fundamental concerns of Western culture abruptly emerged. The presence and absence of the gods, their withdrawal and imminence, defined the central and empty space where European culture discovered, as linked to a single investigation, the finitude of man and the return of time. The nineteenth century is commonly thought to have discovered the historical dimension; it could only open it up from out of the *circle*, the spatial form that negates time, the form in which the gods manifest their arrival and flight and men manifest their return to their native ground of finitude. More than simply an event that affected our emotions, that gave rise to the fear of nothingness, the death of God profoundly influenced our language; at the source of language it placed a silence that no work, unless it be pure chatter, can mask. Language thus assumes a sovereign position; it comes to us from elsewhere, from a place of which no one can speak, but it can be transformed into a work only if, in ascending to its proper discourse, it directs its speech towards this absence. In this sense, every work is an attempt to exhaust language; eschatology has become of late a structure of literary experience, and literary experience, by right of birth, is now of paramount importance. This was René Char's meaning: "When the dam built by men finally collapsed, torn along the giant fault line created by the abandonment of the gods, words in the distance, immemorial words, tried to resist the exorbitant thrust. In this moment was decided the dynasty of their meaning. I rushed to the very end of this diluvian night."[13]

In relation to this event, Hölderlin occupies a unique and exemplary position: he forged and manifested the link between a work and the absence of a work, between the flight of the gods and the perdition of language. He stripped the artist of his magnificent powers – his timelessness, his capacity to guarantee the truth and to raise every event to the heights of language. Hölderlin's language replaced the epic unity commemorated by Vasari with a division that is responsible for every work in our culture, a division that links it to its own absence and to its dissolution in the madness that had accompanied it from the beginning. He made it possible for us, positivist quadrupeds, to climb the slopes of an inaccessible summit which he had reached and which marked the *limit*, and, in doing so, to ruminate upon the psychopathology of poets.

NOTES

a   The French title of this essay, "*Le 'non' du père,*" contains a verbal pun, which plays off the homonymy of *non* [no] and *nom* [name]. – Ed.

1   In *Dichter und Helden* (Heidelberg: Weiss, 1921), pp. 5 – 22.

2   Heinrich Lange, *Hölderlin: Eine Pathographie* (Munich, 1942).

3 Friedrich Beissner, *Hölderlin: Reden und Aufsätze* (Weimar, 1961); L. Liegler, "Der gefesselte Strom und Ganymed . . . ," *Hölderlin Jahrbuch* 2 (1947), pp. 62–77; A. Müller, "Die beiden Fassungen von Hölderlins Elegie 'Der Wanderer,' *Hölderlin Jahrbuch* 3 (1948–1949), pp. 103–31.

4 Beck has published many articles in the *Hölderlin Jahrbuch.*

5 Hölderlin's *Hyperion,* trans. William R. Trask (New York: Ungar, 1965), reflects his relationship to Schiller; see Michael Hamburger, *Friedrich Hölderlin: Poems and Fragments* (Ann Arbor: University of Michigan Press, 1967), pp. 4–7.

6 For example, *Strindberg und Van Gogh: Versuch einer pathographischen Analyse unter vergleichender Heranziehung von Swedenborg und Hölderlin* (Bern: E. Bircher, 1922).

7 Jean Vinchon, *L'Art et la folie* (Paris: Stock, 1924); Jean Fretet, *L'Aliénation poétique: Rembrandt, Mallarmé, Proust* (Paris: J. B. Janin, 1946).

8 See *Hyperion,* p. 23, for the "All-in-One"; for the genius of Hellas, see pp. 88–96.

9 The *Thalia-Fragment* has not been translated into English.

10 Hamburger, *Poems and Fragments,* p. 355.

11 Ibid., p. 353.

12 Maurice Blanchot, "La folie par excellence," *Critique* 45 (1951), pp. 99–118.

13 "Seuil," in *Fureur et mystère* [1948], in *Oeuvres complètes* (Paris: Gallimard, 1983), p. 255.

SPEAKING AND SEEING
IN RAYMOND ROUSSEL*

———

The oeuvre is given to us divided just before the end by a statement that undertakes to explain how . . . This *How I Wrote Certain of My Books*,[1] which came to light after everything else was written, bears a strange relationship to the oeuvre whose mechanism it reveals by covering it in an autobiographical narrative at once hasty, modest, and meticulous.

Roussel seems to respect chronological order; in explaining his work he follows the thread leading directly from his early stories to the just-published *Nouvelles impressions d'Afrique* [*New Impressions of Africa*]. Yet the arrangement of the discourse seems to be contradicted by its internal space. In the foreground, writ large, is the process he used to compose his early writings; then, in ever-narrowing degrees, come the mechanisms he used to create the novels *Impressions d'Afrique* [*Impressions of Africa*] and *Locus solus* [*Solitary Place*], which is barely outlined. On the horizon, where language disappears in time, his most recent texts—the plays *La Poussière de soleils* [*Motes in Sunbeams*] and *L'Étoile au front* [*Star on the Forehead*]—are mere specks. As for the poem *Nouvelles impressions*, which has retreated to the far side of the horizon, it can be identified only by what it is not. The basic geometry of this "revelation" reverses the triangle of time. By a complete revolution, the near becomes distant, as if only in the

———

*Originally published in *Lettre ouverte* 4 (Summer 1962), pp. 38–51, this essay is a variant of the first chapter of Foucault's *Raymond Roussel* (Paris: Gallimard, 1963). The English translation of the latter has been used as a reference, but it has been extensively modified.

first turns of the labyrinth can Roussel play the guide. He leaves off just as the path approaches the center where he himself stands. At the moment of his death, in a gesture both cautious and illuminating, Roussel holds up to his work a mirror possessed of a bizarre magic: it pushes the central figure into the background where the lines are blurred, placing the point of revelation at the farthest distance, while bringing forward, as if for extreme myopia, whatever is farthest from the moment of its utterance. Yet as the subject approaches, the mirror deepens in secrecy.

A redoubled secret: the solemn finality of its form and the care with which it was withheld throughout the body of his work, only to be given up at the moment of his death, transforms what is revealed into an enigma. Lyricism, carefully excluded from *How I Wrote Certain of My Books* (the quotations from Dr. Janet that Roussel used to speak about what was undoubtedly the pivotal experience of his life attest to the rigor of this exclusion), appears inverted – at once denied and purified – in this strange form of the secret that death would preserve and make known. The "how" that Roussel inscribes in the title of his last, revelatory work introduces not only the secret of his language, but also the secret of his relationship with such a secret, not to lead us to it but, rather, to leave us disarmed and completely confused when it comes to determining the nature of the reticence that held the secret in a reserve suddenly abandoned.

His first sentence, "I have always intended to explain how I wrote certain of my books," clearly shows that his statements were not accidental, nor made at the last minute, but made up instead a part of the oeuvre itself, and of what was most constant, and best hidden, in its intention. Since his final revelation and original intention now becomes the inevitable and ambiguous threshold through which we are initiated into his work while forming its conclusion, there is no doubt it is deceptive: by giving us a key to explain the work, it poses a second enigma. It dictates an uneasy awareness for the reading of the work: a restless awareness since the secret cannot be found in the riddles and charades that Roussel was so fond of; it is carefully detailed for a reader who willingly lets the cat take his tongue before the end of the game, but it is Roussel who takes the reader's tongue for the cat. He forces the reader to learn a secret that he had not recognized, and to feel trapped in an anonymous, amorphous, now-you-see-it-now-you-don't, never really demonstrable type of secret. If Roussel of his own free will said that there *was* a secret, one could suppose that he completely suppressed it by admitting it and saying that it was, or else he shifted it, extended and multiplied it, while withholding the principle of the secret and its suppression. Here the impossibility of coming to a decision links all discourse about Roussel not only with the common risk of being mistaken but also with the more refined risk of being at one with it—and by one's very consciousness of the secret, which is always inclined to close in on itself and abandon the oeuvre to an easy night, altogether contrary to the day that traverses it.

In 1932, Roussel sent his printer a portion of the text that would become, after his death, *How I Wrote Certain of My Books*.[2] It was understood that these pages would not be published during his lifetime. The pages were not awaiting his death; rather, this decision was already within them, no doubt because of the immediacy of the revelation they contained. When, on May 30, 1933, he decided what the structure of the book would be, he had long since made plans never to return to Paris. During the month of June he settled in Palermo, where he spent every day drugged and in an intense state of euphoria. He attempted to kill himself, or to have himself killed, as if now he had acquired "the taste for death which hitherto he feared." On the morning he was due to leave his hotel for a drug cure at Kreuzlingen, he was found dead: in spite of his extreme weakness, he had dragged himself and his mattress against the door communicating with the adjoining room of his companion Charlotte Dufresne.

This door, which had been open at all times, was locked from the inside. The death, the lock, and this closed door formed, at that moment and for all time, an enigmatic triangle where Roussel's work is both offered to and withdrawn from us. Whatever is understandable in his language speaks to us from a threshold where access is inseparable from what constitutes its barrier—access and barrier in themselves equivocal, since in this indecipherable act the question remains, to what end? To release this death so long dreaded and now so suddenly desired? Or perhaps also to discover anew this life from which he had attempted furiously to free himself, but which he had also long dreamed of prolonging into eternity through his work and through the ceaseless, meticulous, fantastic constructions of the works themselves? Is there any other key, apart from the one in this last text, which is there, standing right up against the door? Is it signaling to open – or motioning to close? Is it holding a simple key that is marvelously ambiguous, ready in one turn either to lock in or to open up? Is it carefully shut on an irrevocable death, or is it transmitting beyond that death the exalted state of mind whose memory had stayed with Roussel since he was nineteen, and whose illumination he had always sought to recover in vain – except perhaps on this one night?

It is curious that Roussel, whose language is extremely precise, said that *How I Wrote Certain of My Books* was a "secret and posthumous" text. No doubt he meant several things other than the obvious meaning, which is secret until death: that death was a ritual part of the secret, its prepared threshold and its solemn conclusion. Perhaps he meant that the secret would remain secret even in death, giving it an added twist, by which the "posthumous" intensified the "secret" and made it definitive; or even better, death would reveal that there is a secret without showing what it hides, only what makes it opaque and impenetrable. He would keep the secret by revealing the substance. We are left with nothing, questioning a perplexing indiscretion, a key that is itself locked up, a cipher that deciphers and yet is encoded.

How I Wrote Certain of My Books hides as much, if not more, than it promises to reveal. It only gives us fragments of a breakdown of memory, which makes it necessary, as Roussel said, to use "ellipsis." However general this lacuna may be, it is only superficial compared to a more fundamental one, arbitrarily indicated by his simple exclusion, without comment, of a whole series of works. "It goes without saying that my other books, *La Doublure* [*The Lining/The Rehearsal/The Understudy*], *La Vue* [*The View/The Lens/The Vision*], and *Nouvelles impressions d'Afrique*, are absolutely outside of this process." Also outside of the secret are three poetical texts. *L'Inconsolable* [*The Inconsolable*], *Les Têtes de carton du carnaval de Nice* [*Cardboard Heads of the Carnival in Nice*], and the first poem written by Roussel, *Mon Âme* [*My Soul*]. What secret underlies his action of setting them aside, satisfied with a simple reference but without a word of explanation? Do these works hide a key of a different nature, or is it the same, but doubly hidden, to the extent of denying its existence? Could there perhaps be a master key that would reveal a silent law to identify the works coded and decoded by Roussel, and those whose code is not to have any evident code? The idea of a key, as soon as it is formulated, eludes its promise, or rather takes it beyond what it can deliver to a point where all of Roussel's language is placed in question.

There is a strange power in this text whose purpose is to "explain." So doubtful is its status, its point of origin, where it makes its disclosures and defines its boundaries, the space that at the same time it upholds and undermines, that after its initial dazzling it has but one effect: to create doubt, to disseminate it by a concerted omission when there was no reason for it, to insinuate it into what ought to be protected from it, and to plant it even in the solid ground of its own foundation. *How I Wrote Certain of My Books* is, after all, one of *his* books. Doesn't this text of the unveiled secret also hold its own secret, exposed and masked at the same time by the light it sheds on the other works?

Every esoteric interpretation of Roussel's language places the "secret" on the side of an objective truth. But this language means nothing but what it means [*veut dire*]: the marvelous flying machine that, equipped with magnets, sails, and wheels, bends to calculated breaths of air and deposits little enamel cobblestones on the sand, from which a mosaic emerges, wants to say and to show forth only the extraordinary meticulousness of its construction; it signifies itself, in a self-sufficiency by which Roussel's positivism, which Michel Leiris loved to point out, was certainly enchanted. The apparatuses of *Locus solus*, like the memorable flora of *Impressions d'Afrique*, are not *weapons* but—exactly and above all when they are alive, like Fogar's gyratory medusa or memory tree—*machines*. They do not speak; they work serenely in a gestural circularity in which the silent glory of their automatism is affirmed. Not one symbol, not one proper hieroglyph in all this minuscule, measured agitation, prolix with details but sparing of adornments. Not a hidden meaning, but a secret form.

The law of the construction of this flying "pile driver" is at once the mechanism that allows an old Germanic soldier to take shape out of a stippling of teeth stuck in the ground and the phonetic decomposition of an arbitrary sentence fragment that dictates the ordering of elements (spinster, old soldier, teeth). It is morphological, not a semantic displacement. The enchantment is not the result of a secret deposited in the folds of language by an external hand; it emerges from the very forms of this language when it opens out from itself in line with the

set of its possible nervures. In that visible contingency the secret culminates: not only did Roussel withhold, with only rare exceptions, the
key to formal genesis, but each phrase read could harbor a considerable number of such keys, virtually an infinitude, since the number of
words come is much greater than the number of words gone. Math-
ematically, there is no chance of finding the real solution; one is simply limited, by the revelation enacted in the final moment, to sense
beneath each of his sentences a provisional morphological field of
events, all of which are possible without a single one being assignable. It is the contrary of occult reticence, which leads, under multiple
but cleverly convergent forms, to a unique secret whose obstinate
presence is repeated and ends by asserting itself without ever being
clearly stated. Roussel's enigma is that each element of his language is
caught up in an indenumerable series of contingent configurations. A
secret much more manifest but also much more difficult than that
suggested by Breton: it does not reside in a ruse of meaning or in the
play of unveilings but in a concerted incertitude of morphology, or
perhaps in the certitude that a variety of constructions can articulate
the same text, authorizing incompatible but mutually possible systems of reading—a rigorous and uncontrollable polyvalence of forms.

Hence a structure worth remarking: at that moment when words
open out onto the things they say, without ambiguity or residuum,
they also have an invisible and multiform effect on other words,
which they link or dissociate, support and destroy in unavoidable
combinations. There, symmetrical with the threshold of meaning, is a
secret threshold, curiously open, and impassable, impassable precisely in being an immense opening, as if the key forbade crossing the
door it fits, as if the gesture creating this fluid, uncertain space were
one of definitive immobilization; as if, having come upon this internal
door by which it communicates with the dizziness of all its possibilities, language would linger over a gesture of both opening and closing. *How I Wrote Certain of My Books*—with death, suddenly and
obstinately sought by Roussel, at the center of its project—gives shape
to this ambiguous threshold: the internal space of language is designated very precisely there, but access to it is immediately refused in
an ellipsis whose accidental appearance hides its inevitable nature.
Like the cadaver at Palermo, the insoluble explication rests on an
internal threshold, unblocked and closed. It sets up Roussel's lan-

guage at its own limit, a language so immobile and finally so silent that it is just as comprehensible that Roussel himself might bar the threshold open as that he might force it closed. Here, death and language are isomorphic.

In which we care to see not one of those "thematic" laws which are said to govern both lives and oeuvres at the same time, discreetly and from on high but, rather, an experience in which language takes on one of its extreme and most poorly attended significations.

This labyrinth of words, constructed according to an inaccessible architecture and subject only to its own play, is at the same time a positive language: without vibrations, fine, discreet, obstinately attached to things, altogether close to them, faithful to the point of obsession to their detail, to their distances, to their colors, to their imperceptible rips, it is the neutral discourse of objects themselves, stripped of complicity or of any sentimental cousinship, as if entirely absorbed by the external. Spread over a world of possible forms that hollow out a void in it, this language is, more than any other, proximate to the being of things. And, just there, one is near what is really "secret" in Roussel's language–that it is so open when its construction is so closed, that it has so much ontological weight when its morphology is so provisional, that it looks out over a detailed discursive space when, with decided purpose, it is enclosed within a narrow fortress; in short, that it has the precise structure of that minuscule photograph which, encased in a fountain pen, opens to the attentive gaze "a whole beach of sand" whose immobile and sunstruck plethora the hundred and thirteen pages of *La Vue* hardly begin to exhaust. This language of internal artifice is a language that faithfully offers up much to see. The intimate secret of the secret is thus the power of making appear–itself hidden within a basic movement that communicates with the visible, and comes without problem or deformation to an understanding with things. The fountain pen of *La Vue* (instrument for constructing words which additionally offers up much to see) is, as it were, the most immediate shape of this relationship: in a thin piece of white ivory, long and cylindrical, perhaps also bizarrely carved, and extending toward the top, after a superposition of spirals and balls, in a sort of palette marked with a slightly faded and barely decipherable inscription, terminating at the bottom in a metal casing that different inks have stained like a multicolored rust, its smudged stem already slightly yellowed—a lens hardly wider than a brilliant point opens up a luminous space of simple, innumerable, and patient things in this instrument—designed for sketching arbitrary signs, no less distorted than itself, on paper.

How I Wrote Certain of My Books excludes *La Vue* from the procedural works, but it is evident that there is a fundamental connection between the photograph inserted in the fountain pen and the construction of *Locus solus* or the *Impressions*, which put so many marvels on view through an extravagance of writing. Both speak of the same secret—not of the secret that veils what it speaks of but, rather, of the much more naive, if little divulged, secret that in speaking and in obeying the arbitrary rules of language, one brings forth into the full light of appearance a whole generous world of things, which goes with the grain of poetic art internal to language and burrows beneath the familiar vegetation of wondrous galleries. A poetic art of quite extensive rites, quite close in its ontological signification to great destructive experience of language.

In truth, this world lacks the full existence that seems at first sight to illumine it from top to bottom. In *La Vue*, it is entirely a miniature, without proportions, of interrupted acts, of waves whose crests never reach unfurling, of balloons attached to the sky like leather suns, of children frozen into a track meet of statues. In *Impressions d'Afrique* and *Locus solus* there are machines to repeat things in time, to prolong in them a monotone, circular, and exhausted existence, to introduce them in the ceremonial of a representation, to maintain them, like the boneless head of Danton, in the automatism of a lifeless resurrection. As if a language thus ritualized could accede only to things already dead and disburdened of their time; as if it could not at all reach the being of things, but only their vain repetition and that double in which they might faithfully be recovered without ever recovering the freshness of their being. The narrative hollowed out from the interior by the communicative process with things hollowed out from the exterior by their own death, and so separated from themselves: on the one hand, with the apparatus of their repetition pitilessly described, and on the other hand, with their existence definitively inaccessible. At the level of the "signified" there is thus a symmetrical undoubling of what separates the description of things and the secret architecture of words in the "signified."

A figure of four terms is thus outlined: narrative, process, event, repetition. The event is hidden–present and at the same time beyond reach–in the repetition, as the process is in the narrative (which structures and evades it); so initial existence, in all its freshness, has the same function as the artificial machinery of the process; but inversely, the process plays the same role as the apparatuses of repetition: a subtle architecture that communicates with the first presence of things, throwing light upon them in the morning of their epiphany. And at the intersection of these four terms, whose play determines the possibility of language–of its marvelously overt artifice–death serves as relay and as limit. As threshold: it separates the event and its quasi-identical iteration by an infinitesimal distance, making them communicate in a life as paradoxical as that of Fogar's trees, whose growth is the unfolding of what is dead; in Roussel's language, it has separated the narrative and the invisible process in the same manner, making them live, once Roussel was gone, with an enigmatic life. In this sense the last text could well be only one manner of putting the whole oeuvre back into place in that water crystal in which Canterel had immersed Danton's flayed head in order that it repeat his discourses without end in the grip of a depilated, electrified, aquatic cat.

It is among these four cardinal points, which death dominates and shields like a great spider, that language weaves its precarious surface, that thin network within which rites and meaning intertwine.

And perhaps *La Doublure*, a text written during the first great crisis, in "a sensation of universal glory of extraordinary intensity," provides the most exact shape of the Secret, and to the very extent that it lacks process, the masks of the Nice carnival lend themselves to being seen even while hiding: but beneath that multicolored papier mâché, with the huge blue and red heads, the bonnets, the wigs, in the immobile separation of lips or the blind almond of eyes, a night menaces. What is seen is viewed only in the manner of a sign beyond measure, which designates the emptiness onto which it was thrown even while masking it. The mask is hollow and masks that hollowness. Such is the fragile and privileged situation of language: the word acquires its ambiguous volume in the interstices of the mask, denouncing the derisory, ritual double of the papier mâché visage and the dark presence of an inaccessible face. Its place is that impassable emptiness–a floating space, an absence of earth, an "incredulous sea"–in which death surges forth between concealed being and disarmed appearance, but in which, just as much, speaking has the marvelous power of offering up much to see. Here the birth and the death of language, it capacity to mask and to lead death in a dance of multicolored papier mâché, realize themselves.

The entirety of Roussel's language—and not only his last text—is "posthumous and secret." Secret since, without hiding anything, it is the hidden ensemble of all its possibilities, all its forms, which are sketched out and disappear across its transparency, like the personages sculpted by Fuxier in grape seeds. Posthumous, since it circulates amidst the immobility of things, and since, once their death comes to pass, it recounts the rites of their resurrection. From its birth, it is the other side of time. The intersecting structure of the "secret" and the "posthumous" is the most commanding figure of Roussel's language. Proclaimed at the moment of death, it is the visible secret of the unveiled secret; it makes the strange process communicate with all the other works; it designates a marvelous and pained experience of language that opens up for Roussel in the undoubling of *La Doublure*, and is closed again when the "double" of the work was made manifest in the undoubling of the final revelation. Royalty without the mystery of the Rite, which sovereignly organizes the relations of language, of existence, and of repetition—all this long procession of masks.

All these perspectives—it would be comforting to close them off, to suppress all the openings, and to allow Roussel to escape by the one exit that our conscience, seeking respite, will grant him. André Breton wrote, in "*Fronton Virage*" ["*The Wall at the Bend in the Road*"], "Is it likely that a man outside of all traditions of initiation should consider himself bound to carry to his grave a secret of another order . . . is it not more tempting to assume that Roussel obeyed, in the capacity of an initiate, a word of irrefutable command?"[3] Of course—everything would be strangely simplified then, and the work would close upon a secret whose forbidden nature alone would indicate its existence, essence, content, and necessary ritual. And in relation to this secret all of Roussel's texts would be just so much rhetorical skill, revealing, to whoever knows how to read what they say, the simple, extraordinarily generous fact that they do not say it. At the absolute limit it could be that the "chain of events" of *La Poussière de soleils* has something

in common–in its form–with the progression in the practice of al-
chemy, even if there is little chance that the twenty-two changes of
scenes dictated by the staging of the play correspond to the twenty-
two cards of the Major Arcana in a tarot deck. It is possible that certain outward signs of the esoteric process might have been used as
models for the double play on words, coincidence, and encounters at
the opportune moment, the linking of the twists and turns of the plot,
and the didactic voyages through banal objects having marvelous stories that define their true value by describing their origins, revealing
in each of them mythical avatars that lead them to the promise of
actual freedom. But if Roussel did use such material, and it is not at all
certain that he did, it would have been in the way he used stanzas of
"*Au clair de la lune*" and "*J'ai du bon tabac*" in his *Impressions
d'Afrique*, not to convey the content through an external and symbolic
language in order to disguise it, but to set up an additional barrier
within the language, part of a whole system of invisible paths, evasions, and subtle defenses.

Like an arrow, Roussel's language is opposed–by its direction
more than by its substance–to an occult language. It is not built on
the certainty that there is secrecy, only one secret that is wisely kept
silent; on the surface, it sparkles with a glaring doubt and hides an
internal void–it is impossible to know whether there is a secret, or
none, or several, and what they are. Any affirmation that a secret
exists, any definition of its nature, dries up Roussel's work at its
source, preventing it from coming to life out of this void which it
animates without ever satisfying our troubled ignorance. In the reading, his works promise nothing. There is only an inner awareness
that by reading the words, so smooth and aligned, we are exposed to
the unallayed danger of reading other words that are both different
and the same. His work as a whole, supported by *How I Wrote Certain
of My Books* and all the undermining doubts sown by that text, systematically imposes a formless anxiety, diverging and yet centrifugal,
directed not toward the most withheld secrets but toward the imitation and the transmutation of the most visible forms: each word at the
same time energized and drained, filled and emptied by the possibility
of there being yet another meaning, this one or that one, or neither
one nor the other, but a third, or more.

NOTES

1   Raymond Roussel, *How I Wrote Certain of My Books*, trans. with notes by Trevor Winkfield (New York: State University of New York Press, 1975, 1977).

2   One can say nothing about Roussel today that does not make manifest a flagrant debt to Michel Leiris: his articles, but also his entire oeuvre, are the indispensable threshold for a reading of Roussel.

3   André Breton, "Fronton Virage," in *Une Etude sur Raymond Roussel*, ed. J. Ferry (Paris: Arcones, 1953).

INTRODUCTION TO ROUSSEAU'S *DIALOGUES**

T hese are anti-*Confessions*. And they come as if from the latter's arrested monologue, from a surge of language that breaks forth from having encountered an obscure barrier. At the beginning of May 1771, Rousseau finishes reading from the *Confessions* at the home of the Count d'Egmont: "Anyone, even if he has not read my writings, who will examine my nature, my character, my morals, my likings, my pleasures, and my habits with his own eyes and can still believe me a dishonorable man, is a man who deserves to be stifled [*un homme à étouffer*]." There begins a game of suffocation which will not end before the rediscovery of the open, breathable, irregular domain – tangled but without snares [*enlacement*] – of the walk and the reverie.[1] The man who does not believe that Rousseau is decent is to be stifled, then: a severe caveat, since he is not to base his conviction on a reading of Rousseau's books but on a knowledge of the man, that knowledge which is offered up plain in the book of *Confessions*, but which, through the book, must be affirmed without it. One must believe what the written word says, but not believe it because one has read it. And the injunction is read by the author. In this way, one will be able to

---

*In J.-J. Rousseau, *Rousseau juge de Jean-Jacques: Dialogues* (Paris: A. Colin, coll. "Bibliothèque de Cluny," 1962), pp. vii–xxiv [*Rousseau, Judge of Jean-Jacques: Dialogues, The Collected Writings of Rousseau*, Vol. I, ed. Roger D. Masters and Christopher Kelly, trans. Judith R. Bush, Christopher Kelly, and Roger D. Masters (Hanover, N.H.: University Press of New England, 1990)]. I have made use of this translation for many of the passages cited by Foucault. For quotations from the *Confessions* I have relied on the translation by J. J. Cohen: *The Confessions* (Baltimore: Penguin, 1971). In both instances I have occasionally made slight alterations – R.H.

hear it, embracing its meaning and not contesting it by making an issue of the place from which it is pronounced. So there opens up a space of light, faithful, indefinitely transmissible speech where belief and truth communicate without hindrance, that space no doubt of the immediate voice in which the Savoyard vicar, at his listening post, had once placed his profession of faith. The *Confessions* is read on several occasions, at M. du Perzay's, at Dorat's, before the royal prince of Sweden, at the Egmonts' finally. A confidential reading, before a restricted audience, but whose quasi secrecy relates at bottom only to the text that supports it; the truth it aims to transmit will be freed for an indefinite and direct path, already idealized for becoming a belief. In the ether where the voice finally triumphs, the unbelieving wretch will not be able to breathe any more; there will no longer be any need of hands or cords to choke him.

This light voice, this voice that with its gravity thins down to the last degree the text from which it arises, falls into silence. The great meeting of convictions whose instantaneous effect Rousseau expected is not heard: "Everyone was silent. Mme d'Egmont was the only person who seemed moved. She trembled visibly but quickly controlled herself and remained quiet, as did the rest of the company. Such was the advantage I derived from my reading and my declaration." The voice is muted, and the only echo that it awakens in response is nothing but a repressed shudder, an emotion visible for a moment, quickly brought back to silence.

It was probably during the following winter that Rousseau started writing the *Dialogues*, with an absolutely different use of the voice. From the beginning, it is a voice already stifled and enclosed in a "profound, universal silence, no less inconceivable than the mystery it veils . . . this terrifying and terrible silence." It no longer evokes the circle of an attentive audience around it, but only the labyrinth of a writing whose message is completely embedded in the material density of the sheets of paper that it covers. From the depths of its existence, the conversation of the *Dialogues* is written in the same sense that the *Confessions* in their monologue are spoken. For this man who always complained of not knowing how to speak, and who made the ten years during which he practiced the craft of writing into a kind of unfortunate parenthesis in his life, the discourses, letters (real or fictional), addresses, declarations—the operas, too—defined, throughout his existence, a language space in which speech and writing cross, contest, and reinforce each other. This interweaving challenges the one by the other but justifies them by opening them up to one another: speech to the text that determines it ("I shall come forward with this work in my hand . . ."), writing to the speech that makes it into an immediate, burning confession.

But precisely there, at the junction of sincerities, in that first opening of language, is where the peril originates: without a text, speech is spread around, deformed, endlessly travestied, and maliciously twisted (as was the confession of the children's abandonment). Written, one's discourse is reproduced; altered, its authorship is questioned; the booksellers sell bad proofs; false attributions circulate. Language is no longer sovereign in its space. Whence the great anxiety that hangs over Rousseau's existence from 1768 to 1776 – that his voice might be lost. And in two possible ways: that the manuscript of the *Confessions* might be read and destroyed, leaving that voice in suspense and without justification; and that the text of the *Dialogues* might be passed over and remain in a definitive abandonment in which the voice would be suffocated by the pages on which it was transcribed: "If I dared to make some request of those into whose hands this writing will fall, it would be to read all of it." We know of the famous gesture by which Rousseau meant to deposit the manuscript of the *Dialogues* at Notre-Dame, meant to lose it by passing it on, wished to entrust this text of distrust to an anonymous place, so that it would be transformed into speech. Here we see, according to a strict coherence, the symmetrical counterpart of the care given to protecting the manuscript of the *Confessions*; that work, the fragile, indispensable support of a voice, had been desecrated by a reading addressed "to ears the least prepared to hear it"; the text of the *Dialogues* confines a voice that is walled in by darkness and that might make itself heard as a living voice only with the help of an all-powerful intercessor: "It could happen that the noise of this action would bring my manuscript to the eyes of the King."

And failure is lodged in the systematic necessity of the event. The reading of the *Confessions* gives rise only to a long silence, opening up, under the passionate voice and in front of it, an empty space into which it rushes, giving up the idea of making itself heard, and in which it is gradually stifled by the muffled pressure of the murmurs that deflect it toward the contrary of what is said, the contrary of what it was. On the other hand, the depositing of the *Dialogues* runs up against a barred space. The marvelous place where writing might make itself heard is forbidden; it is surrounded by a grillwork fence so light that it remained invisible up to the moment of passing through it, but so strongly padlocked that this place from which one might be heard is just as closed off as the one where speech was resolved into writing. During this whole period the space of language was covered by four linked figures: the voice of the *Confessions* that rises out of an imperiled text, a voice always threatened with being cut off from its support and thereby suffocated; this same voice that plunges into silence and is stifled by the absence of an echo; the text of the *Dialogues* which confines an unheard voice and offers it up, lest it die, to an absolute listening; that same text expelled from the place where it might become speech and perhaps itself condemned to "be ensnared" in the impossibility of making itself heard. The only recourse is to surrender peacefully, and from the depths of a consenting tenderness, to the universal embrace: "To yield henceforth to my destiny, not to go on struggling against it, to let my persecutors do as they will with their prey, to remain their unresisting plaything for the remainder of my sad old days . . . this is my final resolution."

And these four figures of suffocation will not be resolved until the day when the free space of the Lake of Bienne will return to life in memory, with the slow rhythm of the water and that unbroken sound that, being neither speech nor text, takes the voice back to its source, to the murmur of reverie: "There the sound of the waves and the tossing of the water, holding my senses and ridding my soul of any other agitation, plunged it into a delicious reverie in which darkness often surprised me without my noticing it." In this absolute and original murmuring, all human speech regains its immediate truth and its confidence: "The first fires of love emerged from the pure crystal of the fountains."

The suffocation that is wished upon the enemy at the end of the *Confessions* has become an obsession with entrapment by the "Gentlemen" throughout the *Dialogues*: Jean-Jacques and the one who believes him to be dishonest are joined in the same mortal embrace. A single cord presses them against each other, breaks off the voice, and from its melody calls forth the disorder of internal words that are at odds with themselves and doomed to the written silence of fictional dialogues.

More often than not, Rousseau's language is linear. In the *Confessions*, the flashbacks, the anticipations, the interference of themes derive from a free use of melodic writing. A genre of writing that was always privileged by him, because he saw it–in music and in language–as the most natural kind of expression, the one in which the speaking subject is fully present, without reserve or reticence, in each of the forms of what it says: "In the venture that I have undertaken to display myself in full to the public, nothing about me must remain obscure or hidden; I must constantly reveal myself to its eyes, so that it may observe me in all the aberrations of my heart, in all the recesses of my life." A continuous expression, indefinitely faithful to the course of time, and following it like a thread; "finding the least gap in my story, the least omission, and asking himself: what did he do during that period of time?" the reader must not "accuse me of not having wanted to tell everything." A perpetual variation in style is necessary, then, in order to sincerely follow this sincerity of every moment. Each event and the emotion accompanying it will need to be restored in their freshness, and presented now for what they were. "I will tell each thing as I feel it, as I see it, without affectation, without constraint, without concerning myself about its motley appearance." For this diversity is that of things only in one perspective: in its perpetual and constant origin it is the perspective of the soul that experiences them, rejoices in them, and suffers from them; it conveys, without distance, without interpretation, not what occurs but the person to whom the event occurs. "I write not so much the history of these events as that of the state of my soul as they took place." When it is that of nature, language traces out a line of immediate reversibility, such that there is no secrecy, no fortress, no real interior, but an externalized sensibility that is immediately expressed: "By relating in simple detail everything that happened to me, everything that I did, everything that I thought, everything that I felt, I cannot mislead unless I mean to; and even if I meant to, I would not easily succeed in this manner."

It is here that this linear language assumes its amazing powers. From that diversity of passions, impressions, and style, from its faithfulness to so many unconnected events ("without having any condition myself, I have experienced every condition; I have lived in every one, from the lowest to the highest"), he creates a design that is both unified and unique–"myself alone." This signifies an inseparable proximity to oneself, and an absolute difference from others. "I am made unlike anyone I have ever met; I will even venture to say that I am like no one in existence. If I am no better, at least I am different." And yet, this marvelous unity, so different, can only be reconstituted by others, like the readiest and most necessary of hypotheses. It is the reader who transforms this nature, always external to itself, into truth: "It is for him to assemble these elements and to determine the being that they compose; the result must be his work; if he should go wrong, then the whole mistake will be his own making." In this sense the language of the *Confessions* finds its philosophical dwelling place (just like the melodic language of music) in the dimension of the original, that is, in that hypothesis which founds what appears in the being of nature.

The *Dialogues*, on the contrary, are constructed on a vertical writing. The subject that speaks in that disciplined, harmonically structured language is a disunited subject, superimposed on itself, lacunar, and incapable of being made present except through an addition that is never completed—as if it appeared at a receding point that only a certain convergence would enable one to locate. Instead of being gathered into the surfaceless point of a sincerity where error, hypocrisy, and mendacity would not even have room to lodge themselves, the subject that speaks in the *Dialogues* covers a surface of language that is never closed, and on which others will be able to intervene through their tenacity, their spitefulness, their stubborn decision to falsify everything.

From 1767 to 1770, during the time he was completing the *Confessions*, Rousseau went by the name of Jean-Joseph Renou. While he is writing the *Dialogues* he has abandoned the pseudonym and again signed his name. Now, it is this Jean-Jacques Rousseau who in his concrete unity is absent from the *Dialogues*—or, rather, through them, and perhaps by them, is disunited. The discussion involves an anonymous Frenchman, representative of those who have stolen Rousseau's name; facing him, a certain Rousseau, who, without any concrete determination other than his honesty, bears the name that the public has robbed from the real Rousseau, and he knows precisely what belongs to Rousseau—his works. Lastly, a third but constant presence, one who is no longer called anything but *le* Jean-Jacques with a lordly familiarity, as if he no longer had the right to the proper name that individualizes him, but only to the singularity of his first name. But this Jean-Jacques is not even presented in the unity to which he is entitled: there is a Jean-Jacques-for-Rousseau who is the "author of the books," and another for the Frenchman, who is the "author of the crimes." But since the author of the crimes cannot be the author of books whose sole purpose is to win hearts over to virtue, Jean-Jacques-for-Rousseau will cease to be the author of the books, becoming nothing but the criminal of public opinion, and Rousseau, denying that Jean-Jacques wrote the books, will assert that he is only a falsifier. Conversely, if Jean-Jacques-for-the-Frenchman has committed all the crimes that one knows he has, then he was able to give would-be moral lessons only by concealing a secret "venom." Those books are therefore other than what they appear to be, and their truth is manifested only in a displaced form, in those texts which Jean-Jacques does not sign but knowledgeable people are right to attribute to him; the author of the crimes thus becomes the author of criminal books. It is through these four characters that the real Jean-Jacques Rousseau (the one who said so simply and supremely "myself alone" in the *Confessions*) is gradually identified. Even so, he is never presented in flesh and blood, and he never speaks (except in the always-elided form of the author of the *Dialogues*, in the irruption of a few notes, and in fragments of discourse reported by Rousseau or by the Frenchman). If he was seen or heard, this was only by Rousseau (that second self, the bearer of his true name). The Frenchman declares himself satisfied, without even having met him; he does not have the courage and hardly recognizes the utility of speaking for him – at most he is willing to be the trustee of his papers and his mediator for a posthumous recognition. That is how distant and inaccessible that character is now whose immediate presence made possible the language of the *Confessions*; henceforth he will be positioned at the outer limit of speech, already beyond it, at the virtual, never-perceived vertex of the triangle formed by the two interlocutors and the four characters defined by their dialogue.

The apex of the triangle, the moment when Rousseau, having rejoined Jean-Jacques, will be recognized for what he is by the Frenchman, and when the author of the true books will have routed the false author of the crimes, can be reached only in a beyond, when, death having quelled the hatreds, time will be able to resume its original course. This figure that is virtually traced out in the text of the *Dialogues*, and all the lines of which converge toward a unity regained in its truth, sketches a kind of reverse image of another figure, the one that, from the outside, has directed the drafting of the *Dialogues* and the moves that immediately followed it. Jean-Jacques Rousseau, the author of his books, had seen himself reproached by the French for having written criminal books (the denunciation of *Emile* and the *Contract*), or accused of not having written them at all (the dispute concerning the *The Village Soothsayer*), or suspected of having written libels. In any case, he became, through his books, and because of them, the author of countless crimes. The *Dialogues* are intended, by taking up the hypothesis of the enemies, to rediscover the author of the books and consequently to do away with the author of the crimes; and this was to be accomplished by means of a deposit so extraordinary and so impressive that its very brilliance would reveal the secret; hence the idea of placing the manuscript on the great altar of Notre-Dame (then the substitutive ideas: the visit to Condillac, and the circular letter). But an obstacle always looms up: the public's indifference, the incomprehension of the man of letters, and, above all, model and symbol of all the others, the fence, so visible but unnoticed, that surrounds the choir of the church. All these barriers are themselves only the reflection, in the real world, of that limit which indefinitely postponed, in the fiction of the *Dialogues*, the rediscovery of J.-J. Rousseau. The God from whom Jean-Jacques expected the restitution of his indivisible and triumphant unity eludes him behind the fence, just as that endless posterity, in which people will see the memory of Rousseau "reestablished in the honor it deserves" and his books recognized as being "useful through the esteem that is due to their Author," shines beyond death.

It is only in that grilled-off and mortal beyond that the simple evil which spoke in the *Confessions* can be reconstituted. That is, unless all at once a lateral shift occurs (what Rousseau calls "withdrawal into oneself"). Unless language again becomes melodic and linear, the simple tracking of an ego [*moi*] that is punctual and therefore true. So the "myself alone" that opens the first book of the *Confessions* will be answered, in the first line of the *Reveries*, by its strict equivalent: "So here I am, alone on the earth." This "so" envelops in its logical curve the whole necessity that organized the *Dialogues*, the painful dispersion of the one who is both their "subject" and their "object," the yawning space of their language, the anxious setting-down of their letter, their resolution, finally, in a speech that again says "I,"

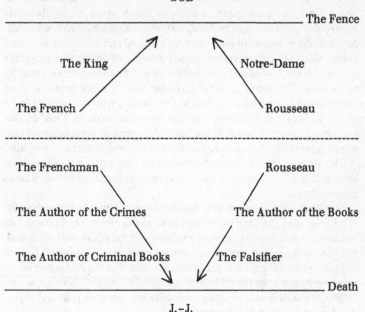

GOD

The Fence

The King   Notre-Dame

The French   Rousseau

The Frenchman   Rousseau

The Author of the Crimes   The Author of the Books

The Author of Criminal Books   The Falsifier

Death

J.–J.

naturally and originally, and restores the possibility of dreaming after so many haunting thoughts, and the free and idle expansiveness of the walk, after so many desperate moves.

The *Dialogues*, an autobiographical text, has the basic structure of great theoretical texts: it is a matter of establishing nonexistence, and of justifying existence, in a single burst of thought. To establish, according to the readiest, most economical, and most probable hypothesis, everything that pertains to illusion, untruth, distorted passions, to a neglected nature, driven to self-estrangement, everything that assails our existence and our tranquility with a discord that is no less pressing for being apparent, is at the same time to reveal its nonbeing and to show its inevitable genesis. To justify existence is to bring it back to its natural truth, at that immobile point where all impulses arise, take effect, and subside according to a spontaneity that is both a necessity of character and the freshness of an untrammeled freedom.

In this way the justification tends, little by little, to vitiate existence into a figure without space or time, so that it owes its fragile being only to the impulses that incite it, traverse it against its will, and indicate it in the evanescent form, always external to itself, of the sensitive being. Whereas nonexistence, in the process of establishment, finds its ground, the law of its organization, and even the internal necessity of its being. Existence is never anything but an innocence that does not manage to be virtuous; and nonexistence, without ceasing to be illusion, darkens, thickens into an essential malice. This double movement is never taken to the limit of incompatibility, because language intervenes with a dual function: to express innocence and bind it with its sincerity; to form the system of conventions and laws that limit self-interest, organize their consequences, and establish it in its general forms.

But what happens then in a world where one can no longer speak? What restraint [*mesure*] will be able to check the excessiveness [*démesure*] of each impulse, prevent existence from being only an indefinitely sensitive point, and nonexistence from organizing itself into an indefinite conspiracy? It is this excessiveness that the *Dialogues* experience through a world without language, just as the *Contract* would define, through man's language, the possible measure [*mesure*] of justified existence and necessary malice.

Silence is the primary experience of the *Dialogues*, both the silence that made them necessary with their writing and their peculiar organization, and that which, from within, serves as a thread for the dialectics, the proof, and the assertion. The *Confessions* were intended to mark out a path of truth amid the world's noisy rumors in order to silence them. The *Dialogues* strive to engender a language inside a space in which everything is quiet. Below is a rough characterization of the moments of that language, and the way in which that failure develops:

1. Certain individuals have given my contemporaries false ideas about me. And yet my entire work should have justified my existence (*La nouvelle Héloïse* proving the purity of my heart; *Emile*, my interest in virtue).

2. Faced with the growing danger, I yielded and attempted to restore language at a subsequent moment. I supposed that I had the same opinions about myself as others have (so I assume all those illusions to be well founded): How would I have acted toward that

dark character which I've become in my own fictitious opinion? I would have gone to visit him, I would have questioned him, I would have listened to and read his *Confessions*.

3. But what I would have done, they haven't done at all; they haven't even tried to ascertain what my behavior would have been if I had in front of me this character they have made me into. So I yield again, and I seek, still in order to avoid the utter excessiveness of innocence and malice, a third, higher and deeper, form of language. Since people have not questioned me to learn my answers, I shall give an answer that will question others, forcing them to give me an answer that will show me, perhaps, that I am mistaken, that the excessiveness between nonexistence based in malice and existence found innocent is not total; and by compelling them to break their silence I will rediscover the language that limits excessiveness.

The language of the *Dialogues* is a third-degree language, therefore, since it is a matter of overcoming three forms of silence: that "triple wall of silence" which is alluded to several times and which should not be understood simply as a turn of phrase – it is the basic structure from which the *Dialogues* draw their existence. And an internal necessity, since the three characters represent, in reverse order, the different levels of this thwarted language: the Frenchman (who has spoken first, but offstage, and draws the monster's portrait before the opening of the *Dialogues*) defines that response which J.-J. Rousseau gives – only as a last resort and because he has not obtained it – instead of the French. Rousseau represents the person who would have spoken at the second level, the man who, after having read the works, but believed in the monster, would go to listen to the confessions of J.-J. Rousseau. Finally, Jean-Jacques himself is the first-level man, the one who is just as his books and his life prove him to be, the one whose language was not understood from the very start. But in the *Dialogues* he does not himself appear, he is merely promised, so difficult is it, at a level of language so complex, to recover the first speech by which existence innocently justifies itself while founding nonexistence.

The dialogue is a writing convention that is rather rare in Rousseau: he prefers correspondence, a slow and lengthy exchange where silence is vanquished the more easily as the partners break through it in a freedom that reflects its own image from one to the other and becomes the mirror of itself. But here, the form of an imaginary dialogue is required by the conditions of possibility of the language that is deployed therein. It is a matter of making other voices speak in a harmonic structure; it is a language that must necessarily pass through others in order to address them, since if one speaks to them without forcing them to speak, they reduce what one says to silence by remaining silent themselves. They have to speak if I am to make myself understood, and make it understood, in my language, that they must finally cease being silent. This language of theirs, with which I address them (and by which I establish the hypocrisy of their un- truth), is a structural necessity if I am to speak to them of that silence to which, by saying nothing, they wish to reduce my language and the justification of my existence.

This basic structure is reflected at the thematic surface of the text by the indefinite significance that is attributed to silence. The silence that Rousseau's enemies surround him with signifies all the vile ru- mors about him that are circulating. The silence in which these ru- mors are cloaked signifies the plot that organizes them. The silence in which this conspiracy is cloaked signifies the relentless vigilance of those responsible for it. In this absence of speech one can read the marvelous effectiveness of a secret sect—that of the "Gentlemen," in which the Enlightenment philosophers who have just triumphed over the Jesuits explicitly take up the role of the Reverend Fathers of the *Provinciales,* and silence Speech just as they did. The silence from which their venture benefits on all sides signifies a universal complic- ity, the unbroken chain that links together in the same criminal spirit all people of high society, then all the French, England, the whole world. It is a paradox, of course, that such a network stays hidden, that there does not exist in this association of the wicked any man who in spite of everything is honorable enough to speak, or who has that extra degree of perversity that would make him betray. But this silence signifies that the plot is organized by a very small leadership, a few men, perhaps just one, Diderot assisted at most by Grimm. These are probably the only ones to be informed about everything, to be familiar with each element of the undertaking; but no one knows this because they keep quiet, and reveal themselves only by making sure the others do not talk (witness d'Alembert going to impose si- lence on the noisy Voltaire). It is in their hands that absolute silence, which is to say, absolute conspiracy, is ensured; they are the summit from which silence imperiously falls; all the others are instruments rather than agents, partial, indifferent accomplices who are not told the essentials of the project, and who keep quiet in turn. And gradually silence settles even on the person who is its object and its purpose. It reaches the individual who speaks tirelessly in these *Dialogues*, and speaks there only because people keep quiet and in order to reactivate as language the silence that weighs on him.

The point is that if silence for him is the monotonous signifier of the plot, for the conspirators it is the thing that is unanimously signified to the victim. It is intimated to him that he is not the author of his books; it is intimated that, whatever one might say, his purpose will be distorted; it is intimated that his speech no longer belongs to him, that his voice will be stifled; that he will no longer make any word of justification understood; that his manuscripts will be taken; that he will not find any legible ink to write with, but "lightly tinted water"; that posterity will not know his real face or his true heart; that he will not be able to convey what he meant to say to future generations; and that it is finally in his own interest to shut up, since he is not called upon to speak. And this silence is signified to him in the most ponderous and imperious manner by the apparent kindnesses that are done to him. What does he have to say when he is given a party, and when Thérèse is offered a gift of charity? What does he have to say seeing that people do not denounce his vices, that they keep silent concerning his crimes, that they do not even talk about the ones he has admitted? What could he protest against, seeing that our Gentlemen let him live, and "even pleasantly, insofar as it is possible for a wretch to live without doing harm"? What does he have to say when we keep silent?

A whole world is constructed, which is that silent world of Surveillance and Sign. From all directions, J.-J. is being watched: "He has been pointed out, described, recommended everywhere to deliverymen, Clerks, guards, spies, Chimney-sweeps, at all the Theaters, in all the cafés, to the barbers, the merchants, the peddlers, the booksellers." The walls, the floors have eyes that follow him. This silent observation has no direct expression that is transformed into an accusing language. Nothing but signs, none of which is a spoken word. When he goes walking, people spit on his path, when he goes in to see a show, people move away from him or, on the contrary, gather round him with fists held out, sticks threatening him; people talk about him loudly, but in a mute, icy language that is not addressed to him, passing slantwise from one to the other all around his anxious ears, so that he feels in question, and not questioned. Rocks are thrown at him in Môtiers, and in Paris a straw dummy resembling him is burned under his windows: a double sign—that people would like to burn him, but that he will be burned in mockery, for he would have the right to speak if it were decided to condemn him. Thus he is condemned to that world of signs which deprived him of speech.[2]

That is why, against the Surveillance-Signs system, he demands admittance into the Trial-Punishment system as a liberation. The trial presupposes the bright display of speech: its edifice is not entirely solid unless it culminates in the confession of the accused, in that spoken acknowledgment of the crime by the criminal. No one has the right to deprive anyone of a trial; a person is entitled to be tried and sentenced, since to undergo punishment is to have spoken. Punishment always implies prior speech. Ultimately, the closed world of the tribunal is less perilous than the empty space where the accusatory word does not meet with any opposition since it propagated in silence, and where the defense is never convincing since it responds only to a stubborn silence. Prison walls would be preferable if they would manifest a *declared* injustice. The prison cell would be the contrary of that surveillance and those signs which appear, circulate, fade away, and reappear indefinitely in a space where they float freely; it would be a surveillance tied to punishment, a sign that would finally signify the clear speech of a judgment. For his part, Rousseau has agreed to be the *judge* of Jean-Jacques.

But the appeal for prison is only a dialectical moment (just as it was a tactical moment when Rousseau actually formulated it in 1765, after being expelled from the island of Saint-Pierre). There are other ways to convert Surveillance back into a free gaze, and the Sign into an immediate expression.

That is the function of the initial myth, the myth of an "ideal world similar to ours, yet altogether different," where everything is a little sharper and somehow more appealing to the senses: "Forms are more elegant, colors more vivid, odors sweeter, all objects more interesting." Nothing needs to be scrutinized, pondered, interpreted: everything asserts itself with a force that is gentle and lively at the same time; hearts are prompted by a direct, quick impulse that no obstacle can deflect or distort, and that dies away as soon as one's interest disappears. It is a world without mystery, without concealment, hence without hypothesis, without mystery or intrigue. Reflection does not have to fill the empty spaces of a blurred and myopic gaze; the images of things are automatically reflected in clear gazes where they directly trace the original simplicity of their lines. In contrast to Surveillance, which squints its eyes, tracks down its object and silently encloses it, there is from the outset an indefinitely open gaze that lets the free expanse offer its forms and colors.

In this world, which delights in reality itself, the signs are, from the origin, replete with what they mean to say. They form a language only to the extent that they hold an immediate expressive value. Each one can tell, and has to tell, nothing else but its being: "It can never act except at the level of its source." So it does not have the ability to dissemble or mislead, and it is received just as it is transmitted – in the vivacity of its expression. It does not signify a more or less well-founded judgment, it does not bring about the circulation of an opinion in the space of nonexistence, it conveys, from one heart to another, "the imprint of its modifications." It expresses what is imprinted, being of a piece, absolutely, with what the gaze offers. In the world of Surveillance, the Sign signified opinion, hence nonexistence, hence malice; in that of the Gaze, it signifies what is seen, and so the world in its innocent freshness. In the course of a walk one day, Rousseau stops in front of an engraving; he takes it in, enjoying its lines and colors. His absorbed look, his set eyes, his whole motionless body signify nothing else than what is given to his gaze, and the sudden imprint that is stamped in his soul: this is what happens in that marvelous world. But as he is looking, Rousseau is being watched: some agents of the plot see that he is looking at the plan of a fortress; he is suspected of spying and of contemplating an act of treason. In this world of reflection, what else could so much attention given to a simple engraving mean?

At the beginning of the *Dialogues* the universe of the Gaze and of Expression scarcely have anything but a fictive existence: like the state of nature, it is a hypothesis for understanding, and for understanding what is the opposite of itself or at least its distorted truth. It represents our world methodically reduced to an unreal truth, which explains it precisely by that discrepancy, by a tiny but decisive difference. It keeps this explanatory value throughout the *Dialogues,* enabling one to understand how Rousseau was made a nonperson, but a famous object of slander, how the plot originated, how it was developed, how a return has become impossible now. But, at the same time, the myth of this unreal world gradually loses its fictive quality along with its universal scope to become more and more limited and more and more real. When all is said and done, it will only define the soul of Jean-Jacques.

Quite early in the *Dialogues* Rousseau already imagines that world impinging on ours, merging with it in a single space and forming with it a tangle so inextricable that in order to recognize one another its inhabitants are obliged to use a system of signs, those signs which happen to have a truthfulness of expression imperceptible to others, so that they form more of a sect than a world. In the shadow of real society such signs delineate a barely recognizable web of initiates whose very existence is hypothetical, since the only example of them given is the author of the works of Jean-Jacques Rousseau. In the second dialogue, Jean-Jacques is actually brought into the myth, but with great precautions. From the outside, first of all, Rousseau has been able to recognize him as a being of the Gaze. He was able to note in him the three characteristic behaviors of such men. In solitude, he contemplates his *fictions,* that is, objects of which he has complete control and which cannot be hidden from his gaze by any shadow. When he is tired of imagining (for he has a "lazy disposition"), he *dreams,* calling for the help of sensible objects and in turn populating nature with "creatures after his very heart." Lastly, if he wishes to take a rest from his reverie, he passively surrenders to "relaxation," opening himself without the least activity to the most ordinary spectacles: "a boat that passes by, a windmill that turns, a cowherd at work, people bowling or playing with a racquet, the flowing river, the flying bird." As for Jean-Jacques's soul, it is deduced a priori so to speak, as if it were a matter of inserting it through reasoning in the society to which it is entitled: "Let us set all the facts aside for a moment." Let us suppose a temperament made up of an extreme sensitivity and a lively imagination: in this type of man reflection will have a small part, dissimulation will not be possible—he will immediately show what he experiences at the moment he experiences it. There will be in this man no other signs than those of the most lively and immediate expression. Is this still-abstract man Jean-Jacques? Yes, "he is just the sort of man I have studied."

But is he the only individual of that sort? Apparently so; at any rate, he is the only cited exemplar of that utterly sincere and totally secret family. But, truth be told, the character in the *Dialogues* who bears the name Rousseau is also a man in keeping with the myth: he had been able to recognize the author of the *Héloïse* and *Emile*, he was able to detect the immediate expressive value of signs in him, he was able to look at Jean-Jacques without preconception or reflection, he opened his soul to Jean-Jacques's. As for the Frenchman, he entered the delightful garden later; first he had to leave the universe of Signs and Surveillance, of which he was more the confidant than the agent; but through Rousseau he learned to look at Jean-Jacques, through his books he learned to read him. The Frenchman, Rousseau, and Jean-Jacques will all three, but all by themselves, form that real society which the beginning of the *Dialogues* constructed as a great systematic myth, giving it the whole breadth of a world. That universe *à trois* (whose structure is so highly privileged in Rousseau's entire work) is promised at the end of the *Dialogues* as the imminent dream that will be able to lead, if not to happiness, at least to final peace: "Let us add," Rousseau suggests to the Frenchman, "the sweetness of seeing two decent and true hearts once again open themselves to his own. Let us thus temper the horror of this solitude . . . let us mete out this consolation to him in his final hour, in which the least friends shut their eyes to him."

But whatever may have been gained by reducing the myth to an enchanted trinity, it is still a dream. To become completely real it will have to contract even more, and no longer invoke the blessed trinity and its golden age; it will have to cease appealing to the Frenchman and invoking his third-party presence; Rousseau and Jean-Jacques will have to be one and the same. Surveillance will then recede into the depths of a calm and indifferent sky; the Signs will fade away; there will only remain an indefinitely sensitive Gaze, always invited into confidence—a gaze that is wonderfully open to things but gives no other sign of what it sees than the completely interior expression of the pleasure of existing. A gaze without surveillance and an expression below the threshold of signs will be based on the pure act of enjoyment in which the envisioned trinity will reunite with supreme solitude, already divine, in reality at last: "What does one enjoy in such a situation? Nothing outside oneself, nothing but oneself and one's own existence, as long as this state endures one suffices to oneself like God."

The myth that opened up the space of the *Dialogues*, and in which their three characters took their places and attempted to reunite, finally encounters the reality toward which speech and dream were advancing only in that first person of the *Reveries*, who is the only one to dream, the only one to speak.

—So the *Dialogues* are not the work of a madman?

—That question would be important if it made any sense, but by definition a work is nonmadness.

—The structure of a work can allow the pattern of an illness to appear.

—It is crucial that the converse not be true.

—You have prevented it from being true by refusing to speak of delirium, persecution, morbid belief, and so on.

—I have even pretended not to know that the madness was present elsewhere, before the *Dialogues*: one sees it taking form, and one can follow it in the whole correspondence from 1765 onward.

—You have placed the work ahead of the possibility of madness, as if to better expunge madness from the work; you have not mentioned the points at which the delirium breaks forth. Who in his right mind can believe that Corsica was annexed in order to make things difficult for Rousseau?

—What work demands that we believe it, if it is a work?

—How is it diminished if it is delirious?

—It's a strange and barbarous combination of words, frequent as it is (and so laudatory nowadays), that associates a work with delirium. A work cannot have its place in delirium; it may just be that language, which from deep within itself makes the work possible, also opens it to the empirical space of madness (as it may also have opened it to that of eroticism or mysticism).

—So, a raving work can exist, provided it is not "raved."

—Only language can be raving. Here, raving is a present participle.

—The language of a work? Well, then once again . . .

—The language that prescribes to a work its space, its formal structure, and its very existence as a work of language, can confer on the secondary language, which resides within the work, a structural analogy with delirium. Distinctions need to be drawn: the language of the work is what it is aiming for beyond itself, that which it says; but this side of itself it is also that on the basis of which it speaks. The categories of the normal and the pathological, of madness and delirium, cannot be applied to this language; for it is a primary breakthrough [*franchissement*], a pure transgression.

– It was Rousseau who was delirious, and his whole language as a result.

– We were talking about the work.

– But what about Rousseau at the precise moment when, pen in hand, he traced the lines of his complaint, his sincerity, and his suffering?

– That is a psychologist's question. Not mine, consequently.

NOTES

1 Concerning this theme, see Jean Starobinski's remarkable pages in his *J.-J. Rousseau* (Paris: Plon, 1958), p. 25 ff.

2 During the period when Rousseau is living in this world of signs without words he has resumed his activity as a copyist, having transcribed perhaps twelve thousand pages of music. Throughout the *Dialogues* he emphasizes that this is not an affected poverty but a real necessity, and that he risks losing his health and his eyesight by doing it.

SO CRUEL A KNOWLEDGE*

Révéroni de Saint-Cyr (1767–1829) was an engineer officer who played a rather important role at the beginning of the Revolution and under the Empire. He was Narbonne's adjutant in 1792, then Marshal Berthier's aide-de-camp. He wrote a large number of plays, ten or so novels (such as *Sabina d'Herfeld* in 1797, *Nos folies* in 1799) and several theoretical treatises: *Essai sur le perfectionnement des beaux-arts, ou Calculs et hypothèses sur la poésie, la peinture et la musique* (1804); *Essai sur le mécanisme de la guerre* (1804); *Examen critique de l'equilibre social européen, ou Abrégé de statistique politique et littéraire* (1820).

The scene takes place in Poland, which is to say everywhere. A disheveled countess flees a burning castle. Soldiers have hastily disemboweled the chambermaids and pages among the statues, which, before crashing down, have slowly turned their beautiful empty heads to the sky. The screams, reverberating for a long time, have faded off into the mirrors. A veil slips over a woman's chest, a veil that hands tie again and tear loose again with the same awkward movements. The dangers, the looks, the desires, and the fear intercross, forming a swift lattice of blades, more unexpected, more fatal than the shards of collapsing stucco. Perhaps this salon wall will long remain

---

*This commentary on Claude-Prosper Crébillon's *Les Egarements du coeur et d'esprit* (text presented by Etiemble [Paris: A. Colin, 1961] and J.-A. Révéroni de Saint-Cyr's *Pauliska ou la Perversité* (Paris: 1798) appeared in *Critique* 4 (July 1962), pp. 597–611. Robert Hurley's translation.

standing, where a blue naiad tries to escape from Neptune, her head held very straight, front-facing, her eyes fixed on the gaping doorway, her bust and her arms turned to the rear, where they are engaged in an undecided struggle with the indulgent, agile, enormous hands of an old man crouched on a seat of light shells and tritons. Pauliska abandons her scorched lands to the Cossacks of the empress, her countrywomen bound to the pale trunks of the maples, her servants mutilated and their mouths covered with blood. She seeks refuge in old Europe, a Europe of bad sleep which sets all its traps for her at one go. Strange traps, in which it is hard to recognize the familiar ones of male flattery, worldly pleasures, scarcely intended falsehoods, and jealousy. What is taking form is an evil much less "metaphysical," much more "English" than "French," as the translator of Hawkesworth put it,[1] an evil very close to the body and meant for it. "A modern perversity."

Like the convent, the forbidden castle, the forest, the inaccessible island, the "sect" has become, beginning in the second half of the eighteenth century, one of the great reserves of the Western fantastical imagination. Pauliska runs through the whole cycle: political associations, clubs of libertines, bands of brigands or counterfeiters, guilds of crooks or science mystics, orgiastic societies of women without men, sbirros of the College of Cardinals, and finally, as every novel of terror seems to require, the most secret and most illustrious order, the indefinite conspiracy, the Holy Inquisition. In this underground world the misfortunes lose their chronology and link up with the world's most ancient cruelties. In reality, Pauliska is fleeing a millennial conflagration, and the partition of 1795 casts her into an ageless cycle. She falls into the castle of evil spells where the corridors close up, where the mirrors tell lies and watch what passes before them, where the air distills strange poisons—labyrinth of the Minotaur or Circe's cave. She descends into the Underworld where she encounters a prostitute Jocasta who violates a child under motherly caresses, a dionysian castration, an accursed town in flames. It is a paradoxical initiation not into the lost secret but into all those agonies that man never forgets.[2]

Sixty years earlier, *Les Egarements du coeur et de l'esprit*, which Etiemble had the very good judgment to republish in a new edition, told about another initiation that was not that of misfortune. Meilcour was introduced into the most brilliant "society," but perhaps the one most difficult to decipher, the most open and the best defended, the one that invents sham evasions to show itself to advantage, when the novice has a big name, a fortune, a pretty face, a ravishing figure, and he is not yet eighteen years old. The "world" is also a sect; or rather, secret societies at the end of the century have kept the role that the social hierarchy and its facile mysteries had played since the beginning of the Classical period. The sect is the social world in the other dimension, its ground-level Saturnalia.

What Versac teaches the neophyte, in the next-to-last scene of the *Egarements* (final error, first truth), is a "science of the world." A science that cannot be learned by oneself, since it involves knowledge not of nature but of arbitrariness and the strategy of ridicule; an initiatory science, since its main strength lies in the condition that one feigns ignorance of it, and the person who divulged it would be disgraced and excluded if he were found out: "But I trust that you will keep the utmost secrecy about what I have said, and about what I am going to say." This didactics of the world has three parts: a theory of *impertinence* (a game of servile imitation with a contrived eccentricity, in which the unexpected does not go beyond the customary, and the improper is proper from the start, because its game is to please); a theory of *self-conceit*, with its three main tactics (assert oneself; be the first, spontaneously, to adopt the latest absurdity; "hold" a conversation by keeping it in the first person); a system of *good form* that requires thoughtlessness, slander, and presumption. But this is still only a "heap of minutiae." The essential thing, no doubt, is in a diagonal lesson that teaches what Crébillon knows best–the use of speech.

The language of the world is seemingly without content, overloaded with useless formal expressions, both ritualized into a mute decoration–"a few favorite words, a few involved phrases, a few exclamations"–and multiplied by unexpected finds that are more certain to diminish meaning, "put finesse into one's turns and peril into one's ideas." And yet it is a language saturated and rigorously functional: every phrase must be a brief form of judgment; devoid of meaning, it must take on the greatest possible load of valuation–"see nothing . . . that one does not scorn or praise to excess." This garrulous, incessant, diffuse speech always has an economic aim–a certain effect on the value of people and things. Thus, it takes its risks: it attacks or protects; it always exposes itself; it has its courage and its skill; it has to hold untenable positions, lay itself open to the retort, to ridicule, and dodge them; it is belligerent. What gives weight to this language is not what it means to *say* but to *do*. Saying nothing, it teems with implications, and refers to positions that supply its meaning, since by itself it has none; it indicates a whole silent world that never gains access to words. That indicative distance is propriety. As it shows everything that one does not say, language can and must cover up everything; it is never quiet, since it is the living economy of situations, their visible nervure. "You have noticed that people in society never run dry of words. . . . That is because there is nothing in the well." Bodies themselves are not silent at the moment of their most intense pleasure. The alert Sopha had already noticed this, when his indiscretion watched the ardors of his guests: "Though Zulica never stopped speaking, I could no longer hear what she said."

No sooner has Meilcour escaped from the captious discourse of Versac than he falls into the arms of Madame de Lursay, where he rediscovers his stammerings, his candor, his indignation, and his naïveté, of which he is finally disburdened in spite of himself. And yet the lesson has not been useless, since it yields us the narrative in its form and its irony. In relating the adventure of his innocence, Meilcour no longer perceives it anywhere but in that distance where it is already lost: all of Versac's knowledge has slipped in between his naïveté and the imperceptibly different consciousness he has of it, with that practice of the world in which "the heart and the mind are forced to spoil themselves."

Pauliska's initiation, on the other hand, is achieved through great silent myths. The world's secret was in language and its rules of warfare; that of the sects is in its wordless complicities. That is why their victim, never truly initiated, is always kept in the harsh and monotonous condition of the object. Pauliska, the stubborn novice, indefinitely escapes the evil whose barriers she unintentionally passes through; her hands that crush her deliverer, that body which she offers to her tormentor in an extreme madness are only the inert instruments of her torture. The incorruptible Pauliska is fully enlightened since, all things considered, she knows—but she is never initiated, since she always refuses to become the sovereign subject of what she knows. She is completely familiar with the sorrow of experiencing with the same innocence the good fortune of being *aware* and the misfortune of remaining an *object*.

From the start of this brutal game, its trap was announced. One evening Pauliska is taken to a meeting of Polish émigrés whose goal is precisely what she has her heart set on—restoring the fatherland and establishing the reign of a better order there. Through half-open shutters she spies a strange conventicle: the gigantic shadow of grand master swings against the wall; leaning slightly toward the audience, he remains silent with a beast's dreamy seriousness; around him crawl feverish acolytes; the room is full of silhouettes. Inside, there is undoubtedly talk of reestablished justice, shared lands, and of that general will which, in a free nation, gives rise to free men. Men? Pauliska moves closer: in the dim light, she recognizes an assembly of dogs presided over by an ass; they bark, throw themselves upon one another, tear at the miserable donkey. A benevolent society of men, a riot of animals. This Goyaesque scene shows the novice the savage and anticipated truth about what will happen to her: in society (in societies, plural), man is nothing but a dog to man; law is the appetite of the beast.

No doubt the initiation story owes its strongest erotic appeal to the link that it intimates between Knowledge and Desire. An obscure, essential link that we are mistaken to recognize only in "Platonism," that is, in the exclusion of one of the two terms. In actual fact, each epoch has its system of "erotic knowledge" which brings into play (in one and the same game) the experience of the Limit and that of the Light. This game obeys a deep geometry that is manifested, anecdotally, by precarious situations or trivial objects like the veil, the chain, the mirror, the cage (figures in which the luminous and the impassible are combined).

The knowledge that is employed, in Crébillon, against the pretty innocents by those who are no longer pretty or innocent has several faces:

- being experienced and subtly leading ignorance while pretending to go astray along with it (*to seduce*);

- having recognized the evil there where innocence still discerns nothing but purity, and making the latter serve the former (*to corrupt*);

- anticipating and arranging the outcome, as the profligate does when he prepares all the lures of the trap he sets for naïveté (*to deceive*);

- being "in the know" and playing along, the better to spoil the game, when one has perfectly grasped the stratagem by which prudence, with its feigned simplicity, resists (*to tempt*).

These four poisonous figures—they all flourish in the garden of the *Egarements*—creep up the sides of the fine, simple forms of ignorance, innocence, naïveté, and prudence, clinging to their contours, covering them with a disturbing vegetation. Around their nakedness they form a redoubled modesty—a strange clothing, secret words with a double meaning, a sheath that guides the blows. They are all related to the eroticism of the veil (that veil which the last episode of *The Sopha* misuses to such advantage).

The veil is that thin surface which chance, haste, and modesty have placed and do their best to maintain; but its line of force is dictated by the vertical of the drop. The veil unveils, through a fatality which is that of its light fabric and its supple form. To play its role, which is to cover and to be exact, the veil must conform precisely to the surfaces, repeat the lines, course over the volumes without superfluous discourse, and highlight the forms with a glittering whiteness, stripping them of their shadow. Its folds add a hint of disturbance, but this ruffling of underlinen only foretells a nakedness soon to come: it is something like the already-rumpled image, the molested tenderness of the body that it conceals. All the more so because it is transparent— with a functional transparence that is unbalanced and artful. It plays its opaque and protective role well, but only for the one who uses it to cover herself, for the groping, fumbling, and feverish hand that defends itself. But for the one who witnesses all these efforts and who remains on the watch from a distance, this veil is revealing. Paradoxically, the veil hides modesty from itself and draws its attention away from its main object of caution; but in manifesting this caution to the indiscreet, it allows him to see indiscreetly that which it withholds. Doubly traitorous, the veil shows what it averts and conceals, from what it is meant to hide, the fact that it unveils it.

Standing in contrast to the veil there is the cage. An outwardly simple form, without any ruses, cut out according to relations of force in which the game is already over: here the vanquished, there, on all sides, all around, the victor. The cage, however, has multiple functions: the person inside is nude, since the transparency is without remedy or any possible hiding; through a disequilibrium peculiar to that space of closure, the object is always, for the tormentors, within reach, whereas they are themselves inaccessible; one is at a distance from one's chains, captive within a whole range of actions, none of which is impossible, but none of which has any protective or emancipatory value. The cage is the space where freedom is mimicked, but where its chimera is annihilated by the presence of the tormentors. The irony of the veil is a redoubled game; that of the cage, a game that is unplayed. Perfidiously, the veil establishes a communication; the cage is the simple figure of an unmediated division – subject utterly against object, power utterly against powerlessness. The cage is linked to a triumphant knowledge that reigns over an enslaved ignorance. It makes little difference how the closure was obtained: it opens the era of an instrumental knowledge connected no longer to the somewhat shady ambiguity of consciousness but, rather, to the meticulous order of technical persecution.

Let us pause for a moment at the bounds of that cage in which Pauliska's lover was confined, naked.

1. He was captured by a society of Amazons who make a profession of detesting men, their violence, their rough bodies. The caging is carried out in the form of all against one.

2. The young man was placed in a zoological gallery where, alongside other animals, he is used for a natural history demonstration: the priestess of these heinous vestals enumerates for her companions all the imperfections of that rustic body, without charm or attractiveness.

3. The initiates have proudly bared their breasts; the novices must do likewise, to show that no palpitation, no blush betrays the disorder of a heart surreptitiously invaded by desire. Here, the figure becomes complicated: are the women really such mistresses of that icy body which they set against the masculine animal? And does it not give rise, in the man, to a visible desire to which the most innocent of the women does not fail to respond with signs of emotion? And so, in this manner, desire binds inverse chains.

4. But by helping each other the women can protect themselves against that danger. Are they not capable, the one leaning on the other's shoulder, of counterposing to the beastly body shown to them this other body which is all softness, downy volume, smooth sand for caressing? A strange desire based on comparison and the excluded middle. This confined male must not be completely exorcised, since a pejorative contemplation is necessary before the women's desire,

pure at last, is able to go without betrayal, from themselves to their exact equivalents.

5. As a matter of fact, they reconstitute the image of the detested man by means of a strange statue and they make it the object of their desire. But the cleverest of them will be imprisoned in this game. Taking him for a marvelous machine, she will quite genuinely desire the handsome boy she thinks she has locked up and who plays at being as cold as a statue. In her ecstasy she falls down unconscious, while he, coming out of his feigned inertia, springs back to life and escapes. A modern version and a term-by-term reversal of the myth of Pygmalion.

Further, though, of the Labyrinth as well. Theseus becomes a captive therein of an Ariadne-Minotaur, whom he escapes only by becoming threatening and desirable himself, and by abandoning the sleeping woman on her lovely island. In the simple form of the cage, a strange knowledge is at work, changing the roles, transmuting images and reality, metamorphosing the figures of desire – a whole in-depth labor of which one finds two variants in the underground and in the machine.

The underground is the endoscopic form of the cage; but also its direct contradiction, since nothing it contains is visible. Its very existence is hidden from view. An absolute prison against which no assault is possible: it is Hell, minus its profound justice. By its nature, the cells of the Inquisition are underground. What goes on there is absolutely unseen, but there reigns an absolute, nocturnal, unavoidable gaze that contrasts, in its erotic structure, with the oblique and luminous gaze of the mirror.

The mirror has two modes, near and far. Through the effect of its lines, it can observe from afar – that is, offer everything to the gaze without allowing any hold on it, a parodic inversion of consciousness. In its near mode, it is a tricked gaze. The observer surreptitiously occupies the camera obscura that the looking glass harbors; he slips into immediate self-satisfaction. He places himself there where the closed volume of the body has just opened up, but only to close again immediately from the other side of that surface it inhabits by making itself as unspatial as possible; a cunning geometer, a two-dimensional Cartesian devil that now lodges its invisible presence in the visibility of the observed to himself.

The magic mirror, true and false "psyche," combines these two modes. It is placed in the hands of the observer, of whom it allows a supreme observation; but it has that strange property of watching the observed in the belated and somewhat hesitant gesture that he has in front of the mirror. That is the role of the enchanted "Sopha," an enveloping and tepid space in which the body surrenders to the pleasure of being alone and in the presence of itself: a secretly inhabited space that quietly worries and soon, in its turn, begins to desire the first innocent body that slips away from it by offering itself absolutely.

What does Crébillon's strange magician see, in the depths of his silk mirror? Nothing else, really, but his desire and the secret of his greedy heart. It reflects, and nothing more. But precisely here is the absolute subterfuge of the observed. In looking, the one does not know that, at bottom, he is seeing himself; the other, not knowing he is being looked at, is vaguely aware of being seen. Everything is organized by this awareness that is at once skin-deep and beneath words. On the other side of the treacherous mirror one is alone and deceived, but with a solitude so watchful that the other's presence is mimed concavely by gestures that, enabling one to defend oneself from him, reverently, fearfully, invoke him. Thus, at the meeting's surface, on the smooth plane of the mirror, the limit-gesture par excellence takes form in a momentary pause of delight: laying bare, it masks what it reveals. A figure in which the slender threads of the reciprocal knowledges are knitted together, but where the soul of the desirable eludes desire in a definitive way, just as Zeinis eludes the Sopha's heart.

But all these corridors collapse in Pauliska's adventure. The leader of the brigands, she says, "stamps the floor with his heel; I feel my chair fall very quickly through a trap door that immediately closes shut again above my head; and I find myself in the midst of eight to ten men with a greedy, astonished, terrifying look on their faces." Innocence is in the presence of the gaze itself. The voracity of desire does not need an unreal image in order to reach the other's nakedness; it presses heavily, subjecting what can no longer defend itself to a deliberate examination. It does not steal its pleasure, it serenely promises violence.

If so rough a situation holds strong erotic powers nonetheless, this is because it is less *perverse* than *subversive*. The fall into the forgers' cave symbolizes its movement. This is not yet the Saturnalia of the wretched—an optimistic dream, hence of no value to desire; it is the fall of the fortunate into the abyss where they become just so many prey. One does not want to possess Pauliska's former happiness but to possess her, because she was happy—a project belonging not to a revolutionary will, but to a desire for subversion. Pauliska is placed at the level of a desire that manifests the people's bestial virility. In the novels of the eighteenth century, the popular element only formed a mediation in the economy of Eros (procuress, valet). In the inverted world of the underground, it shows a majestic vigor that was unsuspected. The chthonian serpent awakened.

In actual fact, it acquired this masculinity through conspiracy; it did not naturally belong to it. The underground is a realm of scoundrels, a negative image of the social contract. Each is a prisoner of the others, of whom he may become the betrayer and the administrator of justice. The underground is the cage that has solidified, been made completely opaque (being dug out of the ground) and liquified at the same time, become transparent to itself, precarious, since it is caught up in enveloping, mutual, distrustful consciousnesses. The tormentors are just as much prisoners as their victim, who is just as interested in their salvation as they are: she shares their fate in that piece of solidary and constricted space. The Danube, whose water can be seen rolling above the sealed slabs of glass, symbolically indicates, to everyone, to Pauliska and the brigands alike, that they will be drowned at the first breach of their contract. The cage carefully separated the sovereign lords and the objects; the underground brings them together in a stifling knowledge. At the center of this circle stands, as a symbol, the grandiose printing machine, from which Pauliska, knowing and not knowing, extracts a "groan" which is not that of the press but the cry of her crushed deliverer.

In most eighteenth-century novels, the machinations outweigh the machines. They are all the techniques of illusion that construct an artful supernature out of little or nothing: images that rise from the depths of mirrors, invisible designs whose phosphorus flares up in the darkness, trompe l'oeil that gives rise to false, yet true, passions. Potions for the senses. There is also the whole insidious apparatus of the poisonings: camphor, snakeskins, charred turtledove bones, and, above all, the terrible eggs of Java ants. And lastly there is the inoculation of unavowable desires, which disturb the most faithful hearts— illusory delights, real enjoyments. All these potions without magic, these true-illusion machines, are not different, by nature or function, from that dream which the soul held prisoner by the Sopha instilled with a kiss into the innocent heart of Zeinis. All convey this same lesson: that images have the same warmth for the heart as what they represent, and that the most unreal artifice cannot arouse false passions when it causes a true intoxication. Nature can accommodate every mechanism of desire if it is able to build those marvelous machines in which the borderless fabric of the true and the false is woven.

The electric wheel described at the end of *Pauliska* is a very different kind of machinery. Bound back to back and naked, the two women victims, opposite and complementary to one another (like two terminals: the Polish blonde and the Italian brunette, the passionate and the ardent, the virtuous and the wayward, the one who burns with love and the one who is consumed with desire), are separated, where their bodies meet, only by a thin glass flywheel. As soon as it turns, sparks fly, with a burst of suffering and cries. The bristling bodies electrify, the nerves revulse: desire, horror? Over there, having reached the last degree of exhaustion by going to the extreme limit of his lust, the persecutor receives, via the cake of wax on which he sits enthroned, the fluid of those young exasperated bodies. And, little by little, Salviati feels himself imbued with the grand and majestic desire that promises his victims endless agonies.

On a first examination, this strange machine appears rather elementary: a mere putting of desire into a discursive form, it imprisons its object in a suffering that multiplies the latter's charms, so that the object itself strengthens the desire, and thereby its own pain, in a more and more intense circle that will be broken only by the final fulguration. However, Pauliska's machine has greater, and stranger, powers. Unlike the machination machine, it keeps a maximum distance between the partners which only an impalpable fluid can cross. This fluid extracts from the body that suffers, and because it suffers, its desirability—a blend of its youthfulness, its flawless flesh, its spasmodic tremors. Now, the agent of this blend is the electric current that gives rise to all the physical movements of desire in the victim. The desirability the fluid conveys to the persecutor is the persecuted's desire, while the inert, enervated tormentor receives, as if in a first suckling, that desire which he immediately makes his own; or rather, which he transmits, without retaining it, to the motion of the wheel, thus forming a simple relay in the persecuted desire that comes back to itself as an accelerated persecution. The tormentor is no longer anything but a neutral moment in the appetite of his victim; and the machine reveals what it is—not a working-class objectification of desire but a projection of the desired in which the wheelwork mechanism detaches the desiring. Which is not a defeat for the latter, far from it: his passivity is the ruse of knowledge that, being familiar with all the moments of desire, experiences them in an impersonal game whose cruelty sustains both a keen awareness and a heartless mechanics.

The economy of this machine is quite peculiar. In Sade, the apparatus delineates, in its meticulousness, the architecture of a desire that remains sovereign. Even when he is exhausted and the machine is constructed for reviving him, the desiring individual maintains his absolute rights as a subject, the victim never being anything more than the remote, enigmatic, and narrative unity of an object of desire and a subject of suffering—so that, at the limit of perfection of a torturing machine, there is the tortured body as the point of application of a cruel will (for example, Minski's living tables). In contrast, the "electrodynamic" machine of the *Supermale* is vampiric in nature: the crazy wheels carry the mechanism to that point of delirium where it becomes a monstrous beast whose jaws crush and set fire to the hero's inexhaustible body. Révéroni's machine also consecrates the apotheosis of the weary warriors, but in another sense: it is set up at the end of an initiatory passage, as the terminal object par excellence. It transforms the desiring into an immobile, inaccessible figure, toward whom advance all the motions that he immediately reverses without leaving his dominion: God finally at rest, who knows absolutely and who is absolutely desired. As for the object of desire (whom the potion finally allowed to escape), it is transmuted into an infinitely generous source of desire itself. At the end point of this initiation it also finds repose and light; not the illumination of consciousness nor the repose of detachment, but the white light of knowledge and that inertia which allows the anonymous violence of desire to take its course.

All these objects are much more, no doubt, than the theatrical props of license. Their form gathers the fundamental space in which the relations of Desire and Knowledge are enacted; they give shape to an experience in which the transgression of the prohibition releases the light. One easily recognizes, in the two groups they form, two opposite, and perfectly coherent, structures of that space and of the experience that is connected to it.

Some, familiar to Crébillon, constitute what might be called "situation objects." They are visible forms that capture a moment and give a new impetus to the imperceptible interrelations of subjects: meeting surfaces, places of exchange where the refusals, the looks, the consents, the evasions cross one another, they function as light relays whose material density decreases in proportion to the complexity of the meaning they convey. Their value is that of the combination of relations they establish, which are established through them. Their fragile and transparent pattern is only the nervure of situations: thus the *veil* in the relation of indiscretion to the secret; the *mirror* in that of surprise and self-absorption; the *potion* in the games of truth and illusion. So many traps in which the consciousnesses remain captive. But only for a moment, for these situation objects have a centrifugal dynamic: one is lost there while knowing oneself to be lost and already in search of the way out. Their helpful perils mark out the path of return from the labyrinth. This is the Ariadne aspect of the erotic consciousness–the thread held at its two ends by consciousnesses that look for each other, escape each other, capture each other, and rescue each other; and now they are again separated from each other by that thread which, indissociably, links them together. All these Ariadne objects play with the stratagems of truth at the threshold of light and illusion.

Opposite, in Révéroni, one finds objects that are enveloping, imperious, unavoidable: the subjects are caught there without remedy, their position altered, their consciousness detained and changed from top to bottom. Escape is inconceivable; the only way out is in the direction of that dark point which indicates the center, the infernal fire, the law of the figure. No longer threads that one ties and unties but corridors in which one is swallowed up, they are "configuration objects," of the type underground, cage, and machine–the labyrinth's inward path. There, error and truth are no longer in question: one may miss Ariadne, one cannot miss the Minotaur. She is the uncertain, the improbable, the distant; he is the certain, the quite-close. And yet, in contrast to Ariadne's traps, where everyone finds his bearings at the moment of being lost, the figures of the Minotaur are utterly foreign; together with death, whose threat they bear, they mark the boundaries of the unhuman and the inhuman–the jaws of the cage close shut on a world of bestiality and predation. The underground harbors a whole swarm of infernal beings, and that inhumanity which is peculiar to the corpses of men.

But the secret of this erotic Minotaur is not so much that he is more than half-animal, nor that he forms an ill-defined figure, badly divided between two adjacent areas. His secret covers a much more incestuous rapprochement: in him, the devouring labyrinth and Daedalus who made him are superposed. He is at the same time the blind machine, the passageways of desire with their fatality, and the skillful, calm, and free architect who has already left the unavoidable trap. The Minotaur is Daedalus's presence and absence at the same time, in the indecipherable and dead sovereignty of his knowledge. All the previous figures that symbolize the monster convey, as he does, that languageless alliance between an anonymous desire and a knowledge whose reign conceals the empty face of the Master. Ariadne's slender threads get tangled up in consciousness; here, with a pure knowledge and a subjectless desire, there only remains the brutal duality of beasts without a species.

All of Ariadne's traps revolve around the most central, the most exemplary of erotic situations—the transvestite. Indeed, the latter gets lost in a redoubled game in which nature is not profoundly transmuted but evaded in place. Like the veil, the transvestite conceals and betrays; like the mirror, he presents reality in an illusion that snatches it away in offering it. He is a potion as well, since he arouses illusory and natural sentiments based on falsely true impressions. He is the unnatural mimicked and thereby conjured away. The space symbolized by the Minotaur is, on the contrary, a space of transmutation; as cage, it makes man into an animal of desire—desiring like a wild beast, desired like a prey; as underground chamber, it contrives, underneath the states, a counter city-state that vows to destroy the oldest laws and pacts; as machine, its meticulous movement, supported by nature and reason, gives rise to Antiphysis and all the volcanoes of madness. It is no longer a matter of the deceptive surfaces of disguise but, rather, of a nature metamorphosed into a depth by the powers of the counternatural.

It is here no doubt that "modern perversity," as Révéroni put it, finds its proper space. Shifted toward the regions of a light eroticism, the initiations of Ariadne, so important in the erotic discourse of the eighteenth century, are for us no longer anything but playful—let us say, rather, along with M. Etiemble who is clear about this, "love, love in all its forms." The truly transgressive forms of eroticism are now found in the space covered by Pauliska's initiation: in the direction of the counternatural, there where Theseus is headed when he approaches the center of the labyrinth, toward that corner of darkness where, voracious architect, Knowledge keeps watch.

NOTES

1 John Hawkesworth, *Ariana ou la Patience récompensée*, trans. M. Hawkesworth (Paris, 1757).

2 Révéroni presented a theory of modern mythology in his *Essai sur le perfectionnement des beaux-arts.*

A PREFACE TO TRANSGRESSION*

We like to believe that sexuality has regained, in contemporary experience, its truth as a process of nature, a truth that has long been lingering in the shadows and hiding under various disguises—until now, that is, when our positive awareness allows us to decipher it so that it may at last emerge in the clear light of language. Yet never did sexuality enjoy a more immediately natural understanding, and never did it know a greater "felicity of expression," than in the Christian world of fallen bodies and of sin. The proof is its whole tradition of mysticism and spirituality, which was incapable of dividing the continuous forms of desire, of rapture, of penetration, of ecstasy, of that outpouring which leaves us spent: all of these experiences seemed to lead, without interruption or limit, right to the heart of a divine love of which they were both the outpouring and the source returning upon itself. What characterizes modern sexuality from Sade to Freud is not its having found the language of its logic or of its nature, but, rather, through the violence done by such languages, its having been "denatured"—cast into an empty zone in which it achieves whatever meager form is bestowed upon it by the establishment of its limits, and in which it points to nothing beyond itself, no prolongation, except the frenzy that disrupts it. We have not in the least liberated sexuality, though we have, to be exact, carried it to its limits: the limit of consciousness, because it ultimately dictates the

*This essay first appeared in a special issue of *Critique* (195–96 [Aug.–Sept. 1963], pp. 751–69] devoted to Georges Bataille. This translation, by Donald F. Bouchard and Sherry Simon, has been slightly amended.

only possible reading of our unconscious; the limit of the law, since it seems the sole substance of universal taboos; the limit of language, since it traces that line of foam showing just how far speech may advance upon the sands of silence. Thus, it is not through sexuality that we communicate with the orderly and pleasingly profane world of animals; rather, sexuality is a fissure—not one that surrounds us as the basis of our isolation or individuality but one that marks the limit within us and designates us as a limit.

Perhaps we could say that it has become the only division possible in a world now emptied of objects, beings, and spaces to desecrate. Not that it proffers any new content for our millenary exploit, rather, it permits a profanation without object, a profanation that is empty and turned inward upon itself, whose instruments are brought to bear on nothing but each other. Profanation in a world that no longer recognizes any positive meaning in the sacred—is this not more or less what we may call transgression? In that zone which our culture affords for our gestures and speech, transgression prescribes not only the sole manner of discovering the sacred in its unmediated substance, but also a way of recomposing its empty form, its absence, through which it becomes all the more scintillating. A rigorous language, as it arises from sexuality, will not reveal the secret of man's natural being, nor will it express the serenity of anthropological truths, but rather, it will say that he exists without God; the speech given to sexuality is contemporaneous, both in time and in structure, with that through which we announced to ourselves that God is dead. From the moment that Sade delivered its first words and marked out, in a single discourse, the boundaries of what suddenly became its kingdom, the language of sexuality has lifted us into the night where God is absent, and where all of our actions are addressed to this absence in a profanation that at once identifies it, dissipates it, exhausts itself in it, and restores it to the empty purity of its transgression.

There indeed exists a modern form of sexuality: it is that which offers itself in the superficial discourse of a solid and natural animality, while obscurely addressing itself to Absence, to this high region where Bataille placed, in a night not soon to be ended, the characters of *Eponine*:

> In this strained stillness, through the haze of my intoxication, I seemed
> to sense that the wind was dying down; a long silence flowed from the

immensity of the sky. The priest knelt down softly. He began to sing in a despondent key, slowly as if at someone's death: *Miserere mei Deus, secondum misericordiam magnam tuam.* The way he moaned this sensuous melody was highly suspicious. He was strangely confessing his anguish before the delights of the flesh. A priest should conquer us by his denials but his efforts to humble himself only made him stand out more insistently; the loveliness of his chant, set against the silent sky, enveloped him in a solitude of morose pleasures. My reverie was shattered by a felicitous acclamation, an infinite acclamation already on the edge of oblivion. Seeing the priest as she emerged from the dream which still visibly dazed her senses, Eponine began to laugh and with such intensity that she was completely shaken; she turned her body and, leaning against the railing, trembled like a child. She was laughing with her head in her hands and the priest, barely stifling a clucking noise, raised his head, his arms uplifted, only to see a naked behind: the wind had lifted her coat and, made defenseless by the laughter, she had been unable to close it.[1]

Perhaps the importance of sexuality in our culture, the fact that since Sade it has persistently been linked to the most profound decisions of our language, derives from nothing else than this correspondence which connects it to the death of God. Not that this death should be understood as the end of his historical reign, or as the finally delivered judgment of his nonexistence, but as the now-constant space of our experience. By denying us the limit of the Limitless, the death of God leads to an experience in which nothing may again announce the exteriority of being, and consequently to an experience that is *interior* and *sovereign.* But such an experience, for which the death of God is an explosive reality, discloses as its own secret and clarification, its intrinsic finitude, the limitless reign of the Limit, and the emptiness of those excesses in which it spends itself and where it is found wanting. In this sense, the inner experience is, throughout, an experience of the *impossible* (the impossible being both that which we experience and that which constitutes the experience). The death of God is not merely an "event" that gave shape to contemporary experience as we now know it: it continues indefinitely tracing its great skeletal outline.

Bataille was perfectly conscious of the possibilities of thought that could be released by this death, and of the impossibilities in which it entangled thought. What, indeed, is the meaning of the death of God, if not a strange solidarity between the stunning realization of his nonexistence and the act that kills him? But what does it mean to kill God if he does not exist, to kill God *who has never existed?* Perhaps it means to kill God both because he does not exist and to guarantee that he will not exist—certainly a cause for laughter: to kill God to liberate life from this existence that limits it, but also to bring it back to those limits that are annulled by this limitless existence—as a sacrifice; to kill God to return him to this nothingness he is and to manifest his existence at the center of a light that blazes like a presence—for the ecstasy; to kill God in order to lose language in a deafening night and because this wound must make him bleed until there springs forth "an immense alleluia lost in the interminable silence"—and this is communication. The death of God restores us not to a limited and positivistic world but to a world exposed by the experience of its limits, made and unmade by that excess which transgresses it.

Undoubtedly it is excess that discovers that sexuality and the death of God are bound to the same experience; or that again shows us, as if in "the most incongruous book of all," that "God is a whore." And from this perspective the thought that relates to God and the thought that relates to sexuality are linked in a common form, since Sade to be sure, but never in our day with as much insistence and difficulty as in Bataille. And if it were necessary to give, in opposition to sexuality, a precise definition of eroticism, it would have to be the following: an experience of sexuality which links, for its own ends, an overcoming of limits to the death of God. "Eroticism can say what mysticism never could (its strength failed when it tried): God is nothing if not the surpassing of God in every sense of vulgar being, in that of horror or impurity; and ultimately in the sense of nothing."[2]

Thus, at the root of sexuality, of the movement that nothing can ever limit (because it is, from its origin and in its totality, constantly involved with the limit), and at the root of this discourse on God which Western culture has maintained for so long—without any sense of the impropriety of "thoughtlessly adding to language a word which surpasses all words" or any clear sense that it places us at the limits of all possible languages—a singular experience is shaped: that of transgression. Perhaps one day it will seem as decisive for our culture, as much a part of its soil, as the experience of contradiction was at an earlier time for dialectical thought. But in spite of so many scattered signs, the language in which transgression will find its space and the illumination of its being lies almost entirely in the future.

It is surely possible, however, to find in Bataille its calcinated roots, its promising ashes.

Transgression is an action that involves the limit, that narrow zone of a line where it displays the flash of its passage, but perhaps also its entire trajectory, even its origin; it is likely that transgression has its entire space in the line it crosses. The play of limits and transgression seems to be regulated by a simple obstinacy: transgression incessantly crosses and recrosses a line that closes up behind it in a wave of extremely short duration, and thus it is made to return once more right to the horizon of the uncrossable. But this play is considerably more complex: these elements are situated in an uncertain context, in certainties that are immediately upset so that thought is ineffectual as soon as it attempts to seize them.

The limit and transgression depend on each other for whatever density of being they possess: a limit could not exist if it were absolutely uncrossable and, reciprocally, transgression would be pointless if it merely crossed a limit composed of illusions and shadows. But can the limit have a life of its own outside of the act that gloriously passes through it and negates it? What becomes of it after this act and what might it have been before? For its part, does transgression not exhaust its nature when it violates the limit, being nothing beyond this point in time? And this point, this curious intersection of beings that do not exist outside it but totally exchange what they are within it – is it not also everything that overflows from it on all sides? It serves as a glorification of what it excludes: the limit opens violently onto the limitless, finds itself suddenly carried away by the content it had rejected and fulfilled by this alien plenitude that invades it to the core of its being. Transgression carries the limit right to the limit of its being; transgression forces the limit to face the fact of its imminent disappearance, to find itself in what it excludes (perhaps, to be more exact, to recognize itself for the first time), to experience its positive truth in its downward fall. And yet, toward what is transgression unleashed in its movement of pure violence, if not that which imprisons it, toward the limit and those elements it contains? What bears the brunt of its aggression, and to what void does it owe the unrestrained fullness of its being, if not that which it crosses in its violent act and which, as its destiny, it crosses out in the line it effaces?

Transgression, then, is not related to the limit as black to white, the prohibited to the lawful, the outside to the inside, or as the open area of a building to its enclosed spaces. Rather, their relationship takes the form of a spiral that no simple infraction can exhaust. Perhaps it is like a flash of lightning in the night which, from the beginning of time, gives a dense and black intensity to the night it denies; which lights up the night from the inside, from top to bottom, and yet owes to the dark the stark clarity of its manifestation, its harrowing and poised singularity. The flash loses itself in this space it marks with its sovereignty and becomes silent now that it has given a name to obscurity.

Since this existence is both so pure and so complicated, it must be detached from its questionable association to ethics if we want to understand it and to begin thinking from it and in the space it denotes; it must be liberated from the scandalous or subversive, that is, from anything aroused by negative associations. Transgression does not seek to oppose one thing to another, nor does it achieve its purpose through mockery or by upsetting the solidity of foundations; it does not transform the other side of the mirror, beyond an invisible and uncrossable line, into a glittering expanse. Transgression is neither violence in a divided world (in an ethical world) nor a victory over limits (in a dialectical or revolutionary world); and, exactly for this reason, its role is to measure the excessive distance that it opens at the heart of the limit and to trace the flashing line that causes the limit to arise. Transgression contains nothing negative, but affirms limited being—affirms the limitlessness into which it leaps as it opens this zone to existence for the first time. But, correspondingly, this affirmation contains nothing positive: no content can bind it, since, by definition, no limit can possibly restrict it. Perhaps it is simply an affirmation of division; but only insofar as division is not understood to mean a cutting gesture, or the establishment of a separation or the measuring of a distance, only retaining that in it which may designate the existence of difference.

Perhaps when contemporary philosophy discovered the possibility of nonpositive affirmation, it began a process of reorientation whose only equivalent is the shift instituted by Kant when he distinguished the *nihil negativum* and the *nihil privativum*—a distinction known to have opened the way for the advance of critical thought.[3] This philosophy of nonpositive affirmation, in other words of the testing of the limit, is, I believe, what Blanchot was defining through his principle of "contestation." Contestation does not imply a generalized negation, but an affirmation that affirms nothing, a radical break of transitivity. Rather than being a process of thought for denying existences or values, contestation is the act that carries them all to their limits and, from there, to the Limit where an ontological decision achieves its end; to contest is to proceed until one reaches the empty core where being achieves its limit and where the limit defines being. There, at the transgressed limit, the "yes" of contestation reverberates, leaving without echo the hee-haw of Nietzsche's braying ass.

Thus, contestation shapes an experience that Bataille wanted to circumscribe through every detour and repetition of his work, an experience that has the power "to implicate (and to question) everything without possible respite" and to indicate, in the place where it occurs and in its most essential form, "the immediacy of being." Nothing is more alien to this experience than the demonic character who, true to his nature, "denies everything." Transgression opens onto a scintillating and constantly affirmed world, a world without shadow or twilight, without that serpentine "no" that bites into fruits and lodges their contradictions at their core. It is the solar inversion of satanic denial. It was originally linked to the divine, or rather, from this limit marked by the sacred it opens the space where the divine functions. The discovery of such a category by a philosophy that questions itself about the existence of the limit is evidently one of the countless signs that our path is a path of return and that, with each day, we are becoming more Greek. Yet this motion should not be understood as the promised return to a homeland or the recovery of an original soil that produced and will naturally resolve every opposition. In reintroducing the experience of the divine at the center of thought, philosophy has been well aware since Nietzsche (or it should very well know) that it questions an origin without positivity and an opening indifferent to the patience of the negative. No form of dialectical movement, no analysis of constitutions and of their transcendental ground can serve as support for thinking about such an experience or even as access to this experience. In our day, would not the instantaneous play of the limit and of transgression be the essential test for a thought that centers on the "origin," for that form of thought to which Nietzsche dedicated us from the beginning of his works and one that would be, absolutely and in the same motion, a Critique and an Ontology, an understanding that comprehends both finitude and being?

What possibilities generated this thought from which everything, up until our time, has seemingly diverted us, but as if to lead us to the point of its returning? From what impossibilities does it derive its hold on us? Undoubtedly, it can be said that it comes to us through that opening made by Kant in Western philosophy when he articulated, in a manner that is still enigmatic, metaphysical discourse and reflection on the limits of our reason. However, Kant ended by closing this opening when he ultimately relegated all critical investigations to an anthropological question; and undoubtedly, we have subsequently interpreted Kant's actions as the granting of an indefinite respite to metaphysics, because dialectics substituted for the questioning of being and limits the play of contradiction and totality. To awaken us from the confused sleep of dialectics and of anthropology, we required the Nietzschean figures of tragedy, of Dionysus, of the death of God, of the philosopher's hammer, of the Superman approaching with the steps of a dove, of the Return. But why, in our day, is discursive language so ineffectual when asked to maintain the presence of these figures and to maintain itself through them? Why is it so nearly silent before them, as if it were forced to yield its voice so that they may continue to find their words, to yield to these extreme forms of language in which Bataille, Maurice Blanchot, and Pierre Klossowski have made their home, which they have made the summits of thought?

The sovereignty of these experiences must surely be recognized some day, and we must try to assimilate them: not to reveal their truth—a ridiculous pretension with respect to words that form our limits—but to serve as the basis for finally liberating our language. But our task for today is to direct our attention to this nondiscursive language, this language which, for almost two centuries, has stubbornly maintained its disruptive existence in our culture; it will be enough to examine its nature, to explore the source of this language which is neither complete nor fully in control of itself, even though it is sovereign for us and hangs above us, this language which is sometimes immobilized in scenes we customarily call "erotic" and suddenly volatized in a philosophical turbulence, when it seems to lose its very basis.

The parcelling out of philosophical discourse and descriptive scenes in Sade's books is undoubtedly the product of complex architectural laws. It is quite probable that the simple rules of alternation, of continuity, or of thematic contrast are inadequate for defining the space of the language where descriptions and demonstrations are articulated, where a rational order is linked to an order of pleasures, and where, especially, subjects are located both in the movement of various discourses and in a constellation of bodies. Let us simply say that this space is completely covered by a language that is discursive (even when it involves a narrative), explicit (even when it denotes nothing), and continuous (especially at the moment the thread passes from one character to another): a language that nevertheless does not have an absolute subject, that never discovers the one who ultimately speaks and incessantly maintains its *hold* on speech from the announcement of the "triumph of philosophy" in Justine's first adventure to Juliette's corpseless disappearance into eternity. Bataille's language, on the other hand, continually breaks down at the center of its space, exposing in his nakedness, in the inertia of ecstasy, a visible and insistent subject who had tried to keep language at arms length, but who now finds himself thrown by it, exhausted, upon the sands of that which he can no longer say.

How is it possible to discover, under all these different figures, that form of thought we carelessly call "the philosophy of eroticism," but in which it would be necessary to recognize (which is no less, but also much more) an essential experience for our culture since Kant and Sade—the experience of finitude and being, of the limit and transgression? What is the proper space of this form of thought and what language can it adopt? Undoubtedly, no form of reflection, yet developed, no established discourse, can supply its model, its foundation, or even the riches of its vocabulary. Would it be of help, in any case, to argue by analogy that we must find a language for the transgressive which would be what dialectics was, in an earlier time, for contradiction? Our efforts are undoubtedly better spent in trying to speak of this experience and in making it speak from the depths where its language fails, from precisely the place where words escape it, where the subject who speaks has just vanished, where the spectacle topples over before an upturned eye—from where Bataille's death has recently placed his language. We can only hope, now that his death has sent us to the pure transgression of his texts, that they will protect those who seek a language for the thought of the limit, that they will serve as a dwelling place for what may already be a ruined project.

In effect, do we not grasp the possibility of such thought in a language that necessarily strips it of any semblance of thought and leads it to the very impossibility of language? Right to this limit where the existence of language becomes problematic? The reason is that philosophical language is linked beyond all memory (or nearly so) to dialectics; and the dialectic was able to become the form and interior movement of philosophy from the time of Kant only through a redoubling of the millenary space from which philosophy had always spoken. We know full well that reference to Kant has invariably addressed us to the most formative elements of Greek thought: not to recapture a lost experience but to bring us closer to the possibility of nondialectical language. This age of commentary in which we live, this historical redoubling from which there seems no escape, does not indicate the velocity of our language in a field now devoid of new philosophical objects, which must be constantly recrossed in a forgetful and always rejuvenated glance. But far more to the point, it indicates the inadequacy, the profound silence, of a philosophical language that has been chased from its natural element, from its original dialectics, by the novelists found in its domain. If philosophy is now experienced as a multiple desert, it is not because it has lost its proper object or the freshness of its experience but because it has been suddenly divested of that language which is historically "natural" to it. We experience not the end of philosophy but a philosophy that regains its speech and finds itself again only in the marginal region that borders its limits—that is, one that finds itself either in a purified metalanguage or in the thickness of words enclosed by their darkness, by their blind truth. The prodigious distance that separates these alternatives and manifests our philosophical dispersion marks, more than a disarray, a profound coherence. This separation and real incompatibility is the actual distance from whose depths philosophy addresses us. It is here that we must focus our attention.

But what language can arise from such an absence? And, above all, who is the philosopher who will now begin to speak? "What of us when, having become sobered, we learn what we are? Lost among idlers in the night, where we can only hate the semblance of light coming from their small talk."[4] In a language stripped of dialectics, at the heart of what it says but also at the root of its possibility, the philosopher is aware that "we are not everything"; he learns as well that even the philosopher does not inhabit the whole of his language like a secret and perfectly fluent god. Next to himself, he discovers the existence of another language that also speaks and of which he is not the master, one that strives, fails, and falls silent, one that he cannot manipulate, the language he spoke at one time and has now separated itself from him, now gravitating in a space increasingly silent. Most of all, he discovers that he is not always lodged in his language in the same fashion, and that in the location from which a subject had traditionally spoken in philosophy—one whose obvious and garrulous identity has remained unexamined from Plato to Nietzsche—a void has been hollowed out in which a multiplicity of speaking subjects are joined and severed, combined and excluded. From the lessons on Homer to the cries of a madman in the streets of Turin, who can be said to have spoken this continuous language, so obstinately the same? Was it the Wanderer or his shadow? The philosopher or the first of the nonphilosophers? Zarathustra, his monkey, or already the Superman? Dionysus, Christ, their reconciled figures, or finally this man right here? The breakdown of philosophical subjectivity and its dispersion in a language that dispossesses it while multiplying it within the space created by its absence is probably one of the fundamental structures of contemporary thought. Again, this is not the end of philosophy but, rather, the end of the philosopher as the sovereign and primary form of philosophical language. And perhaps to all those who strive above all to maintain the unity of the philosopher's grammatical function—at the price of the coherence, even of the existence of philosophical language—we could oppose Bataille's exemplary enterprise: his desperate and relentless attack on the preeminence of the philosophical subject as it confronted him in his own work, in his experience and his language that became his private torment, in the first reflected torture of that which speaks in philosophical language—in the dispersion of stars that encircle a median night, allowing voiceless words to be born. "Like a flock chased by an infinite shepherd, we, the bleating wave, would flee, endlessly flee from the horror of reducing being to totality."[5]

It is not only the juxtaposition of reflective and novelistic texts in the language of thought that makes us aware of the shattering of the philosophical [*philosophant*] subject. The words of Bataille define the situation in far greater detail: in the constant movement to different levels of speech and a systematic disengagement from the "I" who has begun to speak and is already on the verge of deploying his language and installing himself in it; temporal disengagements ("I was writing this," or similarly, "in retrospect, if I return to this matter"); shifts in the distance separating a speaker from his words (in a diary, note-books, poems, stories, meditations, or discourses intended for demon-stration); an inner detachment from the assumed sovereignty of thought or writing (through books, anonymous texts, prefaces to his books, footnotes). And it is at the center of the philosophical subject's disappearance that philosophical language proceeds as if through a labyrinth, not to recapture him, but to test (and through language itself) the extremity of its loss. That is, it proceeds to the limit and to this opening where its being surges forth, but where it is already lost, completely overflowing itself, emptied of itself to the point where it becomes an absolute void—an opening which is communication: "at this point there is no need to elaborate; as my rapture escapes me, I immediately reenter the night of a lost child, anguished in his desire to prolong his ravishment, with no other end than exhaustion, no way of stopping short of fainting. It is such excruciating bliss."[6]

This experience forms the exact reversal of the movement that has sustained the wisdom of the West at least since the time of Socrates, that is, the wisdom to which philosophical language promised the serene unity of a subjectivity that would triumph in it, having been fully constituted by it and through it. But if the language of philosophy is one in which the philosopher's torments are tirelessly repeated and his subjectivity is discarded, then not only is wisdom meaningless as the philosopher's form of composition and reward, but in the expira-tion of philosophical language a possibility inevitably arises (that upon which it falls—the face of the die; and the place into which it falls—the void into which the die is cast): the possibility of the mad philosopher. In short, the experience of the philosopher who finds, not outside his language (the result of an external accident or imagi-nary exercise) but at the inner core of its possibilities, the transgres-sion of his philosophical being; and thus, the nondialectical language of the limit that only arises in transgressing the one who speaks. This play of transgression and being is fundamental for the constitution of philosophical language, which reproduces and undoubtedly produces it.

Essentially the product of fissures, abrupt descents, and broken contours, this misshapen and craglike language describes a circle; it refers to itself and is folded back on a questioning of its limits—as if it were nothing more than a small night lamp that flashes with a strange light, signaling the void from which it arises and to which it addresses everything it illuminates and touches. Perhaps, it is this curious configuration that explains why Bataille attributed such obstinate prestige to the Eye. Throughout his career (from his first novel to *Larmes d'Eros*), the eye was to keep its value as a figure of inner experience: "When at the height of anguish, I gently solicit a strange absurdity, an eye opens at the summit, in the middle of my skull."[7] This is because the eye, a small white globe that encloses its darkness, traces a limiting circle that only sight can cross. And the darkness within, the somber core of the eye, pours out into the world like a fountain which sees, that is, which lights up the world; but the eye also gathers up all the light of the world in the pupil, that small black spot, where it is transformed into the bright night of an image. The eye is mirror and lamp: it discharges its light into the world around it, while in a movement that is not necessarily contradictory, it precipitates this same light into the transparency of its well. Its globe has the expansive quality of a marvelous seed—like an egg imploding toward the center of night and extreme light, which it is and which it has just ceased to be. It is the figure of being in the act of transgressing its own limit.

The eye, in a philosophy of reflection, derives from its capacity to observe the power of becoming always more interior to itself. Lying behind each eye that sees, there exists a more tenuous one, an eye so discreet and yet so agile that its all-powerful glance can be said to eat away at the flesh of its while globe; behind this particular eye, there exists another and, then, still others, each progressively more subtle until we arrive at an eye whose entire substance is nothing but the pure transparency of a vision. This inner movement is finally resolved in a nonmaterial center where the intangible forms of truth are created and combined, in this heart of things which is the sovereign subject. Bataille reverses this entire direction: sight, crossing the globular limit of the eye, constitutes the eye in its instantaneous being; sight carries it away in this luminous stream (an outpouring fountain, streaming tears and, shortly, blood), hurls the eye outside of itself, conducts it to the limit where it bursts out in the immediately extinguished flame of its being. Only a small white ball, veined with blood, is left behind, only an exorbitated eye to which all sight is now denied. And in the place from which sight had once passed, only a

cranial cavity remains, only this black globe which the uprooted eye
has made to close upon its sphere, depriving it of vision but offering to
this absence the spectacle of that indestructible core which now imprisons the dead glance. In the distance created by this violence and
uprooting, the eye is seen absolutely but denied any possibility of
sight: the philosophizing subject has been dispossessed and pursued
to its limit, and the sovereignty of philosophical language can now be
heard from the distance, in the measureless void left behind by the
exorbitated subject.

But perhaps the eye accomplishes the most essential aspect of its
play when forced from its ordinary position, it is made to turn upward
in a movement that leads it back to the nocturnal and starred interior
of the skull and it is made to show us its usually concealed surface,
white and unseeing: it shuts out the day in a movement that manifests
its own whiteness (whiteness being undoubtedly the image of clarity,
its surface reflection, but for this very reason it cannot communicate
with it or communicate it); and the circular night of the pupil is made
to address the central absence that it illuminates with a flash, revealing it as night. The upturned orb suggests both the most open and the
most impenetrable eye: causing its sphere to pivot, while remaining
exactly the same and in the same place, it overturns day and night,
crosses their limit, but only to find it again on the same line and from
the other side; and the white hemisphere that appears momentarily at
the place where the pupil once opened is like the being of the eye as it
crosses the limit of its vision—when it transgresses this opening to the
light of day which defined the transgression of every sight. "If man did
not imperiously close his eyes, he would finally be unable to see the
things worth seeing."[8]

But what we need to see does not involve any interior secret or the
discovery of a more nocturnal world. Torn from its ordinary position
and made to turn inward in its orbit, the eye now only pours its light
into a bony cavern. This turning up of its globe may seem a betrayal of
"la petite mort," but more exactly, it simply indicates the death that it
experiences right where it is, in this springing up in place that causes
the eye to rotate. Death, for the eye, is not the always elevated line of
the horizon, but the limit it ceaselessly transgresses in its natural location, in the hollow where every vision originates, and where this
limit is elevated into an absolute limit by an ecstatic movement that
allows the eye to spring up from the other side. The upturned eye

discovers the bond that links language and death at the moment it acts out this relationship of the limit and being; and it is perhaps from this that it derives its prestige, in permitting the possibility of a language for this play. Thus, the great scenes that interrupt Bataille's stories invariably concern the spectacle of erotic deaths, where upturned eyes display their white limits and rotate inward in gigantic and empty orbits. *Le Bleu du ciel* gives a singularly precise outline of this movement: early in November, when the earth of German cemeteries is alive with the twinkling light of candles and candle stubs, the narrator is lying with Dorothy among the tombstones; making love among the dead, the earth around him appears like the sky on a bright night. And the sky above forms a great hollow orbit, a death mask, in which he recognizes his inevitable end at the moment that pleasure overturns the four globes of flesh, causing the revolution of his sight. "The earth under Dorothy's body was open like a tomb, her belly opened itself to me like a fresh grave. We were struck with stupor, making love on a starred cemetery. Each light marked a skeleton in a grave and formed a wavering sky as perturbed as our mingled bodies. I unfastened Dorothy's dress, I dirtied her clothes and her breast with the fresh earth which was stuck to my fingers. Our bodies trembled like two rows of chattering teeth."[9]

But what might this mean at the heart of a system of thought? What significance has this insistent eye which appears to encompass what Bataille successively designated *the inner experience, the extreme possibility, the cosmic process,* or simply *meditation*? It is certainly no more metaphoric than Descartes's phrasing of the "clear perception of sight" or this sharp point of the mind which he called *acies mentis*. In point of fact, the upturned eye has no meaning in Bataille's language, can have no meaning, since it marks its limit. It indicates the moment when language, arriving at its confines, overleaps itself, explodes and radically challenges itself in laughter, tears, the eyes rolled back in ecstasy, the mute and exorbitated horror of sacrifice, and where it remains fixed in this way at the limit of its void, speaking of itself in a second language in which the absence of a sovereign subject outlines its essential emptiness and incessantly fractures the unity of its discourse. The enucleated or rolled-back eye marks the zone of Bataille's philosophical language, the void into which it pours and loses itself, but in which it never stops talking—somewhat like the interior, diaphanous, and illuminated eye of mystics and spiritualists that marks the point at which the secret language of prayer is embedded and choked by a marvellous communication that silences it. Similarly, but in an inverted manner, the eye in Bataille delineates the zone shared by language and death, the place where language discovers its being in the crossing of its limits – the nondialectical form of philosophical language.

This eye, as the fundamental figure of the place from which Bataille speaks and in which his broken language finds its uninterrupted domain, establishes the connection, prior to any form of discourse, that exists between the death of God (a sun that rotates and the great eyelid that closes upon the world), the experience of finitude (springing up in death twisting the light that is extinguished as it discovers that the interior is an empty skull, a central absence), and the turning-back of language upon itself at the moment that it fails – a conjunction that undoubtedly has no other equivalent than the association, well known in other philosophies, of sight to truth or of contemplation to the absolute. Revealed to this eye, which in its pivoting conceals itself for all time, is the being of the limit: "I will never forget the violent and marvellous experience that comes from the will to open one's eyes, facing what exists, what happens."

Perhaps in the movement that carries it to a total night, the experience of transgression brings to light this relationship of finitude to being, this moment of the limit that anthropological thought, since Kant, could only designate from the distance and from the exterior through the language of dialectics.

The twentieth century will undoubtedly have discovered the related categories of exhaustion, excess, the limit, and transgression – the strange and unyielding form of these irrevocable movements that consume and consummate us. In a form of thought that considers man as worker and producer – that of European culture since the end of the eighteenth century – consumption was based entirely on need, and need based itself exclusively on the model of hunger. When this element was introduced into an investigation of profit (the appetite of those who have satisfied their hunger), it inserted man into a dialectic of production which had a simple anthropological meaning: if man was alienated from his real nature and immediate needs through his labor and the production of objects with his hands, it was nevertheless through its agency that he recaptured his essence and achieved the indefinite gratification of his needs. But it would undoubtedly be misguided to conceive of hunger as that irreducible anthropological factor in the definition of work, production, and profit; and similarly, need has an altogether different status, or it responds at the very least to a code whose laws cannot be confined to a dialectic of production. The discovery of sexuality – the discovery of that firmament of indefinite unreality where Sade placed it from the beginning, the discovery of those systematic forms of prohibition we now know imprison it, the discovery of the universal nature of transgression in which it is both object and instrument – indicates in a sufficiently forceful way the impossibility of attributing the millenary language of dialectics to the major experience that sexuality forms for us.

Perhaps the emergence of sexuality in our culture is an event of multiple values: it is tied to the death of God and to the ontological void that His death fixed at the limit of our thought; it is also tied to the still-silent and groping apparition of a form of thought in which the interrogation of the limit replaces the search for totality, and the act of transgression replaces the movement of contradictions. Finally, it involves the questioning of language by language in a circularity that the "scandalous" violence of erotic literature, far from ending, displays from its first use of words. Sexuality is only decisive for our culture as spoken, and to the degree it is spoken. Not that it is our language that has been eroticized now for nearly two centuries; rather, since Sade and the death of God, the universe of language has absorbed our sexuality, denatured it, placed it in a void where it establishes its sovereignty and where it incessantly sets up as the Law the limits it transgresses. In this sense, the appearance of sexuality as a fundamental problem marks the slippage of a philosophy of man as worker to a philosophy based on a being who speaks; and insofar as philosophy has traditionally maintained a secondary role to knowledge and work, it must be admitted, not as a sign of crisis but of essential structure, that it is now secondary to language. Not that philosophy is now fated to a role of repetition or commentary, but that it experiences itself and its limits in language and in this transgression of language which carries it, as it did Bataille, to the faltering of the speaking subject. On the day that sexuality began to speak and to be spoken, language no longer served as a veil for the infinite; and in the density it acquired on that day, we now experience finitude and being. In its dark domain, we now encounter the absence of God, our death, limits, and their transgression. But perhaps it is also a source of light for those who have liberated their thought from all forms of dialectical language, as it became for Bataille, on more than one occasion, when he experienced the loss of his language in the dead of night. "What I call night differs from the darkness of thoughts: night possesses the violence of light. Yes, night: the youth and the intoxication of thinking."[10]

Perhaps this "difficulty with words" that now hampers philosophy, a condition fully explored by Bataille, should not be identified with the loss of language that the closure of dialectics seemed to indicate. Rather, it follows from the actual penetration of philosophical experience in language and the discovery that the experience of the limit, and the manner in which philosophy must now understand it, is realized in language and in the movement where it says what cannot be said.

Perhaps this "difficulty with words" also defines the space given over to an experience in which the speaking subject, instead of expressing himself, is exposed, goes to encounter his finitude and, under each of his words, is brought back to the reality of his own death: that zone, in short, which transforms every work into the sort of "tauromachy" suggested by Michel Leiris, who was thinking of his own actions as a writer but undoubtedly also of Bataille.[11] In any event, it is on the white beach of an arena (a gigantic eye) where Bataille experienced the fact—crucial for his thought and characteristic of all his language—that death *communicated with communication*, and that the uprooted eye, a white and silent sphere, could become a violent seed in the night of the body, that it could render present this absence of which sexuality has never stopped speaking and from which it is made to speak incessantly. When the horn of the bull (a glittering knife that carries the threat of night, and an exact reversal of the image of light that emerges from the night of the eye) penetrates the eyeball of the toreador, who is blinded and killed, Simone performs an act we have come to expect: she swallows a pale and skinless seed and returns to its original night the luminous virility that has just committed murder. The eye is returned back to its night, the globe of the arena turns upward and rotates; but it is the moment in which being necessarily appears in its immediacy and in which *the act that crosses the limit touches absence itself*: "Two globes of the same color and consistency were simultaneously activated in opposite directions. A bull's white testicle had penetrated Simone's black and pink flesh; an eye had emerged from the head of the young man. This coincidence, linked until death to a sort of urinary liquefaction of the sky, gave me Marcelle for a moment. I seemed, in this ungraspable instant, to touch her."[12]

NOTES

1   Georges Bataille, *L'Abbé C.*, part two: "Récit de Charles" [1950], in *Oeuvres complètes* (Paris: Gallimard, 1971), vol. 3, pp. 263–64.

2   Bataille, *L'Erotisme*, part two: "Etudes diverses," VII: "Préface to *Madame Edwards*" [1957], in *Oeuvres complètes*, vol. 3, pp. 263–64 (*Eroticism*, trans. M. Dalwood [San Francisco: City Lights, 1986], p. 269).

3   See *Immanuel Kant's Critique of Pure Reason* [1781], trans. and ed. Norman Kemp Smith (London: MacMillan, 1933), p. 295 – Ed.

4   Bataille, *Somme athéologique*, part one: *L'Expérience intérieure* [1943] (6th ed., Paris: Gallimard, 1954), Preface, p. 10.

5   Bataille, *L'Expérience intérieure*, part two: *Le Supplice*, p. 54.

6   Ibid., p. 74.

7   Bataille, *L'Expérience intérieure*, part three: *Le Bleu du ciel*, p. 101.

8   Bataille, *La Littérature et le mal: Baudelaire* [1957], in *Oeuvres complètes* [*Literature and Evil*, trans. Alastair Hamilton (London: Martin Boyars, 1973), p. 40].

9   Bataille, *Le Bleu du ciel* [1957], in *Oeuvres complètes*, vol. 3 (1971), p. 481–82.

10 Bataille, *Le Coupable: la divinité du rire* [1961], in *Oeuvres complètes*, vol. 5 (1973), p. 354 [*Guilty*, trans. B. Boone (San Francisco: Lapis, 1988), p. 108].

11 Michel Leiris, *De la Littérature considérée comme une tauromachie* (Paris: Gallimard, 1946) [*Manhood*, trans. Richard Howard (London: Jonathan Cape, 1968)].

12 Bataille, *Histoire de l'oeil: sous le soleil de Saville*, new version, in *Oeuvres complètes*, vol. 1 (1970), appendix, p. 598 [*Story of the Eye*, trans. Joachim Nevgroschel (San Francisco: City Lights, 1987), pp. 65–66].

LANGUAGE TO INFINITY*

W riting so as not to die, as Maurice Blanchot said, or perhaps
even speaking so as not to die, is a task undoubtedly as old as the
word. The most fateful decisions are inevitably suspended during the
course of a story. We know that discourse has the power to arrest the
flight of an arrow in a recess of time, in the space proper to it. It is
quite likely, as Homer has said, that the gods send disasters to men so
that they can tell of them, and that in this possibility speech finds its
infinite resourcefulness; it is quite likely that the approach of death —
its sovereign gesture, its prominence within human memory —
hollows out in the present and in existence the void toward which
and from which we speak. But the *Odyssey*, which affirms this gift of
language in death, tells the inverted story of how Ulysses returns
home: it repeats, each time death threatened him and in order to ward
off its dangers, exactly how (by what wiles and intrigues) he had
succeeded in maintaining this imminence that returns again the moment he begins to speak, in the form of a menacing gesture or a new
danger. And when, as a stranger among the Phaeacians, he hears in
another's voice the tale, already a thousand years old, of his own history, it is as if he were listening to his own death: he covers his face
and cries, in the gesture of a woman to whom the dead body of a hero
is brought after a battle. Against this speech which announces his
death and arises from deep within the new *Odyssey* as from an older

---

*This essay was originally published in *Tel quel* 15 (1963), pp. 44–53. The translation, by
Donald F. Bouchard and Sherry Simon, has been slightly amended.

time, Ulysses must sing the song of his identity and tell of his misfortunes to escape the fate presented to him by a language before language. And he pursues this fictive speech, confirming and dissipating its powers at the same time, into this space, which borders death but is also poised against it, where the story locates its natural domain. The gods send disasters to mortals so that they can tell of them, but men speak of them so that misfortunes will never be fully realized, so that their fulfillment will be averted in the distance of words, at the place where they will be stilled in the negation of their nature. Boundless misfortune, the resounding gift of the gods, marks the point where language begins; but the limit of death opens before language, or rather within language, an infinite space. Before the imminence of death, language rushes forth, but it also starts again, tells of itself, discovers the story of the story and the possibility that this interpenetration might never end. Headed toward death, language turns back upon itself; it encounters something like a mirror; and to stop this death which would stop it, it possesses but a single power—that of giving birth to its own image in a play of mirrors that has no limits. From the depths of the mirror where it sets out to arrive anew at the point where it started (at death), but so as finally to escape death, another language can be heard—the image of actual language, but as a minuscule, interior, and virtual model; it is the song of the bard who had already sung of Ulysses before the *Odyssey* and before Ulysses himself (since Ulysses hears the song), but who will also sing of him endlessly after his death (since, for the bard, Ulysses is already as good as dead); and Ulysses, who is alive, receives this song as a wife receives her slain husband.

Perhaps there exists in speech an essential affinity between death, endless striving, and the self-representation of language. Perhaps the figure of a mirror to infinity erected against the black wall of death is fundamental for any language from the moment it determines to leave a trace of its passage. Not only since the invention of writing has language pretended to pursue itself to infinity; but neither is it because of its fear of death that it decided one day to assume a body in the form of visible and permanent signs. Rather, somewhat before the invention of writing, a change had to occur to open the space in which writing could flow and establish itself, a change, symbolized for us in its most original figuration by Homer, that forms one of the most decisive ontological events of language: its mirrored reflection upon death and the construction, from this reflection, of a virtual space where speech discovers the endless resourcefulness of its own image, and where it can represent itself as already existing behind itself, already active beyond itself, to infinity. The possibility of a work of language finds its original fold in this duplication. In this sense, death is undoubtedly the most essential of the accidents of language (its limit and its center): from the day that men began to speak toward death and against it, in order to grasp and imprison it, something was born, a murmuring that repeats, recounts, and redoubles itself endlessly, has undergone an uncanny process of amplification and thickening, in which our language is today lodged and hidden.

(A hypothesis that is hardly indispensable: alphabetical writing is already, in itself, a form of duplication, since it represents not the signified but the phonetic elements by which it is signified; the ideogram, on the other hand, directly represents the signified, independently from a phonetic system, which is another mode of representation. Writing, in Western culture, automatically dictates that we place ourselves in the virtual space of self-representation and reduplication; since writing refers not to a thing but to speech, a work of language only advances more deeply into the intangible density of the mirror, calls forth the double of this already-doubled writing, discovers in this way a possible and impossible infinity, ceaselessly strives after speech, maintains it beyond the death that condemns it, and frees a murmuring stream. This presence of repeated speech in writing undeniably gives to what we call a work of language an ontological status unknown in those cultures where the act of writing designates the thing itself, in its proper and visible body, stubbornly inaccessible to time.)

Jorge Luis Borges tells the story of a condemned writer to whom God grants, at the precise instant of his execution, another year of life to complete the work he had begun.[1] Suspended between life and death, this work is a drama where everything is necessarily repeated: the end (as yet unfinished) taking up word for word the (already-written) beginning, but in such a way as to show the main character, whom we know and who has spoken since the first scenes, to be not himself but an impostor. And during this impending death, during the year that passes while a drop of rain streaks the condemned man's cheek, as the smoke of his last cigarette disappears, Hladik writes—but with words that no one will be able to read, not even God—the great, invisible labyrinth of repetition, of language that divides itself and becomes its own mirror. When the last epithet is found (also the first since the drama begins again), the volley of rifle fire, released less than a second before, strikes his silence at its heart.

I wonder if it is not possible to construct or, at the very least, to outline from a distance an ontology of literature beginning from these phenomena of self-representation in language; such figures, which seemingly belong to the level of guile or entertainment, conceal, that is, betray the relationship that language establishes with death—with this limit to which language addresses itself and against which it is poised. It would be necessary to begin with a general analysis of all the forms of reduplication of language to be found in Western literature. These forms, there is no reason to doubt, are limited in number, and it should be possible to list them in their entirety. Their often-extreme discretion, the fact that they are occasionally hidden and surface through what seems chance or inadvertance, should not deceive us; or, rather, we must recognize in them the very power of illusion, the possibility for language (a single stringed instrument) to stand upright as a work. The reduplication of language, even if it is concealed, constitutes its being as a work, and the signs that might appear from this must be read as ontological indications.

These signs are often imperceptible, bordering on the futile. They manage to present themselves as faults—slight imperfections at the surface of a work: we might say that they serve as an involuntary opening to the inexhaustible depths from which they come to us. I am reminded of an episode in *The Nun* where Suzanne explains the history of a letter to a correspondent (its composition, hiding place, attempted theft, and finally its custody by a friend who was able to return it)—of precisely this letter in which she explains to her correspondent, and so on.[2] Proof, to be sure, that Diderot was distracted, but, more important, a sign that language is speaking of itself, that the letter is not the letter, but the language that doubles it within the same system of reality (because they speak at the same time, use the same words, and identically share the same body; language is the letter's flesh and blood); and yet, language is also absent, but not as a result of the sovereignty we ascribe to a writer; rather, it renders itself absent by crossing the virtual space where language is made into an image of itself and transgresses the limit of death through its reduplication in a mirror. Diderot's "blunder" is not the result of his eagerness to intervene, but is due to the opening of language to its system of self-representation: the letter in *The Nun* is only an analogue of a letter, resembling it in every detail with the exception of being its imperceptibly displaced double (this displacement made visible only because of a tear in the fabric of language). In this lapsus (in the exact sense of the word), we find a figure which is quite similar to – but exactly the inverse of – that found in *The Thousand and One Nights*, where an episode recounted by Scheherazade tells why she was obliged for a thousand and one nights, and so on. In this context, the mirrored structure is explicitly given: at its center, the work holds out a mirror ("*psyche*": a fictive space, a real soul) where it appears like a miniature of itself and preceding itself, since it tells its own story as one among the many wonders of the past, among so many other nights. And in this privileged night, so much like the others, a space is opened that seems to be that in which it merely forms an insignificant aberration, and it reveals the same stars in the same sky. We could say that there is one night too many, that a thousand would have been enough; we could say, inversely, that a letter is missing in *The Nun* (the one that should tell the history of the letter so that it would no longer be required to tell of its own adventure). It seems clear, in any event, that in the same dimension there exists, from the one, a missing day and, from the other, one night too many – the fatal space in which language speaks of itself.

It is possible that in every work language is superimposed upon itself in a secret verticality; where the double is exactly the same as the thin space between – the narrow, black line that no perception can divulge except in those fortuitous and deliberately confusing moments when the figure of Scheherazade surrounds itself with fog, retreats to the origins of time, and arises infinitely reduced at the center of a brilliant, profound, and virtual disc. A work of language is the body of language crossed by death in order to open this infinite space where doubles reverberate. And the forms of this superimposition, essential to the construction of any work, can undoubtedly only be deciphered in these adjacent, fragile, and slightly monstrous figures where a division into two signals itself; their exact listing and classification, the establishment of the laws that govern their functioning or transformations, could well lead to a formal ontology of literature.

It seems to me that a change was produced in the relationship of language to its indefinite repetition at the end of the eighteenth century – nearly coinciding with the moment in which works of language became what they are now for us, that is, literature. This is the time (or very nearly so) when Hölderlin became aware, to the point of blindness, that he could only speak in the space marked by the disappearance of the gods, and that language could only depend on its own power to keep death at a distance. Thus, an opening was traced on the horizon toward which our speech has ceaselessly advanced.

For a long time – from the advent of the Homeric gods to the remoteness of the divine in the fragment of *Empedocles* – speaking so as not to die had a meaning now alien to us. To speak of heroes or as a hero, to desire to construct something like a work, to speak so that others speak of it to infinity, to speak for "glory," was indeed to move toward or against this death maintained by language; to speak as a sacred orator warning of death, to threaten men with this end beyond any possible glory, was also to disarm death and promise immortality. In other words, every work was intended to be completed, to still itself in a silence where the infinite Word reestablished its supremacy. Within a work, language protected itself against death through this invisible speech, this speech before and after any possible time from which it made itself into its self-enclosed reflection. The mirror to infinity, to which every language gives birth once it erects itself vertically against death, was not displayed without an evasion: the work placed the infinite outside of itself – a real and majestic infinity in which it became a virtual and circular mirror, completed in a beautifully closed form.

Writing, in our day, has moved infinitely closer to its source, to this disquieting sound which announces from the depths of language – once we attend to it – the source against which we seek refuge and toward which we address ourselves. Like Franz Kafka's beast, language now listens from the bottom of its burrow to this inevitable and growing noise.[3] To defend itself it must follow its movements, become its loyal enemy, and allow nothing to stand between them except the contradictory thinness of a transparent and unbreakable partition. We must ceaselessly speak, for as long and as loudly as this indefinite and deafening noise – longer and more loudly so that in mixing our voices with it we might succeed – if not in silencing and mastering it – in modulating its futility into the endless murmuring we call literature. From this moment, a work whose only meaning resides in its being a self-enclosed expression of its glory is no longer possible.

The date of this transformation is roughly indicated by the simultaneous appearance at the end of the eighteenth century of the works of Sade and the tales of terror. It is not their common predilection for cruelty which concerns us here; nor is it the discovery of the link between literature and evil, but something more obscure and paradoxical at first sight. These languages which are constantly drawn out of themselves by the overwhelming, the unspeakable, by thrills, stupefaction, ecstasy, dumbness, pure violence, wordless gestures, and are calculated with the greatest economy and precision to produce effects (so that they make themselves as transparent as possible at this limit of language toward which they hurry, erasing themselves in their writing for the exclusive sovereignty of what they wish to say and lies outside of words)—these languages very strangely represent themselves in a slow, meticulous, and infinitely extended ceremony. These simple languages, which name and make one see, are curiously double.

Undoubtedly, it would still take a long time to understand the language of Sade as it exists for us today: I am not referring to the possible meaning of this prisoner's purpose in endlessly writing books that could not be read (somewhat on the order of Borges's character who boundlessly extends the second of his death through the language of a repetition addressed to no one); but to the nature of these words in the present and to the existence in which they prolong their life to our day. This language's claim to tell all is not simply that of breaking prohibitions but of seeking the limits of the possible; the design, in a systematically transformed network, of all the branchings, insertions, and overlappings that are deduced from the human crystal in order to give birth to great, sparkling, mobile, and infinitely extendable configurations; the lengthy passage through the underground of nature to the double lightning flash of the spirit (the first, derisive and dramatic, which blasts Justine, and the second, invisible and absolutely slow, which—in the absence of a charnel house—causes Juliette to disappear into a kind of eternity asymptotic to death)—these elements designate the project of subjecting every possible language, every future language, to the actual sovereignty of this unique Discourse which no one, perhaps, will be able to hear. Through so many bodies consummated in their actual existence, this Saturnine language devours all eventual words, all those words which have yet to be born. And if each scene in its visible aspect is doubled by a demonstration that repeats it and gives it value as a universal element, it is because what is being consumed in this second discourse, and upon another mode, is not all future languages but every language that has been effectively pronounced: everything, before Sade and in his time, that could have been thought, said, practiced, desired, honored, flouted, or condemned in relation to man, God, the soul, the body, sex, nature, priests, or women finds itself meticulously repeated (from this arise the interminable enumerations on the historical or ethnographic level, which do not support Sade's reasoning but delineate the space where his reason functions)—thus, repeated, combined, dissociated, reversed, and reversed once again, not in view of a dialectical reward but toward a radical exhaustion. Saint-Fond's wonderful negative cosmology, the punishment that reduces it to silence, Clairville thrown into a volcano, the wordless apotheosis of Juliette are moments that register the calcination of every language. Sade's impossible book stands in the place of every book—of all these books it makes impossible from the beginning to the end of time. Under this obvious pastiche of all the philosophies and stories of the eighteenth century, beneath this immense double that is not without analogy to *Don Quixote*, the totality of language finds itself sterilized by the single and identical movement of two inseparable figures: the strict, inverted repetition of what has already been said and the simple naming of that which lies at the limit of what we can say.

The precise object of "sadism" is not the other, neither his body, nor his sovereignty: it is everything that might have been said. Furthermore and still somewhat at a distance, it is the mute circle where language deploys itself: to a world of captive readers, Sade, the captive, denies the possibility of reading. This is done so effectively that if we asked to whom the works of Sade were addressed (and address themselves today), there is only one answer: no one. The works of Sade inhabit a strange limit, which they nevertheless persist in transgressing—or, rather, which they transgress because of the fact that they speak: they deny themselves the space of their language—but by confiscating it in a gesture of repetitive appropriation; and they evade not only their meaning (a meaning constructed at every turn) but their possible being; the indecipherable play of ambiguity within them is nothing but the serious sign of this conflict which forces them to be the double of every language (which, in their repetition, they set to fire) and of their own absence (which they constantly manifest). These works could and should, in a strict sense, continue without interruption, in a murmuring that has no other ontological status than that of a similar conflict.

In spite of appearances, the simplicity of the novels of terror achieves much the same ends. They were meant to be read and were in effect: *Coelina or The Child of Mystery* sold 1.2 million copies from its publication in 1798 to the Restoration.[4] This means that every person who knew how to read, and had read at least one book in his life, had read *Coelina.* It was the Book—an absolute text whose readership exactly corresponded to the total domain of possible readers. It was a book without a future, without a fringe exposed to deaf ears, since almost instantaneously and in a single movement it was able to achieve its goal. Historical conditions were necessary to foster this new phenomenon (as far as I know, it has never been repeated). It was especially necessary that the book possess an exact functional efficiency and that it coincide, without any screening or alteration, without dividing itself into two, with its objective, which was very simply to be read. But novels of this type were not meant to be read at the level of their writing or in the specific dimensions of their language; they wished to be read for the things they recounted, for this emotion, fear, horror, or pity that words were charged to communicate, but only through their pure and simple transparency. Language should acquire the thinness and absolute seriousness of the story; in making itself as gray as possible, it was required to transmit an event to its docile and terrorized reader, to be nothing but the neutral element of pathos. That is to say, it never offered itself in its own right; there was no mirror, wedged into the thickness of its discourse which might open the unlimited space of its own image. Rather, it erased itself between the things it said and the person to whom it spoke, accepting with absolute seriousness and according to the principle of strict economy its role as horizontal language, its role of communication.

Yet these novels of terror are accompanied by an ironic movement that doubles and divides them, which is not the result of historical repercussions or an effect of tedium. In a phenomenon quite rare in the history of literary language, satire in this instance is exactly contemporaneous with the situation it parodies.[5] It is as if two twin and complementary languages were born at once from the same central source: one existing entirely in its naïveté, the other within parody; one existing solely for the reader's eyes, the other moving from the reader's simpleminded fascination to the easy tricks of the writer. But in actuality, these two languages are more than simply contemporaneous; they lie within each other, share the same dwelling, constantly intertwine, forming a single verbal network and, as it were, a forked language that turns against itself from within, destroying itself in its own body, poisonous in its very density.

The native thinness of the story is perhaps firmly attached to a secret annihilation, to an internal struggle that is the very law of its development, proliferation, and inexhaustible flora. This "too-muchness" functions somewhat like the excess in Sade, but the latter proceeds to the simple act of naming and to the recovery of all language, while the former relies on two different figures. The first is an ornamental superabundance, where nothing is shown without the explicit, simultaneous, and contradictory indication of all its attributes at once: it is not a weapon that shows itself under a word and cuts through it but an inoffensive and complete panoply (let us call this figure, after an often repeated episode, the effect of the "bloody skeleton": the presence of death is manifested by the whiteness of the rattling bones and, at the same time, on this smooth skeleton, by the dark and contradictory streaks of blood). The second figure is that of a "wavelike succession to infinity": each episode must follow the preceding one in keeping with the simple but absolutely essential law of increment. It is necessary to approach always closer to the moment when language will reveal its absolute power, by giving birth, through each of its feeble words, to terror; but this is the moment in which language inevitably becomes impotent, when its breath is cut short, when it should still itself without even saying that it stops speaking. Language must push back to infinity this limit it bears with itself, which indicates, at once, its kingdom and its limit. Thus, in each novel, an exponential series of endless episodes; and then, beyond this, an endless series of novels. The language of terror is dedicated to an endless expense, even though it only seeks to achieve a single effect. It drives itself out of any possible resting place.

Sade and the novels of terror introduce an essential imbalance within works of language: they force them of necessity to be always excessive and deficient. Excessive because language can no longer avoid multiplying itself—as if struck from within by a disease of proliferation; it is always beyond the limit in relation to itself; it only speaks as a supplement starting from a displacement such that the language from which it separates itself and which it recovers is the one that appears useless and excessive, and deserves to be expunged; but, as a result of the same shift, it sheds in turn all ontological weight; it is at this point excessive and of so little density that it is fated to extend itself to infinity without ever acquiring the weight that might immobilize it. But does this not also imply that it suffers a deficiency, or, rather, that it is struck by the wound of the double? That it challenges language to reproduce it in the virtual space (in the real transgression) of the mirror, and to create a new mirror in the first, and again another, and always to infinity? The actual infinity of illusion which forms, in its vanity, the thickness of a work—that absence in the interior from which the work paradoxically erects itself.

Perhaps what we should rigorously define as "literature" came into existence at precisely the moment, at the end of the eighteenth century, when a language appeared that appropriates and consumes all other languages in its lightning flash, giving birth to an obscure but dominant figure where death, the mirror and the double, and the wavelike succession of words to infinity enact their roles.

In "The Library of Babel," everything that can possibly be said has already been said:[6] it contains all conceived and imagined languages, and even those which might be conceived or imagined; everything has been pronounced, even those things without meaning, so that the odds of discovering even the smallest formal coherence are extremely slight, as witnessed by the persevering search of those who have never been granted this dispensation. And yet standing above all these words is the rigorous and sovereign language that recovers them, tells their story, and is actually responsible for their birth: a language that is itself poised against death, because it is at the moment of falling into the shaft of an infinite Hexagon that the most lucid (and consequently the last) of the librarians reveals that even the infinity of language multiplies itself to infinity, repeating itself without end in the divided figures of the Same.

This configuration is exactly the reverse of that found in classical rhetoric. Rhetoric did not enunciate the laws or forms of a language; it established the relationship between two forms of speech: the first, mute, indecipherable, fully present to itself, and absolute; the other, garrulous, had only to voice this first speech according to forms, operations, and conjunctions whose space measured its distance from the first and inaudible text. For finite creatures and for men who would die, rhetoric ceaselessly repeated the speech of the Infinite that would never come to an end. Every figure of rhetoric betrayed a distance in its own space, but in signaling the first speech it lent the provisional density of a revelation to the second: it showed. The space of language today is not defined by rhetoric, but by the Library—by the ranging to infinity of fragmentary languages, substituting for the double chain of Rhetoric the simple, continuous, and monotonous line of language left to its own devices, a language fated to be infinite because it can no longer support itself upon the speech of infinity. But within itself, it finds the possibility of its own division, of its own repetition, the power to create a vertical system of mirrors, self images, analogies. A language that repeats no other speech, no other Promise, but postpones death indefinitely by ceaselessly opening a space where it is always the analogue of itself.

Libraries are the enchanted domain of two major difficulties. They have been resolved, we know, by mathematicians and tyrants (but perhaps not altogether). There is a dilemma: either all these books are already contained within the Word [*la Parole*] and they must be burned, or they are contradictory and, again, they must be burned. Rhetoric is a means of momentarily postponing the burning of libraries (but it holds out this promise for the near future, that is, for the end of time). And thus the paradox: If we make a book that tells of all the others, would it or would it not be a book itself? Must it tell its own story as if it were a book among others? And if it does not tell its story, what could it possibly be, since its objective was to be a book? Why should it omit its own story, since it is required to speak of every book? Literature begins when this paradox is substituted for the dilemma; when the book is no longer the space where speech adopts a form (forms of style, forms of rhetoric, forms of language) but the site where books are all recaptured and consumed: a site that is nowhere, since it gathers all the books of the past in this impossible "volume" whose murmuring will be shelved among so many others—after all the others, before all the others.

NOTES

1   "The Secret Miracle," in Jorge Luis Borges, *Labyrinths*, ed. Donald A. Yates and James E. Irby, trans. Donald A. Yates and others (New York: New Directions, 1962), pp. 88–94.

2   Denis Diderot, *La Religeuse* [1796] (Paris: Colin, 1961) [*The Nun*, trans. Leonard Tancock (London: Folio Society, 1922)].

3   Franz Kafka, "The Burrow," in *The Complete Stories*, ed. Nahum M. Glazer (New York: Schocken, 1971), pp. 325–59.

4   René-Charles Guibert de Piérécourt, *Coelina ou L'Enfant du Mystère* (Paris: Le Prieur, 1798), 3 vols.

5   A text such as Bellin de Labordière's *Une Nuit anglaise* [*An English Night*] was meant to have the same relation to tales of terror as *Don Quixote* had to chivalric romances; but it is their exact comtemporary.

6   Borges, "The Library of Babel," in *Labyrinths*, pp. 51–58.

AFTERWORD TO
*THE TEMPTATION OF ST. ANTHONY**

I

The Temptation of Saint Anthony was rewritten on three different
occasions: in 1849, before *Madame Bovary*; in 1856, before *Salammbô;*
and in 1872, while Flaubert was writing *Bouvard et Pécuchet.* He published extracts in 1856 and 1857. Saint Anthony accompanied Flaubert
for twenty-five or thirty years—for as long, in fact, as the hero of the
Sentimental Education. In these twin and inverted figures, the old
anchorite of Egypt, still besieged by desires, responds through the
centuries to a young man of eighteen, seized by the apparition of Madame Arnoux while travelling from Paris to Le Havre. Moreover, the
evening when Frédéric—at this stage, a pale reflection of himself—
turns away, as if in fear of incest, from the woman he continues to
love recalls the shadowed night when the defeated hermit learns to
love even the substance of life in its material form. "Temptation"
among the ruins of an ancient world populated by spirits is transformed into an "education" in the prose of the modern world.

The Temptation was conceived early in Flaubert's career—perhaps
after attending a puppet show—and it influenced all of his works.
Standing alongside his other books, standing behind them, *The Temptation* forms a prodigious reserve: for scenes of violence, phantasmagoria, chimeras, nightmares, slapstick. Flaubert successively

---

*This essay originally appeared in *Cahiers Renaud Barrault,* No. 59 (March 1967), pp.
7-30. This translation, by Donald F. Brouchard and Sherry Simon, has been slightly
amended.

transformed its inexhaustible treasure into the gray provincial reveries of *Madame Bovary,* into the sculpted sets of *Salammbô,* and into the eccentricities of everyday life in *Bouvard. The Temptation* seems to represent Flaubert's unattainable dream: what he wanted his works to be—supple, silky, delicate, spontaneous, harmoniously revealed through rapturous phrases—but also what they must never be if they were to see the light of day. *The Temptation* existed before any of Flaubert's books (its first sketches are found in *Mémoires d'un fou, Rêve d'enfer, Danse des morts,* and, particularly, in *Smahr*),[1] and it was repeated—as ritual, purification, exercise, a "temptation" to overcome—prior to writing each of his major texts. Suspended over his entire work, it is unlike all his other books by virtue of its prolixity, its wasted abundance, and its overcrowded bestiary; and set back from his other books, it offers, as a photographic negative of their writing, the somber and murmuring prose which they were compelled to repress, to silence gradually, in order to achieve their own clarity. The entire work of Flaubert is dedicated to the conflagration of this primary discourse: its precious ashes, its black, unmalleable coal.

II

We readily understand *The Temptation* as setting out the formal progression of unconfined reveries. It would be to literature what Bosch, Breughel, or the Goya of the *Caprichos* were at one time to painting. The first readers (or audience) were bored by the monotonous progression of grotesques: Maxime Du Camp remarked: "We listened to the words of the Sphinx, the chimera, the Queen of Sheba, of Simon the Magician. . . . A bewildered, somewhat simpleminded, and, I would even say, foolish Saint Anthony sees, parading before him, different forms of temptation."[2] His friends were enraptured by the "richness of his vision" (François Coppée), "by its forest of shadows and light" (Victor Hugo), and by its "hallucinatory mechanism" (Hippolyte Taine). But stranger still, Flaubert himself invoked madness, phantasms; he felt he was shaping the fallen trees of a dream: "I spend my afternoons with the shutters closed, the curtains drawn, and without a shirt, dressed as a carpenter. I bawl out! I sweat! It's superb! There are moments when this is decidedly more than delirium." As the book nears completion: "I plunged furiously into *Saint*

Anthony and began to enjoy the most terrifying exaltation. I have never been more excited."

In time, we have learned as readers that *The Temptation* is not the product of dreams and rapture, but a monument to meticulous erudition.[3] To construct the scene of the heresiarchs, Flaubert drew extensively from Tillemont's *Mémoires ecclésiastiques*, Matter's four-volume *Histoire du gnosticisme*, the *Histoire de Manichée* by Beausobre, Reuss's *Théologie chrétienne*, and also from Saint Augustine and, of course, from Migne's *Patrologia* (Athanasius, Jerome, and Epiphanus). The gods that populate the text were found in Burnouf, Anquetil-Duperron, in the works of Herbelot and Hottinger, in the volumes of the *Univers Pittoresque*, in the work of the Englishman, Layard, and, particularly, in Creutzer's translation, the *Religions de l'Antiquité*. For information on monsters, he read Xivrey's *Traditions tératologiques*, the *Physiologus* re-edited by Cahier and Martin, Boaistuau's *Histoires prodigieuses*, and the Duret text devoted to plants and their "admirable history." Spinoza inspired his metaphysical meditation on extended substance. Yet, this list is far from exhaustive. Certain evocations in the text seem totally dominated by the machinery of dreams: for example, the magisterial Diana of Ephesus, with lions at her shoulders and with fruits, flowers, and stars interlaced on her bosom, with a cluster of breasts, and griffins and bulls springing from the sheath which tightly encircles her waist. Nevertheless, this "fantasy" is an exact reproduction of plate 88 in Creutzer's last volume: if we observe the details of the print, we can appreciate Flaubert's diligence. Cybele and Atys (with his languid pose, his elbow against a tree, his flute, and his costume cut into diamond shapes) are both found in plate 58 of the same work; similarly, the portrait of Ormuz is in Layard and the medals of Oraios, Sabaoth, Adonaius, and Knouphus are easily located in Matter. It is indeed surprising that such erudite precision strikes us as a phantasmagoria. More exactly, we are astounded that Flaubert experienced the scholar's patience, the very patience necessary to knowledge, as the liveliness of a frenzied imagination.

Possibly, Flaubert was responding to an experience of the fantastic which was singularly modern and relatively unknown before his time, to the discovery of a new imaginative space in the nineteenth century. This domain of phantasms is no longer the night, the sleep of reason, or the uncertain void that stands before desire, but, on the contrary, wakefulness, untiring attention, zealous erudition, and constant vigilance. Henceforth, the visionary experience arises from the black and white surface of printed signs, from the closed and dusty volume that opens with a flight of forgotten words; fantasies are carefully deployed in the hushed library, with its columns of books, with its titles aligned on shelves to form a tight enclosure, but within confines that also liberate impossible worlds. The imaginary now resides between the book and the lamp. The fantastic is no longer a property of the heart, nor is it found among the incongruities of nature; it evolves from the accuracy of knowledge [*savoir*] and its treasures lie dormant in documents. Dreams are no longer summoned with closed eyes, but in reading; and a true image is now a product of learning [*connaissance*]: it derives from words spoken in the past, exact recensions, the amassing of minute facts, monuments reduced to infinitesimal fragments, and the reproductions of reproductions. In the modern experience, these elements contain the power of the impossible. Only the assiduous clamor created by repetition can transmit to us what only happened once. The imaginary is not formed in opposition to reality as its denial or compensation; it grows among signs, from book to book, in the interstice of repetitions and commentaries; it is born and takes shape in the interval between books. It is a phenomenon of the library.

Both Jules Michelet (in the *Sorcière*) and Edgar Quinet (in *Ahasvérus*) had explored these forms of erudite dreams, but *The Temptation* is not a scholarly project which evolved into an artistically coherent whole. As a work, its form relies on its location within the domain of knowledge: it exists by virtue of its essential relationship to books. This explains why it may represent more than a mere episode in the history of Western imagination; it opens a literary space wholly dependent on the network formed by the books of the past: as such, it serves to circulate the fiction of books. Yet, we should not confuse it with apparently similar works, with *Don Quixote* or the works of Sade, because the link between the former and the tales of knight-errantry or between the *Nouvelle Justine* and the virtuous novels of the eighteenth century is maintained through irony; and, more importantly, they remain books regardless of their intention. *The Temptation,* however, is linked in a completely serious manner to the vast world of print and develops within the recognizable institution of writing. It may appear as merely another new book to be shelved alongside all the others, but it serves, in actuality, to extend the space that existing books can occupy. It recovers other books; it hides and displays them and, in a single movement, it causes them to glitter and disappear. It is not simply the book that Flaubert dreamed of writing for so long; it dreams other books, all other books that dream and that men dream of writing–books that are taken up, fragmented, displaced, combined, lost, set at an unapproachable distance by dreams, but also brought closer to the imaginary and sparkling realization of desires. In writing *The Temptation*, Flaubert produced the first literary work whose exclusive domain is that of books: following Flaubert, Stéphane Mallarmé and his *Le Livre* become possible, then James Joyce, Raymond Roussel, Franz Kafka, Ezra Pound, Jorge Luis Borges. The library is on fire.

Déjeuner sur l'herbe and *Olympia* were perhaps the first "museum" paintings, the first paintings in European art that were less a response to the achievement of Giorgione, Raphael, and Velasquez than an acknowledgment (supported by this singular and obvious connection, using this legible reference to cloak its operation) of the new and substantial relationship of painting to itself, as a manifestation of the existence of museums and the particular reality and interdependence that paintings acquire in museums. In the same period, *The Temptation* was the first literary work to comprehend the greenish institutions where books are accumulated and where the slow and incontrovertible vegetation of learning quietly proliferates. Flaubert is to the library what Edouard Manet is to the museum. They both produced works in a self-conscious relationship to earlier paintings or texts–or rather to the aspect in painting or writing that remains indefinitely open. They erect their art within the archive. They were not meant to foster the lamentations–the lost youth, the absence of vigor, and the decline of inventiveness–through which we reproach our Alexandrian age, but to unearth an essential aspect of our culture: every painting now belongs within the squared and massive surface of painting and all literary works are confined to the indefinite murmur of writing. Flaubert and Manet are responsible for the existence of books and paintings within works of art.

III

The presence of the book in *The Temptation*, its manifestation and concealment, is indicated in a strange way: it immediately contradicts itself as a book. From the start, it challenges the priority of its printed signs and takes the form of a theatrical presentation: the transcription of a text that is not meant to be read, but recited and staged. At one time, Flaubert had wanted to transform *The Temptation* into a kind of epic drama, a *Faust* capable of swallowing the entire world of religion and gods. He soon gave up this idea but retained within the text the indications marking a possible performance: division into dialogues and scenes, descriptions of the place of action, the scenic elements, and their modifications, blocking directions for the "actors" on stage— all given according to a traditional typographical arrangement (smaller type and wider margins for stage directions, a character's name in large letters above the speeches, etc.). In a significant redoubling, the first indicated setting—the site of all future modifications— has the form of a natural theater: the hermit's retreat has been placed "at the top of a mountain, on a platform rounded in the form of a half-moon and enclosed by large boulders." The text describes a stage which, itself, represents a "platform" shaped by natural forces and upon which new scenes will in turn impose their sets. But these indications do not suggest a future performance (they are largely incompatible with an actual presentation); they simply designate the specific mode of existence of the text. Print can only be an unobtrusive aid to the visible; an insidious spectator takes the reader's place and the act of reading is dissolved in the triumph of another form of sight. The book disappears in the theatricality it creates.

But it will immediately reappear within a scenic space. No sooner have the first signs of temptation emerged from the gathering shadows, no sooner have the disquieting faces appeared in the night, than Saint Anthony lights a torch to protect himself and opens a "large book." This posture is consistent with the iconographic tradition: in the painting of Breughel the Younger, the painting that so impressed Flaubert when he visited the Balbi collection in Genoa and that he felt had incited him to write *The Temptation*, the hermit, in the lower right-hand corner of the canvas, is kneeling before an immense volume, his head slightly bowed, and his eyes intent on the written lines. Surrounding him on all sides are naked women with open arms, lean Gluttony stretching her giraffe's neck, barrel-like men creating an uproar, and nameless beasts devouring each other; at his back is a procession of the grotesques that populate the earth—bishops, kings, and tyrants. But this assembly is lost on the saint, absorbed in his reading. He sees nothing of this great uproar, unless perhaps through the corner of his eye, unless he seeks to protect himself by invoking the enigmatic powers of a magician's book. It may be, on the contrary, that the mumbling recitation of written signs has summoned these poor shapeless figures that no language has ever named, that no book can contain, but that anonymously invade the weighty pages of the volume. It may be, as well, that these creatures of unnatural issue escaped from the book, from the gaps between the open pages or the blank spaces between the letters. More fertile than the sleep of reason, the book perhaps engenders an infinite brood of monsters. Far from being a protection, it has liberated an obscure swarm of creatures and created a suspicious shadow through the mingling of images and knowledge. In any case, setting aside this discussion of the open folio in Breughel's painting, Flaubert's Saint Anthony seizes his book to ward off the evil that begins to obsess him and reads at random five passages from Scriptures. But, by a trick of the text, there immediately arises in the evening air the odors of gluttony, the scent of blood and anger, and the incense of pride, aromas worth more than their weight in gold, and the sinful perfumes of Oriental queens. The book – but not any book – is the site of temptation. Where the first passage read by the hermit is taken from the "Acts of the Apostles," the last four, significantly, come from the Old Testament[4] – from God's Scripture, from the supreme book.

In the two earlier versions of *The Temptation* reading of sacred texts played no role. Attacked by the canonical figures of evil, the hermit immediately seeks refuge in his chapel; goaded by Satan, the Seven Deadly Sins are set against the Virtues and, led by Pride, they make repeated assaults upon the protected enclosure. This imagery of the portal and the staging of a mystery are absent from the published text. In the final version, evil is not given as the property of characters, but incorporated in words. A book intended to lead to the gates of salvation also opens the gates of Hell. The full range of fantastic apparitions that eventually unfold before the hermit – orgiastic palaces, drunken emperors, unfettered heretics, misshapen forms of the gods in agony, abnormalities of nature – arise from the opening of a book, as they issued from the libraries that Flaubert consulted. It is appropriate, in this context, that Flaubert dropped from the definitive text the symmetrical and opposing figures of Logic and the swine, the original leaders of the pageant, and replaced them with Hilarion, the learned disciple who was initiated into the reading of sacred texts by Saint Anthony.

The presence of the book, first hidden under a fantastic theater, then exalted anew as the site of a spectacle that will end up rendering it once again imperceptible, constitutes for *The Temptation* an exceptionally complex space. We are apparently presented with a frieze of colorful characters set against cardboard scenery; on the edge of the stage, in a corner, sits the hooded figure of the motionless saint. The scene is reminiscent of a puppet theater. As a child, Flaubert saw *The Mystery of Saint Anthony* performed numerous times by Père Legrain in his puppet theater; he later brought George Sand to a performance. The first two versions of *The Temptation* retained elements from this source (most obviously, the pig, but also the personification of sin, the assault on the chapel, and the image of the Virgin). In the definitive text, only the linear succession of the visions remains to suggest an effect of "marionnettes": sins, temptations, divinities, and monsters are paraded before the laconic hermit–each emerging, in turn, from the hellish confines of the box where they were kept. But this is only a surface effect constructed upon a staging in depth (it is the flat surface that is deceptive in this context).

As support for these successive visions, to set them up in their illusory reality, Flaubert arranged a limited number of relays, which extend, in a perpendicular direction, the pure and straightforward reading of the printed phrases. The first intersection is the reader (1)–the actual reader of the text–and the book lies before him (1*a*); from the first lines (*it is in the Thebaid . . . the hermit's cabin appears in the background*) the text invites the reader to become a spectator (2) of a stage whose scenery is carefully described (2*a*); at center stage, the spectator sees the hermit (3) seated with his legs crossed: he will shortly rise and turn to his book (3*a*) from which disturbing visions will gradually escape–banquets, palaces, a voluptuous queen, and finally Hilarion, the insidious disciple (4). Hilarion leads the saint into a space filled with visions (4*a*); this opens a world of heresies and gods, and a world where improbable creatures proliferate (5). Moreover, the heretics are also capable of speech and recount their shameless rites; the gods recall their past glories and the cults that were devoted to them; and the monsters proclaim their proper bestiality. Derived from the power of their words or from their mere presence, a new dimension is realized, a vision that lies within that produced by the satanic disciple (5a), a vision that contains the abject cult of the Ophites, the miracles of Apollonius, the temptations of Buddha, and the ancient and blissful reign of Isis (6). Beginning as actual readers, we successively encounter five distinct levels, five different orders of language (indicated by *a*): that of the book, a theater, a sacred text, visions, and visions of visions. There are also five series of characters, of figures, of landscapes, and of forms: the invisible spectator, Saint Anthony in his retreat, Hilarion, the heretics, the gods and the monsters, and, finally, the shadows propagated by their speeches or through their memories.

This organization, which develops through successive enclosures, is modified by two others. (In actuality, it finds its confirmation and completion in two others.) The first is that of a retrospective encasement. Where the figures on the sixth level (visions of visions) should be the palest and least accessible to direct perception, they appear forcefully on the scene, as dense, colorful, and insistent as the figures that precede them or as Saint Anthony himself. It is as if the clouded memories and secret desires, which produced these visions from the first, have the power of acting without meditation in the scenic space, upon the landscape where the hermit pursues his imaginary dialogue with his disciple, or upon the stage that the fictitious spectator is meant to behold during the acting out of this semi-mystery. Thus, the fictions of the last level fold back upon themselves, envelop the figures from which they arose, quickly surpass the disciple and the anchorite, and finish by inscribing themselves within the supposed materiality of the theater. Through this retrospective envelopment, the most ephemeral fictions are presented in the most direct language, through the stage directions, indicated by the author, whose task is an external definition of the characters.

This arrangement allows the reader (1) to see Saint Anthony (3) over the shoulder of the implied spectator (2) who is an accomplice to the dramatic presentation: the effect is to identify the reader with the spectator. Consequently, the spectator sees Anthony on the stage, but he also sees over his shoulder the apparitions presented to the hermit, apparitions that are as substantial as the saint: Alexandria, Constantinople, the Queen of Sheba, Hilarion. The spectator's glance dissolves into the hallucinated gaze of the hermit. Anthony then leans over Hilarion's shoulder, and sees with his eyes the figures evoked by the evil disciple; and Hilarion, through the arguments of the heretics, perceives the face of the gods and the snarling monsters, contemplates the images that haunt them. Developed from one figure to another, a wreath is constructed which links the characters in a series of knots independent of their proper intermediaries, so that their identities are gradually merged and their different perceptions blended into a single dazzling sight.

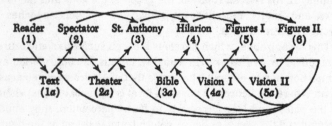

An immense distance lies between the reader and the ultimate visions that entrance the imaginary figures: orders of language placed according to degrees of subordination, relay-characters gazing over each other's shoulders and withdrawing to the depths of this "text-presentation," and a population abounding in illusions. But two movements counter this distance: the first, affecting the different orders of language, renders the invisible elements visible through a direct style, and the second, which concerns the figures, gradually adopts the vision and the light fixed upon the characters and brings forward the most distant imagines until they emerge from the sides of the scene. It is this double movement that makes a vision actually tempting: the most indirect and encased elements of the vision are given with a brilliance compatible with the foreground; and the visionary, attracted by the sights placed before him, rushes into this simultaneously empty and overpopulated space, identifies himself with this figure of shadow and light, and begins to see, in turn, with unearthly eyes. The profundity of these boxed apparitions and the linear and naive succession of figures are not in any way contradictory. Rather, they form the perpendicular intersections that constitute the paradoxical shape and the singular domain of *The Temptation.* The frieze of marionnettes and the stark, colored surface of these figures who jostle one another in the shadows offstage are not the effects of childhood memories or the residue of vivid impressions: they are the composite result of a vision that develops on successive and gradually more distant levels and a temptation that attracts the visionary to the place he has seen and that suddenly envelops him in his own visions.

IV

The Temptation is like a discourse whose function is to maintain not a single and exclusive meaning (by excising all the others), but the simultaneous existence of multiple meanings. The visible sequence of scenes is extremely simple: first, the memories of the aging monk, the hallucinations and sins summarized by the figure of an ancient queen who arrives from the Orient (Chapters I and II); then, the disciple who initiates the rapid multiplication of heresies through his debate on Scripture (III and IV); followed by the emergence of the gods who successively appear on the stage (V); with the depopulation of the earth, Anthony is free to return to it guided by his disciple who has become both Satan and Knowledge, free to gauge its expanse and to observe the tangled and infinite growth of monsters (VI, VII). This visible sequence is supported by a number of underlying series.

1. Temptation is conceived in the hermit's heart; it hesitantly evokes his companions during his retreat and the passing caravans; from this, it extends into vaster regions; overpopulated Alexandria, the Christian Orient torn by theological conflicts, all those Mediterranean civilizations ruled by gods who emerged from Asia, and, finally, the limitless expanse of the universe—the distant stars at night, the imperceptible cell from which life awakens. But this ultimate scintillation only serves to return the hermit to the material principle of his first desires. Having reached the limits of the world, the grand and tempting itinerary returns to its point of departure. In the first two versions of the text, the Devil explained to Anthony "that sins were in his heart and sorrows in his mind." These explanations are now inessential: pushed to the limits of the universe, the arching waves of the temptation return to those things that are nearest. In the minute or-

ganism where the primordial desires of life are awakened, Anthony recaptures his ancient heart, his badly controlled appetites, but no longer experiences their charged fantasies. Before his eyes, there lies the material truth. Under this red light, the larva of desire is gently formed. The center of temptation has not shifted: or rather, it has been displaced very slightly from the top to the bottom—passing from the heart to the sinews, from a dream to the cell, from a bright image to matter. Those things that haunted the imagination of the hermit from inside can now become the object of enraptured contemplation; and where he had pushed them aside in fear, they now attract and invite him to a dormant identification: "to descend to the very depths of matter, to become matter."[5] It is only in appearance that the temptation wrenches the hermit from his solitude and populates his field of vision with men, gods, and monsters, for along its curved expanse, it gives rise to a number of distinct movements: a progressive expansion to the confines of the universe; a loop bringing desire back to its truth; a shift that causes a violent phantasm to subside in the soft repose of matter; a passage from the inside to the outside—from heartfelt nostalgia to the vivid spectacle of life; the transformation of fear into the desire for identification.

2. Sitting on the doorstep of his cabin, the hermit is obsessed by the memories of an old man: formerly, isolation was less painful, work less tedious, and the river was not as distant as now. He had enjoyed his youth—the young girls who congregated at the fountain—and also his retreat, and the opportunity for companionship, particularly with his favorite disciple. His memories flood back upon him in this slight wavering of the present at the hour of dusk. It is a total inversion of time: first, the images of twilight in the city humming with activity before dark—the port, shouting in the streets, the tambourines in the taverns; followed by Alexandria in the period of the massacres, Constantinople during the Council; this suddenly gives way to the heretics whose affronts originated with the founding of Christianity; behind them are the gods who once had a following of faithful and whose temples range from India to the Mediterranean; and finally, the appearance of figures as old as time itself—the distant stars, brute matter, lust and death, the recumbent Sphinx, chimeras, all those things that, in a single movement, create life and its illusions. Further, beyond this primordial cell from which life evolved, Anthony desires an impossible return to the passive stage prior to life: the whole of his

existence is consequently laid to rest where it recovers its innocence and awakens once again to the sounds of animals, the bubbling fountain, and the glittering stars. The highest temptation is the longing to be another, to be all others; it is to renew identifications and to achieve the principle of time in a return that completes the circle. The vision of Engadine approaches.

An ambiguous figure – simultaneously a form of duration and eternity, acting as conclusion and a fresh start – introduces each stage of this return through time. The heresies are introduced by Hilarion – as small as a child and withered like an old man, as young as awakening cognition and as old as well-pondered knowledge. Apollonius introduces the gods: he is familiar with their unending metamorphoses, their creation and death, but he is also able to regain instantly "the Eternal, the Absolute, and Being."[6] Lust and Death lead the dance of life because they undoubtedly control the end and new beginnings, the disintegration of forms and the origin of all things. The larva-skeleton, the eternal Thaumaturge, and the old child each function within the book as "alternators" of duration; through the time of history, myth, and the entire universe, they guarantee the hermit's recapture of the cellular principle of life. The night of *The Temptation* can greet the unchanged novelty of a new day, because the earth has turned back upon its axis.

3. The resurgence of time also produces a prophetic vision of the future. Within his recollections, Anthony encountered the ancient imagination of the Orient: deep within this memory, which no longer belongs to him, he saw a form arising that represented the temptation of the wisest of the kings of Israel – the Queen of Sheba. Standing behind her, he recognized, in the shape of an ambiguous dwarf, her servant and his own disciple, a disciple who is indissociably linked to Desire and Wisdom. Hilarion is the incarnation of all the dreams of the Orient, but he possesses as well a perfect knowledge of Scriptures and their interpretation. Greed and science are united in him – covetous knowledge and damnable facts. This gnome increases in size throughout the course of the liturgy; by the last episode, he has become gigantic, "beautiful as an archangel and luminous as the sun." His kingdom now includes the universe as he becomes the Devil in the lightning flash of truth. Serving as an embryonic stage in the development of Western thought, he first introduces theology and its infinite disputes; then, he revives ancient civilizations and their

gods whose rule was so quickly reduced to ashes; he inaugurates a rational understanding of the world; he demonstrates the movement of the stars and reveals the secret powers of life. All of European culture is deployed in this Egyptian night, haunted by the past of the Orient: the Middle Ages with their theology, the Renaissance with its erudition, the modern age with its sciences of the world and the living. *The Temptation* acts as a nocturnal sun whose trajectory is from east to west, from desire to knowledge, from imagination to truth, from the oldest longings to the findings of modern science. The appearance of Egypt converted to Christianity (and with it Alexandria) and the appearance of Anthony represent the zero point between Asia and Europe; both seem to arise from a fold in time, at the point where Antiquity, at the summit of its achievement, begins to vacillate and collapses, releasing its hidden and forgotten monsters; they also plant the seed of the modern world with its promise of endless knowledge. We have arrived at the hollow of history.

The "temptation" of Saint Anthony is the double fascination exercised upon Christianity by the sumptuous spectacle of its past and the limitless acquisitions of its future. The definitive text excludes Abraham's God, the Virgin, and the virtues (who appear in the first two versions), but not to save them from profanation; they were incorporated in figures that represent them—in Buddha, the tempted god, in Apollonius the thaumaturge who resembles Christ, and in Isis the mother of sorrows. *The Temptation* does not mask reality in its glittering images, but reveals the image of an image in the realms of truth. Even in its state of primitive purity, Christianity was formed by the dying reflections of an older world, formed by the feeble light it projected upon the still grey shadows of a nascent world.

4. The two earlier versions of *The Temptation* began with the battle of the Seven Deadly Sins against the three theological virtues (Faith, Hope, and Charity), but this traditional imagery of the mysteries disappears in the published text. The sins appear only in the form of illusions and the virtues are given a secret existence as the organizing principles of the sequences. The endless revival of heresies places Faith at the mercy of overpowering error; the agony of the gods, which makes them disappear as glimmers of imagination, transforms Hope into a futile quest; and nature in repose or with its savage forces unleashed reduces Charity to a mockery. The three supreme virtues have been vanquished; and turning away from Heaven, the saint "lies

flat on his stomach, and leaning upon his elbows, he watches breath-
lessly. Withered ferns begin to flower anew."[7] At the sight of this small
palpitating cell, Charity is transformed into dazzling curiosity ("O joy!
O bliss! I have seen the birth of life; I have seen motion begin"),[8] Hope
is transformed into an uncontrollable desire to dissolve into the violence of the world ("I long to fly, to swim, to bark, to shout, to howl"),[9]
and Faith becomes an identification with brute nature, the soft and
somber stupidity of things ("I wish to huddle upon these forms, to
penetrate each atom, to descend to the depths of matter—to become
pure matter").[10]

This book, which initially appears as a progression of slightly inco-
herent fantasies, can claim originality only with respect to its meticulous organization. What appears as fantasy is no more than the simple
transcription of documents, the reproductions of drawings or texts,
but their sequence conforms to an extremely complex composition.
By assigning a specific location to each documentary element, it is
also made to function within several simultaneous series. The linear
and visible sequence of sins, heresies, divinities, and monsters is
merely the superficial crest of an elaborate vertical structure. This
succession of figures, crowded like puppets dancing the farandole,
also functions as: a trinity of canonical virtues; the geodesic line of a
culture born in the dreams of the Orient and completed in the knowledge of the West; the return of History to the origin of time and the
beginning of things; a pulsating space that expands to the outer limits
of the universe and suddenly recedes to return to the simplest element of life. Each element and each character has its place not only in
the visible procession, but in the organization of Christian allegories,
the development of culture and knowledge, the reverse chronology of
the world, and the spatial configurations of the universe.

In addition, *The Temptation* develops the encapsulated visions in
depth as they recede, through a series of stages, to the distance; it
constitutes a volume behind the thread of its speeches and under its
line of successions. Each element (setting, character, speech, alteration of scenery) is effectively placed at a definite point in the linear
sequence, but each element also has its vertical system of correspon-
dences and is situated at a specific depth in the fiction. This explains
why *The Temptation* can be the book of books: it unites in a single
"volume" a series of linguistic elements that derive from existing
books and that are, by virtue of their specific documentary character,

the repetition of things said in the past. The library is opened, catalogued, sectioned, repeated, and rearranged in a new space; and this "volume" into which Flaubert has forced it is both the thickness of a book that develops according to the necessarily linear thread of its text and a procession of marionnettes that, in deploying its boxed visions, also opens a domain in depth.

V

Saint Anthony seems to summon *Bouvard et Pécuchet*, at least to the extent that the latter stands as its grotesque shadow, its tiny, yet boundless, double. As soon as Flaubert completed *The Temptation*, he began his last book. It contains the same elements: a book produced from other books; the encyclopedic learning of a culture; temptation experienced in a state of withdrawal; an extended series of trials; the interplay of illusions and belief. But the general shape is altered. First, the relationship of the Book to the indefinite series of all other books has changed. *The Temptation* was composed of fragments drawn from invisible volumes and transformed into a display of pure phantasms: only the Bible–the supreme Book–shows the sovereign presence of the written word in the text and on the center of its stage; it announced, once and for all, the powers of temptation possessed by the Book. Bouvard and Pécuchet are directly tempted by books, by their endless multiplicity, by the frothing of works in the grey expanse of the library. In *Bouvard et Pécuchet*, the library is clearly visible–classified and analysed. It can exert its fascination without being consecrated in *a* book or transformed into images. Its powers stem from its singular existence–from the unlimited proliferation of printed paper.

The Bible has become a bookstore, and the magic power of the image has become a devouring appetite for reading. This accounts for the change in the form of temptation. Saint Anthony had withdrawn into idle seclusion in his desire to avoid the disturbing presence of others; yet, neither a living grave nor a walled fortress are sufficient protection. He had exorcised every living form but they returned with a vengeance, testing the saint by their proximity but also by their remoteness. These forms surround him on every side, possess him, but disappear as he extends his hand. Their operation places the saint in a state of pure passivity: his only function was to localize them in the Book through happy memories or the force of imagination. All of his gestures, every word of compassion, and any show of violence, dissipate the mirage—proving that he had suffered a temptation (that only in his heart did an illusory image take on reality). Bouvard and Pécuchet, on the other hand, are indefatigable pilgrims: they try everything, they touch and are drawn to everything; they put everything to the test of their marginal industry. If they withdraw from the world as the Egyptian monk did, it is an active retreat, an enterprising use of their leisure where they summon, with constant recourse to their extensive reading, all the seriousness of science and the most solemnly printed truths. They wish to put into practice everything they read, and if success eludes them, as the images dissipate before Saint Anthony, it is not as a result of their initial gesture but of their persistent search. Their temptation arises from zealousness.

For these two simple men, to be tempted is to believe. It is to believe in the things they read, to believe in the things they overhear; it is to believe immediately and unquestioningly in the persistent flow of discourse. Their innocence is fully engaged in this domain of things already said. Those things that have been *read* and *heard* immediately become things *to do*. But their enterprise is so pure that no setback can alter their belief: they do not measure their truths by their success; they do not threaten their beliefs with the test of action. Possible disasters always remain outside the sovereign field of belief and their faith remains intact. When Bouvard and Pécuchet abandon their quest, they renounce not their faith but the possibility of applying their beliefs. They detach themselves from works to maintain the dazzling reality of their faith in faith. They repeat, for the modern world, the experiences of Job; stricken through their knowledge and not their possessions, abandoned by science and not by God, they persist, like him, in their fidelity—they are saints. For Saint Anthony, unlike these modern-day saints, temptation lies in the sight of the things without belief: it is to perceive error mixed with truth, the spectre of false gods resembling the true God, a nature abandoned without providence to the immensity of its spaces or the unleashing of its vital forces. And paradoxically, as these images are relegated to the shadows from which they emerged, they carry with them some of the belief that Saint Anthony had invested in them, if only for an instant—a part of the faith he had invested in the Christian God. The disappearance of those fantasies that seemed most inimical to his

faith does not forcefully reinstate his religion, but gradually undermines it until it is completely taken from him. In their fanatical blood-
shed, the heretics dissolve the truth; and the dying gods gather into
their darkness part of the image of the true God. Anthony's saintliness
was broken in the defeat of those things in which he had no faith; and
that of Bouvard and Pécuchet triumphs in the downfall of their faith.
They are the true elect. They were given the grace denied the saint.

The relationship between sainthood and stupidity was undoubtedly of fundamental importance for Flaubert; it can be found in
Charles Bovary; it is visible in *Un coeur simple*, and perhaps as well,
in the *Sentimental Education*; it is essential to *The Temptation* and
Bouvard, but it adopts symmetrically opposite forms in these books.
Bouvard and Pécuchet link sainthood to stupidity on the basis of the
will-to-act, the dimension where they activate their desires: they had
dreamed of being rich, of being men of leisure and independent
means, men of property, but in achieving these goals, they discover
that these new roles necessitate an endless cycle of tasks and not a
pure and simple existence; the books that should have taught them
how to exist dissipated their energies by telling them what they must
do. Such is the stupidity and virtue, the sanctity and simplemindedness of those who zealously undertake to make of themselves what
they already are, who put into practice received ideas, and who silently endeavor throughout their lives to achieve union with their
inner selves in a blind and desperate eagerness. On the other hand,
Saint Anthony links simplemindedness to sainthood on the basis of a
will-to-be: he wished to be a saint through a total deadening of his
senses, intelligence, and emotions, and by dissolving himself into the
images that come to him through the mediation of the Book. It is from
this that the temptations increase their hold upon him: he refuses to
be a heretic, but takes pity on the gods; he recognizes himself in the
temptations of Buddha, secretly shares the raptures of Cybele, and
weeps with Isis. But his desire to identify with the things he sees
triumphs when faced with pure matter: he wishes to be blind, drowsy,
greedy, and as stupid as the "Catoblepas";[11] he wishes that he were
unable to lift his head higher than his stomach and that his eyelids
would become so heavy that no light could possibly reach his eyes. He
wishes to be a dumb creature–an animal, a plant, a cell. He wishes to
be pure matter. Through this sleep of reason and in the innocence of

desires that have become pure movement, he could at least be re-
united to the saintly stupidity of things.

As Anthony is about to accomplish his desire, the day returns and
the face of Christ shines in the sun: the saint kneels and returns to his
prayers. Has he triumphed over his temptations; has he been defeated
and, as a punishment, must the same cycle be indefinitely repeated?
Or has he achieved purity through the dumbness of matter; is this the
moment when he achieves a true saintliness by discovering, through
the dangerous space of books, the pulsation of innocent things; is he
now able to *perform*, through his prayers, prostrations, and readings,
this mindless sanctity he has become?

Bouvard and Pécuchet also make a new start: having been put to
the test, they are now made to abandon the performance of those
actions they had undertaken to become what they were initially. They
can now be purely and simply themselves: they commission the construction of a large double desk to reestablish the link to their essential nature, to begin anew the activity which had occupied them for
over ten years, to begin their copying. They will occupy themselves by
copying books, copying their own books, copying every book; and
unquestionably they will copy *Bouvard et Pécuchet.* Because to copy is
to do nothing; it is *to be* the books being copied. It is to be this tiny
protrusion of redoubled language, of discourse folded upon itself; this
invisible existence transforms fleeting words into an enduring and
distant murmur. Saint Anthony was able to triumph over the Eternal
Book in becoming the languageless movement of pure matter; Bouvard and Pécuchet triumph over everything alien to books, all that
resists the book, by transforming themselves into the continuous
movement of the book. The book opened by Saint Anthony, the book
that initiated the flight of all possible temptations, is indefinitely extended by these two simple men; it is prolonged without end, without
illusion, without greed, without sin, without desire.

NOTES

1 Flaubert's juvenilia. -Ed.

2 *Souvenirs littéraires* (Paris, 1882); Du Camp, who was among the first to listen to Flaubert's
recitation, discouraged his efforts.

3 As a result of the remarkable studies by Jean Seznec [see *Les Sources de l'épisode des dieux dans
La Tentation de Saint Antoine* (Paris: Vrin, 1940)].

4 Acts of the Apostles 10:11; Daniel 2:46; 2 Kings 20:15; 1 Kings 10:1.

5   *The Temptation of Saint Anthony*, trans. Lafcadio Hearn (New York: Grosset & Dunlap, 1943), p. 164.

6   *The Temptation*, p. 97.

7   Ibid., p. 163.

8   Ibid.

9   Ibid.

10 Ibid., p. 164.

11 Ibid., p. 159.

THE PROSE OF ACTAEON*

Pierre Klossowski reconnects with a long-lost experience. Today only a few vestiges of that experience are left to evoke it; and they would remain enigmatic no doubt if they had not been reanimated and made manifest in this language. And if they had not then begun to speak once more, saying that the Demon is not the Other, the pole far removed from God, the Antithesis without remedy (or almost), evil matter, but something strange, bewildering, which leaves one speechless and immobile–the Same, the exact Likeness.

Despite all the denials and persecutions, dualism and gnosticism weighed substantially on the Christian conception of Evil: their binary thought (God and Satan, Light and Darkness, Good and Heaviness, the great combat, a certain radical and stubborn malice) arranged the order of disorders for our thought. Western Christianity condemned gnosticism but retained a light and promising reconciliation that belonged to it. For a long time Christianity continued to enact the simplified contests of the Temptation in its phantasms. Through the world's cracks a crowd of strange animals rise up before the half-closed eyes of the kneeling anchorite–ageless figures of matter.

But what if, on the contrary, the Devil, the Other, were the Same? And what if the Temptation were not one of the episodes of the great antagonism but the subtle insinuation of the Double? What if the contest unfolded in a mirror space? What if eternal History (of which our

*This essay originally appeared in *La Nouvelle revue française* 135 (March 1964), pp. 444–59. Robert Hurley's translation.

own is but the visible form, soon to be effaced) were not simply always the same, but the identity of that Same, both an imperceptible displacement and an embrace of the nondissociable? There was a whole Christian experience that knew this danger well—the temptation to experience temptation in the form of the indistinguishable. The quarrels of demonology are structured by this profound peril; and undermined, or rather driven and multiplied by it, they endlessly renew an interminable debate: to go to the Sabbath is to surrender oneself to the Devil, or perhaps it is to devote oneself to the simulacrum of the Devil that God sends to men of little faith in order to tempt them—or to those of too much faith, the credulous who imagine there is another god than God. And the judges who burn the devil-possessed are themselves victims of this temptation, of this trap in which their justice is confounded: for the possessed are but a true image of the false power of the demons; an image by which the Demon takes hold not of the bodies of the sorcerers but of the souls of their tormentors. That is, if God has not himself put on the face of Satan in order to cloud the minds of those who do not believe in his solitary omnipotence; so that God, simulating the Devil, would have arranged the strange nuptials of the witch and her persecutor, of those two condemned figures: doomed therefore to Hell, to the reality of the Devil, to that true simulacrum of God simulating the Devil. In these twists and turns the perilous games of extreme similitude are multiplied: God who so closely resembles Satan who imitates God so well . . .

It took nothing less than Descartes's Evil Genius to put an end to this great peril of Identities in which sixteenth-century thought had not ceased to "subtilize" itself. The Evil Genius of the Third Meditation is not the slightly enhanced epitome of the deceitful powers residing in man but what most resembles God, what can imitate all His powers, pronounce eternal truths like Him, and if he wishes, arrange it that $2 + 2 = 5$. He is His marvelous twin—except for a certain maliciousness, which made him fall immediately from any possible existence. Thereafter the anxiety over simulacra entered into silence. It was forgotten that up to the start of the Classical age (look at baroque literature and especially baroque theater) they were one of the major occasions of giddiness for Western thought. One continued to be concerned about Evil, about the reality of images and representation, about synthesis of the diverse. One no longer thought that the Same could make one's head spin.

Incipit Klossowski, like Zarathustra. And in this somewhat obscure and secret face of Christian experience, he suddenly discovers (as if it were its double, perhaps its simulacrum), the resplendent theophany of the Greek gods. Between the ignoble Goat who shows up on the Sabbath and the virgin goddess who slips out of reach into the coolness of the water, the game is reversed. At Diana's bath the simulacrum is presented in the receding of extreme proximity and not in the brash emergence of the other world; but the doubt is the same, as is the risk of dividing in two: "Diana makes a pact with a daemon intermediary between the gods and men in order to appear to Actaeon. With its aerial body, the daemon *simulates* Diana in her theophany and inspires Actaeon with the desire and the foolish hope to possess the goddess. It becomes Actaeon's imagination and Diana's mirror." And Actaeon's final metamorphosis does not transform him into a stag that is torn apart but into a lewd, frantic, and delightfully profaning goat. As if, in the complicity of the divine with sacrilege, some of the Greek light flashed through the depths of the Christian night.

Klossowski is placed at the intersection of two roads very far apart yet very similar, both coming from the Same, and both perhaps leading there: that of the theologians and that of the Greek gods, whose imminent scintillating return Nietzsche announced. A return of the gods that is also, and without any possible dissociation, the stealing of the Demon into the dubious tepidity of the night: "What if some day or night a *demon* were to steal after you into your loneliest loneliness and say to you: 'This life as you now live it and have lived it, you will have to live once more and innumerable times more; and there will be nothing new in it, but every pain and every joy and every thought and sigh and everything unutterably small or great in your life will have to return to you, all in the same succession and sequence—even this spider and this moonlight between the trees, and even this moment and *I myself*. The eternal hourglass of existence is turned upside down again and again, and you with it, speck of dust!' Would you not throw yourself down and gnash your teeth and curse the demon who spoke thus? Or have you once experienced a tremendous moment when you would have answered him: 'You are a *god* and never have I heard anything more divine.'"[1]

Klossowski's experience is situated approximately there, in a world ruled by an evil genius who would not have found his god, or who might also pose as God, or who might be God himself. This world would not be Heaven, or Hell, or limbo, but quite simply our world – a world, finally, that would be the same as ours except that, precisely, it is the same. In this imperceptible divergence of the same, an infinite movement finds its place of emergence. This movement is completely foreign to dialectics, for it does not involve the proof of a contradiction, or the game of an identity affirmed then negated. The $A = A$ equation is stirred by an endless internal movement that diverts each of the two terms from its own identity and refers them to each other through the action (the force, the treachery) of this divergence itself. So that no truth can be engendered from this affirmation, but a perilous space is cleared where Klossoski's discourse and his fables, his ensaring and ensnared ruses, will find their language. A language as essential for us as those of Blanchot and Bataille, since in its turn it teaches us how the gravest dimension of thought must find its illuminated lightness outside of dialectics.

Actually, neither God nor Satan ever appear in this space. A strict absence that is also their entanglement. But neither one is named, perhaps because they are "invokers" and not invoked. It is a narrow, numinous area in which the figures are all on some Index of the condemned. There one crosses the paradoxical space of real presence – a presence that is real only insofar as God has absented himself from the world, leaving behind only a trace and a void, so that the reality of this presence is the absence where it takes its place and where it derealizes itself through transubstantiation. *Numen quod habitat simulacro.*

That is why Klossowski hardly approves of Paul Claudel's or Charles Du Bos's urging André Gide to convert; he knows very well that those who placed God at one end and the Devil at the other, pitting them against each other in flesh and blood (a god of blood and a devil of flesh), were mistaken, and that Gide was closer to being right when by turns he drew near and withdrew, playing the simulacrum of the Devil at the bidding of others, but not at all knowing, in doing so, whether he was the Devil's plaything, object, instrument, or whether he might be the chosen one of an attentive and artful god.[2] Perhaps it is of the essence of salvation not to announce itself with signs but to come about in the profundity of simulacra.

And since all the figures that Klossowski delineates and brings to life in his language are "simulacra," we need to understand this word in the resonance we can now give to it: a vain image (as opposed to reality), a representation of something (in which this thing delegates and manifests itself, but withdraws and in a sense conceals itself), a falsehood that causes one to take one sign for another, a sign of the presence of a deity (and the converse possibility of taking this sign for its opposite, the simultaneous coming of the Same and the Other (originally, to simulate meant to come together).[3] In this way, that constellation peculiar to Klossowski, and wonderfully rich, is established: simulation, similitude, simultaneity, simulation, and dissimulation.

For linguists the sign derives its meaning only from the interplay and the sovereignty of all other signs. It does not have any autonomous, natural, or immediate relation with what it signifies. It owes its validity not only to its context but also to a whole virtual expanse that spreads out in a kind of dotted array on the same plane as it: through this set of all the signifiers that define the language at a given moment, it is constrained to say what it does say. In the religious domain one often finds a sign with a completely different structure. It says what it says through a profound appurtenance to the origin, through a consecration. There is not a tree in the Scripture, not a living or withered plant that does not refer to the tree of the Cross—to that timber carved out of the First Tree at the foot of which Adam succumbed. A figure like this is tiered in depth across shifting forms, which endows it with it that strange, dual property of designating no meaning but referring to a model (to a single of which it would be the double, but which would reclaim it as its diffraction and its transitory duplication) and of being tied to the history of a manifestation that is never completed. In this history the sign can always be referred to a new episode in which a simpler single, a more primary model (but ulterior in the Revelation) will appear, giving it an entirely contrary meaning. Thus the tree of the Fall one day became what it always was, that of the Reconciliation. This type of sign is always prophetic and ironic: completely suspended from a future that it rehearses and that will repeat it in the full light of day. It says this, then that, or rather it already said this and that, without anyone's being able to know it. In essence it is a simulacrum, saying everything at the same time, and constantly simulating something other than what it says. It offers an image dependent on a truth that is always receding: *Fabula.* In its form, as in a riddle, it links together the transformations of the light that will come to it: *Fatum.* A *Fabula* and a *Fatum* that both refer to the first enunciation from which they spring, to that root which the Latins understand as speech, and in which the Greeks see, moreover, the essence of luminous visibility.

No doubt it is necessary to draw a rigorous distinction between signs and simulacra. They do not belong to the same experience at all, even if they often happen to be superimposed. For, in fact, the simulacrum does not determine any meaning: it is of the order of appearance in the shattering of time—the light of Noon and eternal recurrence. Perhaps Greek religion only knew simulacra. The Sophists first, then the Stoics and Epicureans insisted on reading these simulacra as signs, a late reading in which the Greek gods are effaced. Christian exegesis, fathered on Alexandrian soil, inherited that interpretation.

In the great detour that is ours today and through which we attempt to circumvent all the Alexandrianism of our culture, Klossowski is the one who, from the depths of the Christian experience, has rediscovered the marvels and the depths of the simulacrum, beyond all of yesterday's games: those of sense and nonsense, of signifier and signified, of symbol and sign. This is doubtless what gives his work its sacral and solar allure as soon as one rediscovers in it that Nietzschean impulse where it is a question of Dionysus and the Crucified (since they are, as Nietzsche saw, simulacra of one another).

In Klossowski's work the reign of simulacra obeys precise rules. The reversal of situations occurs in a moment, with a switching of sides almost as in a detective novel (the good become wicked, the dead come back to life, rivals reveal themselves to be accomplices, executioners are subtle rescuers, encounters are prepared long in advance, the most banal phrases have a double meaning). Each reversal seems to point to an epiphany; but in reality each discovery deepens the enigma, increases the uncertainty, and unveils one element only to veil the relations between all the others. But the most peculiar and most difficult aspect of the matter is that the simulacra are not at all things or traces or those beautiful motionless forms that the Greek statues were. Here the simulacra are human beings.

Klossowski's world is sparing of objects, and such objects as there are only form scant relays between the men for whom they serve as stand-ins and precarious spacers, so to speak: portraits, photographs, stereoscopic views, signatures on checks, open wasp-waisted corsets that are like the empty, still rigid shell of a woman's torso. On the other hand, the Simulacra Men proliferate: still few in *Roberte*,[4] they multiply in *La Révolution*,[5] and especially in *Le Souffleur*,[6] so much so that that text, almost relieved of any setting, of any materiality that might convey stable signs offered to interpretation, forms little more than a successive nesting of dialogues. This is understandable, for men are much more vertiginous simulacra than the painted faces of the deities. They are utterly ambiguous, since they speak, gesture, wink, shake their fingers and appear at windows like semaphores (to give out signs or give the impression that they constitute only the simulacra of signs?).

Such characters as these are not the deep and continuous beings of reminiscence, but beings destined, like those of Nietzsche, for a deep oblivion, for that oblivion which makes possible, in the "subvening" moment, the sudden appearance of the Same. In them everything fragments, splinters, offers itself and withdraws in an instant; they may be living or dead, it hardly matters; the oblivion in them watches over the Identical. They do not signify anything; they simulate themselves–Vittorio and von A., Uncle Florence and the monstrous husband, Théodore who is also K., Roberte above all, simulating Roberte in the tiny, uncrossable distance by means of which Roberte is the way she is, *this* evening.

All these simulacra-figures swivel in place: the debauchees become inquisitors, the seminarists Nazi officers, the uneasy persecutors of Théodore Lacase are encountered again in a friendly half circle around K.'s bed. These twists are produced by the action of the "alternators" of experience. In Klossowski's novels these alternators are the only peripeties, but in the strict sense of the word–what ensures the turning and returning. Thus the test-provocation (the rock of truth that is at the same time the temptation of the worst, the fresco of *La Vocation*,[7] or the sacrilegious task assigned by von A.); the dubious inquisition (the censors who claim to be former debauchees, like Malagrida, or the psychiatrist with dishonorable intentions); the double-faced conspiracy (the "resistance" network that executes Dr. Rodin). But above all, the two great configurations that make appearance alternate are hospitality and theater–two structures that face each other in reverse symmetry.

The *hôte* (already the word rotates on its internal axis, saying the thing and its complementary at the same time[a]) – the host offers what he possesses because he can only possess what he proposes, what is there before his eyes and for everybody. He is, as they say with a word that is marvelous with ambiguity, a "*regardant*." Surreptitiously and full of avarice, this giving look takes its share of delights and appropriates in full sovereignty an aspect of the things that *regard* only it. But this look has the power to absent itself, to vacate the place it occupies and to offer what it envelops with its avidity. So that its gift is the semblance of an offering, once it preserves only the feeble, distant silhouette, the visible simulacrum of the thing that it gives. In *Le Souffleur* the theater has replaced this giving look, as it reigned in *Roberte* and *La Révocation.*[8] The theater imposes on Roberte the role of Roberte, that is, it tends to reduce the interior distance that opened up within the simulacrum (through the effect of the giving look) and to make Roberte herself inhabit the double that Theodore (perhaps K.) has severed from it. But if Roberte plays her role in a natural way (which is the case at least for one replica), it is no longer anything but a simulacrum of theater; and if, on the other hand, Roberte mumbles her lines, it is Roberte-Roberte who hides behind a pseudoactress (and who is bad insofar as she is is not an actress but Roberte). That is why this role can only be played by a simulacrum of Roberte who resembles her so closely that Roberte is perhaps that simulacrum herself. So it is necessary either for Roberte to have two existences or for there to be two Robertes with one existence: she must be a pure simulacrum of herself. With the look it is the Regardant who is divided in two (and to the point of death); on the stage of the false theater, it is the Regarded who is irreparably, ontologically split.[9]

But behind this whole great game of alternating experiences that makes the simulacra flash on and off, is there an absolute Operator who in this way addresses enigmatic signs? In *La Vocation suspendue* it seems that all the simulacra and their alternations are organized around a major call that makes itself heard in them, or that may, for that matter, remain silent. In the subsequent texts, this imperceptible but calling God has been replaced by two visible figures, or rather two series of figures that are at once on an equal footing and in perfect disequilibrium with the simulacra – doublers and doubled. At one extremity, the dynasty of monstrous characters, at the boundary of life and death: Professor Octave, or the "old master" that one sees at

the beginning of *Le Souffleur*, operating the switches of a suburban
train station, in a vast windowed hall located before or after existence.
But does this "Operator" really intervene? How does it bring the plot
to a climax? What is it in fact? The Master, Roberte's uncle (the one
with two faces), Dr. Rodin (the one who is dead and resuscitated), the
fancier of stereoscopic shows, the chiropractor (who shapes and
kneads the body), K. (who steals the works and perhaps the wives of
others, unless he gives his own) or Théodore Lacase (who makes
Roberte act). Or Roberte's husband? An immense genealogy that goes
from the Almighty to the one who is crucified in the simulacrum that
he is (since he, who is K., says "I" when Théodore speaks). But, at the
other extremity, Roberte too is the great operator of simulacra. Relentlessly, she caresses shoulders and hair with her long, beautiful hands,
arouses desire, recalls former lovers, unfastens a spangled corset or a
Salvation Army uniform, devotes herself to soldiers, collects money
for hidden miseries. Beyond doubt, it is she who diffracts her husband
in all the monstrous or pitiful characters in which he is scattered. She
is legion. Not the one who always says no, but the opposite, she who
constantly says yes. A forked yes that gives rise to that in-between
space where everyone is beside himself. Let us not say Roberte-the-
Devil and Théodore-God; rather, let us say that one is the simulacrum
of God (the same as God, hence the Devil) and that the other is the
simulacrum of Satan (the same as the Malicious One, hence God). But
one is the Snubbed Inquisitor (ridiculous seeker of signs, stubborn
and always disappointed interpreter, for there are no signs but only
simulacra), and the other is the Sorceress Saint (always on her way to
a Sabbath in which her desire invokes beings to no avail, for there are
never any men but only simulacra). It is of the nature of simulacra not
to sustain either the exegesis that believes in signs or the virtue that
loves beings.

Catholics scrutinize signs. Calvinists put no trust in them, because
they believe only in the election of souls. But what if we were neither
signs nor souls but simply the same as ourselves (neither the visible
children of our works nor predestined) and thus spread-eagled in the
simulacrum's distance from itself? This being the case, signs and
men's destiny would no longer have any common ground. The Edict
of Nantes would have been revoked. We would be in the void left by
Christian theology's division.[10] On this forsaken soil (or perhaps rich
soil, owing to that abandonment) we could give heed to the words of

Hölderlin: "*Zeichen sind wir, deutungslos,*" and perhaps, further still, to all those great and fleeting simulacra that made the gods scintillate in the rising sun, or like great silver arcs in the dead of night.

That is why *Le Bain de Diane* is doubtless, of all the texts of Klossowski, the one closest to that brilliant light–but very dim for us–from whence the simulacrum come to us.[11] In this exegesis of a legend one reencounters a configuration similar to that which organizes the other narratives, as if they all found their great mythical model there: an annunciative fresco as in *La Vocation*; Actaeon, Artemis's nephew, just as Antoine is Roberte's; Dionysus, Actaeon's uncle and old master of intoxication, of heartbreak, of constantly recurring death, of perpetual theophany; Diana doubled by her own desire, Actaeon metamorphosed both by her own and by that of Artemis. And yet, in this text devoted to the interpretation of a distant legend and a myth of distance (the man punished for having tried to approach the naked deity), the offering is close at hand. There, the bodies are young, beautiful, undamaged; they run to one another in complete certainty, for the simulacrum is still presented in its sparkling freshness, without recourse to the enigma of signs. The phantasms are the welcoming of appearance in the original light. But it is an origin that, of its own movement, recedes into an inaccessible distance. Diana at her bath, the goddess slipping into the water just as she offers herself to the gaze, is not only the detour of the Greek gods, it is the moment when the intact unity of the divine "reflects its divinity" in a virginal body, and thereby doubles itself in a demon that makes her, distant from herself, appear chaste, and at the same time offers her to the violence of the Goat. And when divinity ceases to sparkle in the clearings, and doubles itself in appearance where it succumbs while justifying itself, it leaves mythical space and enters the time of the theologians. The desirable trace of the gods is collected (is perhaps lost) in the tabernacle and the ambiguous game of signs.

So the pure speech of myth ceases to be possible. How then does one transcribe into a language such as ours the lost but insistent order of simulacra? A necessarily impure speech, one that draws such shadows toward the light and aims to restore to all those simulacra, beyond the river, something that would be a visible body, a sign or a being. *Tam dira cupido*. It is this desire that the goddess has placed in Actaeon's heart at the moment of metamorphosis and death: If you can describe Diana's nakedness, feel free.

The language of Klossowski is the prose of Actaeon – a transgressive speech. Is not all speech transgressive, when it has to do with silence? Gide and many others along with him wanted to transcribe an impure silence into a pure language, no doubt failing to see that such a speech derives its purity only from a deeper silence that it does not name and that speaks in it, in spite of it – thus rendering it turbid and impure.[12] We know now, since Georges Bataille and Maurice Blanchot, that language owes its transgressive power to an inverse relation, that of an impure speech to a pure silence, and that it is in the space indefinitely covered by this impurity that speech can address such a silence. In Bataille, writing is an undone consecration – a transubstantiation ritualized in the opposite direction, where real presence again becomes a recumbent body and finds itself brought back to silence in a vomiting. Blanchot's language addresses death – not to triumph over it in words of glory but to remain in that Orphic dimension where the song, made possible and necessary by death, can never look death in the face nor make it visible, so that it speaks to death and speaks of it in an impossibility that condemns it to a perpetual mutter.

Klossowski knows these forms of transgression. But he modifies them in an initiative that is his alone: he treats his own language as a simulacrum. *La Vocation suspendue* is the simulated commentary of a narrative that is itself a simulacrum, since it does not exist or, rather, it resides entirely in this commentary that is made of it. So that in a single sheet of language that internal distance opens up which makes it possible for the commentary of an inaccessible work to be conveyed in the very presence of the work and for the work to slip away in the commentary that is nevertheless its only form of existence – mystery of real presence and enigma of the Same. The Roberte trilogy is treated in a different way, apparently at least: diary fragments, dialogued scenes, long conversations that seem to make speech tilt towards the actuality of an immediate language without any overview. But a complex relationship is established between these three texts. *Roberte, ce soir* already exists within the text itself, since the latter tells about Roberte's decision to censor one of the episodes of the novel. But this first narrative also exists in the second that contests it from within through Roberte's diary, then in the third, when one sees the preparations for its theatrical performance, a performance that escapes into the very text of *Le Souffleur*, where Roberte, urged to animate Roberte with her identical presence, doubles herself in an irreducible hiatus. At the same time, the narrator of the first story, Antoine, disperses in the second between Roberte and Octave, then scatters in the multiplicity of *Le Souffleur*, where the one who speaks is, without our being able to decide, either Théodore Lacase or K., his double, who passes himself off as Théodore, tries to lay claim to his works and finds himself finally in Théodore's place; or perhaps the Old Man, who presides over the switches and remains the invisible Prompter of all this language. Prompter already dead, Prompted Prompter, perhaps Octave speaking from beyond death?

None of these, no doubt, but rather that superimposition of voices that "prompt" each other – insinuating their words in the other's discourse and constantly animating it with a movement, a "pneuma" that does not belong to it, but "*soufflant*" also in the sense of a breath, an *expiration* that blows out the light of a candle; *soufflant*, finally, in the sense in which one takes possession of a thing meant for another (steals his place, his role, his position, his wife). Thus, as Klossowski's language recasts itself, projects back over what it has just said in the helix of a new narrative (there are three, as many as there are turns in the spiral staircase that embellishes the cover of *Le Souffleur*), the speaking subject scatters into voices that prompt one another, suggest one another, extinguish one another, replace one another – dispersing the act of writing and the writer into the distance of the simulacrum where it loses itself, breathes, and lives.

Usually, when an author talks about himself as an author, he does so in the confessional mode of the "journal" that speaks the everyday truth – that impure truth expressed in a spare and pure language. Klossowski invents, in this recasting of his own language, in this detachment that does not tend toward any intimacy, a simulacral space that is doubtless the still-hidden contemporary locus of literature. Klossowski writes a work, one of the rare works, that discovers. In it one perceives that literature's being concerns neither men nor signs but this space of the double, this hollow of the simulacrum where Christianity became enchanted with its Demon, and where the Greeks feared the glittering presence of the gods with their arrows. Distance and proximity of the Same, where we others now find our only language.

NOTES

1 I have emphasized *demon, myself,* and *god.* The text is quoted in *Un si funeste désir* (Paris: Gallimard, 1963), an essential collection that contains deeply interesting pages on Nietzsche and makes possible a whole new reading of Klossowski. [The Nietzsche passage is taken from *The Gay Science;* trans. Walter Kaufman (New York: Vintage, 1974), p. 225.]

2 Klossowski, "Gide, De Bos, et le Démon," in *Un si funeste désir,* pp. 37 – 54, and "En Marge de la correspondance de Claudel et de Gide," ibid., pp. 55 – 58.

3 Jean-François Marmontel said, in a wonderful phrase, "Feigning would express the untruths of sentiment and thought" (*Oeuvres* [Paris: Verdiere, 1819], vol. 10, p. 431.

4 Klossowski, *Roberte, ce soir,* in *Les Lois de l'hospitalité* (Paris: Gallimard, 1965).

5 Klossowski, "Sade et la Révolution," lecture at the Collège de Sociologie, February, 1939, in Sade, *Oeuvres complètes* (Paris: Pauvert, 1960), vol. 3.

6 Klossowski, *Le Souffleur ou le Théâtre de société* (Paris: Pauvert, 1960).

7 Klossowski, *La Vocation suspendue* (Paris: Gallimard, 1950).

a The word *hôte* can mean either host or guest – R.H.

8 Klossowski, "La Révocation de l'édit de Nantes," in *Les Lois de l'hospitalité.*

9 Here one reencounters, but as a pure form and in the stripped-down game of the simulacrum, the problem of real presence and of transubstantiation.

10 When, in order to save a man, the Calvinist Roberte violates a tabernacle where real presence is *not* hidden from her, she is suddenly seized, across this tiny temple, by two hands that are her own: the simulacrum of a doubled Roberte triumphs in the emptiness of the sign and of the work.

11 Klossowski, *Le Bain de Diane* (Paris: Pauvert, 1956).

12 Concerning speech and purity, see "La Messe de Georges Bataille," in *Un si funeste désir* (Paris: Gallimard, 1963), pp. 123 – 25.

BEHIND THE FABLE*

I
n every work with a narrative form one needs to distinguish between *fable* and *fiction*. The fable is what is related (episodes, characters, functions they exercise in the narrative, events). Fiction is the
narrative system, or rather the various systems according to which it
is "narrated" ["*récité*"] – the narrator's stance toward what he is relating (depending on whether he is part of the adventure, or contemplates it as a slightly detached observer, or is excluded from it and
comes upon it from the outside), the presence or absence of a neutral
gaze that surveys things and people, providing an objective description of them; an involvement of the whole narrative in the perspective
of one character or several in succession or none in particular; a discourse repeating the events after the fact or dubbing them as they
unfold, and so on. The fable is made up of elements placed in a certain
order. Fiction is the weaving of established relations, through the discourse itself. Fiction, an "aspect" of the fable.

When one speaks in reality, one can very well say "fabulous"
things, but the triangle formed by the speaking subject, his discourse,
and what he tells is determined from the outside by the situation, so
there is no fiction. In that analagon of discourse that the work constitutes, this relation can only be established within the very act of
speaking; what is recounted must indicate, by itself, who is speaking,
and at what distance, and according to what perspective, and using

*This essay appeared in an issue of *L'Arc* devoted to the writings of Jules Verne (*L'Arc*
29 [May 1966], pp. 5–12). Robert Hurley's translation.

what mode of discourse. The work is defined less by the elements of the fable or their ordering than by the modes of fiction, indicated as if obliquely by the very wording [*énoncé*] of the fable. A narrative's fable resides in the mythical possibilities of the culture; its writing resides in the possibilities of the language; its fiction, in the possibilities of the speech act.

No epoch has used simultaneously all the modes of fiction that can be defined abstractly: certain ones are always excluded and treated as parasites; others, by the same token, are privileged and define a norm. The discourse of the author, interrupting his narrative and lifting his eyes from the text to appeal to the reader, inviting him to serve as a judge or witness of what is happening, was frequent in the eighteenth century; it all but disappeared in the course of the last century. On the other hand, the discourse that is linked to the act of writing, that is contemporaneous with its unfolding and enclosed in it, made its appearance less than a century ago. Perhaps it has exerted a very strong tyranny, banishing with the accusation of naïveté, artifice, or crude realism an entire fiction that would not have its locus in the discourse of a single subject and in the very act of its writing.

Since new modes of fiction were admitted into the literary work (a neutral language speaking by itself and without a locus, in an unbroken flow of language, unfamiliar words streaming in from the outside, a patchwork of discourses each having a different mode), it again becomes possible to read, according to their own architecture, texts that, because they were peopled with "parasitic discourses," had been excluded from literature.

The narratives of Jules Verne are wonderfully full of those discontinuities in the fictional mode. Time after time, the relationship established between narrator, discourse, and fable comes undone and reconstitutes itself according to a new design. The storytelling text continually breaks off, changes signs, reverses itself, moves away, comes from elsewhere and as if from a different voice. Speakers, appearing out of nowhere, introduce themselves, silence those who came before, hold forth for a moment in their own discourse, and then suddenly yield the floor to another of those anonymous faces, those grey silhouettes. An organization completely contrary to that of *The Thousand and One Nights*: there, each narrative, even if it is related by a third party, is constructed – fictionally – by the one who lived the story; to each fable its voice, to each voice a new fable. The whole "fiction" consists in the movement by which a character disconnects from the fable to which he belongs and becomes a teller of the next fable. In Jules Verne, a single fable per novel, but related by different, tangled, obscure voices, contending with one another.

Behind the characters of the fable—those one sees, who have a name, hold dialogues, and to whom adventures happen—there reigns a whole shadow theater, with its rivalries and its nocturnal contests, its jousts and its triumphs. Bodyless voices jostle each other to recount the fable.

1. Right beside the main characters,[1] sharing their familiarity, knowing their faces, their habits, their civil status, but also their thoughts and the secret folds of their nature, listening to their retorts but experiencing their feelings as if from within, a shadow speaks. It is in the same boat as the essential characters, sees things as they do, shares their adventures, worries along with them about what might happen. It is what transforms the adventure into a narrative. Although this narrator is endowed with great powers, it has its limits and its constraints: it slipped into the lunar cannonball, next to Ardan, Barbicane and Nicholl, and yet there are secret meetings at the Gun Club that it was unable to attend. Is it the same narrator or another that is here and there, in Baltimore and at Kilimanjaro, in the sidereal rocket, on earth, and in the submarine probe? Are we to assume a kind of supernumerary character throughout the story, continually wandering around in the limbo of the narration, an empty silhouette that would have the gift of ubiquity? Or, rather, should we imagine attentive, singular, and talkative spirits in each place, for each group of persons? In any case, these shadow figures are in the first row of invisibility: they are very nearly true characters.

2. Set back from these intimate "narrators," more discrete, more furtive characters make speeches telling about their movements or indicating a change from one to the other. "On that evening," say these voices, "a stranger who might have chanced to be in Baltimore could not have gained admission for love or money into the great hall . . ."; and yet an invisible stranger (a level-one narrator) was able to pass through the doors and give an account of the auction "as if he were there." Such voices also pass the turn to speak from one narrator to another, thus ensuring that the hide-the-slipper game of the discourse keeps moving. "Though the honorable Mr. Maston did

not hear the cheers given in his honor" (he has just been applauded in the gigantic shell), "at least his ears buzzed" (and the speaker is now in Baltimore).

3. A discourse even more exterior to the visible forms of the fable recaptures it in its entirety and refers it to another narrative system, to an objective chronology or, in any case, to a time which is that of the reader himself. That voice completely "*hors fable*" indicates historical markers ("During the War of Rebellion, a new and influential club . . ."); it recalls the other narratives published by Jules Verne on an analogous subject (in a note appearing in *Sans dessus dessous*, it carries exactitude to the point of differentiating between real polar expeditions and the one recounted in *Le Désert de glace*); it also sometimes refreshes the reader's memory throughout the narrative ("Remember that . . ."). This voice is that of the absolute narrator: the writer's first person (but neutralized) noting in the margins of his narrative what one needs to know in order to read it comfortably.

4. Behind it, and even more distant, another voice is raised from time to time. It contests the narrative, underscores the latter's improbabilities, points out everything that might be impossible. But it immediately replies to this contestation that it has fostered. You must not think, it says, that a person would have to be insane to undertake such an adventure: "This fact need surprise no one. The Yankees, the first mechanicians in the world. . . ." The characters confined in the lunar rocket are stricken with strange feelings of malaise, but do not be surprised: "During the last twelve hours the atmosphere of the projectile had become charged with this deleterious gas, the final product of expiration." And, as an added precaution, this justificatory voice itself raises problems that it must resolve: "We may, perhaps, be astonished to find Barbicane and his companions so little occupied with the future. . . ."

5. There exists a last mode of discourse even more exterior. A completely toneless voice, articulated by no one, without any support or point of origin, coming from an indeterminate elsewhere and arising within the text through an act of pure irruption. Anonymous language deposited there in large sheets. Immigrant discourse. Now, this discourse is always a technical discourse. To be sure, there are long scientific treatises in the dialogues, or expositions, or letters or telegrams attributed to various characters; but they are not in that

position of exteriority which marks the fragments of "automatic information" by which the narrative is occasionally interrupted. A table of simultaneous schedules in the principal cities of the world; a table in three columns indicating the name, location, and height of the great mountain masses of the Moon; measurements of the Earth introduced by the simple formula, "Let one judge by the following figures. . . ." Deposited there by a voice that cannot be assigned, these moraines of knowledge remain at the external border of the narrative.

These voices behind the fable, whose interchange guides the weave of the fiction, would need to be studied for themselves, in their interplay and their struggles. Let us limit ourselves to the one mentioned above.

It is strange that in these "scientific novels" the technical discourse comes from elsewhere, like a reported language. Strange that it speaks by itself in an anonymous murmur. Strange that it appears in the form of irruptive and autonomous fragments. Now, an analysis of the fable reveals the same arrangement, as if it reproduced, in the relationships of the characters, the entanglement of the discourses that recount their imaginary adventures.

1. In the novels of Jules Verne the scientist remains on the fringe. It is not to him that the adventure occurs, or at least he is not the main protagonist. He imparts information, deploys a knowledge, states the possibilities and the limits, observes the results, calmly waits to make sure that what he said was true, and that knowledge was not misrepresented by him. Maston has directed all the operations, but he is not the one who goes to the Moon; he is not the one who will fire the Kilimanjaro cannon. A recording cylinder, he reels out an already-constituted knowledge, obeys impulses, functions all alone in the secrecy of his automatism, and produces results. The scientist does not discover: he is the one in whom knowledge has been inscribed, the smooth scrawl of a science done elsewhere. In *Hector Servadac* the scientist is only an inscription stone; he is called, appropriately, Palmyrin *Rosette*.

2. Jules Verne's scientist is a pure intermediary. An arithmetician, he measures, multiplies, and divides (like Maston or Rosette); a pure technician, he utilizes and constructs (like Schultze or Camaret). He is a *Homo calculator*, nothing more than a meticulous "πR^2". That is why he is distracted, not only with that heedlessness attributed to scientists by tradition but with a deeper distraction: withdrawn from

the world and from adventure, he arithmetizes; withdrawn from inventive knowledge, he works it out and figures it out. Which exposes him to all the accidental distractions that manifest his profoundly *abstract* being.

3. The scientist is always placed at the weakest point. At worst he embodies evil (*Face au drapeau*); or he allows it without intending it or seeing it (*L'Etonnante aventure de la mission Barsac*); or he is an exile (*Robert*); or he is a gentle maniac (as are the artillerists of the Gun Club); or, if he is likeable and on the verge of being a positive protagonist, then it is in his very calculations that the snag is hit (Maston makes a mistake in recopying the measurements of the Earth). In any case, the scientist is the one who is defective in something (the fractured skull and artificial arm of the Gun Club secretary declare this clearly enough). From this, a general principle: knowledge and defect are linked together, and a law of proportionality: the less the scientist is mistaken, the more he is perverse, or demented, or a stranger to the world (Camaret); the more he is positive, the more he is mistaken (Maston, as his name indicates and as the story shows, is only a web of errors: he was mistaken about the *masses* when he began to search the sea bottom for the rocket that was floating, and about the *tons* when he tried to calculate the weight of the Earth). Science speaks only in an empty space.

4. Opposite the scientist, the positive hero is ignorance itself. In some cases (Michel Ardan) he slips into the adventure that knowledge authorizes, and if he penetrates into the space that is provided by calculation it is as though he were in a kind of game – in order to see. In other cases he falls unwittingly into the trap that is set. To be sure, he learns as the episodes succeed one another, but his role is never to acquire this knowledge and become its master and possessor in his turn. Either, as a simple witness, he is there to relate what he has seen; or his function is to destroy the infernal knowledge and to obliterate its traces (that is the case with Jane Braxton in *L'Etonnante aventure de la mission Barsac*). Looking closely, moreover, one sees that the two functions merge: in both cases it is a matter of reducing the (fabulous) reality to the pure (and imaginary) truth of the narrative. Maston, the innocent scientist, aided by the innocent and ignorant Evangelina Scorbitt, is the one whose "flaw" makes possible the impossible undertaking and yet dooms it to failure, obliterates it from reality only to offer it to the useless fiction of the narrative.

It should be noted that in general Jules Verne's great calculators assign themselves and are given a very definite task: to prevent the world from coming to a halt through the effect of a fatal equilibrium; to recover energy sources, to discover the central source, to provide for a planetary colonization, to escape the monotony of the human reign. In short, it is a matter of fighting against entropy. Which explains (if we go from the level of the fable to that of the themes) the persistent recurrence of the adventures of cold and hot, of ice and volcano, of blazing planets and dead stars, of heights and depths, of propulsive energy and declining motion. Time and again, against the most probable world – neutral, blank, homogeneous, anonymous – the calculator (whether he is brilliant, mad, mean, or distracted) makes it possible to discover a fiery heat source that ensures disequilibrium and secures the world against death. The fault in which the calculator is lodged, the pitfall that his foolishness or his error arranges on the great surface of knowledge hurls truth into the fabulous event where it becomes visible, where the energies again break forth in profusion, where the world is restored to a new youth, where all the fires flare up and illuminate the darkness. Until the moment (infinitely near to the first one) when error is dissipated, when madness does away with itself, and when truth is restored to its all-too-probable frothing, its indefinite babble.

Now we can grasp the coherence that exists between the modes of fiction, the forms of the fable, and the content of the themes. The great play of shadows that unfolded behind the fable was the struggle between the neutral probability of scientific discourse (that smooth, anonymous, monochord voice that comes from who knows where and inserts itself in the fiction, imposing the certainty of its truth) and the birth, triumph, and death of the improbable discourses in which the figures of the fable took shape, in which they also disappeared. In defiance of scientific truths and breaking their icy voice, the discourses of fiction constantly proceeded upstream toward the greatest improbability. Above that monotonous hum in which the end of the world was expressed, they spread the asymmetrical fervor of risk, of unlikely chance, of impatient unreason. Jules Verne's novels constitute the negentropy of knowledge. Not science turned recreative, but re-creation based on the uniform discourse of science.

This function of scientific discourse (a hum that must be returned to its improbability) reminds one of the role that Raymond Roussel assigned to the readymade phrases that he found and shattered, pulverized, shook, to make them stream forth with the miraculous strangeness of the impossible narrative. What disturbs the din of language and restores it to the disequilibrium of its sovereign powers is not knowledge (always more and more probable); it is not the fable (which has its obligatory forms); it is, between the two, as if in a limbolike invisibility, the ardent games of fiction.

In their themes and their fable Jules Verne's narratives are quite close to novels of "initiation" or "education." In their fiction they are diametrically opposite. No doubt, the naive protagonist goes through his own adventures like so many tests marked by ritual events — purification by fire, icy death, journey across a dangerous region, climb and descent, passage to the point of no return, near-miraculous return to the starting point. But, in addition, every initiation or education regularly obeys the twofold law of disappointment and metamorphosis. The protagonist came in search of a truth that he knew from a distance, and that flickered before his innocent eyes. He does not find that truth, because it was the truth of his desire or his idle curiosity. In return, a reality that he never suspected is revealed to him, a reality that is deeper, more reticent, more beautiful or darker than the one with which he was familiar: that reality is himself and the world transfigured by each other; the coal and the diamond have exchanged their blackness, their brilliancy. Jules Verne's *Voyages* obey a completely opposite law: a truth unfolds, according to its autonomous laws, before the astonished eyes of the ignorant, the impassive eyes of those who know. That smooth sheet, that discourse without a speaking subject would have remained in its essential retreat if the scientist's "deviation" (his defect, his mediocrity, his distraction, the snag that he constitutes in the world) had not provoked it to reveal itself. Thanks to that slender crack, the characters pass through a world of truth that remains indifferent and closes back in on itself once they have gone by. When they return, they have seen and learned, to be sure, but nothing has changed, either on the face of the world or in the depths of their being. The adventure has left no scar. And the "distracted" scientist withdraws into the essential retreat of knowledge. "In compliance with its author's wishes, the work of Camaret was completely dead, and nothing would convey the name of that brilliant and mad inventor to future ages." The multiple voices of fiction are reabsorbed into the disembodied hum of science; and the great undulations of the most probable erase the bones of the most improbable from their infinite sands. And that goes so far as the probable disappearance and reappearance of all science, which Jules Verne predicts, at the time of his death, in *L'eternel Adam*.

"Mademoiselle Mornas has her own way of accosting you with an Ini-tiate (good day), that's all I have to say to you." But in the sense in which one says: Initiate, good night.

NOTES

1   For the sake of convenience I shall take as a privileged example the three books: *De la Terre à la lune, Autour de la lune,* [*From the Earth to the Moon*; including the sequel, *Around the Moon*, trans. Louis Mercier and Eleanor E. King, rev. Charles Hull (New York: Didier, 1947)] and *Sans dessus dessous*.

THE THOUGHT OF THE OUTSIDE*

I LIE, I SPEAK

In ancient times, this simple assertion was enough to shake the foundations of Greek truth: "I lie, I speak," on the other hand, puts the whole of modern fiction to the test.

The force of these assertions is not in fact the same. As we know, Epimenides' argument can be mastered if, discourse having been slyly folded back upon itself, a distinction is made between two propositions, the first of which is the object of the second. The grammatical configuration of the paradox cannot suppress this essential duality, try as it might to dodge it (particularly if the paradox is locked into "I lie" in its simple form). Every proposition must be of a higher "type" than that which serves as its object. That the object-proposition recurs in the proposition that designates it; that the Cretan's sincerity is compromised the instant he speaks by the content of his assertion; that he may indeed be lying about lying—all this is less an insurmountable logical obstacle than the result of a plain and simple fact—the speaking subject is also the subject about which it speaks.

In forthrightly saying "I speak" I am exposed to none of these perils; the two propositions hidden in the statement ("I speak" and "I say that I speak") in no way compromise each other. I am protected by the impenetrable fortress of the assertion's self-assertion, by the way it coincides exactly with itself, leaving no jagged edges, averting all dan-

---

*This essay originally appeared in *Critique* 229 (June 1966), pp. 523–46. The translation, by Brian Massumi, has been slightly amended.

ger of error by saying no more than that I am speaking. Neither in the words in question nor in the subject that pronounces them is there an obstacle or insinuation to come between the object-proposition and the proposition that states it. It is therefore true, undeniably true, that I am speaking when I say that I am speaking.

But things may not be that simple. Although the formal position of "I speak" does not raise problems of its own, its meaning opens a potentially unlimited realm of questions, in spite of its apparent clarity. "I speak" refers to a supporting discourse that provides it with an object. That discourse, however, is missing; the sovereignty of "I speak" can only reside in the absence of any other language; the discourse about which I speak does not preexist the nakedness articulated the moment I say, "I speak"; it disappears the instant I fall silent. Any possibility of language dries up in the transitivity of its execution. The desert surrounds it. In what extreme delicacy, at what slight and singular point, could a language come together in an attempt to recapture itself in the stripped-down form, "I speak"? Unless, of course, the void in which the contentless slimness of "I speak" is manifested were an absolute opening through which language endlessly spreads forth, while the subject – the "I" who speaks – fragments, disperses, scatters, disappearing in that naked space. If the only site for language is indeed the solitary sovereignty of "I speak," then in principle nothing can limit it – not the one to whom it is addressed, not the truth of what it says, not the values or systems of representation it utilizes. In short, it is no longer discourse and the communication of meaning, but a spreading forth of language in its raw state, an unfolding of pure exteriority. And the subject that speaks is less the responsible agent of a discourse (what holds it, what uses it to assert and judge, what sometimes represents itself in it by means of a grammatical form designed to have that effect) than a nonexistence in whose emptiness the unending outpouring of language uninterruptedly continues.

It is a widely held belief that modern literature is characterized by a doubling-back that enables it to designate itself; this self-reference supposedly allows it both to interiorize to the extreme (to state nothing but itself) and to manifest itself in the shimmering sign of its distant existence. In fact, the event that gave rise to what we call "literature" in the strict sense is only superficially an interiorization; it is far more a question of a passage to the "outside": language escapes the mode of being of discourse – in other words, the dynasty of representation—and literary speech develops from itself, forming a network in which each point is distinct, distant from even its closest neighbors, and has a position in relation to every other point in a space that simultaneously holds and separates them all. Literature is not language approaching itself until it reaches the point of its fiery manifestation; it is, rather, language getting as far away from itself as possible. And if, in this setting "outside of itself," it unveils its own being, the sudden clarity reveals not a folding-back but a gap, not a turning back of signs upon themselves but a dispersion. The "subject" of literature (what speaks in it and what it speaks about) is less language in its positivity than the void that language takes as its space when it articulates itself in the nakedness of "I speak."

This neutral space is what characterizes contemporary Western fiction (which is why it is no longer mythology or rhetoric). The reason it is now so necessary to think through this fiction—while in the past it was a matter of thinking the truth—is that "I speak" runs counter to "I think." "I think" led to the indubitable certainty of the "I" and its existence; "I speak," on the other hand, distances, disperses, effaces that existence and lets only its empty emplacement appear. Thought about thought, an entire tradition wider than philosophy, has taught us that thought leads us to the deepest interiority. Speech about speech leads us, by way of literature as well as perhaps by other paths, to the outside in which the speaking subject disappears. No doubt, that is why Western thought took so long to think the being of language: as if it had a premonition of the danger that the naked experience of language poses for the self-evidence of "I think."

THE EXPERIENCE OF THE OUTSIDE

The breakthrough to a language from which the subject is excluded, the bringing to light of a perhaps irremediable incompatibility between the appearing of language in its being and consciousness of the self in its identity, is an experience now being heralded at diverse points in culture: in the simple gesture of writing as in attempts to formalize language; in the study of myths as in psychoanalysis; in the search for a Logos that would be like the birthplace of all of Western reason. We are standing on the edge of an abyss that had long been invisible: the being of language only appears for itself with the disappearance of the subject. How can we gain access to this strange rela-

tion? Perhaps through a form of thought whose still vague possibility
was sketched by Western culture in its margins. A thought that stands
outside subjectivity, setting its limits as though from without, articulating its end, making its dispersion shine forth, taking in only its
invincible absence; and that, at the same time, stands at the threshold
of all positivity, not in order to grasp its foundation or justification but
in order to regain the space of its unfolding, the void serving as its site,
the distance in which it is constituted and into which its immediate
certainties slip the moment they are glimpsed – a thought that, in relation to the interiority of our philosophical reflection and the positivity
of our knowledge, constitutes what in a phrase we might call "the
thought of the outside."

It will one day be necessary to try to define the fundamental forms
and categories of this "thought of the outside." It will also be necessary to try to retrace its path, to find out where it comes to us from and
in what direction it is moving. One might assume that it was born of
the mystical thinking that has prowled the confines of Christianity
since the texts of the Pseudo-Dionysus: perhaps it survived for a mil-
lennium or so in the various forms of negative theology. Yet nothing is
less certain: although this experience involves going "outside of oneself," this is done ultimately in order to find oneself, to wrap and
gather oneself in the dazzling interiority of a thought that is rightfully
Being and Speech, in other words, Discourse, even if it is the silence
beyond all language and the nothingness beyond all being.

It is less rash to suppose that the first rending to expose the thought
of the outside was, paradoxically, the recursive monologue of the
Marquis de Sade. In the age of Kant and Hegel, at a time when the
interiorization of the law of history and the world was being imperiously demanded by Western consciousness as never before, Sade
never ceases speaking of the nakedness of desire as the lawless law of
the world. In the same period Hölderlin's poetry manifested the shimmering absence of the gods and pronounced the new law of the obligation to wait, infinitely long no doubt, for the enigmatic succor of
"God's failing." Can it be said without stretching things that Sade and
Hölderlin simultaneously introduced into our thinking, for the coming century, but in some way cryptically, the experience of the
outside – the former by laying desire bare in the infinite murmur of
discourse, the latter by discovering that the gods had wandered off
through a rift in language as it was in the process of losing its bear-

ings? That experience was afterward to remain not exactly hidden, because it had not penetrated the thickness of our culture, but afloat, foreign, exterior to our interiority, for the entire time the demand was being formulated, most imperiously, to interiorize the world, to erase alienation, to move beyond the false moment of alienation [*Entäusserung*], to humanize nature, to naturalize man, and to recover on earth the treasures that had been spent in heaven.

The same experience resurfaced in the second half of the nineteenth century at the very core of language, which had become—even though our culture was still seeking to mirror itself in it as if it held the secret of its interiority—the sparkle of the outside. It resurfaces in Nietzsche's discovery that all of Western metaphysics is tied not only to its grammar (that had been largely suspected since Schlegel) but to those who, in holding discourse, have a hold over the right to speak; and in Mallarmé when language appears as a leave-taking from that which it names, but especially—beginning with *Igitur* and continuing through the aleatory and autonomous theatricality of *Le Livre*—as the movement of the speaker's disappearance; and in Artaud, when all of discursive language is constrained to come undone in the violence of the body and the cry, and when thought, forsaking the wordy interiority of consciousness, becomes a material energy, the suffering of the flesh, the persecution and rending of the subject itself; and in Bataille, when thought ceases to be the discourse of contradiction or the unconscious, becoming the discourse of the limit, of ruptured subjectivity, transgression; and in Klossowski, with the experience of the double, of the exteriority of simulacra, of the insane theatrical multiplication of the Me.

Blanchot is perhaps more than just another witness to this thought. So far has he withdrawn into the manifestation of his work, so completely is he, not hidden by his texts, but absent from their existence and absent by virtue of the marvelous force of their existence, that for us he is that thought itself—its real, absolutely distant, shimmering, invisible presence, its necessary destiny, its inevitable law, its calm, infinite, measured strength.

REFLECTION, FICTION

It is extremely difficult to find a language faithful to this thought. Any purely reflexive discourse runs the risk of leading the experience of the outside back to the dimension of interiority; reflection tends irresistibly to repatriate it to the side of consciousness and to develop it into a description of living that depicts the "outside" as the experience of the body, space, the limits of the will, and the ineffaceable presence of the other. The vocabulary of fiction is equally perilous: due to the thickness of its images, sometimes merely by virtue of the transparency of the most neutral or hastiest figures, it risks setting down readymade meanings that stitch the old fabric of interiority back together in the form of an imagined outside.

Hence the necessity of converting reflexive language. It must be directed not toward any inner confirmation–not toward a kind of central, unshakable certitude–but toward an outer bound where it must continually content itself. When language arrives at its own edge, what it finds is not a positivity that contradicts it but the void that will efface it. Into that void it must go, consenting to come undone in the rumbling, in the immediate negation of what it says, in a silence that is not the intimacy of a secret but a pure outside where words endlessly unravel. That is why Blanchot's language does not use negation dialectically. To negate dialectically brings what one negates into the troubled interiority of the mind. To negate one's own discourse, as Blanchot does, is to cast it ceaselessly outside of itself, to deprive it at every moment not only of what it has just said, but of the very ability to speak. It is to leave it where it lies, far behind one, in order to be free for a new beginning–a beginning that is a pure origin because its only principles are itself and the void, but that is also a rebeginning because what freed that void was the language of the past in the act of hollowing itself out. Not reflection, but forgetting; not contradiction, but a contestation that effaces; not reconciliation, but droning on and on; not mind in laborious conquest of its unity, but the endless erosion of the outside; not truth finally shedding light on itself, but the streaming and distress of a language that has always already begun. "Not speech, barely a murmur, barely a tremor, less than silence, less than the abyss of the void; the fullness of the void, something one cannot silence, occupying all of space, the uninterrupted, the incessant, a tremor and already a murmur, not a murmur but speech, and not just any speech, distinct speech, precise speech, within my reach."[1]

This kind of symmetrical conversion is required of the language of fiction. It must no longer be a power that tirelessly produces images and makes them shine but, rather, a power that undoes them, that lessens their overload, that infuses them with an inner transparency that illuminates them little by little until they burst and scatter in the lightness of the unimaginable. Blanchot's fictions are, rather than the images themselves, their transformation, displacement, and neutral interstices. They are precise; the only figures they outline are in the gray tones of everyday life and the anonymous. And when wonder overtakes them, it is never in themselves but in the void surrounding them, in the space in which they are set, rootless and without foundation. The fictitious is never in things or in people but in the impossible verisimilitude of what lies between them–encounters, the proximity of what is most distant, the absolute dissimulation in our very midst. Therefore, fiction consists not in showing the invisible, but in showing the extent to which the invisibility of the visible is invisible. Thus, it bears a profound relation to space; understood in this way, space is to fiction what the negative is to reflection (whereas dialectical negation is tied to the fable of time). No doubt, this is the role that houses, hallways, doors, and rooms play in almost all of Blanchot's narratives: placeless places, beckoning thresholds, closed, forbidden spaces that are nevertheless exposed to the winds, hallways fanned by doors that open rooms for unbearable encounters and create gulfs between them, across which voices cannot carry, and that even muffle cries; corridors leading to more corridors where the night resounds, beyond sleep, with the smothered voices of those who speak, with the cough of the sick, with the death rattle of the dying, with the suspended breath of those who ceaselessly cease living; a long and narrow room, like a tunnel, in which approach and distance–the approach of forgetting, the distance of the wait–draw near to one another and unendingly move apart.

Thus reflexive patience, always directed outside itself, and a fiction that cancels itself out in the void where it undoes its forms intersect to form a discourse appearing with no conclusion and no image, with no truth and no theater, with no proof, no mask, no affirmation, free of any center, unfettered to any native soil; a discourse that constitutes its own space as the outside toward which, and outside of which, it speaks. This discourse, as speech of the outside whose words welcome the outside it addresses, has the openness of a commentary: the repetition of what continually murmurs outside. But this discourse, as a speech that is always outside what it says, is an incessant advance toward that whose absolutely fine-spun light has never received language. This singular mode of being of discourse–a return to the ambiguous hollowness of undoing and origin–no doubt defines the common ground of Blanchot's "novels" and "narratives," and of his "criticism." From the moment discourse ceases to follow the slope of self-interiorizing thought and, addressing the very being of language, returns thought to the outside; from that moment, in a single stroke, it becomes a meticulous narration of experiences, encounters, and improbable signs–language about the outside of all language, speech about the invisible side of words. And it becomes attentiveness to what in language already exists, has already been said, imprinted, manifested–a listening less to what is articulated in language than to the void circulating between its words, to the murmur that is forever taking it apart; a discourse on the nondiscourse of all language; the fiction of the invisible space in which it appears. That is why the distinction between "novels," "narratives," and "criticism" is progressively weakened in Blanchot until, in *L'Attente l'oubli*, language alone is allowed to speak–what is no one's, is neither fiction nor reflection, neither already said nor never yet said, but is instead "between them, this place with its fixed open expanse, the retention of things in their latent state."[2]

BEING ATTRACTED AND NEGLIGENT

Attraction is no doubt for Blanchot what desire is for Sade, force for Nietzsche, the materiality of thought for Antonin Artaud, and transgression for Georges Bataille: the pure, most naked, experience of the outside. It is necessary to be clear about what the word designates: "attraction," as Blanchot means it, does not depend on any charm. Nor does it break one's solitude or found any positive communication. To be attracted is not to be beckoned by the allure of the exterior, rather, it is to suffer–in emptiness and destitution–the presence of the outside and, tied to that presence, the fact that one is irremediably outside the outside. Far from calling on one interiority to draw close to another, attraction makes it imperiously manifest that the outside is there, open, without depth, without protection or reserve (how could it have any when it had no interiority, and, instead, infinitely unfolds outside any enclosure?), but that one cannot gain access to that opening because the outside never yields its essence. The outside cannot

offer itself as a positive presence – as something inwardly illuminated
by the certainty of its own existence – but only as an absence that pulls
as far away from itself as possible, receding into the sign it makes to
draw one toward it, as though it were possible to reach it. Attraction,
the marvelous simplicity of opening, has nothing to offer but the infinite void that opens beneath the feet of the person it attracts, the indifference that greets him as if he were not there, a silence too insistent
to be resisted and too ambiguous to be deciphered and definitively
interpreted – nothing to offer but a woman's gesture in a window, a
door left ajar, the smile of a guard before a forbidden threshold, a gaze
condemned to death.

Negligence is the necessary correlate of attraction. The relations
between them are complex. To be susceptible to attraction a person
must be negligent – essentially negligent, with total disregard for what
one is doing (in *Aminadab*, Thomas enters the fabulous boardinghouse only because he neglects to enter the house across the street)
and with the attitude that one's past and kin and whole other life is
nonexistent, thus relegating them to the outside (neither in the boardinghouse in *Aminadab* nor in the city in *Le Très-Haut*, nor in the
"sanatorium" of *Le Dernier Homme*, nor in the apartment in *Le Moment voulu* does one know what is going on outside, or care to know:
one is outside the outside, which is never figured, only incessantly
hinted at by the whiteness of its absence, the pallor of an abstract
memory, or at most by the glint of snow through a window). This kind
of negligence is in fact the flip side of a zealousness – a mute, unjustified, obstinate diligence in surrendering oneself, against all odds, to
being attracted by attraction, or more precisely (since attraction has
no positivity) to being, in the void, the aimless movement without a
moving body of attraction itself. Pierre Klossowski was so right to
emphasize that in *Le Très-Haut* Henri's last name is "Sorge" (Care)
although it is mentioned only once or twice in the text.

But is this zeal always alert? Does it not commit an oversight that
may seem trifling but is in fact more crucial than that massive forgetting of an entire life, of all prior attachments and relations? Is not the
stride that tirelessly carries the attracted person forward precisely distraction and error? Was it not necessary to "hold back, stay put," as is
suggested several times in *Celui qui ne m'accompagnait pas* and in *Le
Moment voulu*? Is it not in the nature of zeal to weigh itself down with
its own solicitude, to hold it too far, to multiply steps, to grow dizzy

with stubbornness, to advance toward the attraction, when attraction speaks imperiously from the depths of its withdrawal only to what is itself withdrawn? It is of the essence of zeal to be negligent, to believe that what is concealed lies elsewhere, that the past will repeat itself, that the law applies to it, that it is awaited, watched over, spied upon. Who will ever know if Thomas—perhaps "Doubting Thomas" should come to mind—had more faith than the others in his questioning of his own belief and in his demands to see and touch? And is what he touched on a body of flesh really what he was after when he asked for a resurrected presence? And was not the illumination suffusing him as much shadow as light? Perhaps Lucie was not who he was looking for; perhaps he should have questioned the person who was thrust on him for a companion; perhaps, instead of trying to get to the upper stories to find the implausible woman who had smiled at him, he should have followed the simple path, taken the gentlest slope, and abandoned himself to the vegetal powers below. Perhaps it was not he who had been called, perhaps someone else was awaited.

All this uncertainty, which makes zeal and negligence two indefinitely reversible figures, undoubtedly has as its principle "the carelessness ruling the house."[5] This negligence is more visible, more concealed, more ambiguous yet more fundamental than any other. Everything in it can be deciphered as an intentional sign, as secret diligence, as spying or entrapment: perhaps the lazy servants are hidden powers; perhaps the wheel of fortune dispenses fates recorded long ago in books. But now zeal does not envelop negligence as its necessary allotment of shadow; rather, negligence remains so indifferent to what can manifest or conceal it that any gesture pertaining to it takes on the value of a sign. It was out of negligence that Thomas was called: the opening of attraction and the negligence welcoming the person who is attracted are one and the same. The constraint it creates is not simply blind (which is why it is absolute, and absolutely nonreciprocal). It is illusory; it binds no one because it itself is bound to that bond and can no longer be pure and open attraction. How could attraction not be essentially negligent—leaving things what they are, letting time pass and repeat, letting people advance toward it? For it is the infinite outside, for it is nothing that does not fall outside it, for it undoes every figure of interiority in pure dispersion.

One is attracted precisely to the extent that one is neglected. This is why zeal can only consist in neglecting that negligence, in oneself becoming a courageously negligent solicitude, in going toward the light in negligence of shadow, until it is discovered that the light itself is only negligence, a pure outside equivalent to a darkness that disperses, like a blown-out candle, the negligent zeal it had attracted.

WHERE IS THE LAW, AND WHAT DOES THE LAW DO?

Being negligent, being attracted, is a way of manifesting and concealing the law – of manifesting the withdrawal with which it conceals itself, of consequently attracting it in a light that hides it.

If it were self-evident and in the heart, the law would no longer be the law, but the sweet interiority of consciousness. If, on the other hand, it were present in a text, if it were possible to decipher it between the lines of a book, if it were in a register that could be consulted, then it would have the solidity of external things: it would be possible to follow or disobey it. Where then would its power reside, by what force or prestige would it command respect? In fact, the presence of the law is its concealment. Sovereignly, the law haunts cities, institutions, conduct, and gestures; whatever one does, however great the disorder and carelessness, it has already applied its might: "The house is always, at every instant, in proper order."[4] Taking liberties is not enough to interrupt it; you might think that you have detached yourself from it and can observe its exercise from without. The moment you believe that you can read its decrees from afar, and that they apply only to other people, is the moment you are closest to the law; you make it circulate, you "contribute to the enforcement of a public decree."[5] Yet this perpetual manifestation never illuminates what the law says or wants: the law is not the principle or inner rule of conduct. It is the outside that envelops actions, thereby removing them from all interiority; it is the darkness beyond their borders; it is the void that surrounds them, converting, unknown to anyone, their singularity into the gray monotony of the universal and opening around them a space of uneasiness, of dissatisfaction, of multiplied zeal.

And of transgression. How could one know the law and truly experience it, how could one force it to come into view, to exercise its powers clearly, to speak, without provoking it, without pursuing it into its recesses, without resolutely going even farther into the outside

into which it is always receding? How can one see its invisibility unless it has turned into its opposite, punishment, which, after all, is
only the law overstepped, irritated, beside itself? But, if punishment
could be provoked merely by the arbitrary actions of those who violate the law, then the law would be in their control: they would be
able to touch it and make it appear at will; they would be masters of
its shadow and light. That is why transgression endeavors to overstep
prohibition in an attempt to attract the law to itself; it always surrenders to the attraction of the essential withdrawal of the law; it obstinately advances into the opening of an invisibility over which it will
never triumph; insanely, it endeavors to make the law appear in order
to be able to venerate it and dazzle it with its own luminous face; all it
ends up doing is reinforcing the law in its weakness – the lightness of
the night that is its invincible, impalpable substance. The law is the
shadow toward which every gesture necessarily advances; it is itself
the shadow of the advancing gesture.

Aminadab and *Le Très-haut* form a diptych, one on each side of the
invisibility of the law. In the first novel, the strange boardinghouse
Thomas enters (attracted, called, perhaps elected, although not without being constrained to cross many forbidden thresholds) seems
subject to an unknown law: its nearness and absence are continually
recalled by doors open and prohibited, by the great wheel handing out
blank or undecipherable fates, by the overhang of an upperstory from
which the appeal originates, from which anonymous orders fall, but
to which no one can gain access. The day some people decide to track
the law into its lair is the day they encounter the monotony of the
place where they are already, as well as violence, blood, death, and
collapse, and finally resignation, despair, and a voluntary, fatal disappearance into the outside: for the outside of the law is so inaccessible
that anyone who tries to conquer and penetrate it is consigned not to
punishment which would be the law finally placed under restraint;
but to the outside of that outside – to the profoundest forgetting of all.
What it is that is served by the "domestics" – those *guards* and *servants*
who, unlike the "boarders," "belong to the house" and must represent
the law, enforcing it and submitting silently to it – is known to no one,
not even to themselves (do they serve the house or the will of the
guests?). As far as anyone knows, they could even be former boarders
who became servants. They are simultaneously zeal and indifference,

drunkenness and attentiveness, slumber and tireless activity, the twin figures of wickedness and solicitude: what conceals concealment and what makes it manifest.

In *Le Très-haut* the law itself (somewhat like the upper story in *Aminadab*, in its monotonous resemblance and exact identity with every other law) is manifested in its essential concealment. Sorge ("care" for and of the law: the solicitude one feels for the law, and the solicitude of the law for those to whom it is applied, even, especially, if they wish to escape it), Henri Sorge, is a bureaucrat: he works at city hall, in the office of vital statistics; he is only a tiny cog in a strange machine that turns individual existences into an institution; he is the first form of the law, because he transforms every birth into an archive. But then he abandons his duty (but is it really an abandonment? He takes a vacation and extends it—unofficially, it is true, but with the complicity of the administration, which tacitly arranges this essential idleness). This quasi retirement—is it a cause or an effect?—is enough to throw everyone's existence into disarray, and for death to inaugurate a reign that is no longer the classifying reign of the municipal register but the dishonored, contagious, anonymous reign of the epidemic; not the real death of decease and its certification, but a hazy charnel house where no one knows who is a patient and who is a doctor, who is a guard and who is a victim, whether it is a prison or a hospital, a safe house or a fortress of evil. All dams have burst, everything overflows its bounds: the dynasty of rising waters, the kingdom of dubious dampness, oozing, abscesses, and vomiting: individualities dissolve; sweating bodies melt into the walls; endless screams blare through the fingers that muffle them. Yet when Sorge leave state service, where he was responsible for ordering other people's existence, he does not go outside the law; quite the opposite, he forces it to manifest itself at the empty place he just abandoned. The movement by which he effaces his singular existence and removes it from the universality of the law in fact exalts the law; through that movement he serves the law, shows its perfection, "obliges" it, while at the same time linking it to its own disappearance (which is, in a sense, the opposite of transgressive existence exemplified by Bouxx and Dorte); he has become one with the law.

The law can only respond to this provocation by withdrawing: not by retreating into a still deeper silence, but by remaining immobile in its identity. One can, of course, plunge into the open void: plots can hatch, rumors of sabotage can spread, arson and murder can replace the most ceremonious order; the order of the law was never so sovereign than at this moment, when it envelops precisely what had tried to overturn it. Anyone who attempts to oppose the law in order to found a new order, to organize a second police force, to institute a new state, will only encounter the silent and infinitely accommodating welcome of the law. The law does not change: it subsided into the grave once and for all, and each of its forms is only a metamorphosis of that never-ending death. Sorge wears a mask from Greek tragedy—he has a threatening and pitiful mother like Clytemnestra, a dead father, a sister relentless in her mourning, an all-powerful and insidious father-in-law. He is Orestes in submission, an Orestes whose concern is to escape the law in order better to submit himself to it. In that he insists on living in the plague quarter, he is also a god who consents to die among humans, but who cannot succeed in dying and therefore leaves the promise of the law empty, creating a silence rent by the profoundest of screams: where is the law, what does the law do? And when, by virtue of a new metamorphosis or a new sinking into his own identity, he is recognized, named, denounced, venerated, ridiculed by a woman bearing a strange resemblance to his sister, at that moment, he, the possessor of every name, is transformed into something unnameable, an absent absence, the amorphous presence of the void and the mute horror of that presence. But perhaps this death of God is the opposite of death (the ignominy of a limp and slimy thing twitching for all eternity); and the gesture with which he kills her finally liberates his language—a language that has nothing more to say than the "I speak, I am speaking now" of the law, indefinitely prolonged by the simple fact of that language's proclamation in the outside of its muteness.

EURYDICE AND THE SIRENS

The law averts its face and returns to the shadows the instant one looks at it; when one tries to hear its words, what one catches is a song that is no more than the fatal promise of a future song.

The Sirens are the elusive and forbidden form of the alluring voice. They are nothing but song. Only a silvery wake in the sea, the hollow of a wave, a cave in the rocks, the whiteness of the beach—what are they in their very being if not a pure appeal, if not the mirthful void of listening, if not attentiveness, if not an invitation to pause? Their music is the opposite of a hymn: no presence shimmers in their immortal words; only the promise of a future song accompanies their melody. What makes them seductive is less what they make it possible to hear than what sparkles in the remoteness of their words, the future of what they say. Their fascination is due not to their current song but to what it promises to be. What the Sirens promise to sing to Ulysses is his own past exploits, transformed into a poem for the future: "We know all the suffering, all the suffering inflicted by the gods on the people of Argos and Troy on the fields of Troad." Presented as though in negative outline, the song is but the attraction of song; yet what it promises the hero is nothing other than a duplicate of what he has lived through, known, and suffered, precisely what he himself is. A promise at once deceptive and truthful. It lies because all those who surrender to seduction and steer their ships toward the beach will only meet death. But it speaks the truth in that it is death that enables the song to sound and endlessly recount the heroes' adventure. Yet one must refuse to hear this song so pure—so pure that it says nothing more than its own devouring withdrawal—that one must plug one's ears, pass by it as if one were deaf, in order to live and thus begin to sing. Or, rather, in order for the narrative that will never die to be born, one must listen but remain at the mast, wrists and ankles tied; one must vanquish all desire by a trick that does violence to itself; one must experience all suffering by remaining at the threshold of the alluring abyss; one must finally find oneself beyond song, as if one had crossed death while still alive only to restore it in a second language.

Then there is the figure of Eurydice. She would seem to be the exact opposite, since she must be summoned back from the shadows by the melody of a song capable of seducing and lulling death, and since the hero is unable to resist Eurydice's power of enchantment, of which she herself is the saddest victim. Yet she is a close relative of the Sirens: just as they sing only the future of a song, she shows only the promise of a face. Orpheus may have succeeded in quieting barking dogs and beguiling sinister forces, but on the return trip he should have been chained like Ulysses or as unperceiving as his sailors. In fact, he was the hero and his crew combined in a single character: he was seized by the forbidden desire and untied himself with his own hands, letting the invisible face disappear into the shadows, just as Ulysses let the song he did not hear vanish in the waves. Each of their voices is then freed: Ulysses' with his salvation and the possibility of telling the tale of his marvelous adventure; Orpheus's with his absolute loss and never-ending lament. But it is possible that behind Ulysses' triumphant narrative there prevails the inaudible lament of not having listened better and longer, of not having ventured as close as possible to the wondrous voice that might have finished the song. And that behind Orpheus's laments shines the glory of having seen, however fleetingly, the unattainable face at the very instant it turned away and returned to darkness – a nameless, placeless hymn to the light.

These two figures are profoundly interwoven in Blanchot's work.[6] Some of his narratives, for example *L'Arrêt de mort*, are dedicated to the gaze of Orpheus: the gaze that at the wavering threshold of death goes in search of the submerged presence and tries to bring its image back to the light of day, but secures only the nothingness in which the poem can subsequently appear. In Blanchot, however, Orpheus does not see Eurydice's face in a movement that conceals it and makes it visible: he is able to contemplate it face to face; he sees with his own eyes the open gaze of death, "the most terrible gaze a living thing can encounter." It is that gaze, or rather the narrator's gaze into that gaze, that exerts an extraordinary power of attraction; it is what makes a second woman appear in the middle of the night in an already-captive state of stupefaction and forces her to wear the plaster mask allowing one to contemplate "face to face that which lives eternally." The gaze of Orpheus acquires the fatal power that sang in the voice of the Sirens. Similarly, the narrator of *Au Moment voulu* goes in search of Judith in the forbidden place where she is imprisoned; against all expectations, he easily finds her, like an overly close Eurydice who offers herself in an impossible, happy return. But the figure lurking in the background who guards her, and from which Orpheus comes to wrest her, is less a dark and inflexible goddess than a pure voice: "Indifferent and neutral, withdrawn into a vocal realm where she is so completely stripped of superfluous perfections that she seems deprived of herself: just, but in a way reminiscent of justice ruled by every negative destiny."[7] Is not this voice – which "sings blankly" and

offers so little to be heard–the voice of the Sirens, whose seductive-
ness resides in the void they open, in the fascinated immobility seizing all who listen?

THE COMPANION

At the first signs of attraction, when the withdrawal of the desired face
remains sketchy, when the firmness of the solitary voice is just beginning to stand out against the blur of the murmur, something like a
sweet and violent movement intrudes on interiority, drawing it out of
itself, turning it around, bringing forth next to it–or rather right behind it–the background figure of a companion who always remains
hidden but always makes it patently obvious that he is there; a double
that keeps his distance, an accosting resemblance. The instant that
interiority is lured out of itself, an outside empties the place into
which interiority customarily retreats and deprives it of the possibility
of retreat: a form arises–less than a form, a kind of stubborn, amorphous anonymity–that divests interiority of its identity, hollows it out,
divides it into noncoincident twin figures, divests it of its unmediated
right to say *I*, and pits against its discourse a speech that is indissociably echo and denial. To lend an ear to the silvery voice of the Sirens, to
turn toward the forbidden face that has already concealed itself, is not
simply to abandon the world and the distraction of appearance; it is
suddenly to feel grow within oneself a desert at the other end of which
(but this immeasurable distance is also as thin as a line) gleams a
language without an assignable subject, a godless law, a personal pronoun without a person, an eyeless expressionless face, an other that is
the same. Does the principle of attraction secretly reside in this tear
and this bond? When one thought that one was being drawn out of
oneself by an inaccessible remoteness, was it not simply that this
mute presence was bearing down in the shadows with all its inevitable weight? The empty outside of attraction is perhaps identical to
the nearby outside of the double. That would make the companion
attraction at the height of its dissimulation: it is dissimulated because
it presents itself as a pure, close, stubborn, redundant presence, as
one figure too many; and because it repels more than it attracts, because one must keep it at a distance, because there is always the
danger that one will be absorbed by it and compromised by it in
boundless confusion. This means that the companion acts both as a

demand to which one is never equal and a weight of which one would like to rid oneself. One is irretrievably bound to the companion with a familiarity that is hard to bear; yet one must draw still closer to him and create a bond with him different from the absence of ties that attaches one to him through the faceless form of absence.

This figure is infinitely reversible. Is the companion an unacknowledged guide? Is he a law that is manifest but is not visible as law? Or does he constitute a heavy mass, an encumbering inertia, a slumber threatening to engulf all vigilance? No sooner does Thomas enter the house to which he has been attracted by a half-made gesture and an ambiguous smile than he receives a strange double (is this what, according to the meaning of the title, is "God-given"?): the double's apparently wounded face is only the outline of a face tattooed over his, and in spite of hideous flaws, he retains something like "a reflection of former beauty." Does he know the secrets of the house better than anyone else, as he will boast at the end of the novel? Is not his apparent fatuousness but a silent awaiting of the question? Is he a guide or a prisoner? Does he count among the inaccessible powers that dominate the house, or is he only a domestic? His name is *Dom*. He is invisible and falls silent whenever Thomas addresses a third party, and soon disappears entirely; but when Thomas seems to have finally gained entry to the house, when he thinks he has found the face and voice he was seeking, when he is being treated as a domestic, Dom reappears in possession of, or claiming to be in possession of, the law and speech: Thomas had been wrong to have had so little faith, to have failed to question he who was there to respond, to have squandered his zeal on his wish to gain access to the upper stories, when it would have been enough for him to allow himself to go down. The more choked Thomas's voice becomes, the more Dom speaks, assuming the right to speak and to speak for him. All of language totters; when Dom uses the first person, it is actually Thomas's language that is speaking, without him, in the void that the wake of his visible absence leaves in a darkness connected to dazzling light.

The companion is also indissociably what is closest and farthest away. In *Le Très-haut* he is represented by Dorte, the man from "down there"; he is a stranger to the law and stands outside the order of the city; he is illness in its raw state, disseminated death infusing life; by contrast to the "Most High" of the title he is "Most Low"; and yet he is obsessively close; he is unreservedly familiar; he freely confides; he is inexhaustibly and multiply present; he is the eternal neighbor; the sound of his cough carries across doors and walls; his death throes resound through the house; and in this world oozing moisture, water rising on all sides, Dorte's flesh itself, his fever and sweat, cross the partition to stain Sorge's room next door. When he finally dies, howling in one last transgression that he is not dead, his scream goes out into the hand that muffles it, forever vibrating in Sorge's fingers. Sorge's flesh and bones, his body, will long remain that death, and the cry that contests and confirms it.

It is in this movement which is the pivot of language that the essence of the stubborn companion is most clearly manifested. The companion is not a privileged interlocutor, some other speaking subject; he is the nameless limit language reaches. That limit, however, is in no way positive; it is instead the deep into which language is forever disappearing only to return identical to itself, the echo of a different discourse that says the same thing, of the same discourse saying something else. "*Celui qui ne m'accompagnait pas*" ("he who did not accompany me") has no name (and wishes to be kept in that essential anonymity); he is a faceless, gazeless *he* who can only see through the language of another whom he submits to the order of his own night; he edges as close as can be to the *I* that speaks in the first person, and whose words and phrases he repeats in an infinite void. Yet there is no bond between them; an immeasurable distance separates them. That is why he who says *I* must continually approach him in order finally to meet the companion who does not accompany him and who forms no bond with him that is positive enough to be manifested by being untied. There is no pact to tie them to each other; yet they are powerfully linked by a constant questioning (describe what you see, are you writing now?) and by the uninterrupted discourse manifesting the impossibility of responding. It is as if this withdrawal, this hollowness that is perhaps nothing more than the inexorable erosion of the person who speaks, cleared a neutral space of language. The narrative plunges into the space between the narrator and the inseparable companion who does not accompany him; it runs the full length of the straight line separating the speaking *I* from the *he* he is in his spoken being; it unfolds a placeless place that is the outside of all speech and writing, that brings them forth and dispossesses them, that imposes its law on them, that manifests through its infinite unraveling their momentary gleaming and sparkling disappearance.

NEITHER ONE NOR THE OTHER

Despite several consonances, we are quite far from the experience through which some are wont to lose themselves in order to find themselves. The characteristic movement of mysticism is to attempt to join—even if it means crossing the night—the positivity of an existence by opening a difficult line of communication with it. Even when that existence contents itself, hollows itself out in the labor of its own negativity, infinitely withdrawing into a lightless day, a shadowless night, a visibility devoid of shape, it is still a shelter in which experience can rest. The shelter is created as much by the law of a Word as by the open expanse of silence. For in the form of the experience, silence is the immeasurable, inaudible, primal breath from which all manifest discourse issues; or speech is a reign with the power to hold itself in silent suspense.

The experience of the outside has nothing to do with that. The movement of attraction and the withdrawal of the companion lay bare what precedes all speech, what underlies all silence: the continuous streaming of language. A language spoken by no one: any subject it may have is no more than a grammatical fold. A language not resolved by any silence: any interruption is only a white stain on its seamless sheet. It opens a neutral space in which no existence can take root. Mallarmé taught us that the word is the manifest nonexistence of what it designates; we now know that the being of language is the visible effacement of the one who speaks: "Saying that I hear these words would not explain for me the dangerous strangeness of my relations with them. . . . They do not speak, they are not inside; on the contrary, they lack all intimacy and lie entirely outside. What they designate consigns me to this outside of all speech, seemingly more secret and more inward than the inner voice of conscience. But that outside is empty, the secret has no depth, what is repeated is the emptiness of repetition, it does not speak and yet has always been said."[8] The experiences Blanchot narrates lead to this anonymity of language liberated and opened to its own boundlessness. What they find in that murmuring space is less an endpoint than the site without geography of their possible rebeginning: hence the direct and luminous, at last serene, question Thomas asks at the end of *Aminadab* when all speech seems to be denied him; and the pure flash of the empty promise—"now I am speaking"—in *Le Très-Haut*; and the appearance in the final pages of *Celui qui ne m'accompagnait pas* of a smile that has no face but is worn at last by a silent name; or the first contact with the words of the subsequent rebeginning at the end of *Le Dernier Homme.*

Language is then freed from all of the old myths by which our awareness of words, discourse, and literature has been shaped. For a long time it was thought that language had mastery over time, that it acted both as the future bond of the promise and as memory and narrative; it was thought to be prophecy and history; it was also thought that in its sovereignty it could bring to light the eternal and visible body of truth; it was thought that its essence resided in the form of words or in the breath that made them vibrate. In fact, it is only a formless rumbling, a streaming; its power resides in dissimulation. That is why it is one with the erosion of time; it is depthless forgetting and the transparent emptiness of waiting.

Language, its every word, is indeed directed at contents that preexist it; but in its own being, provided that it holds as close to its being as possible, it only unfolds in the pureness of the wait. Waiting is directed at nothing: any object that could gratify it would only efface it. Still, it is not confined to one place, it is not a resigned immobility; it has the endurance of a movement that will never end and would never promise itself the reward of rest; it does not wrap itself in interiority; all of it falls irremediably outside. Waiting cannot wait for itself at the end of its own past, nor rejoice in its own patience, nor steel itself once and for all, for it was never lacking in courage. What takes it up is not memory but forgetting. This forgetting, however, should not be confused with the scatteredness of distraction or the slumber of vigilance; it is a wakefulness so alert, so lucid, so new that it is a goodbye to night and a pure opening onto a day to come. In this respect forgetting is extreme attentiveness – so extreme that it effaces any singular face that might present itself to it. Once defined, a form is simultaneously too old and too new, too strange and too familiar, not to be instantly rejected by the purity of the wait, and thereby condemned to the immediacy of forgetting. It is in forgetting that the wait remains a waiting: an acute attention to what is radically new, with no bond of resemblance or continuity with anything else (the newness of the wait drawn outside of itself and freed from any past); attention to what is most profoundly old (for deep down the wait has never stopped waiting).

Language–in its attentive and forgetful being, with its power of dissimulation that effaces every determinate meaning and even the existence of the speaker, in the gray neutrality that constitutes the essential hiding place of all being and thereby frees the space of the image–is neither truth nor time, neither eternity nor man; it is instead the always undone form of the outside. It places the origin in contact with death, or rather brings them both to light in the flash of their infinite oscillation–a momentary contact in a boundless space. The pure outside of the origin, if that is indeed what language is eager to greet, never solidifies into a penetrable and immobile positivity; and the perpetually rebegun outside of death, although carried toward the light by the essential forgetting of language, never sets the limit at which truth would finally begin to take shape. They immediately flip sides. The origin takes on the transparency of the endless; death opens interminably onto the repetition of the beginning. And what language *is* (not what it means, not the form in which it says what it means), what language is in its being, is that softest of voices, that nearly imperceptible retreat, that weakness deep inside and surrounding every thing and every face–what bathes the belated effort of the origin and the dawnlike erosion of death in the same neutral light, at once day and night. Orpheus's murderous forgetting, Ulysses' wait in chains, are the very being of language.

At a time when language was defined as the place of truth and the bond of time, it was placed in absolute peril by the Cretan Epimenides' assertion that all Cretans were liars: the way in which that discourse was bound to itself undid any possibility of truth. On the other hand, when language is revealed to be the reciprocal transparency of the origin and death, every single existence receives, through the simple assertion "I speak," the threatening promise of its own disappearance, its future appearance.

NOTES

1   Maurice Blanchot, *Celui qui ne m'accompagnait pas* (Paris: Gallimard, 1953), p. 125 [*The One Who Was Standing Apart From Me*, trans. Lydia Davis (Barrytown, N.Y.: Station Hill, 1993), pp. 66–67].

2   Blanchot, *L'Attente l'oubli* (Paris: Gallimard, 1962), p. 162.

3   Blanchot, *Aminadab* (Paris: Gallimard, 1942), p. 235.

4   Ibid., p. 122.

5　Blanchot, *Le Très-Haut* (Paris: Gallimard, 1948), p. 81.

6　See Blanchot, *L'Espace littéraire* (Paris: Gallimard, 1955), pp. 179–184; and *Le Livre à venir* (Paris: Gallimard, 1955), pp. 9–17 [cf. "The Gaze of Orpheus" and "The Song of the Sirens," in Blanchot, *The Gaze of Orpheus*, trans. Lydia Davis (Barrytown, N.Y.: Station Hill, 1981), pp. 99–104 and 105–13].

7　Blanchot, *Au Moment voulu* (Paris: Gallimard, 1951), pp. 68–69.

8　Blanchot, *Celui qui ne m'accompagnait pas*, pp. 136–37 [*The One Who Was Standing Apart From Me*, p. 72].

C.B. What do André Breton and Surrealism represent for a philosopher of 1966 who concerns himself with language and with knowledge?

M.F. I have the impression that there are two great families of founders. There are the builders who place the first stone, and there are the diggers and excavators. Perhaps in our uncertain space, we are closer to those who excavate: to Nietzsche (instead of Husserl), to Klee (instead of Picasso). Breton belongs to that family. To be sure, the Surrealist institution masked the silent gestures that cleared the space in front of them. Perhaps that was only the Surrealist game, the Surrealist mystification: to clear the ground by means of rituals that seemed to exclude, to enlarge the wilderness by laying down boundaries that looked imperious. In any case, we are presently in the hollow space that Breton left behind him.

C.B. Is that hollow space already old?

M.F. For a long time I experienced Breton's image as that of a dead man; not that he would have ceased to be alive or to affect us, but because his admirable existence created around it and radiating from it the immense void in which we are now lost. I have the impression that we have lived, walked, run, danced, made signs and gestures to which there was no response in the sacred space that surrounded the shrine of Breton, stretched out immobile and covered with gold. I

---

*This interview, conducted by C. Bonnefoy, originally appeared in *Arts et loisirs* 54(5–11 October 1966), pp. 8–9. Robert Hurley's translation.

don't mean to say that he was far away from us, but that we were close to him, in the power of his dark specter. Breton's death, now, is like the reduplication of our own birth. Breton was, is, an all-powerful dead man who is quite close, as Agamemnon was for the Atridae (that is, for every Greek). There you have Breton's profile as it looks to me.

c.b.   That quasi-sacred presence of Breton, that hollow left by Surrealism do not belong to magic or the imaginary, but presuppose an essential contribution to contemporary thought. What does the latter owe to Breton?

m.f.   The most important thing, in my view, is that Breton established a clear communication between these two figures which had long been estranged, writing and knowledge. Before him, French literature could well be concocted of observations, analysis, ideas; it was never—except in Diderot—a literature of knowledge. That is the big difference, I think, between German and French culture. Breton bringing knowledge into expression (with psychoanalysis, ethnology, art history, and so on) is, in a sense, our Goethe. There is an image that needs to be obliterated, I think—that of Breton as a poet of unreason. A different one should be placed, not over against it, but on top of it, that of Breton as a writer of knowledge.

But this dismissal of literature as a delectable ignorance (in the manner of Gide) is affirmed by Breton in a singular way. For the Germans (Goethe, Thomas Mann, Hermann Broch), literature is knowledge when it is an enterprise of internalization, of memory: it is a matter of making a calm and exhaustive recollection of what has been learned [*connaissance*], of appropriating the world, of reducing it to the measure of man. For Breton, on the contrary, writing become knowledge (and knowledge become writing) is a means of pushing man beyond his limits, of forcing him to face the insuperable, of placing him near to what is farthest away from him. Hence the interest he brought to bear on the unconscious, on madness, on dreams.

c.b.   Like the German Romantics?

m.f.   Yes, but the dreams of the German Romantics are the night illuminated by the light of wakefulness, whereas for Breton dreams are the unbreakable core of the night placed at the heart of the day. I have the impression that this wonderful abolition of the division between knowledge and writing has been very important for contemporary expression. As a matter of fact, we are in a time when the activity of writing [*l'écrire*] and knowledge are profoundly intermingled, as is shown by the works of Michel Leiris, Pierre Klossowski, Michel Butor, Jean-Pierre Faye, and others.

C.B.   Isn't there, for Breton, a power of writing?

M.F.   For Breton, I think, writing in itself, the book in its white flesh have the power to change the world. Up to the end of the nineteenth century, language and writing were transparent instruments in which the world was reflected, decomposed, and recomposed; in any case, writing and discourse formed part of the world. But perhaps there is a writing so radical and so sovereign that it manages to face up to the world, to counterbalance it, to offset it, even to utterly destroy it and scintillate outside it. Actually, this experience begins to appear rather clearly in *Ecce homo* and in Stéphane Mallarmé. This experience of the book as an antiworld is reencountered in Breton and it has contributed substantially to changing the status of writing. And it has done so in two ways. First, Breton remoralized writing, as it were, by demoralizing it completely. The ethic of writing no longer comes from what one has to say, from the ideas that one expresses, but from the very act of writing. In that raw and naked act, the writer's freedom is fully committed at the same time as the counteruniverse of words takes form.

Further, at the same time that writing is remoralized, it begins to exist in a kind of rocklike solidity. It asserts itself apart from everything that might be said through it. Which explains, no doubt, the rediscovery by Breton of the whole dynasty of imagination that French literature had driven out: the imagination is not so much what is born in the obscure heart of man as it is what arises in the luminous thickness of discourse. And Breton, a swimmer between two words, traverses an imaginary space that had never been discovered before him.

C.B.   But how do you explain the fact that in certain periods Breton was taken up with political commitment?

M.F.   I was always struck by the fact that what is at issue in his work is not history but revolution; not politics but the absolute power to change life. The deep incompatibility between Marxists and existentialists of the Sartean type, on the one hand, and Breton on the other, comes no doubt from the fact that for Marx or Sartre writing forms part of the world, whereas for Breton a book, a sentence, a word may by themselves constitute the antimatter of the world and counterbalance the whole universe.

C.B.   But didn't Breton grant as much importance to life as he did to writing? Isn't there, in *Nadja*, in *L'Amour fou*, in *Les Vases communicants* a sort of continuous osmosis between writing and life, between life and writing?

M.F.   While Breton's other discoveries were already at least prefigured in Goethe, in Nietzsche, Mallarmé or others, what we really owe to him alone is the discovery of a space that is not that of philosophy, nor of literature, nor of art, but that of experience. We are now in a time when experience – and the thought that is inseparable from it – are developing with an extraordinary richness, in both a unity and a dispersion that wipe out the boundaries of provinces that were once well established.

There is no doubt that the whole network connecting the works of Breton, Georges Bataille, Leiris, and Blanchot, and extending through the domains of ethnology, art history, the history of religions, linguistics, and psychoanalysis, are effacing the rubrics in which our culture classified itself, and revealing unforeseen kinships, proximities, and relations. It is very probable that we owe this new scattering and this new unity of our culture to the person and the work of André Breton. He was both the spreader and the gatherer of all this agitation in modern experience.

This discovery of the domain of experience enabled Breton to be completely outside literature, to contest not only all the existing literary works, but the very existence of literature; but it also enabled him to open up to possible languages domains that had remained silent and marginal until then.

DIFFERENT SPACES*

As we know, the great obsession of the nineteenth century was history: themes of development and arrest, themes of crisis and cycle, themes of accumulation of the past, a great overload of dead people, the threat of global cooling. The second principle of thermodynamics supplied the nineteenth century with the essential core of its mythological resources. The present age may be the age of space instead. We are in an era of the simultaneous, of juxtaposition, of the near and the far, of the side-by-side, of the scattered. We exist at a moment when the world is experiencing, I believe, something less like a great life that would develop through time than like a network that connects points and weaves its skein. Perhaps we may say that some of the ideological conflicts that drive today's polemics are enacted between the devoted descendants of time and the fierce inhabitants of space. Structuralism, or at least what is grouped under that somewhat general name, is the effort to establish, between elements that may have been distributed over time, a set of relations that makes them appear juxtaposed, opposed, implied by one another, that makes them appear, in short, like a kind of configuration. And this does not really amount to a denial of time; it is a certain way of handling what is called time and what is called history.

It should be made clear, however, that the space now appearing on the horizon of our concerns, of our theory, of our systems, is not an

---

*This is the text of a lecture presented to the Architectural Studies Circle 14 March 1967; it was first published until 1984. (See *Architecture, Mouvement, Continuité* 5 [October 1984], pp. 46–49). Robert Hurley's translation.

innovation. Space itself, in the Western experience, has a history, and one cannot fail to take note of this inevitable interlocking of time with space. It could be said, to retrace very crudely this history of space, that in the Middle Ages there was a hierarchized ensemble of places: sacred places and profane places, protected places and, on the contrary, places that were open and defenseless, urban places and country places (speaking of people's real life); for cosmological theory, there were supracelestial places as opposed to the celestial place, which contrasted in turn with the terrestrial place. There were places where things were placed because they had been violently displaced and then places, on the contrary, where things found their natural emplacement and their natural rest. It was this whole hierarchy, this opposition, this interconnection of places that constituted what might be called, very roughly, medieval space–a space of localization.

This space of localization opened up with Galileo, for the real scandal of Galileo's work was not so much in having discovered, or rather rediscovered, that the earth revolves around the sun, but in having constituted a space that was infinite, and infinitely open–so that the medieval place was dissolved in it, as it were. A thing's place was no longer anything but a point in its motion, just as a thing's rest was nothing more than its motion indefinitely slowed down. To put it differently, starting from Galileo, from the seventeenth century, extension supplanted localization.

In our day, emplacement is supplanting extension which itself replaced localization. Emplacement is defined by the relations of proximity between points or elements. In formal terms these can be described as series, trees, lattices.

Further, we are aware of the importance of problems of emplacement in contemporary engineering: the storage of information or of the partial results of a calculation in the memory of a machine, the circulation of discrete elements, with a random output (such as, quite simply, automobiles or in fact the tones on a telephone line), the identification of tagged or coded elements in an ensemble that is either distributed haphazardly or sorted in a univocal classification, or sorted according to a plurivocal classification, and so on.

More concretely still, for people the problem of place or emplacement is posed in terms of demography; and this last problem of human emplacement is not just the question of knowing if there will be enough space for man in the world–a problem that is very important after all – but also the problem of knowing what relations of proximity, what type of storage, of circulation, of identification, of classification of human elements are to be preferentially retained in this or that situation to obtain this or that result. We are in an age when space is presented to us in the form of relations of emplacement.

In any case, I think that today's anxiety concerns space in a fundamental way, no doubt much more than time. Time probably only appears as one of the possible games of distribution between the elements that are spread out in space.

Now, in spite of all the techniques of investment, in spite of the whole network of knowledge that enable us to determine it or formalize it, contemporary space is perhaps not yet entirely desacralized – unlike time, no doubt, which was desacralized in the nineteenth century. To be sure, there was a certain theoretical desacralization of space (signaled at the start by the work of Galileo), but perhaps we have not yet arrived at a practical desacralization of space. And perhaps our life is still dominated by a certain number of oppositions that cannot be tampered with, that institutions and practices have not ventured to change – oppositions we take for granted, for example, between private space and public space, between the family space and social space, between cultural space and useful space, between the space of leisure activities and the space of work. All these are still controlled by an unspoken sacralization.

The enormous work of Gaston Bachelard and the descriptions of the phenomenologists have taught us that we are living not in a homogeneous and empty space but, on the contrary, in a space that is laden with qualities, a space that may also be haunted by fantasy. The space of our first perception, that of our reveries, that of our passions harbors qualities that are all but intrinsic; it is a light, ethereal, transparent space, or rather a somber, harsh, cluttered space. It is a space from on high, it is a space of peaks, or, on the contrary, it is a space from below, a space of mire, it is a space that can be fluid like running water, it is a space that can be fixed, solidified like stone or crystal.

And yet these analyses, though they are fundamental for contemporary reflection, are concerned primarily with internal space. I would like to speak now of the space outside [*du dehors*].

The space in which we are living, by which we are drawn outside ourselves, in which, as a matter of fact, the erosion of our life, our time, and our history takes place, this space that eats and scrapes away at us, is also heterogeneous space in itself. In other words, we do not live in a kind of void, within which individuals and things might be located. We do not live in a void that would be tinged with shimmering colors, we live inside an ensemble of relations that define emplacements that are irreducible to each other and absolutely nonsuperposable.

Of course, one could attempt to describe these different emplacements, looking for the set of relations by which a particular emplacement might be defined. For example, describe the set of relations that define emplacements of transit, streets, trains (a train is an extraordinary bundle of relations, since it's something through which one passes; it is also something by which one can pass from one point to another, and then it is something that passes by). One could describe, through the bundle of relations that make it possible to define them, those way stations that cafés, movie theaters, and beaches constitute. One could also describe, through their web of relations, the emplacement of repose, closed or semiclosed, formed by the house, the room, the bed, and so on. But what interests me among all these emplacements are certain ones that have the curious property of being connected to all the other emplacements, but in such a way that they suspend, neutralize, or reverse the set of relations that are designated, reflected, or represented [*réflechis*] by them. Those spaces which are linked with all the others, and yet at variance somehow with all the other emplacements, are of two great types.

First, there are the utopias. Utopias are emplacements having no real place. They are emplacements that maintain a general relation of direct or inverse analogy with the real space of society. They are society perfected or the reverse of society, but in any case these utopias are spaces that are fundamentally and essentially unreal.

There are also, and probably in every culture, in every civilization, real places, actual places, places that are designed into the very institution of society, which are sorts of actually realized utopias in which the real emplacements, all the other real emplacements that can be found within the culture are, at the same time, represented, contested, and reversed, sorts of places that are outside all places, although they are actually localizable. Because they are utterly different from all the emplacements that they reflect or refer to, I shall call these places "heterotopias," as opposed to utopias; and I think that between utopias and these utterly different emplacements, these heterotopias, there must be a kind of mixed, intermediate experience, that would be the mirror. The mirror is a utopia after all, since it is a placeless place. In the mirror I see myself where I am not, in an unreal space that opens up virtually behind the surface; I am over there where I am not, a kind of shadow that gives me my own visibility, that enables me to look at myself there where I am absent – a mirror utopia. But it is also a heterotopia in that the mirror really exists, in that it has a sort of return effect on the place that I occupy. Due to the mirror, I discover myself absent at the place where I am, since I see myself over there. From that gaze which settles on me, as it were, I come back to myself and I begin once more to direct my eyes toward myself and to reconstitute myself there where I am. The mirror functions as a heterotopia in the sense that it makes this place I occupy at the moment I look at myself in the glass both utterly real, connected with the entire space surrounding it, and utterly unreal – since, to be perceived, it is obliged to go by way of that virtual point which is over there.

As for heterotopias, properly speaking, how might they be described? What meaning do they have? One could imagine, I won't say a "science," because that word is too compromised now, but a sort of systematic description that would have the object, in a given society, of studying, analyzing, describing, "reading," as people are fond of saying now, these different spaces, these other places, a kind of contestation, both mythical and real, of the space in which we live. This description could be called "heterotopology." As a first principle, let us submit that there is probably not a single culture in the world that does not establish heterotopias: that is a constant of every human group. But heterotopias obviously take forms that are very diverse, and perhaps one would not find a single form of heterotopia that is absolutely universal. They can be classed, however, into two major types.

In so-called primitive societies, there is a certain form of heterotopias that I would call "crisis heterotopias"; that is, there are privileged or sacred or forbidden places reserved for individuals who are in a state of crisis with respect to society and the human milieu in which they live. Adolescents, menstruating women, women in labor, old people, and so on.

In our society these crisis heterotopias have all but disappeared, though one still finds a few remnants of them. For example, the private secondary school, in its nineteenth-century form, or military service certainly played such a role for boys, the first manifestations of male sexuality needing to take place "elsewhere" than in the family. For girls there existed, until the middle of the twentieth century, a tradition that was called the "honeymoon trip" [*voyage des noces*]; this was an ancestral theme. The girl's deflowering could not take place "anywhere," and so the train, the honeymoon hotel, was indeed this anywhere place, this heterotopia without geographical coordinates.

But these crisis heterotopias are now disappearing and being replaced, I believe, by what could be called heterotopias of deviation: those in which individuals are put whose behavior is deviant with respect to the mean or the required norm. These are the rest homes, the psychiatric hospitals; they are also, of course, the prisons, to which we should probably add old people's homes, which are on the borderline, as it were, between the crisis heterotopia and the deviation heterotopia, since after all old age is a crisis and also a deviation, seeing that in our society, where leisure activity is the rule, idleness forms a kind of deviation.

The second principle of this description of heterotopias is that, in the course of its history, a society can make a heterotopia that exists and has not ceased to exist operate in a very different way; in fact, each heterotopia has a precise and specific operation within the society, and the same heterotopia can have one operation or another, depending on the synchrony of the culture in which it is found.

I will take as an example the curious heterotopia of the cemetery. The cemetery is certainly a different place compared with ordinary cultural spaces, and yet it is a space that is connected to all the other emplacements of the city or the society or the village, since every individual, every family happens to have relatives in the cemetery. The cemetery has practically always existed in Western culture, but it has undergone substantial mutations. Up to the end of the eighteenth century, the cemetery was placed in the very heart of the city, next to the church. A whole hierarchy of burial places existed there. You had the charnel house in which the corpses lost every trace of individuality; there were a few individual tombs; and then there were tombs inside the church. These tombs were themselves of two kinds. Either nothing more than slabs with an inscription or mausoleums with statues. This cemetery, which was lodged in the sacred space of the church, took on an altogether different look in modern civilizations; and, curiously, it was during the time when civilization became, as we say very roughly, "atheist," that Western culture inaugurated what is called the cult of the dead.

Basically, it was quite natural that at a time when people really believed in the resurrection of bodies and the immorality of the soul they did not attribute a cardinal importance to mortal remains. On the contrary, from the moment that one is no longer quite sure of having a soul, that the body will return to life, it may be necessary to devote much more attention to those mortal remains, which are finally the only trace of our existence in the midst of the world and in the midst of words.

In any case, it was in the nineteenth century that each person began to have the right to his little box for his little personal decomposition; but, further, it was only then that people began putting cemeteries at the edge of cities. In correlation with this individualization of death and the bourgeois appropriation of the cemetery, there emerged an obsession with death as a "disease." It was thought that the dead brought illness to the living, and that the presence and proximity of the dead right next to the houses, right next to the church, almost in the middle of the street, was responsible for the propagation of death itself. This great theme of disease spread by the contagion of cemeteries persisted at the end of the eighteenth century; and it was only in the course of the nineteenth century that cemeteries began to be moved toward outlying districts. Cemeteries then no longer constituted the sacred and immortal wind of the city, but the "other city" where each family possessed its dark dwelling.

A third principle. The heterotopia has the ability to juxtapose in a single real place several emplacements that are incompatible in themselves. Thus the theater brings onto the rectangle of the stage a whole succession of places that are unrelated to one another; in the same way, the cinema is a very curious rectangular hall at the back of which one sees a three-dimensional space projected onto a two-dimensional screen; but perhaps the oldest example of these heterotopias, in the form of contradictory emplacements, is the garden. One should bear in mind that in the East the garden, an amazing creation now thousands of years old, was deeply symbolic, with meanings that were superimposed, as it were. The traditional garden of the Persians was a sacred space that is said to have joined together within its rectangle four parts representing the four parts of the world, with a space even more sacred than the others which was like the umbilicus, the navel of the world at its center (this was the location of the basin and the fountain); and all the garden's vegetation was supposed to be distributed within that space, within that figurative microcosm. As for carpets, originally they were reproductions of gardens. The garden is a carpet in which the entire world attains its symbolic perfection, and the carpet is a kind of garden that moves through space. The garden is the smallest parcel of the world and the whole world at the same time. Since early antiquity the garden has been a sort of blissful and universalizing heterotopia (hence our zoological gardens).

Fourth principle. More often than not, heterotopias are connected with temporal discontinuities [*découpages du temps*]; that is, they open onto what might be called, for the sake of symmetry, heterochronias. The heterotopia begins to function fully when men are in a kind of absolute break with their traditional time; thus, the cemetery is indeed a highly heterotopian place, seeing that the cemetery begins with that strange heterochronia that loss of life constitutes for an individual, and that quasi eternity in which he perpetually dissolves and fades away.

Generally speaking, in a society like ours heterotopias and heterochronias are organized and arranged in a relatively complex way. First, there are heterotopias of time that accumulates indefinitely—for example, museums and libraries. Museums and libraries are heterotopias in which time never ceases to pile up and perch on its own summit, whereas in the seventeenth century, and up to the end of the seventeenth century still, museums and libraries were the expression of an individual choice. By contrast, the idea of accumulating everything, the idea of constituting a sort of general archive, the desire to contain all times, all ages, all forms, all tastes in one place, the idea of constituting a place of all times that is itself outside time and protected from its erosion, the project of thus organizing a kind of perpetual and indefinite accumulation of time in a place that will not move—well, in fact, all of this belongs to our modernity. The museum and the library are heterotopias that are characteristic of Western culture in the nineteenth century.

Opposite these heterotopias, which are linked to the accumulation of time, there are heterotopias that are linked, rather, to time in its most futile, most transitory and precarious aspect, and in the form of the festival. These are heterotopias that are not eternitary but absolutely chronic. Such are the fairs, those marvelous empty emplacements on the outskirts of cities that fill up once or twice a year with booths, stalls, unusual objects, wrestlers, snake ladies, fortune tellers. And, just recently, a new chronic heterotopia has been invented, the vacation village, those Polynesian villages which offer three short weeks of a primitive and eternal nudity to city dwellers. And you can see, moreover, that the two forms of heterotopia, the heterotopia of the festival and that of an eternity of accumulating time are combined: the straw huts of Djerba are in one sense akin to the libraries and the museums, for, by rediscovering Polynesian life one abolishes time, but time is also regained, the whole history of humanity goes back to its source as if in a kind of grand immediate knowledge.

A fifth principle. Heterotopias always presuppose a system of opening and closing that isolates them and makes them penetrable at the same time. In general, one does not gain entry to a heterotopian emplacement as if to a windmill. Either one is constrained to enter, which is the case with barracks and prisons, or one has to submit to rituals and purifications. One can enter only with a certain permission and after a certain number of gestures have been performed. There are even heterotopias that are entirely devoted to those purification activities, a half-religious half-hygienic purification as in Muslim baths, or an apparently purely hygienic purification as in Scandinavian saunas.

There are others, on the contrary, that look like pure and simple openings, but which generally conceal curious exclusions. Everybody can enter these heterotopian emplacements, but actually this is only an illusion: one believes he is going inside and, by the very fact of entering, one is excluded. I am thinking, for example, of those famous rooms that existed in the large farms of Brazil and, in general, of South America. The door for entering did not open onto the central room where the family lived, and every individual who passed by, every traveler had the right to push that door open, enter the room and sleep there one night. Now, these rooms were such that the individual who visited there never gained access to the heart of the family; he was absolutely the chance guest, he was not really the invited guest. This type of heterotopia, which has practically disappeared in our civilizations, might be reencountered in the famous American motel rooms where one enters with one's car and one's mistress and where unlawful sexuality is both absolutely sheltered and absolutely hidden, kept out of public view, and yet without being left to the open air.

Finally, the last trait of these heterotopias is that they have a function in relation to the remaining space. This function is spread between two extreme poles. Either the heterotopias have the role of creating a space of illusion that denounces all real space, all real emplacements within which human life is partitioned off, as being even more illusory. Perhaps it is this role that was played for a long time by those famous brothels which we are now deprived of. Or, on the contrary, creating a different space, a different real space as perfect, as meticulous, as well-arranged as ours is disorganized, badly arranged, and muddled. This would be the heterotopia not of illusion but of compensation, and I wonder if it is not somewhat in that manner that certain colonies functioned.

In some cases they played a heterotopian role at the level of the general organization of terrestrial space. I am thinking, for example, of those Puritan societies which the English founded in America during the first wave of colonization, which were other absolutely perfect places.

I'm also thinking of those extraordinary colonies of Jesuits that were founded in South America: marvelous, absolutely regulated colonies in which human perfection was effectively achieved. The Jesuits of Paraguay established colonies in which existence was regulated in every particular. The village was laid out according to a strict arrangement around a rectangular plaza with a church at the far end; on one side the secondary school, on the other the cemetery, and then, opposite the church, there began an avenue that a second avenue intersected at a right angle. The families each had their little hut along these two axes, and in this way the sign of Christ was exactly reproduced. Christianity thus marked the space and the geography of the American world with its fundamental sign.

The daily life of individuals was regulated not with the whistle but with the bell. Reveille was set for everybody at the same hour and work began for everybody at the same hour; meals were at noon and five o'clock; then one went to bed, and at midnight there was something called the conjugal wakeup, meaning that when the convent bell rang, everybody did his duty.

Brothels and colonies were two extreme types of heterotopia, and if you consider, for example, that the ship is a piece of floating space, a placeless place, that lives by its own devices, that is self-enclosed and, at the same time, delivered over to the boundless expanse of the ocean, and that goes from port to port, from watch to watch, from brothel to brothel, all the way to the colonies in search of the most precious treasures that lie waiting in their gardens, you see why for our civilization, from the sixteenth century up to our time, the ship has been at the same time not only the greatest instrument of economic development, of course (I'm not talking about that subject today), but the greatest reservoir of imagination. The sailing vessel is the heterotopia par excellence. In civilizations without ships the dreams dry up, espionage takes the place of adventure, and the police that of the corsairs.

THIS IS NOT A PIPE *

_____

TWO PIPES

The first version, that of 1926 I believe: a carefully drawn pipe, and underneath it (handwritten in a steady, painstaking, artificial script, a script from the convent, like that found heading the notebooks of schoolboys or on a blackboard after an object lesson), this note: "This is not a pipe."

The other version—the last, I assume—can be found in _Aube à l'antipode_.[a] The same pipe, same statement, same handwriting. But instead of being juxtaposed in a neutral, limitless, unspecified space, the text and the figure are set within a frame. The frame itself is placed upon an easel, and the latter in turn upon the clearly visible slats of the floors. Above everything, a pipe exactly like the one in the picture, but much larger.

The first version disconcerts us by its very simplicity. The second multiplies intentional ambiguities before our eyes. Standing upright against the easel and resting on wooden pegs, the frame indicates that this is an artist's painting: a finished work, exhibited and bearing for an eventual viewer the statement that comments on or explains it. And yet this naive handwriting, neither precisely the work's title nor one of its pictorial elements; the absence of any other trace of the artist's presence; the roughness of the ensemble; the wide slats of the

*This essay originally appeared in _Les Cahiers du chemin_ 2 (15 January 1968), pp. 79–105; the issue was devoted to René Magritte, who had died in the preceding year. The translation, by James Harkness, has been modified (see endnote b).

floor—everything suggests a blackboard in a classroom. Perhaps a swipe of the rag will soon erase the drawing and the text. Perhaps it will erase only one or the other, in order to correct the "error" (drawing something that will truly not be a pipe, or else writing a sentence affirming that this indeed is a pipe). A temporary slip (a "miswriting" suggesting a misunderstanding) that one gesture will dissipate in white dust?

But this is still only the least of the ambiguities; here are some others. There are two pipes. Or rather must we not say, two drawings of the same pipe? Or yet a pipe and the drawing of that pipe, or yet again two drawings each representing a different pipe? Or two drawings, one representing a pipe and the other not, or two more drawings yet, of which neither the one nor the other are or represent pipes?[b] And so I am surprised to find myself confusing *being* and *representing* as if they were equivalent, as if a sketch were what it represents; and I see well that were I to have to—and I must—dissociate carefully (as the Port Royal *Logic* has asked me to do for more than three centuries) a representation from what it represents, I should have to take up all the hypotheses I just proposed again, and multiply them by two.

But it still strikes me that the pipe represented in the drawing—blackboard or canvas, little matter—this "lower" pipe is wedged solidly in a space of visible reference points: width (the written text, the upper and lower borders of the frame) and depth (the grooves of the floor). A stable prison. On the other hand, the higher pipe lacks coordinates. Its enormous proportions render uncertain its location (an opposite effect to that found in *Tombeau des lutteurs* [*The Wrestlers' Tomb*], where the gigantic is caught inside the most precise space). Is the disproportionate pipe drawn in front of the painting, which itself rests far in back? Or, indeed, is it suspended just above the easel like an emanation, a mist just detaching itself from the painting—pipe smoke taking the form and roundness of a pipe, thus opposing and resembling the pipe (according to the same play of analogy and contrast found between the vaporous and the solid in the series *La Bataille de l'Argonne* [*The Battle of the Argonne*])? Or might we not suppose, in the end, that the pipe floats behind the painting and the easel, more gigantic than it appears? In that case, would it be its uprooted depth, the inner dimension rupturing the canvas (or panel) and slowly, in a space henceforth without reference point, expanding to infinity?

About even this ambiguity, however, I am ambiguous. Or, rather, what appears to me very dubious is the simple opposition between the higher pipe's dislocated buoyancy and the stability of the lower one. Looking a bit more closely, we easily discern that the feet of the easel, supporting the frame where the canvas is held and where the drawing is lodged – these feet, resting upon a floor made certain and visible by its own coarseness, are in fact beveled. They touch only by three tiny points, robbing the ensemble, itself somewhat ponderous, of all stability. An impending fall? The collapse of easel, frame, canvas or panel, drawing, text? Splintered wood, fragmented shapes, letters scattered one from another until words can perhaps no longer be reconstituted? All this litter on the ground, while above, the large pipe without measure or reference point will linger in its inaccessible, balloonlike immobility?

THE UNRAVELED CALLIGRAM

Magritte's drawing (for the moment I speak only of the first version) is as simple as a page borrowed from a botanical manual: a figure and the text that names it. Nothing is easier to recognize than a pipe, drawn thus; nothing is easier to say – our language knows it well in our place – than the "name of a pipe."[c] Now, what lends the figure its strangeness is not the "contradiction" between the image and the text. For a good reason: contradiction could exist only between two statements, or within one and the same statement. Here there is clearly but one, and it cannot be contradictory because the subject of the proposition is a simple demonstrative. False, then? But who would seriously contend that the collection of intersecting lines above the text *is* a pipe? Must we say: My God, how simpleminded! What misleads us is the inevitability of connecting the text to the drawing (as the demonstrative pronoun, the meaning of the word *pipe*, and the likeness of the image all invite us to do here) – and the impossibility of defining a perspective that would let us say that the assertion is true, false, or contradictory.

I cannot dismiss the notion that the sorcery here lies in an operation rendered invisible by the simplicity of its result, but which alone can explain the vague uneasiness provoked. The operation is a calligram that Magritte has secretly constructed, then carefully unraveled. Each element of the figure, their reciprocal position, and their relationship derive from this process, annulled as soon as it has been accomplished.

In its time-honored tradition, the calligram has a triple role: to augment the alphabet, to repeat something without the aid of rhetoric, to trap things in a double cipher. First, it brings a text and a shape as close together as possible. It is composed of lines delimiting the form of an object while also arranging the sequence of letters. It lodges statements in the space of a shape, and makes the text *say* what the drawing *represents.* On the one hand, it alphabetizes the ideogram, populates it with discontinuous letters, and thus interrogates the silence of uninterrupted lines. But, on the other hand, it distributes writing in a space no longer possessing the neutrality, openness, and inert blankness of paper. It forces the ideogram to arrange itself accordingly to the laws of a simultaneous form. For the blink of an eye, it reduces phoneticism to a mere gray murmur completing the contours of the shape; but it renders outline as a thin skin that must be pierced in order to follow, word for word, the outpouring of its internal text.

The calligram is thus tautological—but in opposition to rhetoric. The latter toys with the fullness of language. It uses the possibility of repeating the same thing in different words, and profits from the extra richness of language that allows us to say different things with a single word. The essence of rhetoric is in allegory. The calligram uses that capacity of letters to signify both as linear elements that can be arranged in space and as signs that must unroll according to a unique chain of sound. As a sign, the letter permits us to fix words; as line, it lets us give shape to things. Thus the calligram aspires playfully to efface the oldest oppositions of our alphabetical civilization: to show and to name; to shape and to say; to reproduce and to articulate; to imitate and to signify; to look and to read.

Pursuing its quarry by two paths, the calligram sets the most perfect trap. By its double function, it guarantees capture, as neither discourse alone nor a pure drawing could do. It banishes the invincible absence that defeats words, imposing on them, by the ruses of a writing at play in space, the visible form of their reference. Cleverly arranged on a sheet of paper, signs invoke the very thing of which they speak—from outside, by the margin they outline, by the emergence of their mass on the blank space of the page. And in return, visible form is excavated, furrowed by words that work at it from within, and which, dismissing the immobile, ambiguous, nameless presence, spin forth the web of significations that christen it, determine it, fix it in the universe of discourse. A double trap, unavoidable snare: How, henceforth, would the flight of birds, the transitory form of flowers, the falling rain escape?

And now Magritte's drawing. It seems to be created from the fragments of an unraveled calligram. Under the guise of reverting to a previous arrangement, it recovers its three functions – but in order to pervert them, thereby disturbing all the traditional bonds of language and the image.

After having invaded the figure in order to reconstitute the old ideogram, the text has now resumed its place. It has returned to its natural site – below the image, where it serves to support it, insert it in the series of texts and in the pages of the book. Once more it becomes a "legend." Form itself reascends to the ethereal realm from which the complicity of letters with space had forced it for an instant to descend. Free from all discursive attachment, it can float anew in its natural silence. We return to the page, and to its old principle of distribution – but only apparently. Because the words we now can read underneath the drawing are themselves drawn – images of words the painter has set apart from the pipe, but within the general (yet still undefinable) perimeter of the picture. From the calligraphic past, which I am quite obliged to extend to them, the words have conserved their logical relationship to the drawing, and their state as something drawn. Consequently, I must read them superimposed upon themselves. At the surface of the image, they form the reflection of a sentence saying that this is not a pipe. The image of a text. But, conversely, the represented pipe is drawn by the same hand and with the same pen as the letters of the text: it extends the writing more than it illustrates it or fills its void. We might imagine it brimming with small, chaotic letters, graphic signs reduced to fragments and dispersed over the entire surface of the image. A figure in the shape of writing. The invisible, preliminary calligraphic operation intertwined the writing and the drawing – and when Magritte restored things to their own places, he took care that the shape remain written, and that the text never be anything more than the drawn representation of itself.

The same for tautology. From calligraphic doubling, Magritte seemingly returns to the simple correspondence of the image with its legend. Without saying anything, a mute and adequately recognizable figure displays the object in its essence; from the image, a name written below receives its "meaning" or rule for usage. Now, compared to the traditional function of the legend, Magritte's text is doubly paradoxical. It sets out to name something that evidently does not need to be named (the form is too well known, the label too familiar). And at the moment when he should reveal the name, Magritte does so by denying that the object is what it is. Whence comes this strange game, if not from the calligram? From the calligram that says things twice (when once would doubtless do); from the calligram that, without seeming to do so, introduced a negative relationship between what it shows and what it represents. For, in sketching out a bouquet, a bird, or a downpour by a scattering of letters, the calligram never says of those hypocritically spontaneous forms that "this is a dove, a flower, a crashing downpour"; it avoids naming what the disposition of letters sketches. Show what happens through words, in the half silence of letters; do not say what these lines are which, at the borders of the text, limit it and carve it up. Once Magritte makes the text fall outside the image, it is up to the statement, for its own part, to recapture that negative relation, and to make it, in the syntax that belongs to it, a negation. The "not to say" that animates the calligram silently from inside is now said from the outside, in the verbal form of "not." But the text that runs beneath the pipe must simultaneously be able to say several things to the calligram that is hidden behind it.

"This" (the drawing, whose form you doubtless recognize and whose calligraphic heritage I have just traced) "is not" (is not substantially bound to . . . , is not constituted by . . . , does not cover the same material as . . .) "a pipe" (that is, this word from your language, made up of pronounceable sounds that translate the letters you are reading). Therefore, *This is not a pipe* can be read thus:

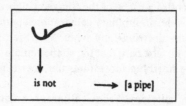

But, at the same time, the text states an entirely different thing: "This" (the statement arranging itself beneath your eyes in a line of discontinuous elements, of which *this* is both the signifier and the first word) "is not" (could neither equal nor substitute for . . . , could not adequately represent . . .) "a pipe" (one of the objects whose possible rendering can be seen above the text—interchangeable, anonymous, inaccessible to any name). Then we must read:

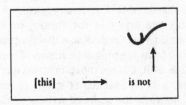

Now, on the whole, it easily seems that Magritte's statement is negated by the immediate and reciprocal dependency between the drawing of the pipe and the text by which the pipe can be named. Designation and design do not overlap one another, save in the calligraphic play hovering in the ensemble's background and conjured away simultaneously by the text, the drawing, and their current separation. Hence the third function of the statement: "This" (this ensemble constituted by a written pipe and a drawn text) "is not" (is incompatible with) "a pipe" (this mixed element springing at once from discourse and the image, whose ambiguous being the verbal and visual play of the calligram wants to evoke).

$$\text{This} \left\{ \begin{array}{c} \smallsmile \\ \text{[This is not a} \\ \text{pipe]} \end{array} \right\} \text{ is not } \left\{ \text{a} \quad \text{ipe} \right.$$

A third perturbation: Magritte reopened the trap the calligram had sprung on the thing it described. But in the act the object itself escaped. On the page of an illustrated book, we seldom pay attention to the small space running above the words and below the drawings, forever serving them as a common frontier for ceaseless crossings. It is there, on these few millimeters of white, the calm sand of the page, that are established all the relations of designation, nomination, description, classification. The calligram absorbed that interstice; but, once opened, it does not restore it. The trap shattered on emptiness: image and text fall each to its own side, of their own weight. No longer do they have a common ground nor a place where they can meet, where words are capable of taking shape and images of entering into lexical order. The slender, colorless, neutral strip, which in Magritte's drawing separates the text and the figure, must be seen as a crevasse—an uncertain, foggy region now dividing the pipe floating in its imagistic heaven from the mundane tramp of words marching in their successive line. Still, it is too much to claim that there is a blank or lacuna: instead, it is an absence of space, an effacement of the "common place" between the signs of writing and the lines of the image. The "pipe" that was at one with both the statement naming it and the drawing representing it—this shadow pipe knitting the lineaments of form with the fiber of words—has utterly vanished. A disappearance that from the other side of this chasm the text confirms sadly: This is not a pipe. In vain the now-solitary drawing imitates as closely as possible the shape ordinarily designated by the word *pipe*; in vain the text unfurls below the drawing with all the attentive fidelity of a label in a scholarly book. No longer can anything pass between them save the decree of divorce, the statement at once contesting the name of the drawing and the reference of the text.

On this basis, we can understand Magritte's second version of *This Is Not a Pipe*. In placing the drawing of the pipe and the statement serving as its legend on the very clearly defined surface of a picture (insofar as it is a painting, the letters are but the image of letters; insofar as it is a blackboard, the figure is only the didactic continuation of a discourse), in placing the picture on a thick, solid wood tripod, Magritte does everything necessary to reconstruct (either by the permanence of a work of art or else by the truth of an object lesson) the space common to language and the image. But this surface is contested at once: for the pipe that Magritte had, with so many precautions, brought near the text, that he had enclosed with the text in the institutional rectangle of the printing, has indeed taken flight. It is above, floating without reference, leaving between the text and the shape that one might have said to be at once the tie and the point of convergence to the horizon only a small empty space, the narrow furrow of its absence as the unsignaled mark of its escape. So, on its beveled and visibly unstable mounts, the easel had any longer but to tilt, the frame to loosen, the picture and the pipe to roll on the ground, the letters to be scattered. The commonplace – banal œuvre or mundane lesson – has disappeared.

KLEE, KANDINSKY, MAGRITTE

Two principles, I believe, ruled Western painting from the fifteenth to the twentieth century. The first asserts the separation between plastic representation (which implies resemblance) and linguistic reference (which excludes it). This distinction is typically made in such a way that it allows for one or the other of two forms of subordination. Either the text is ruled by the image (as in those paintings where a book, an inscription, a letter, or the name of a person are represented); or else the image is ruled by the text (as in books where a drawing completes, as if it were merely taking a short cut, the message that words are charged to represent). True, the subordination remains stable only very rarely. What happens to the text of the book is that it becomes merely a commentary on the image, and the linear channel, through words, of its simultaneous forms; and what happens to the picture is that it is dominated by a text, all of whose significations it figuratively illustrates. But no matter the meaning of the subordination or the manner in which it prolongs, multiplies, and reverses itself. What is essential is that verbal signs and visual representations are never given at once. An order always hierarchizes them. This is the principle whose sovereignty Klee abolished, by showing the juxtaposition of shapes and the syntax of signs in an uncertain, reversible, floating space (simultaneously page and canvas, plane and volume, notebook graph and ground survey, map and chronicle). He produced both systems of representation in the interweaving of just one fabric. In so doing (in contrast to the calligraphers, who reinforced the play of reciprocal subordinations even while multiplying it), he overturned their common space and undertook to build a new one.

The second principle posits an equivalence between the fact of resemblance and the affirmation of a representative bond. Let a figure resemble an object (or some other figure), let there be a relation of analogy between them, and that alone is enough for there to slip into the pure play of the painting a statement – obvious, banal, repeated a thousand times yet almost always silent. (It is like an infinite murmur – haunting, enclosing the silence of figures, investing it, mastering it, extricating the silence from itself, and finally reversing it within the domain of things that can be named.) "What you see is *that*." No matter, again, in what sense the representative relation is posed – whether the painting is referred to the visible world around it, or whether it independently establishes an invisible world that resembles itself. The essential point is that resemblance and affirmation cannot be dissociated. The rupture of this principle can be ascribed to Kandinsky: not because he had dissociated the terms but because he gave leave simultaneously to resemblance and the representation function.

No one, apparently, is further from Klee and Kandinsky than Magritte. More than any other his painting seems wedded to exact resemblances, to the point where they willfully multiply as if to assert themselves. It is not enough that the drawing of the pipe so closely resembles a pipe which in turn . . . and so on. A painting more committed than any other to the careful and cruel separation of graphic and plastic elements. If they happen to be superimposed within the painting like a legend and its image, it is on condition that the statement contest the obvious identity of the figure, and the name we are prepared to give it. And yet Magritte's art is not foreign to the enterprise of Klee and Kandinsky. Rather it constitutes, on the basis of a system common to them all, a figure at once opposed and complementary.

THE MUFFLED WORK OF WORDS

The exteriority of written and figurative elements, so obvious in Magritte, is symbolized by the nonrelation – or in any case by the very complex and problematic relation – between the painting and its title. This gulf, which prevents us from being both the reader and the viewer at the same time, brings the image into abrupt relief above the horizontal line of words. "The titles are chosen in such a way as to keep anyone from assigning my paintings to the familiar region that habitual thought appeals to in order to escape perplexity." A little like the anonymous hand that designated the pipe by the statement, "This is not a pipe," Magritte names his paintings in order to focus attention upon the very act of naming. And yet in this split and drifting space, strange bonds are knit, there occur intrusions, brusque and destructive invasions, avalanches of images into the milieu of words, and verbal lightning flashes that streak and shatter the drawings. Patiently, Klee constructed a space without name or geometry, tangling the chain of signs with the fiber of figures. Magritte secretly mines a space he seems to maintain in the old arrangement. But he excavates it with words: and the old pyramid of perspective is no more than a molehill about to cave in.

In any reasonable drawing a subscript such as "This is not a pipe" is enough immediately to divorce the figure from itself, to isolate it from its space, and to set it floating—whether near or apart from itself, whether similar to or unlike itself, no one knows. Against *Ceci n'est pas une pipe* there is *L'Art de la conversation* [*The Art of Conversation*]: in a landscape of battling giants or of the beginning of the world, two tiny persons are speaking—an inaudible discourse, a murmur instantly reabsorbed into the silence of the stones, into the silence of a wall whose enormous blocks overhang the two garrulous mutes. Jumbled together, the blocks form at their base a group of letters where it is easy to make out the word: REVE [dream]—as if all these airy, fragile words had been given the power to organize the chaos of stones. Or as if, on the contrary, behind the alert but immediately lost chatter of men, things could in their silence and sleep compose a word—a permanent word no one could efface; yet this word now designates the most fleeting of images. But this is not all: because it is in dream that men, at last reduced to silence, commune with the signification of things and allow themselves to be touched by enigmatic, insistent words that come from elsewhere. *Ceci n'est pas une pipe* exemplifies the penetration of discourse into the form of things; it reveals discourse's ambiguous power to deny and to redouble. *L'Art de la conversation* marks the anonymous attraction of things that form their own words in the face of men's indifference, insinuating themselves, without men even being aware of it, into their daily chatter.

Between the two extremes, Magritte's work deploys the play of words and images. The countenance of an absolutely serious man, unsmiling, unblinking, "breaks up" with a laughter that comes from nowhere. The "might that falls" cannot fall without shattering a windowpane whose fragments (still retaining, on their sharp edges and glass shards, the sun's reflections) are scattered on the floor and sill. Referring to the sun's disappearance as a "fall," the words have swept along, with the image they evoke, not only the windowpane but the other sun, the twin sun perfectly outlined on the smooth and transparent glass. Like a clapper in a bell, the key stands vertically "in the keyhole": it rings forth the familiar expression until it becomes absurd. Moreover, listen to Magritte: "Between words and objects one can create new relations and specify characteristics of language and objects generally ignored in everyday life." Or again: "Sometimes the name of an object takes the place of an image. A word can take the place of an object in reality. An image can take the place of a word in a proposition." And the following statement, conveying no contradiction but referring to the inextricable tangle of words and images and to the absence of a common ground to sustain them: "In a painting, words are of the same cloth as images. Rather one sees images and words differently in a painting."[1]

Make no mistake–in a space where every element seems to obey the sole principle of resemblance and plastic representation, linguistic signs (which had an excluded aura, which prowled far around the image, which the title's arbitrariness seemed to have banished forever) have surreptitiously reapproached. Into the solidity of the image, into its meticulous resemblance, they have introduced a disorder–an order pertaining to the eyes alone. They have routed the object, revealing its filmy thinness.

In order to deploy his plastic signs, Klee wove a new space. Magritte allows the old space of representation to rule, but only at the surface, no more than a polished stone, bearing words and shapes: beneath, nothing. It is a gravestone: the incisions that drew figures and those that marked letters communicate only by void, the nonplace hidden beneath marble solidity. I will note that this absence reascends to the surface and impinges upon the painting itself. When Magritte offers his version of *Madame Récamier* or *Le Balcon* [*The Balcony*], he replaces the traditional paintings' characters with coffins. Invisibly contained between waxen oak planks, emptiness undoes the space composed by the volume of living bodies, the arrangement of clothing, the direction of the gaze and all the faces that are about to speak. The "nonplace" emerges "in person"–in place of persons and where no one is present any longer.

SEVEN SEALS OF AFFIRMATION

With a sovereign and unique gesture, Kandinsky dismissed the old equivalence between resemblance and affirmation, freeing painting from both. Magritte proceeds by dissociating the two: disrupting their bonds, establishing their inequality, bringing one into play without the other, maintaining that which stems from painting, and excluding that which is closest to discourse – pursuing as closely as possible the indefinite continuation of the similar, but excising from it any affirmation that would attempt to say what is resembled. An art of the "Same," liberated from the "as if." We are farthest from trompe-l'œil. The latter seeks to support the weightiest burden of affirmation by the ruse of a convincing resemblance: "What you see on the wall's surface is not an aggregate of lines and colors. It is depth, sky, clouds that have shaded your house, a real column around which you could walk, a stairway that continues the steps you have begun to climb (already you start toward it, despite yourself), a stone balustrade over which lean the attentive faces of ladies and courtiers, wearing clothes identical to your own, to the very ribbons, smiling at your astonishment and your own smiles, gesturing to you in a fashion that is mysterious because they have answered you without even waiting for your own gestures to them."

Magritte's text, which speaks right next to that pipe most like a pipe, stands opposed to such affirmations, resting upon such analogies. But who speaks in their singular text, in which the most elementary of affirmations is conjured?

First the pipe itself: "What you see here, the lines I form or that form me, is not a pipe as you doubtless believe; but only a drawing, while the real pipe, reposing in its essence quite beyond every artificial gesture, floating in the element of its ideal truth, is above – look, just above the painting where I am, a simple and solitary similitude." To which the higher pipe responds in the same statement: "What you see floating before your eyes, beyond space and without fixed foundation, this mist that settles neither on canvas nor on a page, how could it really be a pipe? Don't be misled: I am mere similarity – not something similar to a pipe, but the cloudy similitude that, referring to nothing, traverses texts and makes texts such as the one you can read and drawings such as the one below communicate." But the statement, already articulated twice by different voices, in turn comes for-

ward to speak for itself. "The letters that form me and that you see—
the moment you try to read them as naming the pipe, how can they
say that they are a pipe, these things so divorced from what they
name? This is a graphism that resembles only itself, and that could
never replace what it describes." But there is more. Two by two the
voices mingle to say a third element is not a pipe. Bound together by
the frame of the painting enclosing them, the text and the lower pipe
enter into complicity: The designating power of words and the illus-
trative power of drawing denounce the higher pipe, and refuse the
abstract apparition the right to call itself a pipe, because its unan-
chored existence renders it mute and invisible. Bound together by
their reciprocal similitude, the two pipes contest the written statement's right to call itself a pipe, for it is composed of signs with no
resemblance to the thing they designate. Bound together by the fact
that they each come from elsewhere, that one is a discourse capable
of conveying truth while the other is like the ghost of a thing-in-itself,
the text and the higher pipe join to assert that the pipe in the painting
is not a pipe. And perhaps it must be supposed that, beside these three
elements, a siteless voice speaks in this statement, and that a formless
hand wrote it; it would be in speaking at once of the painting's pipe, of
the pipe that rises up above, and of the text that is writing, that this
anonym would say: "None of these is a pipe, but rather a text that
simulates a pipe; a drawing of a pipe that simulates a drawing of a
pipe; a pipe (drawn other than as a drawing) that resembles a pipe
(drawn after a pipe that itself would be other than a drawing)." Seven
discourses in a single statement—more than enough to demolish the
fortress where similitude was the prisoner of the assertion of resemblance.

Henceforth similitude is restored to itself—unfolding from itself and
folding back upon itself. It is no longer the finger perpendicularly
crossing the surface of the canvas in order to refer to something else.
It inaugurates a play of analogies that run, proliferate, propagate, and
correspond within the layout of the painting, affirming and representing nothing. Thus in Magritte's art we find infinite games of purified
similitude that never overflow the painting. They establish
metamorphoses—but in what sense? Is it the plant whose leaves take
flight and become birds, or the birds that drown and slowly botanize
themselves, sinking into the ground with a final quiver of greenery
(*Les Grâces naturelles* [*The Natural Graces*], *La Saveur des larmes* [*The*

Flavor of Tears])? Is it a woman who "takes to the bottle" or the bottle that feminizes itself by becoming a "nude study"[d] (here composing a disturbance of plastic elements because of the latent insertion of verbal signs and the play of an analogy that, affirming nothing, is doubly activated by the playfulness of the statement)? Instead of blending identities, it happens that similitude also has the power to destroy them: a woman's torso is sectioned into three parts (increasingly large as we move from top to bottom). While holding back all affirmation of identity, the shared proportions guarantee analogy: three segments lacking a fourth in just the same fashion, though the fourth element is incalculable. The head (final element = x) is missing: *Folie des grandeurs* [*Delusions of Grandeur*], says the title.

Another way analogy is freed from its old complicity with representative affirmation: perfidiously mixing (and by a ruse that seems to indicate just the opposite of what it means) the painting and what it is supposed to represent. Evidently, this is a way of affirming that the painting is indeed its own model. But, in fact, such an affirmation would imply an interior distance, a divergence, a disjuncture between the canvas and what it is supposed to mimic. For Magritte, on the contrary, there exists from the painting to the model a perfect continuity of scene, a linearity, a continuous overflowing of one into the other. Either by gliding from left to right (as in *La Condition humaine* [*The Human Condition*], where the sea's horizon follows the horizon on the canvas without a break); or by the inversion of distances (as in *La Cascade* [*The Waterfall*], where the model invades the canvas, envelops it on all sides, and gives it the appearance of being behind what ought to be on its far side). Opposed to this analogy that denies representation by erasing duality and distance, there is the contrary one that evades or mocks it by means of the snare of doubling. In *Le Soir qui tombe* [*Night Fall*] the windowpane bears a red sun analogous to the one hung in the sky (against Descartes and the way in which he resolved the two suns of appearance within the unity of representation). This is the converse of *La Lunette d'approche* [*Telescope*]: through the transparence of a window can be seen the passing of clouds and the sparkle of a blue sea; but the window opens onto black void, showing this to be a reflection of nothing.

TO PAINT IS NOT TO AFFIRM

Rigorous separation between linguistic signs and plastic elements: equivalence of resemblance and affirmation. These two principles constituted the tension in classical painting, because the second reintroduced discourse (affirmation exists only where there is speech) into an art from which the linguistic element was rigorously excluded. Hence the fact that classical painting spoke – and spoke constantly – while constituting itself entirely outside language; hence the fact that it rested silently in a discursive space; hence the fact that it provided, beneath itself, a kind of common ground where it could restore the bonds of signs and the image.

Magritte knits verbal signs and plastic elements together, but without referring them to a prior isotopism. He skirts the base of affirmative discourse on which resemblance calmly reposes, and he brings pure similitudes and nonaffirmative verbal statements into play within the instability of a disoriented volume and an unmapped space. A process whose formulation is, in some sense, given by *Ceci n'est pas une pipe.*

1. To employ a calligram where are all found, simultaneously present and visible, image, text, resemblance, affirmation, and their common ground.

2. Then suddenly to open it up, so that the calligram immediately decomposes and disappears, leaving as a trace only its own absence.

3. To allow discourse to collapse of its own weight and to acquire the visible shape of letters. Letters which, insofar as they are drawn, enter into an uncertain, indefinite relation, confused with the drawing itself – but minus any area to serve as a common ground.

4. To allow similitudes, on the other hand, to multiply of themselves, to be born from their own vapor and to rise endlessly into an ether where they refer to nothing other than themselves.

5. To verify clearly, at the end of the operation, that the precipitate has changed color, that it has gone from black to white, that the "This is a pipe" has become "This is not a pipe." In short, that painting has stopped affirming.

NOTES

a "Dawn at the Ends of the Earth," the title of a book with illustrations by Magritte. Actually, Magritte's pipe and its wry subscript appear in a whole series of paintings and drawings. There is also a pun on the word *aube*, which can mean either "dawn" or "float." – J.H.

b At this point, the original version of the essay, which appears in *Dits et écrits*, begins to vary from the augmented version that appeared as a monograph. Here and throughout, we follow the *Dits et écrits* text. – Ed.

c   An untranslatable pun. Le "*nom d'une pipe*" is a mild or euphemistic oath on the order of "for Pete's sake" substituted for "for God's sake." – J.H.

1   I cite all these quotations from P. Waldberg's *Magritte*. They illustrated a series of drawings in the twelfth issue of *Révolution surréaliste*.

d   A bizarre pun. Literally, *corps nu*, "naked body." Spoken aloud, the phrase sounds like *cornu*, "horned" – slang for cuckoldry, or more generally any sexual betrayal. – J.H.

WHAT IS AN AUTHOR?*

The coming into being of the notion of "author" constitutes the privileged moment of individualization in the history of ideas, knowledge, literature, philosophy, and the sciences. Even today, when we reconstruct the history of a concept, literary genre, or school of philosophy, such categories seem relatively weak, secondary, and superimposed scansions in comparison with the solid and fundamental unit of the author and the work.

I shall not offer here a sociohistorical analysis of the author's persona. Certainly, it would be worth examining how the author became individualized in a culture like ours, what status he has been given, at what moment studies of authenticity and attribution began, in what kind of system of valorization the author was involved, at what point we began to recount the lives of authors rather than of heroes, and how this fundamental category of "the-man-and-his-work criticism" began. For the moment, however, I want to deal solely with the relationship between text and author and with the manner in which the text points to this figure that, at least in appearance, is outside it and antecedes it.

Beckett nicely formulates the theme with which I would like to begin: "'What does it matter who is speaking,' someone said, 'what does it matter who is speaking.'" In this indifference appears one of the fundamental ethical principles of contemporary writing [écriture].

---

*This essay is the text of a lecture presented to the Société Française de philosophie on 22 February 1969 (Foucault gave a modified form of the lecture in the United States in 1970). This translation, by Josué V. Harari, has been slightly modified.

I say "ethical" because this indifference is really not a trait characterizing the manner in which one speaks and writes but, rather, a kind of immanent rule, taken up over and over again, never fully applied, not designating writing as something completed, but dominating it as a practice. Since it is too familiar to require a lengthy analysis, this immanent rule can be adequately illustrated here by tracing two of its major themes.

First of all, we can say that today's writing has freed itself from the theme of expression. Referring only to itself, but without being restricted to the confines of its interiority, writing is identified with its own unfolded exteriority. This means that it is an interplay of signs arranged less according to its signified content than according to the very nature of the signifier. Writing unfolds like a game [*jeu*] that invariably goes beyond its own rules and transgresses its limits. In writing, the point is not to manifest or exalt the act of writing, nor is it to pin a subject within language; it is, rather, a question of creating a space into which the writing subject constantly disappears.

The second theme, writing's relationship with death, is even more familiar. This link subverts an old tradition exemplified by the Greek epic, which was intended to perpetuate the immortality of the hero: if he was willing to die young, it was so that his life, consecrated and magnified by death, might pass into immortality; the narrative then redeemed this accepted death. In another way, the motivation, as well as the theme and the pretext of Arabian narratives—such as *The Thousand and One Nights*—was also the eluding of death: one spoke, telling stories into the early morning, in order to forestall death, to postpone the day of reckoning that would silence the narrator. Scheherazade's narrative is an effort, renewed each night, to keep death outside the circle of life.

Our culture has metamorphosed this idea of narrative, or writing, as something designed to ward off death. Writing has become linked to sacrifice, even to the sacrifice of life: it is now a voluntary effacement that does not need to be represented in books, since it is brought about in the writer's very existence. The work, which once had the duty of providing immortality, now possesses the right to kill, to be its author's murderer, as in the cases of Flaubert, Proust, and Kafka. That is not all, however: this relationship between writing and death is also manifested in the effacement of the writing subject's individual characteristics. Using all the contrivances that he sets up between himself and what he writes, the writing subject cancels out the signs of his particular individuality. As a result, the mark of the writer is reduced to nothing more than the singularity of his absence; he must assume the role of the dead man in the game of writing.

None of this is recent; criticism and philosophy took note of the disappearance – or death – of the author some time ago. But the consequences of their discovery of it have not been sufficiently examined, nor has its import been accurately measured. A certain number of notions that are intended to replace the privileged position of the author actually seem to preserve that privilege and suppress the real meaning of his disappearance. I shall examine two of these notions, both of great importance today.

The first is the idea of the work [*oeuvre*]. It is a very familiar thesis that the task of criticism is not to bring out the work's relationships with the author, nor to reconstruct through the text a thought or experience, but rather to analyze the work through its structure, its architecture, its intrinsic form, and the play of its internal relationships. At this point, however, a problem arises: What is a work? What is this curious unity which we designate as a work? Of what elements is it composed? Is it not what an author has written? Difficulties appear immediately. If an individual were not an author, could we say that what he wrote, said, left behind in his papers, or what has been collected of his remarks, could be called a "work"? When Sade was not considered an author, what was the status of his papers? Simply rolls of paper onto which he ceaselessly uncoiled his fantasies during his imprisonment.

Even when an individual has been accepted as an author, we must still ask whether everything that he wrote, said, or left behind is part of his work. The problem is both theoretical and technical. When undertaking the publication of Nietzsche's works, for example, where should one stop? Surely everything must be published, but what is "everything"? Everything that Nietzsche himself published, certainly. And what about the rough drafts for his works? Obviously. The plans for his aphorisms? Yes. The deleted passages and the notes at the bottom of the page? Yes. What if, within a workbook filled with aphorisms, one finds a reference, the notation of a meeting or of an address, or a laundry list: is it a work, or not? Why not? And so on, ad infinitum. How can one define a work amid the millions of traces left by someone after his death? A theory of the work does not exist, and the empirical task of those who naively undertake the editing of works often suffers in the absence of such a theory.

We could go even further: Does *The Thousand and One Nights* constitute a work? What about Clement of Alexandria's *Miscellanies* or Diogenes Laërtes' *Lives*? A multitude of questions arises with regard to this notion of the work. Consequently, it is not enough to declare that we should do without the writer (the author) and study the work itself. The word *work* and the unity that it designates are probably as problematic as the status of the author's individuality.

Another notion which has hindered us from taking full measure of the author's disappearance, blurring and concealing the moment of this effacement and subtly preserving the author's existence, is the notion of writing [*écriture*]. When rigorously applied, this notion should allow us not only to circumvent references to the author, but also to situate his recent absence. The notion of writing, as currently employed, is concerned with neither the act of writing nor the indication—be it symptom or sign—of a meaning that someone might have wanted to express. We try, with great effort, to imagine the general condition of each text, the condition of both the space in which it is dispersed and the time in which it unfolds.

In current usage, however, the notion of writing seems to transpose the empirical characteristics of the author into a transcendental anonymity. We are content to efface the more visible marks of the author's empiricity by playing off, one against the other, two ways of characterizing writing, namely, the critical and the religious approaches. Giving writing a primal status seems to be a way of retranslating, in transcendental terms, both the theological affirmation of its sacred character and the critical affirmation of its creative character. To admit that writing is, because of the very history that it made possible, subject to the test of oblivion and repression, seems to represent, in transcendental terms, the religious principle of the hidden meaning (which requires interpretation) and the critical principle of implicit significations, silent determinations, and obscured contents (which give rise to commentary). To imagine writing as absence seems to be a simple repetition, in transcendental terms, of both the religious principle of inalterable and yet never fulfilled tradition, and the aesthetic principle of the work's survival, its perpetuation beyond the author's death, and its enigmatic excess in relation to him.

This usage of the notion of writing runs the risk of maintaining the author's privileges under the protection of the a priori: it keeps alive, in the gray light of neutralization, the interplay of those representations that formed a particular image of the author. The author's disappearance, which, since Mallarmé, has been a constantly recurring event, is subject to a series of transcendental barriers. There seems to be an important dividing line between those who believe that they can still locate today's discontinuities [*ruptures*] in the historico-transcendental tradition of the nineteenth century and those who try to free themselves once and for all from that tradition.

It is not enough, however, to repeat the empty affirmation that the author has disappeared. For the same reason, it is not enough to keep repeating that God and man have died a common death. Instead, we must locate the space left empty by the author's disappearance, follow the distribution of gaps and breaches, and watch for the openings this disappearance uncovers.

First, we need to clarify briefly the problems arising from the use of the author's name. What is an author's name? How does it function? Far from offering a solution, I shall only indicate some of the difficulties that it presents.

The author's name is a proper name, and therefore it raises the problems common to all proper names. (Here I refer to Searle's analyses, among others.[1]) Obviously, one cannot turn a proper name into a pure and simple reference. It has other than indicative functions: more than an indication, a gesture, a finger pointed at someone, it is the equivalent of a description. When one says "Aristotle," one employs a word that is the equivalent of one, or a series, of definite descriptions, such as "the author of the *Analytics*," "the founder of ontology," and so forth. One cannot stop there, however, because a proper name does not have just one signification. When we discover that Arthur Rimbaud did not write *La Chasse spirituelle*, we cannot pretend that the meaning of this proper name, or that of the author, has been altered. The proper name and the author's name are situated between the two poles of description and designation: they must have a certain link with what they name, but one that is neither entirely in the mode of designation nor in that of description; it must be a specific link. However–and it is here that the particular difficulties of the author's name arise–the links between the proper name and the individual named and between the author's name and what it names are not isomorphic and do not function in the same way. There are several differences.

If, for example, Pierre Dupont does not have blue eyes, or was not born in Paris, or is not a doctor, the name Pierre Dupont will still always refer to the same person; such things do not modify the link of designation. The problems raised by the author's name are much more complex, however. If I discover that Shakespeare was not born in the house we visit today, this is a modification that, obviously, will not alter the functioning of the author's name. But if we proved that Shakespeare did not write those sonnets which pass for his, that would constitute a significant change and affect the manner in which the author's name functions. If we proved that Shakespeare wrote Bacon's *Organon* by showing that the same author wrote both the works of Bacon and those of Shakespeare, that would be a third type of change that would entirely modify the functioning of the author's name. The author's name is not, therefore, just a proper name like the rest.

Many other facts point out the paradoxical singularity of the author's name. To say that Pierre Dupont does not exist is not at all the same as saying that Homer or Hermes Trismegistus did not exist. In the first case, it means that no one has the name Pierre Dupont; in the second, it means that several people were mixed together under one name, or that the true author had none of the traits traditionally ascribed to the personae of Homer or Hermes. To say that X's real name is actually Jacques Durand instead of Pierre Dupont is not the same as saying that Stendhal's name was Henri Beyle. One could also question the meaning and functioning of propositions like "Bourbaki is so-and-so, so-and-so, and so forth," and "Victor Eremita, Climacus, Anticlimacus, Frater Taciturnus, Constantine Constantius, all of these are Kierkegaard."

These differences may result from the fact that an author's name is not simply an element in a discourse (capable of being either subject or object, of being replaced by a pronoun, and the like); it performs a certain role with regard to narrative discourse, assuring a classificatory function. Such a name permits one to group together a certain number of texts, define them, differentiate them from and contrast them to others. In addition, it establishes a relationship among the texts. Hermes Trismegistus did not exist, nor did Hippocrates—in the sense that Balzac existed—but the fact that several texts have been placed under the same name indicates that there has been established among them a relationship of homogeneity, filiation, authentication of some texts by the use of others, reciprocal explication, or concomitant utilization. The author's name serves to characterize a certain mode of being of discourse: the fact that the discourse has an author's name, that one can say "this was written by so-and-so" or "so-and-so is its author," shows that this discourse is not ordinary everyday speech that merely comes and goes, not something that is immediately consumable. On the contrary, it is a speech that must be received in a certain mode and that, in a given culture, must receive a certain status.

It would seem that the author's name, unlike other proper names, does not pass from the interior of a discourse to the real and exterior individual who produced it; instead, the name seems always to be present, marking off the edges of the text, revealing, or at least characterizing, its mode of being. The author's name manifests the appearance of a certain discursive set and indicates the status of this discourse within a society and a culture. It has no legal status, nor is it located in the fiction of the work; rather, it is located in the break that founds a certain discursive construct and its very particular mode of being. As a result, we could say that in a civilization like our own there are a certain number of discourses endowed with the "author function" while others are deprived of it. A private letter may well have a signer – it does not have an author; a contract may well have a guarantor – it does not have an author. An anonymous text posted on a wall probably has an editor – but not an author. The author function is therefore characteristic of the mode of existence, circulation, and functioning of certain discourses within a society.

Let us analyze this "author function" as we have just described it. In our culture, how does one characterize a discourse containing the author function? In what way is this discourse different from other discourses? If we limit our remarks to the author of a book or a text, we can isolate four different characteristics.

First of all, discourses are objects of appropriation. The form of ownership from which they spring is of a rather particular type, one that has been codified for many years. We should note that, historically, this type of ownership has always been subsequent to what one might call penal appropriation. Texts, books, and discourses really began to have authors (other than mythical, sacralized and sacralizing figures) to the extent that authors became subject to punishment, that is, to the extent that discourses could be transgressive. In our culture (and doubtless in many others), discourse was not originally a product, a thing, a kind of goods; it was essentially an act—an act placed in the bipolar field of the sacred and the profane, the licit and the illicit, the religious and the blasphemous. Historically, it was a gesture fraught with risks before becoming goods caught up in a circuit of ownership.

Once a system of ownership for texts came into being, once strict rules concerning author's rights, author–publisher relations, rights of reproduction, and related matters were enacted—at the end of the eighteenth and the beginning of the nineteenth century—the possibility of transgression attached to the act of writing took on, more and more, the form of an imperative peculiar to literature. It is as if the author, beginning with the moment at which he was placed in the system of property that characterizes our society, compensated for the status that he thus acquired by rediscovering the old bipolar field of discourse, systematically practicing transgression and thereby restoring danger to a writing that was now guaranteed the benefits of ownership.

The author function does not affect all discourses in a universal and constant way, however. In our civilization, it has not always been the same types of texts that have required attribution to an author. There was a time when the texts we today call "literary" (narratives, stories, epics, tragedies, comedies) were accepted, put into circulation, and valorized without any question about the identity of their author; their anonymity caused no difficulties since their ancientness, whether real or imagined, was regarded as a sufficient guarantee of their status. On the other hand, those texts we now would call scientific—those dealing with cosmology and the heavens, medicine and illnesses, natural sciences and geography—were accepted in the Middle Ages, and accepted as "true," only when marked with the name of their author. "Hippocrates said," "Pliny recounts," were not really formulas of an argument based on authority; they were the markers inserted in discourses that were supposed to be received as statements of demonstrated truth.

A switch takes place in the seventeenth or eighteenth century. Scientific discourses began to be received for themselves, in the anonymity of an established or always redemonstrable truth; their membership in a systematic ensemble, and not the reference to the individual who produced them, stood as their guarantee. The author function faded away, and the inventor's name served only to christen a theorem, proposition, particular effect, property, body, group of elements, or pathological syndrome. By the same token, literary discourses came to be accepted only when endowed with the author function. We now ask of each poetic or fictional text: From where does it come, who wrote it, when, under what circumstances, or beginning with what design? The meaning ascribed to it and the status or value accorded it depend on the manner in which we answer these questions. And if a text should be discovered in a state of anonymity— whether as a consequence of an accident or the author's explicit wish—the game becomes one of rediscovering the author. Since literary anonymity is not tolerable, we can accept it only in the guise of an enigma. As a result, the author function today plays an important role in our view of literary works. (These are obviously generalizations that would have to be refined insofar as recent critical practice is concerned. Criticism began some time ago to treat works according to their genre and type, following the recurrent elements that are enfigured in them, as proper variations around an invariant that is no longer the individual creator. Even so, if in mathematics reference to the author is barely anything any longer but a manner of naming theorems or sets of propositions, in biology and medicine the indication of the author and the date of his work play a rather different role. It is not simply a manner of indicating the source, but of providing a certain index of "reality" in relation to the techniques and objects of experience made use of in a particular period and in such-and-such a laboratory.)

The third characteristic of this author function is that it does not develop spontaneously as the attribution of a discourse to an individual. It is, rather, the result of a complex operation that constructs a certain being of reason that we call "author." Critics doubtless try to give this being of reason a realistic status, by discerning, in the individual, a "deep" motive, a "creative" power, or a "design," the milieu in which writing originates. Nevertheless, these aspects of an individual which we designate as making him an author are only a projection, in more or less psychologizing terms, of the operations we force texts to undergo, the connections we make, the traits we establish as pertinent, the continuities we recognize, or the exclusions we practice. All these operations vary according to periods and types of discourse. We do not construct a "philosophical author" as we do a "poet," just as in the eighteenth century one did not construct a novelist as we do today. Still, we can find through the ages certain constants in the rules of author construction.

It seems, for example, that the manner in which literary criticism once defined the author–or, rather, constructed the figure of the author beginning with existing texts and discourses–is directly derived from the manner in which Christian tradition authenticated (or rejected) the texts at its disposal. In order to "rediscover" an author in a work, modern criticism uses methods similar to those that Christian exegesis employed when trying to prove the value of a text by its author's saintliness. In *De Viris illustribus*, Saint Jerome explains that homonymy is not sufficient to identify legitimately authors of more than one work: different individuals could have had the same name, or one man could have, illegitimately, borrowed another's patronymic. The name as an individual trademark is not enough when one works within a textual tradition.

How, then, can one attribute several discourses to one and the same author? How can one use the author function to determine if one is dealing with one or several individuals? Saint Jerome proposes four criteria: (1) if among several books attributed to an author one is inferior to the others, it must be withdrawn from the list of the author's works (the author is therefore defined as a constant level of value); (2) the same should be done if certain texts contradict the doctrine expounded in the author's other works (the author is thus defined as a field of conceptual or theoretical coherence); (3) one must also exclude works that are written in a different style, containing words and expressions not ordinarily found in the writer's production (the author is here conceived as a stylistic unity); (4) finally, passages quoting statements made or mentioning events that occurred after the author's death must be regarded as interpolated texts (the author is here seen as a historical figure at the crossroads of a certain number of events).

Modern literary criticism, even when–as is now customary–it is not concerned with questions of authentication, still defines the author in much the same way: the author provides the basis for explaining not only the presence of certain events in a work, but also their transformations, distortions, and diverse modifications (through his biography, the determination of his individual perspective, the analysis of his social position, and the revelation of his basic design). The author is also the principle of a certain unity of writing—all differences having to be resolved, at least in part, by the principles of evolution, maturation, or influence. The author also serves to neutralize the contradictions that may emerge in a series of texts: there must be—at a certain level of his thought or desire, of his consciousness or unconscious—a point where contradictions are resolved, where incompatible elements are at last tied together or organized around a fundamental or originating contradiction. Finally, the author is a particular source of expression that, in more or less completed forms, is manifested equally well, and with similar validity, in works, sketches, letters, fragments, and so on. Clearly, Saint Jerome's four criteria of authenticity (criteria that seem totally insufficient for today's exegetes) do define the four modalities according to which modern criticism brings the author function into play.

But the author function is not a pure and simple reconstruction made secondhand from a text given as inert material. The text always contains a certain number of signs referring to the author. These signs, well known to grammarians, are personal pronouns, adverbs of time and place, and verb conjugation. Such elements do not play the same role in discourses provided with the author function as in those lacking it. In the latter, such "shifters" refer to the real speaker and to the spatio-temporal coordinates of his discourse (although certain modifications can occur, as in the operation of relating discourses in the first person). In the former, however, their role is more complex and variable. Everyone knows that, in a novel offered as a narrator's account, neither the first-person pronoun nor the present indicative refers exactly to the writer or to the moment in which he writes but, rather, to an alter ego whose distance from the author varies, often changing in the course of the work. It would be just as wrong to equate the author with the real writer as to equate him with the fictitious speaker; the author function is carried out and operates in the scission itself, in this division and this distance.

One might object that this is a characteristic peculiar to novelistic or poetic discourse, a game in which only "quasi discourses" participate. In fact, however, all discourses endowed with the author function possess this plurality of self. The self that speaks in the preface to a treatise on mathematics—and that indicates the circumstances of the treatise's composition – is identical neither in its position nor in its functioning to the self that speaks in the course of a demonstration, and that appears in the form of "I conclude" or "I suppose." In the first case, the "I" refers to an individual without an equivalent who, in a determined place and time, completed a certain task; in the second, the "I" indicates an instance and a level of demonstration which any individual could perform provided that he accepted the same system of symbols, play of axioms, and set of previous demonstrations. We could also, in the same treatise, locate a third self, one that speaks to tell the work's meaning, the obstacles encountered, the results obtained, and the remaining problems; this self is situated in the field of already existing or yet-to-appear mathematical discourses. The author function is not assumed by the first of these selves at the expense of the other two, which would then be nothing more than a fictitious splitting in two of the first one. On the contrary, in these discourses the author function operates so as to effect the dispersion of these three simultaneous selves.

No doubt, analysis could discover still more characteristic traits of the author function. I will limit myself to these four, however, because they seem both the most visible and the most important. They can be summarized as follows: (1) the author function is linked to the juridical and institutional system that encompasses, determines, and articulates the universe of discourses; (2) it does not affect all discourses in the same way at all times and in all types of civilization; (3) it is not defined by the spontaneous attribution of a discourse to its producer but, rather, by a series of specific and complex operations; (4) it does not refer purely and simply to a real individual, since it can give rise simultaneously to several selves, to several subjects – positions that can be occupied by different classes of individuals.

Up to this point I have unjustifiably limited my subject. Certainly the author function in painting, music, and other arts should have been discussed; but even supposing that we remain within the world of discourse, as I want to do, I seem to have given the term "author" much too narrow a meaning. I have discussed the author only in the limited sense of a person to whom the production of a text, a book, or a work can be legitimately attributed. It is easy to see that in the sphere of discourse one can be the author of much more than a book – one can be the author of a theory, tradition, or discipline in which other books and authors will in their turn find a place. These authors are in a position that I will call "transdiscursive." This is a recurring phenomenon—certainly as old as our civilization. Homer, Aristotle, and the Church Fathers, as well as the first mathematicians and the originators of the Hippocratic tradition, all played this role. Furthermore, in the course of the nineteenth century, there appeared in Europe another, more uncommon, kind of author, whom one should confuse with neither the "great" literary authors, nor the authors of religious texts, nor the founders of science. In a somewhat arbitrary way we shall call those who belong in this last group "founders of discursivity."

They are unique in that they are not just the authors of their own works. They have produced something else: the possibilities and the rules for the formation of other texts. In this sense they are very different, for example, from a novelist, who is, in fact, nothing more than the author of his own text. Freud is not just the author of *The Interpretation of Dreams* or *Jokes and Their Relation to the Unconscious*; Marx is not just the author of the *Communist Manifesto* or *Das Kapital*: they both have established an endless possibility of discourse. Obviously, it is easy to object. One might say that it is not true that the author of a novel is only the author of his own text; in a sense, he also, provided that he acquires some "importance," governs and commands more than that. To take a very simple example, one could say that Ann Radcliffe not only wrote *The Castles of Athlin and Dunbayne* and several other novels but also made possible the appearance of the Gothic horror novel at the beginning of the nineteenth century; in that respect, her author function exceeds her own work. But I think there is an answer to this objection. These founders of discursivity (I use Marx and Freud as examples, because I believe them to be both the first and the most important cases) make possible something altogether different from what a novelist makes possible. Ann Radcliffe's texts opened the way for a certain number of resemblances and analogies which have their model or principle in her work. The latter contains characteristic signs, figures, relationships, and structures that could be reused by others. In other words, to say that Ann Radcliffe founded the Gothic horror novel means that in the nineteenth-century Gothic novel one will find, as in Ann Radcliffe's works, the theme of the heroine caught in the trap of her own innocence, the hidden castle, the character of the black, cursed hero devoted to making the world expiate the evil done to him, and all the rest of it. On the other hand, when I speak of Marx or Freud as founders of discursivity, I mean that they made possible not only a certain number of analogies but also (and equally important) a certain number of differences. They have created a possibility for something other than their discourse, yet something belonging to what they founded. To say that Freud founded psychoanalysis does not (simply) mean that we find the concept of the libido or the technique of dream analysis in the works of Karl Abraham or Melanie Klein; it means that Freud made possible a certain number of divergences—with respect to his own texts, concepts, and hypotheses—that all arise from the psychoanalytic discourse itself.

This would seem to present a new difficulty, however, or at least a new problem: is the above not true, after all, of any founder of a science, or of any author who has introduced some transformation into a science that might be called fecund? After all, Galileo made possible not only those discourses which repeated the laws he had formulated, but also statements very different from what he himself had said. If Georges Cuvier is the founder of biology, or Ferdinand de Saussure the founder of linguistics, it is not because they were imitated, nor because people have since taken up again the concept of organism or sign; it is because Cuvier made possible, to a certain extent, a theory of evolution diametrically opposed to his own fixism; it is because Saussure made possible a generative grammar radically different from his structural analyses. Superficially, then, the initiation of discursive practices appears similar to the founding of any scientific endeavor.

Still, there is a difference, and a notable one. In the case of a science, the act that founds it is on an equal footing with its future transformations; this act becomes in some respects part of the set of modifications that it makes possible. Of course, this belonging can take several forms. In the future development of a science, the founding act may appear as little more than a particular instance of a more general phenomenon that unveils itself in the process. It can also turn out to be marred by intuition and empirical bias; one must then reformulate it, making it the object of a certain number of supplementary theoretical operations that establish it more rigorously, and so on. Finally, it can seem to be a hasty generalization that must be retraced. In other words, the founding act of a science can always be reintroduced within the machinery of those transformations which derive from it.

In contrast, the initiation of a discursive practice is heterogeneous to its subsequent transformations. To expand a type of discursivity, such as psychoanalysis as founded by Freud, is not to give it a formal generality it would not have permitted at the outset but, rather, to open it up to a certain number of possible applications. To limit psychoanalysis as a type of discursivity is, in reality, to try to isolate in the founding act an eventually restricted number of propositions or statements to which, alone, one grants a founding value, and in relation to which certain concepts or theories accepted by Freud might be considered as derived, secondary, and accessory. In addition, one does not declare certain propositions in the work of these founders to be false: instead, when trying to seize the act of founding, one sets aside those statements that are not pertinent, either because they are deemed inessential, or because they are considered "prehistoric" and derived from another type of discursivity. In other words, unlike the founding of a science, the initiation of a discursive practice does not participate in its later transformations. As a result, one defines a proposition's theoretical validity in relation to the work of the founders–while, in the case of Galileo and Newton, it is in relation to what physics or cosmology is in its intrinsic structure and normativity that one affirms the validity of any proposition those men may have put forth. To phrase it very schematically: the work of initiators of discursivity is not situated in the space that science defines; rather, it is the science or the discursivity which refers back to their work as primary coordinates.

In this way we can understand the inevitable necessity, within these fields of discursivity, for a "return to the origin." This return, which is part of the discursive field itself, never stops modifying it. The return is not a historical supplement that would be added to the discursivity, or merely an ornament; on the contrary, it constitutes an effective and necessary task of transforming the discursive practice itself. Reexamination of Galileo's text may well change our understanding of the history of mechanics, but it will never be able to change mechanics itself. On the other hand, reexamining Freud's texts modifies psychoanalysis itself, just as a reexamination of Marx's would modify Marxism.

What I have just outlined regarding these "discursive instaurations" is, of course, very schematic; this is true, in particular, of the opposition I have tried to draw between discursive initiation and scientific founding. It is not always easy to distinguish between the two; moreover, nothing proves that they are two mutually exclusive procedures. I have attempted the distinction for only one reason: to show that the author function, which is complex enough when one tries to situate it at the level of a book or a series of texts that carry a given signature, involves still more determining factors when one tries to analyze it in larger units, such as groups of works or entire disciplines.

To conclude, I would like to review the reasons why I attach a certain importance to what I have said.

On the one hand, an analysis in the direction that I have outlined might provide for an approach to a typology of discourse. It seems to me, at least at first glance, that such a typology cannot be constructed solely from the grammatical features, formal structures, and objects of discourse: more likely, there exist properties or relationships peculiar to discourse (not reducible to the rules of grammar and logic), and one must use these to distinguish the major categories of discourse. The relationship (or nonrelationship) with an author, and the different forms this relationship takes, constitute—in a quite visible manner—one of these discursive properties.

On the other hand, I believe that one could find here an introduction to the historical analysis of discourse. Perhaps it is time to study discourses not only in terms of their expressive value or formal transformations but according to their modes of existence. The modes of circulation, valorization, attribution, and appropriation of discourses vary with each culture and are modified within each. The manner in which they are articulated according to social relationships can be more readily understood, I believe, in the activity of the author function and in its modifications than in the themes or concepts that discourses set in motion.

It would seem that one could also, beginning with analyses of this type, reexamine the privileges of the subject. I realize that in undertaking the internal and architectonic analysis of a work (be it a literary text, philosophical system, or scientific work), in setting aside biographical and psychological references, one has already called back into question the absolute character and founding role of the subject. Still, perhaps one must return to this question, not in order to reestablish the theme of an originating subject but to grasp the subject's points of insertion, modes of functioning, and system of dependencies. Doing so means overturning the traditional problem, no longer raising the questions: How can a free subject penetrate the density of things and give it meaning? How can it activate the rules of a language from within and thus give rise to the designs that are properly its own? Instead, these questions will be raised: How, under what conditions, and in what forms can something like a subject appear in the order of discourse? What place can it occupy in each type of discourse, what functions can it assume, and by obeying what rules? In short, it is a matter of depriving the subject (or its substitute) of its role as originator, and of analyzing the subject as a variable and complex function of discourse.

Second, there are reasons dealing with the "ideological" status of the author. The question then becomes: How can one reduce the great peril, the great danger with which fiction threatens our world? The answer is: One can reduce it with the author. The author allows a limitation of the cancerous and dangerous proliferation of significations within a world where one is thrifty not only with one's resources and riches but also with one's discourses and their significations. The author is the principle of thrift in the proliferation of meaning. As a result, we must entirely reverse the traditional idea of the author. We are accustomed, as we have seen earlier, to saying that the author is the genial creator of a work in which he deposits, with infinite wealth and generosity, an inexhaustible world of significations. We are used to thinking that the author is so different from all other men, and so transcendent with regard to all languages that, as soon as he speaks, meaning begins to proliferate, to proliferate indefinitely.

The truth is quite the contrary: the author is not an indefinite source of significations that fill a work; the author does not precede the works; he is a certain functional principle by which, in our culture, one limits, excludes, and chooses; in short, by which one impedes the free circulation, the free manipulation, the free composition, decomposition, and recomposition of fiction. In fact, if we are accustomed to presenting the author as a genius, as a perpetual surging of invention, it is because, in reality, we make him function in exactly the opposite fashion. One can say that the author is an ideological product, since we represent him as the opposite of his historically real function. When a historically given function is represented in a figure that inverts it, one has an ideological production. The author is therefore the ideological figure by which one marks the manner in which we fear the proliferation of meaning.

In saying this, I seem to call for a form of culture in which fiction would not be limited by the figure of the author. It would be pure romanticism, however, to imagine a culture in which the fictive would operate in an absolutely free state, in which fiction would be put at the disposal of everyone and would develop without passing through something like a necessary or constraining figure. Although, since the eighteenth century, the author has played the role of the regulator of the fictive, a role quite characteristic of our era of industrial and bourgeois society, of individualism and private property, still, given the historical modifications that are taking place, it does not seem necessary that the author function remain constant in form, complexity, and even in existence. I think that, as our society changes, at the very moment when it is in the process of changing, the author function will disappear, and in such a manner that fiction and its polysemous texts will once again function according to another mode, but still with a system of constraint—one that will no longer be the author but will have to be determined or, perhaps, experienced [*expérimenter*].

All discourses, whatever their status, form, value, and whatever the treatment to which they will be subjected, would then develop in the anonymity of a murmur. We would no longer hear the questions that have been rehashed for so long: Who really spoke? Is it really he and not someone else? With what authenticity or originality? And what part of his deepest self did he express in his discourse? Instead, there would be other questions, like these: What are the modes of existence of this discourse? Where has it been used, how can it circulate, and who can appropriate it for himself? What are the places in it where there is room for possible subjects? Who can assume these various subject functions? And behind all these questions, we would hear hardly anything but the stirring of an indifference: What difference does it make who is speaking?

NOTES

1   John Searle, *Speech Acts: An Essay in the Philosophy of Language* (Cambridge, Eng.: Cambridge University Press, 1969), pp. 162–74. – ED.

SADE: SERGEANT OF SEX*

G.D.   When you go to the movies, are you struck by the sadism of some recent films, whether they take place in a hospital, or, as in the last Pasolini, in a false prison?

M.F.   I have been struck – at least until recently – by the absence of sadism, and the absence of Sade, the two not being equivalent. There can be Sade without sadism and sadism without Sade. But let's leave aside the problem of sadism, which is more delicate, and focus on Sade. I believe that there is nothing more allergic to the cinema than the work of Sade. Among the numerous reasons, this one first: the meticulousness, the ritual, the rigorous ceremonial form that all the scenes of Sade assume exclude the supplementary play of the camera. The least addition or suppression, the smallest ornament, are intolerable. No open fantasy, but a carefully programmed regulation. As soon as something is missing or superimposed, all is lost. There is no place for an image. The blanks must not be filled except by desires and bodies.

G.D.   In the first part of Alexandro Jodorowsky's *El Topo* there is a bloody orgy, a rather revealing cutting up of bodies. Isn't the cinema's sadism first a way of treating actors and their bodies? And particularly women in the cinema – are they not (mis)treated as appendages of a male body?

M.F.   The way in which the body is treated in contemporary cin-

*This interview, conducted by G. Dupont, appeared in *Cinématographe* 16 (Dec. 1975), pp. 3–5. This translation, by John Johnston, has been slightly amended.

ema is something very new. Look at the kisses, the faces, the cheeks, the eyebrows, the teeth in a film like Werner Schroeter's *The Death of Maria Malibran.* To call that sadism seems to me completely false, except through the detour of a vague psychoanalysis involving a partial object, a body in pieces, the *vagina dentata.* It's a rather vulgar Freudianism that reduces to sadism this way of celebrating the body and its wonders. What Schroeter does with a face, a cheekbone, the lips, an expression of the eyes has nothing to do with sadism. It's a question of the multiplying and burgeoning of the body, an exaltation, in some way autonomous, of its least parts, of the least possibilities of a body fragment. There is an anarchizing of the body, in which hierarchies, localizations and designations, organicity if you like, is being undone. Whereas in sadism it's very much the organ as such that is relentlessly targeted. You have an eye that looks, I tear it from you. You have a tongue that I have taken between my lips and bitten, I'm going to cut it off. With these eyes you will no longer be able to see, with this tongue you will no longer be able to eat or speak. The body in Sade is still strongly organic, anchored in this hierarchy – the difference being, of course, that the hierarchy is not organized, as in the old fable, from the head but from sex.

Whereas in some contemporary films, the way of making the body escape itself is of a completely different type. The goal is to dismantle this organicity: this is no longer a tongue but something completely different that comes out of the mouth. It's not the organ of a mouth that has been soiled and meant for someone else's pleasure. It's an "unnameable," "unusual" thing, outside of all programs of desire. It's the body made entirely malleable by pleasure: something that opens itself, tightens, palpitates, beats, gapes. In *The Death of Maria Malibran,* the way in which the two women kiss each other, what is it? Sand dunes, a desert caravan, a voracious flower that advances, insect mandibles, a grassy crevice. All that is antisadism. The cruel science of desire has nothing to do with these unformed pseudopods, which are the slow movements of pleasure-pain.

G.D.   Have you seen the "snuff films" in New York? There's one in which a woman is cut into pieces.

M.F.   No, but apparently the woman is really cut up alive.

G.D.   It's purely visual, without any words. A cold medium in relation to cinema, which is a hot medium. No more literature on the subject of the body: it's only a body in the act of dying.

M.F.   It's no longer cinema. It's part of a private erotic circuit, made only to kindle desire. It's just a matter of being "turned on," as Americans say, by a kind of stimulation that comes only from images but is no less potent than reality – although of another kind.

G.D.   Would you say that the camera is the master who treats the actor's body as the victim? I am thinking of Marilyn Monroe falling over and over again at Tony Curtis's feet in *Some Like It Hot.* Surely the actress experienced that as a sadistic sequence.

M.F.   The relationship between the camera and the actress in the film you're talking about seems to me still very traditional. One finds it in the theater: the actor taking upon himself the sacrifice of the hero and accomplishing it even in his own body. What seems new in the cinema I was speaking about is the discovery-exploration of the body by means of the camera. I imagine that the cinematography in these films is very intense. It's an encounter at once calculated and aleatory between the bodies and the camera, discovering something, breaking up an angle, a volume, a curve, following a trace, a line, possibly a ripple. And then suddenly the body derails itself, becomes a landscape, a caravan, a storm, a mountain of sand, and so on. It's the contrary of sadism, which cuts up the unity. What the camera does in Schroeter's films is not to detail the body for desire but to knead the body like dough out of which images are born, images of pleasure and images for pleasure. At the point of an always-unforseen encounter between the camera (and its pleasure) and the body (throbbing with its own pleasure) these images and pleasures with multiple entries are born.

Sadism was anatomically wise, and, if it gave way to mania, it was within a very reasonable manual of anatomy. There is no organic madness in Sade. To try to adapt Sade, this meticulous anatomist, in precise images does not work. Either Sade disappears or one makes old-fashioned family entertainment.

G.D.   An old-fashioned cinema, in the proper sense, since recently one tends to associate fascism and sadism, in the name of "retro" or a nostalgic return. Thus Liliana Cavani in *The Night Porter* and Pier Paolo Pasolini in *Salo.* Yet this representation is not history. The bodies are dressed up in period costumes. They would have us believe that Himmler's henchmen correspond to the Duke, the Bishop, and his Excellency in Sade's text.

M.F.   It's a complete historical error. Nazism was not invented by the great erotic madmen of the twentieth century but by the most sinister, boring, and disgusting petit-bourgeois imaginable. Himmler was a vaguely agricultural type and married a nurse. We must understand that the concentration camps were born from the conjoined imagination of a hospital nurse and a chicken farmer. A hospital plus a chicken yard – that's the phantasm behind the concentration camps. Millions of people were murdered there, so I don't say it to diminish the blame of those responsible for it, but precisely to disabuse those who want to superimpose erotic values upon it.

The Nazis were charwomen in the bad sense of the term. They worked with brooms and dusters, wanting to purge society of everything they considered unsanitary, dusty, filthy; syphilitics, homosexuals, Jews, those of impure blood, Blacks, the insane. It's the foul petit bourgeois dream of racial hygiene that underlies the Nazi dream. Eros is absent.

That said, it's not impossible that locally, within this structure, there were erotic relationships that formed in the bodily confrontation between victim and executioner. But it was accidental.

The problem raised is why we imagine today to have access to certain erotic phantasms through Nazism. Why these boots, caps, and eagles that are found to be so infatuating, particularly in the United States? Is it our incapacity to live out this great enchantment of the disorganized body that we project onto a meticulous, disciplinary, anatomical sadism? Is the only vocabulary that we possess for transcribing the grand pleasure of the body in explosion this sad fable of a recent political apocalypse? Are we unable to think the intensity of the present except as the end of the world in a concentration camp? You see how poor our treasure of images really is! And how urgent it is to fabricate another instead of whining about "alienation" and vilifying the "spectacle."

G.D.   Directors see Sade like the maidservant, the night porter, the floorscrubber. At the end of Pasolini's film the victims are seen through a glass. The floorscrubber sees through a glass what happened far off in a medieval courtyard.

M.F.   You know that I am not for Sade's absolute sacralization. After all, I would be willing to admit that Sade formulated an eroticism proper to a disciplinary society: a regulated, anatomical, hierarchical society whose time is carefully distributed, its spaces partitioned, characterized by obedience and surveillance.

It's time to leave all that behind, and Sade's eroticism with it. We must invent with the body, with its elements, surfaces, volumes, and thicknesses, a nondisciplinary eroticism—that of a body in a volatile and diffused state, with its chance encounters and unplanned pleasures. It bothers me that in recent films certain elements are being used to resuscitate through the theme of Nazism an eroticism of the disciplinary type. Perhaps it was Sade's. Too bad then for the literary deification of Sade, too bad for Sade: he bores us. He's a disciplinarian, a sergeant of sex, an accountant of the ass and its equivalents.

THE GRAY MORNINGS OF TOLERANCE*

Where do children come from? From the stork, from a flower, from God, from the Calabrian uncle. But look rather at the faces of these kids: they do not do anything that gives the impression they believe what they are saying. Delivered with smiles, silences, a distant tone, looks that dart to the left and the right, the answers to these adult questions have a treacherous docility; they assert the right to keep for oneself those things that one likes to whisper. The stork is a way of making fun of grownups, of paying them back in their own false coin; it is the ironic, impatient sign that the question will go no further, that the adults are nosy, they will not get into the circle, and the child will continue to tell the "rest" to himself.

So begins the film by Pier Paolo Pasolini.

Enquête sur la sexualité [inquiry into sexuality] is an odd translation for *Comizi d'amore*: love conference, meeting, or perhaps forum. This is the ancient game of the "symposium," but out of doors on the beaches and the bridges, the street corner, with ball-playing children, boys hanging out, bored bathers, clusters of prostitutes on the boulevard, or workers after the factory job. Very far from the confessional, very far, too, from an inquiry where the most secret things are examined under an assurance of discretion, this is *Street Talk about Love*. After all, the street is the most spontaneous form of Mediterranean conviviality.

*This review appeared in *Le Monde* 9998 (23 March 1977), p. 24. Robert Hurley's translation.

As if in passing, Pasolini offers the microphone to the strolling or sunbathing group: he asks an undirected question about "love," about that vague area where sex, the couple, pleasure, the family, marital engagement with its customs, and prostitution with its rates all intersect. Someone makes up her mind, replies with a little hesitation, gains confidence, speaks for the others; they gather round, approve or grumble, arms on shoulders, face against face. Laughter, affection, a bit of fever quickly circulate among these bodies that bunch together or lightly touch one another. And that speak of themselves with all the more restraint and distance as their contact is livelier and warmer. The adults arrange themselves side by side and speechify; the young people speak briefly and intertwine. Pasolini the interviewer fades out: Pasolini the filmmaker watches, all ears.

The document is negligible when one is more interested in these things that are said than in the mystery that is not said. After the long reign of what is called (too hastily) "Christian morality," one might expect, in this Italy of the early sixties, some sort of sexual effervescence. Not at all. Persistently, the replies are given in terms of right: for or against divorce, for or against the preeminence of the husband, for or against compulsory virginity for girls, for or against the condemnation of homosexuals. As if Italian society of that time, between the secrets of penance and the prescriptions of the law, had not yet found a voice for that public confiding of the sexual which our media currently propagate.

"You say they don't talk? It's because they are afraid," explains Musatti, the run-of-the-mill psychiatrist whom Pasolini questions from time to time, along with Moravia, regarding the inquiry that is underway. But Pasolini obviously does not believe a word of it. What pervades the entire film is not, in my opinion, the obsession with sex but a kind of historical apprehension, a kind of premonitory and confused hesitation with regard to a new system that was emerging in Italy – that of tolerance. And this is where the divisions are clearly visible, in that crowd that agrees to speak about rights when it is questioned about love. Divisions between men and women, country people and city dwellers, rich and poor? Yes, of course, but especially between young people and the others. The latter fear a regime that will upset all the painful and subtle adjustments that have ensured the ecosystem of sex (with the prohibition of divorce that binds the man and the woman unequally, with the brothel that figures as a complement to the family, with the price of virginity and the cost of marriage). The young people approach this change in a very different way—not with shouts of joy but with a mixture of gravity and mistrust, because they know that it is tied to economic transformations likely to renew the inequalities of age, fortune, and status. At bottom, the gray mornings of tolerance do not appeal to anyone, and no one feels that they promise a celebration of sex. With resignation or rage, the older people express their anxiety: What will happen to the law? And the "young" stubbornly reply: What will happen to rights, to *our* rights?

This film, fifteen years old, can serve as a reference mark. One year after *Mamma Roma* Pasolini continues what will become, in his films, a great saga of young people. Of those young people in whom he did not at all see adolescents for psychologists but the current form of a "youth" which our societies, since the Middle Ages, since Rome and Greece, have never been able to integrate, which they have feared or rejected, which they have never managed to subdue, except by getting it killed from time to time in war.

And then, 1963 was the period when Italy had just made a noisy entry into that movement of expansion-consumption-tolerance of which Pasolini was to give us the balance sheet, ten years later, in the *Ecrits corsaires.* The book's vehemence corresponds to the film's anxiety.

1963 was also the period when there began almost everywhere in Europe and the United States that new questioning of the myriad forms of power which the wise men tell us is "in fashion." Very well, then! The "fashion" risks being worn for awhile yet, as it is these days in Bologna.

THE FOUR HORSEMEN OF THE APOCALYPSE
AND THE EVERYDAY WORMS*

B.S.   When I saw the film [*Hitler: A View from Germany*] for the first time, in Germany, I was spellbound, as if by a witch. I was moved because I'm somewhat familiar with Germany, with its culture. And I was disturbed. I thought this film had something perverse about it. Actually, everyone is a bit suspicious of this film. What was your reaction? Did you say to yourself, "That's exactly what needed to be done!"

M.F.   No, because there is not *one* thing to do about what occurred during the years 1930–1945, there are a thousand, ten thousand, and there will be for some time to come. It is certain that the cloak of silence that, for political reasons, has covered post-1945 Nazism is such that one could not fail to raise the question, "What does that become in the minds of Germans? What does that become in their hearts? What does that become in their bodies?" It was bound to become something, and one waited a little anxiously to see how it would come out the other end of the tunnel—in the form of what myth, of what story, of what wound it was going to appear. Syberberg's film is a beautiful monster. I say "beautiful" because that's what struck me the most—and maybe it's what you have in mind when you speak of the perverse quality of the film. I'm not talking about the aesthetic of the film, which I don't know anything about. It manages to bring a certain beauty out of this history without masking any of its sordid, ignoble, and routinely abject aspects. Perhaps that is where it has

---

*This interview, conducted by B. Sobel, appeared in a special issue of the *Cahiers du cinéma* devoted to the work of Hans-Jürgen Syberberg (6 [Feb. 1980], pp. 95–96). Robert Hurley's translation.

grasped the most bewitching facet of Nazism, a certain intensity of abjection, a certain sheen of mediocrity, which was doubtless a power of sorcery that Nazism exerted.

B.S.   When I saw the film, I had a strange feeling myself: I had the startling revelation that young people experienced Nazism as a utopia, as a real utopia. I thought it was very important that Syberberg does not judge or condemn but makes us aware of the fact that a "normally constituted" man, in terms of conventional norms, could have been a Nazi.

M.F.   Simone Weil said of the film that was made about Eva Braun, which was shown a few days ago on television, that it "renders horror commonplace." That is completely true, and the film about Eva Braun, which was made by Frenchmen, was positively stupefying by that very fact. Now, the film by Syberberg does the opposite; it makes the commonplace ignoble. It brings out a potential for ignominy in the banality of a certain way of thinking, a certain way of life, a certain number of daydreams of the European of the everyday thirties. In that respect, this film is the exact opposite of the films that Simone Weil rightly denounced. I hope that eventually it will be possible to sandwich the film on Eva Braun between parts of Syberberg's film. The former seems to be made with an old-fashioned, appropriate, pleasant, and boring postcard depicting a respectable middle-class European family on vacation in the thirties. The value of Syberberg's film is precisely in its saying that horror is commonplace, that the commonplace bears dimensions of horror within itself, that there is a reversibility between horror and banality. The problem of tragic literature and of philosophy is what status should be given to the four horsemen of the Apocalypse. Are they those extravagant and dark heroes who await the end of the world to burst forth? In what form do they suddenly appear, with what countenance? The plague, the great massacres of war, a famine? Or might they be four little worms that we all have in our brains, deep inside our heads, at the bottom of our hearts?

That is the strength of Syberberg's film, I believe. It has done a good job of bringing out the moments when what happens in Europe during the years 1930–1945 is indeed the great dark horsemen of the Apocalypse, and then, it has shown very convincingly the biological kinship, so to speak, between those four horsemen and the everyday worms.

THE IMAGINATION
OF THE NINETEENTH CENTURY*

The *Ring* of the century, conducted by Pierre Boulez and directed by Patrice Chéreau, ended in its fifth and last year. One and a half hours of applause, as once again Valhalla went down in flames. Again and again the artists are called back on the stage. The boos of the first year, the departure of some of the musicians, the unwillingness of the orchestra and of some singers are forgotten; forgotten are the Action Committee for the Preservation of Richard Wagner's Work, the leaflets and the anonymous letters calling for the head of the conductor and director.

To be honest, there are still some unsuccessfully conspiring ghosts left on the green hill. This unexpected *Ring*, produced by foreigners, probably upset them. But they were pale enough, just like the fallen gods. In the bookstore windows of Bayreuth there is, among hundreds of works about, for, or against Wagner (it seems that after Jesus Christ, Wagner has the most extensive list of annual bibliographies) a thin volume whose cover bears a curious photograph: Winifred, Wagner's daughter-in-law, raising her hand above a small man, who is bowing his head to give her a respectful kiss. One can only see his back, but even though his face is turned away, the little mustache is clearly recognizable. Who is doing whom the honor: Is the heiress-directress honoring the painter-dictator, or is he honoring her? I had the impression that very few were interested in such problems.

---

*This commentary originally appeared in Italian translation in *Corriere della sera* 105:225 (30 Sept. 1980), p. 5. This translation, by Alex Susteric, has been amended.

The times have changed. Don't they want to know what those who had sent the race of blond warriors, the massacred slaughterers, into the slaughterhouse, have made out of Wagner? Instead, they want to know what to make out of the unavoidable Wagner today.

Most of all, what to do with this tetralogy which dominates and is the most sullied of Wagner's entire work. If it weren't for the *Ring*, the life of the directors would be simpler. Simpler, too, would be our relation to the culture which is nearest to us.

There was an elegant solution immediately after the war: Wieland Wagner's symbolic purge, the motionless forms of ageless and outcast myths. There was Joachim Herz's parsimonious, political solution for East Germany: he anchored the *Ring* to the historic shores of the 1848 Revolution. And finally there was Peter Stein's "ingenious" solution, discovering the secret of the "Ring" in the theater of the nineteenth century: his Valhalla was revealed as the center of dance of the Paris opera. In all of these solutions a direct encounter with Wagner's mythology, this inflammable, dangerous, and also somewhat ridiculous content, is avoided.

Boulez, Chéreau, and the scenic designer Peduzzi took a more daring approach. They wanted, quite correctly, to revive this mythology. Against all expectations the old guard of Bayreuth screamed of treason, whereas in reality it was a return to Wagner, the Wagner of the "music drama," something that has to be clearly differentiated from opera. Back to the Wagner who wanted to give an imaginary to the nineteenth century, who wanted not a commemoration festival but a celebration where every time the ritual was meant to have the novelty of an event.

Boulez is the strictest and most creative heir of the Vienna School, one of the most important representatives of that strong current which permeated and renewed all the art (and not only the music) of the nineteenth century; and there he stands conducting the tetralogy as if it were a matter of "accompanying" a scene full of noises, horrors, and images. Some wondered about so much passion for musical structures devoted to such an imagery.

And yet Boulez rediscovered the meaning of Wagner's "music drama" by looking through the eyes of the music of the entire nineteenth century.

Accompaniment? Naturally, says Boulez, that is precisely what Wagner wanted. Of course, one has to know what kind of accompaniment. He conducts more clearly, brightly, more intelligently, and more intelligibly than others. He did not impose such reserve on the orchestra to assign a supporting role to the music. On the contrary, the music wasn't meant only to underline, emphasize or announce what happens on the stage. Boulez took seriously Wagner's idea of a "drama" in which music and text do not repeat each other, do not both restate the same thing in their own way. Here the orchestra, the singing, the recitation, the rhythms of the music, the movements on the stage, and the decor must come together as the basic elements in order to first constitute the time of the production, a unified form, a singular event.

Boulez thus acted on the simple fact that spectators aren't deaf and listeners aren't blind. When he attempts to let "everything" be sensed, he does so not to suggest to the ear what the eye can clearly see but because the dramatic development of the music is interwoven with that of the text. Boulez does not consider Wagner's leitmotif to be a tonal doubling of the figure, a mere costume made out of notes. It is itself an individual, albeit a musical one. Rather than a coined, repeatedly stamped-out figure, it is a flexible, ambiguous, proliferating structure, a developmental principle of a tonal world. If the drama has to work itself out in the music, and if the music may not be reduced to a repetition of the drama, a conductor like Boulez is absolutely necessary: a conductor who analyzes, who dissects every moment with a scalpel—Nietzsche spoke about Wagner's "miniatures"—and who in every instant unfolds the increasingly complex dynamic of the work.

One has to have heard Boulez's interpretation on the last evening of "Twilight." One was reminded of what he once said about the tetralogy: "Wagner's gigantic construction," his "intimate diary." Right up to the last pause, he constructs with extraordinary precision the enormous musical forest; it was as if Boulez was retracing his own itinerary. And also the whole movement of a century of modern music, which, beginning with Wagner, found its way through the great adventure and arrived at the intensity and movement of drama. The perfectly deciphered form wove itself into the image.

One can again find in the *Ring* that tension characteristic of Chéreau: an infallible logic in the relations between the characters, the perspicuity of all the elements of the text, a particular sensibility for every single movement and gesture, in brief, the absence of anything gratuitous; and an intentional uncertainty as far as time and place are concerned, an extreme diffusion of the elements of reality. The daughters of the Rhine are prostitutes who tuck up their clothes at the base of a dam. The old bespectacled Jew Mime digs in his trunks to find the holy sword wrapped in newspaper. The gods pace back and forth like exiled princes of a melancholy eighteenth century or like members of an entrepreneurial family threatened with bankruptcy after too much embezzling. The Valkyrie has a helmet, whereas Siegfried will be married in tails.

The same goes for Peduzzi's scenery: big, immobile architectures, huge upright boulders like eternal ruins, gigantic wheels that nothing could set in motion again. But the wheels stand in the heart of a forest, two busts of angels on the rock, and an imperturbable Dorian capital on the walls of Valhalla over the Valkyrie's fire bed, or in the palace of the Gibichungen, which sometimes resembles a harbor in twilight painted by Claude Lorrain, other times the neoclassicist palaces of the Wilhelminian bourgeoisie.

Not that Chéreau and Peduzzi, like Brecht, might have wanted to play with various time references (the epoch to which the work refers, in which it was written, in which it was produced). They, too, took Wagner seriously, even at the cost of having to show the opposite of what Wagner wanted to show. Wagner wanted to give the nineteenth century a mythology? Very well. Did he choose to assemble it from Indo-European legends? Fine. Did he thus want to give his epoch the imaginary that it lacked? It is precisely at this point that Chéreau says no. The nineteenth century was full of images that were the true reason for those great mythological reconstructions, which they changed and concealed. Chéreau did not want to elevate the bazaar of Wagnerian mythology into the sky of eternal myths, nor did he want to reduce it to concrete historical reality. He wanted to unearth those truly living images that were able to give it its force.

Thus Chéreau dug out the images buried under Wagner's text. Forcibly disparate: fragments of utopia, machine parts, elements of engravings, social types, glimpses of oneiric towns, dragons for children, domestic scenes in the manner of Strindberg, the profile of a ghetto Jew. But his successful tour de force lies in the perfect integration of all these elements into the tense dramatics of personal relations and the embodiment of the broad, picturesque visions suggested by Peduzzi. Chéreau's production is always humorous, never malignly reductive. "Wagner's mythology was nothing more than frumpery for bourgeois parvenus." He subjects all this material to a metamorphosis of beauty and to the power of dramatic tension. In a certain sense, he thus descends from Wagner's mythology to the bustling images that populated it and recreates for us a new myth out of them, while simultaneously showing their paradoxical splendor and total logic.

On the stage of Bayreuth, where Wagner wanted to create a mythology for the nineteenth century, Chéreau and Peduzzi again resurrected the imaginary of that century that Wagner probably shared with Bakhunin, Marx, Dickens, Jules Verne, Boecklin, the architects of bourgeois factories and villas, with the illustrators of children's books, and the agents of antisemitism. These images appear to them as mythology, closely related to the one dominating us today. Thus they give the imagination of the nineteenth century, whose mark we still bear in our wounds, the formidable magnitude of a mythology.

From Wagner up to today Boulez stretched the tightly woven fabric of contemporary musical development. Simultaneously, Chéreau and Peduzzi let the Wagnerian *universa* ascend into the firmament of a mythology, which we must recognize as ours. Thanks to the rediscovered contemporaneity of his music, Wagner's mythology doesn't first have to be painfully translated for us, for it is part of our own.

Wolfgang Wagner asked himself on the last evening of this *Ring* what other *Ring* may still be possible. If that cannot be known, it is because Bayreuth is no longer that conservatorium of a mythically ever-identical Wagner–since tradition, as we know, is nothing but "carelessness." Bayreuth will finally be the place where Wagner himself will be treated as one of our contemporary myths.

PIERRE BOULEZ,
PASSING THROUGH THE SCREEN*

Y ou ask me what it was like to have glimpsed, by accident and through the privilege of chance friendship, a little of what was happening in music nearly thirty years ago. I was just a passerby held by affection, a certain perplexity, curiosity, the strange feeling of witnessing something I was incapable of being contemporaneous with. It was a lucky meeting: at the time, music was deserted by discourses from the outside.

Painting in those days was something to be talked about; at any rate, aesthetics, philosophy, reflection, taste–and politics, as I recall–felt they had a right to say something about the matter, and they applied themselves to it as if it were a duty: Piero della Francesca, Venice, Cézanne, or Braque. Silence protected music, however, preserving its insolence. What was doubtless one of the great transformations of twentieth-century art remained out of reach for those forms of reflection, which had established their quarters all around us, places where we risked picking up our habits.

I'm not any more capable of talking about music than I was then. I only know that my having pieced together–through the mediation of another person, most of the time–what was happening in Boulez's camp enabled me to feel like a stranger in the world of thought where I had been trained, to which I still belonged and which was still compelling, for me and for many others. Perhaps things are better that

*This commentary appeared in *Dix ans et après: album souvenir du festival d'automne*, ed. M. Colin, J.-P. Léonardini, J. Markovits (Paris: Messidor, 1982), pp. 232–36. Robert Hurley's translation.

way: if I had had around me the means to understand this experience, I may have only found an occasion to make a place for it where it did not belong.

One is apt to think that a culture is more attached to its values than to its forms, that these can easily be modified, abandoned, taken up again; that only meaning is deeply rooted. This is to overlook how much hatred forms have given rise to when they have come apart or come into existence. It is to ignore the fact that people cling to ways of seeing, saying, doing, and thinking, more than to what is seen, to what is thought, said, or done. In the West the combat of forms has been just as hard fought, if not more so, than that of ideas or values. But in the twentieth century things have taken an unusual turn: the "formal" itself, serious work on the system of forms, has become an issue. And a remarkable object of moral hostilities, of aesthetic debates and political clashes.

During a time in which we were being taught the privileges of meaning, of the lived-through [*du vécu*], the sensuous [*du charnel*], of foundational experience [*de l'expérience originaire*], subjective contents or social significations, to encounter Boulez and music was to see the twentieth century from an unfamiliar angle—that of the long battle around the "formal." It was to recognize how in Russia, in Germany, in Austria, in Central Europe, through music, painting, architecture, or philosophy, linguistics and mythology, the work of the formal had challenged the old problems and overturned the ways of thinking. A whole history of the formal in the twentieth century remains to be done: attempting to measure it as a power of transformation, drawing it out as a force for innovation and a locus of thought, beyond the images or the "formalism" behind which some people tried to hide it. And also recounting its difficult relations with politics. We have to remember that it was quickly designated, in Stalinist or fascist territory, as enemy ideology and detestable art. It was the great adversary of the academic and party dogmatisms. Battles around the formal have been one of the major features of twentieth-century culture.

Boulez only needed a straight line, without any detour or mediation, to go to Stéphane Mallarmé, to Paul Klee, to René Char, to Henri Michaux, and later to e. e. cummings. Often a musician goes to painting, a painter to poetry, a playwright to music, via an encompassing figure and through a universalizing aesthetic: romanticism, expressionism, and so on. Boulez went directly from one point to another, from one experience to another, drawn by what seemed to be not an ideal kinship but the necessity of a conjuncture.

At a stage in his work, and because his progress had led him to a particular point (that point and that stage remaining completely internal to music), a chance encounter suddenly occurred, a flash proximity. It is no use wondering what common aesthetic, what analogous worldview the two *Visage nuptial*, the two *Marteau sans maître*, that of Char and that of Boulez, might have shared.[1] There wasn't one. From the first such event there began a work by one on the other; the music elaborated the poem which elaborated the music. A work all the more exact and all the more dependent on a painstaking analysis because it did not rely on any prior mutuality.

This coming into correlation, daring and deliberate at the same time, was a singular lesson against the categories of the universal. It is not the ascent toward the highest place, it is not access to the most enveloping viewpoint, that gives the most light. The bright light comes laterally, from the breaching of a compartment, the piercing of a wall, two intensities brought together, a distance crossed at one stroke. It is good to prefer the meeting of edges to the large fuzzy lines that blur faces and blunt angles in order to bring out the general meaning. Let's leave it to anyone so inclined to see that nothing is justified without a common discourse and a comprehensive theory. In art as in thought, encounters are justified only by the new necessity they have established.

Boulez's relation to history—I mean the history of his own practice—was intense and combative. For many, and I am one of them, he remained enigmatic, I believe, for a long time. Boulez hated the attitude that chose a fixed module in the past and sought to make it vary across contemporary music: a "classicist" attitude, as he put it. He had just as much antipathy for the "archaistic" attitude that takes present-day music as a reference and tries to graft the artificial youth of past elements onto it. I think his object, in this attention to history, was to make it so that nothing remains fixed, neither the present nor the past. He wanted them both to be in perpetual motion relative to each other. When he focused closely on a given work, rediscovering its dynamic principle, on the basis of a decomposition that was as subtle as possible, he was not trying to make a monument of it; he attempted to traverse it, to "pass through" it, to undo it with an action such that the present itself might move as a result. "Punch through it like a screen," he is fond of saying now, thinking, as in *Les Paravents*,[2] of the action that destroys, by which one dies oneself and which enables one to pass to the other side of death.

There was something baffling in this relation to history: the values that it implied did not indicate a polarity in time (progress or decline); they did not define sacred places. They marked points of intensity that were also objects "to consider." Musical analysis was the form taken by this relation to history – an analysis that did not look for the rules of use of a canonical form but sought to discover a principle of multiple relations. Through this practice, one saw the emergence of a relation to history which disregarded cumulations and scorned totalities. Its law was the dual simultaneous transformation of the past and the present by the movement that detaches one from the other through an elaboration of the one by the other.

Boulez has never accepted the idea that any thought, in the practice of art, would be unwelcome if it was not reflection on the rules of a technique or on their proper application. So he did not have much use for Paul Valéry. What he expected from thought was precisely that it always enable him to do something different from what he was doing. He demanded that it open up, in the highly regulated, very deliberate game that he played, a new space of freedom. One heard some people accuse him of technical gratuitousness, others, of too much theory. But for him the main thing was to conceive of practice strictly in terms of its internal necessities without submitting to any of them as if they were sovereign requirements. What is the role of thought, then, in what one does if it is to be neither a mere savoir-faire nor pure theory? Boulez showed what it is – to supply the strength for breaking the rules with the act that brings them into play.

NOTES

1   René Char, "Le Visage nuptial," in *Fureur et mystère* (Paris: Gallimard, 1948); *Le Marteau sans maître* (Paris: J. Corti, 1934 and 1945) ["The Nuptial Countenance," in *Poems of René Char*, trans. Mary Ann Caws and Jonathon Griffin (Princeton: Princeton University Press, 1976), p. 67; *The Hammer with no Master*, in *Poems of René Char*, pp. 3–31].

2   Jean Genet, *Les Paravents* (Lyon: L'Arbalète, 1961) [*The Screens*, trans. Bernard Frechtman (New York: Grove Press, 1962)].

PART TWO

METHODOLOGY AND EPISTEMOLOGY

PHILOSOPHY AND PSYCHOLOGY*

A.B. What is psychology?

M.F. Let me say that I don't think we should try to define psychology as a science but perhaps as a cultural form. It fits into a whole series of phenomena with which Western culture has been familiar for a long time, and in which there emerged such things as confession, casuistry, dialogues, discourses, and argumentations that could be articulated in certain milieus of the Middle Ages, love courtships or whatnot in the mannered circles of the seventeenth century.

A.B. Are there internal or external relations between psychology as a cultural form and philosophy as a cultural form? And is philosophy a cultural form?

M.F. You're asking two questions:

1. Is philosophy a cultural form? I have to say that I'm not much of a philosopher, so I'm not really in a position to know. I think that's the great problem being debated now; perhaps philosophy is in fact the most general cultural form in which we might be able to reflect on the reality of the West.

2. Now, what are the relations between psychology as a cultural form and philosophy? Well, I believe that we are looking at a point of conflict that for five hundred years has set philosophers and psychologists against one another, a problem that is given a new pertinence by all the questions that revolve around educational reform.

*This interview, conducted by Alain Badiou, appeared in *Dossiers pédagogiques de la radio-télévision scolaire* (27 Feb. 1965), pp. 65-71. Robert Hurley's translation.

I think we can say this: first, that psychology and, through psychology, the human sciences have indeed been in a very tangled relationship with philosophy since the nineteenth century. What is one to make of this entanglement of philosophy and the human sciences? One can tell himself that philosophy in the Western world delimited a domain, blindly and in the void as it were, in darkness, in the obscurity of its own consciousness and its methods—the domain that it called the "soul" or "thought," and that now serves as a legacy that the human sciences have to cultivate in a clear, lucid, and positive manner. So the human sciences would be legitimately occupying that rather vague domain which was marked off but left fallow by philosophy.

That is what one might reply. I think it is what would be said, rather willingly, by people who can be thought of as the defenders of the human sciences, people who consider that the ancient philosophical task, which originated in the West with Greek thought, should now be resumed using the tools of the human sciences. I don't think that defines the exact dimensions of the problem. It seems to me that such a way of analyzing things is clearly tied to a philosophical perspective, which is positivism.

One might also say something else—the contrary. It may be part of the destiny of Western philosophy that, since the nineteenth century, something like an anthropology became possible; when I say "anthropology" I am not referring to the particular science called anthropology, which is the study of cultures exterior to our own; by "anthropology" I mean the strictly philosophical structure responsible for the fact that the problems of philosophy are now all lodged within the domain that can be called that of human finitude.

If one can no longer philosophize about anything but man insofar as he is a *Homo natura*, or insofar as he is a finite being, to that extent isn't every philosophy at bottom an anthropology? This being the case, philosophy becomes the cultural form within which all the sciences of man in general are possible.

That is what could be said, and it would be, if you will, the opposite analysis to the one I outlined a moment ago, so that in the great destiny of Western philosophy it could co-opt the human sciences, just as previously one could co-opt philosophy as a kind of blank program of what the human sciences should be. That is the entanglement, which is what we have to think through, both now, here where we are, and generally in the coming years.

A.B. You said in the first perspective that, on the whole, philosophy was conceived as prescribing its domain to a positive science that would later ensure its actual elucidation. In this perspective what can ensure the specificity of psychology, in comparison with other types of investigation? Can positivism, by its own means, ensure that specificity and does it intend to do so?

M.F. Well, at a time when the human sciences did in fact receive their problematic, their domain, and their concepts from a philosophy that was mainly that of the eighteenth century, I think that psychology could be defined either as a science, let's say, of the soul, or as a science of the individual. To that extent, I think the differentiation from the other human sciences that existed then, and that was already possible, could be made in a rather clear manner: one could oppose psychology to the sciences of the physiological order, just as one opposed the soul to the body; one could oppose psychology to sociology, just as one opposed the individual to the collectivity or the group, and if one defines psychology as the science of consciousness, to what is one going to oppose it? Well, for a period extending roughly from Arthur Schopenhauer to Nietzsche, it could be said that psychology was opposed to philosophy, just as consciousness was opposed to the unconscious. I think, moreover, that it was precisely around the elucidation of the nature of the unconscious that the reorganization and the repartitioning of the human sciences were carried out, essentially around Freud, and the positive definition, inherited from the eighteenth century, of psychology as a science of consciousness and of the individual can no longer stand, now that Freud has existed.

A.B. Now let's place ourselves in the other perspective: the problematic of the unconscious, which you see as the source of the restructuring of the domain of the human sciences. What meaning do you assign to it, given that the human sciences are regarded as a moment in the destiny of Western philosophy?

M.F. This problem of the unconscious is really very difficult, because apparently one can say that psychoanalysis is a form of psychology that is added to the psychology of consciousness, doubling the psychology of consciousness with a supplementary layer that would be that of the unconscious. And, as a matter of fact, it was realized immediately that by discovering the unconscious one pulled in at the same time a lot of problems that no longer involved either the individual, exactly, or the soul opposed to the body; but that one brought back inside the strictly psychological problematic what had previously been excluded from it, either on the grounds that it was physiology, reintroducing the problem of the body, or sociology, reintroducing the problem of the individual with his milieu, the group to which he belongs, the society in which he is caught, the culture in which he and his ancestors have always thought. With the result that the simple discovery of the unconscious is not an addition of domains: it is not an extension of psychology, it is actually the appropriation, by psychology, of most of the domains that the human sciences covered—so that one can say that, starting with Freud, all the human sciences became, in one way or another, sciences of the psyche. And the old realism à la Emile Durkheim—conceiving of society as a substance in opposition to the individual who is also a kind of substance incorporated into society—appears to me to be unthinkable now. In the same way, the old distinction of the soul and the body, which was still valid even for the psychophysiology of the nineteenth century, that old opposition no longer exists, now that we know that our body forms part of our psyche, or forms part of that experience, conscious and unconscious at once, which psychology addresses—so that all there is now, basically, is psychology.

A.B. This restructuring, which culminates in a sort of psychological totalitarianism, is carried out around the theme of the discovery of the unconscious, to repeat your expression. Now, the word discovery is usually linked to a scientific context. How do you understand the discovery of the unconscious, then? What type of discovery is involved?

M.F. Well, the unconscious was literally discovered by Freud as a thing; he perceived it as a certain number of mechanisms that existed at the same time in man in general and in a given particular man.

Did Freud thereby commit psychology to a radical concretification [*chosification*], against which the entire subsequent history of modern psychology never ceased to react, up to Maurice Merleau-Ponty, up to contemporary thinkers? Possibly so; but it may be precisely in that absolute horizon of things that psychology was made possible, if only as criticism.

Then again, for Freud the unconscious has a languagelike structure; but one should bear in mind that Freud is an exegete and not a semiologist; he is an interpreter and not a grammarian. His problem, finally, is not a problem of linguistics, it is a problem of decipherment. Now, what is it to interpret, what is it to treat a language not as a linguist does but as an exegete or hermeneut does—if not in fact to grant that there exists a kind of absolute graphy that we will have to discover in its very materiality—and go on to recognize that this materiality is meaningful, a second discovery; and then to find out what it means, a third discovery; and finally, fourthly, to discover the laws according to which these signs mean what they do. It is then, and only then, that one encounters the layer of semiology, that is, for example, the problem of metaphor and metonymy, that is, the ways in which a group of signs may be able to say something. But this fourth discovery is fourth only in relation to three more fundamental ones, and these three primary discoveries are the discovery of something that is there in front of us, the discovery of a text to be interpreted—the discovery of a kind of absolute ground for a possible hermeneutic.

A.B.   The specialists of decipherment of texts distinguish decipherment and decoding: decipherment consisting in deciphering a text to which one has the key, and decoding, a text to which one doesn't have the key, the very structure of the message. Would psychological methods be in the category of decipherment or that of decoding?

M.F.   I'll say that it's decoding, and yet not entirely, because there again the concepts of decipherment and decoding are concepts that linguists have essentially defined in order to co-opt what is, in my view, unco-optable for any linguistics—that is, hermeneutics, interpretation. Let us accept, if you will, the notion of decoding: I would say that Freud in effect decodes, which is to say, he recognizes that there is a message there. He doesn't know what that message means; he doesn't know the laws according to which the signs can mean what they mean. So he has to discover at one go both what the message means and what the laws are by which the message means what it means. In other words, the unconscious must convey not only what it says but the key to what it says. And it is for that reason, moreover, that psychoanalysis, the experience of psychoanalysis, psychoanalytic language have always intrigued literature. There is a kind of fascination of contemporary literature, not only with psychoanalysis but with all the phenomena that are connected with madness: because what is madness now, in the contemporary world, if not a message, if not language, signs that one hopes—because it would be too dreadful otherwise—mean something, signs whose meaning is not known and whose means of conveying it is not known. And, consequently, madness must be treated as a message that would have its own key within itself. That is what Freud does when he's faced with a hysterical symptom; that is what is done by people who are now trying to address the problem of psychosis.

And, after all, what is literature if not a certain language about which we know very well that it does not say what it says. For if literature meant to say what it says, it would simply say: "The marquise went out at five o'clock. . . ." We know very well that literature doesn't say that, so we know that it is a second-order language, folded back on itself, which means something other than what it says. We don't know what that other language is that's underneath; we know just that, at the end of our reading of the novel, we should have discovered what it means and in terms of what, of what laws the author was able to say what he meant. We need to have done both an exegesis and a semiology of the text.

Hence there is a kind of symmetrical structure of literature and madness that consists in the fact that one cannot do their semiology except by doing their exegesis, their exegesis except by doing their semiology, and this reciprocal tie absolutely cannot be undone, I think. Let us say simply that up to 1950 it had merely been understood, very poorly moreover, very approximately, with regard to psychoanalysis or literary criticism, that something like an interpretation was at issue. It had not been seen that there was a whole dimension of semiology, of analysis of the very structure of signs. This semiological dimension is now being uncovered and, consequently, the interpretive dimension is being hidden—and, in point of fact, it is the structure of envelopment, of wrapping, which characterizes the language of madness and the language of literature, and that is why we would arrive at a situation where not only all the human sciences are psychologized, but even literary criticism and literature are psychologized.

A.B.　If the unconscious presents itself on the whole as a text-object, to preserve your concretist [*chosiste*] perspective, in which the message is discovered as always adhering to a code—so that there is no general code within which the message might disclose its meaning in an a priori fashion, as it were—then a psychology cannot be a general science: it never deals with anything but texts that are radically singular, being the bearers of their own specific code. And psychology is, therefore, a science of the individual, not only by virtue of its object but ultimately by virtue of its method. Or is there a general hermeneutic?

M.F. One needs to distinguish, in this instance and elsewhere, between the general and the absolute; there is no absolute hermeneutic, in the sense that one can never be sure that one has obtained the final text, that what one has obtained doesn't mean something else behind what it means. And one can never be sure, on the other hand, of doing an absolute linguistics. So, whatever the approach, one is never sure of reaching either the absolutely general form or the absolutely primary text.

That being said, I still think that there are relatively large generalized structures, and that, for example, there may be among several individuals a certain number of identical processes [*procédés*] that may be encountered in all of them alike; and there is no reason why structures you have discovered for one would not apply to the other.

A.B. Will psychology be, in the last instance, the science of these structures or knowledge of the individual text?

M.F. Psychology will be the knowledge of structures; and the eventual therapeutics, which cannot fail to be tied to psychology, will be knowledge of the individual text—that is, I don't think psychology can ever dissociate itself from a certain normative program. Psychology may well be, like philosophy itself, a medicine and a therapeutics—actually, there is no doubt that it's a medicine and a therapeutics. And the fact that in its most positive forms psychology happens to be separated into two subsciences, which would be psychology and pedagogy for example, or psychopathology and psychiatry, separated into two moments as isolated as these, is really nothing but the sign that they must be brought together. Every psychology is a pedagogy, all decipherment is a therapeutics: you cannot know without transforming [*sans transformer*].

A.B. Several times you have seemed to say that psychology is not satisfied with establishing relations, structures, no matter how rigorous and complex, between given elements, but that it always involves interpretations—and that the other sciences, on the contrary, when they encountered data to be interpreted, were no longer adequate to the task. And you seem to be saying that psychology had to appear on the scene. If that is the case, does the word "psychology" seem to you to have the same meaning in expressions like "human psychology" and "animal psychology?"

M.F.   I'm glad you've asked that question, because as a matter of fact I'm responsible for a shift. First, I said that the general articulation of the human sciences had been completely remodeled by the discovery of the unconscious, and that psychology had paradoxically assumed a kind of imperative over the other sciences; and then I started talking about psychology in a strictly Freudian perspective–as if all psychology could only be Freudian. There was a general repartitioning of the human sciences starting with Freud; that's an undeniable fact, I believe, one that even the most positivist psychologists couldn't deny. This doesn't mean that all psychology, in its most positive developments, became a psychology of the unconscious or a psychology of the relations of consciousness to the unconscious. There remained a certain physiological psychology; there remained a certain experimental psychology. After all, the laws of memory, as they were established by my namesake fifty, sixty years ago, have absolutely nothing to do with Freudian forgetting. That remains what it is, and I don't think that at the level of positive, quotidian knowledge the presence of Freudianism has really changed the observations that can be made either about animals, or even about certain aspects of human behavior. Freudianism involves a kind of archaeological transformation; it is not a general metamorphosis of all psychological knowledge.

A.B.   But then, if the term "psychology" encompasses aspects that are so different, what meaning do these aspects share? Is there a unity of psychology?

M.F.   Yes, if we grant that when a psychologist studies the behavior of a rat in a maze, what he is trying to define is the general form of behavior that might be true for a man as well as a rat; it is always a question of what can be known about man.

A.B.   Then would you agree with the statement that the object of psychology is knowledge of man, and the different "psychologies" are so many ways of gaining that knowledge?

M.F.   Yes, basically, I would agree with that–but I wouldn't want to repeat it too often, because it sounds too simple . . . But it's much less simple if one considers that, at the beginning of the nineteenth century, there appeared the very curious project of knowing man. That is probably one of the fundamental facts in the history of European culture–because even though there were, in the seventeenth and eighteenth centuries, books titled *Traité de l'homme*[1] or *A Treatise of Human Nature*,[2] they absolutely did not treat of man in the way that we do when we do psychology. Until the end of the eighteenth century–that is, until Kant–every reflection on man is a secondary reflection with respect to a thought that is primary, and that is, let's say, the thought of the infinite. It was always a matter of answering questions like these: Given that the truth is what it is, or that mathematics or physics have taught this thing or that, why is it that we perceive in the way that we perceive, that we know in the way that we know, that we are wrong in the way that we are wrong?

Starting with Kant, there is a reversal: the problem of man will be raised as a kind of cast shadow, but this will not be in terms of the infinite or the truth. Since Kant, the infinite is no longer given, there is no longer anything but finitude; and it's in that sense that the Kantian critique carried the possibility–or the peril–of an anthropology.

A.B. During a certain period, in our classes, much was made of the distinction between "explain" and "understand" in the human sciences. Does that distinction have any meaning in your view?

M.F. I'm afraid to say yes, but it does seem to me that the first time "explain" and "understand" were distinguished and put forward in that way–as radical, absolute, and mutually incompatible epistemological forms–it was by Wilhelm Dilthey. Now, all the same, it is something very important, and it was precisely Dilthey who wrote, to my knowledge, the only history of hermeneutics in Western history, a work that was a bit rough but extremely interesting. Now, I think what is profound in him is the feeling he had that hermeneutics represented a quite particular mode of reflection, whose meaning and value risked being hidden by different modes of knowledge more or less borrowed from the natural sciences. And he had a strong feeling that the epistemological model of the natural sciences was going to be imposed as a norm of rationality on the human sciences, whereas these same sciences were probably just one of the avatars of the hermeneutic techniques that had always existed in the Western world, since the first Greek grammarians, in the exegetes of Alexandria, in the Christian and modern exegetes. And I think that Dilthey intuited the historically general context that psychology and the human sciences in general belonged to in our culture. That is what he defined, in a rather mystical way, by understanding as opposed to explanation. Explanation would be the bad epistemological model;

understanding is the mythical figure of a human science restored to its radical meaning as exegesis.

A.B.   Do you think that what is said of the exact and rigorous sciences can be said of psychology as a science and a technique—that it carries out its own critique of its methods, its concepts, and so on?

M.F.   I believe that what is currently taking place in psychoanalysis and in certain other sciences such as anthropology is something similar to that. The fact that after Freud's analysis something like Jacques Lacan's analysis is possible, that after Durkheim something like Claude Lévi-Strauss is possible—all of that proves, in fact, that the human sciences are establishing in and for themselves a certain critical relationship that calls to mind the relationship that physics or mathematics maintain towards themselves. The same is true of linguistics.

A.B.   But not of experimental psychology?

M.F.   Well, no, not up to now. But, after all, when psychologists do studies on learning and they look at the data, determining the extent to which their informational analyses may enable them to formalize the results obtained, that is also a kind of reflexive and generalizing—and foundational—relationship that psychology establishes for itself. Now, it cannot be said that cybernetics or information theory is the philosophy or the psychology of learning, just as it cannot be said that what Lacan is doing, or what Lévi-Strauss is doing, is the philosophy of psychoanalysis or of anthropology. It is instead a certain reflexive relationship of science with itself.

A.B.   If you were in a philosophy class, the kind that we have now, what would you teach on the subject of psychology?

M.F.   The first precaution I would take, if I were a philosophy professor and I had to teach psychology, would be to buy myself the most realistic mask I can imagine and the one farthest from my normal face, so that my students would not recognize me. I would try, like Anthony Perkins in *Psycho*, to adopt another voice so that none of my speech patterns would appear. That is the first precaution I would take. Next I would try, as far as possible, to introduce the students to the techniques that are currently being used by psychologists, laboratory methods, social psychology methods. I would try to explain to them what psychoanalysis consists in. And then, the following hour, I would remove my mask, I would take up my own voice again, and we would do philosophy, even if this meant reencountering psychology, at that moment, as a kind of absolutely unavoidable and inevitable impasse that Western thought entered into in the nineteenth century. But when I would say that it's an absolutely unavoidable and inevitable impasse, I would not criticize it as a science; I would not say that it is not really a positive science; I wouldn't say that it's something that ought to be more philosophical or less philosophical. I would say simply that there was a kind of anthropological slumber in which philosophy and the human sciences were enchanted, as it were, and put to sleep by one another—and that we need to awake from this anthropological slumber, just as in the past people awoke from the dogmatic slumber.

NOTES

1   René Descartes, *Traité de l'homme* (Paris: Clerselier, 1664), in *Oeuvres et lettres*, ed. A. Bridoux (Paris: Gallimard, 1953), pp. 805–75 [*Treatise of Man*, trans. Thomas Steele Hall (Cambridge, Mass.: Harvard University Press, 1972)].

2   David Hume, *A Treatise of Human Nature, Being an Attempt to Introduce the Experimental Method of Reasoning into Moral Subjects* (London: J. Noon, 1739–1740), 3 vols., trans. by A. Leroy as *Traité de la nature humaine: essai pour introduire la méthode expérimentale dans les sujets moraux* (Paris: Aubier-Montagne, 1973), 2 vols.

THE ORDER OF THINGS *

R.B. How is *The Order of Things* related to *Madness and Civilization?*

M.F. *Madness and Civilization,* roughly speaking, was the history of a division, the history above all of a certain break that every society finds itself obliged to make. On the other hand, in this book I wanted to write a history of order, to state how a society reflects upon resemblances among things and how differences between things can be mastered, organized into networks, sketched out according to rational schemes. *Madness and Civilization* is the history of difference, *The Order of Things* the history of resemblance, sameness, and identity.

R.B. The book's subtitle once again includes this word "archaeology." It appeared in the subtitle of *The Birth of the Clinic* and again in the preface to *Madness and Civilization.*

M.F. By "archaeology" I would like to designate not exactly a discipline but a domain of research, which would be the following: in a society, different bodies of learning, philosophical ideas, everyday opinions, but also institutions, commercial practices and police activities, mores—all refer to a certain implicit knowledge [*savoir*] special to this society. This knowledge is profoundly different from the bodies of learning [*des connaissances*] that one can find in scientific books, philosophical theories, and religious justifications, but it is what makes possible at a given moment the appearance of a theory, an opinion, a practice. Thus, in order for the big centers of internment to

*This interview, conducted by Raymond Bellours, appeared in *Les Lettres françaises* 1125 (31 March–6 April 1966), pp. 3–4. This translation, by John Johnston, has been slightly amended.

be opened at the end of the seventeenth century, it was necessary that a certain knowledge of madness be opposed to nonmadness, of order to disorder, and it's this knowledge that I wanted to investigate, as the condition of possibility of knowledge [*connaissance*], of institutions, of practices.

This style of research has for me the following interests: it allows me to avoid every problem concerning the anteriority of theory in relation to practice, and the reverse. In fact, I deal with practices, institutions and theories on the same plane and according to the same isomorphisms, and I look for the underlying knowledge [*savoir*] that makes them possible, the stratum of knowledge that constitutes them historically. Rather than try to explain this knowledge from the point of view of the practico-inert, I try to formulate an analysis from the position of what one could call the "theoretico-active."[a]

R.B. You find yourself therefore confronting a double problem – of history and formalization.

M.F. All these practices, then, these institutions and theories, I take at the level of traces, that is, almost always at the level of verbal traces. The ensemble of these traces constitutes a sort of domain considered to be homogeneous: one doesn't establish any differences a priori. The problem is to find common traits between these traces of orders different enough to constitute what logicians call "classes," aestheticians call "forms," social scientists call "structures," which are the invariants common to a certain number of traces.

R.B. How have you raised the problem of choice and nonchoice?

M.F. I will say that, in fact, there should not be any privileged choice. One should be able to read everything, to know all the institutions and all the practices. None of the values traditionally recognized in the history of ideas and philosophy should be accepted as such. One is dealing with a field that will ignore the differences and traditionally important things. Which means that one will take up *Don Quixote*, Descartes, and a decree by Pomponne de Bellièvre about houses of internment in the same stroke. One will perceive that the grammarians of the eighteenth century have as much importance as the recognized philosophers of the same period.

R.B. It is in this sense that you say, for example, that Cuvier and Ricardo have taught you as much or more than Kant and Hegel. But then the question of information becomes the pressing one: how do you read everything?

M.F. One can read all the grammarians, and all the economists. For *The Birth of the Clinic* I read every medical work of importance for the methodology of the period 1780–1820. The choices that one could make are inadmissible and shouldn't exist. One ought to read everything, study everything. In other words, one must have at one's disposal the general archive of a period at a given moment. And archaeology is, in a strict sense, the science of this archive.

R.B. What determines the choice of historic period (here, as in *Madness and Civilization*, you go from the Renaissance to the present), and its relationship with the "archaeological" perspective that you adopt?

M.F. This kind of research is only possible as the analysis of our own subsoil. It's not a defect of these retrospective disciplines to find their point of departure in our own actuality. There can be no doubt that the problem of the division between reason and unreason became possible only with Nietzsche and Artaud. And it's the subsoil of our modern consciousness of madness that I have wanted to investigate. If there were not something like a fault line in this soil, archaeology would not have been possible or necessary. In the same way, if the question of meaning and of the relation between meaning and the sign had not appeared in European culture with Freud, Saussure, and Husserl, it is obvious that it would not have been necessary to investigate the subsoil of our consciousness of meaning. In the two cases these are the critical analysis of our own condition.

R.B. What has brought you to adopt the three axes that orient your whole analysis?

M.F. Roughly this. The human sciences that have appeared since the end of the nineteenth century are caught, as it were, in a double obligation, a double and simultaneous postulation: that of hermeneutics, interpretation, or exegesis—one must understand a hidden meaning. And the other: one must formalize, discover the system, the structural invariant, the network of simultaneities. Yet these two questions seemed to comfort each other in a privileged fashion in the human sciences, to the point that one has the impression that it is necessary that they be one or the other, interpretation or formalization. What I undertook was precisely the archaeological research of what had made this ambiguity possible. I wanted to find the branch that bore this fork. Thus I had to respond to a double question concerning the Classical period—that of the theory of signs, and that of the empirical order, of the constitution of empirical orders.

It appeared to me that, in fact, the Classical age, usually considered as the age of the radical mechanization of nature, of the mathematization of the living, was in reality something entirely different—that there existed a very important domain that included general grammar, natural history and the analysis of wealth; and that this empirical domain is based on the project of an ordering of things, and this thanks not to mathematics and geometry but to a systematics of signs, a sort of general and systematic taxonomy of things.

R.B.   It's thus a return to the Classical age that has determined the three axes. How, then, is the passage in these three domains from the Classical age to the nineteenth century effected?

M.F.   It revealed one thing that came to me as a complete surprise—that man didn't exist within Classical knowledge [*savoir*]. What existed in the place where we now discover man was the power special to discourse, to the verbal order, to represent the order of things. In order to study grammar or the system of wealth, there was no need to pass through a human science, just through discourse.

R.B.   Yet, apparently, if ever a literature seemed to speak of man, it was our literature of the seventeenth century.

M.F.   Insofar as what existed in Classical knowledge were representations ordered in a discourse, all the notions that are fundamental for our conception of man—such as those of life, work, and language—had no basis in that period, and no place.

At the end of the seventeenth century, discourse ceased to play the organizing role that it had in Classical knowledge. There was no longer any transparency between the order of things and the representations that one could have of them; things were folded somehow onto their own thickness and onto a demand exterior to representation. It's for this reason that languages with their history, life with its organization and its autonomy, and work with its own capacity for production appeared. In the face of that, in the lacuna left by discourse, man constituted himself, a man who is as much one who lives, who speaks and who works, as one who experiences [*connaît*] life, language and work, as one finally who can be known to the extent that he lives, speaks and works.

R.B.   Against this background, how does our situation today present itself?

M.F.   At the moment we find ourselves in a very ambiguous situation. Man has existed since the beginning of the nineteenth century only because discourse ceased to have the force of law over the empirical world. Man has existed where discourse was silenced. Yet with Saussure, Freud, and Hegel, at the heart of what is most fundamental in the knowledge of man, the problem of meaning and the sign reappeared. Now, one can wonder if this return of the great problem of the sign and meaning, of the order of signs, constitutes a kind of superimposition in our culture over what had constituted the Classical age and modernity–or, rather, if it's a question of omens announcing that man is disappearing–since, until the present, the order of man and that of signs have in our culture been incompatible with each other. Man would die from the signs that were born in him–that's what Nietzsche, the first one to see this, meant.

R.B.   It seems to me that this idea of an incompatibility between the order of signs and the order of man must have a certain number of consequences.

M.F.   Yes. For example: (1) It makes an idle fancy of the idea of a science of man that would be at the same time an analysis of signs. (2) It announces the first deterioration in European history of the anthropological and humanist episode that we experienced in the nineteenth century, when one thought that the sciences of man would be at the same time the liberation of man, of the human being in his plenitude. Experience has shown that the human sciences, in their development, led to the disappearance of man rather than to his apotheosis. (3) Literature, whose status changed in the nineteenth century when it ceased to belong to the order of discourse and became the manifestation of language in its thickness, must no doubt now assume another status, is assuming another status; and the hesitation that it manifests between the vague humanisms and the pure formalism of language is, no doubt, only one of the manifestations of this phenomenon, which is fundamental for us and makes us oscillate between interpretation and formalizations, man and signs.

C.B.   Thus one sees clearly the great determination of French literature since the Classical age take form–in particular, the scheme that leads from a first humanism, that of Romanticism, to Flaubert, then to this literature of the subject embodied in the generation of the *Nouvelle revue française*, to the new humanism, of before and after the war, and today to the formation of the *nouveau roman*. Yet German literature holds this kind of evolutionary scheme in check, however one envisages it.

M.F. Perhaps insofar as German classicism was contemporary with this age of history and interpretation, German literature found itself from its origins in this confrontation we are experiencing today. That would explain why Nietzsche didn't do anything but become aware of this situation; and now he's the one who serves as a light for us.

R.B. That would explain why he can appear throughout your book as the exemplary figure, the nonarchaeologizable subject (or not yet); since it is starting from what he opened that the question is raised in all its violence.

M.F. Yes, he is the one who through German culture understood that the rediscovery of the dimension proper to language is incompatible with man. From that point, Nietzsche has taken on a prophetic value for us. And then, on the other hand, it is necessary to condemn with the most complete severity all the attempts to dull the problem. For example, the use of the most familiar notions of the eighteenth century, the schemes of resemblance and contiguity, all of that which is used to build the human sciences, to found them, all that appears to me to be a form of intellectual cowardice that serves to confirm what Nietzsche signified to us for almost a century—that where there is a sign, there man cannot be, and that where one makes signs speak, there man must fall silent.

What appears to me to be deceiving and naive in reflections on and analyses of signs is that one supposes them to be always already there, deposited on the figure of the world, or constituted by men, and that one never investigates their being. What does it mean, the fact that there are signs and marks of language? One must pose the problem of the being of language as a task, in order not to fall back to a level of reflection that would be that of the eighteenth century, to the level of empiricism.

R.B. One thing in your book struck me very sharply—the perfect singularity of its position toward philosophy, the philosophical tradition and history, on the one hand, and, on the other, toward the history of ideas, methods, and concepts.

M.F. I was shocked by the fact that there existed on one side a history of philosophy which gave itself as a privileged object the philosophical edifices that the tradition signaled as important (at the very most it meant accepting, since it was a little trendy, that it had to do with the birth of industrial capitalism); and, on the other side, a history of ideas, that is to say subphilosophies, which took for their privileged object the texts of Montesquieu, Diderot or, Fontenelle.

If one adds to that the histories of the sciences, one cannot fail to be struck by the impossibility of our culture of raising the problem of the history of its own thought. It's why I have tried to make, obviously in a rather particular style, the history not of thought in general but of all that "contains thought" in a culture, of all in which there is thought. For there is thought in philosophy, but also in a novel, in jurisprudence, in law, in an administrative system, in a prison.

NOTES

a   The "practico-inert" is a historical category developed by Jean-Paul Sartre in *The Critique of Dialectical Reason* (Atlantic Highlands, N.J: Humanities Press, 1976). The practico-inert field is a structure that unifies individuals from without (for example, by common interest). – Ed.

NIETZSCHE, FREUD, MARX*

T his project of a "round table," when it was proposed to me, seemed very interesting but obviously rather imposing. I suggest an expedient: some themes concerning *the techniques of interpretation* of Marx, Nietzsche, and Freud.

In reality, behind these themes, there is a dream: to be able one day to compile a kind of general corpus, an encyclopedia of all the techniques of interpretation that we have come to know from the Greek grammarians to our own day. I believe that, until now, few chapters of this great corpus of all the techniques of interpretation have been edited.

It seems to me that it would be possible, by way of general introduction to this idea of a history of the techniques of interpretation, to say this: Language—in any case, language in the Indo-European cultures—has always given birth to two kinds of suspicions:

- First of all, the suspicion that language does not mean exactly what it says. The meaning that one grasps, and that is immediately manifest, is perhaps in reality only a lesser meaning that protects, confines, and yet in spite of everything transmits another meaning, the latter being at once the stronger meaning and the "underlying" meaning. This is what the Greeks called *allēgoria* and *huponoia*.

*This essay originally appeared in *Cahiers de Royaumont* (Paris: Minuit, 1967), vol. 4: *Nietzsche*, pp. 183-200. It stems from the July 1964 Royaumont colloquium. This translation, by Jon Anderson and Gary Hentzi, has been slightly amended.

• On the other hand, language gives birth to this other suspicion: It exceeds its merely verbal form in some way, and there are indeed other things in the world which speak and which are not language. After all, it could be that nature, the sea, the rustling of trees, animals, faces, masks, crossed swords, all of these speak; perhaps there is language that articulates itself in a manner that is not verbal. This would be, if you like, very roughly, the Greek's *sēmainon*.

These two suspicions, which one sees already appearing with the Greeks, have not disappeared, and they are still with us, since we have once again begun to believe, specifically since the nineteenth century, that mute gestures, that illnesses, that all the tumult around us can also speak; and more than ever we are listening in on all this possible language, trying to intercept, beneath the words, a discourse that would be more essential.

I believe that each culture—I mean to say each cultural form in Western civilization—has had its system of interpretation, its techniques, its methods, its own ways of suspecting that language means something other than what it says, and of suspecting that there is language other than in language. It seems, then, that one could inaugurate the enterprise of making the system, or the "table," as they used to say in the seventeenth century, of all these systems of interpretation.

In order to understand what system of interpretation the nineteenth century founded, and so in turn what system of interpretation we, too, even now are involved in, it seems to me necessary to take a remote reference point, a type of technique that could exist, for example, in the sixteenth century. In that period, what provided a *place* for interpretation, both its general site and the minimal unity that interpretation had to maintain, was resemblance. Whenever things resembled each other, wherever *that* was similar, something wanted to be said and could be deciphered; the important role that resemblance, and all the notions that revolve around it like satellites, played in the cosmology, in the botany, in the zoology, in the philosophy of the sixteenth century is well known. Actually, to twentieth-century eyes, this whole network of similitudes is rather confused and tangled. In fact, the corpus of resemblance in the sixteenth century was perfectly organized. There were at least five perfectly defined notions:

- The notion of conformability, *convenientia*, which is adjustment (for example, of the soul to the body, or of the animal series to the vegetable series).

- The notion of *sympatheia*, sympathy, which is the identity of accidents in distinct substances.

- The notion of *emulatio*, which is the very curious parallelism of attributes in distinct substances or beings, such that the attributes of one are like the reflections of those of another. (Thus Porta explains that the human face is, with its seven distinguishable parts, the emulation of the sky with its seven planets.)

- The notion of *signatura*, signature, which is, among the visible properties of an individual, the image of an invisible and hidden property.

- And then, of course, the notion of *analogy*, which is the identity of relations between two or more distinct substances.

In this period, then, the theory of the sign and the techniques of interpretation were based on a perfectly clear definition of all the possible types of resemblance, and they formed the basis of two perfectly distinct types of knowledge: *cognitio*, which was the transition, in some lateral fashion, from one resemblance to another; and *divinatio*, which was knowledge in depth, going from a superficial resemblance to a deeper resemblance. All these resemblances manifest the *consensus* of the world that grounds them; they are opposed to the *simulacrum*, the false resemblance, which is based on the dissension between God and the Devil.

If these sixteenth-century techniques of interpretation were left in suspension by the evolution of Western thought in the seventeenth and eighteenth centuries, if the Baconian critique, the Cartesian critique of resemblance certainly played a major role in bracketing them, the nineteenth century—and particularly Marx, Nietzsche, and Freud—have put us back into the presence of a new possibility of interpretation; they have founded once again the possibility of a hermeneutic.

The first volume of *Capital*, texts like *The Birth of Tragedy* and *The Genealogy of Morals*, and *The Interpretation of Dreams*, put us back into the presence of interpretive techniques. And the shock effect, the kind of wound caused in Western thought by these works, probably comes from what they reconstituted before our eyes, something, moreover, that Marx himself called "hieroglyphs." This has put us into an uncomfortable position, since these techniques of interpretation concern us ourselves, since we, the interpreters, have begun to interpret ourselves by these techniques. With these techniques of interpretation, in turn, we must interrogate those interpreters who were Freud, Nietzsche, and Marx, so that we are perpetually sent back in a perpetual play of mirrors.

Freud says somewhere that there are three great narcissistic wounds in Western culture:[1] the wound inflicted by Copernicus; the one made by Darwin, when he discovered that man descended from the ape; and the wound made by Freud himself, when he in turn discovered that consciousness rests on the unconscious. I wonder whether one could not say that Freud, Nietzsche, and Marx, by involving us in a task of interpretation that always reflects back on itself, have not constituted around us, and for us, these mirrors in which we are given back images whose perennial wounds form our narcissism today. In any case—and it is to this end that I would like to make some suggestions—it seems to me that Marx, Nietzsche, and Freud have not in some way multiplied the signs in the Western world. They have not given a new meaning to things that had no meaning. They have in reality changed the nature of the sign and modified the fashion in which the sign can in general be interpreted.

The first question that I wanted to pose is this: Have not Marx, Freud, and Nietzsche profoundly modified the space of distribution in which signs can be signs?

In the period that I have taken as a point of reference, in the sixteenth century, signs were disposed in a homogeneous fashion in a space that was itself homogeneous in all directions. The signs of the earth referred to the sky, but they referred to the subterranean world as well; they referred from man to animal, from animal to plant, and reciprocally. Beginning in the nineteenth century, with Freud, Marx, and Nietzsche, signs were ranged in a much more differentiated space, according to a dimension that could be called that of depth [*profondeur*], as long as this is not taken to mean interiority, but on the contrary exteriority.

I think in particular of the long debate that Nietzsche never ceased to carry on with depth. There is in Nietzsche a critique of ideal depth, of depth of conscience, which he denounces as an invention of philosophers; this depth would be the pure and interior search for truth. Nietzsche shows how it implies resignation, hypocrisy, the mask; so that the interpreter must, when he examines signs in order to denounce them, descend along the vertical line and show that this depth of interiority is in reality something other than what it says. Consequently, it is necessary that the interpreter descend, that he be, as Nietzsche says, "the good excavator of the lower depths."[2]

But, in reality, when one interprets one can trace this descending line only to restore the glittering exteriority that was covered up and buried. For if the interpreter must go to the bottom himself, like an excavator, the movement of interpretation is, on the contrary, that of a projection [*surplomb*], of a more and more elevated projection, which always leaves depth above it to be displayed in a more and more visible fashion; and depth is now restored as an absolutely superficial secret, in such a way that the flight of the eagle, the ascension of the mountain, all the verticality that is so important in Zarathustra is in the strict sense the reversal of depth, the discovery that depth was only a game and a surface fold. To the extent that the world becomes deeper under our gaze, we perceive that everything which elicited man's depth was only child's play.

I wonder whether this spatiality, this game with depth of Nietzsche's spatiality cannot be compared to the apparently different game that Marx carried on with platitude. The concept of platitude in Marx is very important; at the beginning of *Capital*, he explains how, unlike Perseus, he must plunge into the fog to show that, in fact, there are no monsters or profound enigmas, because everything profound in the conception that the bourgeoisie has of money, capital, value, and so on, is in reality nothing but platitude.

And, of course, it would be necessary to recall the space of interpretation that Freud constituted, not only in the famous topology of consciousness and the unconscious, but equally in the rules that he formulated for psychoanalytic treatment, and the analyst's deciphering of what is said in the course of the spoken "chain." It would be necessary to recall the spatiality, very material after all, to which

Freud attached such importance and which lays out the patient under the overhanging gaze [*regard surplombant*] of the psychoanalyst.

The second theme—which I would like to propose to you is, moreover, somewhat related to the first—is to point out that, beginning with the three men of whom we are now speaking, interpretation has at last become an infinite task.

In truth, it already was in the sixteenth century, but signs referred [*se renvoyaient*] to each other quite simply because resemblance can only be limited. Beginning in the nineteenth century, signs are linked together in an inexhaustible network, itself also infinite, not because they are based on a resemblance without borders but because there is irreducible gaping and openness.

The incompleteness of interpretation, the fact that it is always lacerated and that it remains suspended on its own brink, is found once again, I believe, in a somewhat analogous fashion in Marx, Nietzsche, and Freud in the form of the refusal of beginning. Refusal of the "Robinsonade," said Marx; a distinction, so important in Nietzsche, between the beginning and the origin; and the always-incomplete character of the regressive and analytic process in Freud. It is, above all, in Nietzsche and Freud, moreover, and to a lesser degree in Marx, that one sees delineated this experience, which I believe so important to modern hermeneutics: the farther one goes in interpretation, the closer one comes at the same time to an absolutely dangerous region where interpretation not only will find its point of return but where it will disappear as interpretation, perhaps involving the disappearance of the interpreter himself. The existence that always approached the absolute point of interpretation would be at the same time that of a point of rupture.

It is well known how, in Freud, the discovery of this structurally open, structurally gaping character of interpretation was progressively made. It was made first in a very allusive manner, quite veiled by itself, in *The Interpretation of Dreams*, when Freud analyzes his own dreams and invokes reasons of modesty or of nondisclosure of a personal secret in order to interrupt himself.

In the analysis of Dora, the idea appears that interpretation must indeed be halted, not be allowed to go through to the end in consideration of something that will be called "transference" some years later. Furthermore, the inexhaustibility of analysis asserts itself across the entire study of transference in the infinite and infinitely problematic character of the relationship of analysand to analyst, a relationship that is clearly constitutive for psychoanalysis, which opens the space in which psychoanalysis never ceases to deploy itself without ever being able to complete itself.

In Nietzsche, too, it is clear that interpretation is always incomplete. What is philosophy for him if not a kind of philology continually in suspension, a philology without end, always farther unrolled, a philology that would never be absolutely fixed? Why? As he says in *Beyond Good and Evil*, it is because "to perish from absolute knowledge could well form part of the basis of being."[3] And yet he has shown in *Ecce homo* how near he was to this absolute knowledge that forms part of the basis of Being. Likewise, in the course of the autumn of 1888 at Turin.

If in Freud's correspondence one deciphers his perpetual worries from the moment that he discovered psychoanalysis, one can wonder whether Freud's experience is not, after all, rather similar to that of Nietzsche. What is in question in the point of rupture of interpretation, in this convergence of interpretation on a point that renders it impossible, could well be something like the experience of madness.

An experience against which Nietzsche fought and by which he was fascinated; an experience against which Freud himself struggled, not without anguish, all of his life. This experience of madness would be the sanction of a movement of interpretation that approaches its center at infinity and that collapses, charred.

This essential incompleteness of interpretation is, I believe, linked to two other principles, also fundamental, which would constitute, with the first two of which I have just spoken, the postulates of modern hermeneutics. First of all, if interpretation can never be completed, this is quite simply because there is nothing to interpret. There is nothing absolutely primary to interpret, for after all everything is already interpretation, each sign is in itself not the thing that offers itself to interpretation but an interpretation of other signs.

There is never, if you like, an *interpretandum* that is not already *interpretans*, so that it is as much a relationship of violence as of elucidation that is established in interpretation. Indeed, interpretation does not clarify a matter to be interpreted, which offers itself passively; it can only seize, and violently, an already-present interpretation, which it must overthrow, upset, shatter with the blows of a hammer.

One sees this already in Marx, who interprets not the history of the relations of production but a relation already offering itself as an interpretation, since it appears as nature. Likewise, Freud interprets not signs but interpretations. Indeed, what does Freud discover beneath symptoms? He does not discover, as is said, "traumas"; he brings to light *phantasms* with their burden of anguish, that is, a kernel that is itself already in its own being an interpretation. Anorexia, for example, does not refer to weaning, as the signifier refers to the signified; rather, anorexia, as a sign, a symptom to be interpreted, refers to phantasms of the bad maternal breast, which is itself an interpretation, which is already in itself a speaking body. This is why Freud has nothing to interpret other than what in the language of his patients is offered to him as symptoms; his interpretation is the interpretation of an interpretation, in the terms in which this interpretation is given. It is well known that Freud invented the "superego" [*surmoi*] the day that a patient said to him: "I feel a dog over me" ["*je sens un chien sur moi*"].

In the same manner, Nietzsche seizes interpretations that have already seized each other. For Nietzsche, there is no original signified. Words themselves are nothing but interpretations, throughout their history they interpret before being signs, and ultimately they signify only because they are essentially nothing but interpretations. Witness the famous etymology of *agathos*.[4] This is also what Nietzsche means when he says that words have always been invented by the ruling classes; they do not denote a signified, they impose an interpretation. Consequently, it is not because there are primary and enigmatic signs that we are now dedicated to the task of interpreting but because there are interpretations, because there is always the great tissue of violent interpretations beneath everything that speaks. It is for this reason that there are signs, signs that prescribe to us the interpretation of their interpretation, that enjoin us to overturn them as signs. In this sense one can say that allēgoria and *huponoia* are at the bottom of language and before it, not just what slipped after the fact from beneath words in order to displace them and make them vibrate but what gave birth to words, what makes them glitter with a luster that is never fixed. This is also why the interpreter, for Nietzsche, is the "authentic one"; he is the "true one," not just because he seizes a sleeping truth in order to proclaim it but because he pronounces the interpretation that all truth functions to cover up. Perhaps this primacy of interpretation with respect to signs is what is most decisive in modern hermeneutics.

The idea that interpretation precedes the sign implies that the sign is not a simple and benevolent being, as was still the case in the sixteenth century, when the plethora of signs, the fact that things resembled each other, simply proved the benevolence of God and separated the sign from the signifier by only a transparent veil. On the contrary, beginning with the nineteenth century, beginning with Freud, Marx, and Nietzsche, it seems to me that the sign becomes malevolent; I mean that there is in the sign an ambiguous and somewhat suspicious form of ill will and "malice" ["*malveiller*"]. And this is to the extent that the sign is already an interpretation that does not appear as such. Signs are interpretations that try to justify themselves, and not the reverse.

Thus money functions in the way that one sees it defined in the *Critique of Political Economy* and above all in the first volume of *Capital.* Thus symptoms function in Freud. And in Nietzsche, words, justice, binary classifications of Good and Evil, and consequently signs, are masks. In acquiring this new function of covering up interpretation, the sign loses its simple signifying being, which is still possessed in the Renaissance; its own density comes as though to open itself up, and all the negative concepts that had until then remained foreign to the theory of the sign can hurl themselves into the opening. The theory of the sign knew only the transparent and scarcely negative moment of the veil. Now a whole play of negative concepts, of contradictions, of oppositions, in short, the whole play of reactive forces that Deleuze has analyzed so well in his book on Nietzsche will be able to organize itself in the interior of the sign.

"To stand the dialectic back on its feet": if this expression must have a meaning, would it not be precisely to have put back into the density of the sign, into this open space, without end, gaping, into this space without real content or reconciliation, all this play of negativity that the dialectic, at last, had unleashed by giving it a positive meaning?

Finally, the last characteristic of hermeneutics: interpretation finds itself with the obligation to interpret itself to infinity, always to resume. From which, two important consequences. The first is that interpretation will henceforth always be interpretation by "whom?"

One does not interpret what is in the signified, but one interprets after all: *who* posed the interpretation. The basis of interpretation is nothing but the interpreter, and this is perhaps the meaning that Nietzsche gave to the word "psychology." The second consequence is that interpretation must always interpret itself and cannot fail to turn back on itself. In opposition to the time of signs, which is a time of definite terms [*l'echeance*], and in opposition to the time of dialectic, which is linear in spite of everything, there is a time of interpretation, which is circular. This time is obliged to go back over where it has already been, which after all constitutes the only risk that interpretation really runs – but it is a supreme risk, which signs paradoxically cause it to run. The death of interpretation is to believe that there are signs, signs that exist primarily, originally, actually, as coherent, pertinent, and systematic marks.

The life of interpretation, on the contrary, is to believe that there are only interpretations. It seems to me necessary to understand what too many of our contemporaries forget, that hermeneutics and semiology are two fierce enemies. A hermeneutic that in effect falls back on a semiology believes in the absolute existence of signs: it abandons the violence, the incompleteness, the infinity of interpretations in order to enthrone the terror of the index or to suspect language. Here we recognize Marxism after Marx. On the contrary, a hermeneutic that wraps itself in itself enters the domain of languages which do not cease to implicate themselves, that intermediate region of madness and pure language. It is there that we recognize Nietzsche.

NOTES

1   See Sigmund Freud, "Eine Schwierigkeit der Psychoanalyse" ["One of the Difficulties of Psychoanalysis" (1917), in *Sigmund Freud; Collected Papers*, ed. Ernest Jones, trans. Joan Riviere, (London: Hogarth Press, 1925), pp. 347–56)].

2   See Friedrich Nietzsche, *Morgenröthe* (Leipzig: Naumann 1881 [*The Dawn of Day*, trans. J. M. Kennedy, in *The Complete Works of Friedrich Nietzsche*, ed. Oscar Levy, vol. 9 (London: Foulis, 1911), p. 230].

3   See Friedrich Nietzsche, *Jenseits von Gut und Böse* (Leipzig: Nauman, 1886) (*Beyond Good and Evil*, in *The Complete Works of Friedrich Nietzsche*, vol. 12, ed. Oscar Levy, trans. Helen Zimmern (London: Foulis; 1911), pp. 53–54].

4   See Friedrich Nietzsche, *Zur Genealogie der Moral* (Leipzig: Naumann, 1887) [*On the Genealogy of Morals*, in *Basic Writings of Nietzsche*, ed. and trans. Walter Kaufmann (New York: Modern Library, 1968), pp. 4–5].

ON THE WAYS OF WRITING HISTORY*

R.B. The dual reception, critical and public, enthusiastic and guarded, that your book met with warrants a sequel to the interview in which, over a year ago in this same publication, you explained the nature and scope of your investigations. Which of the reactions provoked by *Les Mots et les Choses* [*The Order of Things*] was the most striking to you?

M.F. I was struck by the following fact: professional historians recognized it as being a work of history, and many others, who have an antiquated and no doubt completely obsolete idea of history, clamored that history was being murdered.

R.B. Doesn't it seem to you that the book's form – by which I mean both the absence of extensive notes and bibliographies, of accumulated and acknowledged references, customary for this kind of work, and the mirror play constituted by *Las Meninas* – together with your very style may have helped to mask its nature?

M.F. The book's presentation has something to do with it no doubt, but I think the main factor is that many people are unaware of the very important mutation in historical knowledge that has been underway for more than twenty years now. People know that the books of Georges Dumézil, Claude Lévi-Strauss, and Jacques Lacan are among the major books of our time; but do they also know that among the works that are making possible a new adventure in knowledge we

---

*This interview, conducted by Raymond Bellour, appeared in *Les Lettres françaises* 1187 (15–21 June 1967), pp. 6–9. Robert Hurley's translation.

have to place the books of Fernand Braudel, François Furet, Denis Richet, and Emmanuel Le Roy Ladurie, along with the research of the historical school of Cambridge and the Soviet school?

R.B.　You situate yourself deliberately as a historian, then. What do you attribute the misunderstanding to?

M.F.　I think history has been the object of a curious sacralization. For many intellectuals the distant, uninformed, and conservative respect for history was the simplest way to reconcile their political consciousness and their research or writing activity. Under the sign of the history cross, all discourse became a prayer to the god of just causes. There is also a more technical reason. One has to recognize, in fact, that in fields such as linguistics, ethnology, the history of religions, sociology, the concepts that were formed in the nineteenth century, which can be categorized as dialectical, were largely abandoned. Now, in the eyes of some people, history as a discipline constituted the final refuge of the dialectical order; through it one could save the reign of the rational contradiction . . . Many intellectuals were thus able to maintain, for these two reasons and against all probability, a conception of history organized on the model of the narrative as a great sequence of events taken up in a hierarchy of determinations: individuals are caught within that totality which transcends them and trifles with them, but of which they are perhaps at the same time the unwitting authors. So that for some people, this history, both an individual project and a totality, became untouchable: to refuse that form of historical assertion [*dire*] would be to attack the great cause of the revolution.

R.B.　What does the newness of the historical works that you invoke consist in exactly?

M.F.　They can be characterized a bit schematically in this way:

1. These historians address the very difficult problem of periodization. It was noticed that the manifest periodization that is punctuated by political revolutions was not always methodologically the best possible form of demarcation [*découpe*].

2. Every periodization carves out in history a certain level of events, and, conversely, each layer of events calls for its own periodization. This is a set of delicate problems, since, depending on the level that one selects, one will have to delimit different periodizations, and, depending on the periodization one provides, one will reach dif-

ferent levels. In this way one arrives at the complex methodology of discontinuity.

3. The old traditional opposition between the human sciences and history (the first studies the synchronic and nondevelopmental, the second analyzes the dimension of great constant change) disappears: change can be an object of analysis in terms of structure, and historical discourse is full of analyses borrowed from ethnology and sociology, from the human sciences.

4. Historians are bringing into historical analysis types of relationship and modes of connection that are more numerous than the universal relation of causality by which people tried to define the historical method.

So, for the first time perhaps, we have the possibility of analyzing as an object a set of materials that were deposited in the course of time in the form of signs, traces, institutions, practices, works, and so on. There are two essential manifestations of all these changes:

- as concerns the historians, the works of Braudel, of the Cambridge school and the Russian school, and so on.

- the quite remarkable critique and analysis of the notion of history developed by Louis Althusser at the beginning of *Reading Capital.*[1]

R.B. You're pointing to a direct kinship between your works and those of Althusser?

M.F. Having been his student and owing him a great deal, I may have a tendency to credit to his influence an effort that he might question, so I can't answer for his part. But I would still say: Open the books of Althusser and see what he says.

However, there does remain an obvious difference between Althusser and me: he employs the phrase "epistemological break" in connection with Marx, and I assert to the contrary that Marx does not represent an epistemological break.

R.B. Isn't this divergence with respect to Marx precisely the most evident sign of what appeared to be questionable in your analyses of the structural mutations of knowledge during the nineteenth century?

M.F. What I said about Marx concerns the specific domain of political economy. Whatever the importance of Marx's modifications of

Ricardo's analyses, I don't think his economic analyses escape from the epistemological space that Ricardo established. On the other hand, we can assume that Marx inserted a radical break in people's historical and political consciousness, and that the Marxist theory of society did inaugurate an entirely new epistemological field.

My book carried the subtitle *An Archaeology of the Human Sciences*. It implies a second one that would be *An Analysis of Knowledge and of Historical Consciousness in the West Since the Sixteenth Century*. And even before I've advanced very far in this work, it looks to me as if this time the great break should be situated at the level of Marx. We're brought back to what I was saying earlier: the periodization of fields of knowledge cannot be carried out in the same way according to the levels at which one is placed. One encounters a kind of layering of bricks and what is interesting, strange, curious, will be to find out precisely how and why the epistemological break for the sciences of life, economy, and language is situated at the beginning of the nineteenth century, and for the theory of history and of politics in the middle of the nineteenth century.

R.B.   But that is to deliberately reject the privilege of history as a harmonic science of totality, as the Marxist tradition presents it to us.

M.F.   As far as I can tell, that idea, which is widespread, is not actually found in Marx. But I will reply by emphasizing that in this domain, where we are only beginning to outline the possible principles, it is still quite early to be addressing the problem of reciprocal determinations of these layers. It is not out of the question that we may find forms of determinations such that all the levels agree to march in step on the bridge of historical development. But those are only hypotheses.

R.B.   In the articles that attack your book one notices the words "to freeze history," which recur like a leitmotif and seem to formulate the most important accusation, calculated to question your conceptual framework as well as the narrative technique it implies—indeed the very possibility of formulating a logic of mutation as you mean to do. What do you think about this?

M.F.   In what is called the "history of ideas," one generally describes change by giving oneself two expedients that make things easier:

1. One uses concepts that seem rather magical to me, such as influence, crisis, sudden realization [*prise de conscience*], the interest taken

in a problem, and so on – convenient concepts that don't work, in my view.

2. When one encounters a difficulty, one goes from the level of analysis which is that of the statements themselves to another, which is exterior to it. Thus, faced with a change, a contradiction, an incoherence, one resorts to an explanation by social conditions, mentality, worldview, and so on.

I wanted to try, by playing a systematic game, to forgo these two conveniences, and so I made an effort to describe statements, entire groups of statements, while bringing out the relations of implication, opposition, exclusion that might connect them.

I was told, for example, that I had granted or invented an absolute break between the end of the eighteenth century and the beginning of the nineteenth century. As a matter of fact, when one looks carefully at the scientific discourses of the end of the eighteenth century, one notes a very rapid and, in fact, quite puzzling change. I wanted to describe that change in a precise way, establishing the set of necessary and sufficient transformations to pass from the initial form of scientific discourse, that of the eighteenth century, to its final form, that of the nineteenth century. The set of transformations that I defined preserves a certain number of theoretical elements, displaces certain others, sees old ones disappear and appear anew. All this makes it possible to define the rule of passage in the domains that I considered. So it's the complete contrary of a discontinuity that I tried to establish, since I showed the very form of the passage from one state to another.

R.B. I wonder if the misunderstanding doesn't come from the difficulty of conceptualizing the terms "change" and "passage" on the one hand, side by side with "table" and "description" on the other.

M.F. All the same, it's been more than fifty years since it was realized that the tasks of description were essential in domains like history, ethnology, and linguistics. After all, mathematical language since Galileo and Newton functions not like an explanation of nature but like a description of processes. I don't see why one might question the need for unformalized disciplines such as history to also undertake the primary tasks of description.

R.B. How do you conceive of these primary tasks in terms of method?

M.F. (1) If what I said is true, one should be able to account for and analyze texts that I didn't talk about, according to the same schemas exactly, while bringing a few supplementary transformations to bear. (2) The texts that I spoke of could easily be taken up again, along with the very material that I treated, in a description that would have a different periodization and would be situated at a different level. For example, when the archaeology of historical knowledge is done, obviously it will be necessary to again use the texts on language, and it will be necessary to relate them to the techniques of exegesis, of the criticism of sources, and to all the knowledge concerning sacred scripture and the historical tradition. Their description will be different then. But if they are exact, these descriptions should be such that one can define the transformations that make it possible to go from one to the other.

In one sense, description is infinite, therefore; in another, it is closed, insofar as it tends to establish the theoretical model of accounting for the relations that exist between the discourses being studied.

R.B. This twofold character of the description would seem to be the very thing that is apt to cause reticence or bewilderment, since history is thus directly tied into the infinity of its archives—hence into the meaninglessness that characterizes all infinity—and, at the same time, captured in models whose formal character reveals with its very logic the meaninglessness of all internal and circular closure. And the effect is all the stronger because your book stays utterly distant from what could be called "living history," the history in which practice—whatever the theoretical level where it is solicited and the models in which one may enclose its inexhaustible diversity—turns meaninglessness into a kind of familiarity, in the "natural" world of actions and institutions. How do you understand that break on which *The Order of Things* is based?

M.F. In trying to play the game of a rigorous description of the statements themselves, it became apparent to me that the domain of statements did obey formal laws, that, for example, one could find a single theoretical model for different epistemological domains; and in this sense one could conclude that there was an autonomy of discourses. But there is nothing to be gained from describing this autonomous layer of discourses unless one can relate it to other layers, practices, institutions, social relations, political relations, and so on. It is that relationship which has always intrigued me, and in *Histoire de la folie* [*Madness and Civilization*] and *Naissance de la clinique* [*Birth of the Clinic*], I tried to define the relations between these different domains. I considered, for example, the epistemological domain of medicine and that of institutions of repression, hospitalization, unemployment relief, public health administration, and so on. But I noticed that things were more complicated than I had thought in those first two works, that the discursive domains did not always conform to structures they had in common with their associated practical and institutional domains, that they obeyed, rather, structures they shared with other epistemological domains – that there was a kind of isomorphism of discourses among themselves in a given period. So one is presented with two perpendicular axes of description: that of the theoretical models common to several discourses, and that of the relations between the discursive domain and the nondiscursive domain. In *The Order of Things* I covered the horizontal axis, in *Madness and Civilization*, the vertical dimension of the figure.

Regarding the first, let someone demonstrate to me, with texts in support, that no such theoretical coherence between discourses exists, and a real discussion can begin. As for minimizing the domain of practice, my previous books are there to show that I did nothing of the sort, and by way of comparison I will refer to an illustrious example. When Dumézil demonstrates that Roman religion is in a relation of isomorphism with Scandinavian or Celtic legends, or some Iranian ritual, he doesn't mean that Roman religion doesn't have its place inside Roman history, that Roman history doesn't exist, but that one cannot describe the history of Roman religion, its relations with the institutions, the social classes, the economic conditions, except by taking the internal morphology into account. In the same way, to demonstrate that the scientific discourses of an era come under a common theoretical model is not to say that they escape from history and float in the air like disembodied and solitary entities, but that one cannot do a history, an analysis of the functioning of that knowledge, its role, the conditions that are laid down for it, the way in which it is rooted in society, without considering the strength and consistency of those isomorphisms.

R.B. This objectivity that you grant to theoretical models for an extensive analysis of history as a science, and to descriptive logic in the construction of these models, makes one wonder about the starting point of that description, its source, so to speak – which means, in the case of a book as personal as yours, trying to understand the relationship of the author and his text, exactly what place he expects to occupy therein, what place he can and must occupy.

M.F.   The only way I can reply to that is by plunging into the book itself. If the style of analysis that I tried to formulate in it is admissible, it should be possible to define the theoretical model to which not only my book belongs but also those which belong to the same configuration of knowledge [*savoir*]. It is doubtless the one that now allows us to treat history as a set of actually articulated statements, and language as an object of description and an ensemble of relations linked to discourse, to the statements that are the object of interpretation. It is our age and it alone that makes possible the appearance of that ensemble of texts which treat grammar, natural history, or political enonomy as so many objects.

So, in that respect and only in that respect, the author is constitutive of the thing he is talking about. My book is a pure and simple fiction: it is a novel, but it is not I who invented it, it is the relationship of our age and its epistemological configuration with that whole mass of statements. So the subject is, in fact, present in the whole book, but it is the anonymous "one" who speaks today in everything that is said.

R.B.   How do you understand the status of this anonymous "one"?

M.F.   Perhaps one is gradually, but not without difficulty, getting rid of a great allegorical distrust. By that I mean the simple idea, with regard to a text, that consists in asking oneself nothing else but what that text is *really* saying underneath what it is *actually* saying. No doubt, that is the legacy of an ancient exegetical tradition: concerning anything that is said, we suspect that something else is being said. The secular version of this allegorical distrust had the effect of assigning to every commentator the task of recovering the author's true thought everywhere, what he had said without saying it, meant to say without being able to, meant to conceal and yet allowed to appear. It is clear that today there are many other possible ways of dealing with language. Thus contemporary criticism – and this is what differentiates it from what was still being done quite recently – is formulating a sort of new combinative scheme [*combinatoire*] with regard to the diverse texts that it studies, its object texts. Instead of reconstituting the immanent secret, it treats the text as a set of elements (words, metaphors, literary forms, groups of narratives) among which one can bring out absolutely new relations, insofar as they have not been controlled by the writer's design and are made possible only by the work itself as such. The formal relations that one discovers in this way were not present in anyone's mind; they don't constitute the latent content of the statements, their indiscreet secret. They are a construction, but an accurate construction provided that the relations described can actually be assigned to the material treated. We've learned to place people's words in relationships that are still unformulated, said by us for the first time, and yet objectively accurate.

So contemporary criticism is abandoning the great myth of interiority: *Intimior intimio ejus.* It is completely detached from the old themes of nested boxes, of the treasure chest that one is expected to go look for at the back of the work's closet. Placing itself outside the text, it constructs a new exteriority for it, writing texts of texts.

R.B. It seems to me that, with its very inventiveness and its multiple contributions, modern literary criticism, for example, as you describe it, in a sense displays a curious regression relative to the man who provided it with its basic requirements. I mean Maurice Blanchot. For while Blanchot has, in fact, conquered an imperious exteriority of the text for modern thought, calling it "literature," he doesn't at all offer himself the convenience that tends to dodge the violence of the work as the site of a name and a biography whose secret, precisely, is in being traversed in various ways by the irreducible and abstract force of literature. In each case, Blanchot retraces its severe itinerary without worrying, as a more scholarly criticism would require, about describing it as such in the logic of its forms.

M.F. It's true that Blanchot made possible all discourse about literature. First of all, because he was the first to show that works are connected to each other by that external face of their language where "literature" appears. Literature is thus what constitutes the outside of every work, what furrows all written language and leaves an empty claw mark on every text. It is not a mode of language, but a groove that runs like a great impulse through all the literary languages. By bringing to light this agency [*instance*] of literature as a "common place," an empty space where works come to be lodged, I believe he assigned to contemporary criticism what ought to be its object, what makes possible its work both of accuracy and invention.

One can assert, moreover, that Blanchot made it possible by establishing between the author and the work a mode of relation that had not been imagined. Now we know that the work does not belong to an author's design, nor even to that of his own existence, that it maintains with him relations of negation, of destruction, that for him it is the streaming of the eternal outside; and yet there is that primordial function of the name. Because of the name, the work is marked by a modality that cannot be reduced to the anonymous babble of all other languages. There is no doubt that contemporary criticism has not yet really questioned this exigency of the name that Blanchot has suggested to it. It will have to deal with the matter, since the name marks for the work its relations of opposition to other works, of difference from them, and it absolutely characterizes the literary work's mode of being in a culture and in institutions like ours. After all, it has been centuries, six or seven, since anonymity, with very few exceptions, completely disappeared from literary language and its operation.

R.B.   I think that is why Blanchot's lesson is finding among technical critics—from whom, for his part, he maintains an equal distance—a clearer echo in a psychoanalytic type of interpretation, which by definition operates in a subjective space, than in a linguistic type of interpretation, in which there is often the risk of mechanistic abstraction.

From this standpoint what is important, problematical, in certain investigations of a scientific type like yours, is a certain familiarity, rather new, that they appear to maintain with the more explicitly "subjective" works of literature.

M.F.   It would be very interesting to know what the assignable, "nameable" individuality of a scientific work consists in; those of Niels Heinrik Abel or Joseph-Louis Lagrange, for example, are marked by writing traits that individualize them as surely as a painting by Titian or a page by Chateaubriand. The same is true of philosophical writings or descriptive writings such as those of Linnaeus or Georges Buffon. And yet they are caught within a network of all those which speak of the "same thing," which are contemporaneous and succeed them: this network that envelops them delineates those great figures without a civil status that we call "mathematics," "history," "biology."

The problem of singularity, or of relationship between the name and the network, is an ancient one, but in the past there were sorts of channels, marked paths that separated literary works, physical or mathematical works, historical works, from each other. Each developed at its appropriate level and, as it were, in the portion of territory assigned to it, despite a whole set of overlaps, borrowings, resemblances. Today one notes that all this sectioning-off, this partitioning is fading or reconstituting itself in a completely different way. Thus the relationships between linguistics and literary works, between music and mathematics, the discourse of historians and that of economists, are not characterized simply by borrowing, imitation, or unintentional analogy, or even by structural isomorphism; these works, these initiatives, are formed in relation to one another, exist for one another. There is a literature of linguistics, and not an influence by grammarians on the grammar and vocabulary of novelists. In the same way, mathematics is not applicable to the construction of musical language, as it was at the end of the seventeenth and the beginning of the eighteenth century; it now constitutes the formal universe of the musical work itself. So we are witnessing a general and vertiginous obliteration of the old distribution of languages.

People are fond of saying that nothing else but language interests us today, and that it has become the universal object. Make no mistake: this supremacy is the temporary supremacy of a migrating tribe. It's true that we are interested in language; yet it's not that we come to possess it at last but that, on the contrary, it eludes us more than it has ever eluded us. Its boundaries are collapsing, and its calm universe is starting to melt; and if we are submerged, this is not so much by its timeless rigor as by the present motion of its wave.

R.B.   How do you situate yourself personally in this mutation that draws the most exacting works of knowledge into a kind of novelistic adventure?

M.F.   Unlike those who are labeled "structuralists," I'm not really interested in the formal possibilities afforded by a system such as language. Personally, I am more intrigued by the existence of discourses, by the fact that words were spoken. Those events functioned in relation to their original situation, they left traces behind them, they continue to exist, and they exercise, in that very subsistence in history, a certain number of manifest or secret functions.

R.B.   In that way, you surrender to the characteristic passion of the historian, who wants to respond to the endless murmur of the archives.

M.F.   Yes, because my object is not language but the archive, which is to say, the accumulated existence of discourses. Archaeology, as I understand it, is not akin either to geology (as the analysis of

substrata) or to genealogy (as the description of beginnings and successions); it is the analysis of discourse in its *archival* form.

A nightmare has haunted me since my childhood: I am looking at a
text that I can't read, or only a tiny part of it decipherable. I pretend to
read it, aware that I'm inventing; then suddenly the text is completely
scrambled, I can no longer read anything or even invent it, my throat
tightens and I wake up.

I'm not blind to the personal investment there may be in this obsession with language that exists everywhere and escapes us in its very
survival. It survives by turning its looks away from us, its face inclined toward a darkness we know nothing about.

How can these discourses on discourses I am undertaking be justified? What status can they be given? People have begun to realize—
one thinks of logicians above all, students of Bertrand Russell and
Ludwig Wittgenstein—that language can be analyzed in its formal
properties only if one takes its concrete functioning into account. Language is indeed a set of structures, but discourses are functional units,
and analysis of language in its totality cannot fail to meet that essential requirement. In this context, what I'm doing is placed in the general anonymity of all the investigations currently revolving around
language—that is, not only the language that enables us to say things
but discourses that have been said.

R.B.   What do you mean more exactly by this idea of anonymity?

M.F.   I wonder if people are not currently reencountering, in the
form of the relation of the name to anonymity, a certain transposition
of the old Classical problem of the individual and truth, or the individual and beauty. How is it that an individual born at a given moment,
having a particular history and a particular face, can discover, he
alone and he first, a particular truth, perhaps even truth itself? That is
the question to which Descartes's *Meditations* replies: How was I able
to discover the truth?[2] Well, many years later one reencounters it in
the Romantic theme of genius: How can an individual lodged in a fold
of history discover forms of beauty in which the whole truth of an age
or a civilization is expressed? Today the problem is no longer posed in
those terms. We are no longer inside truth but inside the coherence of
discourses, no longer inside beauty, but inside complex relations of
forms. Now it is a question of how an individual, a name, can be the
medium for an element or group of elements that, integrating itself
into the coherence of discourses or the indefinite network of forms,

effaces, or at least renders vacuous and useless, that name, that individuality whose mark it carries for a certain time and in certain regards. We have to conquer anonymity, to prove we are justified in having the enormous presumption of becoming anonymous one day, a bit like the classical thinkers needing to justify the enormous presumption of having found the truth, and of having attached their name to it. In the past, the problem for the person who wrote was to pull himself out of the anonymity of all; in our time, it is to manage to obliterate one's proper name and to lodge one's voice in that great din of discourses which are pronounced.

R.B.   Doesn't it seem to you that, once the impulse is pushed to the limit, this amounts to playing the double, reciprocal game of assertion and effacement, of speech and silence, which Blanchot makes into the essence of the literary act when he assigns the work the chosen function of being a rich abode of silence in the face of the unbearable spoken immensity without which, however, the work would not exist? When Claude Lévi-Strauss says, concerning *Le Cru et le cuit* (*The Raw and the Cooked*), "So this book about myths is, in its own way, a myth," he is thinking of the sovereign impersonality of myth–and yet few books, by that very fact, are as personal as his *Mythologiques.*[3] In a very different way, you are a similar case in relation to history.

M.F.   What gives such books, which only aspire to be anonymous, so many marks of singularity and individuality, are not the privileged signs of a style or the mark of a singular or individual interpretation, but the mania for the eraser stroke with which one carefully obliterates everything that might indicate a written individuality. Between writers [*écrivains*] and those who happen to write [*écrivants*] there are obliterators.

Nicolas Bourbaki is the basic model.[4] All of us dream of doing something, each in his own domain, like Bourbaki, where mathematics is constructed under the anonymity of a whimsical name. Perhaps the irreducible difference between mathematical investigators and our activities is that the eraser strokes applied with a view to anonymity mark the signature of a name more surely than ostentatious fountain pens. And it could be said, too, that Bourbaki has its style and its own particular way of being anonymous.

R.B.   Like your reference to classical individuality, this implies that the position of the author in this type of research might actually be a reduplication of the philosopher's position–a perennially ambiguous one, between science and literature. In that sense, what does the modern status of philosophy appear to be?

M.F. It seems to me that philosophy no longer exists –which is not to say that it has disappeared but that it has spread through a large quantity of diverse activities. Thus, the activities of the axiomatician, the linguist, the ethnologist, the historian, the revolutionary, the politician may be forms of philosophical activity. In the nineteenth century the reflection that concerned itself with the conditions of possibility of objects was philosophical; today every activity that reveals a new object for knowledge or practice is philosophy, whether that activity comes under mathematics, linguistics, ethnology, or history.

R.B. Yet, in the last chapter of *The Order of Things*, where you discuss the human sciences today, you grant history a privilege over all the other disciplines. Might that be a new way of recovering that power of synthetic legislation which used to be the peculiar privilege of philosophical thought, and which Martin Heidegger already recognized as being no longer that of traditional philosophy, but of "history of philosophy"?

M.F. It's true that history holds a privileged position in my inquiry. The fact is that in our culture, at least for several centuries now, discourses are linked in a historical fashion: we acknowledge things that were said as coming from a past in which they were succeeded, opposed, influenced, replaced, engendered, and accumulated by others. Cultures "without history" are obviously not those in which there was no event, or development, or revolution, but in which the discourses do not accumulate in the form of history. They exist side by side; they replace one another, they forget one another; they transform one another. On the other hand, in a culture like ours, every discourse appears against a background where every event vanishes.

That is why in studying an ensemble of theoretical discourses concerning language, economy, and living beings, I didn't try to establish the a priori possibilities or impossibilities of such knowledges [*connaissances*]. I tried to do a historian's work by showing the simultaneous functioning of these discourses and the transformations that accounted for their visible changes.

But this doesn't mean that history has to play the role of a philosophy of philosophies here, that it can claim to be the language of languages, as was thought by a nineteenth-century historicism that tended to endow history with the lawgiving and critical power of philosophy. If history possesses a privilege, it would be, rather, insofar as it would play the role of an internal ethnology of our culture and our rationality, and consequently would embody the very possibility of any ethnology.

R.B. After that long detour, I would like to return to the book, and ask you the reason for the gap [*écart*] that people sense in your formulation when one goes from the analysis of the seventeenth and eighteenth centuries to that of the nineteenth and twentieth centuries – a gap that has been the object of some of the strongest reservations stated concerning your work.

M.F. Something does seem to change with the nineteenth century in the distribution of the book. The same thing in *Madness and Civilization*, people assumed that I mean to attack modern psychiatry, and in *The Order of Things*, that I was engaging in polemics using the thought of the nineteenth century. Actually, there is a clear difference in the two analyses. I can, in fact, define the Classical age in its particular configuration by the twofold difference that contrasts it with the sixteenth century, on the one hand, with the nineteenth century, on the other. But I can define the modern age in its singularity only by contrasting it with the seventeenth century, on the one hand, and with us, on the other hand; so, in order to effect this transition, it is necessary bring out in all our statements the difference that separates us from it. It is a matter of pulling oneself free of that modern age which begins around 1790 to 1810 and goes up to about 1950, whereas for the Classical age it's only a matter of describing it.

Thus the apparently polemical character is owing to the fact that one has to delve into the mass of accumulated discourse under our own feet. Through gentle digging one can uncover the old latent configurations, but when it comes to determining the system of discourse on the basis of which we still live, as soon as we are obliged to question the words that still resonate in our ears, that are mingled with those we are trying to speak, then archaeology, like Nietzschean philosophy, is forced to work with hammer blows.

R.B. Isn't the unique and impassioned status that you give to Nietzsche more precisely the most obvious sign of that unbridgeable gap [*écart*]?

M.F. If I had to recommence this book, which was finished two years ago, I would try not to give Nietzsche that ambiguous, utterly privi-

leged, metahistorical status I had the weakness to give him. It is due to
the fact, no doubt, that my archaeology owes more to Nietzschean
genealogy than to structuralism properly so called.

R.B.   But, in that case, how can one restore Nietzsche to archaeology without the risk of being false to both? There seems to be an
insurmountable contradiction in that very fact. In your book I would
see it in the figurative form of a basic conflict between Nietzsche and
Las Meninas. For, without resorting to the facile games with regard to
your preference for spatial metaphors, it is clear that the table [*tab-
leau*] turns out to be the privileged locus for your book, as it is in a
sense for every structuralism; which in my view accounts for the way
that you compare the present anonymity with that of the seventeenth
century, on behalf of an idea of reading which can lay out history in a
table as well as locate it in the Borges text on the Chinese encyclopedia, which was your book's "birthplace." That's why the nineteenth
century, where history is invented in the form of an incongruity between signs and men, is the object of the debate, and our era has the
hope of a new resolution through an attempt to bring the historical
subject back into the space of the table, in a new anonymity.

Isn't Nietzsche precisely the locus where all signs converge in the
irreducible dimension of the subject, anonymous by dint of being itself, anonymous by the fact that it incorporates the totality of voices in
the form of fragmentary discourse? And in that way, is it not the extreme and exemplary form of thought and of all expression as autobi-
ography, without anything left out or left over, which is always
lacking in the space of the table—just as it is lacking in the time of
history, where it is and is not, for one can say it only in the sense of
one's own madness, and not by recourse to an exterior law? Thus
doesn't the fact that Nietzsche—and with him a certain truth of
literature—is missing, so to say, from your book, which owes and
brings so much to him, doesn't this fact attest to the impossibility of
treating all discourses at the same level? And doesn't that very thing,
in the form of your presence in the book, correspond exactly to the
impossible anonymity you dream of, an anonymity that, being told,
can only signify a world without written speech or, to the point of
madness, the circular literature of Nietzsche?

M.F.   It's hard for me to answer, because all your questions basically come from that one, as does our whole dialogue, therefore. It's
that question which supports the passionate, somewhat distant inter-

est you have in what is happening around us, in the generations that precede you. Your desire to write and to question comes from that question. So here begins the interview of Raymond Bellour by Michel Foucault, an interview that has lasted for several years and of which *Les Lettres françaises* may one day publish a fragment.

NOTES

1 Louis Althusser, "Du Capital à la philosophie de Marx," in Althusser, P. Macherey, and J. Rancière, *Lire Le Capital* (Paris: Maspero, 1965), vol. 1, pp. 9–89 ["From *Capital* to Marx's Philosophy," in Althusser and Etienne Balibar, *Reading Capital*, trans. Ben Brewster (New York: Pantheon, 1970), pp. 11–69].

2 René Descartes, *Meditationes de prima philosophia* (Paris: Soly, 1641). See *Méditations touchant la Première Philosophie, dans lesquelles l'existence de Dieu et la distinction réelle entre l'âme et le corps de l'homme sont démontrées*, in *Oeuvres et lettres*, ed. André Bridoux (Paris: Gallimard, 1953), pp. 253–547 [*Discourse on Method*; and *Meditations on First Philosophy*, trans. Donald A. Cross (Indianapolis: Hackett, 1993)].

3 Claude Lévi-Strauss, *Mythologiques*, vol. 1: *Le Cru et le cuit* (Paris, Plon, 1964) [*Introduction to a Science of Mythology*, vol. 1: *The Raw and the Cooked*, trans. John and Doreen Weightman (Chicago: University of Chicago Press, 1983)].

4 Nicolas Bourbaki, the collective pseudonym taken by a group of French mathematicians (Henri Cartan, Claude Chevalley, Jean Dieudonné, Charles Ehresmann, André Weyl, and others) who have undertaken to reconstruct mathematics on rigorous axiomatic foundations. – Ed.

ON THE ARCHAEOLOGY OF THE SCIENCES:
RESPONSE TO THE EPISTEMOLOGY CIRCLE*

———

Our sole intention in asking these questions of the author of *Madness and Civilization, Birth of the Clinic,* and *The Order of Things,* was to get him to state the critical propositions on which the possibility of his theory and the implications of his method are founded. The Circle[1] proceeded by requesting him to define his replies in relation to the status, the history, and the concept of science.

ON THE EPISTEME AND
EPISTEMOLOGICAL RUPTURE

Since the work of Gaston Bachelard the notion of epistemological rupture has served to designate the discontinuity, which the history and philosophy of the sciences claim to detect, between the birth of every science and the "tissue of tenacious positive, solidary errors" which in retrospect is recognized to have preceded it. The prototypical examples of Galileo, Newton, and Lavoisier, but also those of Einstein and Mendeleev, illustrate the horizontal perpetuation of that rupture.

The author of *The Order of Things* detects a vertical discontinuity between the epistemic configuration of one epoch and the next.

We ask him: What relations are maintained between that horizontality and that verticality?[2]

The archaeological periodization delimits within the continuum

---

*This "response" to the Paris Epistemology Circle originally appeared in *Cahiers pour L'analyse* 9 (Summer 1968): *Genealogy of the Sciences,* pp. 9–40. The translation has been extensively amended.

synchronic sets which group learnings together in the pattern of unitary systems. Would he accept the alternative that was proposed to him between a radical historicism (archaeology could predict its own reinscription into a new discourse) and a sort of absolute knowledge (of which some authors could have had the presentiment independently of epistemic constraints)?

FOUCAULT'S REPLY

A curious intersection. For decades now historians have preferred to devote their attention to long periods of time. As if, beneath the political peripeties and their episodes, historians undertook to bring to light the stable and resilient equilibria, the imperceptible processes, constant readjustments, the tendential phenomena that culminate, then reverse after secular continuities, the movements of accumulation and slow saturations, the great immobile and mute bases that the tangle of traditional narratives had hidden beneath a thick coating of events. To conduct this analysis, historians deploy the instruments they have partly fashioned and partly received: models of economic growth, quantitative analysis of the flows of exchange, profiles of demographic growth and regression, and the study of climatic fluctuations. These tools have enabled them to distinguish, in the field of history, various sedimentary strata; the linear successions, which until then had been the object of research, were replaced by a set of deeper uncouplings. From political instability to the dilatoriness proper to "material civilization," the levels of analysis have multiplied; each level has its specific ruptures; each contains a periodicity that belongs only to itself. And the units become broader the further one descends toward the deeper strata. The old historical question (what link to establish between discontinuous events) is replaced, from now on, by a series of difficult interrogations: Which layers should be isolated from each other? What type and criteria of periodization need to be adopted for each of them? What system of relations, (hierarchy, dominance, tier-arrangement, univocal determination, circular causality), can be established between them.

Now, in about the same period, in those disciplines which are called the history of ideas, of the sciences, of philosophy, of thought and also literature (their specificity can be left aside for the moment), in those disciplines which, in spite of their titles, on the whole escape the work of the historian and his methods, attention was displaced from the vast units forming an "epoch" or "century" toward phenomena of rupture. Beneath the great continuities of thought, beneath the massive and homogeneous manifestations of the mind, and beneath the stubborn development of a science struggling from its beginnings to exist and complete itself, attempts have been made to detect the occurrence of interruptions. Gaston Bachelard has charted out the epistemological thresholds that interrupt the indefinite accumulation of knowledges [*connaissances*]; Martial Geroult has described the enclosed systems, the closed conceptual architectures that partition the space of philosophical discourse; Georges Canguilhem has analyzed the mutations, displacements, and transformations in the field of validity and the rules for the use of concepts. As for literary analysis, it is the internal structure of the oeuvre — on a still smaller scale the text — that it examines.

But this intersection should not give us any illusions. We should not accept on trust the appearance that certain historical disciplines have moved from continuity to discontinuity, while others — really history as such — were moving from the swarm of discontinuities to broad and uninterrupted units. In fact, what has happened is that the notion of discontinuity has changed in status. For history in its classical form, discontinuity was both the given and the unthinkable: it was both what presented itself in the form of scattered events, institutions, ideas, or practices; and what had to be evaded, reduced, effaced by the historian's discourse in order to reveal the continuity of the concatenations. Discontinuity was that stigma of temporal dispersion which it was the historian's duty to suppress from history.

It has now become one of the fundamental elements of historical analysis. It appears in this analysis with a triple role. First it constitutes a deliberate operation of the historian (and no longer what he receives willy-nilly from the material he has to deal with): for he must, at least as a systematic hypothesis, distinguish between the possible levels of his analysis, and establish the periodizations that suit them. It is also the result of his description (and no longer what has to be eliminated by the action of his analysis): for what he undertakes to discover is the limits of a process, the point of change of a curve, the reversal of a regulatory movement, the bounds of an oscillation, the threshold of a function, the emergence of a mechanism, the moment a circular causality is upset. Finally, it is a concept that his work constantly specifies. It is no longer a pure and uniform void interposing a single blank between two positive patterns; it has a different form and function, according to the domain and level to which it is assigned. A notion that cannot but be rather paradoxical: since it is both instrument and object of the investigation, since it delimits the field of an analysis of which it is itself an effect; since it makes it possible to individualize the domains but can only be established by comparing them; since it only breaks down units in order to establish new ones; since it punctuates series and duplicates levels; and, in the last analysis, since it is not just a concept present in the historian's discourse but one that he secretly presupposes. On what basis could he speak if not on that of this rupture which offers him history as an object—and its own history?

To be schematic, we could say that history and, in a general way, historical disciplines have ceased to be the reconstitution of the concatenations behind the apparent sequences; they now practice the systematic introduction of discontinuity. The great change that characterizes them in our epoch is not the extension of their domain to economic mechanisms with which they have long been familiar nor is it the integration of ideological phenomena, forms of thought, or types of mentality: they were already being analyzed in the nineteenth century. It is, rather, the transformation of discontinuity: its transition from obstacle to practice; an internalization into the discourse of the historian which means it need no longer be an external fatality that has to be reduced but, rather, an operational concept to be utilized; an inversion of signs thanks to which it is no longer the negative of historical reading (its underside, its failure, the limits of its power) but the positive element that determines its object and validates its analysis. We must be prepared to understand what has become history in the real work of the historians: a certain controlled use of discontinuity for the analysis of temporal series.

It is clear that many remain blind to this fact which is contemporaneous with us and yet which historical knowledge has born witness to for nearly half a century. Indeed, if history could remain the chain of uninterrupted continuities, if it ceaselessly linked together concatenations that no analysis could undo without abstraction, if it wove obscure syntheses always in the process of reconstitution around men, their words and their deeds, it would be a privileged shelter for consciousness: what it takes away from the latter by bringing to light material determinations, inert practices, unconscious processes, forgotten intentions in the silence of institutions and things, it would restore in the form of a spontaneous synthesis; or rather, it would allow it to pick up once again all the threads that had escaped it, to reanimate all those dead activities, and to become again the sovereign subject in a new or restored light. Continuous history is the correlate of consciousness: the guarantee that what escapes from it can be restored to it; the promise that it will some day be able to appropriate outright all those things which surround it and weigh down on it, to restore its mastery over them, and to find in them what really must be called – leaving the word all its overload of meaning – its home. The desire to make historical analysis the discourse of continuity, and make human consciousness the originating subject of all knowledge and all practice, are the two faces of one and the same system of thought. Time is conceived in terms of totalization, and revolution never as anything but a coming to consciousness.

However, since the beginning of this century, psychoanalytical, linguistic, and then ethnological research has dispossessed the subject of the laws of its desire, the forms of its speech, the rules of its action, and the systems of its mythical discourses. Those in France who are securely in control, constantly reply: "Yes, but history . . . history, which is not a structure, but becoming; not simultaneity, but succession; not a system but a practice; not a form, but a never-ending effort of a consciousness coming back to itself, and attempting to regain control of itself right down to the most basic of its conditions; history, which is not discontinuity but long and uninterrupted patience." But in order to chant this contestatory litany, it was essential to divert attention from the work of historians, that is, refuse to see what is actually happening in their practice and discourse; close one's eyes to the great mutation of their discipline; remain obstinately blind to the fact that perhaps history is not a better shelter for the sovereignty of consciousness, less perilous than that of myths, language or sexuality; in short, for the sake of salvation, it was essential to reconstitute a history that is no longer being done. And if this history could not offer enough security, the development of thought, knowledges [*connaissances*], knowledge [*savoir*], and the development of a consciousness forever close to itself, indefinitely bound to its past and present in all its moment, was asked to save what had to be saved: Who dares strip the subject of its recent history? Every time the use of discontinuity becomes too visible in an historical analysis (particularly if it is concerned with knowledge) the cry goes up: History murdered! But do not make a mistake here: what is mourned for so loudly is in no sense the obliteration of history but the disappearance of that form of history which was secretly, but in its entirety, transferred to the synthetic activity of the subject. All the treasure of the past had been hoarded in the ancient citadel of this history. It was believed to be strong, because it was sanctified, and it was the last bastion of philosophical anthropology [*de la pensée anthropologique*]. But historians went elsewhere long ago. They can no longer be counted on to protect the privileges or to reaffirm once again—however necessary it might be in the present troubles—that history at least is living and continuous.

THE FIELD OF DISCURSIVE EVENTS

If one wants to apply the concept of discontinuity systematically (that is, to define it, to use it in as general a way as possible and to validate it) to these domains—so uncertain of their frontiers and so indecisive in their content—which are called the history of ideas, thought, science, knowledges [*connaissances*], a certain number of problems arise.

First, the negative tasks. It is essential to break free of a set of notions connected with the postulate of continuity. Doubtless, they do not have a very rigorous structure, but their function is very precise. Such is the notion of tradition, which makes it possible both to register all innovations with respect to a system of permanent coordinates and to give a status to an ensemble of constant phenomena. Such is the notion of influence, which gives a more mystical than substantial support to the facts of transmission and communication. Such is the notion of development, which makes it possible to describe a sequence of events as the manifestation of one and the same organizing principle. Such is the symmetrical and inverse notion of teleology or evolution toward a normative stage. Such are the notions of the mentality or spirit of an age, which make it possible to establish a community of meanings, of symbolic ties or a play of resemblances and mirrors between simultaneous or successive phenomena. It is necessary to abandon those readymade syntheses, those groupings which are admitted before any examination, those links of which the validity is accepted at the outset; to drive out the obscure forms and forces by which it is customary to link together the thoughts of men and their discourses; to accept having no other business in the first instance than with a population of dispersed events.

There is no longer any need to consider as valid the lines of demarcation between disciplines or the groups with which we have become familiar. As they stand, one cannot accept either the distinction between the broad types of discourse, or that between forms of genres (science, literature, philosophy, religion, history, fiction, and so on). The reasons are blindingly obvious. We are ourselves uncertain of the use of these distinctions in the world of our own discourse. This is true a fortiori when one is concerned to analyze sets of statements which were distributed, scattered, and generally characterized in a completely different manner; after all, "literature" and "politics" are recent categories that can only be applied to medieval or even Classical culture by means of a retrospective hypothesis and by a play of new analogies or semantic resemblances. Neither literature nor politics nor, consequently, philosophy and the sciences were articulated in the field of discourse in the seventeenth and eighteenth centuries as they were in the nineteenth century. Anyway, it is clearly necessary to recognize that these divisions—those which we accept today, or those which are contemporary to the discourses studied—are always themselves reflexive categories, principles of classification, normative rules and institutionalized types; they are, in turn, facts of discourse which merit analysis alongside other facts, which certainly have complex relations with them, but do not have intrinsic characteristics that are autonomous and universally recognizable.

But, above all, the unities that must be questioned are those which appear most immediately—those of the book and the oeuvre. At first sight they cannot be removed without extreme artificiality; they are given in a most certain manner, either by a material individualization (a book is a thing that occupies a determinate space, has its economic value, and itself marks the limits of its beginning and end with a number) or by an assignable relation (even if in certain cases it is rather problematic) between discourses and the individual who has put them forward. And yet, as soon as one looks at them more closely, the difficulties begin. They are no less than those that the linguist encounters when he seeks to define the unity of a sentence, or the historian encounters when he seeks to define the unity of literature or science. The unity of a book is not a homogeneous unity: the relations that exist between different mathematical treatises are not the same as those existing between different philosophical texts. The difference between one of Stendhal's novels and one of Dostoyevsky's novels cannot be superposed upon that which separates two volumes of *The Human Comedy*; and the latter, in its turn, cannot be superposed upon that which separates *Ulysses* from *The Portrait of the Artist as a Young Man*. Further, the edges of a book are neither clear nor rigorously delineated. No book exists by itself, it is always in a relation of support and dependence vis-à-vis other books; it is a point in a network – it contains a system of indications that point, explicitly or implicitly, to other books, other texts, or other sentences. If one is concerned with a book of physics, or with a collection of political speeches, or with a science fiction novel, the system of indications and consequently the complex relations of autonomy and heteronomy will differ. However much the book is given as an object one might have in hand, however much it is constrained within the little paralleliped that encloses it, its unity is variable and relative; the latter is neither constructed nor indicated, and consequently cannot be described except from out of a discursive field.

As for the oeuvre, the problems it raises are still more difficult. On the face of it, the oeuvre is merely the sum of the texts that can be designated by the sign of a proper name. But the designation (even if one leaves aside the problems of attribution) is not a homogeneous function: an author's name does not designate a text that he published himself under his own name, another that he presented under a pseudonym, another that might be discovered after his death in crude form, still another that is no more than scribbling, a notebook of jottings, a "paper," in the same fashion. The constitution of a complete oeuvre or an opus presumes a number of theoretical choices that are easy neither to justify nor even to formulate. Is it enough to add to the texts published by an author those he projected putting into print but which remained incomplete only by the fact of his death? Must one add abandoned outlines? And what status to give to letters, to notes, to reported conversations, to remarks recorded by auditors – in short, to the immense swarm of verbal traces that an individual leaves around him at the moment of death, which speak so many different languages in an indefinite intersection, and which will linger for centuries, perhaps for millennia, before being effaced? In any case, the designation of a text by the name "Mallarmé" is doubtless not of the same type if it is a matter of English themes, translations of Edgar Allan Poe, poems, or responses to inquiries. The same relation does not exist between the name of Nietzsche, on the one hand, and the youthful autobiographies, the scholarly dissertations, the philological articles, *Zarathustra*, *Ecce homo*, the letters, the last postcards signed by Dionysos or Kaiser Nietzsche, the innumerable notebooks in which laundry lists are entangled with sketches of aphorisms, on the other.

In fact, the only unity that can be recognized in the "oeuvre" of an author is a certain function of expression. The presumption is that there must be a level (as deep as it is necessary to presume it to be) at which the oeuvre reveals itself, in all its fragments, even the most minuscule and inessential, as the expression of the thought, or the experience, or the imagination, or the unconscious of the author, or of historical determinations in which he was caught. But one soon sees that the unity of the opus, far from being immediately given, is constituted by an operation; that this operation is interpretative (in the sense that it deciphers, in the text, the expression or transcription of something at once hidden and manifest); that, in the end, the operation that determines the opus, in its unity – and consequently the oeuvre itself as the result of that operation – will not be the same for the author of *Theater and Its Double* or for the author of the *Tractatus logico-philosophicus*. The oeuvre cannot be considered either an immediate unity, or a certain unity, or a homogeneous unity.

Finally, as a last measure to put out of circulation the unreflected continuities by means of which the discourse that one seeks to analyze is half-secretly organized in advance, it is crucial to renounce two postulates that are bound together, facing one another. The one assumes that it is never possible to find the irruption of a genuine event in the order of discourse; that, beyond every apparent beginning, there is always a secret origin – so secret and primordial that it can never be entirely recaptured in itself. So much so that one is led fatefully through the naïveté of chronologies, toward an indefinitely distant point, never present in any history. The point itself could only be its own emptiness; all beginnings from that point could only be recommencements or occultations (strictly speaking both, in one and the same gesture). Linked to this is the thesis that every manifest discourse secretly rests on an "already said"; but that this "already said" is not just a phrase already pronounced, a text already written, but a "never said" – a disembodied discourse, a voice as silent as a breath, a writing that is only the void left by its own trace. It is thus presumed that all that discourse happens to put into words is already found articulated in that half silence which precedes it, which continues to run obstinately underneath it, but which it uncovers and renders quiet. In the final account, manifest discourse would only be the depressive presence of what it does not say; and the nonsaid would be a hollow that animates from the interior all that is said. The first motif dedicates the historical analysis of discourse to being a quest for and repetition of an origin that escapes all determination of origin. The second dedicates it to being an interpretation or monitoring of an already-said that would at the same time be a nonsaid. These two themes, which function to guarantee the infinite continuity of discourse and its secret presence to itself in the action of an absence that is always one stage farther back, must be renounced. Each moment of discourse must be welcomed in its irruption as an event; in the punctuation where it appears; and in the temporal dispersion that allows it to be repeated, known, forgotten, transformed, wiped out down to its slightest traces, and buried far from every eye in the dust of books. There is no need to retrace the discourse to the remote presence of its origin; it must be treated in the play of its immediacy.

Once these preliminary forms of continuity, these unregulated syntheses of discourse are set aside, a whole domain is set free. An immense domain, but one that can be defined; it is constituted by the set of all effective statements (whether spoken or written) in their dispersion as events and in the immediacy that is proper to each. Before it is dealt with as a science, a novel, a political discourse, or the work of an author, or even a book, the material to be handled in its initial neutrality is a population of events in the space of discourse in general. Hence the project of a *pure description of the facts of discourse.* This description is easily distinguished from a linguistic analysis. Of course, one can establish a linguistic system (if one does not construct it artificially) only by utilizing a corpus of statements [*énoncés*], or a collection of discursive acts. But it is then an issue of defining, on the basis of an ensemble that has the value of a sample, rules that permit the eventual construction of different statements. Even if it disappeared a long time ago, even if no one speaks it anymore and it is reestablished on rare fragments, a language always constitutes a system for possible statements. It is a finite ensemble of rules which authorizes an infinite number of performances. Discourse, in constrast, is the always-finite and temporally limited ensemble of those statements alone which were formulated. They might be innumerable; they might, by their mass, exceed any capacity for registration; they nevertheless constitute a finite ensemble. The question asked by linguistic analysis, concerning a discursive act, is always: According to what rules has this statement been constituted and consequently, according to what rules could other similar statements be constructed? The description of discourse asks a different question: How is it that this statement appeared, rather than some other one in its place?

Similarly, it is clear why this description of discourse is opposed to the analysis of thought. There, too, a system of thought can only be reconstituted from a definite ensemble of discourses. But this ensemble is treated in such a manner that one attempts to rediscover, beyond the statements themselves, the intention of the speaking subject, his conscious activity, what he meant, or even the unconscious pattern that emerges against his will in what he says or in the hardly discernible cracks in his explicit utterances. At any rate, it is a matter of reconstituting another discourse, rediscovering the barely audible, murmuring, endless utterance that animates the voice heard from within and reestablishing the tenuous and invisible text that skims through the interstices of the written lines and occasionally jostles them. The analysis of thought is always *allegorical* in relation to the discourse which it uses. Its question is invariably: What, then, was being said in what was said? But the analysis of discourse is directed to another end: it is concerned to grasp the statement in the narrowness and singularity of its event; to determine the conditions of its existence, to fix its limits as accurately as possible, to establish its correlations with the other statements with which it may be linked, and to show what other forms of articulation it excludes. It does not look beneath what is manifest for the barely heard mutterings of another discourse. It must show why the discourse could not be other than it was, what makes it exclusive of other discourses, and how it takes up a position among other discourses and in relation to them which no other could occupy. The real question of the analysis of discourse could, therefore, be formulated as follows: What is this regular existence that comes to the fore in what is said – and nowhere else?

One might ask what is the ultimate purpose of this suspension of all accepted units, this obstinate pursuit of discontinuity, if it is no more than a matter of releasing a cloud of discursive events, of collecting them and preserving them in their absolute dispersion. In fact, the systematic effacement of merely given units makes it possible, first, to restore to the statement its singularity as an event. It is no longer regarded merely as the intervention of a linguistic structure, nor as the episodic manifestation of a deeper significance than itself; it is dealt with at the level of its historical irruption; an attempt is made to direct attention at the incision it constitutes, this irreducible—and often minute—emergence. However banal it is, however unimportant its consequences may seem, however quickly it is forgotten after its appearance, however little understood or badly deciphered one would think it, however quickly it may be devoured by the night, a statement is always an event that neither language nor meaning can completely exhaust. A strange event, certainly: first, because, on the one hand, it is linked to an act of writing or to the articulation of a speech but, on the other hand, opens for itself a residual existence in the field of a memory or in the materiality of manuscripts, books, and any other form of record; then because it is unique like every other event, but is open to repetition, transformation, and reactivation; finally, because it is linked both to the situations that give rise to it, and to the consequences it gives rise to, but also at the same time and in quite another modality, to the statements that precede it and follow it.

But the instance of the enunciative event has been isolated with respect to language and thought not in order to deal with it in itself as if it were independent, solitary, and sovereign. On the contrary, the aim is to grasp how these statements, as events and in their so peculiar specificity, can be articulated to events that are not discursive in nature, but may be of a technical, practical, economic, social, political, or other variety. To reveal in its purity the space through which discursive events are scattered is not to undertake to establish it inside a break [*coupure*] that nothing could cross; it is not to close it in on itself; nor, a fortiori, to open it to a transcendence; on the contrary, it is to acquire the freedom to describe a series of relations between it and other systems outside it. Relations that have to be established—without recourse to the general form of language or to the individual consciousness of the speaking subjects—in the field of events.

The third advantage of such a description of discursive acts is that releasing them from all the groupings that present themselves as natural, immediate, and universal unities makes it possible to describe other unities, but this time by a set of controlled decisions. Given that the conditions are clearly defined, it might be legitimate, on the basis of correctly described relations, to constitute discursive ensembles that would not be new but would, however, have remained invisible. Those ensembles would not be at all new, because they would be made up of already-formulated statements, between which a certain number of well-determined relations could be recognized. But these relations would never have been formulated for themselves in the statements in question (unlike, for example, those explicit relations which are posed and pronounced by the discourse itself when it adopts the form of the novel, or is inscribed in a series of mathematical theorems). But these invisible relations would in no way constitute a kind of secret discourse animating the manifest discourses from within; it is not therefore an interpretation that could make them come to light but, rather, the analysis of their coexistence, of their succession, of their mutual dependence, of their reciprocal determination, of their independent or correlative transformation. All together (though they can never be analyzed exhaustively), they form what might be called, by a kind of play on words—for consciousness is never present in such a description—the "unconscious," not of the speaking subject, but of the thing said.

Finally, a more general theme might be outlined on the horizon of all these investigations—the theme of the mode of existence of discursive events in a culture. What has to be brought out is the set of conditions which, at a given moment and in a determinate society, govern the appearance of statements, their preservation, the links established between them, the way they are grouped in statutary sets, the role they play, the action of values or consecrations by which they are affected, the way they are invested in practices or attitudes, the principles according to which they come into circulation, are repressed, forgotten, destroyed or reactivated. In short, it is a matter of the discourse in the system of its institutionalization. I shall call an *archive*, not the totality of texts that have been preserved by a civilization or the set of traces that could be salvaged from its downfall, but the series of rules which determine in a culture the appearance and disappearance of statements, their retention and their destruction, their paradoxical existence as *events* and *things*. To analyze the facts of discourse in the general element of the archive is to consider them,

not at all as *documents* (of a concealed significance or a rule of construction), but as *monuments*;[5] it is—leaving aside every geological
metaphor, without assigning any origin, without the least gesture toward the beginnings of an *archē*—to do what the rules of the etymo-
logical game allow us to call something like an *archaeology*.

Such, more or less, is the problematic of *Madness and Civilization*,
of *The Birth of the Clinic*, and of *The Order of Things*. None of these
texts is autonomous or sufficient by itself; they all depend upon one
another, to the extent that each involves the very partial exploration of
a limited region. They should be read as an ensemble of descriptive
experiments still in basic outline. However, if it is not necessary to
apologize for their being quite so partial and full of gaps, the choices
to which they are obedient must be explained. For if the general field
of discursive events permits of no a priori parceling, it is nevertheless
out of the question that all the relations characteristic of the archive
might be described in one block. As a first approximation, a provisional parceling must be accepted; an initial region, which analysis
will overturn and reorganize once it has been able to define an ensemble of relations. How to delimit that region? On the one hand, it is
necessary to choose a domain empirically in which the relations have
a chance of being numerous, dense, and relatively easy to describe.
And in what other region do discursive events seem most linked to
one another, and in the most decipherable relations, than what is
generally designated by the term "science"? But, on the other hand,
how to have the greatest chance of capturing in a statement not the
moment of its formal structure and its laws of construction but,
rather, that of its existence and its rules of manifestation, except by
addressing oneself to little formalized groups of discourses in which
the statements do not appear to be engendered according to the rules
of pure syntax? Finally, how to be sure that one will not fall prey to all
those unreflective unities or syntheses which refer to the speaking
subject, the subject of discourse, the author of a text—in short, to all
these anthropological categories? If not perhaps by considering precisely the ensemble of the statements through which these categories
are constituted—the ensemble of the statements that have chosen the
subject of discourses (their proper subject) as "object," and have undertaken to deploy it as a field of knowledges [*connaissances*]?

Hence the privilege accorded de facto to that discourse set which
might, very schematically, be said to define the "sciences of man." But

this privilege is only one of a point of departure. One must keep two facts well in mind: that the analysis of discursive events and the description of the archive are not in any way limited to the same domain; and that the dividing-up of the domain itself can be considered neither definitive nor absolutely valid. It is a matter of a first approximation, which should permit relations to be made apparent that have a chance of effacing the limits of that first sketch. Now, I should indeed acknowledge that such a project of description as I am trying at present to circumscribe is itself caught up in that region that I am trying, by way of an initial approach, to analyze, and that it runs the risk of being dissociated under the effect of analysis. I am investigating that strange and quite problematic configuration of human sciences to which my own discourse is tied. I am analyzing the space in which I speak. I am laying myself open to undoing and recomposing that space which indicates to me the first indices of my discourse. I am seeking to disassociate its visible coordinates and shake up its surface immobility. I thus risk raising, at each instant and beneath each of my resolutions, the question of knowing whence it can arise, for everything I say could well have the effect of displacing the place from which I am saying it. So though I might have responded to the question of whence I claimed to be speaking—I, who want, from such a height and from so far away, to describe the discourses of others—simply by saying that I believed myself to have been speaking from the same place as those discourses, I must now acknowledge that I can myself no longer speak from where I showed them to be speaking without saying it, but instead only from that difference, that infinitesimal discontinuity which my discourse already left in its wake.

DISCURSIVE FORMATIONS AND POSITIVITIES

I thus undertook to describe relations of coexistence among statements. I took care not to pay heed to any of those unities that could be presumed of them, and that tradition placed at my disposal—whether the work of an author, the cohesion of an epoch, or the evolution of a science. I did not go beyond the presence of events close to my own discourse—certain to be dealing with a coherent system from that point forward if I managed to describe a system of relations among them.

Initially, it seemed to me that certain statements could form a set insofar as they referred to one and the same object. After all, statements concerning madness, for example, are not all on the same formal level (they are far from all obeying the criteria required for a scientific statement): they do not all belong to the same semantic field (some come from medical semantics, others from legal or administrative semantics; others use a literary vocabulary), but they are all related to that object outlined in different ways in individual or social experience which can be designated as madness. Yet it is easy to see that the unity of the object does not allow the individualization of a set of statements and the establishment of a descriptive and constant relation between them. This for two reasons. First, the object, far from being that in relation to which it is possible to define a set of statements is, rather, constituted by the set of those formulations; it would be wrong to look for the unity of the discourse of psychopathology or psychiatry in "mental illness"; it would certainly be wrong to ask of the very being of this illness, of its hidden content, of its truth, dumb and shut in on itself, what it has been possible to say of it at any given moment: rather, mental illness has been constituted by the set of what it has been possible to say in the group of all the statements that named it, delineated it, described and explained it, gave account of its developments, indicated its diverse correlations, judged it, and eventually allowed it to speak by articulating, in its name, discourses which were to pass for its speech. But there is more: That ensemble of statements which concern madness, and in truth constitute it, is far from being related only to a single object, from having formed it once and for all and conserved it indefinitely as its inexhaustible horizon of ideality. The object that the medical statements of the seventeenth or eighteenth century posed as their correlate is not identical to the object that takes form through juridical sentences or police measures. So, too, all the objects of psychopathological discourse were modified from Phillipe Pinel or Etienne Esquirol to Eugen Bleuler; the same illnesses are not at all in question for the former and the latter—at once because the code of perceiving and the techniques of description changed, because the designation of madness and its general parceling no longer follow the same criteria, and because the function and role of medical discourse, the practices it sanctions and in which it is invested, and the distance at which it keeps the patient, were profoundly modified.

One could, perhaps should, conclude of this multiplicity of objects that it is not possible to admit, as a unity that would validly constitute an ensemble of statements, the "discourse concerning madness." It would perhaps be necessary to restrict oneself only to those groups which have one and the same object—the discourse on melancholy, or on neurosis. But one would soon become aware that each of these discourses, in turn, constituted its object and worked on it up to the point of transforming it entirely. So much so that the problem arises of knowing whether the unity of a discourse is wrought not by the permanence and singularity of an object but, rather, by the common space in which diverse objects stand out and are continuously transformed. The characteristic relation that permits the individualization of a general unity of statements concerning madness would therefore be the rule of the simultaneous or successive appearance of the various objects that are named, described, analyzed, valued, or judged in it; the law of their exclusion or mutual implication; the system that governs their transformation. The unity of the discourses on madness is not founded on the existence of the object "madness," or on the constitution of a unique horizon of objectivity; it is the series of rules which make possible, during a given period, the appearance of medical descriptions (with their object), the appearance of a series of discriminatory and repressive measures (with their particular object), and the appearance of a set of practices codified in prescriptions or medical treatments (with their specific objects). It is thus the set of rules which takes account of the object's noncoincidence with itself, its perpetual difference, its deviation and dispersion rather than of the object itself in its identity. Over and above the unity of discourses on madness, it is the pattern of the rules which define the transformations of these different objects, their nonidentity through time, the break that is produced in them, and the internal discontinuity that suspends their permanence. Paradoxically, to define the individuality of a set of statements does not consist of individualizing its object, fixing its identity, or describing the characteristics that it permanently retains; on the contrary, it is to describe the dispersion of these objects, to grasp all the interstices that separate them, to measure the distances reigning between them—in other words, to formulate their law of distribution. I will not call this system the "domain" of objects (since that word implies unity, closure, close proximity rather than scattering and dispersion). A bit arbitrarily, I will give it the name "referential"; and I will say, for example, that "madness" is not the object (or referent) common to a group of propositions but is, rather, the referential or law of dispersion of different objects or referents put into play by an ensemble of statements whose unity this law defines precisely.

The second criterion that could be used to constitute discursive sets is the type of enunciation used. It had seemed to me, for example, that from the beginning of the nineteenth century medical science was characterized less by its objects or concepts (of which the former remained the same while the latter were entirely transformed) than by a certain *style*, a certain constant form of enunciation: a descriptive science could be seen coming into existence. For the first time, medicine is constituted no longer by an ensemble of traditions, of observations, of heterogeneous recipes but by a corpus of knowledge which assumes that but one way of seeing is brought to the same things, that there is but one graphing of the perceptual field, one analysis of the pathological phenomenon in accord with the visible space of the body, one system of transcribing what is seen into what is said (one vocabulary, one set of metaphors). In short, medicine seemed to be formalizing itself as a series of descriptive statements. But here, too, it proved necessary to abandon this initial hypothesis. I had to admit that clinical medicine was just as much a set of political prescriptions, economic decisions, institutional settlements and educational models as it was a set of descriptions; that, at any rate, the latter could not be abstracted from the former, and that descriptive enunciation was only one of the formulations present in clinical discourse as a whole. Recognize that this description has not ceased to be displaced: whether because, from Xavier Bichat to cellular pathology, the same things stopped being described; or because, from visual examination, auscultation, and palpation to the use of the microscope and biological tests, the system of information was modified; or yet because, from simple anatomo-clinical correlation to the minute analysis of physiopathological processes, the lexicon of signs and their decipherment was entirely reconstituted; or finally, because the doctor had little by little ceased himself to be the site of recording and interpretation, and because beside him, outside of him, masses of documentation, instruments of correlation, and techniques of analysis came to be constituted, of which he of course had to make use, but which modified his position as inspecting subject with respect to the patient.

All these alterations, which perhaps today take us out of clinical medicine, were put into place slowly, in the course of the nineteenth century, in the interior of clinical discourse and in the space that it outlined. If one wanted to define that discourse by a codified form of enunciation (for example, the description of a certain number of determinate elements on the surface of the body, inspected by the eye, the ear, and the fingers of the doctor; the identification of descriptive unities and of complex signs; the estimation of their probable significance; the prescription of the corresponding course of therapy), it would be necessary to acknowledge that clinical medicine was unmade as soon as it appeared, and that it had hardly been formulated except with Bichat and René Laënnec. In fact, the unity of the clinical discourse is not a determinate form of statements, but the set of rules which simultaneously or successively made possible not only purely perceptual descriptions but also observations mediated through instruments, protocols of laboratory experiments, statistical calculations, epidemiological or demographic observations, institutional settlements, and political decisions. This whole set cannot be subject to a unique model of linear concatenation. It is, rather, a question of a group of diverse enunciations which are far from obeying the same formal rules, from having the same exigencies of proof, from maintaining a constant relation to truth, and from having the same operational function. What must be characterized as clinical medicine is the coexistence of those dispersed and heterogeneous statements; it is the system that governs their distribution, the support they give to each other, the way in which they imply or exclude each other, the transformation they undergo, and the pattern of their arisal, disposition, and replacement. A temporal coincidence can be established between the appearance of the discourse and the introduction of a privileged type of enunciation in medicine; but the latter does not have a constituent or normative role. A set of diverse enunciative forms are unfolded beside and around this phenomenon; and it is the general ordering of this unfolding that constitutes, in its individuality, clinical discourse. The rule of formation of these statements in their heterogeneity, in the very impossibility of their integration into a single syntactic chain, is what I shall term enunciative divergence [*l'écart énonciatif*]. And I shall say that clinical medicine is characterized, as an individualized discursive set, by the divergence or the law of dispersion which governs the diversity of its statements.

The third criterion by which unitary groups of statements could be established is the existence of a series of permanent and internally consistent concepts. It might be supposed, for example, that the analysis of language and of grammatical facts made from Lancelot to the end of the eighteenth century depended on a definite number of concepts whose content and use were established once and for all: the concept of judgment defined as the general and normative form of every sentence, the concepts of subject and attribute grouped together in the more general category of the noun, the concept of the verb used as the equivalent of the logical copula, the concept of the word defined as the sign of a representation. In this way it would seem possible to reconstitute the conceptual architecture of Classical grammar. But here again limitations appear immediately. One could hardly make use of such elements in describing the analyses done by the authors of Port Royal. One has to admit that new concepts appear, some of which may be derived from the ones I have listed, but others of which are heterogeneous, and some even incompatible with them. The notions of natural or inverted syntactic order, of the complement (introduced at the beginning of the eighteenth century by Beauzée), can no doubt be integrated into the conceptual system of the Port Royal grammar. But neither the idea of a value originally expressive of sounds, nor that of a primitive knowledge enveloped in words and obscurely transmitted by them, nor that of a regularity of the historical evolution of consonants, can be deduced from the set of concepts used by the grammarians of the eighteenth century. Even more, the conception of the verb as a simple name allowing the designation of an action or an operation; the definition of the sentence no longer as an attributive proposition but as a series of designative elements the ensemble of which produced a representation—all of this is rigorously incompatible with the collection of concepts of which Claude Lancelot or Nicolas Beauzeé could make use. Must we then admit that grammar only apparently constitutes a consistent set; and that this set of statements, analyses, descriptions, principles and consequences, and deductions is a false unity, though it survived under this name for more than a century?

In fact, it is possible to define a common system beneath all the more or less heterogeneous concepts of Classical grammar, which explains not only their emergence but also their dispersion and, eventually, their incompatibility. This system is not constituted by concepts any more general and abstract than those which appear on the surface and are openly manipulated there; it is constituted, rather, by a set of rules of formation of concepts. This set is itself divided into four subordinate groups. There is the group that governs the formation of those concepts which permit the description and analysis of the sentence as a unit in which the elements (the words) are not merely juxtaposed but related to one another. This set of rules may be called the theory of *attribution*; and without it itself being modified, this theory was able to make a place for the concepts of the verb-copula, or the verb-name specific to an action, or the verb-tie of the elements of representation. There is also the group that governs the formation of those concepts which permit a description of the relations between the different signifying elements of the sentence and the different elements of what is represented by these signs. This is the theory of *articulation*, which can, in its specific unity, render an account of concepts as different as that of the word as the result of an analysis of thought and that of the word as an instrument by which such an analysis can be made. The theory of *designation* governs the emergence not only of such concepts as that of the arbitrary and conventional sign but also that of the spontaneous and natural sign, immediately charged with expressive value (thus permitting the reintroduction of the action of language in the real or ideal becoming of humanity). Finally, the theory of *derivation* accounts for the formation of a very dispersed and heterogeneous series of notions; the idea of an immobility of language which is only subject to change as a result of external accidents; the idea of a historical correlation between the development of language and the individual's capacities for analysis, reflection, and understanding [*connaissance*] the idea of a circular determination between the forms of language, those of writing, knowledge and science, those of social organization, and, finally, those of historical progress; the idea of poetry understood not only as a particular use of vocabulary and grammar but as the spontaneous movement of language shifting in the space of human imagination, which is, by its very nature, metaphorical. These four "theories" – which are four formative schemata of concepts – have describable relations between them: they assume each other; they oppose each other in pairs; they derive one from the other and, in elaborating their logical sequence, they link up the discourses, which can neither be unified nor superposable, into a single pattern. They form what may be called a *theoretical network*. This term must not be understood to mean a group of fundamental concepts which could regroup all the others and permit their replacement in the unity of a deductive architecture but, rather, the general law of their dispersion, heterogeneity, and incompatibility (whether simultaneous or successive) – the rule of their insurmountable plurality. And it is only permissible to recognize an individualizable set of statements in general grammar insofar as all the concepts that appear are interconnected, intersect, interfere with and follow each other, are hidden and scattered in it, are formed from one and the same theoretical network.

Finally, one might attempt to constitute units of discourse on the basis of an identity of opinions. The "human sciences" are so condemned to polemic, so open to the play of preferences or interests, so permeable by philosophical or ethical themes, so apt in certain cases to political utilization, also so near to certain religious dogmas that it is legitimate in the first instance to suppose that a certain thematic might be capable of binding together a set of discourses, of balancing it like an organism that has its needs, its internal power and its survival capacities. For example, might not one constitute everything that belonged to evolutionist discourse from Buffon to Darwin as a unit? First, this theme is more philosophical than scientific, closer to cosmology than to biology; it has, rather, guided investigations from afar than named, discovered and explained results; it always presupposed more than was known, but on the basis of this fundamental choice, it made obligatory the transformation into discursive knowledge [*savoir*] what was outlined as a hypothesis or as an exigency. Might one not speak in the same way of the physiocratic idea? An idea that postulated the natural character of the three ground rents beyond any proof and before any analysis; which therefore presupposed the political and economic primacy of landed property; which ruled out any analysis of the mechanisms of industrial production; which implied, in return, the description of the circulation of money inside a state, of its distribution between different social categories, and of the channels whereby it returned to production; which finally led Ricardo to consider the cases in which this triple rent did not appear, the conditions in which its formation was possible, and therefore to denounce the arbitrary character of the physiocratic theme?

But such an attempt leads one to make two opposing but complementary observations. In one case, the same fact of opinion, the same thematic, the same choice is articulated on the basis of two completely different series of concepts, two completely different types of discourse and two completely different fields of objects: the evolutionist idea, in its most general formulation, is perhaps the same in Benoît de Maillet, Théophile de Bordeau or Diderot, and in Darwin; but in fact what makes it possible and consistent is not at all of the same order in both cases. In the eighteenth century the evolutionist idea is a choice made on the basis of two well-determined possibilities: either it is admitted that the common ancestry of species forms a completely pregiven continuity interrupted and in some sense torn apart only by natural catastrophes, by the dramatic history of the earth, by the upheavals of an extrinsic time (in which case it is this time which creates the discontinuity, ruling out evolutionism); or, on the other hand, it is admitted that it is time that creates the continuity, the changes in nature that compel species to take characters different from those which were pregiven–such that the more or less continous table of the species is like the outcrop of a whole stratum of time beneath the eyes of the naturalist. In the nineteenth century, the evolutionist idea is a choice that no longer involves the constitution of a table of species but, rather, the modalities of the interaction between an organism, all of whose elements are solidary, and an environment that provides it with its real conditions of life. One "idea" only, but based on two systems of choices.

On the other hand, in the case of physiocracy, one can say Quesnay's choice depends on exactly the same system of concepts as the contrary opinion upheld by those who might be called the "utilitarians." In this period, the analysis of wealth contained a relatively limited series of concepts, and one that was generally agreed upon (everyone defined money in the same way, as a mere sign without any value except through the practically necessary materiality of that sign; everyone explained price in the same way, by the mechanism of barter and by the quantity of labor necessary to obtain the commodity; everyone determined the price of a given labor in the same way, by the cost of the upkeep of a worker and his family while the work was being done). But on the basis of this single conceptual system, there were two methods of explaining the formation of value, depending on whether the analysis was made on the basis of exchange or on that of the remuneration of the working day. These two possibilities inscribed in economic theory and in the rules of its conceptual system gave rise to two different opinions on the basis of the same elements.

It would finally be quite incorrect to look for the principles of the individualization of a discourse in matters of opinion. What defines the unity of natural history, for example, is not the permanence of particular ideas such as that of evolution; what defines the unity of economic discourse in the eighteenth century is not the conflict between the physiocrats and the utilitarians, or between the owners of landed property and the partisans of commerce and industry. What permits the individualization of a discourse and gives it an independent existence is the system of points of choice which it offers from a field of given objects, from a determinate enunciative scale; and from a series of concepts defined in their content and use. Therefore, it would be inadequate to look for the general foundations of a discourse and the overall form of its historical identity in a theoretical option; for a similar option can reappear in two types of discourse, and a single discourse can give rise to several different options. Neither the permanence of opinions through time nor the dialectic of their conflicts is sufficient to individualize a set of statements. To do that, one must be able to register the distribution of points of choice, and define, behind every option, a *field of strategic possibilities*. If the physiocrats' analysis is a part of the same discourse as the utilitarians' analysis, it is not because they lived during the same period, nor because they confronted one another in the same society, nor because their interests were entangled in the same economy, but because their two options derive from one and the same distribution of points of choice, in one and the same strategic field. This field is not the total of all the conflicting elements, nor is it an obscure unity divided against itself and refusing to recognize itself in the mask of each of its opponents; it is the law of formation and dispersion of all possible options.

To sum up, we have here four criteria enabling us to recognize discursive units that are not at all the traditional unities (whether "text," "work," "science"; whatever the domain or form of the discourse, whatever the concepts it uses or the choices it manifests). These four criteria are not only not incompatible, they demand one another: the first defines the unity of a discourse by the rule of formation of all its *objects*; the next by the rule of formation of all its *syntactic* types; the third by the rule of formation of all its *semantic* elements; the fourth by the rule of formation of all its *operational* eventualities.

All the aspects of discourse are thus covered. And when it is possible, in a group of statements, to register and describe *one* referential, *one* type of enunciative divergence, *one* theoretical network, *one* field of strategic possibilities, then one can be sure that they belong to what can be called a *discursive formation*. This formation groups together a whole population of statement-events. Obviously, neither in its criteria, in its limits, nor in its internal relations, does it coincide with the immediate and visible unities into which statements are conventionally grouped. It brings to light relations between the phenomena of enunciation which had hitherto remained in darkness and were not immediately transcribed on the surface of discourses. But what it brings to light is not a secret, the unity of a hidden meaning, nor a general and unique form; it is a controlled system of differences and dispersions. This four-level system which governs a discursive formation and has to explain, not its common elements but the play of its divergences, its interstices, its distances—in some sense its blanks rather than its full surfaces—that is what I propose to call its *positivity*.

KNOWLEDGE

At the outset the problem was to define unities that could be legitimately installed in such a disproportionate domain as that of statement-events other than the hastily admitted forms of synthesis. I tried to give an answer to this question which would be empirical (and articulated in precise inquiries) and critical (since it concerned the place from which I was posing the question, the region which situated it, the spontaneous unity within which I could believe I was talking). Hence the investigations into the domain of the discourses which installed, or claimed to install, a "scientific" knowledge [*connaissance*] of living, speaking, and working men. These investigations have brought to light sets of statements which I have called "discursive formations" and systems that should explain these sets called "positivities." But have I not purely and simply produced a history of the human "sciences"—or, if you will, of the inexact knowledges [*connaissances*] whose accumulation has not yet managed to constitute a science? Am I not still caught in their apparent divisions and in the system they pretend to adopt for themselves? Have I not made a kind of critical epistemology of these patterns which cannot firmly be said really to deserve the name of sciences?

In fact, the discursive formations I have separated or described do not precisely coincide with the delimitation of these sciences (or pseudo-sciences). Undoubtedly I opened my inquiry into the history of madness on the basis of the existence at present of a discourse that calls itself psychopathology (which some may regard as having pretensions to be scientific); undoubtedly I undertook to analyze what it was possible to say about wealth, money, exchange, about linguistic signs and the functioning of words, in the seventeenth and eighteenth centuries on the basis of the existence of an economics and a linguistics (whose criteria of scientific rigor may well be contested by some). But the positivities obtained at the end of the analysis and the discursive formations that they group together do not cover the same space as these disciplines, and are not articulated as they are; to go further, they cannot be superimposed on what it was possible to regard as a science or as an autonomous form of discourse in the period under study. Thus the system of positivity analyzed in *Madness and Civilization* does not explain, either exclusively or in a privileged way, what doctors were able to say about mental disease at the time; rather, it defines the referential, the enunciative scale, the theoretical network, the points of choice which made possible the very dispersion of medical statements, institutional controls, administrative measures, literary expressions, and philosophical formulations. The discursive formation constituted and described by the analysis goes far beyond the account that might have been given of the prehistory of psychopathology or of the genesis of its concepts.

In *The Order of Things* this situation is inverted. The positivities obtained by description isolate discursive formations which are narrower than the scientific domains recognized in the first instance. The system of natural history permits the explanation of a certain number of statements about the resemblances and differences between beings, the constitutions of specific and generic characteristics, the distribution of relationship in the general space of the table; but it does not govern the analysis of involuntary movement, nor the theory of genera, nor the chemical explanations of growth. The existence, the autonomy, the internal consistency and the limitation of this discursive formation precisely constitute one of the reasons why a general science of life was not formulated in the Classical age. Similarly, the positivity that governed the analysis of wealth in the same period did not determine every statement about exchange, commercial transactions and prices: it left out "political arithmetic," which did not enter the field of economic theory until much later, when a new system of positivity had made the introduction of that kind of discourse into economic analysis both possible and necessary. Nor does general grammar explain all that it was possible to say about language in the Classical age (whether by exegetes of religious texts, by philosophers, or by theoreticians of literary works). In none of those three cases was it a matter of discovering what men could have thought about language, wealth or life at a time when a biology, an economics, and a philology were slowly and stealthily constituting themselves; nor was it a matter of finding out the errors, prejudices, confusions, or even fantasies still mixed up with the concepts on their way to formation; nor was it a matter of knowing the price in breaks and repressions which a science, or at least a discipline with scientific pretensions, had to pay in order to constitute itself at last on such impure ground. It was a matter of bringing out the system of that "impurity" – or rather, for the word can have no meaning in this analysis, of explaining the simultaneous appearance of a certain number of statements whose level of scientificity, form, and degree of elaboration may well seem heterogeneous to us in retrospect.

The discursive formation analyzed in *The Birth of the Clinic* represents a third case. It is much broader than medical discourse, in the strict sense of the term (the scientific theory of illness, of its forms, of its determinations and of therapeutic instruments): it encompasses a whole series of political reflections, reform programs, legislative measures, administrative settlements, and ethical considerations; but, on the other hand, it does not include everything it was possible to know in the period studied about the human body, about its workings, its anatomico-physiological correlations, and about the disturbances that may occur in it. The unity of clinical discourse is in no sense the unity of a science or of a set of knowledges attempting to acquire a scientific status. It is a complex unity: the criteria by which we can – or think we can – distinguish one science from another (for example, physiology from pathology), a more developed science from one which is less so (for example, biochemistry from neurology), a really scientific discourse (such as hormonology) from a mere codification of experience (such as semiology), a real science (such as microbiology) from a science that was not a science (such as phrenology), could not be applied to it. Clinical medicine constitutes neither a false science nor a true one, although in the name of present-day criteria we may assume the right to recognize the truth of certain of its statements and the falsity of certain others. It is an enunciative ensemble both theoretical and practical, descriptive and institutional, analytical and prescriptive, made up of inferences as well as decisions, of assertions as well as degrees.

Discursive formations are neither current sciences in gestation, nor sciences formerly recognized as such, then fallen into desuetude and abandoned as a result of the new requirements of our criteria. They are unities of a different kind and on a different level from what is called today (or was once called) a "science." In order to characterize them, the distinction between scientific and nonscientific is not pertinent: they are epistemologically neutral. As for the systems of positivity which ensure unitary grouping, they are not rational structures, nor are they forces, equilibria, oppositions or dialectics between forms of rationality and irrational constraints; the distinction between the rational and its opposite is not pertinent in describing these unities; they are not the laws of intelligibility but the laws of the formation of a whole set of objects, types of formulation, concepts, and theoretical options which are invested in institutions, techniques, collective and individual behavior, political operations, scientific activities, literary fictions and theoretical speculations. The set thus formulated from the system of positivity, and manifested in the unity of a discursive formation, is what might be called a knowledge [*savoir*]. Knowledge is not the sum of scientific knowledges [*connaissances*], since it should always be possible to say whether the latter are true or false, accurate or not, approximate or definite, contradictory or consistent; none of these distinctions is pertinent in describing knowledge, which is the set of the elements (objects, types of formulation, concepts and theoretical choices) formed from one and the same positivity in a field of a unitary discursive formation.

We are now dealing with a complex pattern. It can and must be analyzed both as a formation of statements (when considering the population of discursive events that are part of it); as a positivity (when considering the system that governs the dispersion of the objects, the types of formulation, the concepts and the opinions that come into play in these statements); as a knowledge (when considering these objects, types of formulation, concepts and opinions as they are invested in a science, a technical recipe, an institution, a fictional narrative, a legal or political practice, and so on). *Knowledge* cannot be analyzed in terms of knowledges; nor can positivity in terms of rationality; nor can the discursive formation in terms of science. And one cannot ask that their description be equivalent to a history of knowledges, a genesis of rationality or the epistemology of a science.

It remains true, nonetheless, that it is possible to describe a certain number of relations between the sciences (with their structures of rationality and the sum of their knowledges) and the discursive formations (with their system of positivity and the field of their knowledge). For it is true that only formal criteria can decide about the scientificity of a science, that is, can define the conditions that make it possible as a science; but they can never account for its factual existence, that is, its historical appearance, the events, episodes, obstacles, dissensions, expectations, delays, and facilitations that have been able to stamp its actual destiny. If, for example, it was necessary to wait for the end of the eighteenth century for the concept of life to become fundamental in the analysis of living beings, or if the registering of the resemblances between Latin and Sanskrit could not have given birth before Franz Bopp to a comparative and historical grammar, or again, if the established fact of intestinal lesions in "feverous" ailments could not give rise before the beginning of the nineteenth century to an anatomo-pathological medicine, the reason is to be sought neither in the epistemological structure of biology in general, nor of grammatical science, nor of medical science; nor, moreover, in the error that would sustain men's blindness for so long. It resides instead in the morphology of knowledge, in the system of positivities, in the internal disposition of discursive formations. Even more, it is in the element of knowledge that the conditions of the appearance of a science, or at least of a discursive ensemble that acquires or claims the models of scientificity, are determined. If, toward the beginning of the nineteenth century, one witnesses the formation, under the name of political economy, of a discursive ensemble that gives itself the signs of scientificity, and imposes a certain number of formal rules; if, at about the same period, certain discourses are organized on the model of medical, clinical, and semiological discourses in order to be constituted as psychopathology, the cause of these "sciences"–whether for their actual equilibrium, or for the ideal form toward which they supposedly aim–cannot be demanded retrospectively. Nor can cause be demanded for a project of rationalization that would take form then in

the minds of men but be unable to take charge of what these discourses had in the way of specificity. It is in the field of knowledge that
the analysis of these conditions of appearance must be undertaken – at
the level of discursive ensembles and the play of positivities.

Under the general term of the "conditions of possibility" of a science, two heteromorphous systems must be distinguished. The first
defines the conditions of the science as a science: it is relative to its
domain of objects, to the type of language it uses, to the concepts it has
at its disposal or it is seeking to establish; it defines the formal and
semantic rules required for a statement to belong to the science; it is
instituted either by the science in question, insofar as it poses its own
norms for itself, or by another science, insofar it imposes itself on the
former as a model of formalization; at any rate, these conditions of
scientificity are internal to scientific discourse in general and cannot
be defined other than through it. The other system is concerned with
the possibility of a science in its historical existence. It is external to
the former system, and the two cannot be superposed. It is constituted
by a field of discursive sets which have neither the same status, units,
organization, nor the same functioning as the sciences to which they
give rise. These discursive sets should not be seen as a rhapsody of
false knowledges, archaic themes, and irrational figures which the
sciences, in their sovereignty, definitively thrust aside into the night of
a prehistory. Nor should they be imagined as the outline of future
sciences that are still confusedly wrapped around their futures, veg-
etating for a time in the half sleep of silent germination. Finally, they
should not be conceived as the only epistemological system to which
those supposedly false, quasi- or pseudo-sciences, the human sciences, are susceptible. In fact, the system is concerned with patterns
that have their own consistency, laws of formation and autonomous
disposition. To analyze discursive formations, positivities, and the
knowledge which corresponds to them is not to assign forms of scientificity but, rather, to run through a field of historical determination
which must account for the appearance, retention, transformation,
and, in the last analysis, the erasure of discourses, some of which are
still recognized today as scientific, some of which have lost that status,
some have never pretended to acquire it, and finally, others have
never attempted to acquire it. In a word, knowledge is not science in
the successive displacement of its internal structures; it is the field of
its actual history.

SEVERAL REMARKS

The analysis of discursive formations and of their system of positivity in the element of knowledge concerns only certain determinations of discursive events. There can be no question of constituting a unitary discipline replacing all other descriptions of discourses and invalidating them *en bloc.* Rather, it is a question of giving a place to different, already-familiar, and often long-practiced types of analyses: of determining their level of functioning and effectivity; of defining their points of application, and, finally, of avoiding the illusions to which they can give rise. To bring into existence the dimension of knowledge as a specific dimension is not to reject the various analyses of science; it is to unfold as broadly as possible the space in which they can come to rest. Above all, it is to give free rein to two forms of extrapolation which have symmetrical and inverse reductive roles: epistemological extrapolation and genetic extrapolation.

Epistemological extrapolation should not be confused with the (always-legitimate and possible) analysis of the formal structures that may characterize a scientific discourse. But it does suggest that these structures are enough to define for a science the historical law of its appearance and unfolding. *Genetic* extrapolation should not be confused with the (always-legitimate and possible) description of the context – whether discursive, technical, economic, or institutional – in which a science appeared. But it does suggest that the internal organization of a science and its formal norms can be described on the basis of its external conditions. In one case, the science is given the responsibility of explaining its own historicity; in the other, various historical determinations are required to explain a scientificity. But this is to ignore the fact that the place in which a science appears and unfolds is neither this science itself distributed according to a teleological sequence, nor a set of mute practices or extrinsic determinations, but the field of knowledge, with the set of relations which traverse it. This misconstrual can, in fact, be explained by the privilege granted to two types of sciences, which serve in general as models whereas they are surely limit cases. There are indeed sciences of such a type that every episode of their historical development can be taken up again in the interior of their deductive system; their history can, in fact, be described as a movement of lateral extension, then of repetition and generalization at a higher level, such that each moment appears either as a special region, or as a definite degree of formalization; sequences are abolished in favor of proximities that do not reproduce them; and dates are removed in order to reveal synchronies that know no calendar. This is clearly the case with mathematics, in which Cartesian algebra defines a special region in a field that was generalized by Joseph-Louis Lagrange, Niels Henrik Abel, and Evariste Galois; in which the Greek method of exhaustion seems to be contemporary with the calculus of definite integrals. On the other hand, there are sciences that can only secure their unity through time by the narration or critical repetition of their own history: if there has been one and only one psychology since Gustav Fechner, if there has been only one sociology since Auguste Comte, or even since Emile Durkheim, it is not insofar as it is possible to assign a single epistemological structure (as tenuous as is conceivable) to so many diverse discourses; it is insofar as sociology or psychology have at each moment located their discourse in a historical field they themselves had traversed in the critical mode of confirmation or invalidation. The history of mathematics is always on the point of crossing the boundary of epistemological description; the epistemology of "sciences" such as psychology or sociology is always on the edge of a genetic description.

That is why, far from constituting privileged examples for the analysis of all other scientific domains, these two extreme cases instead threaten to lead to an error: the failure to reveal, at once in their specificity and in their relations, the level of epistemological structures and the level of determinations of knowledge; the fact that all sciences (even ones as highly formalized as mathematics) presuppose a space of historicity that does not coincide with the interaction of its forms; but that all sciences (even ones as heavy with empiricity as psychology and as far from the norms required to constitute a science) exist in the field of a knowledge which does not merely prescribe the sequence of their episodes, but which determines their laws of formation according to a describable system. On the other hand, there are "intermediate" sciences – such as biology, physiology, political economy, linguistics, philology – that ought to provide the models: for with them it is impossible to fuse the instance of knowledge and the form of science into a false unity, or to elide the moment of knowledge.

It is possible, on this basis, to situate a certain number of legitimate descriptions of scientific discourse in their possibility, but also to define them in their limits. Descriptions that are directed not toward knowledge as an instance of formation but to the objects, forms of enunciation, concepts, and, finally, to the opinions to which they give rise; descriptions that will, nevertheless, only remain legitimate on the condition that they do not pretend to discover the conditions of existence of something as a scientific discourse. It is thus perfectly legitimate to describe the series of opinions or theoretical options which emerge in a science and à propos a science: one should be able to define, for a historical period or determinate domain, what the principles of choice are, in what way (by what rhetoric or dialectic) they are manifested, hidden, or justified, how the field of the polemic is organized and institutionalized, what the motivations that may characterize the individuals are; in short, there is room for a *doxology*, the description (sociological or linguistic, statistical or interpretative) of the facts of opinion. But there is also *doxological illusion* each time one sets forth description as the analysis of the conditions of the existence of a science. This illusion has two aspects. It admits that the actuality of opinions, instead of being determined by the strategic possibilities of conceptual games, refers directly to the divergences of interests or mental habits among individuals; opinion would be the irruption of the nonscientific (of the psychological, of the political, of the social, of the religious) in the specific domain of science. But, on the other hand, it presumes that opinion constitutes the central nucleus, the fulcrum from which the entire ensemble of scientific statements is deployed; opinion would manifest the impact of fundamental choices (metaphysical, religious, political) of which the diverse concepts of biology, or of economics, or of linguistics, would only be the positive, superficial version, the transcription into a determinate vocabulary, the mask blind to itself. The doxological illusion is one manner of eliding the field of a mode of knowledge as the site and law of formation of theoretical opinions.

Similarly, it is perfectly legitimate to describe, for a given science, certain of its concepts or its conceptual ensembles: the definition given them, the use made of them, the field in which the attempt is made to validate them, the transformations to which they are made subject, the way in which they are generalized or transferred from one domain to another. It is equally legitimate to describe, in connection with a science, the forms of propositions that it recognizes as valid, the types of inference to which it has recourse, the rules to which it appeals in order to link statements to one another or to render them equivalent, the laws that it lays down in order to govern their transformations or their substitutions. In short, one can always establish the semantics and the syntax of a scientific discourse. But it is necessary to protect oneself from what one would call the *formalist illusion:* that is, from imagining that these laws of construction are at the same time and with full title the conditions of existence; that valid concepts and propositions are nothing more than the giving of form to an undomesticated experience, or the result of reworking concepts and propositions already in place. One must guard against imagining that science is launched into existence out of a certain degree of conceptualization and a certain way of proceeding in the construction and the concatenation of propositions; that it is enough, in describing its emergence within the field of discourses, to register the linguistic level that characterizes it. The formalist illusion elides knowledge (the theoretical network and enunciative repartition) as the site and law of formation of concepts and propositions.

Finally, it is possible and legitimate to define, by a regional analysis, the domain of objects to which a science addresses itself. And to analyze it either on the horizon of ideality which the science constitutes (by a code of abstraction, by rules of manipulation, by a system of presentation and potential representation) or in the world of things to which those objects refer. For if it is true that the object of biology or of political economy is indeed defined by a particular structure of ideality peculiar to these two sciences, and if these objects are not purely and simply the life in which individual human beings participate, or the industrialization they have fashioned, nevertheless, these objects refer to experience or to a definite phase of capitalist evolution. But it would be incorrect to believe (through an *illusion of experience*) that there are regions or domains of things which present themselves spontaneously to an activity of idealization and to the work of scientific language; that these things unfurl themselves in the order in which history, technology, discoveries, institutions, and human instruments have managed to constitute them or bring them to light; that all scientific elaboration is only a certain way of reading, deciphering, abstracting, decomposing, and recomposing what is given either in a natural (and consequently generally valid) experience or in a cultural (and consequently relative and historical) experience. There is an illusion that consists of the supposition that science is grounded in the plenitude of a concrete and lived experience; that geometry elaborates a perceived space, that biology gives form to the intimate experience of life, or that political economy translates the processes of industrialization at the level of theoretical discourse; therefore, that the referent itself contains the law of the scientific object. But it is equally illusory to imagine that science is established by an act of rupture and decision, that it frees itself at one stroke from the qualitative field and from all the murmurings of the imaginary by the violence (serene or polemical) of a reason that founds itself by its own assertions—that is, that the scientific object brings itself into existence of itself in its own identity.

If there are, at the same time, both relations and a break between the analysis of life and the familiarity of the body, suffering, sickness, and death; if there are ties and separations between political economy and a particular form of production; if, in a general way, science refers to experience and yet detaches itself from it, it is not a matter of univocal determination, nor of a sovereign, constant, and definitive break. In fact, these relations of reference and separation are specific to each scientific discourse, and their form varies through history. This is because they are themselves determined by the specific instance of knowledge. The latter defines the laws of formation of scientific objects and by the same action specifies the connections or oppositions between science and experience. Their extreme proximity and their unbridgeable distance is never given at the outset; it finds its principle in the morphology of the referential; this is what defines the reciprocal disposition—the confrontation, opposition, their system of communication—of the referent and the object. Between science and experience, there is knowledge no longer as an invisible mediation, or as a secret complicit pander between two distances so difficult to reconcile and unravel at the same time. In fact, knowledge determines the space in which science and experience can be separated and situated one in relation to the other.

What the archaeology of knowledge places out of bounds is thus not the possibility of diverse descriptions to which scientific discourse can give rise; it is, rather, the general thematic of "understanding" [*connaissance*]. Understanding is the continuity of science and experience, their indissociable interlinkage, their indefinite reversibility. It is a play of forms that anticipate all contents insofar as they have already rendered them possible. It is a field of originary contents that silently outline the forms through which they can be read. It is the peculiar instauration of the formal within a successive order, that of psychological or historical geneses; but it is the ordering of the empirical by a form whose teleology is imposed upon it. Understanding confers upon experience the charge of giving an account of the effective existence of science; it confers upon scientificity the charge of giving an account of the historical emergence of the forms and of the system it follows. The thematic of understanding is tantamount to the denegation of knowledge.

To this major thematic, several others are linked. One, that of a constituent activity that would assure – by a series of fundamental operations anterior to all explicit acts, to all concrete manipulations, to all given contents – the unity of a science defined by a system of formal requisites and a world defined as the horizon of all possible experiences. Another, that of a subject who assures, in its reflexive unity, the synthesis of the successive diversity of the given with the ideality that profiles itself, in its identity, through the course of time. Finally, and above all, the great historico-transcendental thematic that ran through the nineteenth century and barely exhausts itself even today in the tireless repetition of these two questions: What should history be, what absolutely archaic project did it need to have traversed, what fundamental telos established it from its first moment forward (or rather, from whatever it was that made its first moment possible) and directs it, in shadow, toward a conclusion yet withheld in order that the truth might see the light of day, or that it might recognize, in that always-remote brightness, the return of what its origin had already obscured? And the other question immediately arises: What must this truth, or perhaps this more than originary opening be in order that history might not unfold without covering it over, hiding it, plunging it into an oblivion by whose repetition, whose recall, and so whose ever-incomplete memory history would always be marked? One can do whatever one likes to make these questions as radical as possible. They would still remain tied, in spite of every effort to effect a separation, to an analytics of the subject and to a problematics of understanding.

In opposition to all these themes, it might be said that knowledge, as the field of historicity in which the sciences appear, is free of any constituent activity, disengaged from any reference to an origin or to a historico-transcendental teleology, detached from any reliance upon a foundational subjectivity. Of all the previous forms of synthesis by which the discontinuous events of discourse were hoped to be unified, these latter were for more than a century the most insistent and most redoubtable; they animated the thematic of a continuous history perceptually linked to itself and put indefinitely to the tasks of reprise and totalization. History had to be continuous in order for the sovereignty of the subject to be safeguarded; but, reciprocally, a constituent subjectivity and a transcendental teleology had to run through history in order that the latter could be thought in its unity. Thus the anonymous discontinuity of knowledge was excluded from discourse and thrown out into the unthinkable.

NOTES

1   The Epistemology Circle consisted of Alain Badiou, Jacques Bouveresse, Yves Duroux, Alain Grosrichard, Thomas Herbert, Patrick Hochart, Jean Malthoit, Jacques-Alain Miller, Jean-Claude Milner, Jean Mosconi, Jacques Nassif, Bernard Pautrat, François Regnault, and Michel Torto – Ed.

2   We refer, in this question, to the following passage from Georges Canguilhem's article on Foucault's book (*Critique* 242 [July 1967], pp. 612 – 13): "Concerning a theoretical knowledge [*savoir*], is it possible to think of it in the specificity of its concept without reference to some norm? Among the theoretical discourses conducted in conformity with the epistemic systems of the seventeenth and eighteenth centuries, some, such as natural history, were discarded by the episteme of the nineteenth century, but others were integrated into it. Newtonian physics did not pass away with the physiology of animal economy, even though the former served the latter as a model. Georges Buffon was refuted by Darwin, if not by Etienne Geoffroy Saint-Hilaire. But Newton is no more refuted by Einstein than by Maxwell; Darwin was not refuted by Mendel and Morgan. The sequence Galileo – Newton – Einstein does not contain ruptures similiar to those in the sequence Tournefort – Linnaeus – Engler in botanical taxonomy."

3   I am indebted to Georges Canguilhem for the idea of using the word in this sense.

MADNESS AND SOCIETY*

In the West the traditional approach to the study of systems of thought has consisted in focusing only on positive phenomena. During the past few years, however, in ethnology, Lévi-Strauss has explored a method that makes it possible to reveal the negative structure in any society or culture. For example, he has demonstrated that if incest is prohibited within a culture this is not due to the affirmation of a certain type of values; it is because there is a checkerboard, as it were, with barely perceptible gray or light blue squares that define a culture's mode of existence. It is the weave [trame] of these squares that I wanted to apply to the study of systems of thought. Thus for me it was a matter not of knowing what is affirmed and valorized in a society or a system of thought but of studying what is rejected and excluded. I merely used a method of working that was already recognized in ethnology.

Madness has always been excluded. Now, during the last fifty years in what are called the "advanced countries," comparative ethnologists and psychiatrists have attempted, first of all, to determine whether the madness that was encountered in their countries – that is, mental disorders such as obsessional neurosis, paranoia, schizophrenia – also existed in so-called primitive societies. They have tried to find out, second, whether those primitive societies did not assign a different status to the mentally disturbed than the one

*This text, a lecture given 29 September 1970 at the Franco-Japanese Institute in Kyoto, first appeared in Japanese translation in *Misuzu* (Dec. 1970), pp. 16–22. Robert Hurley's translation.

seen in their own countries. Whereas in their society the mad were excluded, didn't primitive societies attribute a positive value to them? For example, aren't the shamans in Siberia or North America mental cases? Third, they asked themselves whether certain societies were not ill themselves. For example, Ruth Benedict concluded that the entire Kwakiutl tribe exhibited a paranoiac character.

In speaking to you today, I would like to take an opposite approach to the one taken by these researchers. I would like first to look at the status of the mentally disturbed in primitive societies; second, to see how the matter stands in our industrial societies; third, to reflect on the mutation that occurred in the nineteenth century; and finally, by way of conclusion, to demonstrate that the position the madman is in has not fundamentally changed in modern industrial society.

Roughly, the areas of human activity can be divided into these four categories:

- labor, or economic production;

- sexuality, family; that is, reproduction of society;

- language, speech;

- ludic activities such as games and festivals.

In all societies there are persons who have behaviors different from others that do not conform to the commonly defined rules in these four areas—in short, what are called "marginal individuals." Already in the ordinary population, the relationship to labor varies according to gender and age. In many societies, if the political and ecclesiastical leaders happen to control the labor of others or serve as intermediaries with supernatural power, they do not work directly themselves and are not involved in the production cycle.

There are also persons who are outside the second cycle of social reproduction. Celibates constitute an example, and one sees many of these, among religious devotees in particular. Moreover, among the Indians of North America, we know that there exist homosexuals and transvestites: it has to be said that they occupy a marginal position in social reproduction.

Third, in discourse as well, there are persons who escape the norm. The words they employ have different meanings. In the case of a prophet, words with a symbolic meaning could one day reveal their hidden truth. The words that poets use are of an aesthetic order and also escape the norm.

Fourth, in all societies there are persons excluded from the games and festivals. Sometimes they are excluded because they are considered dangerous; other times they are themselves the object of a festival. Like the scapegoat among the Hebrews, it may happen that someone is sacrificed after taking responsibility for the others' crime; while the ceremony of his exclusion takes place, the people stage a festival.

In all these cases, those who are excluded differ from one area to another, but it may happen that the same person is excluded in every area. I am thinking of the madman. In every society, or almost, the madman is excluded in all things and, depending on the case, he is given a religious, magical, ludic, or pathological status.

For example, in a primitive tribe of Australia, the madman is regarded as an individual to be feared by the society, a man endowed with a supernatural force. In other instances, certain madmen become victims of society. In any case, they are people who have behaviors that are different from the others, in labor, in the family, in discourse, and in games.

What I would now like to address is the fact that in our industrial societies madmen are similarly excluded from ordinary society by an isomorphic system of exclusion and are assigned a marginal condition.

First, as far as labor is concerned, even in our day the first criterion for determining madness in an individual consists in showing that he is unfit for work. Freud said correctly that the madman (he was talking mainly about neurotics) was a person who could neither work nor love. I will come back to the verb "love," but there is a profound truth in this idea of Freud's. In Europe in the Middle Ages, the existence of madmen was accepted. Sometimes they would get excited and unstable, or they would turn out to be lazy, but they were allowed to wander around. Now, beginning in the seventeenth century, roughly, industrial society was formed and the existence of such persons was no longer tolerated. In response to the requirements of industrial society, large establishments for confining them were created almost simultaneously in France and in England. It was not just madmen who were put there, but also the unemployed, sick people, old people, all those who were unable to work.

According to the traditional account of historians, it was at the end of the eighteenth century–that is in 1793 in France–that Philippe Pinel freed madmen from their chains, and it was at about the same time in England that Samuel Tuke, a Quaker, created a psychiatric hospital. It is thought that madmen were treated as criminals until then, and that Pinel and Tuke labeled them "ill" for the first time. But I am obliged to say that this account is erroneous. In the first place, it is not true that before the Revolution madmen were regarded as criminals; second, it is a misconception to think that madmen were freed of their former status.

This second idea probably constitutes a greater misconception than the first. In general, in primitive society and modern society alike, in the Middle Ages as well as in the twentieth century, what might be called a "universal status" was given to madmen. The only difference is that, from the seventeenth century to the nineteenth century, the right to demand the confinement of a madman belonged to the family: it was the family, first of all, that excluded madmen. Now, starting in the nineteenth century, this prerogative was gradually lost to the family and granted to physicians. In order to confine a madman, a medical certificate was required; once confined, the madman was deprived of all responsibility and any rights as a family member–he even lost his citizenship and was the object of a judicial interdiction. It could be said that law prevailed over medicine in endowing madmen with a marginal status.

Second, there is one fact to note in regard to sexuality and the family system. When one consults European documents up to the beginning of the nineteenth century, sexual practices such as masturbation, homosexuality, and nymphomania are not at all treated as belonging to the domain of psychiatry. It was from the beginning of the nineteenth century that these sexual anomalies were identified with madness and considered as disturbances manifested by an individual who was incapable of adapting to the European bourgeois family. The idea that the main cause of madness resided in sexual anomaly was reinforced when Beyle described creeping paralysis and demonstrated that it was due to syphilis. When Freud considered disturbance of the libido as a cause or an expression of madness, this exerted the same type of influence.

Third, the madman's status with respect to language was curious in Europe. On the one hand, the speech of madmen was rejected as being worthless, and, on the other, it was never completely nullified. We may say that the fool was, in a sense, the institutionalization of the speech of madness. Without any relation to morality and politics, and, moreover, under the cover of irresponsibility, he told, in a symbolic form, the truth that ordinary men could not state.

To take a second example, up to the nineteenth century, literature was highly institutionalized for buttressing the social ethic and for entertaining people. Now, in our day, literature has completely rid itself of all that and has become totally anarchic. This suggests a curious affinity between literature and madness. Literary language is not constrained by the rules of everyday language. For example, it is not subject to the severe rule of constant truth-telling, any more than the teller is under the obligation to always remain sincere in what he thinks and feels. In short, unlike the words of politics or the sciences, those of literature occupy a marginal position with respect to everyday language.

As regards European literature, literary language became especially marginal during these three periods:

1. In the sixteenth century it became more marginal than it was in the Middle Ages: the epics and the chivalrous novels were destructive and contentious with respect to society. That is true of Erasmus' *The Praise of Folly*, the work of Tasso, or Elizabethan drama. In France, there is even a literature of madness that appeared. The Duke de Bouillon went so far as to have the text of a madman printed at his own expense, and the French took pleasure in reading it.

2. The second period goes from the end of the eighteenth century to the beginning of the nineteenth century. As to literature by madmen, one notes the publication of the poetry of Hölderlin and Blake, and, later, the work of Raymond Roussel. This last writer entered a psychiatric hospital for obsessional neurosis in order to be treated by the eminent psychiatrist Pierre Janet, but he ended up committing suicide. It is significant that a contemporary author such as Alain Robbe-Grillet took Raymond Roussel as his starting point, dedicating his first book to him.[1] For his part, Antonin Artaud was a schizophrenic: it was he who, after the weakening of surrealism, created a breakthrough in the poetic world, opening up new vistas. For that matter, one has only to consider Nietzsche or Baudelaire to affirm that one

must imitate madness or actually become mad in order to establish new fields in literature.

3. These days, people are paying more and more attention to the relationship between literature and madness. All things considered, madness and literature are marginal in relation to everyday language, and they are looking for the secret of general literary production in a model which is madness.

Finally, let us reflect on the situation the madman is in with respect to games in an industrial society. In the traditional European theater – I imagine the same thing is true in Japan – the fool assumed a central role, from the Middle Ages to the eighteenth century. The madman made the spectators laugh, for he saw what the other actors did not see, and he revealed the ending of the plot before they did. That is, he is an individual who reveals the truth with spirit. Shakespeare's *King Lear* is a good example. The king is a victim of his own fantasy, but at the same time he is someone who tells the truth. In other words, in the theater the madman is a character who expresses with his body the truth that the other actors and spectators are not aware of, a character through whom the truth appears.

Further, in the Middle Ages there were many festivals, but among them there was only one that was not religious. It is called the Festival of Folly. In this festival, the social and traditional roles were completely reversed: a poor man played the role of a rich man, a weak man that of a powerful one. The sexes were inverted, the sexual prohibitions nullified. On the occasion of this holiday, the lower class had the right to say what they wanted to the bishop or the mayor. In general, it was insults . . . In short, during this festival all the social, linguistic, and familial institutions were overturned and called back in question. In church, an irreverent layman celebrated mass, after which he would bring in a donkey whose braying was perceived as a mockery of the litany of mass. In sum, it was a counterholiday in relation to Sunday, Christmas or Easter, one that escaped from the habitual circuit of ordinary festivals.

In our time, the politico-religious meaning of festivals has been lost; instead, we resort to alcohol or drugs as a way of contesting the social order, and we have thus created a kind of artificial madness. Basically, it is an imitation of madness, and it can be seen as an attempt to set society ablaze by creating the same state as madness.

I am absolutely not a structuralist. Structuralism is only a means of analysis. For example, how have the conditions under which the madman lives changed from the Middle Ages to the present day? What were the conditions necessary for that change? I merely make use of the structuralist method to analyze all that.

In the Middle Ages and during the Renaissance madmen were permitted to exist in the midst of society. What is called the "village idiot" did not get married, did not participate in games, and he was fed and supported by others. He would roam from town to town, sometimes he would enter the army, he would become a peddler; but when he became too worked up and dangerous, the others would construct a little house outside town where they would temporarily confine him. Arab society is still tolerant toward madmen. In the seventeenth century European society became intolerant toward them. The cause of this, as I said, is that industrial society began to take form. I also told how, from before 1650 to 1750, in cities such as Hamburg, Lyon, and Paris, large-sized institutions were created for interning not only madmen but old people, the sick, the unemployed, idlers, prostitutes— all those who found themselves outside the social order. Capitalist industrial society could not tolerate the existence of groups of vagabonds. Out of a Parisian population numbering a half-million inhabitants, six thousand were confined. In these establishments there was no therapeutic intention; everyone was subjected to forced labor. In 1665 the police were reorganized in Paris; it was then that a grid of squares for social conditioning [*formation*] was constituted. The police kept constant watch over the confined vagabonds.

The irony is that work therapy is frequently practiced in modern psychiatric hospitals. The logic underlying this practice is obvious. If incapacity for work is the first criterion of madness, one has only to teach the patients to work in the hospital to cure them of their madness.

Now, why did the situation of madmen change from the end of the eighteenth century to the beginning of the nineteenth century? It is said that Pinel liberated the madmen in 1793, but those he liberated were only sick people, old people, idlers, prostitutes; he left the madmen in the institutions. This took place when it did because, at the beginning of the nineteenth century, the speed of industrial development accelerated, and, in accordance with the first principle of capitalism, the hordes of unemployed proletarians were regarded as a reserve army of labor power. For that reason, those who did not work but were able to work were let out of the establishments. But there, too, a second process of selection took effect: not only those who were unwilling to work, but those who did not have the ability to work, namely the mad, were left in the establishments and regarded as patients whose troubles had characterological or psychological causes.

Thus what had previously been a confinement institution became a psychiatric hospital, a treatment organization. In the years that followed, hospitals were set in place: (1) to confine those who were unable to work for physical reasons; (2) to confine those who could not work for nonphysical reasons. In this way, mental disorders had become the object of medicine and a social category called "psychiatry" was born.

I am not trying to deny the validity of psychiatry, but this medicalization of the madman occurred quite late historically, and it does not seem to me that this result exerted a profound influence on his status. Furthermore, if this medicalization occurred, it was, as I said earlier, essentially for economic and social reasons: that was how the madman was made identical to the mentally ill individual and an entity called "mental illness" was discovered and developed. Psychiatric hospitals were created as something symmetrical to hospitals for physical illnesses. It could be said that the madman is an avatar of our capitalist societies, and it seems that, at bottom, the status of the madman does not vary at all between primitive societies and advanced societies. This only demonstrates the primitivism of our societies.

Today, in sum, I wanted to show the traumatizing quality that our societies still possess. If something has slightly revalorized the status of the madman, it would be the emergence of psychoanalysis and the psychotropic drugs. But that breakthrough has only just begun; our society still excludes madmen. As to whether this is the case only in capitalist societies, and as to how things are in socialist societies, my sociological knowledge is not adequate for making a judgment.

NOTES

1   Alain Robbe-Grillet, *Un Régicide* (Paris: Minuit, 1948).

THEATRUM PHILOSOPHICUM*

I must discuss two books of exceptional merit and importance: *Difference and Repetition* and *The Logic of Sense*.[1] Indeed, these books are so outstanding that they are difficult to discuss; this may explain, as well, why so few have undertaken this task. I believe that these words will continue to revolve about us in enigmatic resonance with those of Klossowski, another major and excessive sign, and perhaps one day, this century will be known as Deleuzian.[a]

One after another, I should like to explore the many paths that lead to the heart of these challenging tests. As Deleuze has said to me, however, this metaphor is misleading: there is no heart, but only a problem – that is, a distribution of notable points; there is no center but always decenterings, series, from one to another, with the limp of a presence and an absence – of an excess, of a deficiency. Abandon the circle, a faulty principle of return; abandon our tendency to organize everything into a sphere. All things return on the straight and narrow, by way of a straight and labyrinthine line. Thus, fibrils and bifurcation (Leiris's marvelous series would be well suited to a Deleuzian analysis).

Overturn Platonism: what philosophy has not tried? If we defined philosophy at the limit as any attempt, regardless of its source, to reverse Platonism, then philosophy begins with Aristotle; or better yet, it be-

---

*This review essay originally appeared in *Critique* 282(1970), pp. 885–908. The translation, by Donald F. Brouchard and Sherry Simon, has been slightly amended.

gins with Plato himself, with the conclusion of the *Sophist* where it is impossible to distinguish Socrates from the crafty imitator; or it begins with the Sophists who were extremely vocal about the rise of Platonism and who ridiculed its future greatness with their perpetual play on words.

Are all philosophies individual species of the genus "anti-Platonic"? Would each begin with a declaration of this fundamental rejection? Can they be grouped around this desired and detestable center? Should we instead say that the philosophical nature of a discourse is its Platonic differential, an element absent in Platonism but present in the discourse itself? A better formulation would be: It is an element in which the effect of absence is induced in the Platonic series through a new and divergent series (consequently, its function in the Platonic series is that of a signifier both excessive and absent); and it is also an element in which the Platonic series produces a free, floating, and excessive circulation in that other discourse. Plato, then, is the excessive and deficient father. It is useless to define a philosophy by its anti-Platonic character (as a plant is distinguished by its reproductive organs); but a philosophy can be distinguished somewhat in the manner in which a phantasm is defined, by the effect of a lack when it is distributed into its two constituent series—the "archaic" and the "real"—and you will dream of a general history of philosophy, a Platonic phantasmatology, and not an architecture of systems.

In any event, here is Deleuze. His "reversed Platonism" consists of displacing himself within the Platonic series in order to disclose an unexpected facet: division.[2] Plato did not establish a weak separation between the genus "hunter," "cook," or "politician," as the Aristotelians said; neither was he concerned with the particular characteristics of the species "fisherman" or "one who hunts with snares",[3] he wished to discover the identity of the true hunter. *Who is?* and not *What is?* He searched for the authentic, the pure gold. Instead of subdividing, selecting, and pursuing a productive seam, he chose among the pretenders and ignored their fixed cadastral properties, he tested them with the strung bow, which eliminates all but one (the nameless one, the nomad). But how does one distinguish the false (the simulators, the "so-called") from the authentic (the unadulterated and pure)? Certainly not by discovering a law of the true and false (truth is not opposed to error but to false appearances), but by looking above these manifestations to a model, a model so pure that the actual purity of the "pure" resembles it, approximates it, and measures itself against it; a model that exists so forcefully that in its presence the sham vanity of the false copy is immediately reduced to nonexistence. With the abrupt appearance of Ulysses, the eternal husband, the false suitors disappear. *Exeunt* simulacra.

Plato is said to have opposed essence to appearance, a higher world to this world below, the sun of truth to the shadows of the cave (and it becomes our duty to bring essences back into the world, to glorify the world, and to place the sun of truth within man). But Deleuze locates Plato's singularity in the delicate sorting, in this fine operation that precedes the discovery of essence precisely because it calls upon it, and tries to separate malign simulacra from the masses [*peuple*] of appearance. Thus it is useless to attempt the reversal of Platonism by reinstating the rights of appearances, ascribing to them solidity and meaning, and bringing them closer to essential forms by lending them a conceptual backbone: these timid creatures should not be encouraged to stand upright. Neither should we attempt to rediscover the supreme and solemn gesture that established, in a single stroke, the inaccessible Idea. Rather, we should welcome the cunning assembly that simulates and clamors at the door. And what will enter, submerging appearance and breaking its engagement to essence, will be the event; the incorporeal will dissipate the density of matter; a timeless insistence will destroy the circle that imitates eternity; an impenetrable singularity will divest itself of its contamination by purity; the actual semblance of the simulacrum will support the falseness of false appearances. The sophist springs up and challenges Socrates to prove that he is not the illegitimate usurper.

To reverse Platonism with Deleuze is to displace oneself insidiously within it, to descend a notch, to descend to its smallest gestures—discreet, but *moral*—which serve to exclude the simulacrum; it is also to deviate slightly from it, to open the door from either side to the small talk it excluded; it is to initiate another disconnected and divergent series; it is to construct, by way of this small lateral leap, a dethroned para-Platonism. To convert Platonism (a serious task) is to increase its compassion for reality, for the world, and for time. To subvert Platonism is to begin at the top (the vertical distance of irony) and to grasp its origin. To pervert Platonism is to search out the smallest details, to descend (with the natural gravitation of humor) as far as its crop of hair or the dirt under its fingernails–those things that were never hallowed by an idea; it is to discover the decentering it put into effect in order to recenter itself around the Model, the Identical, and the Same; it is the decentering of oneself with respect to Platonism so as to give rise to the play (as with every perversion) of surfaces at its border. Irony rises and subverts; humor falls and perverts.[4] To pervert Plato is to side with the Sophists' spitefulness, the unmannerly gestures of the Cynics, the arguments of the Stoics, and the fluttering chimeras of Epicurus. It is time to read Diogenes Laertius.

We should be alert to the surface effects in which the Epicurians take such pleasure:[5] emissions proceeding from deep within bodies and rising like the wisps of a fog–interior phantoms that are quickly reabsorbed into other depths by the sense of smell, by the mouth, by the appetites, extremely thin membranes that detach themselves from the surfaces of objects and proceed to impose colors and contours deep within our eyes (floating epiderm, visual idols); phantasms of fear or desire (cloud gods, the adorable face of the beloved, "miserable hope transported by the wind"). It is all this swarming of the impalpable that must be integrated into our thought: we must articulate a philosophy of the phantasm construed not through the intermediary of perception of the image, as being of the order of an originary given but, rather, left to come to light among the surfaces to which it is related, in the reversal that causes every interior to pass to the outside and every exterior to the inside, in the temporal oscillation that always makes it precede and follow itself–in short, in what Deleuze would perhaps not allow us to call its "incorporeal materiality."

It is useless, in any case, to seek a more substantial truth behind the phantasm, a truth to which it points as a rather confused sign (thus, the futility of "symptomatologizing"); it is also useless to contain it within stable figures and to construct solid cores of convergence where we might include, on the basis of their identical properties, all its angles, flashes, membranes, and vapors (no possibility of "phenomenalization"). Phantasms must be allowed to function at the limit of bodies; against bodies, because they stick to bodies and protrude from them, but also because they touch them, cut them, break them into sections, regionalize them, and multiply their surfaces; and equally, outside of bodies, because they function between bodies according to laws of proximity, torsion, and variable distance – laws of which they remain ignorant. Phantasms do not extend organisms into the imaginary; they topologize the materiality of the body. They should consequently be freed from the restrictions we impose upon them, freed from the dilemmas of truth and falsehood and of being and nonbeing (the essential difference between simulacrum and copy carried to its logical conclusion); they must be allowed to conduct their dance, to act out their mime, as "extrabeings."

The Logic of Sense can be read as the most alien book imaginable from *The Phenomenology of Perception*.[6] In this latter text, the body-organism is linked to the world through a network of primal significations which arise from the perception of things, while, according to Deleuze, phantasms form the impenetrable and incorporeal surface of bodies; and from this process, simultaneously topological and cruel, something is shaped that falsely presents itself as a centered organism and distributes at its periphery the increasing remoteness of things. More essentially, however, *The Logic of Sense* should be read as the boldest and most insolent of metaphysical treatises – on the simple condition that instead of denouncing metaphysics as the neglect of being, we force it to speak of extrabeing. Physics: discourse dealing with the ideal structure of bodies, mixtures, reactions, internal and external mechanisms, metaphysics: discourse dealing with the materiality of incorporeal things – phantasms, idols, and simulacra.

Illusion is certainly the misfortune of metaphysics, but not because metaphysics, by its very nature, is doomed to illusion, but because for too long it has been haunted by illusion and because, in its fear of the simulacrum, it was forced to hunt down the illusory. Metaphysics is not illusory – it is not merely another species of this particular genus – but illusion is a metaphysics. It is the product of a particular metaphysics that designated the separation between the simulacrum on one side and the original and the perfect copy on the other. There was a critique whose task was to unearth metaphysical illusion and to establish its necessity; Deleuze's metaphysics, however, initiates the necessary critique for the disillusioning of phantasms. With this grounding, the way is cleared for the advance of the Epicurean and materialist series, for the pursuit of their singular zigzag. And it does not lead, in spite of itself, to a shameful metaphysics; it leads joyously to metaphysics – a metaphysics freed from its original profundity as well as from a supreme being, but also one that can conceive of the phantasm in its play of surfaces without the aid of models, a metaphysics where it is no longer a question of the One Good but of the absence of God and the epidermic play of perversity. A dead God and sodomy are the thresholds of the new metaphysical ellipse. Where natural theology contained metaphysical illusion in itself and where this illusion was always more or less related to natural theology, the metaphysics of the phantasm revolves around atheism and transgression. Sade and Bataille and somewhat later, the palm upturned in a gesture of defense and invitation, Roberte.[7]

Moreover, this series of liberated simulacrum is activated, or mimes itself, on two privileged sites: that of psychoanalysis, which should eventually be understood as a metaphysical practice since it concerns itself with phantasms; and that of the theater, which is multiplied, polyscenic, simultaneous, broken into separate scenes that refer to each other, and where we encounter, without any trace of representation (copying or imitating), the dance of masks, the cries of bodies, and the gesturing of hands and fingers. And throughout each of these two recent and divergent series (the attempt to "reconcile" these series, to reduce them to either perspective, to produce a ridiculous "psychodrama," has been extremely naive), Freud and Artaud exclude each other and give rise to a mutual resonance. The philosophy of representation – of the original, the first time, resemblance, imitation, faithfulness – is dissolving; and the arrow of the simulacrum released by the Epicureans is headed in our direction. It gives birth – rebirth – to a "phantasmaphysics."

Occupying the other side of Platonism are the Stoics. Observing Deleuze in his discussion of Epicurus and Zeno, of Lucretius and Chrysippus, I was forced to conclude that his procedure was rigorously Freudian. He does not proceed – with a drum roll – toward the great Repression of Western philosophy; he registers, as if in passing, its oversights. He points out its interruption, its gaps, those small things of little value neglected by philosophical discourse. He carefully reintroduces the barely perceptible omissions, knowing full well that they imply an unlimited negligence. Through the insistence of our pedagogical tradition, we are accustomed to reject the Epicurean simulacra as useless and somewhat puerile; and the famous battle of Stoicism, which took place yesterday and will reoccur tomorrow, has become cause for amusement in the schools. Deleuze did well to combine these tenuous threads and to play, in his own fashion, with this network of discourses, arguments, replies, and paradoxes, those elements that circulated for many centuries throughout the Mediterranean. We should not scorn Hellenistic confusion or Roman platitudes but listen to those things said on the great surface of the empire; we should be attentive to those things that happened in a thousand instances, dispersed on every side: fulgurating battles, assassinated generals, burning triremes, queens poisoning themselves, victories that invariably led to further upheavals, the endlessly exemplary Actium, the eternal event.

To consider a pure event, it must first be given a metaphysical basis.[8] But we must be agreed that it cannot be the metaphysics of substances, which can serve as a foundation for accidents; nor can it be a metaphysics of coherence, which situates these accidents in the entangled nexus of causes and effects. The event–a wound, a victory-defeat, death–is always an effect produced entirely by bodies colliding, mingling, or separating, but this effect is never of a corporeal nature; it is the intangible, inaccessible battle that turns and repeats itself a thousand times around Fabricius, above the wounded Prince Andrew.[9] The weapons that tear into bodies form an endless incorporeal battle. Physics concerns causes, but events, which arise as its effects, no longer belong to it. Let us imagine a stitched causality: as bodies collide, mingle, and suffer, they create events on their surfaces, events that are without thickness, mixture, or passion; for this reason, they can no longer be causes. They form, among themselves, another kind of succession whose links derive from a quasi-physics of incorporeals–in short, from metaphysics.

Events also require a more complex logic.[10] An event is not a state of things, something that could serve as a referent for a proposition (the fact of death is a state of things in relation to which an assertion can be true or false; dying is a pure event that can never verify anything). For a ternary logic, traditionally centered on the referent, we must substitute an interrelationship based on four terms. "Marc Antony is dead" *designates* a state of things; *expresses* my opinion or belief; *signifies* an affirmation; and, in addition, has a *meaning*: "dying." An intangible meaning with one side turned toward things because "dying" is something that occurs, as an event, to Antony, and the other toward the proposition because "dying" is what is said about Antony in a statement. To die: a dimension of the proposition; an incorporeal effect produced by a sword; a meaning and an event; a point without thickness or substance of which someone speaks, which roams the surface of things. We should not restrict meaning to the cognitive core that lies at the heart of a knowable object; rather, we should allow it to reestablish its flux at the limit of words and things, as what is said of a thing (not its attribute or the thing in itself) and as something that happens (not its process or its state). Death supplies the best example, being both the event of events and meaning in its purest state. Its domain is the anonymous flow of discourse; it is that of which we speak as always past or about to happen, and yet it occurs at the extreme point of singularity. A meaning-event is as neutral as death: "not the end, but the unending; not a particular death, but any death; not true death, but as Kafka said, the snicker of its devastating error."[11]

Finally, this meaning-event requires a grammar with a different form of organization,[12] since it cannot be situated in a proposition as an attribute (to be *dead*, to be *alive*, to be *red*) but is fastened to the verb (to die, to live, to redden). The verb, conceived in this fashion, has two principal forms around which the others are distributed: the present tense, which posits an event, and the infinitive, which introduces meaning into language and allows it to circulate as the neutral element to which we refer in discourse. We should not seek the grammar of events in temporal inflections; nor should we seek the grammar of meaning in fictitious analysis of the type: to live = to be alive. The grammar of the meaning-event revolves around two asymmetrical and hobbling poles: the infinitive mode and the present tense. The meaning-event is always both the displacement of the present and the eternal repetition of the infinitive. To die is never localized in the density of a given moment, but from its flux it infinitely divides the shortest moment. To die is even smaller than the moment it takes to think it, and yet dying is indefinitely repeated on either side of this widthless crack. The eternal present? Only on the condition that we conceive the present as lacking plenitude and the eternal as lacking unity: the (multiple) eternity of the (displaced) present.

To summarize: At the limit of dense bodies, an event is incorporeal (a metaphysical surface); on the surface of words and things, an incorporeal event is the *meaning* of a proposition (its logical dimension); in the thread of discourse, an incorporeal meaning-event is fastened to the verb (the infinitive point of the present).

In the more or less recent past, there have been, I think, three major attempts at conceptualizing the event: neopositivism, phenomenology, and the philosophy of history. Neopositivism failed to grasp the distinctive level of the event; because of its logical error, the confusion of an event with a state of things, it had no choice but to lodge the event within the density of bodies, to treat it as a material process, and to attach itself more or less explicitly to a physicalism ("in a schizoid fashion," it reduced surfaces into depth); as for grammar, it transformed the event into an attribute. Phenomenology, on the other hand, reoriented the event with respect to meaning: either it placed the bare event before or to the side of meaning–the rock of facticity, the mute inertia of occurrences–and then submitted it to the active processes of meaning, to its digging and elaboration; or else it assumed a domain of primal significations which always existed as a disposition of the world around the self, tracing its paths and privileged locations, indicating in advance where the event might occur and its possible form. Either the cat whose good sense precedes the smile or the common sense of the smile that anticipates the cat. Either Sartre or Merleau-Ponty. For them, meaning never coincides with an event; and from this evolves a logic of signification, a grammar of the first person, and a metaphysics of consciousness. As for the philosophy of history, it encloses the event in a cyclical pattern of time. Its error is grammatical; it treats the present as framed by the past and future: the present is a former future where its form was prepared; it is the past to come, which preserves the identity of its content. On the one hand, this sense of the present requires a logic of essences (which establishes the present in memory) and of concepts (where the present is established as a knowledge of the future), and on the other, a metaphysics of a crowned and coherent cosmos, of a hierarchical world.

Thus, three philosophies that fail to grasp the event. The first, on the pretext that nothing can be said about those things which lie "outside" the world, rejects the pure surface of the event and attempts to enclose it forcibly–as a referent–in the spherical plenitude of the world. The second, on the pretext that signification only exists for consciousness, places the event outside and beforehand, or inside and after, and always situates it with respect to the circle of the self. The third, on the pretext that events can only exist in time, defines its identity and submits it to a solidly centered order. The world, the self, and God (a sphere, a circle, and a center): three conditions that make it impossible to think through the event. Deleuze's proposals, I believe, are directed to lifting this triple subjection that, to this day, is imposed on the event: a metaphysics of the incorporeal event (which is consequently irreducible to a physics of the world), a logic of neutral meaning (rather than a phenomenology of signification based on the subject), and a thought of the present infinitive (and not the raising up of the conceptual future in a past essence).

We have arrived at the point where the two series of the event and the phantasm are brought into resonance—the resonance of the incorporeal and the intangible, the resonance of battles, of death that subsists and insists, of the fluttering and desirable idol: it subsists not in the heart of man but above his head, beyond the clash of weapons, of fate and desire. It is not that they converge in a common point, in some phantasmatic event, or in the primary origin of a simulacrum. The event is that which is invariably lacking in the series of the phantasm—its absence indicates its repetition devoid of any grounding in an original, outside of all forms of imitation, and freed from the constraints of similitude. Consequently, it is disguise of repetition, the always-singular mask that conceals nothing, simulacra without dissimulation, incongruous finery covering a nonexistent nudity, pure difference.

As for the phantasm, it is "excessive" with respect to the singularity of the event, but this "excess" does not designate an imaginary supplement adding itself to the bare reality of facts; nor does it form a sort of embryonic generality from which the organization of the concept gradually emerges. To conceive of death or a battle as a phantasm is not to confuse them either with the old image of death suspended over a senseless accident or with the future concept of a battle secretly organizing the present disordered tumult; the battle rages from one blow to the next, and the process of death indefinitely repeats the blow, always in its possession, which it inflicts once and for all. This conception of the phantasm as the play of the (missing) event and its repetition must not be given the form of individuality (a form inferior to the concept and therefore, informal), nor must it be measured against reality (a reality that imitates an image); it presents itself as universal singularity: to die, to fight, to vanquish, to be vanquished.

The Logic of Sense tells us how to think through the event *and* the phantasm, their severed and double affirmation, their affirmation of disjunction. Determining an event on the basis of a concept, by denying any importance to repetition, is perhaps what might be called knowing [*connaître*]; and measuring the phantasm against reality, by going in search of its origin, is judging. Philosophy tried to do both; it dreamed of itself as a science, and presented itself as a critique. Thinking, on the other hand, would amount to effectuating the phantasm in the mime that produces it at a single stroke; it would make the event indefinite so that it repeats itself as a singular universal. Thinking in the absolute would thus amount to thinking through the event *and* the phantasm. A further clarification: If the role of thought is to produce the phantasm theatrically and to repeat the universal event in its extreme point of singularity, then what is thought itself if not the event that befalls the phantasm and the phantasmatic repetition of the absent event? The phantasm and the event, affirmed in disjunction, are the object of thought [*le pensé*], and thought itself [*la pensée*]; on the surface of bodies they place the extrabeing that only thought can think through; and they trace the topological event where thought itself is formed. Thought has to think through what forms it, and is formed out of what it thinks through. The critique–knowledge duality is perfectly useless: thought says what it is.

This formulation, however, is a bit dangerous. It connotes equivalence and allows us once more to imagine the identification of an object and a subject. This would be entirely false. That the object of thought [*le pensé*] forms thought [*la pensée*] implies, on the contrary, a double dissociation: that of a central and founding subject to which events occur while it deploys meaning around itself; and of an object that is a threshold and point of convergence for recognizable forms and the attributes we affirm. We must conceive of an indefinite, straight line that (far from bearing events as a string supports its knots) cuts and recuts each moment so many times that each event arises both incorporeal and indefinitely multiple. We must conceptualize not the synthesizing and synthesized subject but rather a certain insurmountable fissure. Moreover, we must conceptualize a series, without any original anchor, of simulacra, idols, and phantasms which, in the temporal duality in which they are formed are always the two sides of the fissure from which they are made signs and are put into place as signs. The fissure of the I and the series of signifying points do not form a unity that permits thought to be both subject and object, but they are themselves the event of thought [*la pensée*] and the incorporeality of what is thought [*le pensé*], the object of thought [*le pensé*] as a problem (a multiplicity of dispersed points) and thought [*la pensée*] as mime (repetition without a model).

This is why *The Logic of Sense* could have as a subtitle: *What Is Thinking?* A question that Deleuze always inscribes twice through the length of his book – in the text of a stoic logic of the incorporeal, and in the text of a Freudian analysis of the phantasm. What is thinking? Listen to the stoics, who tell us how it might be possible to have thought about *what is thought*. Read Freud, who tells us how *thought* might think. Perhaps we arrive here for the first time at a theory of thought that is entirely disburdened of the subject and the object. The thought-event is as singular as a throw of the dice; the thought-phantasm does not search for truth, but repeats thought.

In any case, we understand Deleuze's repeated emphasis on the mouth in *The Logic of Sense*. It is through this mouth, as Zeno recognized, that cartloads of food pass as well as carts of meaning ("If you say cart, a cart passes through your mouth"). The mouth, the orifice, the canal where the child intones the simulacra, the dismembered parts, and bodies without organs; the mouth in which depths and surfaces are articulated. Also the mouth from which falls the voice of the other giving rise to lofty idols that flutter above the child and from the superego. The mouth where cries are broken into phonemes, morphemes, semantemes: the mouth where the profundity of an oral body separates itself from incorporeal meaning. Through this open mouth, through this alimentary voice, the genesis of language, the formation of meaning, and the flash of thought extend their divergent series.[15] I would enjoy discussing Deleuze's rigorous phonocentrism were it not for the fact of a constant phonodecentering. Let Deleuze receive homage from the fantastic grammarian, from the dark precursor who nicely situated the remarkable facets of this decentering:

Les dents, la bouche
Les dents la bouchent
L'aidant la bouche
Laides en la bouche
Lait dans la bouche, etc.

The Logic of Sense causes us to reflect on matters that philosophy has neglected for many centuries: the event (assimilated in a concept, from which we vainly attempted to extract in the form of a *fact*, verifying a proposition, of *actual experience*, a modality of the subject, of *concreteness*, the empirical content of history); and the phantasm (reduced in the name of reality and situated at the extremity, the pathological pole, of a normative sequence: perception – image – memory – illusion). After all, what most urgently needs thought in this century, if not the event and the phantasm?

We should thank Deleuze for his efforts. He did not revive the tiresome slogans: Freud with Marx, Marx with Freud, and both, if you please, with us. He analyzed clearly the essential elements for establishing the thought of the event and the phantasm. His aim was not reconciliation (to expand the farthest reaches of an event with the imaginary density of a phantasm, or to ballast a floating phantasm by adding a grain of actual history); he discovered the philosophy that permits the disjunctive affirmation of both. Even before *The Logic of Sense*, Deleuze formulated this philosophy with completely unguarded boldness in *Difference and Repetition*, and we must now turn to this earlier work.

Instead of denouncing the fundamental omission that is presumed to have inaugurated Western culture, Deleuze, with the patience of a Nietzschean genealogist, points to the variety of small impurities and paltry compromises.[14] He tracks down the minuscule, repetitive act of cowardice and all those features of folly, vanity, and complacency which endlessly nourish the philosophical mushroom – what Michel Leiris might call "ridiculous rootlets." We all possess good sense, we all make mistakes, but no one is dumb (certainly, none of us). There is no thought without goodwill; every real problem has a solution, because our apprenticeship is to a master who has answers for the questions he poses; the world is our classroom. A whole series of insignificant beliefs. But in reality, we encounter the tyranny of goodwill, the obligation to think "in common" with others, the domination of a pedagogical model, and most important, the exclusion of stupidity – the disreputable morality of thought whose function in our society is easy to decipher. We must liberate ourselves from these constraints; and in perverting this morality, philosophy itself is disoriented.

Take difference. It is generally assumed to be a difference *from or within* something; behind difference, beyond it—but as its support, its site, its delimitation, and consequently, as the source of its mastery— we pose, through the concept, the unity of a group and its breakdown into species in the operation of difference (the organic domination of the Aristotelian concept). Difference is transformed into that which must be specified within a concept, without overstepping its bounds. And yet, above the species, we encounter the swarming of individualities. What is this boundless diversity which eludes specification and remains outside the concept, if not the resurgence of repetition? Underneath the ovine species, we are reduced to counting sheep. This stands as the first form of subjectivation: difference as specification (within the concept) and repetition as the indifference of individuals (outside the concept). But subjectivation to what? To common sense which, turning away from mad flux and anarchic difference, knows how, everywhere and always in the same manner, to recognize what is identical; common sense extracts the generality of an object while it simultaneously establishes the universality of the knowing subject through a pact of goodwill. But what if we gave free rein to ill will? What if thought freed itself from common sense and decided to function only in its extreme singularity? What if it made malign use of the skew of the paradox, instead of complacently accepting its citizenship in the *doxa*? What if it conceived of difference differentially, instead of searching out the common elements underlying difference? Then difference would disappear as a general feature that leads to the generality of the concept, and it would become—a different thought, the thought of difference—a pure event. As for repetition, it would cease to be the dreary succession of the identical, and would become displaced difference. Thought is no longer committed to the construction of concepts once it escapes goodwill and the administration of common sense, concerned as it is with division and characterization. Rather, it produces a meaning-event by repeating a phantasm. The morally good will to think within common sense thought had the fundamental role of protecting thought from its genital singularity.

But let us reconsider the functioning of the concept. For the concept to master difference, perception must apprehend global resemblances (which will then be decomposed into differences and partial identities) at the root of what we call "diversity." Each new representation must be accomplished by those representations which display the full range of resemblances; and in this space of representation (sensation–image–memory), likenesses are put to the test of quantitative equalization and graduated quantities, and in this way the immense table of measurable differences is constructed. In the corner of this graph, on its horizontal axis where the smallest quantitative gap meets the smallest qualitative variation, at this zero point, we encounter perfect resemblance, exact repetition. Repetition which, within the concept, was only the impertinent vibration of identities, becomes, within a system of representation, the organizing principle for similarities. But *what* recognizes these similarities, the exactly alike and the least similar–the greatest and the smallest, the brightest and the darkest–if not good sense? Good sense is the world's most effective agent of division in its recognitions, its establishment of equivalences, its sensitivity to gaps, its gauging of distances, as it assimilates and separates. And it is good sense that reigns in the philosophy of representations. Let us pervert good sense and allow thought to play outside the ordered table of resemblances; then it will appear as the vertical dimension of intensities, because intensity, well before its gradation by representation, is in itself pure difference: difference that displaces and repeats itself, contracts and expands; a singular point that constricts and slackens the indefinite repetitions in an acute event. One must give rise to thought as intensive irregularity. Dissolution of the Me.

A last consideration with respect to the table of representation. The meeting point of the axes is the point of perfect resemblance, and from this arises the scale of differences as so many lesser resemblances, marked identities: differences arise when representation can only partially present what was previously present, when the test of recognition is stymied. For a thing to be different, it must first no longer be the same; and it is on this negative basis, above the shadowy part that delimits the same, that contrary predicates are then articulated. In the philosophy of representation, the relationship of two predicates, like red and green, is merely the highest level of a complex structure: the *contradiction* between red and not-red (based on the model of *being* and *non-being*) is active on the lowest level; the nonidentity of red and green (on the basis of a *negative* test of *recognition*) is situated above this; and this ultimately leads to the *exclusive* position of red and green (in the table where the *genus* color is *specified*). Thus for a third time, but in an even more radical manner, difference is held fast within an oppositional, negative, and contradictory system. For difference to have a place, it was necessary to divide the "same" through contradiction, to limit its infinite identity through nonbeing, to transform its indeterminate positivity through the negative. Given the priority of the same, difference could only arise through these mediations. As for the repetitive, it is produced precisely at the point where the barely launched mediation falls back on itself; when, instead of saying no, it twice pronounces the same yes, and when, instead of distributing oppositions into a system of definitions, it turns back indefinitely to the same position. Repetition betrays the weakness of the same at the moment when it can no longer negate itself in the other, when it can no longer recapture itself in the other. Repetition, at one time pure exteriority and a pure figure of the origin, has been transformed into an internal weakness, a deficiency of finitude, a sort of stuttering of the negative—the neurosis of dialectics. For it was indeed toward dialectics that the philosophy of representation was headed.

And yet, how is it that we fail to recognize Hegel as the philosopher of the greater differences and Leibniz as the thinker of the smallest differences? In actuality, dialectics does not liberate differences; it guarantees, on the contrary, that they can always be recaptured. The dialectical sovereignty of the same consists in permitting differences to exist but always under the rule of the negative, as an instance of nonbeing. They may appear to be the successful subversion of the Other, but contradiction secretly assists in the salvation of identities. Is it necessary to recall the unchanging pedagogical origin of dialectics? What ceaselessly reactivates it, what causes the endless rebirth of the aporia of being and nonbeing, is the humble classroom interrogation, the student's fictive dialogue: "This is red; that is not red. At this moment, it is light outside. No, now it is dark." In the twilight of an October sky, Minerva's bird flies close to the ground: "Write it down, write it down," it croaks, "tomorrow morning, it will no longer be dark."

The freeing of difference requires thought without contradiction, without dialectics, without negation; thought that accepts divergence; affirmative thought whose instrument is disjunction; thought of the multiple—of the nomadic and dispersed multiplicity that is not limited or confined by the constraints of the same; thought that does not conform to a pedagogical model (the fakery of prepared answers) but attacks insoluble problems—that is, a thought which addresses a multiplicity of exceptional points, which is displaced as we distinguish their conditions and which insists upon and subsists in the play of repetitions. Far from being the still incomplete and blurred image of an Idea that would, from on high and for all time, hold the answer, the problem lies in the idea itself, or rather, the Idea exists only in the form of a problem: a distinctive plurality whose obscurity is nevertheless insistent, and in which the question ceaselessly stirs. What is the answer to the question? The problem. How is the problem resolved? By displacing the question. The problem escapes the logic of the excluded third, because it is a dispersed multiplicity; it cannot be resolved by the clear distinctions of a Cartesian idea, because as an idea it is obscure-distinct; it seriously disobeys the Hegelian negative because it is a multiple affirmation; it is not subjected to the contradiction of being and nonbeing, since it is being. We must think problematically rather than question and answer dialectically.

The conditions for thinking of difference and repetition, as we have seen, have undergone a progressive expansion. First, it was necessary, along with Aristotle, to abandon the identity of the concept, to reject resemblance within representation, and simultaneously to free ourselves from the philosophy of representation; and now, it is necessary to free ourselves from Hegel—from the opposition of predicates, from contradiction and negation, from all of dialectics. But there is yet a fourth condition, and it is even more formidable than the others. The most tenacious subjectivation of difference is undoubtedly that maintained by categories. By showing the number of different ways in which being can express itself, by specifying its forms of attribution, by imposing in a certain way the distribution of existing things, categories create a condition where being maintains its undifferentiated repose at the highest level. Categories dictate the play of affirmations and negations, establish the legitimacy of resemblances within representation, and guarantee the objectivity and operation of concepts. They suppress anarchic difference, divide differences into zones, delimit their rights, and prescribe their task of specification with respect to individual beings. On one side, they can be understood as the a priori forms of knowledge, but, on the other, they appear as an archaic morality, the ancient decalogue that the identical imposed upon difference. Difference can only be liberated through the invention of an acategorical thought. But perhaps invention is a misleading word, since in the history of philosophy there have been at least two radical formulations of the univocity of being—those given by Duns Scotus and Spinoza. In Duns Scotus's philosophy, however, being is neutral, while for Spinoza it is based on substance; in both contexts, the elimination of categories and the affirmation that being is expressed for all things in the same way had the single objective of maintaining the unity of being. Let us imagine, on the contrary, an ontology where being would be expressed in the same fashion for every difference, but could only express differences. Consequently, things could no longer be completely covered over, as in Duns Scotus, by the great monochrome abstraction of being, and Spinoza's modes would no longer revolve around the unity of substance. Differences would revolve of their own accord, being would be expressed in the same fashion for all these differences, and being would be no longer a unity that guides and distributes them but their repetition as differences. For Deleuze, the noncategorical univocity of being does not directly attach the multiple to unity itself (the universal neutrality of being, or the expressive force of substance); it puts being into play as that which is repetitively expressed as difference. Being is the recurrence of difference, without there being any difference in the form of its expression. Being does not distribute itself into regions; the real is not subordinated to the possible; and the contingent is not opposed to the necessary. Whether the battle of Actium or the death of Antony were necessary or not, the being of both these pure events—to fight, to die—is expressed in the same manner, in the same way that it is expressed with respect to the phantasmatic castration that occurred and did not occur. The suppression of categories, the affirmation of the univocity of being, and the repetitive revolution of being around difference—these are the final conditions for the thought of the phantasm and the event.

We have not quite reached the conclusion. We must return to this "recurrence," but let us pause a moment.

Can it be said that Bouvard and Pécuchet make mistakes?[15] Do they commit blunders whenever an opportunity presents itself? If they make mistakes, it is because there are rules that underline their failures and under certain definable conditions they might have succeeded. Nevertheless, their failure is constant, whatever their action, whatever their knowledge, whether or not they follow the rules,

whether the books they consulted were good or bad. Everything befalls their undertaking—errors, of course, but also fires, frost, the foolishness and perversity of men, a dog's anger. Their efforts were not
wrong; they were totally botched. To be wrong is to mistake a cause
for another; it is not to foresee accidents; it may derive from a faulty
knowledge of substances or from the confusion of necessities with
possibilities. We are mistaken if we apply categories carelessly and
inopportunely, but it is altogether different to ruin a project completely: it is to ignore the framework of categories (and not simply
their points of application). If Bouvard and Pécuchet are reasonably
certain of precisely those things which are largely improbable, it is
not that they are mistaken in their discrimination of the possible but
that they confuse all aspects of reality with every form of possibility
(this is why the most improbable events conform to the most natural
of their expectations). They confuse or, rather, are confused by the
necessity of their knowledge and the contingency of the seasons, the
existence of things, and the shadows found in books: an accident, for
them, possesses the obstinacy of a substance, and those substances
seized them by the throat in their experimental accidents. Such is
their grand and pathetic stupidity, and it is incomparable to the meager foolishness of those who surround them and make mistakes, the
others whom they rightfully disdain. Within categories, one makes
mistakes; outside of them, beyond or beneath them, one is stupid.
Bouvard and Pécuchet are acategorical beings.

These comments allow us to isolate a use of categories that may not
be immediately apparent; by creating a space for the operation of
truth and falsity; by situating the free supplement of error, categories
silently reject stupidity. In a commanding voice, they instruct us in the
ways of knowledge and solemnly alert us to the possibilities of error,
while in a whisper they guarantee our intelligence and form the a
priori of excluded stupidity. Thus we court danger in wanting to be
freed from categories; no sooner do we abandon them than we face
the magma of stupidity and risk being surrounded not by a marvelous
multiplicity of differences but by equivalences, ambiguities, the "it all
comes down to the same thing," a leveling uniformity, and the ther-
modynamism of every miscarried effort. To think in the form of the
categories is to know the truth so that it can be distinguished from the
false; to think "acategorically" is to confront a black stupidity and, in a
flash, to distinguish oneself from it. Stupidity is contemplated: sight

penetrates its domain and becomes fascinated; it carries one gently along and its action is mimed in the abandonment of oneself; we support ourselves on its amorphous fluidity; we await the first leap of an imperceptible difference, and blankly, without fever, we watch to see the glimmer of light return. Error demands rejection—we can erase it; we accept stupidity—we see it, we repeat it, and softly, we call for total immersion.

This is the greatness of Warhol with his canned foods, senseless accidents, and his series of advertising smiles: the oral and nutritional equivalence of those half-open lips, teeth, tomato sauce, that hygiene based on detergents; the equivalence of death in the cavity of an eviscerated car, at the top of a telephone pole and at the end of a wire, and between the glistening, steel blue arms of the electric chair. "It's the same either way," stupidity says, while sinking into itself and infinitely extending its nature with the things it says of itself; "Here or there, it's always the same thing; what difference if the colors vary, if they're darker or lighter. It's all so senseless—life, women, death! How stupid this stupidity!" But, in concentrating on this boundless monotony, we find the sudden illumination of multiplicity itself—with nothing at its center, at its highest point, or beyond it—a flickering of light that travels even faster than the eyes and successively lights up the moving labels and the captive snapshots that refer to each other to eternity, without ever saying anything: suddenly, arising from the background of the old inertia of equivalences, the zebra stripe of the event tears through the darkness, and the eternal phantasm informs that soup can, that singular and depthless face.

Intelligence does not respond to stupidity, since it is stupidity already vanquished, the categorical art of avoiding error. The scholar is intelligent. It is thought, though, that confronts stupidity, and it is the philosopher who observes it. Their private conversation is a lengthy one, as the philosopher's sight plunges into this candleless skull. It is his death mask, his temptation, perhaps his desire, his catatonic theater. At the limit, thought would be the intense contemplation from close up—to the point of losing oneself in it—of stupidity; and its other side is formed by lassitude, immobility, excessive fatigue, obstinate muteness, and inertia—or, rather, they form its accompaniment, the daily and thankless exercise which prepares it and which it suddenly dissipates. The philosopher must have sufficiently ill will to play the game of truth and error badly: this perversity, which operates in paradoxes, allows him to escape the grasp of categories. But aside from this, he must be sufficiently "ill humored" to persist in the confrontation with stupidity, to remain motionless to the point of stupefaction in order to approach it successfully and mime it, to let it slowly grow within himself (this is probably what we politely refer to as being absorbed in one's thoughts), and to await, in the always-unpredictable conclusion to this elaborate preparation, the shock of difference. Once paradoxes have upset the table of representation, catatonia operates within the theater of thought.

We can easily see how LSD inverts the relationships of ill humor, stupidity, and thought: it no sooner eliminates the supremacy of categories than it tears away the ground of its indifference and disintegrates the gloomy dumbshow of stupidity; and it presents this univocal and acategorical mass not only as variegated, mobile, asymmetrical, decentered, spiraloid, and reverberating but causes it to rise, at each instant, as a swarming of phantasm-events. As it slides on this surface at once regular and intensely vibratory, as it is freed from its catatonic chrysalis, thought invariably contemplates this indefinite equivalence transformed into an acute event and a sumptuous, appareled repetition. Opium produces other effects: thought gathers unique differences into a point, eliminates the background and deprives immobility of its task of contemplating and soliciting stupidity through its mime. Opium ensures a weightless immobility, the stupor of a butterfly that differs from catatonic rigidity; and, far beneath, it establishes a ground that no longer stupidly absorbs all differences but allows them to arise and sparkle as so many minute, distanced, smiling, and eternal events. Drugs—if we can speak of them generally—have nothing at all to do with truth and falsity; only to fortune-tellers do they reveal a world "more truthful than the real." In fact, they displace the relative positions of stupidity and thought by eliminating the old necessity of a theater of immobility. But perhaps, if it is given to thought to confront stupidity, drugs, which mobilize it, which color, agitate, furrow, and dissipate it, which populate it with differences and substitute for the rare flash a continuous phosphorescence, are the source of a partial thought—perhaps.[16] At any rate, in a state deprived of drugs, thought possesses two horns: one is ill will (to baffle categories) and the other ill humor (to point to stupidity and transfix it). We are far from the old sage who invests so much goodwill in his search for the truth that he can contemplate with equanimity the indifferent diversity of changing fortunes and things; far from the irritability of Schopenhauer, who became annoyed with things that did not return to their indifference of their own accord. But we are also distant from the "melancholy" that makes itself indifferent to the world, and whose immobility—alongside books and a globe—indicates the profundity of thought and the diversity of knowledge. Exercising its ill will and ill humor, thought awaits the outcome of this theater of perverse practices: the sudden shift of the kaleidoscope, signs that light up for an instant, the results of the thrown dice, the destiny of another game. Thinking does not provide consolation or happiness. Like a perversion, it languidly drags itself out; it repeats itself with determination upon a stage; at a stroke, it flings itself outside the dice box. At the moment when chance, the theater, and perversions enter into resonance, when chance dictates a resonance among the three, then thought becomes a trance; and it becomes worthwhile to think.

The univocity of being, its singleness of expression, is paradoxically the principal condition that permits difference to escape the domination of identity, frees it from the law of the Same as a simple opposition within conceptual elements. Being can express itself in the same way, because difference is no longer submitted to the prior reduction of categories; because it is not distributed inside a diversity that can always be perceived; because it is not organized in a conceptual hierarchy of species and genus. Being is that which is always said of difference; it is the *Recurrence* of difference.[17]

With this term, we can avoid the use of both *Becoming* and *Return*, because differences are not the elements—not even the fragmentary, intermingled, or monstrously confused elements—of an extended evolution that carries them along in its course and occasionally allows their masked or naked reappearance. The synthesis of Becoming might seem somewhat slack, but it nevertheless maintains a unity—not only and not especially that of an infinite container but also the unity of fragments, of passing and recurring moments, and of the floating consciousness that recognizes it. Consequently, we are led to mistrust Dionysus and his Bacchantes even in their state of intoxication. As for the Return, must it be the perfect circle, the well-oiled millstone that turns on its axis and reintroduces things, forms, and men at their appointed time? Must there be a center and must events occur on its periphery? Even Zarathustra could not tolerate this idea:

"Everything straight lies," murmured the dwarf disdainfully. "All truth is crooked, time itself is a circle."

"Spirit of Gravity," I said angrily, "you do treat this too lightly."

And convalescing, he groans:

"Alas! Man will return eternally, abject man will return eternally."

Perhaps what Zarathustra is proclaiming is not the circle; or perhaps the intolerable image of the circle is the last sign of a higher form of thought; perhaps, like the young shepherd, we must break this circular ruse—like Zarathustra himself, who bit off the head of a serpent and immediately spat it away.

Chronos is the time of becoming and new beginnings. Piece by piece, Chronos swallows the things to which it gives birth and which it causes to be reborn in its own time. This monstrous and lawless becoming—the endless devouring of each instant, the swallowing-up of the totality of life, the scattering of its limbs—is linked to the exactitude of rebeginning. Becoming leads into this great, interior labyrinth, a labyrinth no different in nature from the monster it contains. But from the depths of this convoluted and inverted architecture, a solid thread allows us to retrace our steps and to rediscover the same light of day. Dionysus with Ariadne: you have become my labyrinth. But Aeon is *recurrence* itself, the straight line of time, a splitting quicker than thought and narrower than any instant. It causes the same present to arise—on both sides of this indefinitely splitting arrow—as always existing, as indefinitely present, and as indefinite future. It is important to understand that this does not imply a succession of present instances which derive from a continuous flux and that, as a result of their plenitude, allow us to perceive the thickness of the past and the horizon of a future in which they, in turn, become the past. Rather, it is the straight line of the future that repeatedly cuts the smallest width of the present, that indefinitely recuts it starting from itself. We can trace this schism to its limbs, but we will never find the indivisible atom that ultimately serves as the minutely present unity of time (time is always more supple than thought). On both sides of the wound we invariably find that the schism has already happened (and that it had already taken place, and that it had already happened that it had already taken place), and that it will happen again (and in the future, it will happen again): it is less a cut than a constant fibrillation. Time is what repeats itself; and the present—split by this arrow of the future that carries it forward by always causing its swerving on both sides—endlessly recurs. But it recurs as singular difference; and the analogous, the similar, and the identical never return. Difference recurs; and being, expressing itself in the same manner with respect to difference, is never the universal flux of Becoming; nor is the well-centered circle of the identical. Being is a Return freed from the curvature of the circle; it is Recurrence. Consequently, three deaths of Becoming, the devouring Father—mother in labor; of the circle, by which the gift of life passes to the flowers each springtime; of recurrence—the repetitive fibrillation of the present, the eternal and dangerous fissure fully given in an instant, affirmed in a single stroke once and for all.

By virtue of its splintering and repetition, the present is a throw of the dice. This is not because it forms part of a game in which it insinuates small contingencies or elements of uncertainty. It is at once the chance within the game and the game itself as chance; in the same stroke, both the dice and rules are thrown, so that chance is not broken into pieces and parceled out but is totally affirmed in a single throw. The present as the recurrence of difference, as repetition giving voice to difference, affirms at once the totality of chance. The univocity of being in Duns Scotus led to the immobility of an abstraction, in Spinoza it led to the necessity and eternity of substance; but here it leads to the single throw of chance in the fissure of the present. If being always declares itself in the same way, it is not because being is one but because the totality of chance is affirmed in the single dice throw of the present.

Can we say that the univocity of being has been formulated on three different occasions in the history of philosophy, by Duns Scotus and Spinoza and finally by Nietzsche—the first to conceive of univocity as returning and not as an abstraction or a substance? Perhaps we should say that Nietzsche went as far as the thought of the Eternal Return; more precisely, he pointed to it as an intolerable thought. Intolerable because, as soon as its first signs are perceived, it fixes itself in that image of the circle which carries in itself the fatal threat that all things will return—the spider's reiteration. But this intolerable must be considered because it exists only as an empty sign, a passage-way to be crossed, the formless voice of the abyss whose approach is indissociably both happiness and disgust. In relation to the Return,

Zarathustra is the *Fürsprecher*, the one who speaks for . . . , in the place of . . . , marking the spot of his absence. Zarathustra is not Nietzsche's image but his sign. The sign (which must be distinguished from the symptom) of rupture: the sign closest to the intolerability of the thought of the return, "Nietzsche" allowed the eternal return to be thought. For close to a century the loftiest enterprise of philosophy has been directed to this task, but who has had the arrogance to say that he has seen it through? Should the Return have resembled the nineteenth century's conception of the end of history, an end that circled menacingly around us like a phantasmagoria at the final days? Should we have ascribed to this empty sign, imposed by Nietzsche as an *excess*, a series of mythic contents that disarmed and reduced it? Should we have attempted, on the contrary, to refine it so that it could unashamedly assume its place within a particular discourse? Or should this excessive, this always-misplaced and displaced sign have been accentuated; and instead of finding an arbitrary meaning to correspond to it, instead of constructing an adequate word, should it have been made to enter into resonance with the great signified that today's thought supports as an uncertain and controlled ballast? Should it have allowed recurrence to resound in unison with difference? We must avoid thinking that the return is the form of a content that is difference; rather, from an always-nomadic and anarchic difference to the unavoidably excessive and displaced sign of recurrence, a lightning storm was produced which will bear the name of Deleuze: new thought is possible; thought is again possible.

This thought does not lie in the future, promised by the most distant of new beginnings. It is present in Deleuze's texts—springing forth, dancing before us, in our midst; genital thought, intensive thought, affirmative thought, acategorical thought—each of these an unrecognizable face, a mask we have never seen before; differences we had no reason to expect but which nevertheless lead to the return, as masks of their masks, of Plato, Duns Scotus, Spinoza, Leibniz, Kant, and all other philosophers. This is philosophy not as thought but as theater—a theater of mime with multiple, fugitive, and instantaneous scenes in which blind gestures signal to each other. This is the theater where the laughter of the Sophist bursts out from under the mask of Socrates; where Spinoza's modes conduct a wild dance in a decentered circle while substance revolves about it like a mad planet; where a limping Fichte announces "the fractured I // the dissolved

368 *Aesthetics, Method, and Epistemology*

self"; where Leibniz, having reached the top of the pyramid, can see through the darkness that celestial music is in fact a *Pierrot lunaire*. In the sentry box of the Luxembourg Gardens, Duns Scotus places his head through the circular window; he is sporting an impressive mustache; it belongs to Nietzsche, disguised as Klossowski.

NOTES

1   Gilles Deleuze, *Différence et répétition* (Paris: Presses Universitaires de France, 1968) [*Difference and Repetition*, trans. Paul Patton (New York: Columbia University Press, 1994]; Deleuze, *Logique du sens* (Paris: Minuit, 1969) [*The Logic of Sense*, trans. Mark Lester with Charles Stivale, ed. Constantin V. Bourdas (New York: Columbia University Press, 1990)].

a   For another translation of this last phrase, see the Introduction to this volume, p. XXI.–Ed.

2   *Difference and Repetition*, pp. 126–28; *Logic of Sense*, pp. 253–60.

3   Plato, *The Sophist*, trans. F. M. Cornford, in *Plato: The Collected Dialogues*, ed. E. Hamilton and H. Cairns (Princeton: Princeton University Press, 1961), pp. 957–1017.

4   On the rising of irony and the plunging of humor, see *Difference and Repetition*, p. 5, and *Logic of Sense*, pp. 134–41.

5   *Logic of Sense*, pp. 266–79.

6   Merleau-Ponty, *La Phénoménologie de la perception* (Paris: Gallimard, 1945) [*The Phenomenology of Perception*, trans. Colin Smith [London: Routledge & Kegan Paul, 1962)].

7   A character in Klossowski's *Les Lois de l'hospitalité* (Paris: Gallimard, 1965).

8   *Logic of Sense*, pp. 6–11.

9   Fabricius was a Roman general and statesman (d. 250 B.C.); Prince Andrew is a main character in Tolstoi's *War and Peace*–Ed.

10 *Logic of Sense*, pp. 12–22.

11 Maurice Blanchot, *L'Espace littéraire*, cited in *Difference and Repetition*, p. 112; see also *Logic of Sense*, pp. 148–55.

12 *Logic of Sense*, pp. 148–55.

13 On this subject, see *Logic of Sense*, pp. 185–253. My comments are, at best, an allusion to these splendid analyses.

14 This entire section considers, in a different order from that of the text, some of the themes that intersect within *Difference and Repetition*. I am, of course, aware that I have shifted accents and, far more important, that I have ignored its inexhaustible riches. I have reconstructed one of several possible models. Therefore, I will not apply specific references.

15 A reference to the protagonists of Gustave Flaubert's novel, *Bouvard and Pecuchet*, trans. T. W. Earp and G. W. Stonier (Norfolk, Conn.: New Directions, 1954).–Ed.

16 "What will people think of us?" [Note added by Gilles Deleuze.]

17 On these themes, see *Logic of Sense*, pp. 162–68, 177–80, and *Difference and Repetition*, pp. 35–42, 299–304.

NIETZSCHE, GENEALOGY, HISTORY[*]

1.

Genealogy is gray, meticulous, and patiently documentary. It operates on a field of entangled and confused parchments, on documents that have been scratched over and recopied many times.

On this basis, it is obvious that Paul Ree was wrong to follow the English tendency in describing the history of morality in terms of a linear development—in reducing its entire history and genesis to an exclusive concern for utility. He assumed that words had kept their meaning, that desires still pointed in a single direction, and that ideas retained their logic; and he ignored the fact that the world of speech and desires has known invasions, struggles, plundering, disguises, ploys. From these elements, however, genealogy retrieves an indispensable restraint: it must record the singularity of events outside of any monotonous finality; it must seek them in the most unpromising places, in what we tend to feel is without history—in sentiments, love, conscience, instincts; it must be sensitive to their recurrence, not in order to trace the gradual curve of their evolution but to isolate the different scenes where they engaged in different roles. Finally, genealogy must define even those instances when they are absent, the moment when they remained unrealized (Plato, at Syracuse, did not become Muhammed).

---

[*]This essay originally appeared in *Hommage à Jean Hyppolite* (Paris: Presses Universitaires de France, 1971), pp. 145-72. The translation, by Donald F. Brouchard and Sherry Simon, has been slightly amended.

Genealogy, consequently, requires patience and a knowledge of details, and it depends on a vast accumulation of source material. Its "cyclopean monuments"[1] are constructed from "discreet and apparently insignificant truths and according to a rigorous method"; they cannot be the product of "large and well-meaning errors."[2] In short, genealogy demands relentless erudition. Genealogy does not oppose itself to history as the lofty and profound gaze of the philosopher might compare to the molelike perspective of the scholar; on the contrary, it rejects the metahistorical deployment of ideal significations and indefinite teleologies. It opposes itself to the search for "origins."

2.

In Nietzsche, we find two uses of the word *Ursprung*. The first is unstressed, and it is found alternately with other terms such as *Entstehung, Herkunft, Abkunft, Geburt.* In *The Genealogy of Morals*, for example, *Entstehung* or *Ursprung* serves equally well to denote the origin of duty or guilty conscience;[3] and in the discussion of logic and knowledge in *The Gay Science*, their origin is indiscriminately referred to as *Ursprung, Entstehung,* or *Herkunft.*[4]

The other use of the word is stressed. On occasion, Nietzsche places the term in opposition to another: in the first paragraph of *Human, All Too Human* the miraculous origin [*Wunderursprung*] sought by metaphysics is set against the analyses of historical philosophy, which poses questions *über Herkunft und Anfang. Ursprung* is also used in an ironic and deceptive manner. In what, for instance, do we find the original basis [*Ursprung*] of morality, a foundation sought after since Plato? "In detestable, narrow-minded conclusions. *Pudenda origo.*"[5] Or again, Where should we seek the origin of religion [*Ursprung*], which Schopenhauer located in a particular metaphysical sentiment of the hereafter? It belongs, very simply, to an invention [*Erfindung*], a sleight-of-hand, an artifice [*Kunststück*], a secret formula, in the rituals of black magic, in the work of the *Schwarzkünstler.*[6]

One of the most significant texts with respect to the use of all these terms and to the variations in the use of *Ursprung* is the preface to the *Genealogy*. At the beginning of the text its objective is defined as an examination of the origin of moral preconceptions and the term used is *Herkunft*. Then Nietzsche proceeds by retracing his personal involvement with this question: he recalls the period when he "calligraphied" philosophy, when he questioned if God must be held responsible for the origin of evil. He now finds this question amusing and properly characterizes it as a search for *Ursprung* (he will shortly use the same term to summarize Paul Ree's activity).[7] Farther on he evokes the analyses that are characteristically Nietzschean and that begin with *Human, All Too Human.* Here he speaks of *Herkunft-hypothesen.* This use of the word *Herkunft* cannot be arbitrary, since it serves to designate a number of texts, beginning with *Human, All Too Human*, which deal with the origin of morality, asceticism, justice, and punishment. And yet the word used in all these works had been *Ursprung.*[8] It would seem that at this point in the *Genealogy* Nietzsche wished to validate an opposition between *Herkunft* and *Ursprung* that he had not put into play ten years earlier. But immediately following the use of the two terms in a specific sense, Nietzsche reverts, in the final paragraphs of the preface, to a usage that is neutral and equivalent.[9]

Why did Nietzsche challenge the pursuit of the origin [*Ursprung*], at least on those occasions when he is truly a genealogist? First, because it is an attempt to capture the exact essence of things, their purest possibilities, and their carefully protected identities; because this search assumes the existence of immobile forms that precede the external world of accident and succession. This search is directed to "that which was already there," the "very same" of an image of a primordial truth fully adequate to its nature, and it necessitates the removal of every mask to ultimately disclose an original identity. However, if the genealogist refuses to extend his faith in metaphysics, if he listens to history, he finds that there is "something altogether different" behind things: not a timeless and essential secret but the secret that they have no essence, or that their essence was fabricated in a piecemeal fashion from alien forms. Examining the history of reason, he learns that it was born in an altogether "reasonable" fashion–from chance;[10] devotion to truth and the precision of scientific methods arose from the passion of scholars, their reciprocal hatred, their fanatical and unending discussions, and their spirit of competition–the personal conflicts that slowly forged the weapons of reason.[11] Further, genealogical analysis shows that the concept of liberty is an "invention of the ruling classes"[12] and not fundamental to man's nature or at the root of his attachment to being and truth. What is found at the historical beginning of things is not the inviolable identity of their origin; it is the dissension of other things. It is disparity.

History also teaches us how to laugh at the solemnities of the origin. The lofty origin is no more than "a metaphysical extension which arises from the belief that things are most precious and essential at the moment of birth."[13] We tend to think that this is the moment of their greatest perfection, when they emerged dazzling from the hands of a creator or in the shadowless light of a first morning. The origin always precedes the Fall. It comes before the body, before the world and time; it is associated with the gods, and its story is always sung as a theogony. But historical beginnings are lowly: not in the sense of modest or discreet, like the steps of a dove, but derisive and ironic, capable of undoing every infatuation. "We wished to awaken the feeling of man's sovereignty by showing his divine birth: this path is now forbidden, since a monkey stands at the entrance."[14] Man began with a grimace at what he would become; and Zarathustra himself is plagued by a monkey who jumps along behind him, pulling on his coattails.

The final postulate of the origin is linked to the first two: it would be the site of truth. From the vantage point of an absolute distance, free from the restraints of positive knowledge [*connaissance*], the origin makes possible a field of knowledge [*savoir*] whose function is to recover it, but always in a false recognition due to the excesses of its own speech. The origin lies at a place of inevitable loss, the point where the truth of things is knotted to a truthful discourse, the site of a fleeting articulation that discourse has obscured and finally lost. It is a new cruelty of history that compels a reversal of this relationship and the abandonment of "adolescent" quests: behind the always recent, avaricious, and measured truth, it posits the ancient proliferation of errors. It is now impossible to believe that "in the rending of the veil, truth remains truthful; we have lived long enough not to be taken in."[15] Truth is undoubtedly the sort of error that cannot be refuted because it was hardened into an unalterable form in the long baking process of history.[16] Moreover, the very question of truth, the right it appropriates to refute error and oppose itself to appearance, the manner in which by turns it was initially made available to the wise, then was withdrawn by men of piety to an unattainable world where it was given the double role of consolation and imperative, finally rejected as a useless notion, superfluous and contradicted on all sides—does this not form a history, the history of an error we call truth? Truth, and its original reign, has had a history within history from which we are barely emerging "in the time of the shortest shadow," when light no longer seems to flow from the depths of the sky or to arise from the first moments of the day.[17]

A genealogy of values, morality, asceticism, and knowledge will never confuse itself with a quest for their "origins," will never neglect as inaccessible all the episodes of history. On the contrary, it will cultivate the details and accidents that accompany every beginning; it will be scrupulously attentive to their petty malice; it will await their emergence, once unmasked, as the face of the other. Wherever it is made to go, it will not be reticent—in "excavating the depths," in allowing time for these elements to escape from a labyrinth where no truth had ever detained them. The genealogist needs history to dispel the chimeras of the origin, somewhat in the manner of the pious philosopher who needs a doctor to exorcise the shadow of his soul. He must be able to recognize the events of history, its jolts, its surprises, its unsteady victories and unpalatable defeats—the basis of all beginnings, atavisms, and heredities. Similarly, he must be able to diagnose the illnesses of the body, its conditions of weakness and strength, its breakdowns and resistances, to be in a position to judge philosophical discourse. History is the concrete body of becoming; with its moments of intensity, its lapses, its extended periods of feverish agitation, its fainting spells; and only a metaphysician would seek its soul in the distant ideality of the origin.

3.

Entstehung and *Herkunft* are more exact than *Ursprung* in recording the true object of genealogy; and, though they are ordinarily translated as "origin," we must attempt to reestablish their proper use.

Herkunft is the equivalent of stock or *descent*; it is the ancient affiliation to a group, sustained by the bonds of blood, tradition, or social status. The analysis of *Herkunft* often involves a consideration of race or social type.[18] But the traits it attempts to identify are not the exclusive generic characteristics of an individual, a sentiment, or an idea, which permit us to qualify them as "Greek" or "English"; rather, it seeks the subtle, singular, and subindividual marks that might possibly intersect in them to form a network that is difficult to unravel. Far from being a category of resemblance, this origin allows the setting apart, the sorting out of different traits: the Germans imagined they had finally accounted for their complexity by saying they possessed a double soul; they were fooled by a simple computation, or rather, they were simply trying to master the racial disorder from which they had formed themselves.[19] Where the soul pretends unification or the Me fabricates a coherent identity, the genealogist sets out to study the beginning–numberless beginnings, whose faint traces and hints of color are readily seen by a historical eye. The analysis of descent permits the dissociation of the Me, its recognition and displacement as an empty synthesis, in liberating a profusion of lost events.

An examination of descent also permits the discovery, under the unique aspect of a trait or a concept, of the myriad events through which–thanks to which, against which–they were formed. Genealogy does not pretend to go back in time to restore an unbroken continuity that operates beyond the dispersion of oblivion; its task is not to demonstrate that the past actively exists in the present, that it continues secretly to animate the present, having imposed a predetermined form on all its vicissitudes. Genealogy does not resemble the evolution of a species and does not map the destiny of a people. On the contrary, to follow the complex course of descent is to maintain passing events in their proper dispersion; it is to identify the accidents, the minute deviations–or conversely, the complete reversals–the errors, the false appraisals, and the faulty calculations that gave birth to those things which continue to exist and have value for us; it is to discover that truth or being lies not at the root of what we know and what we are but the exteriority of accidents.[20] This is undoubtedly why every origin of morality from the moment it stops being pious–and *Herkunft* can never be–has value as a critique.[21]

Deriving from such a source is a dangerous legacy. In numerous instances, Nietzsche associates the terms *Herkunft* and *Erbschaft*. Nevertheless, we should not be deceived into thinking that this heritage is an acquisition, a possession that grows and solidifies; rather, it is an unstable assemblage of faults, fissures, and heterogeneous layers that threaten the fragile inheritor from within or from underneath: "injustice or instability in the minds of certain men, their disorder and lack of decorum, are the final consequences of their ancestors' numberless logical inaccuracies, hasty conclusions, and superficiality."[22] The search for descent is not the erecting of foundations: on the contrary, it disturbs what was previously considered immobile; it fragments what was thought unified; it shows the heterogeneity of what was imagined consistent with itself. What convictions and, far more decisively, what knowledge can resist it? If a genealogical analysis of a scholar were made—of one who collects facts and carefully accounts for them—his *Herkunft* would quickly divulge the official papers of the scribe and the pleadings of the lawyer—their father[23]—in their apparently disinterested attention, in their "pure" devotion to objectivity.

Finally, descent attaches itself to the body.[24] It inscribes itself in the nervous system, in temperament, in the digestive apparatus; it appears in faulty respiration, in improper diets, in the debilitated and prostrate bodies of those whose ancestors committed errors. Fathers have only to mistake effects for causes, believe in the reality of an "afterlife" or maintain the value of eternal truths, and the bodies of their children will suffer. Cowardice and hypocrisy, for their part, are the simple offshoots of error: not in a Socratic sense, not that evil is the result of a mistake, not because of a turning away from an original truth, but because the body maintains, in life as in death, through its strength or weakness, the sanction of every truth and error, as it sustains, in an inverse manner, the origin—descent. Why did men invent the contemplative life? Why give a supreme value to this form of existence? Why maintain the absolute truth of those fictions which sustain it? "During barbarous ages . . . if the strength of an individual declined, if he felt himself tired or sick, melancholy or satiated and, as a consequence, without desire or appetite for a short time, he became relatively a better man, that is, less dangerous. His pessimistic ideas only take form as words or reflections. In this frame of mind, he either became a thinker and prophet or used his imagination to feed his superstitions."[25] The body—and everything that touches it: diet, climate, and soil—is the domain of the *Herkunft*. The body manifests the stigmata of past experience and also gives rise to desires, failings, and errors. These elements may join in a body where they achieve a sudden expression, but just as often, their encounter is an engagement in which they efface each other, and pursue their insurmountable conflict.

The body is the surface of the inscription of events (traced by language and dissolved by ideas), the locus of the dissociation of the Me (to which it tries to impart the chimera of a substantial unity), and a volume in perpetual disintegration. Genealogy, as an analysis of descent, is thus situated within the articulation of the body and history. Its task is to expose a body totally imprinted by history and the process of history's destruction of the body.

4.

Entstehung designates *emergence*, the moment of arising. It stands as the principle and the singular law of an apparition. As it is wrong to search for descent in an uninterrupted continuity, we should avoid accounting for emergence by appeal to its final term; the eye was not always intended for contemplation, and punishment has had other purposes than setting an example. These developments may appear as a culmination, but they are merely the current episodes in a series of subjugations: the eye initially responded to the requirements of hunting and warfare; and punishment has been subjected by turns to a variety of needs – revenge, excluding an aggressor, compensating a victim, creating fear. In placing present needs at the origin, the metaphysician would convince us of an obscure purpose that seeks its realization at the moment it arises. Genealogy, however, seeks to reestablish the various systems of subjection: not the anticipatory power of meaning, but the hazardous play of dominations.

Emergence is always produced in a particular state of forces. The analysis of the *Entstehung* must delineate this interaction, the manner of the struggle that these forces wage against each other or against adverse circumstances, and the attempt to avoid degeneration and regain strength by dividing these forces against themselves. It is in this sense that the emergence of a species (animal or human) and its solidification are secured "in an extended battle against conditions which are essentially and constantly unfavorable." In fact, "the species must realize itself as a species, as something – characterized by the durability, uniformity, and simplicity of its form – which can prevail in the perpetual struggle against outsiders or the uprising of those it oppresses from within." On the other hand, individual differences emerge in another state of the relationship of forces, when the species has become victorious and when it is no longer threatened from outside. In this condition, we find a struggle "of egoisms turned against each other, each bursting forth in a splintering of forces and a general striving for the sun and for the light."[26] There are also times when force contends against itself, and not only in the intoxication of an abundance, which allows it to divide itself, but at the moment when it weakens. Force reacts against its growing lassitude and gains strength; it imposes limits, inflicts torments and mortifications; it masks these actions as a higher morality and, in exchange, regains its strength. In this manner, the ascetic ideal was born, "in the instinct of a decadent life which . . . struggles for its own existence."[27] This also describes the movement in which the Reformation arose, precisely where the Church was least corrupt;[28] German Catholicism, in the sixteenth century, retained enough strength to turn against itself, to mortify its own body and history, and to spiritualize itself into a pure religion of conscience.

Emergence is thus the entry of forces; it is their eruption, the leap from the wings to center stage, each in its youthful strength. What Nietzsche calls the *Entstehungsherd* of the concept of goodness is not specifically the energy of the strong or the reaction of the weak, but precisely this scene where they are displayed superimposed or face to face.[29] It is nothing but the space that divides them, the void through which they exchange their threatening gestures and speeches. As descent qualifies the strength or weakness of an instinct and its inscription on a body, emergence designates a place of confrontation, but not as a closed field offering the spectacle of a struggle among equals. Rather, as Nietzsche demonstrates in his analysis of good and evil, it is a "nonplace," a pure distance, which indicates that the adversaries do not belong to a common space. Consequently, no one is responsible for an emergence; no one can glory in it, since it always occurs in the interstice.

In a sense, only a single drama is ever staged in this "nonplace," the endlessly repeated play of dominations. The domination of certain men over others leads to the differentiation of values;[30] class domination generates the idea of liberty;[31] and the forceful appropriation of things necessary to survival and the imposition of a duration not intrinsic to them account for the origin of logic.[32] This relationship of domination is no more a "relationship" than the place where it occurs is a place; and, precisely for this reason, it is fixed, throughout its history, in rituals, in meticulous procedures that impose rights and obligations. It establishes marks of its power and engraves memories on things and even within bodies. It makes itself accountable for debts and gives rise to the universe of rules, which is by no means designed to temper violence, but rather to satisfy it. It would be wrong to follow traditional beliefs in thinking that total war exhausts itself in its own contradictions and ends by renouncing violence and submitting to civil laws. On the contrary, the law is the calculated pleasure of relentlessness. It is the promised blood, which permits the perpetual instigation of new dominations and the staging of meticulously repeated scenes of violence. The desire for peace, the serenity of compromise, and the tacit acceptance of the law, far from representing a major moral conversion or a utilitarian calculation that gave rise to the law, are but its result and, in point of fact, its perversion: "guilt, conscience, and duty had their threshold of emergence in the right to secure obligations; and their inception, like that of any major event on earth, was saturated in blood."[35] Humanity does not gradually progress from combat to combat until it arrives at universal reciprocity, where the rule of law finally replaces warfare; humanity installs each of its violences in a system of rules and thus proceeds from domination to domination.

And it is these rules which allow violence to be inflicted on violence and the resurgence of new forces that are sufficiently strong to dominate those in power. Rules are empty in themselves, violent and unfinalized; they are made to serve this or that, and can be bent to any purpose. The successes of history belong to those who are capable of seizing these rules, to replace those who had used them, to disguise themselves so as to pervert them, invert their meaning, and redirect them against those who had initially imposed them; introducing themselves into this complex mechanism, they will make it function in such a way that the dominators find themselves dominated by their own rules. The isolation of different points of emergence does not conform to the successive configurations of an identical meaning; rather, they result from substitutions, displacements, disguised conquests, and systematic reversals. If interpretation were the slow exposure of the meaning hidden in an origin, then only metaphysics could interpret the development of humanity. But if interpretation is the violent or surreptitious appropriation of a system of rules, which in itself has no essential meaning, in order to impose a direction, to bend it to a new will, to force its participation in a different game, and to subject it to secondary rules, then the development of humanity is a series of interpretations. The role of genealogy is to record its history: the history of morals, ideals, and metaphysical concepts, the history of the concept of liberty or of the ascetic life; as they stand for the emergence of different interpretations, they must be made to appear as events in the theater of procedures.

5.

What is the relationship between genealogy, seen as the examination of *Herkunft* and *Entstehung*, and history in the traditional sense? We could, of course, examine Nietzsche's celebrated apostrophes against history, but we will put these aside for the moment and consider those instances when he conceives of genealogy as *wirkliche Historie*, or its more frequent characterization as historical "spirit" or "sense."[34] In fact, Nietzsche's criticism, beginning with the second of the *Untimely Meditations*, always questioned the form of history that reintroduces (and always assumes) a suprahistorical perspective: a history whose function is to compose the finally reduced diversity of time into a totality fully closed upon itself; a history that always encourages subjective recognitions and attributes a form of reconciliation to all the displacements of the past; a history whose perspective on all that precedes it implies the end of time, a completed development. The historian's history finds its support outside of time and claims to base its judgments on an apocalyptic objectivity. This is only possible, however, because of its belief in eternal truth, the immortality of the soul, and the nature of consciousness as always identical to itself. Once the historical sense is mastered by a suprahistorical perspective, metaphysics can bend it to its own purpose, and, by aligning it to the demands of objective science, it can impose its own "Egyptianism." On the other hand, the historical sense can evade metaphysics and become a privileged instrument of genealogy if it refuses the certainty of absolutes. Given this, it corresponds to the acuity of a glance that distinguishes, separates, and disperses; that is capable of liberating divergence and marginal elements—the kind of dissociating view that is capable of decomposing itself, capable of shattering the unity of man's being through which it was thought that he could extend his sovereignty to the events of his past.

Historical sense reintroduces into the realm of becoming everything considered immortal in man, and just so does it practice *wirkliche Historie*. We believe that feelings are immutable, but every sentiment, particularly the noblest and most disinterested, has a history. We believe in the dull constancy of instinctual life and imagine that it continues to exert its force indiscriminately in the present as it did in the past. But historical knowledge easily disintegrates this unity, points out its avatars, depicts its wavering course, locates its moments of strength and weakness, and defines its oscillating reign. It easily seizes the slow elaboration of instincts and those movements where, in turning upon themselves, they relentlessly set about their self-destruction.[35] We believe, in any event, that the body obeys the exclusive laws of physiology, and that it escapes the influence of history, but this too is false. The body is molded by a great many distinct regimes; it is broken down by the rhythms of work, rest, and holidays; it is poisoned by food or values, through eating habits or moral laws; it constructs resistances.[56] "Effective" history differs from the history of historians in being without constants. Nothing in man–not even his body–is sufficiently stable to serve as the basis for self-recognition or for understanding other men. The traditional devices for constructing a comprehensive view of history and for retracing the past as a patient and continuous development must be systematically dismantled. Necessarily, we must dismiss those tendencies which encourage the consoling play of recognitions. Knowledge [*savoir*], even under the banner of history, does not depend on "rediscovery," and it emphatically excludes the "rediscovery of ourselves." History becomes "effective" to the degree that it introduces discontinuity into our very being–as it divides our emotions, dramatizes our instincts, multiplies our body and sets it against itself. "Effective" history leaves nothing around the self, deprives the self of the reassuring stability of life and nature, and it will not permit itself to be transported by a voiceless obstinacy toward a millennial ending. It will uproot its traditional foundations and relentlessly disrupt its pretended continuity. This is because knowledge is not made for understanding; it is made for cutting.

From these observations, we can grasp the particular traits of the historical sense as Nietzsche understood it–the sense which opposes *wirkliche Historie* to traditional history. The former inverts the relationship ordinarily established between the eruption of an event and necessary continuity. An entire historical tradition (theological or rationalistic) aims at dissolving the singular event into an ideal continuity–as a theological movement or a natural process. "Effective" history, however, deals with events in terms of their most unique characteristics, their most acute manifestations. An event, consequently, is not a decision, a treaty, a reign, or a battle, but the reversal of a relationship of forces, the usurpation of power, the appropriation of a vocabulary turned against those who had once used it, a domination that grows feeble, poisons itself, grows slack, the entry of a masked "other." The forces operating in history do not obey destiny or regulative mechanisms, but the luck of the battle.[57] They do not manifest the successive forms of a primordial intention and their attention is not that of a conclusion, for they always appear through the singular randomness of events. The inverse of the Christian world, spun entirely by a divine spider, and different from the world of the Greeks, divided between the realm of will and the great cosmic folly, the world of effective history knows only one kingdom, without providence or final cause, where there is only "the iron hand of necessity shaking the dice-box of chance."[58] Chance is not simply the drawing of lots but raising the stakes in every attempt to master chance through the will to power, and giving rise to the risk of an even greater chance.[59] The world such as we are acquainted with it is not this ultimately simple configuration where events are reduced to accentuate their essential traits, their final meaning, or their initial and final value. On the contrary, it is a profusion of entangled events. If it appears as a "marvelous motley, profound and totally meaningful," this is because it began and continues its secret existence through a "host of errors and phantasms."[40] We want historians to confirm our belief that the present rests upon profound intentions and immutable necessities. But the true historical sense confirms our existence among countless lost events, without a landmark or a point of reference.

The historical sense can also invert the relationship that traditional history, in its dependence on metaphysics, establishes between proximity and distance. The latter is given to a contemplation of distances and heights: the noblest periods, the highest forms, the most abstract ideas, the purest individualities. It accomplishes this by getting as near as possible, placing itself at the foot of its mountain peaks, at the risk of adopting the famous perspective of frogs. Effective history, on the other hand, shortens its vision to those things nearest to it—the body, the nervous system, nutrition, digestion, and energies; it unearths decadence, and if it chances upon lofty epochs, it is with the suspicion—not vindictive but joyous—of finding a barbarous and shameful confusion. It has no fear of looking down, but it looks from above and descends to seize the various perspectives, to disclose dispersions and differences, to leave things undisturbed in their own dimension and intensity. It reverses the surreptitious practice of historians, their pretension to examine things farthest from themselves, the groveling manner in which they approach this promising distance (like the metaphysicians who proclaim the existence of an afterlife, situated at a distance from this world, as a promise of their reward). Effective history studies what is closest, but in an abrupt dispossession, so as to seize it at a distance (an approach similar to that of a doctor who looks closely, who plunges to make a diagnosis and to state its difference). Historical sense has more in common with medicine than philosophy; and it should not surprise us that Nietzsche occasionally employs the phrase "historically and physiologically,"[41] since among the philosopher's idiosyncracies is a complete denial of the body. This includes, as well, "the absence of historical sense, a hatred for the idea of development, Egyptianism," the obstinate "placing of conclusions at the beginning," of "making last things first."[42] History has a more important task than to be a handmaiden to philosophy, to recount the necessary birth of truth and values; it should become a differential knowledge [*connaissance*] of energies and failings, heights and degenerations, poisons and antidotes. Its task is to become a curative science.[43]

The final trait of effective history is its affirmation of a perspectival knowledge [*savoir*]. Historians take unusual pains to erase the elements in their work which reveal their grounding in a particular time and place, their preferences in a controversy–the unavoidable obstacles of their passion. Nietzsche's version of historical sense is explicit in its perspective and acknowledges its system of injustice. Its perception is slanted, being a deliberate appraisal, affirmation, or negation; it follows the lingering and poisonous traces, prescribes the best antidote. It is not given to a discreet effacement before the objects it observes and does not submit itself to their processes; nor does it seek laws, since it gives equal weight to its own sight and to its objects. Through this historical sense, knowledge is allowed to create its own genealogy in the act of cognition; and *wirkliche Historie* composes a genealogy of history as the vertical projection of its position.

6.

In that genealogy of history he sketches in several versions, Nietzsche links historical sense to the historian's history. They share a beginning that is similarly impure and confused, share the same sign in which the symptoms of sickness can be recognized as well as the seed of an exquisite flower.[44] They arose simultaneously to follow their separate ways, but our task is to trace their common genealogy.

The descent [*Herkunft*] of the historian is unequivocal: he is of humble birth. A characteristic of history is to be without choice: it is prepared to acquaint itself with everything, without any hierarchy of importance; to understand everything, without regard to eminence; to accept everything, without making any distinctions. Nothing must escape it and, more important, nothing must be excluded. Historians argue that this proves their tact and discretion. After all, what right have they to impose their tastes and preferences when they seek to determine what actually occurred in the past? What they in fact exhibit is a total lack of taste, a certain crudity that tries to take liberties with what is most exalted, a satisfaction in meeting up with what is base. The historian is insensitive to all disgusting things; or rather, he especially enjoys those things which should be repugnant to him. His apparent serenity follows from his concerted avoidance of the exceptional and his reduction of all things to the lowest common denominator. Nothing is allowed to stand above him; and underlying his desire for total knowledge is his search for the secrets that belittle everything: "base curiosity." What is the source of history? It comes from the plebs. To whom is it addressed? To the plebs. And its discourse strongly resembles the demagogue's refrain: "No one is greater than you and anyone who presumes to get the better of you—you who are good—is evil." The historian, who functions as his double, can be heard to echo: "No past is greater than your present, and, through my meticulous erudition, I will rid you of your infatuations and transform the grandeur of history into pettiness, evil, and misfortune." The historian's ancestry goes back to Socrates.

This demagoguery, of course, must be masked. It must hide its singular malice under the cloak of universals. As the demagogue is obliged to invoke truth, laws of essences, and eternal necessity, the historian must invoke objectivity, the accuracy of facts, and the permanence of the past. The demagogue denies the body to secure the sovereignty of a timeless idea, and the historian effaces his proper individuality so that others may enter the stage and reclaim their own speech. He is divided against himself: forced to silence his preferences and overcome his distaste, to blur his own perspective and replace it with the fiction of a universal geometry, to mimic death in order to enter the kingdom of the dead, to adopt a faceless anonymity. In this world where he has conquered his individual will, he becomes a guide to the inevitable law of a superior will. Having curbed the demands of his individual will in his knowledge, he will disclose the form of an eternal will in his object of study. The objectivity of historians inverts the relationships of will and knowledge, and it is, in the same stroke, a necessary belief in providence, in final causes and teleology. The historian belongs to the family of ascetics. "I can't stand these lustful eunuchs of history, all the seductions of an ascetic ideal; I can't stand these blanched tombs producing life or those tired and indifferent beings who dress up in the part of wisdom and adopt an objective point of view."[45]

The *Entstehung* of history is found in nineteenth-century Europe: the land of interminglings and bastardy, the period of the "man-of-mixture." We have become barbarians with respect to those rare moments of high civilization: cities in ruin and enigmatic monuments are spread out before us; we stop before gaping walls; we ask what gods inhabited these empty temples. Great epochs lacked this curiosity, lacked our excessive deference; they ignored their predecessors: the Classical period ignored Shakespeare. The decadence of Europe presents an immense spectacle (while stronger periods refrained from such exhibitions), and the nature of this scene is to represent a theater; lacking monuments of our own making, which properly belong to us, we live among a crowd of scenery. But there is more. Europeans no longer know themselves; they ignore their mixed ancestries and seek a proper role. They lack individuality. We can begin to understand the spontaneous historical bent of the nineteenth century: the anemia of its forces and those mixtures that effaced all its individual traits produced the same results as the mortifications of asceticism; its inability to create, its absence of artistic works, and its need to rely on past achievements forced it to adopt the base curiosity of plebs.

If this fully represents the genealogy of history, how could it become, in its own right, a genealogical analysis? Why did it not continue as a form of demogogic or religious knowledge? How could it change roles on the same stage? Only by being seized, dominated, and turned against its birth. And it is this movement which properly describes the specific nature of the *Entstehung*: it is not the unavoidable conclusion of a long preparation but a scene where forces are risked and confront one another where they emerge triumphant, where they can also be confiscated. The locus of emergence for metaphysics was surely Athenian demogoguery, the vulgar spite of Socrates and his belief in immortality, and Plato could have seized this Socratic philosophy to turn it against itself. Undoubtedly, he was often tempted to do so, but his defeat lies in its consecration. The problem was similar in the nineteenth century—to avoid doing for the popular asceticism of historians what Plato did for Socrates. This historical trait should not be founded on a philosophy of history, but dismantled, beginning with the things it produced. It is necessary to master history so as to turn it to genealogical uses, that is, strictly anti-Platonic purposes. Only then will the historical sense free itself from the demands of a suprahistorical history.

7.

The historical sense gives rise to three uses that oppose and correspond to the three Platonic modalities of history. The first is parodic, directed against reality, and opposes the theme of history as reminiscence or recognition; the second is dissociative, directed against identity, and opposes history given as continuity or representative of a tradition; the third is sacrificial, directed against truth, and opposes history as knowledge [*connaissance*]. They imply a use of history that severs its connection to memory, its metaphysical and anthropological model, and constructs a countermemory—a transformation of history into a totally different form of time.

First, the parodic and farcical use. The historian offers this confused and anonymous European, who no longer knows himself or what name he should adopt, the possibility of alternative identities, more individualized and real than his own. But the man with historical sense will see that this substitution is simply a disguise. Historians supplied the Revolution with Roman prototypes, Romanticism with knight's armor, and the Wagnerian era was given the sword of a German hero—ephemeral props whose unreality points to our own. No one kept them from venerating these religions, from going to Bayreuth to commemorate a new afterlife; they were free, as well, to be transformed into street vendors of empty identities. The good historian, the genealogist, will know what to make of this masquerade.

He will not be too serious to enjoy it; on the contrary, he will push the masquerade to its limit and prepare the great carnival of time where masks are constantly reappearing. No longer the identification of our faint individuality with the solid identities of the past, but our "unrealization" through the excessive choice of identities—Frederick of Hohenstaufen, Caesar, Jesus, Dionysus, and possibly Zarathustra. Taking up these masks, revitalizing the buffoonery of history, we adopt an identity whose unreality surpasses that of God, who started the charade. "Perhaps, we can discover a realm where originality is again possible as parodists of history and buffoons of God."[46] In this, we recognize the parodic double of what the second of the *Untimely Meditations* called "monumental history": a history given to reestablishing the high points of historical development and their maintenance in a perpetual presence, given to the recovery of works, actions, and creations through the monogram of their personal essence. But in 1874 Nietzsche accused this history, one totally devoted to veneration, of barring access to the actual intensities and creations of life. The parody of his last texts serves to emphasize that "monumental history" is itself a parody. Genealogy is history in the form of a concerted carnival.

The second use of history is the systematic dissociation of our identity. For this rather weak identity, which we attempt to support and to unify under a mask, is in itself only a parody: it is plural; countless souls dispute its possession; numerous systems intersect and dominate one another. The study of history makes one "happy, unlike the metaphysicians, to possess in oneself not an immortal soul but many mortal ones."[47] And in each of these souls, history will discover not a forgotten identity, eager to be reborn, but a complex system of distinct and multiple elements, unable to be mastered by the powers of synthesis: "It is a sign of superior culture to maintain, in a fully conscious way, certain phases of its evolution which lesser men pass through without thought. The initial result is that we can understand those who resemble us as a completely determined system and as representative of diverse cultures, that is to say, as necessary and capable of modification. And, in return, we are able to separate the phases of our own evolution and consider them individually."[48] The purpose of history, guided by genealogy, is not to discover the roots of our identity, but to commit itself to its dissipation. It does not seek to define our unique threshold of emergence, the homeland to which metaphysi-

cians promise a return; it seeks to make visible all of those discontinuities that cross us. "Antiquarian history," according to the *Untimely
Meditations*, pursues opposite goals. It seeks the continuities of soil,
language, and urban life in which our present is rooted, and, "by cul-
tivating in a delicate manner that which existed for all time, it tries to
conserve for posterity the conditions under which we were born."[49]
This type of history was objected to in the *Meditations* because it
tended to block creativity in support of the laws of fidelity. Somewhat
later–and already in *Human, All Too Human*–Nietzsche reconsiders
the task of the antiquarian, but with an altogether different emphasis.
If genealogy in its own right gives rise to questions concerning our
native land, native language, or the laws that govern us, its intention
is to reveal the heterogeneous systems that, masked by the self, inhibit
the formation of any form of identity.

The third use of history is the sacrifice of the subject of knowledge
[*connaissance*]. In appearance or, rather, according to the mask it
bears, historical consciousness is neutral, devoid of passions, and
committed solely to truth. But if it examines itself and if, more generally, it interrogates the various forms of scientific consciousness in its
history, it finds that all these forms and transformations are aspects of
the will to knowledge [*savoir*]: instinct, passion, the inquisitor's devotion, cruel subtlety, and malice. It discovers the violence of a position
that sides against those who are happy in their ignorance, against the
effective illusions by which humanity protects itself, a position that
encourages the dangers of research and delights in disturbing discoveries.[50] The historical analysis of this rancorous will to knowledge[a]
[*vouloir-savoir*] reveals that all knowledge [*connaissance*] rests upon
injustice (that there is no right, not even in the act of knowing, to truth
or a foundation for truth), and that the instinct for knowledge is malicious (something murderous, opposed to the happiness of mankind).
Even in the greatly expanded form it assumes today, the will to
knowledge does not achieve a universal truth; man is not given an
exact and serene mastery of nature. On the contrary, it ceaselessly
multiplies the risks, creates dangers in every area; it breaks down
illusory defenses; it dissolves the unity of the subject; it releases those
elements of itself that are devoted to its subversion and destruction.
Knowledge [*savoir*] does not slowly detach itself from its empirical
roots, the initial needs from which it arose, to become pure speculation subject only to the demands of reason; its development is not tied

to the constitution and affirmation of a free subject; rather, it creates a progressive enslavement to its instinctive violence. Where religions once demanded the sacrifice of bodies, knowledge now calls for experimentation on ourselves,[51] calls us to the sacrifice of the subject of knowledge [*connaissance*]. "Knowledge [*connaissance*] has been transformed among us into a passion which fears no sacrifice, which fears nothing but its own extinction. It may be that mankind will eventually perish from this passion for knowledge. If not through passion, then through weakness. We must be prepared to state our choice: do we wish humanity to end in fire and light or to end on the sands?"[52] We should now replace the two great problems of nineteenth-century philosophy, passed on by Fichte and Hegel (the reciprocal basis of truth and liberty and the possibility of absolute knowledge [*savoir*]), with the theme that "to perish through absolute knowledge [*connaissance*] may well form a part of the basis of being."[53] This does not mean, in terms of a critical procedure, that the will to truth is limited by the intrinsic finitude of cognition [*connaissance*], but that it loses all sense of limitations and all claim to truth in its unavoidable sacrifice of the subject of knowledge [*connaissance*]. "It may be that there remains one prodigious idea which might be made to prevail over every other aspiration, which might overcome the most victorious: the idea of humanity sacrificing itself. It seems indisputable that if this new constellation appeared on the horizon, only the desire to know truth, with its enormous prerogatives, could direct and sustain such a sacrifice. For to knowledge [*connaissance*], no sacrifice is too great. Of course, this problem has never been posed."[54]

The *Untimely Meditations* discussed the critical use of history: its just treatment of the past, its decisive cutting of the roots, its rejection of traditional attitudes of reverence, its liberation of man by presenting him with other origins than those in which he prefers to see himself. Nietzsche, however, reproached critical history for detaching us from every real source and for sacrificing the very movement of life to the exclusive concern for truth. Somewhat later, as we have seen, Nietzsche reconsiders this line of thought he had at first refused, but he directs it to altogether different ends. It is no longer a question of judging the past in the name of a truth that only we can possess in the present, but of risking the destruction of the subject who seeks knowl-

edge [*connaissance*], in the endless deployment of the will to knowledge [*savoir*].

In a sense, genealogy returns to the three modalities of history that
Nietzsche recognized in 1874. It returns to them in spite of the objections that Nietzsche raised in the name of the affirmative and creative
powers of life. But they are metamorphosed: the veneration of monuments becomes parody; the respect for ancient continuities becomes
systematic dissociation; the critique of the injustices of the past by a
truth held by men in the present becomes the destruction of the man
who maintains knowledge [*connaissance*] by the injustice proper to
the will to knowledge.

NOTES

1 Nietzsche, *The Gay Science* [1882], trans. Walter Kaufmann (New York: Random House, 1974), no. 7.

2 Nietzsche, *Human, All Too Human* [1878], in *Complete Works* (New York: Gordon, 1974), no. 3.

3 Nietzsche, *On the Genealogy of Morals* [1887], in *Basic Writings of Nietzsche*, ed. and trans. Walter Kaufmann (New York: Modern Library, 1968), pt. 2, secs. 6, 8.

4 *Gay Science*, nos. 110, 111, 300.

5 Nietzsche, *The Dawn of Day* [1881], in *Complete Works* (New York: Gordon, 1974), no. 102. *Pudenda origo* is "shameful origin." – Ed.

6 *Gay Science*, nos. 151, 353; also *Dawn*, no. 62; *Genealogy*, pt. 1, sec. 14; Nietzsche, "The Four Great Errors," in *Twilight of the Idols* [1888], in *The Portable Nietzsche*, ed. and trans. Walter Kaufmann (New York: Viking, 1954), sec. 7. *Schwarzkünstler* is a black magician. – Ed.

7 Paul Ree's text was entitled *Ursprung der moralischen Empfindungen*.

8 In *Human, All Too Human*, aphorism 92 was entitled *Ursprung der Gerechtigkeit*.

9 In the main body of the *Genealogy*, *Ursprung* and *Herkunft* are used interchangeably in numerous instances (pt. 1, sec. 2; pt. 2, secs. 8, 11, 12, 16, 17).

10 *Dawn*, no. 123.

11 *Human, All Too Human*, no. 34.

12 Nietzsche, *The Wanderer and His Shadow* [1880], in *Complete Works* (New York: Gordon, 1974), no. 9.

13 Ibid., no. 3.

14 *Dawn*, no. 49.

15 Nietzsche, *Nietzsche Contra Wagner* [1888], in *Portable Nietzsche*, pp. 661–8.

16 *Gay Science*, nos. 110, 265.

17 Nietzsche, "How the True World Finally Became a Fable," *Twilight of Idols*, pp. 485–86.

18 For example, on race, see Nietzsche's *Gay Science*, no. 135; *Beyond Good and Evil* [1886], in *Basic Writings*, nos. 200, 242, 244; *Genealogy*, pt. 1, sec. 5; on social type see *Gay Science*, nos. 348–9; *Beyond Good and Evil*, no. 260.

19 *Beyond Good and Evil*, no. 244.

20 *Genealogy*, pt. 3, sec. 17. The *Abkunft* of feelings of depression.

21 Nietzsche, " 'Reason' in Philosophy," *Twilight of Idols*, pp. 479–84.

22 *Dawn*, no. 247.

23 *Gay Science*, nos. 348–49.

24 Ibid.

25 *Dawn*, no. 42.

26 *Beyond Good and Evil*, no. 262.

27 *Genealogy*, pt. 3, no. 13.

28 *Gay Science*, no. 148. It is also to an anemia of the will that one must attribute the *Entstehung* of Buddhism and Christianity.

29 *Genealogy*, pt. 1, sec. 2.

30 *Beyond Good and Evil*, no. 260; see also *Genealogy*, pt. 2, sec. 12.

31 *Wanderer*, no. 9.

32 *Gay Science*, no. 111.

33 *Genealogy*, pt. 2, no. 6.

34 *Genealogy*, preface, sec. 7, and pt. 1, sec. 2; *Beyond Good and Evil*, no. 224.

35 *Gay Science*, no. 7.

36 Ibid.

37 *Genealogy*, pt. 2, sec. 12.

38 *Dawn*, no. 130.

39 *Genealogy*, pt. 2, sec. 12.

40 *Human, All Too Human*, no. 16.

41 *Twilight of Idols*, no. 44.

42 " 'Reason' in Philosophy," *Twilight of Idols*, nos. 1, 4.

43 *Wanderer*, no. 188.

44 *Gay Science*, no. 337.

45 *Genealogy*, pt. 3, sec. 25.

46 *Beyond Good and Evil*, no. 223.

47 *Wanderer*, "Opinions and Mixed Statements," no. 17.

48 *Human, All Too Human*, no. 274.

49 Nietzsche, *Untimely Meditations* [1873–74] in *Complete Works*, pt. 2, no. 3.

50 See *Dawn*, nos. 429, 432; *Gay Science*, no. 335; *Beyond Good and Evil*, nos. 229–30.

a The French phrase *vouloir-savoir* means both the will to knowledge and knowledge as revenge. – Ed.

51 *Dawn*, no. 501.

52 Ibid., no. 429.

53 *Beyond Good and Evil*, no. 39.

54 *Dawn*, no. 45.

MY BODY, THIS PAPER, THIS FIRE*

On pages 56–59 of *Histoire de la folie* [*Madness and Civilization*] I said that dreams and madness have neither the same status nor the same role in the development of Cartesian doubt: dreams allow me to doubt this place where I am, this sheet of paper I see, this hand I hold out; but madness is not an instrument or stage of doubt; for "*I* who am thinking cannot be mad." Madness is therefore excluded, contrary to the skeptical tradition, which made it one of the reasons for doubting.

To sum up Derrida's objection to this thesis, it is no doubt best to quote the passage where he gives most energetically his reading of Descartes.

> Descartes has just said that all knowledge of sensory origin could deceive him. He pretends to put to himself the astonished objection of the imaginary nonphilosopher who is frightened by such audacity and says: no, not all sensory knowledge, for then you would be mad and it would be unreasonable to follow the example of madmen, to put forward a madman's discourse. Descartes *echoes* this objection: since I am here, writing, and you understand me, I am not mad, nor are you, and we are all sane here. The example of madness is therefore not indicative of the fragility of the sensory idea. So be it. Descartes acquiesces to this natural point of view, or rather he pretends to be sitting back in this

---

*This essay appears as an appendix in the 1972 edition of *Histoire de la folie* (Paris: Plon) but is not included in the English translation (*Madness and Civilization*). It is a response to Jacques Derrida's critique of the *Histoire* in "Cogito and the History of Madness" (see endnote a). This translation, by Geoff Bennington, has been slightly amended.

natural comfort the better, the more radically and the more definitively to spring out of it and unsettle his interlocutor. So be it, he says, you think that I would be extravagant to doubt that I am sitting near the fire, etc., that I would be extravagant to follow the example of madmen. I will therefore propose a hypothesis which will seem much more natural to you, will not disorient you, because it concerns a more common, and more universal experience than that of madness: the experience of sleep and dreams. Descartes then elaborates the hypothesis that will ruin *all* the *sensory* foundations of knowledge and will lay bare only the *intellectual* foundations of certainty. This hypothesis above all will not run from the possibility of extravagances – epistemological ones – much more serious than madness.

The reference to dreams does not, therefore, fall short of a madness potentially respected or even excluded by Descartes: quite the contrary. It constitutes, in the methodical order which here is ours, the hyperbolical exasperation of the hypothesis of madness. This latter affected only certain areas of sensory perception, and in a contingent and partial way. Moreover, Descartes is concerned here not with determining the concept of madness but with utilizing the popular notion of extravagance for juridical and methodological ends, in order to ask questions of principle regarding only the *truth* of ideas. ([Derrida's footnote] *Madness, theme or index*: what is significant is that Descartes, at bottom, never speaks of madness itself in this text. Madness is not his theme. He treats it as the index of a question of principle, and epistemological value. It will be said, perhaps, that this is the sign of a profound exclusion. But this silence on madness itself simultaneously signifies the opposite of an exclusion, since it is not a question of madness in this text, not even to exclude it. It is not in the *Meditations* that Descartes speaks of madness itself.) What must be grasped here is that *from this point of view* the sleeper, or the dreamer, is madder than the madman. Or, at least, the dreamer, insofar as concerns the problem of knowledge which interests Descartes here, is further from true perception than the madman. It is in the case of sleep, and not in that of extravagance, that the *absolute totality* of ideas of sensory origin becomes suspect, is stripped of "objective value" as M. Guéroult puts it. The hypothesis of extravagance is therefore not a good example, a revelatory example, a good instrument of doubt – and for at least two reasons. (a) It does not cover the *totality* of the field of sensory perception. The madman is not always wrong about everything; he is not wrong often enough, is never mad enough. (b) It is not a useful or happy example pedagogically, because it meets the resistance of the non-philosopher who does not have the au-

dacity to follow the philosopher when the latter agrees that he might
indeed be mad at the very moment when he speaks.[a]

Derrida's augmentation is remarkable for its depth and perhaps even
more so for its frankness. The stakes of the debate are clearly indicated: Could there be anything anterior or exterior to philosophical
discourse? Can its condition reside in an exclusion, a refusal, a risk
avoided, and, why not, a fear? Derrida rejects this suspicion passion-
ately. *"Pudenda origo,"* as Nietzsche said, about the religious and their
religion.

Let us confront Derrida's analyses and Descartes's texts.

1. THE PRIVILEGES OF DREAMS OVER MADNESS

Derrida: "Dreaming is a more common, and more universal experience
than that of madness." "The madman is not always wrong about everything." "Madness affects only certain areas of sensory perception, and
in a contingent and partial way."

Now, Descartes does not say that dreaming is "more common and
more universal than madness." Nor does he say that madmen are
only mad from time to time and on particular points. Let us listen
instead to his evocation of people who "insist constantly that they are
kings." Is the madness of these men who think they are kings, or have
a body made of glass, more intermittent than dreams?

Yet it is a fact that in the progression of his doubt, Descartes privileges dreaming over madness. Let us leave undecided for the moment
the problem of whether madness is excluded, merely neglected, or
taken up in a broader and more radical testing.

Scarcely has Descartes cited the example of madness only to abandon it, than he evokes the case of dreams: "However, I must here take
into account the fact that I am a man, and consequently have the habit
of sleeping, and imagining in my dreams the same or sometimes
more unlikely things than these deranged people do when awake."

So dreams have a double advantage. On the one hand, they are
capable of giving rise to extravagances that equal or sometimes exceed those of madness. On the other hand, they have the property of
happening habitually. The first advantage is of a logical and demonstrative order: everything that madness (the example I have just left to
one side) could make me doubt can also be rendered uncertain by

dreams. In their power to make uncertain, dreams are not outdone by madness; and none of the demonstrative force of madness is lost by dreams when I need to convince myself of all that I must call into doubt. The other advantage of dreams is of a quite different order: they are frequent, they happen often; my memories of them are recent, it is not difficult to have access to these vivid memories which they leave. In short, this is a practical advantage when it is no longer a question of demonstrating, but of performing an exercise, and calling up a memory, a thought, a state, in the very movement of meditation.

The extravagance of dreams guarantees their *demonstrative* character as an *example*: their frequency ensures their *accessibility* as an *exercise*. And it is indeed this quality of accessibility which preoccupies Descartes here, certainly more so than the demonstrative quality, which he mentions once and for all, as if to make sure that the hypothesis of madness can be abandoned without regret. On the other hand, the theme that dreams happen very often returns several times. "I am a man, and consequently I am in the habit of sleeping," "how many times has it happened that I have dreamed at night," "what happens in sleep," "thinking about it carefully I remember having often been mistaken while asleep."

I am afraid that Derrida has confused these two aspects of dreaming. It is as if he had covered them both with one word that joins them together by force: "universal." If they could be described as "universal," dreams would happen to everyone and about everything. Dreams would indicate that everything could be doubted by everyone. But this forces the words; it goes far beyond what Descartes's text says; or, rather, it falls far short of the peculiarities of that text; it effaces the clear distinction between the extravagance of dreams and their frequency; it erases the specific role of these two characteristics (demonstration and exercise) in Descartes's discourse; it omits the greater importance accorded to habit than to extravagance.

But why is it important that dreams should be familiar and accessible?

2. MY EXPERIENCE OF DREAMS

Derrida: "The reference to dreams constitutes, in the methodical order which here is ours, the hyperbolical exasperation of the hypothesis of madness."

Before re-reading the paragraph on dreams,[1] let us keep in mind what has just been said: "But just a moment—these are madmen, and I should be no less extravagant if I were to follow their examples."

The discourse then runs as follows: a resolution on the part of the meditating subject to take into consideration that he is a man, that he does sometimes sleep and dream; the appearance of a memory, or rather of a multitude of memories, of dreams that coincide exactly, point by point, with today's perception (sitting here, fully dressed, beside the fire); and yet, a feeling that there is a difference between this perception and that memory, a difference not only noted but brought about by the subject in the very movement of his meditation (I look at this paper; I shake my head, I reach out my hand to make the difference between waking and sleeping stand out sharply); but then come further memories, at a second level (the sharpness of this impression has often formed part of my dreams); with these memories, the vivid feeling that I am awake disappears; it is replaced by the clear vision that there is no certain index that can separate sleep and waking; an observation that provokes in the meditating subject an astonishment such that the lack of differentiation between waking and sleeping provokes the near certainty of being asleep.

It is clear that making sleep and waking into a theme for reflection is not the only consequence of the resolution to think about dreaming. In the very movement that proposes it and makes it vary, this theme *takes effect* in the meditating subject in the form of memories, sharp impressions, voluntary gestures, felt differences, more memories, clear vision, astonishment, and a lack of differentiation very close to the feeling of being asleep. To think of dreams is not to think of something external, whose causes and effects I could know, nor is it to evoke no more than a strange phantasmagoria, or the movements of the brain which can provoke it; thinking about dreams, when one applies oneself to it, is such that its effect is that of blurring the perceived limits of sleeping and waking for the meditating subject at the very heart of his meditation. The subject who thinks of dreaming *is thereby disturbed.* Applying one's mind to dreams is not an indifferent task: perhaps it is indeed in the first place a self-suggested theme; but it quickly turns out to be a risk to which one is exposed. A risk, for the subject, of being modified; a risk of no longer being at all sure of being awake; a risk of *stupor,* as the Latin text says.

And it is here that the example of dreaming shows another of its privileges: dreams may well modify the meditating subject to this extent, but they do not prevent him, in the very heart of this *stupor*, from continuing to meditate, to meditate validly, to see clearly a certain number of things or principles, in spite of the lack of distinction, however deep, between waking and sleeping. Even though I am no longer sure of being awake, I remain sure of what my meditation allows me to see: this is just what is shown by the following passage, which begins, precisely, with a sort of hyperbolic resolution, "let us suppose, then, that we are asleep," or as the Latin text says more forcefully, "*Age somniemus.*" Thinking about dreams had led me to uncertainty; uncertainty, through the astonishment it provoked, led me to the near-certainty of being asleep; this near-certainty is now made by my resolutions into a systematic pretense. The meditating subject is put to sleep by way of artifice: "*Age somniemus,*" and on this basis the meditation will be able to develop anew.

We can now see all the possibilities furnished by the dream's property of being, not universal, certainly, but modestly habitual.

1. It is a possible, immediately accessible experience, the model for which is put forward by countless memories.

2. This possible experience is not only a theme for meditation: it is really and actually produced in meditation, according to the following series: thinking of the dream, remembering the dream, trying to separate the dream from waking, no longer knowing whether one is dreaming or not, acting voluntarily as though one were dreaming.

3. By means of this meditative exercise, thinking about dreaming takes effect in the subject himself: it modifies the subject by striking him with *stupor*.

4. But in modifying him, in making of him a subject uncertain of being awake, thinking about dreams does not disqualify him as meditating subject: even though transformed into a "subject supposedly asleep," the meditating subject can safely pursue the progression of his doubt.

But we must go back and compare this experience of dreams with the example of madness which immediately precedes it.

3. THE 'GOOD' AND THE 'BAD' EXAMPLE

Derrida: "What must be grasped here is that from this point of view the sleeper, or the dreamer, is madder than the madman."

For Derrida, madness is not excluded by Descartes: it is simply neglected. Neglected in favor of a better and more radical example. The example of dreams extends, completes and generalizes what the example of madness indicated so inadequately. To pass from madness to dreams is to pass from a "bad" to a "good" instrument of doubt.

Now I believe that the opposition between dreams and madness is of a quite different type. We must compare Descartes's two paragraphs step by step, and follow the system of their opposition in detail.

1. The *nature* of the meditative exercise. This appears clearly in the *vocabulary* used. In the madness paragraph, a vocabulary of comparison. If I wish to deny that "these hands and this body are mine," I must "compare myself to certain deranged people" (*comparare*) but I would be extravagant indeed "if I followed their examples" (*si quod ab iis exemplum ad me transferrem:* if I applied to myself some example coming from them). The madman: an external term to which I compare myself.

In the dream-paragraph, a vocabulary of memory. "I am in the habit of imagining in my dreams"; "how many times has it happened that I . . ."; "thinking carefully about it, I remember." The dreamer: that which I remember having been; from the depths of my memory rises the dreamer that I was myself, that I will be again.

2. The *themes* of the meditative exercise. They appear in the examples that the meditating subject proposed by himself.

Examples of madness: thinking one is a king when one is poor; imagining one's body is made of glass or that one is a jug. Madness is the entirely other; it deforms and transports; it gives rise to another scene.

Examples of dreams: being seated (as I am at this moment); feeling the heat of the fire (as I feel it today); reaching out my hand (as I decide, at this moment, to do). The dream does not shift the scene; it doubles the demonstratives that point to the scene where I am (this hand? Perhaps a different hand, in image. This fire? Perhaps a different fire, a dream). Dream-imagination pins itself onto present perception at every point.

3. The *central test* of the exercise. This consists in the search for difference; can I take these proposed themes into account in my meditation? Can I seriously wonder whether my body is made of glass, or whether I am naked in my bed? If I can, then I am obliged to doubt

even my own body. On the other hand, my body is saved if my meditation remains quite distinct from madness and dreams.

Distinct from dreams? I put it to the test: I remember dreaming that
I was nodding my head. I will therefore nod my head again, here and
now. Is there a difference? Yes – a certain clarity, a certain distinctness.
But, and this is the second stage of the test, can this clarity and distinctness be found in the dream? Yes, I have a clear memory that it
was so. Therefore what I supposed was the criterion of difference
(clarity and distinctness) belongs indifferently to both dreams and
waking perception; so it cannot make the difference between them.

Distinct from madness? The test is immediately carried out. Or,
rather, looking more closely, the test does not take place as it does in
the case of dreams. There is, in fact, no question of trying to take
myself to be a madman who takes himself to be a king; nor is there
any question of wondering if I am a king (or a captain from Tours)
who takes himself to be a philosopher shut up in a room to meditate.
What is different with madness does not have to be tested, it is established. Scarcely are the themes of extravagance evoked than the distinction bursts out like a shout: *"sed amentes sunt isti."*

4. *The effect of the exercise.* This appears in the sentences, or rather
in the decision-sentences, which end both passages.

Madness-paragraph: "But just a moment – these are madmen"
(third person plural, they, the others, *isti*); "I should be no less extravagant if I followed their example": it would be madness (note the
conditional) even to try the test, to wish to imitate all these delights,
and to play the fool with fools, as fools do. Imitating madmen will not
persuade me that I am mad (as thinking of dreams will in a moment
convince me that I am perhaps asleep); it is the very project of imitating them that is extravagant. The extravagance applies to the very
idea of putting it to the test, and that is why the test fails to take place
and is replaced by a mere registering of difference.

Dream-paragraph: the sentence *"these* are madmen" corresponds
to *"I* am quite astonished" (*obstupescere*: the stupor of indistinctness
responds to the shout of difference); and the sentence "I should be no
less extravagant if . . ." is answered by "my astonishment (*stupor*) is
such that it is almost capable of convincing me that I am asleep." The
test that has been effectively tried has "taken" so well that here I am
(note the present indicative) in uncertainty as to whether I am awake.
And it is in this uncertainty that I decide to continue my meditation.

It would be mad to want to act the madman (and I abandon the idea); but to think about dreaming is already to have the impression of being asleep (and that is what I shall meditate on).

It is extraordinarily difficult to remain deaf to the way these two paragraphs echo one another. Difficult not to be struck by the complex system of oppositions which underlies them. Difficult not to recognize in them two parallel but different exercises: that of the *demens*, and that of the *dormiens*. Difficult not to hear the words and sentences confront each other on both sides of the "however," the importance of which Derrida so deeply underlined, though I think he was wrong not to analyze its function in the play of the discourse. Difficult indeed, to say simply that among the reasons for doubt, madness is an insufficient and pedagogically clumsy example, because the dreamer is in any case much madder than the madman.

The whole discursive analysis shows that the establishment of nonmadness (and the rejection of the test) is not continuous with the test of sleep (and the observation that one is perhaps asleep).

But why this rejection of the test of the *demens*? From the fact that it does not take place, can one draw the conclusion that it is excluded? After all, Descartes speaks so little, and so briefly, about madness . . .

4. THE DISQUALIFICATION OF THE SUBJECT

Derrida: "What is significant is that Descartes, at bottom, never speaks of madness in this text . . . it is not a question of madness in this text, not even to exclude it."

On several occasions Derrida wisely points out that in order to understand Descartes's text properly it is necessary to refer to the original Latin version. He recalls – and he is quite right – the words used by Descartes in the famous sentence: "But just a moment: these are madmen (*sed amentes sunt isti*), and I should be no less extravagant (*demens*) if I were to follow their examples." Unfortunately, he takes the analysis no further than this simple reminder of the words.

Let us return to the passage itself: "How could I deny that these hands and this body are mine, except by comparing myself to certain deranged people . . . ?" (The term used here is *insani*). Now what are these *insani* who take themselves to be kings or jugs? They are *amentes*; and I should be no less *demens* if I were to apply their examples to myself. Why these three terms, or rather why use firstly the term *insanus*, then the couple *amens-demens*? When it is a matter of characterizing them by the implausibility of their imagination, the madmen are called *insani*: a word that belongs as much to current vocabulary as to medical terminology. As far as the signs of it are concerned, to be *insanus* is to take oneself to be what one is not, to believe in fancies, to be the victim of illusions. As for its causes, it comes from having the brain gorged with vapor. But when Descartes wants no longer to characterize madness but to affirm that I ought not to follow the example of madmen, he uses the terms *demens* and *amens*: terms that are in the first place juridical, before being medical, which designate a whole category of people incapable of certain religious, civil, and judicial acts. The *dementes* do not have total possession of their rights when it comes to speaking, promising, pledging, signing, starting a legal action, etc. *Insanus* is a characterizing term; *amens* and *demens* are disqualifying ones. In the former, it is a question of signs; in the others, of capacity.

The two sentences: In order to doubt my body, I must "compare myself to certain deranged people," and "but just a moment—these are madmen," are not the proof of an impatient and annoyed tautology. It is in no way a matter of saying, "one must be mad or act like madmen," but, "these are madmen and I am not mad." It would be a singular flattening of the text to sum it up as Derrida does: "since I am here . . . I am not mad, nor are you, we are all sane here." The development of the text is quite different: to doubt one's body is to be like those with deranged minds, the sick, the *insani*. Can I follow their example and at least feign madness for my own part, and make me uncertain in my own mind whether I am mad or not? I cannot and must not. For these *insani* are *amentes*; and I would be just as *demens* as they, and juridically disqualified if I followed . . .

Derrida has obscurely sensed this juridical connotation of the word. He returns to it several times, insistently and hesitantly. Descartes, he says, "treats madness as an index of a question of principle and epistemological value." Or again: "Descartes is concerned here not with determining the concept of madness but with utilizing the popular notion of extravagance for juridical and methodological ends, in order to ask questions of principle regarding only the truth of ideas." Yes, Derrida is right to emphasize that it is a question of right at this point. Yes, he is right again to say that Descartes did not want to "determine the concept of madness" (and who ever made out that he did?). But he is wrong not to have seen that Descartes's text plays on the gap between two types of determinations of madness (medical on the one hand and juridical on the other). Above all, he is wrong to say hastily that the question of right posed here concerns "the truth of ideas," when in fact, as is clearly stated, it concerns the qualification of the subject.

The problem can, then, be posed thus. Can I doubt my own body, can I doubt my actuality? The example of madmen, of the *insani* invites me to do so. But comparing myself to them and acting like them implies that I, too, will become demented, incapable and disqualified in my enterprise of meditation: I should be no less *demens* if I followed their examples. But if, on the other hand, I take the example of dreaming, if I pretend to dream, then *dormiens* though I am, I will be able to continue meditating, reasoning, seeing clearly. *Demens* I shall be unable to continue: at the hypothesis alone I am obliged to stop, envisage something else, see if another example allows me to doubt my body. *Dormiens*, I can continue with my meditation; I remain qualified to think, and I therefore make my resolution: "*Age somniemus*," which leads to a new stage of meditation.

It would have to be a very distant reading which could assert that "it's not a question of madness in this text."

Alright, you say. Let us admit, in spite of Derrida, that it is necessary to pay such great attention to the text, and to all its little differences. For all that, have you demonstrated that madness is well and truly excluded from the progress of doubt? Does not Descartes refer to it again with reference to the imagination? Will it not be a question of madness when he discovers the extravagance of painters, and all the fantastic illusions they invent?

5. THE EXTRAVAGANCE OF PAINTERS

Derrida: "What [Descartes] seemed previously to exclude . . . as extravagance, he here admits as a possibility in dreams . . . Now, within these representations, these images, these ideas in the Cartesian sense, everything may be fictitious and false, as in the representations of those painters whose imaginations, as Descartes expressly says, "are extravagant enough to invent something so new that its like has never been seen before."

It will indeed be a question of madness several more times in the rest of Descartes's work. And its disqualifying role for the meditating subject will in no way prevent meditation from bearing on it, for it is not for the content of these extravagances that madness is put out of play; that only happens for the subject who wants "to play the fool" and meditate at the same time, when in fact it is a matter of knowing if the subject can take madness in hand, imitate it, feign it, and risk no longer being sure whether or not he is rational. I think I have made this point: madness is excluded by the subject who doubts as a means of qualifying himself as doubting subject. But it is not excluded as an object of reflection and knowledge. Is it not characteristic that the madness talked of by Descartes in the paragraph studied above is defined in medical terms, as the result of a "brain deranged or gorged with the black vapors of bile"?

But Derrida could insist and stress the fact that madness is found again in the movement of doubt, mixed up with the imagination of painters. It is manifestly present as is indicated by the word "extravagant" used to describe the imagination of painters: "If it is possible that their imagination is extravagant enough to invent something so new that we have never seen anything like it . . . certainly at the very least the paints [*couleurs*] with which they compose it must be real." Derrida has realized perfectly what is odd about the expression: "their imagination is extravagant enough." So well has he realized it that he underlines it in his quotation as the peg on which to hang his whole demonstration. And I subscribe wholly to the necessity of isolating these words and keeping them well to one side.

But for a different reason—simply because they *do not appear* in Descartes's text. They are an addition by the translator. The Latin text says only: "*si forte aliquid excogitent ad eo novum ut nihil . . .*"; "if perhaps they invent something so new." It is curious that in support of his thesis Derrida should have spontaneously chosen, retained and underlined what precisely is *only* found in the French translation of the *Meditations*; curious, too, that he should insist, and assert that the word "extravagant" has been "expressly" used by Descartes.

It does not appear, then, that the example of dreaming is for Descartes only a generalization or radicalization of the case of madness. It is not as a feeble, inferior, "unrevealing," "ineffectual" example that madness is distinguished from dreaming; and it is not for its lesser value that, once evoked, it is as if left to one side. The example of madness stands against that of dreaming; they are confronted the one with the other and opposed according to a whole system of differences which are clearly articulated in Descartes's discourse.

And I am afraid that Derrida's analysis neglects many of these differences. Literal differences between words (*comparare/reminiscere; exemplum transferre*/to persuade; conditional/indicative). Thematic differences between images (being beside the fire, holding out one's hand and opening one's eyes/taking oneself to be a king, being covered in gold, having a body made of glass); textual differences in the disposition and opposition of paragraphs (the first plays on the distinction between *insanus* and *demens*, and on the *juridical implication* of *demens* by *insanus*; the second plays on the distinction "remembering being asleep/being persuaded that one is asleep," and on the *real passage* from the one to the other in a mind that applies itself to such a memory). But, above all, differences at the level of what happens in the meditation, at the level of the *events* that follow one another; *acts* carried out by the meditating subject (comparison/reminiscence); *effects* produced in the meditating subject (sudden and immediate perception of a difference/astonishment–stupor–experience of a lack of distinction); the qualification of the meditating subject (invalidated if he were *demens*; validated even if he were *dormiens*).

It is clear that this last set of differences controls all the others; it refers less to the signifying organization of the text than to the series of events (acts, effects, qualifications) which the discursive practice of meditation carries with it: it is a question of the modifications of the subject by the very exercise of discourse. And I have the feeling that if a reader as remarkably assiduous as Derrida has missed so many literary, thematic or textual differences, then this is through having misunderstood those differences which are the principle of these others; namely, the "discursive differences."

We must keep in mind the very title of "meditations." Any discourse, whatever it be, is constituted by a set of utterances which are produced each in its place and time, as so many discursive events. If it is a question of a pure demonstration, these utterances can be read as a series of events linked one to another according to a certain number of formal rules; as for the subject of the discourse, he is not implicated in the demonstration–he remains, in relation to it, fixed, invariable and as if neutralized. On the other hand, a "meditation" produces, as so many discursive events, new utterances that carry with them a series of modifications of the enunciating subject: through what is said in meditation, the subject passes from darkness to light, from impurity to purity, from the constraint of passions to detachment, from uncertainty and disordered movements to the serenity of wisdom, and so on. In meditation, the subject is ceaselessly altered by his own movement; his discourse provokes effects within which he is caught; it exposes him to risks, makes him pass through trials or temptations, produces states in him, and confers on him a status or qualification he did not hold at the initial moment. In short, meditation implies a mobile subject modifiable through the effect of the discursive events that take place. From this one, one can see what a demonstrative meditation would be: a set of discursive events which constitute at once groups of utterances linked one to another by formal rules of deduction, and series of modifications of the enunciating subject which follow continuously one from another. More precisely, in a demonstrative meditation the utterances, which are formally linked, modify the subject as they develop, liberating him from his convictions or on the contrary inducing systematic doubts, provoking illuminations or resolutions, freeing him from his attachments or immediate certainties, including new states. But, inversely, the decisions, fluctuations, displacements, primary or acquired qualifications of the subject make sets of new utterances possible, which are in their turn deduced regularly one from another.

The *Meditations* require this double reading: a set of propositions forming a *system*, which each reader must follow through if he wishes to feel their truth, and a set of modifications forming an *exercise*, which each reader must effect, by which each reader must be affected, if he in turn wants to be the subject enunciating this truth on his own behalf. And if there are indeed certain passages of the *Meditations* which can be deciphered exhaustively as a systematic stringing together of propositions—moments of pure deduction—there exist on the other hand sorts of "chiasmas," where the two forms of discourse intersect, and where the exercise modifying the subject orders the succession of propositions, or controls the junction of distinct demonstrative groups. It seems that the passage on madness and dreaming is indeed of this order.

Let us take it up again now as a whole and as an intersection of the demonstrative and ascetic schemas.

1. The immediately preceding passage presents itself as a practical syllogism.

I ought to be wary of something that has deceived me once

My senses, through which I have received the truest and surest things I possess, have deceived me, and more than once

I ought therefore no longer to trust them.

Clearly, it is here a question of a deductive fragment whose import is completely general: *all* that I have taken to be the most *true* falls under the sway of doubt, along with the senses which furnished it. A fortiori, there can therefore remain nothing that does not become at least as doubtful. Need I generalize any further? Derrida's hypothesis, that the (ineffectual) example of madness, and the (effectual) example of dreaming are summoned to operate this generalization, and to carry the syllogism of doubt farther forward, can thus not be retained. But then by what are they summoned?

2. They are summoned less by an objection or restriction than by a resistance: there are perceptible things that "one cannot rationally doubt." It is the word "*plane*" that the translator renders by "rationally." What then is this "impossibility," given that we have just established a completely binding syllogism? What, then, is this obstacle that opposes our doubting "entirely" "wholly," "completely," (rationally?) given that we've just performed a rationally unassailable piece of reasoning? It is the impossibility of this subject's really effecting such a generalized doubt in the exercise which modifies him; it is the impossibility of constituting oneself as universally doubting subject. What is still a problem, after a syllogism of such general import, is the taking-up of the advice of prudence into effective doubt, the transformation of the subject "knowing he must doubt everything" into a subject "applying his resolution-to-doubt to everything." We see why the translator has rendered "*plane*" as "rationally": by wanting to carry through this qualification "rational" that I brought into play at the very beginning of the meditations (and in at least three forms: having a sufficiently mature mind, being free of cares and passions, being assured of a peaceful retreat). If I am to resolve myself to doubt everything thoroughly, must I first disqualify myself as rational? If I want to maintain my qualification as rational, must I give up carrying out this doubt, or at least carrying it out in general terms?

The importance of the words "being able to doubt completely" consists in the fact that they mark the point of intersection of the two discursive forms – that of the system and that of the exercise: at the level of ascetic discursivity, one cannot yet doubt rationally. It is thus this level that will control the following development, and what is involved in it is not the extent of doubtful things but the status of the doubting subject, the qualificative elaboration that allows him to be at once "all-doubting" yet rational.

But what, then, is the obstacle, the resistance point of the exercise of doubt?

3. My body, and the immediate perception I have of it? More exactly an area defined as "the vivid and the near" (in opposition to all those "distant" and "weak" things which I can *place* in doubt without difficulty): I am here, wearing a dressing gown, sitting beside the fire – in short, the whole system of actuality which characterizes this moment of my meditation. It is of the first importance that Descartes here involves not the certainty that one may have in general of one's own body but, rather, everything that, at this precise *instant* of meditation, resists *in fact* the carrying-out of doubt by the subject who is *currently* meditating. Clearly, it is not certain things that in themselves (by their nature, their universality, their intelligibility) resist doubt but, rather, that which characterizes the actuality of the meditating subject (the place of his meditation, the gesture he is in the process of making, the sensations that strike him). If he really doubted all this system of actuality, would he still be rational? Would he not precisely be renouncing all these guarantees of rational meditation which he gave himself in choosing, as has just been said, the moment of the undertaking (quite late in life, but not too late: the moment that must not be allowed to slip past has come), its conditions (peace and quiet, with no cares to form distractions), its place (a peaceful retreat). If I must begin doubting the place where I am, the attention I am paying to this piece of paper, and this heat from the fire which marks my present moment, how could I remain convinced of the rational character of my undertaking? In placing this actuality in doubt, am I not at the same time going to render impossible all rational meditation and remove all value from my resolution to discover the truth at last?

It is in order to reply to this question that two examples are called on, side by side, both of which force one to call into doubt the subject's system of actuality.

4. First example: madness. Madmen indeed are completely deluded as to what constitutes their actuality: they believe they are

dressed when they are naked, kings when they are poor. But can I take up this example on my own account? Is it through this that I shall be able to transform into an effective resolution the proposition that we must doubt everything which comes to us from dreams? Impossible: "isti sunt dementes," that is, they are juridically disqualified as rational subjects, and to qualify myself among them, following them ("transfer their example to me") would disqualify me in my turn, and I should not be able to be a rational subject of meditation ("I should be no less extravagant" . . .) If one uses the example of madness to move from systems to *askēsis*, from the proposition to the resolution, it is quite possible to constitute oneself as a subject having to call everything into doubt, but it is impossible to remain qualified as a subject conducting rationally his meditation through doubt to an eventual truth. The resistance of actuality to the exercise of doubt is reduced by too strong an example: it carries away with it the possibility of meditating validly; the two qualifications "doubting subject" and "meditating subject" are not in this case simultaneously possible.

That madness is posited as disqualificatory in any search for truth, that it is not "rational" to call it up to carry out necessary doubt, that one cannot feign it even for a moment, that this impossibility is immediately obvious in the assignation of the term *demens*: this is indeed the decisive point at which Descartes parts company with all those for whom madness can be in one way or another the bringer or revealer of truth.

5. Second test: dreaming. Madness has therefore been excluded, not as an insufficient example but as an excessive and impossible test. Dreaming is now invoked: because it renders the actuality of the subject no less doubtful than does madness (one thinks one is sitting at table and one is naked in one's bed); and because it offers a certain number of differences with respect to madness – it forms part of the virtualities of the subject (I am a man), of his frequently actualized virtualities (I often sleep and dream), of his memories (I clearly remember having dreamed), and of his memories, which can return as the most vivid of impressions (to the point where I can compare my present impression validly with my memory of my dream). From these properties of dreaming, it is possible for the subject to conduct the exercise of a calling into doubt of his own actuality. First stage (which defines the test): I remember having dreamed what I now perceive as my actuality. Second stage (which for a moment appears

to invalidate the test): the gesture I make in the very instant of my meditation to find out if I am asleep indeed appears to have the clarity and distinction of waking perception. Third stage (which validates the test): I remember not only the images of my dream, but also their clarity, as great as that of my current impressions. Fourth stage (which concludes the test): at one and the same time *I see manifestly* that there is no certain mark for distinguishing dream from reality; *and* I am so *surprised* that I am no longer sure whether at this precise moment I am asleep or not. These two sides of the successful test (uncertain stupor and manifest vision) indeed constitute the subject as *effectively doubting* his own actuality, and as *validly continuing a meditation* that puts to one side everything that is not manifest truth. The two qualifications (doubting everything that arrives through the senses and meditating validly) are really effected. The syllogism had required that they be simultaneously in play; the subject's consciousness of his actuality had formed an obstacle to the accomplishment of this requirement. The attempt to use the example of madmen as a base had confirmed this incompatibility; the effort made to actualize the vividness of dreams showed, on the one hand, that this incompatibility is not insurmountable. And the meditating subject becomes doubting subject at the end of opposing tests: one that has constituted the subject as rational (as opposed to the disqualified madman), and one that also constituted the subject as doubting (in the lack of distinction between dreaming and waking).

Once this qualification of the subject has finally been achieved ("*Age somniemus*"), systematic discursivity will once again be able to intersect with the discourse of the exercise, take the upper hand, place intelligible truths under examination, until a new ascetic stage constitutes the meditating subject as threatened with universal error by the "great trickster." But even at that stage of the meditation, the qualification as "nonmad" (like the qualification as "potential dreamer") will remain valid.

It seems to me that Derrida has vividly and deeply sensed that this passage on madness has a singular place in the development of the *Meditations.* And he transcribes his feeling into his text, at the very moment at which he attempts to master it.

1. In order to explain that the question of madness should appear at this precise point of the *Meditations,* Derrida invents an alternation of

voices that would displace, reject, and drive out of the text itself the difficult exclamation: "but just a moment—these are madmen."

Derrida did indeed find himself faced with a knotty problem. If, as he supposes, it is true that this whole movement of the first meditation operates a generalization of doubt, why does it pause, if only for a moment, over madness or even over dreaming? Why take pains to demonstrate that vivid and recent sensations are no less doubtful than the palest and most distant ones, once it has been established, *in general terms,* that what comes via the senses must not be trusted? Why make this swerve toward the particular point of my body, this paper, this fire? Why make a detour toward the singular trickeries of madness and dreaming?

Derrida gives to this deviation the status of a break. He imagines a foreign intervention, the scruple or reticence of a straggler worried by the movement overtaking him and fighting a last-minute rearguard action. Descartes has scarcely said that we must not trust the senses when a voice would be raised, the voice of a peasant foreign to all philosophical urbanity; he would, in his simple way, try to broach, or at least to limit the thinker's resolution: "I'm quite happy for you to doubt certain of your perceptions, but . . . that you are sitting here, by the fire, saying these things, holding that paper in your hands and other things of the same nature."[2] You'd have to be mad to doubt them, or rather, only madmen can make mistakes about such certain things. And I'm certainly not mad. It is at this point that Descartes would take over again and say to this obstinate yokel: I'm quite prepared to admit that you're not mad, since you're unwilling to be so; but remember that you dream every night, and that your nightly dreams are no less mad than this madness you refuse. And the naive reticence of the objector who cannot doubt his body because he does not want to be mad would be conquered by the example of dreaming, so much "more natural," "more common," "more universal."

Derrida's hypothesis is a seductive one. It resolves with the utmost nicety his problem, which is to show that the philosopher goes directly to the calling into question of the "totality of beingness" [*la totalité de l'etantité*], that this is precisely the form and philosophical mark of his procedure; if he happens to stop for a moment at a "beingness" as singular as madness, this can only be if some innocent tugs at his sleeves and questions him; by himself he would never have lingered among these stories of jugs and naked kings. In this way the

rejection of madness, the abrupt exclamation "but just a moment—
these are madmen" is itself rejected by Derrida and three times enclosed *outside* philosophical discourse: first, since it is another subject
speaking (not the philosopher of the *Meditations* but the objector raising his scarcely refined voice); second, because he speaks from a
place which is that of nonphilosophical naïveté; and, finally, because
the philosopher takes over again and by quoting the "stronger," more
"telling" example of dreaming disarms the objection and makes the
very man who refuses madness accept something far worse.

But it is now clear what price Derrida has to pay for his skillful
hypothesis. The omission of a certain number of *literal* elements
(which appear as soon as one takes the trouble to compare the Latin
text with the French translation); the elision of *textual* differences (the
whole play of semantic and grammatical opposition between the
dream paragraph and that on madness): finally, and above all, the
erasure of the essential *discursive* determination (the double web of
exercise and demonstration). Curiously, by imagining that other naive objecting voice behind Descartes's writing, Derrida has fudged all
the text's differences; or, rather, in erasing all these differences, in
bringing the test of madness and that of dreaming as close together as
possible, in making the one the first faint failed draft of the other, in
absorbing the insufficiency of the one in the universality of the other,
Derrida is continuing the Cartesian exclusion. For Descartes, the
meditating subject had to exclude madness by qualifying himself as
not mad. And this exclusion is, in its turn, no doubt too dangerous for
Derrida: no longer for the disqualification with which it threatens the
philosophizing subject but for the qualification with which it would
mark philosophical discourse; it would indeed determine it as "other"
than the discourse of madness; it would establish between them a
relationship of exteriority; it would send philosophical discourse
across to the "other side," into the pure presumption of not being mad.
Separation, exteriority, a determination from which the philosopher's
discourse must indeed be saved if it is to be a "project for exceeding
every finite and determinate totality." This Cartesian exclusion must
then be excluded because it is determining. And Derrida is obliged to
proceed to three operations to do this, as we can see: first, he affirms,
against all the visible economy of the text, that the power of doubt
specific to madness is a fortiori included in dreaming; second, he
imagines (to account for the fact that there is any question of madness

in spite of everything) that it is someone else who excludes madness, on his own account and following the oblique line of an objection; finally, he removes all philosophical status from this exclusion by denouncing its naive rusticity. Reverse the Cartesian exclusion and make it an inclusion; exclude the excluder by giving his discourse the status of an objection; exclude the exclusion by rejecting it into prephilosophical naïveté: Derrida has needed to do no less than this to get through Descartes's text and reduce the question of madness to nothing. We can see the result: the elision of the text's differences and the compensatory invention of a difference of voices lead Descartes's exclusion to a second level; philosophical discourse is finally excluded from excluding madness.

2. But madness does not allow itself to be reduced in this way. Even supposing that Descartes was "not speaking" of madness, at the point in his text where it is a question of *insani* and *dementes*, supposing that he gave way for a moment to a yokel in order to raise such a crude question, could it not be said that he proceeds, albeit in an insidious and silent manner, to exclude madness?

Could it not be said that Descartes has *de facto* and constantly avoided the question of madness?

Derrida replies to this objection in advance: Yes indeed, Descartes fully faces up to the risk of madness; not as you pretend in a prefatorial and almost marginal way with reference to some business about jugs and naked kings, but at the very heart of his philosophical enterprise, at the precise moment where his discourse, separating itself from all natural considerations on the errors of the senses or the engorgements of the brain, takes on its radical dimension in hyperbolic doubt and the hypothesis of the evil genius. *That* is where madness is called into question and faced up to; with the evil genius I indeed suppose that I am even more radically mistaken than those who think they have a body made of glass—even go so far as persuading myself that two and three do not perhaps add up to five; then with the *cogito* I reach that extreme point, that excess with respect to any determination which allows me to say, whether mistaken or not, whether mad or not, I am. The evil genius would indeed be the point at which philosophy itself, in the excess proper to it, risks madness; and the *cogito* would be the moment at which madness is erased (not because of an exclusion but because its determination when faced with reason would stop being pertinent). According to Derrida, then, we should not attach too much importance to this little farce of the peasant who interrupts at the beginning of the text with his village idiots: in spite of all their motley, they do not manage to pose the question of madness. On the other hand, all the threats of Unreason would be at play beneath the far more disturbing and gloomy figure of the evil genius. Similarly, the taking up by dreams of the worst extravagances of madmen at the beginning of the text would be an easy victory; on the other hand, after the great panic of the evil genius, we should need no less than the point of the *cogito* (and its excess with respect to the "totality of beingness") to make the determinations of madness and dreams appear to be nonradical. The great solemn theater of the universal trickster and of the "I think" would repeat the still natural fable of the madman and the sleeper, but this time in philosophical radicality.

To hold such an interpretation, Derrida had to deny that it was a question of madness at the point where madness was named (and in specific, carefully differentiated terms); now he has to demonstrate that there is a question of madness at the point where it is not named. Derrida puts this demonstration into operation through two series of semantic derivations. It is enough to quote them:

> *Evil genius:* "total madness," "total panic," "disorder of the body" and "subversion of pure thought," "extravagance," "panic that I cannot master."
>
> *Cogito:* "mad audacity," "mad project," "project which recognizes madness as its freedom," "disorder and inordinate nature of hyperbole," "unheard-of and singular excess," "excess tending toward Zero and Infinity," "hyperbolic point which ought to be, like all pure madness in general, silent."

All these derivations around Descartes's text are necessary for the evil genius and the *cogito* to become, as Derrida wishes, the true scene of confrontation with madness. But more is needed: he has to erase from Descartes's texts themselves everything showing that the episode of the evil genius is a voluntary, controled exercise, mastered and carried out from start to finish by a meditating subject who never lets himself be surprised. If it is true that the hypothesis of the malign genius carries the suspicion of error far beyond those illusions of the senses exemplified by certain madmen, then he who forms this fiction (and by the very fact that he forms it voluntarily and as an exercise) escapes the risk of "receiving them into his belief," as is the case and misfortune of madmen. He is tricked, but not convinced. Perhaps everything is illusion, but no credulity attaches to it. No doubt the evil genius tricks far more than does an engorged brain; he can give rise to all the illusory decors of madness, but he is something quite different from madness. It could even be said that he is the contrary of madness: since in madness *I believe* that an illusory purple covers my nudity and my poverty, while the hypothesis of the evil genius permits *me not to believe* that my body and hands exist. As to the extent of the trap, it is true that the evil genius is not outdone by madness; but, in the position of the subject with respect to the trap, there is a rigorous opposition between evil genius and madness. If the evil genius takes on the powers of *madness*, this is only after the exercise of meditation has excluded the risk of *being mad.*

Let us reread Descartes's text. "I shall think that the sky, the air, the earth, colors, figures, sounds, and all other external things are nothing but illusions and daydreams" (whereas the madman thinks that his illusions and daydreams are really the sky, the air and all external things). "I shall consider myself as having no hands, no eyes . . . but believing falsely that I have all these things" (whereas the madman believes falsely that his body is made of glass, but does *not* consider himself as believing it falsely). "I shall take great care not to receive any falsity into my belief" (whereas the madman receives all falsities).

It is clear: faced with the cunning trickster, the meditating subject behaves not like a madman in a panic at universal error but as a no less cunning adversary, always alert, constantly rational, and remaining in the position of master with respect to his fiction: I shall prepare my mind so well for all the ruses of this great trickster that however powerful and cunning he may be, he will be unable to catch me out. How far we are from Derrida's pretty variations on themes: "total madness, total panic which *I am unable to master,* since it is *inflicted* by hypothesis and *I am no longer responsible for it."* How is it possible to imagine that the meditating subject should no longer be responsible for what he himself calls "this painful and laborious design"?

Perhaps we should ask how it is that an author as meticulous as Derrida, and as attentive to texts, could have been guilty of so many omissions but could also operate so many displacements, transpositions, and substitutions? But perhaps we should ask this to the extent that in his reading Derrida is doing no more than revive an old tradition. He is, moreover, aware of this; and this conformity seems, justifiably, to comfort him. He shies in any case from thinking that the classical interpreters have missed through lack of attention the singularity of the passage on madness and dreaming.

On one fact at least I am in agreement: it is not as an effect of their lack of attention that, before Derrida and in like manner, the classical interpreters erased this passage from Descartes. It is by system. A system of which Derrida is the most decisive modern representative, in its final glory: the reduction of discursive practices to textual traces; the elision of the events produced therein and the retention only of marks for a reading; the invention of voices behind texts to avoid having to analyze the modes of implication of the subject in discourses; the assigning of the originary as said and unsaid in the text to avoid placing discursive practices in the field of transformations where they are carried out.

I will not say that it is a metaphysics, metaphysics itself or its closure which is hiding in this "textualization" of discursive practices. I'll go much farther than that: I shall say that what can be seen here so visibly is a historically well determined little pedagogy. A pedagogy that teaches the pupil there is nothing outside the text, but that in it, in its gaps, its blanks and its silences, there reigns the reserve of the origin; that it is therefore unnecessary to search elsewhere, but that here, not in the words, certainly, but in the words under erasure, in their *grid*, the "sense of being" is said. A pedagogy that gives conversely to the master's voice the limitless sovereignty that allows it to restate the text indefinitely.

Father Bourdin supposed that, according to Descartes, it was impossible to doubt things that were certain, even if one were asleep or mad. With respect to a well-founded certainty, the fact of dreaming or of raving would not be pertinent. Descartes replies very explicitly to this interpretation: "I do not remember having said anything of the sort, nor even having dreamed it while asleep." Indeed – nothing can be clearly or distinctly conceived of which is not true (and at this level, the problem of knowing whether or not the conceiver is dreaming or raving does not need to be asked). But, Descartes adds immediately, who then can *distinguish* "what is clearly conceived and what only seems and appears to be so"? Who, then, as thinking and meditating subject, can know whether he knows clearly or not? Who, then, is capable of not deluding himself as to his own certainty and of not being caught out by it? Except precisely those who are not mad? Those who are "wise." And Descartes retorts, with Father Bourdin in his sights: "But as only the wise can distinguish what is clearly conceived from what only seems and appears to be so, I am not surprised that this fellow can't tell the difference between them."

NOTES

a   Translations of the passages quoted from Derrida are taken, with some modifications, from the version by Alan Bass in *Writing and Difference* (London: Routledge, 1978). The translation of the French words "extravagance" and "extravagant" poses some problems: Bass habitually, but not exclusively, uses "insanity" and "insane," and it is true that the French words carry an overtone of madness absent from most uses of the English cognate forms. However, in the discussion of the "extravagance" of painters, the translation "insanity" is clearly excessive, and Bass resorts to the English "extravagance." I have preferred to use this form throughout in the interests of consistency and clarity and have modified Bass's version of Derrida accordingly. – Ed.

1   I use this term paragraph out of amusement, convenience, and fidelity to Derrida. Derrida says in a picturesque and jocular manner: "Descartes starts a new paragraph" [*va à la ligne*]. We know this is quite mistaken.

2   I am quoting Derrida. In Descartes's text, these things it is so difficult to doubt are characterized not by their "nature," but by their proximity and their vividness – by their relation to the meditating subject.

RETURN TO HISTORY*

Discussions about the relations between structuralism and history have been numerous, highly involved, and often confused—not only in France but in Europe, America, and perhaps Japan as well, I don't know. This has been the case for several reasons that are simple to enumerate.

The first is that no one agrees with anyone else on what structuralism is. Second, in France the word "history" means two things: what historians talk about and what historians do in their practice. The third and most important reason is that many political themes or concerns have run through this discussion about the relations between history and structuralism. It should be said, moreover, that I don't intend to dissociate today's discussion from the political context in which it is situated. On the contrary: in the first part I would like to lay out the general strategy, the battle plan of this debate between the structuralists and their adversaries concerning history.

The first thing to note is that structuralism, at least in its initial form, was an undertaking that aimed to give historical investigations a more precise and rigorous method. Structuralism did not turn away from history, at least not in the beginning; it set out to construct a history, one that was more rigorous and systematic. I will simply take three examples. Franz Boas, an American, can be considered the founder of the structural method in ethnology.[1] Now, what was that

---

*"Rekishi heno kaiki," *Paideia* 11 (1 February 1972), pp. 45–60. This text is based on a French transcription reviewed by Foucault. Robert Hurley's translation.

method as he conceived of it? It was essentially a way of criticizing a certain form of ethnological history that was done in his era. Edward Tylor had provided the model for it.[2] This history assumed that human societies all follow the same evolutionary curve, going from the simplest forms to the most complex. The evolution did not vary from one society to another except in the speed of transformations. Further, the great social forms such as marriage rules or agricultural techniques were seen basically as kinds of biological species, and their extension, their growth, their development, and their distribution were thought to obey the same laws and patterns as the growth and spread of biological species. In any case, the model that Tylor used to analyze the development and history of societies was the biological one. Tylor referred to Darwin, and more generally to evolutionism, in order to tell the story of societies.

Boas's problem was to free ethnological method from that old biological model and to show how human societies, whether simple or complex, obeyed certain internal relations that defined them in their specific organization. That process within each society is what Boas called "social structure," and he thought analysis of the structure would enable him to do a history of human societies which was no longer biological but truly historical. So, for Boas, it was not at all a matter of discarding the historical point of view in favor of, say, an antihistorical or ahistorical point of view.

I took the example of Boas, and in the same way I could have taken the example of linguistics, and phonology in particular. Before Nikolai Trubetskoi, historical phonetics traced the evolution of a phoneme or a sound across a language.[3] It tended not to account for the transformation of an entire state of a language at a given moment. What Trubetskoi wanted to do with phonology was to convert it into the tool that would enable him to go from the individual history of a sound, as it were, to the much more general history of the phonetic system of an entire language.

I could take a third example that I will recall briefly. It's the application of structuralism to literature. When, a few years back, Roland Barthes defined what he called the "level of writing" as against the level of style or the level of language, what was he trying to accomplish?[4] Well, that becomes clear when one looks at how literary history was studied in France from about 1950 to about 1955. During that period, either one did the individual, psychological, and perhaps psychoanalytic history of the writer, or one did a general, overall history of an epoch, of a whole cultural ensemble, a collective consciousness, if you will.

In the first case, one never encountered anything beyond the individual and his personal problems; in the second, one only reached very general levels. What Barthes wanted to do by introducing the notion of writing [*écriture*] was to reveal a certain specific level on the basis of which a history of literature *as* literature might be undertaken, recognizing that it has a particular specificity, that it goes beyond individuals, who reside within its space—and further, that in the midst of all the other cultural productions, it is a perfectly specific element with its own laws of conditioning and transformation. By introducing this notion of writing, Barthes wished to establish a new possibility of literary history.

So I do think we need to bear in mind that, in their initial projects, the different structuralist ventures (whether they were ethnological, linguistic, or literary, and the same could be said regarding mythology and the history of the sciences) at the outset were always attempts to fashion the instrument for a precise historical analysis. Now, one has to acknowledge that this undertaking did not fail—I don't mean to say that at all—but was not recognized for what it was; most of the adversaries of the structuralists agree on this point at least, that structuralism would have missed the very dimension of history and would be in effect antihistorical.

This criticism comes from two different horizons. First of all, there is a theoretical critique whose inspiration is phenomenological or existentialist. It is argued that structuralism was obliged to abandon whatever good intentions it may have had, that in fact it gave an absolute privilege to the study of simultaneous or synchronic relations over the study of developmental relations. When, for example, the phonologists study phonological laws, they study language states, without taking their temporal development into consideration. How can history be done if one fails to take time into account? But that is not all. How could it be said that structural analysis is historical, since it privileges not only the simultaneous over the successive but also the logical over the causal? For example, when Claude Lévi-Strauss analyzes a myth, what he tries to determine is not where the myth comes from, why it came into being, how it was transmitted, why a particular population has recourse to the myth, or what led another population to transform it. He is content, at least in a first phase, with establishing logical relations between the different elements of the myth; temporal and causal relations can be established within the space of that logic. There is another objection, finally: Structuralism does not consider freedom or individual initiative as a factor. Against the linguists, Jean-Paul Sartre objects that language is never anything but the outcome, the crest, the crystallization of a basic, primordial human activity. If there was no speaking subject to continually take up language, inhabit it from within, shape it, deform it, utilize it, if there was not this element of human activity, if there was not speech at the very heart of the language system, how could language evolve? So, as soon as one leaves human practice aside, considering only structure and rules of constraint, it is obvious that one is again missing history.

The objections that have been raised by phenomenologists or existentialists are generally adopted by a certain number of Marxists whom I shall call "summary Marxists," that is, Marxists whose theoretical reference is not Marxism itself but, in fact, contemporary bourgeois ideologies. On the other hand, objections have come from a more serious Marxism, that is, from a truly revolutionary Marxism; these objections are based on the fact that the revolutionary movements that have occurred, that are still occurring among students and intellectuals, owe next to nothing to the structuralist movement. There is perhaps a single exception to this rule; it's the case of Althusser in France. Althusser is a Marxist who has applied certain methods that can be regarded as structuralist to the reading and analysis of Marx, and Althusser's analysis has been very important in the recent history of European Marxism.[5] This importance is tied to the fact that Althusser freed the traditional Marxist interpretation from all the humanism, from all the Hegelianism, and from all the phenomenology that burdened it, and thus made possible once again a reading of Marx that was no longer an academic reading but a truly political one. But as important as these Althusserian readings were at the start, they were quickly outstripped by a revolutionary movement that, although developing among students and intellectuals, is, as you know, an essentially antitheoretical movement. One might add that most of the revolutionary movements that have developed recently in the world have been closer to Rosa Luxemburg than to Lenin. They place more trust in the spontaneity of the masses than in theoretical analysis.

It seems to me that until the nineteenth century the primary aim of historical analysis was to reconstruct the past of the great national ensembles by which industrial capitalist society was divided up or tied together. From the seventeenth and eighteenth centuries onward, industrial capitalist society established itself in Europe and the world according to the schema of the great nationalities. History had the function, within bourgeois ideology, of showing how these great national units, which capitalism needed, came from far back in time and had asserted and maintained their unity through various revolutions.

History was a discipline by means of which the bourgeoisie showed, first, that its reign was only the result, the product, the fruit, of a slow maturation, and that this reign was thus perfectly justified, since it came from the mists of time; next, the bourgeoisie showed that, since this reign came from the dawn of time, it was not possible to threaten it with a new revolution. The bourgeoisie both established its right to hold power and warded off the threats of a rising revolution, and history was indeed what Jules Michelet called the "resurrection of the past." History assigned itself the task of bringing the whole national past back to life. This calling and role of history now must be reconsidered if history is to be detached from the ideological system in which it originated and developed. It is to be understood, rather, as the analysis of the transformations societies are actually capable of. The two fundamental notions of history as it is practiced today are no longer *time* and the *past* but *change* and the *event*. I will cite two examples, the first borrowed from structuralist methods, the second from properly historical methods. The purpose of the first one is to show you how structuralism has given or, at any rate, tries to give a rigorous form to the analysis of changes; and the second aims to show how certain methods of the new history are attempts to give a new status and meaning to the old notion of event.

As the first example, I shall take the analysis that Georges Dumézil did of the Roman legend of Horace.[6] It is, I believe, the first structural analysis of an Indo-European legend. Dumézil found isomorphic versions of this well-known story in several countries, Ireland in particular. There is an Irish narrative in which one sees a character, a hero named Cuchulain, and this Cuchulain is a child who has received from the gods a magical power that gives him an extraordinary strength. One day when the kingdom in which he lived finds itself threatened, Cuchulain leaves on an expedition against the enemies. At the gates of the palace of the opposing leader, he meets a first adversary whom he slays. Then he continues to advance. He meets a second adversary and kills him, then a third, whom he also kills. After this triple victory he can go home, but the combat has brought him to such a pitch of excitement, or rather, the magical power he received from the gods has inflamed him to the point that he becomes red and glowing, so if he returned to his town he would be a danger to everyone there. To quell this burning and seething force, his fellow countrymen, on the way back, decide to send him a woman. But it so happens that this woman is the wife of his uncle. The incest laws prohibit such a sexual relation, so he cannot extinguish his ardor in this way, and they are obliged to plunge him into a bath of cold water—but he is so hot that he makes the bath water boil and they have to soak him in seven different baths before he cools down to a normal temperature and can return home without being a danger to others.

Dumézil's analysis differs from the analyses of comparative mythologies that had been done before him. In the nineteenth century there was a whole school of comparative mythology in which one merely showed the resemblances between one myth and another, and in this way certain historians of religions had managed to find the same solar myth in almost all the world's religions. Dumézil, on the other hand—and this is what makes his analysis structural—compares these two narratives only in order to establish the differences between the first and the second. He identifies these differences in a very precise way. In the case of the Irish Cuchulain, the hero is a child; second, he is charged with a magical power; finally, he is alone. Consider the Roman myth: the hero, Horace, is an adult, is old enough to bear arms, has no magical power—he is simply more clever than the others, since he invents the ruse of pretending to flee and then returning, merely a slight distinction within the strategy, but he has no magical power. There is another set of differences in the case of the Irish legend. The hero has such a strong magical power, and this magical power is so intensified in battle, that his return bears a danger to his own town. In the case of the Roman narrative, the hero returns as a victor, and among those he meets he sees someone who has betrayed her own country in her heart—his sister, who took the side of Rome's enemies. The danger was thus shifted from outside the city to the inside. It is no longer the hero who is the bearer of danger, it is someone different from him, though belonging to the same family. Finally, there is a third set of differences. In the Irish narrative only the magical bath in the seven tanks of cold water can calm the hero, whereas in the Roman narrative a juridical ritual, not a magical or religious one, is required, that is, a trial, then an appeals procedure, then an acquittal, before the hero can regain his place among his contemporaries.

Dumézil's analysis—and this is the first of its features—is therefore the analysis not of a resemblance but of a difference and an interplay of differences. In addition, Dumézil's analysis is not content with drawing up a table of differences; it establishes the system of differences, with their hierarchies and their subordination. For example, he shows that in the Roman narrative, from the moment that the hero is no longer that young child endowed with a magical power, but a soldier like the others, it is clear that he can no longer be alone in the face of his adversaries, because a normal man confronting three normal adversaries would necessarily lose. Consequently, around the hero, Horace, the Roman narrative has added two partners, the two brothers who even things up for the Roman hero facing the three Curiattii. If the hero were charged with a magical power, it would be easy for him to defeat these three adversaries; but once he is a man like the others, a soldier like the others, it is necessary to frame him with two other soldiers, and his victory will be obtained only by a kind of tactical trick. The Roman narrative made the Irish hero's exploit a natural one. When the Romans introduced the difference that consists in putting an adult hero in the place of a child hero, when they presented a normal hero, and no longer a character charged with magical power, there had to be three instead of one against the three. So one has not just the table of differences, but the connection of differences with one another. Finally, Dumézil's structuralist analysis consists in showing what the conditions of such a transformation are.

Through the Irish narrative one makes out the profile of a society in which military organization rests essentially on individuals who have received their power and their strength from their birth: their military strength is tied to a certain magical and religious power. In contrast, what appears in the Roman narrative is a society in which military power is a collective power. There are three Horace heroes, and these three Horace heroes are only functionaries so to speak, since they have been delegated by those in power, whereas the Irish hero had himself taken the initiative of his expedition. The combat unfolds within a common strategy: in other words, the Roman transformation of the old Indo-European myth is the result of the transformation of a society essentially made up, at least as concerns its military stratum, of aristocratic individualities, into a society whose military organization is collective and to a certain extent democratic. And while structural analysis may not solve the problems of the history of Rome, you can see how it ties in directly to the actual history of the Roman world. Dumézil shows that it would be pointless to look in the narrative of the Horaces and the Curiattii for something like the transposition of a real event that would have occurred in the first years of Roman history; but, by showing the schema of transformation of the Irish legend into a Roman narrative, he also reveals the principle of historical transformation of the old Roman society into a state-controlled society. You see that a structural analysis like that of Dumézil can be linked to a historical analysis. On the basis of this example, it could be said that an analysis is structural when it studies a transformable system and the conditions under which its transformations are carried out.

Taking a very different example, I would now like to show how certain methods currently employed by historians make it possible to give a new meaning to the notion of event. People are in the habit of saying that contemporary history concerns itself less and less with events and more and more with certain broad, general phenomena that would extend through time, as it were, and would remain immobile through time. But for several decades historians have been practicing a so-called serial history, in which events and sets of events constitute the central theme.

Serial history does not focus on general objects that have been constituted beforehand, such as feudalism or industrial development; serial history defines its object on the basis of an ensemble of

documents at its disposal. Thus about ten years ago a study was done
of the commercial archive of the port of Seville during the sixteenth
century: everything having to do with the entry and exit of ships, their
number, their cargoes, the selling price of their goods, their national-
ity, the places they came from, the places they were sailing to. It was
all these data, but only these data, that constituted the object of study.
In other words, the object of history is no longer given by a kind of
prior categorization into periods, epochs, nations, continents, forms of
culture . . . One no longer studies Spain and America during the Renaissance; one studies—and that is the sole object—all the documents
relating to the life of the port of Seville at such-and-such a date. The
consequence—and this is the second trait of this serial history—is that
this history doesn't use these documents to immediately decipher the
economic development of Spain; the object of historical research is to
establish, on the basis of these documents, a certain number of relations. In this way it was possible to establish—I'm referring again to
Huguette and Pierre Chaunu's study on Seville—year-by-year statistical estimates of the entries and exits of ships, classifications according
to countries, and distributions in terms of goods.[7] Based on the relations they were able to establish, the Chaunus were also able to plot
the curves of development, the fluctuations, the increases, the stop-
pages, the decreases; they could describe cycles and establish relations, finally, between this group of documents concerning the port of
Seville and other documents of the same type concerning the ports of
South America, the Antilles, England, and the Mediterranean ports.
The historian, you see, does not interpret the document in order to
reach behind it and grasp a kind of hidden social or spiritual reality.
His work consists in manipulating and processing a series of homogeneous documents relating to a particular object and a particular epoch, and the internal or external relations of this corpus of documents
are what constitute the outcome of the historian's work. Using this
method—and this is the third feature of serial history—the historian
can reveal events that would not have appeared in any other way. In
traditional history it was thought that events were what was known,
what was visible, what was directly or indirectly identifiable, and the
work of the historian was to search for their cause or their meaning.
The cause or meaning was essentially hidden. The event, on the other
hand, was essentially visible, even if one sometimes lacked the documents to establish it with certainty. Serial history makes it possible to

bring out different layers of events as it were, some being visible, even immediately knowable by the contemporaries, and then, beneath these events that form the froth of history, so to speak, there are other events that are invisible, imperceptible for the contemporaries, and are of completely different form. Let's take up the example of the Chaunus' work again. In a sense, the entry or exit of a ship from the port of Seville is an event with which the contemporaries inhabiting Seville were perfectly familiar, and which we can reconstruct without too many problems. Beneath this layer of events, there exists another type of events that are a bit more diffuse—events that are not perceived exactly in the same way by the contemporaries, but which they have a certain awareness of all the same, for example, a lowering or an increase in prices which will change their economic behavior. And then, beneath these events as well, you have others that are hard to locate, that are often barely perceptible for the contemporaries but nonetheless constitute decisive breaks. Thus the reversal of a trend, the point at which an economic curve that had been increasing levels off or begins to decline, such a point is a very important event in the history of a town, a country, or possibly a civilization, but the people who are its contemporaries are not aware of it. In our own case, despite a relatively precise national accountancy, we don't exactly know that the reversal of an economic trend has occurred. The economists themselves don't know whether a stop in an economic curve signals a great general economic reversal of the trend or simply a stop, or a little intercycle within a more general cycle. It is history's task to uncover this hidden layer of diffuse, "atmospheric," polycephalic events that determine, finally and profoundly, the history of the world. For it is quite clear to us now that the reversal of an economic trend is much more important than the death of a king.

Population increases, for example, are studied in the same way. The fact that Europe's demographic curve, which was pretty much stationary in the course of the eighteenth century, rose abruptly at the end of the eighteenth century and continued to rise in the nineteenth is, in part, what made possible the industrial development of Europe in the nineteenth century, but no one experienced this event in the way that one might have lived through the revolutions of 1848. An inquiry has begun concerning the modes of alimentation of European populations in the nineteenth century. It was noticed that at a certain moment the quantity of proteins consumed by Europeans started to rise sharply. This is an extremely important event for the history of consumption, for the history of health, for the history of longevity. The abrupt increase in quantities of proteins consumed by a population is, in a sense, much more significant than a change of constitutions or the transition from a monarchy to a republic, for example. It is an event, but an event that cannot be grasped by the classic and traditional methods. It can only be dealt with by an analysis of series of documents that are often neglected, series that are as continuous as possible. So with serial history we don't at all see the event dissolving in favor of a causal analysis or a continuous analysis but, rather, layers of events multiplying.

Two major consequences follow from this, and they are interconnected. The first is that history's discontinuities will multiply. Traditionally, historians dwelled on the discontinuities in events such as the discovery of America or the fall of Constantinople. It's true that such events may involve discontinuities, but the great reversal, for example, of the economic pattern—which was characterized by growth in Europe during the sixteenth century, which stabilized and became regressive in the course of the seventeenth century—marks another discontinuity that is not exactly contemporaneous with the first one. History appears then not as a great continuity underneath an apparent discontinuity, but as a tangle of superimposed discontinuities. The other consequence is that one is led in this way to discover different types of time spans in history. Take prices, for example. There are so-called short cycles: prices rise a little, then, reaching a certain ceiling, they come up against the threshold of consumption and at that moment they go back down a little, then climb again. These are brief cycles that one can isolate without any difficulty. Beneath this short time span, this oscillatory span, as it were, you have more important cycles that last twenty-five to fifty years, and then, farther down, there is what are called, in English, secular "trends" (the word is passing into the French language), which is to say great cycles of expansion or recession that, in general, wherever they have been observed, cover a period of twenty-five to one hundred and twenty years. Then, beneath even these cycles, there is what French historians call "*inerties,*" that is, large-scale phenomena operative over centuries and centuries: for example, agricultural technology in Europe, the ways of living of European farmers that remained largely unchanged from the end of the sixteenth century to the beginning and, in some places, up to the middle of the nineteenth century – an inertia of the peasantry and of the agricultural economy above which one had the great economic cycles and, within the great cycles, smaller cycles, and finally, at the top, the little price and market fluctuations that can be observed. History, then, is not a single time span [*durée*]: it is a multiplicity of time spans that entangle and envelop one another. So the old notion of time should be replaced by the notion of multiple time spans, and when the structuralists' adversaries tell them, "You're neglecting time," these adversaries do not seem to realize that it's been a long time, if I may say so, since history got rid of time, that is, since historians stopped recognizing that great unitary time span which would sweep up all human phenomena in a single movement. At the root of historical time, there is not something like a biological evolution that would carry away all phenomena and all events. In reality there are multiple time spans, and each one of these spans is the bearer of a certain type of events. The types of events must be multiplied just as the types of time span are multiplied. That is the mutation that is occurring at present in the disciplines of history.

And now I will finally arrive at my conclusion, with apologies for reaching it so late. I believe that between the structural analyses of change or transformation and the historical analyses of types of events and types of duration, there is, I won't say exactly an identity nor even a convergence, but a certain number of important points of contact. I will indicate them by way of ending this talk. When they deal with documents, historians do not treat them as something to be interpreted, that is, they don't look behind or beyond them for a hidden meaning. They treat the document with a view to the system of its internal and external relations. In the same way, the structuralist, when he studies myths or literature, doesn't ask those myths or that literature what they may translate or express of the mentality of a civilization or the history of an individual. He makes every effort to bring out the relations and the system of relations characteristic of that text or that myth. Rejection of interpretation of the exegetical approach, which looks behind texts or documents for what they signify, is an element that one encounters both among structuralists and among today's historians.

The second point is, I believe, that structuralists and historians alike are led in the course of their work to abandon the grand old biological metaphor of life and evolution. Starting in the nineteenth century, people have made a lot of use of the idea of evolution and adjacent concepts to retrace or analyze the different changes in human societies or in man's practices and activities. This biological metaphor that enabled one to think about history offered an ideological advantage and an epistemological advantage. The epistemological advantage was that, with biology, one had an explanatory model that had only to be transposed term by term to history. Thus it was hoped that this history, becoming evolutive, would finally be as scientific as biology. As to the ideological advantage—very easy to identify—if history is indeed caught up in a time frame analogous to that of life forms, if the same evolutionary processes are at work in life and in history, then human societies have no particular specificity, and they have no other lawfulness, no other determination or regularity than life itself. And just as there is no violent revolution in life, but simply a slow accumulation of tiny mutations, in the same way human history cannot really have the potential for a violent revolution; it can never harbor within itself anything more than imperceptible changes. By metaphorizing history on the analogy of life, one thus guaranteed that human societies would be incapable of a revolution. I think that structuralism and history make it possible to abandon this great biological mythology of history and duration. Structuralism, by defining transformations, and history, by describing types of events and different types of duration [*durée*], make possible both the appearance of discontinuities in history and the appearance of regular, coherent transformations. Structuralism and contemporary history are theoretical instruments by means of which one can—contrary to the old idea of continuity—really grasp both the discontinuity of events and the transformation of societies.

NOTES

1   Franz Boas, *The Mind of Primitive Man* (New York: Macmillan, 1911); *Race, Language and Culture* (New York: Macmillan, 1940).

2   Edward Tylor, *Researches into the Early History of Mankind and the Development of Civilization* (London: Murray, 1865); *Primitive Culture: Researches into the Development of Mythology, Philosophy, Religion, Art and Custom* (London: Murray, 1871), 2 vols.; *Anthropology: An Introduction to the Study of Man and Civilization* (London: Macmillan, 1881).

3   N. Troubetskoi, *Zur allgemeinen Theorie der phonologischen Vokalsysteme,* Travaux du Cercle linguistique de Prague (Prague, 1929) vol. 1, pp. 39–67; *Grundzüge der Phonologie,* Travaux du

Cercle linguistique de Prague (Prague, 1939), vol. 7. [*Principles of Phonology*, trans. Christiane A. M. Baltaxte (Berkeley: University of California Press, 1969)].

4 Roland Barthes, *Le Degré zéro de l'ecriture* (Paris: Seuil, 1953), [*Writing Degree Zero*, trans. Annette Lavers and Colin Smith (New York: Hill and Wang, 1968)].

5 Louis Althusser, *Pour Marx* (Paris: Maspero, 1965); "Du 'Capital' à la philosophie de Marx," in Althusser, Pierre Macherey, and Jacques Rancière, *Lire "Le Capital"* (Paris: Maspero, 1965); vol. 1. pp. 9–89; "L'Objet du 'Capital,'" in Althusser and Etienne Balibar, ibid., vol 2, pp. 7–185.

6 Georges Dumézil, *Horace et les curiaces* (Paris: Gillimard, 1942).

7 Huguette and Pierre Chaunu, *Séville et l'Atlantique* (Paris: Sevpen, 1955–1960), 12 vols.

STRUCTURALISM AND POST-STRUCTURALISM*

G.R. How should we begin? I have had two questions in mind. First, what is the origin of this global term, "post-structuralism"?

M.F. First, none of the protagonists in the structuralist movement – and none of those who, willingly or otherwise, were dubbed structuralists – knew very clearly what it was all about. Certainly, those who were applying structural methods in very precise disciplines such as linguistics and comparative mythology knew what structuralism was, but as soon as one strayed from these very precise disciplines, nobody knew exactly what it was. I am not sure how interesting it would be to attempt a redefinition of what was known, at the time, as structuralism. It would be interesting, though, to study formal thought and the different kinds of formalism that ran through Western culture during the twentieth century – and if I had the time, I would like to. When we consider the extraordinary destiny of formalism in painting or formal research in music, or the importance of formalism in the analysis of folklore and legend, in architecture, or its application to theoretical thought, it is clear that formalism in general has probably been one of the strongest and at the same time one of the most varied currents in twentieth-century Europe. And it is worth pointing out that formalism has very often been associated at once precisely and in each case interestingly with political situations and even political movements. It would certainly be worth examining

---

*This interview, conducted by Gérard Raulet, originally appeared in *Telos* 16:55 (1983), pp. 195–211. The translation, by Jeremy Harding, has been amended.

more closely the relation of Russian formalism to the Russian Revolution. The role of formalist art and formalist thought at the beginning of the twentieth century, their ideological value, their links with different political movements – all of this would be very interesting.

I am struck by how far the structuralist movements in France and Western Europe during the sixties echoed the efforts of certain Eastern countries – notably Czechoslovakia – to free themselves of dogmatic Marxism; and toward the mid-fifties and early sixties, while countries like Czechoslovakia were seeing a renaissance of the old tradition of prewar European formalism, we also witnessed the birth in Western Europe of what was known as structuralism – which is to say, I suppose, a new modality of this formalist thought and investigation. That is how I would situate the structuralist phenomenon – by relocating it within the broad current of formal thought.

G.R. In Western Europe, Germany was particularly inclined to conceive the student movement, which began earlier there than it did in France (from '64 or '65, there was definite agitation in the universities), in terms of Critical Theory.

MF. Yes.

G.R. Clearly, there is no necessary relation between Critical Theory and the student movement. If anything, the student movement instrumentalized Critical Theory, or made use of it. In the same way, there is no direct connection either between structuralism and '68.

M.F. That is correct.

G.R. But were you not saying, in a way, that structuralism was a necessary preamble?

M.F. No. There is nothing necessary in this order of ideas. But to put it very, very crudely, formalist culture, thought and art in the first third of the twentieth century were generally associated with political, or shall we say, critical – even in some cases revolutionary – movements of the left; and Marxism concealed all that. It was fiercely critical of formalism in art and theory, most clearly from the thirties onward. Thirty years later, you saw people in certain Eastern bloc countries and even in France beginning to circumscribe Marxist dogmatism with types of analysis obviously inspired by formalism. What happened in France in 1968, and in other countries as well, is at once extremely interesting and highly ambiguous – and ambiguous because interesting. It is a case of movements that, very often, have endowed themselves with a strong reference to Marxism and, at the same time, have insisted on a violent critique vis-à-vis the dogmatic Marxism of parties and institutions. Indeed, the range of interplay between a certain kind of non-Marxist thinking and these Marxist references was the space in which the student movements developed—movements that sometimes carried revolutionary Marxist discourse to the height of exaggeration but were often inspired at the same time by an antidogmatic violence that ran counter to this type of discourse.

G.R.   An antidogmatic violence in search of references . . .

M.F.   And looking for them, on occasion, in an exasperated dogmatism.

G.R.   Via Freud or via structuralism.

M.F.   Correct. So, once again, I would like to reassess the history of formalism and relocate this minor structuralist episode in France—relatively short, with diffuse forms—within the larger phenomenon of formalism in the twentieth century, as important in its way as romanticism or even positivism was during the nineteenth century.

G.R.   We will return later to positivism. For now, I want to follow the thread of this French evolution you are almost retracing: a thread of references (both very dogmatic and inspired by a will to antidogmatism) to Marx, Freud, and structuralism, in the hope of discovering in people like Jacques Lacan a figure who would put an end to syncretism and would manage to unify all these strands. This approach, moreover, drew a magisterial response from Lacan to the students at Vincennes, running roughly as follows: "You want to combine Marx and Freud. Psychoanalysis can teach you that you are looking for a master; and you will have this master"—an extremely violent kind of disengagement from this attempt at a combination.[1] I read in Vincent Descombes's book, *Le même et l'autre*, with which you are no doubt familiar . . .[2]

M.F.   No. I know it exists but I have not read it.

G.R.   . . . that fundamentally, it was necessary to wait until 1972 in order to emerge from this vain effort to combine Marxism and Freudianism; and that this emergence was achieved by Gilles Deleuze and Félix Guattari, who came from the Lacanian school. Somewhere, I took the liberty of writing that we had certainly emerged from this fruitless attempt at a combination, but in a way that Hegel would have criticized.[3] In other words, we went in pursuit of the third man—Nietzsche—to bring him into the site of the impossible synthesis, referring to him rather than to the impossible combination of Marx and Freud. In any case, according to Descombes, it seems that this tendency to resort to Nietzsche began in 1972. What do you think?

M.F.   No, I do not think that is quite right. First, you know how I am. I am always a bit suspicious of these forms of synthesis which present French thought as Freudian-Marxist at one stage and then as having discovered Nietzsche at another. Since 1945, for a whole range of political and cultural reasons, Marxism in France was a kind of horizon that Sartre thought for a time was impossible to surpass. At that time, it was definitely a very closed horizon, and a very imposing one. Also, we should not forget that throughout the period from 1945 to 1955 in France, the entire French university—the young French university, as opposed to what had been the traditional university—was very much preoccupied, even occupied, with the task of building something that was not Freudian-Marxist but Husserlian-Marxist—the phenomenology-Marxism relation. That is what was at stake in the debates and efforts of a whole series of people. Maurice Merleau-Ponty and Jean-Paul Sartre, in moving from phenomenology to Marxism, were definitely operating on that axis. Jean Desanti too . . .

G.R.   Mikel Dufrenne, even Jean-François Lyotard.

M.F.   And Paul Ricoeur, who was certainly not a Marxist, but a phenomenologist in no way oblivious to Marxism. So, at first they tried to wed Marxism and phenomenology; and it was later, once a certain kind of structural thinking—structural method—had begun to develop, that we saw structuralism replace phenomenology and become coupled with Marxism. It was a movement from phenomenology toward structuralism, and essentially it concerned the problem of language. That, I think, was a fairly critical point—Merleau-Ponty's encounter with language. And, as you know, Merleau-Ponty's later efforts addressed that question. I remember clearly some lectures in which Merleau-Ponty began speaking of Saussure who, even if he had been dead for fifty years, was quite unknown, not so much to French linguists and philologists but to the cultured public. So the problem of language appeared, and it was clear that phenomenology was no match for structural analysis in accounting for the effects of meaning that could be produced by a structure of the linguistic type, in which the subject (in the phenomenological sense) did not intervene to confer meaning. And quite naturally, with the phenomenological spouse finding herself disqualified by her inability to address language, structuralism became the new bride. That is how I would look at it. Even so, psychoanalysis—in large part under the influence of Lacan—also raised a problem which, though very different, was not unanalogous. For the unconscious could not feature in any discussion of a phenomenological kind; of which the most conclusive proof, as the French saw it anyhow, was the fact that Sartre and Merleau-Ponty—I am not talking about the other—were always trying to break down what they saw as positivism, or mechanism, or Freudian "concretism" in order to affirm a constituting subject. And when Lacan, around the time that questions of language were beginning to be posed, remarked, "Whatever you do, the unconscious as such can never be reduced to the effects of a conferral of meaning to which the phenomenological subject is susceptible," he was posing a problem absolutely symmetrical with that of the linguists. Once again, the phenomenological subject was disqualified by psychoanalysis, as it had been by linguistic theory. And it is quite understandable at that point that Lacan could say the unconscious was structured like a language. For one and all, it was the same type of problem. So we had a Freudian-structuralist-Marxism. And with phenomenology disqualified for the reasons I have just outlined, there was simply a succession of fiancées, each flirting with Marx in turn. Only, all was not exactly going well. Of course, I am describing it as though I were talking about a very general movement. What I describe did undoubtedly take place, and it involved a certain number of individuals; but there were also people who did not follow the movement. I am thinking of those who were interested in the history of science—an important tradition in France, probably since the time of Auguste Comte. Particularly around Georges Canguilhem, an extremely influential figure in the French university—the young French university. Many of his students were neither Marxists nor Freudians nor structuralists. And here I am speaking of myself.

G.R. You were one of those people, then?

M.F. I have never been a Freudian, I have never been a Marxist, and I have never been a structuralist.

G.R. Yes, here too, as a formality and just so the reader is under no misapprehensions, we only need to look at the dates. You began . . .

M.F. My first book was written toward the end of my student days. It was *Madness and Civilization*, written between '55 and '60. This book is neither Freudian nor Marxist nor structuralist. Now, as it happened, I had read Nietzsche in '53 and curious as it may seem, from a perspective of inquiry into the history of knowledge—the history of reason: how does one elaborate a history of rationality? This was the problem of the nineteenth century.

G.R.   Knowledge, reason, rationality.

M.F.   Knowledge, reason, rationality, the possibility of elaborating a history of rationality. I would say that here again, we run across phenomenology, in someone like Koyré, a historian of science, with his German background, who came to France between 1930 and 1935, I believe, and developed a historical analysis of the forms of rationality and knowledge in a phenomenological perspective. For me, the problem was framed in terms not unlike those we mentioned earlier. Is the phenomenological, transhistorical subject able to provide an account of the historicity of reason? Here, reading Nietzsche was the point of rupture for me. There is a history of the subject just as there is a history of reason; but we can never demand that the history of reason unfold as a first and founding act of the rationalist subject. I read Nietzsche by chance, and I was surprised to see that Canguilhem, the most influential historian of science in France at the time, was also very interested in Nietzsche and was thoroughly receptive to what I was trying to do.

G.R.   On the other hand, there are no perceptible traces of Nietzsche in his work . . .

M.F.   But there are; and they are very clear. There are even explicit references; more explicit in his later texts than in his earlier ones. The relation of the French to Nietzsche and even the relation of all twentieth-century thought to Nietzsche was difficult, for understandable reasons . . . But I am talking about myself. We should also talk about Deleuze. Deleuze wrote his book on Nietzsche in the sixties. He was interested in empiricism, in Hume, and again in the question: Is the theory of the subject we have in phenomenology a satisfactory one? He could elude this question by means of the slant of Hume's empiricism. I am convinced that he encountered Nietzsche under the same conditions. So I would say everything that took place in the sixties arose from a dissatisfaction with the phenomenological theory of the subject, and involved different escapades, subterfuges, breakthroughs, according to whether we use a negative or a positive term, in the direction of linguistics, psychoanalysis or Nietzsche.

G.R. At any rate, Nietzsche represented a determining experience for the abolition of the founding act of the subject.

M.F. Exactly. And this is where French writers like Bataille and Blanchot were important for us. I said earlier that I wondered why I had read Nietzsche. But I know very well. I read him because of Bataille, and Bataille because of Blanchot. So, it is not at all true that Nietzsche appeared in 1972. He appeared in 1972 for people who were Marxists during the sixties and who emerged from Marxism by way of Nietzsche. But the first people who had recourse to Nietzsche were not looking for a way out of Marxism. They wanted a way out of phenomenology.

G.R. You have spoken about historians of science, of writing a history of knowledge, a history of rationality and a history of reason. Before returning to Nietzsche, could we briefly define these four terms, which might well be taken–in the light of what you have said–to be synonymous?

M.F. No, no. I was describing a movement that involved many factors and many different problems. I am not saying that these problems are identical. I am speaking about the kinship between the lines of inquiry and the proximity of those who undertook them.

G.R. All the same, could we try to specify their relationships? It is true that this can definitely be found in your books, particularly *The Archaeology of Knowledge*. Nonetheless, could we try to specify these relations between science, knowledge, and reason?

M.F. It is not very easy in an interview. I would say that the history of science has played an important role in philosophy in France. I would say that perhaps if modern philosophy (that of the nineteenth and twentieth centuries) derives in great part from the Kantian question, "*Was ist Aufklärung?*" or, in other words, if we admit that one of the main functions of modern philosophy has been an inquiry into the historical point at which reason could appear in its "adult" form, "unchaperoned," then the function of nineteenth-century philosophy consisted in asking, "What is this moment when reason accedes to autonomy? What is the meaning of a history of reason, and what value can be ascribed to the ascendancy of reason in the modern world, through these three great forms: scientific thought, technical apparatus, and political organization?" I think one of philosophy's great functions was to inquire into these three domains, in some sense, to take stock of things or smuggle an anxious question into the rule of reason. To continue then . . . to pursue the Kantian question, "*Was ist Aufklärung?*" This reprise, this reiteration of the Kantian question in France assumed a precise and perhaps, moreover, an inadequate form: "What is the history of science? What happened, between Greek mathematics and modern physics, as this universe of science was built?" From Comte right through the sixties, I think the philosophical function of the history of science has been to pursue this question. Now, in Germany, this question "What is the history of reason, of rational forms in Europe?" did not appear so much in the history of science but in the current of thought which runs roughly from Max Weber to Critical Theory.

G.R.   Yes, the meditations on norms, on values.

M.F.   From Max Weber to Jürgen Habermas. And the same question arises here. How do matters stand with the history of reason, with the ascendancy of reason, and with the different forms in which this ascendancy operates? Now, the striking thing is that France knew absolutely nothing—or only vaguely, only very indirectly—about the current of Weberian thought. Critical Theory was hardly known in France, and the Frankfurt School was practically unheard of. This, by the way, raises a minor historical problem that fascinates me, and I have not been able to resolve at all. It is common knowledge that many representatives of the Frankfurt School came to Paris in 1935, seeking refuge, and left very hastily, sickened presumably—some even said as much—but saddened anyhow not to have found more of an echo. Then came 1940, but they had already left for England and the U.S. where they were actually much better received. The understanding that might have been established between the Frankfurt School and French philosophical thought—by way of the history of science and, therefore, the question of the history of rationality—never occurred. And when I was a student, I can assure you that I never once heard the name of the Frankfurt School mentioned by any of my professors.

G.R.   It is really quite astonishing.

M.F.   Now, obviously, if I had been familiar with the Frankfurt School, if I had been aware of it at the time, I would not have said a number of stupid things that I did say, and I would have avoided many of the detours I made while trying to pursue my own humble path—when, meanwhile, avenues had been opened up by the Frankfurt School. It is a strange case of nonpenetration between two very similar types of thinking which is explained, perhaps, by that very similarity. Nothing hides the fact of a problem in common better than two similar ways of approaching it.

G.R. What you have just said about the Frankfurt School – about Critical Theory, if you like – which might, under different circumstances, have spared you some fumblings, is even more interesting in view of the fact that one finds an Oskar Negt or a Habermas doffing his hat to you. In an interview I did with Habermas, he praised your "masterly description of the bifurcation of reason": reason had bifurcated at a given moment. But I have still wondered whether you would agree with this bifurcation of reason as conceived by Critical Theory – with the dialectic of reason, in other words, whereby reason becomes perverse under the effects of its own strength, transformed and reduced to instrumental knowledge. The prevailing idea in Critical Theory is the dialectical continuity of reason, and of a perversion that completely transformed it at a certain stage – which it now becomes a question of rectifying. That is what seemed to be at issue in the struggle for emancipation. Basically, to judge from your work, the will to knowledge has never ceased to bifurcate in some way or another – bifurcating hundreds of times in the course of history. Perhaps "bifurcate" is not even the right word. Reason has split knowledge again and again.

M.F. Yes, yes. I think the blackmail that has very often been at work in every critique of reason or every critical inquiry into the history of rationality (either you accept rationality or you fall prey to the irrational) operates as though a rational critique of rationality were impossible, or as though a rational history of all the ramifications and all the bifurcations, a contingent history of reason, were impossible. I think that since Weber, in the Frankfurt School and anyhow for many historians of science such as Canguilhem, it was a question of isolating the form of rationality presented as dominant and endowed with the status of the one-and-only reason, in order to show that it is only *one* possible form among others. In this French history of science – I consider it quite important – the role of Gaston Bachelard, whom I have not mentioned so far, is also crucial.

G.R. Even so, this praise from Habermas is a little barbed. According to Habermas, you provided a masterly description of the "moment reason bifurcated." This bifurcation was unique. It happened once. At a certain point, reason took a turn that led it toward an instrumental rationality, an autoreduction, a self-limitation. This bifurcation, if it is also a division, happened once and once only in history, separating the two realms with which we have been acquainted since Kant. This analysis of bifurcation is Kantian. There is the knowledge of understanding and the knowledge of reason, there is instrumental reason and there is moral reason. To assess this bifurcation, we clearly situate ourselves at the vantage point of practical reason, or moral practical reason. Whence a unique bifurcation, a separation of technique and practice which continues to dominate the entire German history of ideas. And, as you said earlier, this tradition arises from the question, "*Was ist Aufklärung?*" Now, in my view, this praise reduces your own approach to the history of ideas.

M.F. True, I would not speak about *one* bifurcation of reason but more about an endless, multiple bifurcation—a kind of abundant ramification. I do not speak of the point at which reason became instrumental. At present, for example, I am studying the problem of techniques of the self in Greek and Roman antiquity; how man, human life, and the self were all objects of a certain number of *tekhnai* that, with their exacting rationality, could well be compared to any technique of production.

G.R. Without comprising the whole of society.

M.F. Right. And what led the *tekhnē* of self to develop. Everything propitious to the development of a technology of the self can very well be analyzed, I think, and situated as a historical phenomenon—which does not constitute *the* bifurcation of reason. In this abundance of branchings, ramifications, breaks, and ruptures, it was an important event, or episode; it had considerable consequences, but it was not a *unique* phenomenon.

G.R. But directly we cease to view the self-perversion of reason as a unique phenomenon, occurring only once in history, at a moment when reason would seem to have lost something essential, something substantial—as we would have to say after Weber—would you not agree that your work aims to rehabilitate a fuller version of reason? Can we find, for example, another conception of reason implicit in your approach; a project of rationality that differs from the one we have nowadays?

M.F. Yes, but here, once more, I would try to take my distance from phenomenology, which was my point of departure. I do not believe in a kind of founding act whereby reason, in its essence, was discovered or established and from which it was subsequently diverted by such-and-such an event. I think, in fact, that reason is self-created, which is why I have tried to analyze forms of rationality: different foundations, different creations, different modifications in which rationalities engender one another, oppose and pursue one another. Even so, you cannot assign a point at which reason would have lost sight of its fundamental project, or even a point at which the rational becomes the irrational. During the sixties, to put it very, very schematically, I wanted to depart as much from the phenomenological account (with its foundational and essential project of reason, from which we have shifted away on account of some forgetfulness and to which we must return) as from the Marxist account, or the account of Georg Lukács. A rationality existed, and it was the form par excellence of Reason itself, but a certain number of social conditions (capitalism, or rather, the shift from one form of capitalism to another) precipitated this rationality into a crisis, that is, a forgetting of reason, a fall into irrationalism. I tried to take my bearings in relation to these two major models, presented very schematically and unfairly.

G.R. In these models, we see either a unique bifurcation or a forgetfulness, at a given moment, following the confiscation of reason by a class. Thus, the movement across history toward emancipation consists not only in reappropriating what was confiscated (to confiscate it again) but—on the contrary—in giving reason back its truth, intact, investing it with the status of an absolutely universal science. For you, clearly—you have made it plain in your writing—there is no project of a new science, of a broader science.

M.F. Definitely not.

G.R. But you show that each time a type of rationality asserts itself, it does so by a kind of cut-out—by exclusion or by self-demarcation, drawing a boundary between self and other. Does your project include any effort to rehabilitate this other? Do you think, for example, in the silence of the mad person you might discover language that would have much to say about the conditions in which works are brought into existence?

M.F. Yes, what interested me, starting out from the general frame of reference we mentioned earlier, were precisely the forms of rationality applied by the human subject to itself. While historians of science in France were interested essentially in the problem of how a scientific object is constituted, the question I asked myself was this:

How is it that the human subject took itself as the object of possible knowledge? Through what forms of rationality and historical conditions? And, finally, at what price? This is my question: At what price can subjects speak the truth about themselves? At what price can subjects speak the truth about themselves as mad persons? At the price of constituting the mad person as absolutely other, paying not only the theoretical price but also an institutional and even an economic price, as determined by the organization of psychiatry. An ensemble of complex, staggered elements where you find that institutional game-playing, class relations, professional conflicts, modalities of knowledge and, finally, a whole history of the subject and of reason are involved. That is what I have tried to piece back together. Perhaps the project is utterly mad, very complex—and I have only brought a few moments to light, a few specific points such as the problem of the mad subject and what it is. How can the truth of the sick subject ever be told? How can one speak the truth about the mad subject? This is the substance of my first two books. *The Order of Things* asked the price of problematizing and analyzing the speaking subject, the working subject, the living subject. Which is why I attempted to analyze the birth of grammar, general grammar, natural history, and economics. I went on to pose the same kind of question in the case of the criminal and systems of punishment: How to state the truth of oneself, insofar as one might be a criminal subject. I will be doing the same thing with sexuality, only going back much farther: How does the subject speak truthfully about itself, inasmuch as it is the subject of sexual pleasure? And at what price?

G.R.   According to the relation of subjects to whatever they are, in each case, through the constitution of language or knowledge.

M.F.   It is an analysis of the relation between forms of reflexivity—a relation of self to self—and, hence, of relations between forms of reflexivity and the discourse of truth, forms of rationality and effects of knowledge [*connaissance*].

G.R.   In any event, it is not a case of exhuming some prehistorical "archaic" by means of archaeology. (You shall see why I ask this question. It directly concerns certain readings of the so-called French Nietzschean current in Germany.)

M.F.   No, absolutely not. I meant this word "archaeology," which I no longer use, to suggest that the kind of analysis I was using was out-of-phase, not in terms of time but by virtue of the level at which it was situated. Studying the history of ideas, as they evolve, is not my problem so much as trying to discern beneath them how one or another object could take shape as a possible object of knowledge. Why, for instance, did madness become, at a given moment, an object of knowledge corresponding to a certain type of knowledge? By using the word "archaeology" rather than "history," I tried to designate this desynchronization between ideas about madness and the constitution of madness as an object.

G.R. I asked this question because nowadays there is a tendency—its pretext being the appropriation of Nietzsche by the New German Right—to lump everything together; to imagine that French Nietzscheanism, if Nietzscheanism it is—it seems to me that you just confirmed that Nietzsche played a determinant role—is in the same vein. All these elements are associated in order to recreate what are fundamentally the fronts of theoretical class struggle, so hard to find nowadays.

M.F. I do not believe there is a single Nietzscheanism. There are no grounds for believing that there is a true Nietzscheanism, or that ours is any truer than others. But those who found in Nietzsche, more than twenty-five years ago, a means of displacing themselves in terms of a philosophical horizon dominated by phenomenology and Marxism have nothing to do with those who use Nietzsche nowadays. In any case, even if Deleuze has written a superb book about Nietzsche, and although the presence of Nietzsche in his other works is clearly apparent, there is no deafening reference to Nietzsche, nor any attempt to wave the Nietzschean flag for rhetorical or political ends. It is striking that someone like Deleuze has simply taken Nietzsche seriously, which indeed he has. That is what I wanted to do. What serious use can Nietzsche be put to? I have lectured on Nietzsche but written very little about him. The only rather extravagant homage I have rendered Nietzsche was to call the first volume of my *History of Sexuality* "The Will to Know."

G.R. Certainly, as regards the will to know, I think we have been able to see in what you have just said that it was always a *relation*. I suppose you will detest this word with its Hegelian ring. Perhaps we should say "evaluation," as Nietzsche would—a way of evaluating truth. At any rate, a way in which force, neither an archaic instance nor an originary or original resource, is actualized; and so too, a relation of forces and perhaps already a relation of power in the constituting act of all knowledge.

M.F.   I would not say so. That is too involved. My problem is the relation of self to self and of telling the truth. My relation to Nietzsche, or what I owe Nietzsche, derives mostly from the texts of around 1880, where the question of truth, the history of truth and the will to truth were central to his work. Did you know that Sartre's first text–written when he was a young student–was Nietzschean? "The History of Truth," a little paper first published in a *Lycée* review around 1925.[4] He began with the same problem. And it is very odd that his approach should have shifted from the history of truth to phenomenology, while for the next generation–ours–the reverse was true.

G.R.   I think we are now in the process of clarifying what you mean by "will to know"–this reference to Nietzsche. You concede a certain kinship with Deleuze, but only up to a point. Would this kinship extend as far as the Deleuzian notion of desire?

M.F.   No, definitely not.

G.R.   I am asking this question because Deleuzian desire– productive desire–becomes precisely this kind of originary resource which then begins to generate forms.

M.F.   I do not want to take up a position on this, or say what Deleuze may have had in mind. People say what they want or what they can say. The moment a kind of thought is constituted, fixed, or identified within a cultural tradition, it is quite normal that this cultural tradition should take hold of it, make what it wants of it and have it say what it did not mean, by implying that this is merely another form of what it was actually trying to say. Which is all a part of cultural play. But my relation to Deleuze is evidently not that; so I will not say what I think he meant. All the same, I think his task was, at least for a long time, to formulate the problem of desire. And, evidently, the effects of the relation to Nietzsche are visible in his theory of desire, whereas my own problem has always been the question of truth, of telling the truth, the *Wahr-sagen*–what it is to tell the truth– and the relation between telling the truth and forms of reflexivity, of self upon self.

G.R.   Yes, but I think Nietzsche makes no fundamental distinction between will to know and will to power.

M.F.   I think there is a perceptible displacement in Nietzsche's texts between those which are broadly preoccupied with the question of will to know and those which are preoccupied with will to power. But

I do not want to get into this argument for the very simple reason that it is years since I have read Nietzsche.

G.R. It is important to try to clarify this point, I think, precisely because of the hold-all approach that characterizes the way this question is received abroad, and in France for that matter.

M.F. I would say, in any case, that my relation to Nietzsche has not been historical. The actual history of Nietzsche's thought interests me less than the kind of challenge I felt one day, a long time ago, reading Nietzsche for the first time. When you open *The Gay Science* after you have been trained in the great, time-honored university traditions – Descartes, Kant, Hegel, Husserl – and you come across those rather strange, witty, cheeky texts, you say: Well, I won't do what my contemporaries, colleagues or professors are doing; I won't just dismiss this. What is the maximum of philosophical intensity, and what are the current philosophical effects to be found in these texts? That, for me, was the challenge of Nietzsche.

G.R. In the way all this is received at the moment, I think there is a second hold-all concept, that is, postmodernity, which quite a few people refer to and which also plays a role in Germany, since Habermas has taken up the term in order to criticize this trend in all its aspects . . .

M.F. What are we calling postmodernity? I'm not up to date.

G.R. . . . the current of North American sociology (Daniel Bell) as much as what is known as postmodernity in art, which would require another definition (perhaps a return to a certain formalism). Anyway, Habermas attributes the term "postmodernity" to the French current, the tradition, as he says in his text on postmodernity, "running from Bataille to Derrida by way of Foucault." This is an important question in Germany, because reflections on modernity have existed for a long time – ever since Weber. What is postmodernity, as regards the aspect that interests us here? Mainly, it is the idea of modernity, of reason, we find in Lyotard: a "grand narrative" from which we have finally been freed by a kind of salutary awakening. Postmodernity is a breaking apart of reason; Deleuzian schizophrenia. Postmodernity reveals, at least, that reason has only been one narrative among others in history; a grand narrative, certainly, but one of many, which can now be followed by other narratives. In your vocabulary, reason was *one* form of the will to know. Would you agree that this has to do with a certain current? Do you situate yourself within this current; and, if so, how?

M.F.   I must say that I have trouble answering this. First, because I've never clearly understood what was meant in France by the word "modernity." In the case of Baudelaire, yes, but thereafter I think the sense begins to get lost. I do not know what Germans mean by modernity. The Americans were planning a kind of seminar with Habermas and myself. Habermas had suggested the theme of "modernity" for the seminar. I feel troubled here because I do not grasp clearly what that might mean, though the word itself is unimportant; we can always use any arbitrary label. But neither do I grasp the kind of problems intended by this term—or how they would be common to people thought of as being "postmodern." While I see clearly that behind what was known as structuralism, there was a certain problem— broadly speaking, that of the subject and the recasting of the subject—I do not understand what kind of problem is common to the people we call "postmodern" or "poststructuralist."

G.R.   Obviously, reference or opposition to modernity is not only ambiguous, it actually confines modernity. Modernity also has several definitions: the historian's definition, Weber's definition, Theodor Adorno's definition, and Walter Benjamin's of Baudelaire, as you've mentioned. So there are at least some references. Habermas, in opposition to Adorno, seems to privilege the tradition of reason, that is, the Weberian definition of modernity. It is in relation to this that he sees in postmodernity the crumbling-away or the breakup of reason, and allows himself to declare that one of the forms of postmodernity—the one that is in relation with the Weberian definition—is the current that envisages reason as *one* form among others of the will to know—a grand narrative, but *one* narrative among others.

M.F.   That is not my problem, insofar as I am not prepared to identify reason entirely with the totality of rational forms which have come to dominate—at any given moment, in our own era and even very recently—in types of knowledge, forms of technique, and modalities of government or domination; realms where we can see all the major applications of rationality. I am leaving the problem of art to one side; it is complicated. For me, no given form of rationality is actually reason. So I do not see how we can say that the forms of rationality which have been dominant in the three sectors I have mentioned are in the process of collapsing and disappearing. I cannot

see any disappearance of that kind. I can see multiple transformations, but I cannot see why we should call this transformation a "collapse of reason." Other forms of rationality are created endlessly. So
there is no sense at all to the proposition that reason is a long narrative that is now finished, and that another narrative is under way.

G.R. Let us just say that the field is open to many forms of narrative.

M.F. Here, I think, we are touching on one of the forms—perhaps
we should call them "habits"—one of the most harmful habits in contemporary thought, in modern thought even; at any rate, in post-
Hegelian thought: the analysis of the present as being precisely, in
history, a present of rupture, or of high point, or of completion or of a
returning dawn, and so on. The solemnity with which everyone who
engages in philosophical discourse reflects on his own time strikes
me as a flaw. I can say so all the more firmly, since it is something I
have done myself; and since, in someone like Nietzsche, we find this
incessantly—or, at least, insistently enough. I think we should have
the modesty to say to ourselves that, on the one hand, the time we live
in is not *the* unique or fundamental or irruptive point in history where
everything is completed and begun again. We must also have the
modesty to say, on the other hand, that—even without this solemnity—
the time we live in is very interesting; it needs to be analyzed and
broken down, and that we would do well to ask ourselves, "What is
today?" I wonder if one of the great roles of philosophical thought
since the Kantian *"Was ist Aufklärung?"* might not be characterized
by saying that the task of philosophy is to describe the nature of today,
and of "ourselves today." With the proviso that we do not allow ourselves the facile, rather theatrical declaration that this moment in
which we exist is one of total perdition, in the abyss of darkness, or a
triumphant daybreak, and so on. It is a time like any other, or rather, a
time that is never quite like any other.

G.R. This poses dozens of questions; ones that you have posed
yourself in any case. What is the nature of today? Is the era characterized more than others, in spite of everything, by a greater fragmenta-
tion, by "deterritorialization" and "schizophrenia"—no need to take a
position on these terms?

M.F. I would like to say something about the function of any diagnosis concerning what today is. It does not consist in a simple characterization of what we are but, instead—by following lines of fragility in

the present–in managing to grasp why and how that which is might no longer be that which is. In this sense, any description must always be made in accordance with these kinds of virtual fracture which open up the space of freedom understood as a space of concrete freedom, that is, of possible transformation.

G.R. It is here, along the fractures, that the work of the intellectual–practical work, quite clearly–is situated?

M.F. That is my own belief. I would say also, about the work of the intellectual, that it is fruitful in a certain way to describe that which is, while making it appear as something that might not be, or that might not be as it is. Which is why this designation or description of the real never has a prescriptive value of the kind, "because this is, that will be." It is also why, in my opinion, recourse to history–one of the great facts in French philosophical thought for at least twenty years–is meaningful to the extent that history serves to show how that which is has not always been; that is, the things which seem most evident to us are always formed in the confluence of encounters and chances, during the course of a precarious and fragile history. What reason perceives as *its* necessity or, rather, what different forms of rationality offer as their necessary being, can perfectly well be shown to have a history; and the network of contingencies from which it emerges can be traced. Which is not to say, however, that these forms of rationality were irrational; it means that they reside on a base of human practice and human history–and that since these things have been made, they can be unmade, as long as we know how it was that they were made.

G.R. This work on the fractures, both descriptive and practical, is fieldwork.

M.F. Perhaps it is fieldwork and perhaps it is a work which can go farther back in terms of historical analysis, starting with questions posed in the field.

G.R. Would you describe the work on these fracture areas, work in the field, as the microphysics of power, the analytics of power?

M.F. Yes, it is something like that. It has struck me that these forms of rationality–put to work in the process of domination–deserve analysis in themselves, provided we recognize from the outset that they are not foreign to other forms of power which are put to work, for instance, in knowledge [*connaissance*] or technique. On the contrary, there is exchange; there are transmissions, transferences, interferences. But I wish to emphasize that I do not think it is possible to point to a unique form of rationality in these three realms. We come across the same types, but displaced. At the same time, there is multiple, compact interconnection, but no isomorphism.

G.R. In all eras or specifically?

M.F. There is no general law indicating the types of relation between rationalities and the procedures of domination which are put to work.

G.R. I ask this question because there is a scheme at work in a certain number of criticisms made about you. Jean Baudrillard's criticism, for instance, is that you speak at a very precise moment and conceive a moment in which power has become "unidentifiable through dissemination."[5] This unidentifiable dissemination, this necessary multiplication, is reflected in the microphysical approach. Or, again, in the opinion of Alexander Schubert,[6] you address a point where capitalism has dissolved the subject in a way that makes it possible to admit that the subject has only ever been a multiplicity of positions.

M.F. I would like to return to this question in a moment, because I had already begun to talk about two or three things. The first is that, in studying the rationality of dominations, I try to establish interconnections that are not isomorphisms. Second, when I speak of power relations, of the forms of rationality which can rule and regulate them, I am not referring to Power–with a capital P–dominating and imposing its rationality upon the totality of the social body. In fact, there are power relations. They are multiple; they have different forms, they can be in play in family relations, or within an institution, or an administration–or, between a dominating and a dominated class, power relations having specific forms of rationality, forms that are common to them, and so on. It is a field of analysis and not at all a reference to any unique instance. Third, in studying these power relations, I in no way construct a theory of power. But I wish to know how the reflexivity of the subject and the discourse of truth are linked– "How can the subject tell the truth about itself?"–and I think that relations of power exerting themselves upon one another constitute one of the determining elements in this relation I am trying to analyze. This is clear, for example, in the first case I examined, that of madness. It was indeed through a certain mode of domination, exercised by certain people upon certain other people, that the subject could undertake to tell the truth about its madness presented in the form of the other. Thus I am far from being a theoretician of power. At the limit, I would say that power, as an autonomous question, does not interest me. In many instances, I have been led to address the question of power only to the extent that the political analysis of power which was offered did not seem to me to account for the finer, more detailed phenomena I wish to evoke when I pose the question of telling the truth about oneself. If I tell the truth about myself, as I am now doing, it is in part that I am constituted as a subject across a number of power relations that are exerted over me and I exert over others. I say this in order to situate what for me is the question of power. To return to the question you raised earlier, I must admit that I see no grounds for the objection. I am not developing a theory of power. I am working on the history, at a given moment, of the way reflexivity of self upon self established, and the discourse of truth linked to it. When I speak about institutions of confinement in the eighteenth century, I am speaking about power relations as they existed at the time. So I fail utterly to see the objection, unless one imputes to me a project altogether different from my own—either that of developing a general theory of power or, again, that of developing an analysis of power as it exists now. Not at all! I take psychiatry, of course, as it is now. In it, I look at the appearance of certain problems, in the very workings of the institution, which refer us, in my view, to a history—and a relatively long one, involving several centuries. I try to work on the history or archaeology, if you like, of the way people undertook to speak truthfully about madness in the seventeenth and eighteenth centuries. And I would like to bring it to light as it existed at the time. On the subject of criminals, for example, and the system of punishment established in the eighteenth century, which characterizes our own penal system, I have not gone into detail on *all* kinds of power exercised in the eighteenth century. Instead, I have examined, in a certain number of model eighteenth-century institutions, the forms of power exercised and how they were put into play. So I can see no relevance whatever in saying that power is no longer what it used to be.

G.R. Two more rather disconnected questions, which nonetheless strike me as important. Let us begin with the status of the intellectual. We have broadly defined how you conceive of the work, the practice even, of the intellectual. Would you be prepared to discuss here the philosophical situation in France along the following general lines?

The function of the intellectual is no longer either to oppose the state with a universal reason or to provide it with its legitimation. Is there a connection with this rather strange, disconcerting situation we see today—a tacit kind of consensus among intellectuals with regard to the Left, and at the same time, the complete silence of thought on the Left—something one is tempted to see as forcing the powers of the Left to invoke very archaic themes of legitimation? The Socialist Party Congress at Valence with its rhetorical excesses, the class struggle . . .[7]

M.F. The recent remarks of the president of the National Assembly to the effect that we must replace the egoist, individualist, bourgeois cultural model with a new cultural model of solidarity and sacrifice . . . I was not very old when Pétain came to power in France, but this year I recognized in the words of this socialist the very tones that lulled my childhood.

G.R. Yes. Basically, we are witnessing the astonishing spectacle of a power, divested of intellectual logistics, invoking pretty obsolete themes of legitimation. As for intellectual logistics, it seems that as soon as the Left comes to power, no one on the Left has anything to say.

M.F. It is a good question. First, we should remember that if the Left exists in France—the Left in a general sense—and if there are people who have the sentiment of being on the Left, people who vote Left, and if there can be a substantial party of the Left (as the Socialist Party has become), I think an important factor has been the existence of a Left thought and a Left reflection, of an analysis, a multiplicity of analyses, developed on the Left, of political choices made on the Left since at least 1960, which have been made outside the parties. No thanks to the Communist Party, though, or to the old S.F.I.O.—which was not dead until '72 (it took a long time to die)—that the Left is alive and well in France.[8] It is because, through the Algerian war, for example, in a whole sector of intellectual life also, in sectors dealing with the problems of daily life, sectors such as those of political and economic analysis, there was an extraordinarily lively Left thought. And it did not die, even at the moment when the parties of the Left disqualified themselves for different reasons. On the contrary.

G.R. No, at the time, certainly not.

M.F. And we can say that the Left survived for fifteen years—the first fifteen years of Gaullism and then the regime that followed—

because of that effort. Second, it should be noted that the Socialist Party was greeted so responsively in large part because it was reasonably open to these new attitudes, new questions, and new problems. It was open to questions concerning daily life, sexual life, couples, women's issues. It was sensitive to the problems of self-management, for example. All these are themes of Left thought—a Left thought that is not encrusted in the political parties and is not traditional in its approach to Marxism. New problems, new thinking—these have been crucial. I think that one day, when we look back at this episode in French history, we will see in it the growth of a new kind of Left thought that—in multiple and nonunified forms (perhaps one of its positive aspects)—has completely transformed the horizon of contemporary Left movements. We might well imagine this particular form of Left culture as being allergic to any party organization, incapable of finding its real expression in anything but *groupuscules* and individualities. But apparently not. Finally, there has been—as I said earlier—a kind of symbiosis which has meant that the new Socialist Party is now fairly saturated with these ideas. In any case—something sufficiently interesting and attractive to be worthy of note—we have seen a number of intellectuals keeping company with the Socialist Party. Of course, the Socialist Party's very astute political tactics and strategy—and this is not pejorative—account for their coming to power. But here again, the Socialist Party came to power after having absorbed a certain number of Left cultural forms. However, since the Congress of Metz[9] and a fortiori, the Congress of Valence—where we heard things such as we discussed earlier—it is clear that this Left thought is asking itself questions.

G.R. Does this thought itself exist any more?

M.F. I do not know. We have to bear several complex factors in mind. We have to see, for example, that in the Socialist Party, this new Left thought was most active in the circle of someone like Michel Rocard—that Rocard and his group, and of the Rocard current in the Socialist Party, are now hidden under a chimney—flue tile, has had a major effect. The situation is very complex; but I think that the rather wooden pronouncements of many Socialist Party leaders at present are a betrayal of the earlier hopes expressed by a large part of this Left thought. They also betray the recent history of the Socialist Party, and they silence, in a fairly authoritarian manner, certain currents within the party itself. Undoubtedly, confronted with this phenomenon, intellectuals are tending to keep quiet. I say tending, because it is a journalistic error to say that the intellectuals are keeping quiet. Personally, I know several intellectuals who have reacted, who have given their opinion on some measure or on some problem. And I think that if we drew up an exact balance sheet of interventions by intellectuals over the last few months, there would certainly not be any less than before. Anyway, for my part, I have never written as many articles in the press as I have since word went out that I was keeping quiet. Still, let's not worry about me personally. It is true that these reactions are not a kind of fundamental choice. They are finely nuanced interventions — hesitant, slightly doubtful, slightly encouraging, and so on. But they correspond to the present state of affairs — and, instead of complaining about the silence of intellectuals, we should recognize much more clearly their thoughtful reserve in response to a recent event, a recent process, whose outcome we do not yet know for certain.

G.R. No necessary relation, then, between *this* political situation, *this* type of discourse and the thesis, nonetheless very widespread, that reason is power and so we are to divest ourselves of the one and the other?

M.F. No. You must understand that is part of the destiny common to all problems once they are posed: they degenerate into slogans. Nobody has said, "Reason is power." I do not think anyone has said knowledge is power.

G.R. It has been said.

M.F. It has been said, but you have to understand when I read — and I know it was being attributed to me — the thesis "Knowledge is power" or "Power is knowledge," I begin to laugh, since studying their *relation* is precisely my problem. If they were identical, I would not have to study them and I would be spared a lot of fatigue as a result. The very fact that I pose the question of their relation proves clearly that I do not *identify* them.

G.R. Last question. The view that Marxism is doing rather badly today because it drank from the springs of the Enlightenment has dominated thought, whether we like it or not, since the seventies, if only because a number of individuals — intellectuals — known as the New Philosophers have vulgarized the theme. So, Marxism, we are told, is doing fairly badly.

M.F. I do not know if it is doing well or badly. It is an idea that has dominated thought, or philosophy; that is the formula I stop at, if you like. I think you are quite right to put the question, and to put it in that way. I would be inclined to say–I nearly stopped you there–that this view has not dominated thought so much as the "lower depths" of thought. But that would be facile. Uselessly polemical. And it is not really fair. I think we should recognize that in France, toward the fifties, there were two circuits of thought which, if not foreign to one another, were practically independent of one another. There was what I would call the "university circuit"–a circuit of scholarly thought–and then there was the circuit of open thought, or mainstream thought. When I say "mainstream," I do not necessarily mean poor quality. But a university book, a thesis, a course, and so on, were things you found in the academic presses, available to university readers. They scarcely had any influence except in universities. There was the special case of Bergson, that was exceptional. But from the end of the war onward–and no doubt existentialism played a part in this–we have seen ideas of profoundly academic origins, or roots (and the roots of Sartre, after all, are Husserl and Heidegger, who were hardly public dancers) addressed to a much broader public than that of the universities. Now, even though there is nobody of Sartre's stature to continue it, this phenomenon has become democratized. Only Sartre–or perhaps Sartre and Merleau-Ponty–could do it. But then it tended to become something within everybody's range, more or less, and for a certain number of reasons. First, there was the dislocation of the university, the growing number of students and professors, and so on, who came to constitute a kind of social mass; the dislocation of internal structures and a broadening of the university public; also the diffusion of culture (by no means a negative thing). The public's cultural level, on average, has really risen considerably; and, whatever one says, television has played a major role. People come to see that there is a new history, and so forth. Add to this all the political phenomena–the groups and movements half inside and half outside the universities. It all gave university activity an echo that reverberated widely beyond academic institutions or even groups of specialist, professional intellectuals. One remarkable phenomenon in France at the moment is the almost complete absence of specialized philosophy journals. Or they are more or less worthless. So when you want to write something, where do you publish? Where *can* you publish? In the end, you can only manage to slip something into one of the wide-circulation weeklies and general interest magazines. That is very significant. And so what happens—and what is fatal in such situations—is that a fairly evolved discourse, instead of being relayed by additional work which perfects it (either with criticism or amplification), rendering it more difficult and even finer, nowadays undergoes a process of amplification from the bottom up. Little by little, from the book to the review, to the newspaper article, and from the newspaper article to television, we come to summarize a work, or a problem, in terms of slogans. This passage of the philosophical question into the realm of the slogan, this transformation of the Marxist question, which becomes "Marxism is dead," is not the responsibility of any one person in particular, but we can see the slide whereby philosophical thought, or a philosophical issue, becomes a consumer item. In the past, there were two different circuits. Even if it could not avoid all the pitfalls, the institutional circuit, which had its drawbacks—it was closed, dogmatic, academic—nevertheless managed to sustain less heavy losses. The tendency to entropy was less, while nowadays entropy sets in at an alarming rate. I could give personal examples. It took fifteen years to convert my book about madness into a slogan: all mad people were confined in the eighteenth century. But it did not even take fifteen months—it only took three weeks—to convert my book on the will to know into a slogan "Sexuality has never been repressed." In my own experience, I have seen this entropy accelerate in a detestable way for philosophical thought. But it should be remembered that this means added responsibility for people who write.

G.R. I was tempted for a moment to say in conclusion—in the form of a question—not wanting to substitute one slogan for another: Is Marxism not finished, then? In the sense that you say in *The Archaeology of Knowledge* that a "nonfalsified Marxism would help us to formulate a general theory of discontinuity, series, limits, unities, specific orders, autonomies and differentiated dependencies."

M.F. Yes. I am reluctant to make assessments about the type of culture that may be in store. Everything is present, you see, at least as a virtual object, inside a given culture. Or everything that has already featured once. The problem of objects that have never featured in the culture is another matter. But it is part of the function of memory and culture to be able to reactualize any objects whatever that have already been featured. Repetition is always possible, repetition with application, transformation. God knows in 1945 Nietzsche appeared to be completely disqualified. It is clear, even if one admits that Marx will disappear for now, that he will reappear one day. What I wish for–and it is here that my formulation has changed in relation to the one you cited–is not so much the defalsification and restitution of a true Marx but the unburdening and liberation of Marx in relation to party dogma, which has constrained it, touted it, and brandished it for so long. The phrase "Marx is dead" can be given a conjunctural sense. One can say it is relatively true, but to say that Marx will disappear like that . . .

G.R.   But does this reference in *The Archaeology of Knowledge* mean that, in a certain way, Marx is at work in your own methodology?

M.F.   Yes, absolutely. You see, given the period in which I wrote those books, it was good form (in order to be viewed favorably by the institutional Left) to cite Marx in the footnotes. So I was careful to steer clear of that. But I could dredge up–which is of no interest– quite a few passages I wrote referring to Marx, and Marx would not have been that author, functioning that way in French culture, with such a political surcharge. That is the Marx I would have cited at the bottom of the page. I didn't do it: to have some fun, and to set a trap for those among the Marxists who have tacked me to those sentences. That was part of the game.

NOTES

1   The exact quotation can be found in transcript of the proceedings at Vincennes, December 1969, published in *Le Magazine littéraire* 121 (Feb. 1977): "What you as a revolutionary aspire to is a master. You will have one." (See "Impromptu at Vincennes," *October* 40 [Spring 1987], p. 121.– Ed.)

2   See Vincent Descombes, *Le Même et l'Autre: quarante-cinq ans de philosophie française* (Paris: Minuit, 1979). "In fact, when one looks at things a bit more closely, one turns out to be in a plural world, in which phenomena appear out of alignment and produce somewhat unforeseen encounters. Take Freudianism-Marxism."

3   See Gérard Raulet, *Materialien zur Kritischen Theorie* (Frankfurt: Suhrkamp Verlag, 1982).

4   Jean-Paul Sartre, *La Légende de la vérité* [1929], a fragment of which was first published in *Bifur* 8 (June 1931), pp. 77–96.

5   Jean Baudrillard, *Oublier Foucault* (Paris: Galilée, 1977) [*Forget Foucault*, trans. N. Defresne (New York: Semiotext[e], 1987), pp. 7–64].

6   See Alexander Schubert, *Die Decodierung des Menschen* (Frankfurt: Focus, 1981).

7   This took place in 1981.–Ed.

8   *Section française de l'internationale ouvrière.*–Ed.

9   This took place in 1979.–Ed.

FOUCAULT

Maurice Florence*

———

To the extent that Foucault fits into the philosophical tradition, it is the critical tradition of Kant, and his project could be called a Critical History of Thought.[1] This should not be taken to mean a history of ideas that would be at the same time an analysis of errors that might be gauged after the fact; or a decipherment of the misinterpretations linked to them and on which what we think today might depend. If what is meant by thought is the act that posits a subject and an object, along with their various possible relations, a critical history of thought would be an analysis of the conditions under which certain relations of subject to object are formed or modified, insofar as those relations constitute a possible knowledge [savoir]. It is not a matter of defining the formal conditions of a relationship to the object; nor is it a matter of isolating the empirical conditions that may, at a given moment, have enabled the subject in general to become acquainted with an object already given in reality. The problem is to determine what the subject must be, to what condition he is subject, what status he must have, what position he must occupy in reality or in the imaginary, in order to become a legitimate subject of this or that type of knowledge [connaissance]. In short, it is a matter of determining its mode of "subjectivation," for the latter is obviously not the same, ac-

———

*In the early eighties, Denis Huisman asked François Ewald, Foucault's assistant at the Collège de France, to reedit the entry on Foucault for a new edition of the Dictionnaire des philosophes. The text submitted to Huisman was written almost entirely by Foucault himself, and signed pseudonymously "Maurice Florence." Robert Hurley's translation.

cording to whether the knowledge involved has the form of an exegesis of a sacred text, a natural history observation, or the analysis of a mental patient's behavior. But it is also and at the same time a question of determining under what conditions something can become an object for a possible knowledge [*connaissance*], how it may have been problematized as an object to be known, to what selective procedure [*procédure de découpage*] it may have been subjected, the part of it that is regarded as pertinent. So it is a matter of determining its mode of objectivation, which is not the same either, depending on the type of knowledge [*savoir*] that is involved.

This objectivation and this subjectivation are not independent of each other. From their mutual development and their interconnection, what could be called the "games of truth" come into being—that is, not the discovery of true things but the rules according to which what a subject can say about certain things depends on the question of true and false. In sum, the critical history of thought is neither a history of acquisitions nor a history of concealments of truth; it is the history of "veridictions," understood as the forms according to which discourses capable of being declared true or false are articulated concerning a domain of things. What the conditions of this emergence were, the price that was paid for it, so to speak, its effects on reality and the way in which, linking a certain type of object to certain modalities of the subject, it constituted the historical a priori of a possible experience for a period of time, an area and for given individuals.

Now, Michel Foucault did not pose this question—or this series of questions, which are those of an "archaeology of knowledge"—and does not wish to pose it concerning just any game of truth, but concerning only those in which the subject himself is posited as an object of possible knowledge: What are the processes of subjectivation and objectivation that make it possible for the subject qua subject to become an object of knowledge [*connaissance*], as a subject? Of course, it is a matter not of ascertaining how a "psychological knowledge" was constituted in the course of history but of discovering how various truth games were formed through which the subject became an object of knowledge. Michel Foucault attempted to conduct his analysis in two ways. First, in connection with the appearance and insertion of the question of the speaking, laboring, and living subject, in domains and according to the form of a scientific type of knowledge. This had to do with the formation of certain "human sciences," studied in reference to the practice of the empirical sciences, and of their characteristic discourse in the seventeenth and eighteenth centuries (*The Order of Things*). Foucault also tried to analyze the formation of the subject as he may appear on the other side of a normative division, becoming an object of knowledge—as a madman, a patient, or a delinquent, through practices such as those of psychiatry, clinical medicine, and penality (*Madness and Civilization, Birth of the Clinic, Discipline and Punish*).

Foucault has now undertaken, still within the same general project, to study the constitution of the subject as an object for himself: the formation of procedures by which the subject is led to observe himself, analyze himself, interpret himself, recognize himself as a domain of possible knowledge. In short, this concerns the history of "subjectivity," if what is meant by the term is the way in which the subject experiences himself in a game of truth where he relates to himself. The question of sex and sexuality appeared, in Foucault's view, to constitute not the only possible example, certainly, but at least a rather privileged case. Indeed, it was in this connection that through the whole of Christianity, and perhaps beyond, individuals were all called on to recognize themselves as subjects of pleasure, of desire, of lust, of temptation and were urged to deploy, by various means (self-examination, spiritual exercises, admission, confession), the game of true and false in regard to themselves and what constitutes the most secret, the most individual part of their subjectivity.

In sum, this history of sexuality is meant to constitute a third segment, added to the analyses of relations between the subject and truth or, to be exact, to the study of the modes according to which the subject was able to be inserted as an object in the games of truth.

Taking the question of relations between the subject and truth as the guiding thread for all these analyses implies certain choices of method. And, first, a systematic skepticism toward all anthropological universals—which does not mean rejecting them all from the start, outright and once and for all, but that nothing of that order must be accepted that is not strictly indispensable. In regard to human nature or the categories that may be applied to the subject, everything in our knowledge which is suggested to us as being universally valid must be tested and analyzed. Refusing the universal of "madness," "delinquency," or "sexuality" does not imply that what these notions refer to is nothing, or that they are only chimeras invented for the sake of a dubious cause. Something more is involved, however, than the simple observation that their content varies with time and circumstances: It means that one must investigate the conditions that enable people, according to the rules of true and false statements, to recognize a subject as mentally ill or to arrange that a subject recognize the most essential part of himself in the modality of his sexual desire. So the first rule of method for this kind of work is this: Insofar as possible, circumvent the anthropological universals (and, of course, those of a humanism that would assert the rights, the privileges, and the nature of a human being as an immediate and timeless truth of the subject) in order to examine them as historical constructs. One must also reverse the philosophical way of proceeding upward to the constituent subject which is asked to account for every possible object of knowledge in general. On the contrary, it is a matter of proceeding back down to the study of the concrete practices by which the subject is constituted in the immanence of a domain of knowledge. There too, one must be careful: Refusing the philosophical recourse to a constituent subject does not amount to acting as if the subject did not exist, making an abstraction of it on behalf of a pure objectivity. This refusal has the aim of eliciting the processes that are peculiar to an experience in which the subject and the object "are formed and transformed" in relation to and in terms of one another. The discourses of mental illness, delinquency, or sexuality say what the subject is only in a certain, quite particular game of truth; but these games are not imposed on the subject from the outside according to a necessary causality or structural determination. They open up a field of experience in which the subject and the object are both constituted only under certain simultaneous conditions, but in which they are constantly modified in relation to each other, and so they modify this field of experience itself.

Hence a third principle of method: Address "practices" as a domain of analysis, approach the study from the angle of what "was done." For example, what was done with madmen, delinquents, or sick people? Of course, one can try to infer the institutions in which they were placed and the treatments to which they were subjected from the ideas that people had about them, or knowledge that people believed they had about them. One can also look for the form of "true" mental illnesses and the modalities of real delinquency in a given period in order to explain what was thought about them at the time.

Michel Foucault approaches things in an altogether different way. He first studies the ensemble of more or less regulated, more or less deliberate, more or less finalized ways of doing things, through which can be seen both what was constituted as real for those who sought to think it and manage it and the way in which the latter constituted themselves as subjects capable of knowing, analyzing, and ultimately altering reality. These are the "practices," understood as a way of acting and thinking at once, that provide the intelligibility key for the correlative constitution of the subject and the object.

Now, since it is a matter of studying the different modes of objectivation of the subject that appear through these practices, one understands how important it is to analyze power relations. But it is essential to clearly define what such an analysis can be and can hope to accomplish. Obviously, it is a matter not of examining "power" with regard to its origin, its principles, or its legitimate limits, but of studying the methods and techniques used in different institutional contexts to act upon the behavior of individuals taken separately or in a group, so as to shape, direct, modify their way of conducting themselves, to impose ends on their inaction or fit it into overall strategies, these being multiple consequently, in their form and their place of exercise; diverse, too, in the procedures and techniques they bring into play. These power relations characterize the manner in which men are "governed" by one another; and their analysis shows how, through certain forms of "government," of madmen, sick people, criminals, and so on, the mad, the sick, the delinquent subject is objectified. So an analysis of this kind implies not that the abuse of this or that power has created madmen, sick people, or criminals, there where there was nothing, but that the various and particular forms of "government" of individuals were determinant in the different modes of objectivation of the subject.

One sees how the theme of a "history of sexuality" can fit within Michel Foucault's general project. It is a matter of analyzing "sexuality" as a historically singular mode of experience in which the subject is objectified for himself and for others through certain specific procedures of "government."

NOTES

1 The italicized phrase is by François Ewald, who wrote the first part of this statement. – Ed.

LIFE: EXPERIENCE AND SCIENCE[*]

Everyone knows that there are few logicians in France, but that there have been a fair number of historians of science. We also know that they have occupied a considerable place in the philosophic institution, in teaching and research. But people may be less aware of the significance and impact of a work like that of Georges Canguilhem, extending as it has over the past twenty or thirty years, and to the very boundaries of the institution. There have been noisier arenas no doubt – psychoanalysis, Marxism, linguistics, ethnology. But let us not overlook this fact, which pertains, as one prefers, to the sociology of French intellectual milieus, the operation of our university institutions, or our system of cultural values: the role of philosophy – I do not just mean of those who received their university training in philosophy departments – was important in all the political and scientific discussions of those strange years, the sixties. Too important perhaps, in the opinion of some. Now, it so happens that all these philosophers, or nearly all, were affected directly or indirectly by the teaching or the books of Canguilhem.

Whence a paradox: this man, whose work is austere, deliberately delimited and carefully tailored to a particular domain in a history of science that in any case is not regarded as a spectacular discipline, was in some way present in the debates in which he took care never

[*]This essay originally appeared in the *Revue de métaphysique et de morale* 90:1 (Jan.–March 1985), pp. 3–14. It is a modified version of Foucault's introduction to the English translation of Georges Canguilhem's *The Normal and the Pathological*, trans. Carolyn Fawcett with Robert Cohen (New York: Zone, 1989). Robert Hurley's translation.

to appear. But, take away Canguilhem, and you will no longer understand very much about a whole series of discussions that took place among French Marxists; nor will you grasp what is specific about sociologists such as Pierre Bourdieu, Robert Castel, Jean-Claude Passeron, what makes them so distinctive in the field of sociology; you will miss a whole aspect of the theoretical work done by psychoanalysts and, in particular, by the Lacanians. Furthermore, in the whole debate of ideas that preceded or followed the movement of 1968, it is easy to find the place of those who were shaped in one way or another by Canguilhem.

Without ignoring the cleavages that in recent years and since the end of the war have set Marxists against non-Marxists, Freudians against non-Freudians, specialists in a discipline against philosophers, academics against nonacademics, theoreticians against politicians, it seems to me that one could find another dividing line that runs through all these oppositions. It is the one that separates a philosophy of experience, of meaning, of the subject, and a philosophy of knowledge, of rationality, and of the concept. On one side, a filiation which is that of Jean-Paul Sartre and Maurice Merleau-Ponty; and then another, which is that of Jean Cavaillès, Gaston Bachelard, Alexander Koyré, and Canguilhem. Doubtless this cleavage comes from afar, and one could trace it back through the nineteenth century: Henri Bergson and Henri Poincaré, Jules Lachelier and Louis Couturat, Pierre Maine de Biran and Auguste Comte. And, in any case, it was so well established in the twentieth century that, through it, phenomenology was admitted into France. Delivered in 1929, modified, translated and published shortly afterward, the *Cartesian Meditations*[1] soon became the contested object of two possible readings: one that sought to radicalize Husserl in the direction of a philosophy of the subject, and before long was to encounter the questions of *Being and Time*[2]: I have in mind Sartre's article on the "Transcendence of the Ego"[3] in 1935; and the other, that would go back to the founding problems of Husserl's thought, the problems of formalism and intuitionalism; this would be, in 1938, the two theses of Cavaillès on the *Méthode axiomatique* and on *La Formation de la théorie des ensembles*.[4] Whatever the ramifications, the interferences, even the rapprochements may have been in the years that followed, these two forms of thought constituted in France two strains that remained, for a time at least, rather deeply heterogeneous.

On the surface, the second one remained the most theoretical, the most geared to speculative tasks, and the farthest removed from immediate political inquiries. And yet, it was this one that during the war participated, in a very direct way, in the combat, as if the question of the basis of rationality could not be dissociated from an interrogation concerning the current conditions of its existence. It was this one, too, that in the sixties played a crucial part in a crisis that was not just that of the university, but also that of the status and role of knowledge [*savoir*]. One may wonder why this type of reflection turned out to be, in accordance with its own logic, so deeply involved in the present.

One of the main reasons appears to lie in this: the history of the sciences owes its philosophical standing to the fact that it employs one of the themes that entered, somewhat surreptitiously and as if by accident, the philosophy of the seventeenth century. During that era, rational thought was questioned for the first time not only as to its nature, its basis, its powers and its rights, but as to its history and its geography, its immediate past and its conditions of exercise, its time, its place, and its current status. One can take as a symbol of this question, through which philosophy has constructed an essential enquiry concerning its present form and its connection to its context, the debate that was begun in the *Berlinische Monatsschrift* on the theme: *Was ist Aufklärung?* [What is enlightenment?] Moses Mendelssohn, then Immanuel Kant, each on his own account, wrote a reply to this question.[5]

At first it was understood no doubt as a relatively minor query: philosophy was questioned concerning the form it might assume, the shape it had at the moment, and the results that should be expected of it. But it soon became apparent that the reply given risked going far beyond. *Aufklärung* was made into the moment when philosophy found the possibility of establishing itself as the determining figure of an epoch, and when that epoch became the form of that philosophy's fulfillment. Philosophy could also be read as being nothing else than the composition of the particular traits of the period in which it appeared, it was that period's coherent figure, its systematization, or its conceptualized form; but, from another standpoint, the epoch appeared as being nothing less than the emergence and manifestation, in its fundamental traits, of what philosophy was in its essence. Philosophy appears then both as a more or less revealing element of the

significations of an epoch, and, on the contrary, as the general law
that determined the figure that it was to have for each epoch. Reading
philosophy in the context of a general history and interpreting it as
the principle of decipherment of any historical sequence became simultaneously possible. So the question of the "present moment" becomes for philosophy an inquiry it can longer leave aside: to what
extent does this "moment" belong to a general historical process, and
to what extent is philosophy the point where history itself must be
deciphered in its conditions?

In that period, history became one of the major problems of philosophy. It would be necessary no doubt to try and determine why this
question of *Aufklärung* has had, without ever disappearing, such a
different destiny in the traditions of Germany, France, and the Anglo-
Saxon countries; why has it taken hold here and there in so many
and – according to the chronologies – such varied domains? Let us say,
in any case, that German philosophy shaped it into a historical and
political reflection on society, above all (with one central problem, the
religious experience as it related to the economy and the state). From
the post-Hegelians to the Frankfurt School and to Georg Lukács, going
by way of Ludwig Feuerbach, Karl Marx, Friedrich Nietzsche and
Max Weber, all these thinkers give evidence of the same concern. In
France, it is the history of science in particular that has served as a
medium for the philosophical question of historical *Aufklärung*; in a
sense, the critiques of Claude-Henri Saint-Simon, the positivism of
Auguste Comte and his successors were in fact a way of resuming the
inquiry of Mendelssohn and of Kant on the scale of a general history
of societies. Knowledge [*savoir*] and belief, the scientific form of
knowledge [*connaissance*] and the religious contents of representation, or the transition from the prescientific to the scientific, the formation
of a rational power against a background of traditional experience,
the emergence, in the midst of a history of ideas and beliefs, of a type
of history peculiar to scientific knowledge, origin and threshold of
rationality: these were the themes through which, via positivism and
those who opposed it, via the rowdy debates on scientism and the
discussions on medieval science, the question of *Aufklärung* was conveyed into France. And if phenomenology, after a long period in
which it was kept on the fringe, finally joined in, this was no doubt
from the day that Husserl, in the *Cartesian Meditations* and the *Crisis*,
raised the question of the relations between the Western project of a

universal deployment of reason, the positivity of the sciences and the radicality of philosophy.[6]

For a century and a half the history of the sciences has been a bearer of philosophical issues that are easily recognized. Though works like those of Koyré, Bachelard, Cavaillès, or Canguilhem may indeed have had specific, "regional," chronologically well defined areas of the history of the sciences as their centers of reference, they have functioned as hotbeds of philosophical elaboration insofar as they have focused on the different facets of this question of *Aufklärung*, essential to contemporary philosophy.

If one had to look outside France for something corresponding to the work of Koyré, Bachelard, Cavaillès, and Canguilhem, it would be in the vicinity of the Frankfurt School, no doubt, that one would find it. And yet the styles are very different, as are the methods and the areas treated. But both groups ultimately raise the same kind of questions, even if they are haunted, here, by the memory of Descartes and, there, by the ghost of Luther. These are the questions that must be addressed to a rationality that aspires to the universal while developing within a contingency, that asserts its unity and yet proceeds only through partial modifications, that validates itself by its own supremacy but that cannot be dissociated in its history from the inertias, the dullnesses, or the coercions that subjugate it. In the history of the sciences in France, as in German Critical Theory, what is to be examined, basically, is a reason whose structural autonomy carries the history of dogmatisms and despotisms along with it – a reason, therefore, that has a liberating effect only provided it manages to liberate itself.

Several processes that mark the second half of the twentieth century have brought the question of enlightenment back to the center of contemporary concerns. The first one is the importance assumed by scientific and technical rationality in the development of the productive forces and the making of political decisions. The second is the very history of a "revolution" for which the hope had been borne, since the end of the eighteenth century, by a whole rationalism of which we are entitled to ask what part it may have played in the effects of despotism where that hope got lost. The third and last is the movement that caused people in the West to ask it what basis there could be in its culture, its science, its social organization, and finally its very rationality for it to claim a universal validity: is it anything more than a mirage tied to a domination and a political hegemony?

Two centuries after its appearance, *Aufklärung* makes a come-back – as a way for the West to become aware of its present possibilities and of the freedoms it may have access to, but also as a way to question oneself about its limits and the powers it has utilized. Reason as both despotism and enlightenment.

We should not be surprised that the history of the sciences, and especially in the particular form that Georges Canguilhem gave it, was able to occupy such a central place in contemporary debates in France.

To put things very roughly, for a long time the history of the sciences concerned itself (by preference if not exclusively) with a few "noble" disciplines that took their prestige from the antiquity of their founding, their high degree of formalization, their capacity for being mathematized, and the privileged place they occupied in the positivist hierarchy of the sciences. By thus remaining fastened to that knowledge [*connaissance*] which, from the Greeks to Leibniz, had in effect been integral with philosophy, the history of the sciences avoided the question that was central for it and concerned its relation with philosophy. Georges Canguilhem reversed the problem: he centered the main part of his work on the history of biology and on that of medicine, knowing very well that the theoretical importance of the problems raised by the development of a science is not necessarily in direct proportion with the degree of formalization it has attained. So he brought the history of the sciences down from the heights (mathematics, astronomy, Galilean mechanics, Newtonian physics, relativity theory) to regions where the knowledge is much less deductive, where it remained connected, for a much longer time, to the wonders of the imagination, and where it posed a series of questions that were much more foreign to philosophical habits.

But in effecting this displacement, Canguilhem did far more than ensure the revalorization of a relatively neglected domain. He did not just broaden the field of the history of the sciences; he reshaped the discipline itself on a number of essential points.

1. First, he took up the theme of "discontinuity." An old theme that emerged early on, to the point of being contemporaneous, or nearly so, with the birth of a history of the sciences. What marks such a history, as Fontenelle already said, is the sudden formation of certain sciences "out of nothing," the extreme rapidity of certain advances

that were unexpected, the distance separating scientific knowledge from "common custom," and the motifs that stirred up the scientists. The polemical form of this history is responsible for endless accounts of battles against "preconceptions," "resistances" and "obstacles."[7] Taking up this same theme, developed by Koyré and Bachelard, Canguilhem stresses the fact that for him identifying discontinuities does not have to do with postulates or results; it is more a "way of proceeding," a procedure that is integral with the history of the sciences because it is called for by the very object that the latter must deal with. The history of the sciences is not the history of the true, of its slow epiphany; it cannot hope to recount the gradual discovery of a truth that has always been inscribed in things or in the intellect, except by imagining that today's knowledge finally possesses it in such a complete and definitive way that it can use that truth as a standard for measuring the past. And yet the history of the sciences is not a pure and simple history of ideas and of the conditions under which they appeared before they faded away. In the history of the sciences one cannot grant oneself the truth as an assumption, but neither can one dispense with a relation to truth and to the opposition of the true and the untrue. It is this reference to the order of the true and the false that gives this history its specificity and its importance. In what way? By considering that one is dealing with the history of "truthful discourses," that is, with discourses that rectify and correct themselves, and that carry out a whole labor of self-development governed by the task of "truth-telling." The historical connections that the different moments of a science may have with each other necessarily have that form of discontinuity which is constituted by the reformulations, the recastings, the revealing of new foundations, the changes in scale, the transition to a new type of objects – "the perpetual revision of contents by deeper investigation and by erasure," as Cavaillès expressed it. Error is eliminated not by the blunt force of a truth that would gradually emerge from the shadows but by the formation of a new way of "truth-telling."[8] Indeed, one of the conditions of possibility for a history of the sciences to take form at the beginning of the eighteenth century was, as Canguilhem points out, the awareness that people had of the recent "scientific revolutions" – that of algebraic geometry and infinitesimal calculus, that of Copernican and Newtonian cosmology.[9]

2. Whoever says "history of truthful discourse" is also saying recursive method. Not in the sense in which the history of the sciences would say, "Given the truth, finally recognized now, when did people get an inkling of it, what paths did it have to take, what groups did it have to coax into discovering and demonstrating it?" but in the sense in which the successive transformations of this truthful discourse constantly produce reworkings in their own history. What had long remained a dead end one day became a way out; a lateral essay becomes a central problem around which all the others begin to gravitate; a slightly divergent step becomes a fundamental break: the discovery of noncellular fermentation–a side phenomenon in the reign of Pasteurian microbiology–did not mark an essential break until the day when the physiology of enzymes developed.[10] In short, the history of discontinuities is not acquired once and for all; it is "impermanent" by its nature; it is discontinuous; it must constantly be resumed at a new cost.

Must we conclude that science is always making and remaking its own history in a spontaneous way, to the extent that a science's only authorized historian would have to be the scientist himself, reconstructing the past of what he is doing now? For Canguilhem the problem is not of a professional kind; it is a problem of viewpoint. The history of the sciences cannot merely collect what the scientists of the past may have thought or demonstrated; one does not write a history of plant physiology by going back over "everything that people called botanists, physicians, chemists, horticulturalists, agronomists, or economists might have written in regard to conjectures, observations, or experiments with a bearing on the relation between structure and function in objects variously termed herbs, plants, or vegetables."[11] But neither does one do a history of the sciences by refiltering the past through the set of statements or theories that are currently validated, thus detecting the future true in what was "false" and the subsequently manifest error in what was true. This is one of the basic points of Canguilhem's method.

The history of the sciences can be constituted in its specific form only by considering, between the pure historian and the scientist himself, the point of view of the epistemologist. This point of view is that which elicits a "latent orderly progression" from the various episodes of a scientific knowledge [*savoir*]–which means that the processes of elimination and selection of statements, theories, and objects always occur in terms of a certain norm. The latter cannot be identified with a theoretical structure or a current paradigm, for today's scientific truth is itself only an episode of it—let us say, at most, its temporary outcome. One cannot go back to the past and validly trace its history by starting from a "normal science"; it can only be done by rediscovering the "normal" process of which current knowledge is but a moment, and there is no way, short of prophecy, to predict the future. The history of the sciences, Canguilhem says, citing Suzanne Bachelard, cannot construct its object anywhere but in "an ideal space-time."[12] And this space-time is given to it neither by the "realistic" time accumulated by the historians' erudition nor by the space of ideality that partitions science today in an authoritative way but by the viewpoint of epistemology. The latter is not the general theory of every science and of every possible scientific statement; it is the search for the normativity internal to the different scientific activities, as they have actually been carried out. So it involves an indispensable theoretical reflection that enables the history of the sciences to be constituted in a different mode from history in general; and, conversely, the history of the sciences opens up a domain of analysis that is indispensable if epistemology is to be anything else but the simple reproduction of the internal schemas of a science at a given time.[13] In the method employed by Canguilhem, the formulation of "discontinuistic" analyses and the elucidation of the historical relation between the sciences and epistemology go hand in hand.

3. Now, by putting sciences of life back into this historico-epistemological perspective, Canguilhem brings to light a certain number of essential traits that make their development different from that of the other sciences and present their historians with specific problems. At the end of the eighteenth century, it was thought that one could find the common element between a physiology studying the phenomena of life and a pathology devoted to the analysis of diseases, and that this element would enable one to consider the normal processes and the disease processes as a unit. From Xavier Bichat to Claude Bernard, from the analysis of fevers to the pathology of the liver and its functions, there had opened up an immense domain that seemed to promise the unity of a physiopathology and access to an understanding of disease phenomena based on the analysis of normal processes. People expected the healthy organism to provide the general framework in which these pathological phenomena took hold

and assumed, for a time, their own form. It seems that this pathology, grounded in normality, characterized the whole of medical thought for a long time.

But there are phenomena in the study of life which keep it separate from any knowledge that may refer to the physicochemical domains; the fact is that it has been able to find the principle of its development only in the investigation of pathological phenomena. It has not been possible to constitute a science of the living without taking into account, as something essential to its object, the possibility of disease, death, monstrosity, anomaly, and error. Although one may come to know, with increasing exactness, the physicochemical mechanisms that cause them, they have their place nonetheless in a specificity that the life sciences must take into account, lest they obliterate the very thing that forms their object and their particular domain.

There results a paradoxical fact in the sciences of life. While their establishment did come about through the elucidation of physical and chemical mechanisms, through the constituting of domains like the chemistry of cells and molecules, through the use of mathematical models and so on, this process, on the other hand, could unfold only to the extent that the problem of the specificity of disease and the threshold it marks among natural beings was constantly revisited.[14] This does not mean that vitalism, which put so many images in circulation and perpetuated so many myths, is true. Nor does it mean that that notion, which so often became deeply rooted in the least rigorous philosophies, must constitute the unsurpassable philosophy of biologists. But it does mean that it had and no doubt still has an essential role as an "indicator" in the history of biology. And in two ways: as a theoretical indicator of problems to be solved (that is, in a general way, what constitutes the originality of life without the latter's constituting under any circumstances an independent empire in nature); and as a critical indicator of the reductions to be avoided (namely, all those which tend to conceal the fact that the sciences of life cannot do without a certain value assertion that emphasizes conservation, regulation, adaptation, reproduction, and so on); "an exigency rather than a method, an ethic more than a theory."[15]

4. The life sciences call for a certain way of doing their history. They also raise, in a peculiar way, the philosophical question of knowledge [*connaissance*].

Life and death are never problems of physics in themselves, even though the physicist in his work may risk his own life or that of others; for him it is a question of ethics or politics, not a scientific question. As André Lwoff puts it, lethal or not, as far as the physicist is concerned a genetic mutation is neither more nor less than the replacement of one nucleic base by another. But in this difference the biologist recognizes the mark of his own object—and of a type of object to which he himself belongs, since he lives and since he reveals, manipulates, and develops this nature of the living in an activity of knowledge that must be understood as "a general method for the direct or indirect relieving of the tensions between man and the environment." The biologist has to grasp what makes life a specific object of knowledge and, thus, what accounts for the fact that among the living, and because they are living, there are beings capable of knowing, and of knowing, finally, life itself.

Phenomenology expected "lived experience" to supply the originary meaning of every act of knowledge. But can we not or must we not look for it in the "living" itself?

Through an elucidation of knowledge about life and of the concepts that articulate that knowledge, Canguilhem wishes to determine the situation of the *concept in life*. That is, of the concept insofar as it is one of the modes of that information which every living being takes from its environment and by which conversely it structures its environment. The fact that man lives in a conceptually structured environment does not prove that he has turned away from life, or that a historical drama has separated him from it—just that he lives in a certain way, that he has a relationship with his environment such that he has no set point of view toward it, that he is mobile on an undefined or a rather broadly defined territory, that he has to move around in order to gather information, that he has to move things relative to one another in order to make them useful. Forming concepts is a way of living and not a way of killing life; it is a way to live in a relative mobility and not a way to immobilize life; it is to show, among those billions of living beings that inform their environment and inform themselves on the basis of it, an innovation that can be judged as one likes, tiny or substantial: a very special type of information.

Hence the importance that Canguilhem attributes to the encounter, in the life sciences, of the old question of the normal and the pathological with the set of notions that biology, during these last decades, has borrowed from information theory—codes, messages, messengers, and so on. From this viewpoint, *The Normal and the Pathological*, a part of which was written in 1943 and the other part during the period 1963–1966, undoubtedly constitutes Canguilhem's most significant work. It shows how the problem of the specific nature of life has recently been inflected in a direction where one meets with some of the problems that were thought to belong strictly to the most developed forms of evolution.

At the center of these problems one finds that of error. For, at the most basic level of life, the processes of coding and decoding give way to a chance occurrence that, before becoming a disease, a deficiency, or a monstrosity, is something like a disturbance in the informative system, something like a "mistake." In this sense, life—and this is its radical feature—is that which is capable of error. And perhaps it is this datum or rather this contingency which must be asked to account for the fact that the question of anomaly permeates the whole of biology. And it must also be asked to account for the mutations and evolutive processes to which they lead. Further, it must be questioned in regard to that singular but hereditary error which explains the fact that, with man, life has led to a living being that is never completely in the right place, that is destined to "err" and to be "wrong."

And if one grants that the concept is the reply that life itself has given to that chance process, one must agree that error is the root of what produces human thought and its history. The opposition of the true and the false, the values that are attributed to the one and the other, the power effects that different societies and different institutions link to that division—all this may be nothing but the most belated response to that possibility of error inherent in life. If the history of the sciences is discontinuous—that is, if it can be analyzed only as a series of "corrections," as a new distribution that never sets free, finally and forever, the terminal moment of truth—the reason, again, is that "error" constitutes not a neglect or a delay of the promised fulfillment but the dimension peculiar to the life of human beings and indispensable to the duration [*temps*] of the species.

Nietzsche said that truth was the greatest lie. Canguilhem, who is far from and near to Nietzsche at the same time, would perhaps say that on the huge calendar of life it is the most recent error; or, more exactly, he would say that the true/false dichotomy and the value accorded to truth constitute the most singular way of living that has been invented by a life that, from the depths of its origin, bore the potential for error within itself. For Canguilhem, error is the permanent contingency [*aléa*] around which the history of life and the development of human beings are coiled. It is this notion of error that enables him to connect what he knows about biology and the manner in which he does history, without ever intending to deduce the latter from the former, as was done in the time of evolutionism. It is what allows him to bring out the relationship between life and knowledge [*connaissance*] and to follow, like a red thread, the presence of value and the norm within it.

This historian of rationalities, himself so "rationalistic," is a philosopher of error—I mean that error provides him with the basis for posing philosophical problems; or, let us say more exactly, the problem of truth and life. Here we touch on one of the fundamental events, no doubt, in the history of modern philosophy: if the great Cartesian break raised the question of the relations between truth and subjectivity, the eighteenth century introduced a series of questions concerning truth and life, *The Critique of Judgment* and the *Phenomenology of Spirit* being the first great formulations of these.[16] And since that time this has been one of the issues of philosophical discussion. Should life be considered as nothing more than one of the areas that raises the general question of truth, the subject, and knowledge? Or does it oblige us to pose the question in a different way? Should not the whole theory of the subject be reformulated, seeing that knowledge, rather than opening onto the truth of the world, is deeply rooted in the "errors" of life?

One understands why Georges Canguilhem's thought, his work as a historian and a philosopher, has had such a decisive importance in France for all those who, from very different points of view, have tried to rethink the question of the subject. Although phenomenology brought the body, sexuality, death, and the perceived world into the field of analysis, the *cogito* remained central to it; neither the rationality of science nor the specificity of the life sciences could compromise its founding role. In opposition to this philosophy of meaning, the subject, and lived experience, Canguilhem has proposed a philosophy of error, of the concept of the living, as a different way of approaching the notion of life.

NOTES

1   Edmund, Husserl, *Cartesianische Meditationen: Eine Einleitung in die Phänomenologie* [1931], in *Gesammelte Werke*, (The Hague: Nijhoff, 1950), vol. 1 [*Cartesian Meditations: An Introduction to Phenomenology*, trans. Dorion Cairns (The Hague: Martinus Nijhoff, 1960)].

2   Martin Heidegger, *Sein und Zeit* (Tübingen: Niemeyer, 1927) [*Being and Time*, trans. Joan Stambaugh (Albany: State University of New York Press, 1996)].

3   Jean-Paul Sartre, "La Transcendance de l'ego: esquisse d'une description phénoménologique," *Recherches philosophiques* 6 (1935), republished (Paris: Vrin, 1988) [*The Transcendence of the Ego: An Existentialist Theory of Consciousness*, trans. Forrest Williams and Robert Kirkpatrick (New York: Noonday Press, 1957)].

4   Jean Cavaillès, *Méthode axiomatique et formalisme: essai sur le problème du fondement des mathématiques* (Paris: Hermann, 1937); *Remarques sur la formation de la théorie abstraite des ensembles: étude historique et critique* (Paris: Hermann, 1937).

5   Moses Mendelssohn, "Über die Frage: Was heißt Aufklären?," *Berlinische Monatsschrift* 4:3, (Sept. 1784), pp. 193–200; Immanuel Kant, "Beantwortung der Frage: Was ist Aufklärung?" *Berlinische Monatsschrift* 4:6 (Dec. 1784), pp. 491–94 [*Réponse à la question: Qu'est-ce que les Lumières?*, trans. S. Piobetta, in Kant, *La Philosophie de l'histoire [Opuscules]*, (Paris: Aubier, 1947), pp. 81–92].

6   Husserl, *Die Krisis der europäischen Wissenschaft und die transzendentale Phänomenologie: Einleitung in die Phänomenologie* (Belgrade: Philosophia, 1936), vol. 1, pp. 77–176 [*The Crisis of European Sciences and Transcendental Phenomenology: An Introduction to Phenomenological Philosophy*, trans. David Carr (Evanston, IL: Northwestern University Press, 1970)].

7   Fontenelle, B. Le Bovier de, *Préface à l'histoire de l'Académie*, in *Oeuvres*, edition of 1790, vol. 6, pp. 73–74. Georges Canguilhem cites this text in the *Introduction à l'histoire des sciences* (Paris, 1970). vol. 1: *Elements et instruments*, pp. 7–8.

8   On this theme, see Canguilhem, *Idéologie et rationalité dans l'histoire des sciences de la vie* (Paris: Vrin, 1977), p. 21. [*Ideology and Rationality in the History of the Life Sciences*, trans. Arthur Goldhammer (Cambridge, Mass.: MIT Press, 1988), pp. 10–11].

9   *Etudes d'histoire et de philosophie des sciences* (Paris: Vrin, 1968), p. 17.

10 Canguilhem takes up the example discussed by M. Florkin in *A History of Biochemistry* (Amsterdam: Elsevier, 1972–75); cf. Canguilhem, *Idéologie et Rationalité*, p. 15 [*Ideology and Rationality*, p. 5].

11 Canguilhem, *Idéologie et rationalité*, p. 14 [*Ideology and Rationality*, p. 4].

12 Suzanne Bachelard, "Epistémologie et histoire des sciences," in Twelfth International History of the Sciences Conference (Paris: 1968), *Revue de synthèse*, 3rd ser., 49–52 (Jan.–Dec. 1968), p. 51.

13 On the relationship between epistemology and history, see especially the introduction to Canguilhem, *Idéologie et rationalité*, pp. 11–29 [*Ideology and Rationality*, pp. 1–23].

14 Canguilhem, *Études d'histoire et de philosophie des sciences*, p. 239.

15 Canguilhem, *La Connaissance de la vie* [1952], (2d ed., Paris: Vrin, 1965), p. 88.

16 Immanuel Kant, *Kritik der Urteilskraft* [1790], in *Gesammelte Schriften* (Berlin: Königlich Preussiche Akademie der Wissenschaften, 1902), vol. 5, pp. 165–486 [*Critique of Judgment*, trans. Werner S. Pluhar (Indianapolis: Hackett, 1987)]; G. W. F. Hegel, *Phänomenologie des Geistes* (Würzburg: Goebhardt, 1807) [*The Phenomenology of Spirit*, trans. A. V. Miller (New York: Oxford University Press, 1977)].

INDEX

Actaeon, prose of, 125-35
affirmation, 199-202, 208, 353, 359, 360
alienation, 84-85, 151
alternators of experience, 129-31
Althusser, Louis, 281, 422
Aminadab (Blanchot), 155, 156, 158, 159, 164, 166
analogy: notion of, 271
anthropology, 76, 250, 257, 258, 259
antiquarianism, 387
Apollonius, 115, 116
The Archaeology of Knowledge (Foucault), 261-62, 263-64, 444-45, 457, 458, 460.
"Archaeology of the Sciences" (Foucault): and concepts, 329-50; and discursive events, 302-11, 318-21, 324-25, 327; and discursive formations and positivities, 311-26, 327; and epistemological rupture, 297-302; and history, 327-28, 332-33; and illusions, 329, 330-31; and knowledge, 321-33; and objects, 312-14, 320-21, 329, 330-31; and rules, 309-10, 313, 314-15, 317, 330; and semantics, 316-18, 320-21, 329; and statements, 306-10, 312-14, 324-25, 330; and syntax, 314-15, 320-21, 329; and writing history, 284, 289-90, 294
archives, 289-90, 309-10, 311
Aristotle, 217, 343, 344, 356, 359
art/artists, 8-11, 14, 19, 174, 405
Artaud, Antonin, 154, 263, 339, 348
articulation, theory of, 317-18
attraction, 154-57, 160-63, 166
attribution, theory of, 317-18

Aufklärung (enlightenment), 439, 440, 442, 449, 466-70
authentication, 214-15

Bachelard, Gaston, 177, 297, 299, 441, 466, 469, 471
Bataille, Georges, 126, 174, 348, 458, 447; and thought of the outside, 151, 154; transgression in works of, 70-73, 75, 76, 77, 79-87, 153, 151, 154
becoming, 365-66, 373, 379
beginning, refusal of, 274
being, 359-60, 364-68, 380, 588, 411-12, 413
Beyond Good and Evil (Nietzsche), 275
Bichat, Xavier, 314, 315, 473
biology, 328, 330, 470, 473-77
The Birth of the Clinic (Foucault), 263, 284-85, 310, 323-24, 461
Blanchot, Maurice, 17-18, 89, 126, 133, 174, 291, 438; and authorship, 287-88; death in works of, 133, 162, 165; and silence, 291; and thought of the outside, 287-88; thought of the outside in works of, 151-67; transgression in, 74-75, 76, 133, 165; and writing history, 287-88, 291
body, 223-27, 252, 346-47, 375-76, 380, 382, 408, 411
books, 106-13, 117-21, 303-4
Borges, Jorge Luis, 91-92, 95, 99-100, 107, 294
Boulez, Pierre, 235, 236-37, 239, 241-44
Bouvard et Pécuchet (Flaubert), 103, 104, 118, 119, 120, 121, 361
Breton, André, 26, 30, 171-74

cage, 57, 58,-60, 62, 65-66
calligram, 189-95, 202

Canguilhem, Georges, 299, 365-66, 437, 441, 469, 470-77
Cartesian doubt: and Derrida, 393-94, 395-417; and discursive differences, 405-10, 412, 416; and disqualification of subject, 401-3; and dreams and madness, 393, 394, 395-402, 407, 408-15, 416-17; and extravagance of painters, 403-5; and metaphysics, 416; and subjectivity, 477; and truth, 477
Cartesian Meditations (Husserl), 466, 468
categories, 310, 359-60, 361, 365
causality, 281, 421
Cavaillès, Jean, 466, 469, 471
Ceci n'est pas une pipe. See This Is Not a Pipe (Magritte)
Celui qui ne m'accompagnait pas (Blanchot), 155, 167
cemeteries, 180-81
Char, René, 19, 242, 243
Chaunu, Huguette and Pierre, 427, 428
Chéreau, Patrice, 235, 236, 237-38, 239
Christ, 79, 116, 121
Christianity, 69, 150, 184, 214, 230; in Flaubert's works, 115, 116, 117; and Greek thought, 125, 128; and Klossowski's works, 123-24, 128, 151-32, 134
Chronos, 365-66
Classical age, 264, 265, 293, 323
cogito, 271, 412, 413, 477
colonization, 184
Comizi d'amore (film), 229-31
commentaries, 106, 133, 153, 208
companion, 163-65, 166
Comte, Auguste, 328, 437, 440, 466, 468
concepts, 316-18, 320-21, 329-30, 466-67